PRINCIPLES OF RESEARCH IN BEHAVIORAL SCIENCE

SECOND EDITION

BERNARD E. WHITLEY, JR.

BALL STATE UNIVERSITY

Mc
Graw
Hill

Boston   Burr Ridge, IL Dubuque, IA Madison, WI New York
San Francisco St. Louis Bangkok Bogotá Caracas Kuala Lumpur
Lisbon London Madrid Mexico City Milan Montreal New Delhi
Santiago Seoul Singapore Sydney Taipei Toronto

McGraw-Hill Higher Education

A Division of The **McGraw-Hill** *Companies*

Published by McGraw-Hill, an imprint of The McGraw-Hill Companies, Inc., 1221 Avenue of the Americas, New York, NY 10020. Copyright © 2002, 1996 by The McGraw-Hill Companies, Inc. All rights reserved. No part of this publication may be reproduced or distributed in any form or by any means, or stored in a database or retrieval system, without the prior written consent of The McGraw-Hill Companies, Inc., including, but not limited to in any network or other electronic storage or transmission, or broadcast for distance learning.

Library of Congress Cataloging-in-Publication Data

Whitley, Bernard E.
    Principles of research in behavioral science / Bernard E. Whitley, Jr.—2nd ed.
      p.   cm.
    Includes bibliographical references and index.
    ISBN 0-7674-2175-2
    1. Psychology—Research—Methodology.   I. Title.
    BF76.5.W48   2001
    150'.7'2—dc21   2001018329

Manufactured in the United States of America
  2 3 4 5 6 7 8 9 0 VNH/VNH 0 9 8 7 6 5 4 3 2 1

Sponsoring editor, Franklin C. Graham; production, Melanie Field; manuscript editor, Margaret Moore; design manager, Susan Breitbard; text designer, Anna George; cover designer, Linda Robertson; cover art, Naum Gabo, *Linear Construction in Space, Number 4*, 1957–1958, plastic and stainless steel, including base: $40 \times 21\frac{1}{4} \times 28\frac{1}{2}$ in. ($101.6 \times 54 \times 72.4$ cm.). Purchase, with funds from the Friends of the Whitney Museum of American Art. 58.61. Photograph © 1996: Whitney Museum of American Art, New York. Photography by Sandak, Inc. The works of Naum Gabo © Nina Williams; illustrator, Joan Carol; manufacturing manager, Danielle Javier. The text was set in 10/12 Goudy Old Style by G&S Typesetters and printed on 45# Highland Plus by R. R. Donnelley and Sons Company.

Text and illustration credits continue at the back of the book on pages 649–652, which constitute an extension of the copyright page.

www.mhhe.com

BRIEF CONTENTS

PART ONE:
INTRODUCTION

1   BEHAVIORAL SCIENCE: Theory, Research, and Application   *1*
2   RESEARCH STRATEGIES: An Overview   *29*

PART TWO:
FOUNDATIONS
OF RESEARCH

3   THE ETHICAL TREATMENT OF RESEARCH PARTICIPANTS   *57*
4   FORMULATING A RESEARCH QUESTION   *89*
5   DEVELOPING A MEASUREMENT STRATEGY   *121*
6   THE INTERNAL VALIDITY OF RESEARCH   *155*

PART THREE:
RESEARCH
STRATEGIES

7   THE EXPERIMENTAL RESEARCH STRATEGY   *181*
8   THE CORRELATIONAL (PASSIVE) RESEARCH STRATEGY   *221*
9   THE SINGLE-CASE RESEARCH STRATEGY   *263*
10   RESEARCH IN NATURAL SETTINGS   *299*
11   SURVEY RESEARCH   *343*

PART FOUR:
COLLECTING AND
INTERPRETING DATA

12   DATA COLLECTION   *389*
13   INTERPRETING RESEARCH RESULTS   *425*
14   THE EXTERNAL VALIDITY OF RESEARCH   *451*

PART FIVE:
SPECIAL TOPICS

15   EVALUATION RESEARCH   *477*
16   INTEGRATIVE LITERATURE REVIEWING   *515*
17   WRITING RESEARCH REPORTS   *547*
18   THE PROFESSIONAL AND SOCIAL RESPONSIBILITIES
OF SCIENTISTS   *589*

CONTENTS

PREFACE   *xvii*

**PART ONE:
INTRODUCTION**

1   BEHAVIORAL SCIENCE: Theory, Research, and Application   *1*

SCIENCE   *2*
Goals of Science   2
Key Values of Science   5
Scientific Approaches to Knowledge   7

THEORIES   *8*
Components of Theories   9
Characteristics of Theories   15
Purposes of Theories   16
Criteria for Evaluating Theories   21

RESEARCH   *22*
The Research Process   22
Evaluating Research   23
Inference in Research   23

THEORY, RESEARCH, AND APPLICATION   *24*
The Interdependence of Theory, Research, and Application   24
The Uses of Behavioral Science Theory and Research   25

SUMMARY   *27*
QUESTIONS AND EXERCISES FOR REVIEW   *28*

2   RESEARCH STRATEGIES: An Overview   *29*

PURPOSES OF RESEARCH   *30*
Basic and Applied Research   30
Evaluation Research   32
Action Research   32

QUANTITATIVE AND QUALITATIVE RESEARCH   *32*

RESEARCH STRATEGIES   *34*
The Experimental Strategy   35
The Case Study Strategy   37
The Correlational (Passive) Strategy   40
Comparing the Strategies   44

TIME PERSPECTIVES: Short Term Versus Long Term   *44*
Developmental Research   44
Prospective Research   49
Outcome Evaluation   51

RESEARCH SETTINGS: Laboratory Versus Field   *52*
Research Strategies and Research Settings   52
Research Settings and Research Participants   53

RESEARCH AS A SET OF TRADEOFFS   *54*

SUMMARY   *55*

QUESTIONS AND EXERCISES FOR REVIEW   *56*

PART TWO:
FOUNDATIONS
OF RESEARCH

3   THE ETHICAL TREATMENT OF RESEARCH PARTICIPANTS   *57*

RESPONSIBILITY FOR ETHICAL RESEARCH   *59*
The Researcher   59
The Institutional Review Board   60

ETHICAL CONSIDERATIONS IN PLANNING
RESEARCH   *62*
Risk of Harm or Deprivation   62
Voluntary Participation   66
Informed Consent   68
Deception   72

ETHICAL CONSIDERATIONS DURING
DATA COLLECTION   *77*
Avoidance of Harm   77
Withdrawal of Consent   80

ETHICAL CONSIDERATIONS FOLLOWING
DATA COLLECTION   *81*
Alleviating Adverse Effects   81
Debriefing   81
Compensation of Control Groups   84
Confidentiality of Data   84

SUMMARY   *86*

QUESTIONS AND EXERCISES FOR REVIEW   *87*

4   FORMULATING A RESEARCH QUESTION   89

FORMULATING RESEARCH HYPOTHESES   90
Establishing a Background   90
Choosing a Topic   91
Formulating the Question   92
Reviewing the Literature   97
Formulating Hypotheses   104
Designing the Study   107
Writing the Research Proposal   108

REPLICATION RESEARCH   109
Forms of Replication   109
Implications of Replication Research   110
Considerations in Conducting Replication Research   110

DESIGNING RESEARCH FOR UTILIZATION   112
Knowledge Utilization   113
Design Considerations   113

BIAS IN THE FORMULATION OF RESEARCH
QUESTIONS   116
Biased Assumptions   117
Biased Theory   118
Avoiding Bias   118

SUMMARY   119

QUESTIONS AND EXERCISES FOR REVIEW   120

5   DEVELOPING A MEASUREMENT STRATEGY   121

RELIABILITY AND VALIDITY   123
Manifest Variables and Hypothetical Constructs   123
Reliability, Validity, and Measurement Error   124
Assessing Reliability   125
Assessing Validity   128

MODALITIES OF MEASUREMENT   138
Self-Report Measures   138
Behavioral Measures   140
Physiological Measures   142
Choosing a Measurement Modality   143

LOCATING AND EVALUATING MEASURES   146
Categories of Measures   146
Locating Measures   147
Evaluating Measures   148

SUMMARY   152

QUESTIONS AND EXERCISES FOR REVIEW   153

6   THE INTERNAL VALIDITY OF RESEARCH   155

CONFOUNDS   157
Natural Confounds   157
Treatment Confounds   158
Measurement Confounds   159

THREATS TO INTERNAL VALIDITY   159
Time-Related Threats   160
Control Groups in Pretest–Posttest Research   164
Selection Threats   165

REACTIVITY   167
Sources of Reactivity   167
Controlling Reactivity   169

DEMAND CHARACTERISTICS   171
Sources of Demand Characteristics   172
Participant Roles   172
Controlling Demand Characteristics   174

EXPERIMENTER EXPECTANCIES   175
Types of Expectancy Effects   176
Techniques of Control   177

SUMMARY   178

QUESTIONS AND EXERCISES FOR REVIEW   179

**PART THREE:
RESEARCH STRATEGIES**

7   THE EXPERIMENTAL RESEARCH STRATEGY   181

A NOTE ON STATISTICS   183

MANIPULATING THE INDEPENDENT VARIABLE   184
Conditions of the Independent Variable   184
Additional Control and Comparison Conditions   185
Characteristics of a Good Manipulation   187
Using Multiple Stimuli   190

CONTROLLING EXTRANEOUS VARIANCE   191
Holding Extraneous Variables Constant   191
Between-Subjects Designs   192
Within-Subjects Designs   195

MULTIPLE-GROUP DESIGNS   200
Quantitative Independent Variables   200
Qualitative Independent Variables   203
Interpreting the Results of Multiple-Group Experiments   203

FACTORIAL DESIGNS   *204*
The Nature of Factorial Designs   205
Interaction Effects   207
Forms of Factorial Designs   212
Uses for Factorial Designs   214
SUMMARY   *218*
QUESTIONS AND EXERCISES FOR REVIEW   *219*

8   THE CORRELATIONAL (PASSIVE) RESEARCH STRATEGY   *221*

THE NATURE OF CORRELATIONAL RESEARCH   *223*
Assumptions of Linearity and Additivity   223
Factors Affecting the Correlation Coefficient   224
Multifaceted Constructs   228
Some Recommendations   230
SIMPLE AND PARTIAL CORRELATION ANALYSIS   *231*
Simple Correlational Analysis   231
Partial Correlation Analysis   233
MULTIPLE REGRESSION ANALYSIS (MRA)   *236*
Forms of MRA   236
Information Provided by MRA   237
The Problem of Multicollinearity   240
MRA as an Alternative to ANOVA   241
SOME OTHER CORRELATIONAL TECHNIQUES   *243*
Logistic Regression Analysis   244
Multiway Frequency Analysis   244
Data Types and Data Analysis   246
TESTING MEDIATIONAL HYPOTHESES   *246*
Simple Mediation: Three Variables   247
Complex Models   247
Limits on Interpretation   250
FACTOR ANALYSIS   *253*
Uses of Factor Analysis   254
Considerations in Factor Analysis   254
SUMMARY   *259*
QUESTIONS AND EXERCISES FOR REVIEW   *261*

9   THE SINGLE-CASE RESEARCH STRATEGY   *263*

THE ROLE OF SINGLE-CASE RESEARCH
IN PSYCHOLOGY   *264*
Some History   264
Current Status of Single-Case Research   266

VALIDITY CRITERIA IN SINGLE-CASE RESEARCH   266
Measurement Criteria   267
Replication Criteria   269
Control Criteria   269
Impact Criteria   271
Treatment Criteria   272

CASE STUDY RESEARCH   272
Choosing Cases to Study   273
Data Collection   275

SINGLE-CASE EXPERIMENTS   277
Designs for Single-Case Experiments   277
The Importance of a Stable Baseline   288

DATA ANALYSIS IN SINGLE-CASE RESEARCH   291
Qualitative Data   292
Quantitative Data   295

SUMMARY   296

QUESTIONS AND EXERCISES FOR REVIEW   297

10   RESEARCH IN NATURAL SETTINGS   299

THE PROBLEM OF CONTROL IN FIELD SETTINGS   300
Control Over Variables   300
Control Over Research Populations   301

FIELD EXPERIMENTS   301
Choosing a Research Setting   302
Implementing the Independent Variable   304
Problems in Field Experimentation   305

NATURAL EXPERIMENTS AND
QUASI-EXPERIMENTS   306
The Group Comparison Approach   307
The Time Series Approach   312

NATURALISTIC OBSERVATION   315
Categories of Naturalistic Observation   315
Problems in Naturalistic Observation   318

INTERVIEWS   321
Types of Interviews   322
Standardizing Interview Procedures   323
Elements of an Interview   324
Group Interviews   326

ARCHIVAL DATA   326
Types of Archives   326
Advantages of Using Archival Data   327
Limitations of Archival Research   328

ANALYZING OPEN-ENDED DATA   329
Characteristics of Coding Systems   330
Developing Coding Systems   335
Content Analysis   336
SUMMARY   339
QUESTIONS AND EXERCISES FOR REVIEW   340

11   SURVEY RESEARCH   *343*

ASKING QUESTIONS   345
Open- and Closed-Ended Questions   345
Question Wording   346
OBTAINING ANSWERS   350
Levels of Measurement   350
Response Formats   354
Choosing a Response Format   360
MULTI-ITEM SCALES   360
Advantages of Multi-Item Scales   361
Types of Multi-Item Scales   361
RESPONSE BIASES   366
Question-Related Biases   366
Person-Related Biases   368
Interpreting Responses   371
QUESTIONNAIRE DESIGN   371
Question Order   371
Layout of Questionnaires   373
Instructions   374
Using Existing Measures   374
QUESTIONNAIRE ADMINISTRATION   377
Methods of Data Collection   377
Comparing the Methods   381
SURVEY DATA ARCHIVES   383
SUMMARY   384
QUESTIONS AND EXERCISES FOR REVIEW   386

**PART FOUR:
COLLECTING AND
INTERPRETING DATA**

12   DATA COLLECTION   389

RESEARCH PARTICIPANTS   390
Populations and Samples   390
Sampling   391
Sample Size   396

RESEARCH PROCEDURES   399
Effective Research Settings   399
Effective Instructions   402
"Debugging" the Procedure   403
The Data Collection Session   406
The Postexperimental Interview   406
Research Assistants   409

USING THE INTERNET TO COLLECT DATA   411
Forms of Internet Data Collection   411
Advantages of Internet Research   412
Disadvantages of Internet Research   414
Participant Recruitment   416
The Validity of Web-Based Data   418
Ethical Issues   418

SUMMARY   422

QUESTIONS AND EXERCISES FOR REVIEW   423

13   INTERPRETING RESEARCH RESULTS   425

DESCRIBING THE RESULTS OF RESEARCH   426
The Nature of the Relationship   426
Real Versus Chance Relationships   428
Effect Size and Importance   431

INFERENCE IN BEHAVIORAL SCIENCE RESEARCH   434
Knowledge as a Social Construction   434
Making Valid Inferences   438

NULL RESULTS   440
Uses of the Null Hypothesis   440
Prejudice Against the Null Hypothesis   441
Possible Sources of Type II Errors   443
Accepting the Null Hypothesis   444

INTEGRATING THE RESULTS OF RESEARCH   445
Identifying Implications for Theory   445
Identifying Implications for Research   446
Identifying Implications for Application   447

SUMMARY   447

QUESTIONS AND EXERCISES FOR REVIEW   449

14   THE EXTERNAL VALIDITY OF RESEARCH   *451*

THE CONCEPT OF EXTERNAL VALIDITY   452
Aspects of External Validity   452
Components of External Validity   453

THE STRUCTURAL COMPONENT OF EXTERNAL VALIDITY   455
Setting Factors   456
Participant Sample Factors   458
Research Procedure Factors   460
Cultural Factors   462
Time Factors   463

THE FUNCTIONAL AND CONCEPTUAL COMPONENTS OF EXTERNAL VALIDITY   464
The Functional Component   464
The Conceptual Component   465
Relationships Among the Components of External Validity   466

ASSESSING EXTERNAL VALIDITY   466
Assessing Generalizability   466
Assessing Ecological Validity   467

LABORATORY RESEARCH, NATURAL SETTING RESEARCH, AND EXTERNAL VALIDITY   468
Laboratory Research and Ecological Validity   468
External Validity and Internal Validity   473

SUMMARY   474

QUESTIONS AND EXERCISES FOR REVIEW   475

PART FIVE:
SPECIAL TOPICS

15   EVALUATION RESEARCH   *477*

GOAL DEFINITION   479
Needs Assessment   479
Evaluability Assessment   480

PROGRAM MONITORING   487
The Target Population   487
Program Implementation   488
Unintended Effects   490
Program Monitoring and Program Development   492

IMPACT ASSESSMENT   492
Criteria for Evaluating Impact   492
Answering Research Questions   495
Research Strategies   497
Interpreting Null Results   502

EFFICIENCY ANALYSIS   *504*
Cost-Benefit Analysis   505
Cost-Effectiveness Analysis   505

INFORMATION UTILIZATION   *506*
Criteria for Research Utilization   506
The Political Context   507

MEASURING CHANGE   *509*
Difference Scores   509
Reliability of Difference Scores   509
The Reliable Change Index   510

SUMMARY   *511*

QUESTIONS AND EXERCISES FOR REVIEW   *512*

16   INTEGRATIVE LITERATURE REVIEWING   *515*

DEFINING THE RESEARCH QUESTION   *518*
Types of Questions   518
The Scope of the Question   520
Approaches to Answering Questions   520

DATA COLLECTION   *521*

DATA EVALUATION   *521*
Include All Studies   522
Include Only Published Studies   522
Include Only Valid Studies   523
Stratified Sampling   524
Expert Judgment   525

DATA ANALYSIS   *525*
Operationally Defining Study Outcome   525
Classifying Studies   527
Analyzing Patterns of Flaws   528
Level of Analysis   529
Choosing a Technique   530

DATA INTERPRETATION   *536*
The Effects of Judgment Calls   536
The Correlational Nature of Moderator Variable Analyses   537
Publication Biases   537

EVALUATING LITERATURE REVIEWS   538

UNDERSTANDING META-ANALYSIS   539

Defining the Research Question   540

Data Collection   541

Data Evaluation   541

Data Analysis   542

Interpretation   543

SUMMARY   544

QUESTIONS AND EXERCISES FOR REVIEW   545

17   WRITING RESEARCH REPORTS   547

THE RESEARCH REPORT   548

Structure   549

Content   549

Writing for Nonresearchers   571

JOURNAL ARTICLES AND CONVENTION
PRESENTATIONS   574

The Journal Article   574

Convention Presentations   580

Reviewing Manuscripts   581

ETHICAL ISSUES IN PUBLICATION   583

Authorship Credit   583

Plagiarism   585

Multiple Publication   585

SUMMARY   586

QUESTIONS AND EXERCISES FOR REVIEW   587

**18   THE PROFESSIONAL AND SOCIAL RESPONSIBILITIES
OF SCIENTISTS   589**

MALPRACTICE IN RESEARCH   590

Forms of Scientific Malpractice   590

The Extent of the Problem   592

Motivations for Scientific Malpractice   593

Problems of Detection and Enforcement   594

"Quis Custodiet Ipsos Custodes?"   596

MISTAKES AND ERRORS IN RESEARCH   596

Consequences of Error   597

Sources of Culpable Error   598

Correcting Mistakes and Errors   599

USING THE RESULTS OF RESEARCH   600
The Application of Research Results   600
Influencing Decision Makers   602
Researchers' Responsibilities   606

RESEARCH AND THE COMMON GOOD   609
Is Applied Research More Ethical Than Basic Research?   609
Should Research on Some Topics Be Banned or Restricted?   610
Is There an Ethical Obligation to Conduct Research?   612

SUMMARY   612

QUESTIONS AND EXERCISES FOR REVIEW   614

REFERENCES   615

CREDITS   649

NAME INDEX   653

SUBJECT INDEX   661

PREFACE

I was motivated to write the first edition of *Principles of Research in Behavioral Science* because I could not find an appropriate research methods textbook for master's-level students in psychology and related fields. My motivation for preparing this second edition was threefold: new developments in research (such as the growing importance of the Internet), the need for a book such as this as shown by its use at a large number of universities, and the suggestions for improvement sent to me by colleagues who have used the book.

As I did with the first edition, I have tried to produce a book that students will use both as a textbook in their research methods course and as a reference for use later in their careers. The book is, perhaps, still more comprehensive than most research methods books, so most instructors may not want to use all the chapters or all the topics within a chapter. I have tried to support this kind of selectivity by making chapters and sections within chapters as independent as possible, although I do refer to material in earlier chapters when it is relevant.

Within a few minor changes noted later, the sequence of the chapters remains unchanged, generally paralleling the steps of the research process. Part One describes the role of theory in the research process and surveys the major research strategies to provide a context for the following chapters. Part Two discusses issues common to all forms of research: the ethical treatment of research participants, formulating research questions, measurement, and internal validity. Part Three devotes a chapter to each of the major research strategies—experimental, correlational, and single case—one to research in natural settings, and one to survey research. Part Four covers process issues in data collection to supplement the design issues discussed in Part Three, the interpretation of research results, and the problem of external validity. Finally, Part Five covers supplemental topics: evaluation research, the literature review as a form of research, communicating the results of research, and the social responsibility aspects of research ethics.

Each chapter begins with an outline to provide students with a cognitive map of its contents, and ends with a summary to provide closure. Within each chapter, key terms are shown in boldface; the index entry for each term also shows the page on which it is defined in boldface. I chose this approach to defining terms over the traditional glossary because it puts the meaning of a term in the context of how it is used rather than providing only a brief definition. A set of questions and exercises concludes each chapter. Each set includes both factual review questions designed to integrate the topics within the chapter and more philosophical discussion questions designed to highlight controversies and to help students become aware of their own epistemological and scientific values. The exercises are designed to help the students put into practice some of the theory the chapter covers.

Because this book is written for first-year graduate students, it assumes they will have had undergraduate statistics and research methods courses. However, I have tried to keep the book as nonstatistical as possible so that it can be used in courses that precede, are concurrent with, or follow a graduate statistics course. Writing for a first-year graduate student audience has also led to what experienced researchers might find to be a curious mix of basic and advanced topics. However, because many students' undergraduate research methods courses will have been 2 or 3 years in the past, I felt that some review of basic principles was required before more advanced topics were introduced.

Despite the help of colleagues with backgrounds in other areas of behavioral science, my training in social and personality psychology, with additional experience in organizational behavior, still strongly influences two aspects of this book. First, the book focuses on research with human participants; although animal research is crucial to the advancement of behavioral science, I have no experience in that area, so I thought it best to leave that form of research outside the scope of this book. Second, my background influenced the studies I have used as examples: I drew on what I knew best, which tipped the scale in the direction of examples from social, personality, and industrial-organizational research.

CHANGES TO THE SECOND EDITION

The second edition incorporates three changes to the organization of the book. First, the chapter on the ethical treatment of research participants has been moved forward to emphasize its importance. Second, the material from the first edition's Chapter 5 on scaling and coding has been distributed across several chapters of the current edition. Finally, a chapter on survey research has been created, primarily from material previously contained in other chapters.

Information throughout the book has been updated, and a few major content changes have also been made. Qualitative research is now addressed in several relevant chapters, including Chapters 2 (Research Strategies: An Overview) and 10 (Research in Natural Settings). The section in Chapter 4 (Formulating a Research Question) on literature reviewing has been substantially rewritten to include the use and evaluation of on-line resources. The material from the first edition's Chapter 5 on evaluating measures is now part of this edition's Chapter 5 (Developing a Measurement Strategy). Chapter 10 (Research in Natural Settings) has been reorganized to add a section on interviewing (expanding on material from the first edition's Chapter 12), coding open-ended data (from the first edition's Chapter 5), and additional material on archival data.

Finally, Chapter 12 (Data Collection) has a new section on using the Internet to collect data.

Because the book was already rather lengthy, I tried to balance additions of material with cuts. As a result, material from the first edition on the nature of naturalism in research (which would have appeared in the current Chapter 10), alpha, beta, and gamma change (Chapter 15), and media reports of research (Chapter 18) has been dropped from this edition.

Every textbook is a continual work in progress, so I welcome any comments you have for further improvements. Please write to me at the Department of Psychological Science, Ball State University, Muncie, Indiana 47306, or send electronic mail to bwhitley@bsu.edu.

ACKNOWLEDGMENTS

This book would not have been started without the impetus supplied by Mary Kite and David Perkins of Ball State University, who encouraged me to expand the supplemental readings that I wrote into the first edition of this book. Frank Graham, my sponsoring editor at Mayfield Publishing Company, had the faith in my work to take this book on and has supplied advice, support, and encouragement thoughout the long and enlightening experiences of both editions. Ball State University granted me the year-long sabbatical I needed to get a "running start" on the first edition.

A number of people kindly read draft chapters, provided suggestions for improvements, and provided advice, assistance, and support when I needed it. Patricia Keith-Spiegel of Ball State University and Lisa Warren of the O'Berry Center, Goldsboro, North Carolina, read and provided feedback on every chapter. Other help at Ball State University came from Deborah Ware Balogh, Paul Biner, Darrell Butler, William Clark, Judith Gray, and the staff of Bracken Library. The following people all provided invaluable comments and suggestions for improvement: Frank Bernieri, Oregon State University; Gary M. Brosvic, Rider University; Bernardo Carducci, Indiana University Southeast; Charles Collyer, University of Rhode Island; Paul Foos, University of North Carolina, Charlotte; Ellen Girden, Nova University; David Hogan, Northern Kentucky University; Fred Leavitt, California State University, Hayward; M. Christine Lovejoy, Northern Illinois University; Charlotte Mandell, University of Massachusetts, Lowell; Steven Mewaldt, Marshall University; and Lori Temple, University of Nevada, Las Vegas.

Steven Prentice-Dunn of the University of Alabama provided a number of suggestions for the second edition, and Darrell Butler, Patricia Keith-Spiegel, and Wayne Wilkinson of Ball State University were kind enough to comment on drafts of changes to chapters.

Finally, I must thank the production staff at Mayfield Publishing Company, both for putting the book into its final form and for their help and their patience with me.
                                                                    —B. E. W.

1 BEHAVIORAL SCIENCE
Theory, Research, and Application

SCIENCE
Goals of Science
  Description
  Understanding
  Prediction
  Control
Key Values of Science
  Empiricism
  Skepticism
  Tentativeness
  Publicness
Scientific Approaches to
  Knowledge

THEORIES
Components of Theories
  Assumptions
  Hypothetical Constructs
  Definitions
  Propositions
Characteristics of Theories
  Specification
  Scope

Purposes of Theories
  Organizing Knowledge
  Extending Knowledge
  Guiding Action
Criteria for Evaluating Theories

RESEARCH
The Research Process
Evaluating Research
Inference in Research

THEORY, RESEARCH,
AND APPLICATION
The Interdependence of Theory,
  Research, and Application
The Uses of Behavioral Science
  Theory and Research

SUMMARY

QUESTIONS AND EXERCISES
FOR REVIEW

Why do people do what they do? How do biology, personality, personal history, growth and development, other people, and the environment affect the ways people think, feel, and behave? As you have learned from your other behavioral science courses, there are many ways to go about answering questions such as these, ranging from the casual observation of daily life that leads to the development of personal theories of behavior (for example, see Wegner & Vallacher, 1977) to systematic empirical observation leading to the development of formal theories of behavior. As you have also learned, the casual observation approach, also sometimes called "ordinary knowing" (Judd, Smith, & Kidder, 1991), is prone to errors that stem from basic cognitive processes (see, for example, Gilovich, 1991). Therefore, behavioral science takes the more systematic, scientific approach to knowing, which is designed to minimize the effects of these biases.

Behavioral science is composed of three interrelated aspects: research that generates knowledge, theory that organizes knowledge, and application that puts knowledge to use. Most scientists have a greater interest in one of these aspects than in the others (Mitroff & Kilmann, 1978). Nonetheless, complete development as a scientist requires an understanding of all three aspects (Belar & Perry, 1992). As the title of this book indicates, it will explore the research aspect of behavioral science in detail. But before doing so, this chapter will put research into context by reviewing the nature of science and theory, and by examining the interrelationships of research, theory, and application.

SCIENCE

Science is a systematic process for generating knowledge about the world. Three important aspects of science are the goals of science, key values of science, and perspectives on the best way in which science can go about generating knowledge.

Goals of Science

The behavioral sciences have four goals: the description, understanding, prediction, and control of behavior.

DESCRIPTION   As a goal of science, **description** has four aspects. First, it seeks to define the phenomena to be studied and to differentiate among phenomena. If you were interested in studying memory, for example, you would need to start by defining *memory*, by describing what you mean by that term. Do you mean the ability to pick out from a list something previously learned, as in a multiple-choice test, or the ability to recall something with minimal prompting, as in a short-answer test? Description is also used to differentiate among closely related phenomena, to be certain we are studying exactly what we want to study. Environmental psychologists, for example, distinguish between

(1) population density, the number of people per square meter of space, and (2) crowding, an unpleasant psychological state that can result from high population density (Stokols, 1972). High population density does not always lead to feelings of crowding. People who are feeling positive emotions rarely feel crowded in even very densely populated situations—think about the last time you were enjoying a large party in a small house. I return to this definitional aspect of the descriptive goal of science later, when I discuss the components of theories.

The third aspect of the descriptive goal of science is the recording of events that might be useful or interesting to study. Let's assume, for example, your friend has been in an automobile accident, there is a trial to determine liability, and you attend the trial to support your friend. As the trial progresses, something strikes you as interesting: Although four witnesses to the accident had equally good opportunities to see what happened, their memories of the event differ significantly. Two witnesses estimate the car was moving at 30 miles per hour (mph), whereas two others say one car was going about 40 mph when it hit the other car. This inconsistency piques your curiosity, so you attend other trials to see if such inconsistencies are common, and you find they are. You have now described a phenomenon: Eyewitnesses can produce very inconsistent descriptions of an event.

Finally, science works to describe the relationships among phenomena. Perhaps in your courtroom observations you notice that some kinds of questions lead to higher speed estimates than did other kinds of questions. This discovery of relationships among phenomena can help you understand why certain phenomena occur—the second goal of science.

UNDERSTANDING As a goal of science, **understanding** attempts to determine why a phenomenon occurs. For example, once you determine eyewitnesses can be inconsistent, you might want to know why the inconsistencies exist, what causes them. To start answering these questions, you might propose a set of **hypotheses,** or statements about possible causes for the inconsistencies, that you could then test to see which (if any) were correct. For example, given courtroom observations you might hypothesize that the manner in which a lawyer phrases a question might affect a witness's answer so that different ways of phrasing a question cause different, and therefore inconsistent, responses.

But how can you be sure a particular cause, such as question phrasing, has a particular effect, such as inconsistent answers? To deal with this question, the 19th-century philosopher John Stuart Mill developed three rules of, or conditions for, causality; the more closely a test of a hypothesis meets these conditions, the more confident you can be that the hypothesized cause had the observed effect. The first rule is **covariation:** The hypothesized cause must be consistently related to, or correlated with, the effect. In our example, we would want differences in question wording to be consistently related to differences in response. The second rule is **time precedence of the cause:** During the test of the hypothesis, the hypothesized cause must come before the effect. Although this principle seems obvious, you will see in the next chapter that some ways of doing research do not let us establish with certainty that a hypothesized cause did, in fact, come before the effect. The third rule is that there must be no **plausible alternative explanation** for the effect: The hypothesized cause must be the *only* possible cause present during the test of the hypothesis. For example, if you test your question-phrasing hypothesis by having one person phrase a question one way and another person phrase it another way, you have a problem. You have no way of knowing whether any response differences that you observe are caused by the different phrasings (your hypothesis) or by some difference between the people asking the question. For example, perhaps a friendly questioner elicits one kind of response, and an unfriendly questioner, another. In contrast, if the same person asks the question both ways, differences in personality cannot affect the answer given. Chapter 6 will address this problem of alternative explanations in more detail.

Bear these rules of causality closely in mind; they will play an important role in the discussions of research strategies in the next chapter and throughout this book. By the way, if you tested the question-phrasing hypothesis according to these rules, as did Loftus and Palmer (1974), you would find that question phrasing does affect responses. Loftus and Palmer had people watch a film of a moving car running into a parked car. Some of the people were asked how fast they thought the moving car was going when it "smashed" into the other car; other people were asked how fast it was going when it "contacted" the other car. The average speed estimate in response to the "smashed" question was 40.8 mph, whereas the average estimate in response to the "contacted" question was 31.8 mph.

The scientific goal of understanding also looks for relationships among the answers to "why" questions. For example, you might want to know how well your question-phrasing hypothesis fits more general principles of memory (Penrod, Loftus, & Winkler, 1982). An important aspect of scientific understanding is the derivation of general principles from specific observations. Thus, if a thirsty rat is given water after pressing a bar, it will press the bar again; if a hungry pigeon is given a food pellet after pecking a button, it will peck the button again; if a child is praised after putting dirty clothes in a laundry hamper, he or she will do so again. These diverse observations can be summarized with one general principle: Behavior that is rewarded will be repeated. Systems of such general principles are called *theories*, which are discussed later in this chapter. Once general principles are organized into theories, they can be applied to new situations.

PREDICTION   As a goal of science, **prediction** seeks to use our understanding of the causes of phenomena and the relationships among them to predict events. Scientific prediction takes two forms. One form is the forecasting of events. For example, the observed relationship between Graduate Record Examination (GRE) scores and academic performance during the first year of graduate school lets you predict, within a certain margin of error, students' first-year grades from their GRE scores (Educational Testing Service, 1981). When other variables known to be related to graduate school performance, such as undergraduate grade point average (GPA), are also considered, the margin of error is reduced (Goldberg, 1977). Notice that such predictions are made "within a certain margin of error." As you know from your own experience or that of friends, GRE scores and GPA are not perfect predictors of graduate school performance. Prediction in behavioral science deals best with the average outcome of a large number of people: "On the average," the better people do on the GRE, the better they do in graduate school. Prediction becomes much less precise when dealing with individual cases. However, despite their lack of perfection, the GRE (and other standardized tests) and GPA predict graduate school performance better than the alternatives that have been tried (Swets, Dawes, & Monahan, 2000).

The second form taken by scientific prediction is the derivation of research hypotheses from theories. For example, one theory of memory holds that people use information they already have stored in memory to understand, organize, and remember new information (Bransford, 1979). One hypothesis that can be derived from this theory is that people better remember information if they are first given a context that helps them understand it. As an example, consider this sentence: "The haystack was important because the cloth ripped." How meaningful and understandable is that sentence as it stands alone? Now put it in this context: The cloth was the canopy of a parachute. Bransford and his colleagues predicted, on the basis of this theory, that people would be better able to understand and remember new oral, pictorial, and written information, especially ambiguous information, when they were first given a context for it. The experiments they conducted confirmed their hypothesis and thus supported the theory (Bransford, 1979).

This process of hypothesis derivation and testing is important because it tests the validity of the theory on which the hypothesis is based. Ensuring the validity of theories is important because theories are frequently applied in order to influence behavior. If the theory is not valid, the influence attempt will not have the intended effect and could even be harmful.

CONTROL   As a goal of science, **control** seeks to use knowledge to influence phenomena. Thus, practitioners in a number of fields use the principles of behavioral science to influence human behavior. The capability to use behavioral science knowledge to control behavior raises the question of whether we *should* try to control it and, if so, what means we should use. Behavioral scientists have discussed these questions continually since Carl Rogers and B. F. Skinner (1956) first debated them. It is because these questions have no simple answers that all fields of applied behavioral science require students to take professional ethics courses.

Key Values of Science

To achieve its goal of generating knowledge that can be used to describe, understand, predict, and control the world, science needs a way to get there. Value systems reflect traits or characteristics that groups of people hold especially important in achieving their goals. Americans, for example, generally value equality of opportunity (versus class structure) and freedom of individual action (versus government control) as ways of achieving the goal of a good society (Rokeach, 1973). Modern American science tends to value four traits or characteristics that lead to the generation of valid knowledge: Science should be empirical, skeptical, tentative, and public. These values are reflected in the way scientists go about their work. When you think about these values, bear in mind that values are ideals, and so are not always enacted — although we *should* always strive to enact them. Scientists are human, and our human natures occasionally lead us to fall short of our ideals.

EMPIRICISM   The principle of **empiricism** holds that all decisions about what constitutes knowledge are based on objective evidence rather than ideology or abstract logic; when evidence and ideology conflict, evidence should prevail. As an example, let's assume you're a school administrator and must choose between two new reading improvement programs, one of which is consistent with your philosophy of education and the other of which is not. In an empirical approach to choosing between the two programs, you set criteria for evaluating the programs, collect information about how well each program meets the criteria, and choose the one that better meets the criteria. In an ideological approach, you choose the one that best fits your philosophy of education, without seeking evidence about how well it works compared to its competitor. In conducting research, scientists seek evidence concerning the correctness or incorrectness of their theories. In the absence of evidence, the scientist withholds judgment.

The principle of empiricism also holds that all evidence must be objective. To be objective, evidence must be collected in a way that minimizes bias, even accidental bias. The rules for conducting research laid out throughout this book explain how to minimize bias.

SKEPTICISM   The principle of **skepticism** means scientists should always be questioning the quality of the knowledge they have on a topic, asking questions such as, Is there evidence to support this theory or principle? How good is that evidence? Was the research that collected the evidence properly conducted? Is the evidence complete? Have the researchers overlooked any evidence or failed to collect some kinds of evidence bearing on the topic? The purpose of such questions is not to hector the people conducting the research but, rather, to ensure that the theories that describe knowledge are as complete and correct as possible. Consequently, scientists want to see research findings verified before accepting them as correct. This insistence on verification sometimes slows the acceptance of new principles, but it also works to prevent premature acceptance of erroneous results.

TENTATIVENESS   For the scientist, knowledge is tentative and so can change as new evidence becomes available. A principle we consider correct today, we may consider incorrect tomorrow if new evidence appears. This principle grows directly out of the first two: We keep checking the evidence (skepticism), and we give new, valid evidence priority over theory (empiricism). For example, it was long accepted in social psychology that women were more likely than men to change their personal opinions to reflect the opinions of a group to which they belonged. However, when Eagly and Carli (1981) reexamined the evidence, they found the supposed sex difference was really due to gender-based differences in knowledge about the topics used. They found that both men and women were more likely to conform to the group position on topics they knew little about and that most conformity research used opinions on topics, such as professional sports, about which women usually knew less than did men. Consequently, women seemed more likely to conform to group opinion. Social psychologists recognized the validity of the new evidence and now hold that there are no sex differences in conformity.

PUBLICNESS   Finally, science is **public.** Scientists not only make public what they find in their research, but also make public how they conduct their research. This principle has three beneficial effects. First, conducting research in public lets people use the results of research. Second, it lets scientists check the validity of others' research by examining how the research was carried out, as Eagly and Carli did in the example just given. One reason why research reports in scientific journals have such long Method sections is to present the research procedures in enough detail that other scientists can examine them for possible flaws. Third, it lets other scientists replicate, or repeat, the research to see if they get the same results. The outcomes of all behavioral science research are subject to the influence of random error; sometimes that error works so as to confirm a hypothesis. Because the error is random, replication studies should not get the original results and so should reveal the error. Replication can also help detect instances when scientists are overly optimistic in interpreting their research. One example is the case of the chemists who thought they had fused hydrogen atoms at a low temperature—an impossibility, according to current atomic theory. No one could replicate these results, which were finally attributed to poor research procedures (Rousseau, 1992). I discuss replication research in Chapter 4.

Scientific Approaches to Knowledge

The picture of science presented by the goals and values just described represents the dominant view of what science is and how it is conducted. A set of beliefs about the nature of science (and of knowledge in general) is called an **epistemology.** The dominant epistemological position in modern American science is **logical positivism.** Logical positivism holds that knowledge can best be generated through empirical observation, tightly controlled experiments, and logical analysis of data. It also says that scientists must be disinterested observers of nature who are emotionally distant from what or whom they study, and who generate knowledge for its own sake without concern for whether the knowledge is useful or how it might be used.

A contrasting view of science, especially of the social and behavioral sciences, is the **humanistic perspective.** The humanistic epistemology holds that science should produce knowledge that serves people, not just knowledge for its own sake; that people are best understood when studied in their natural environments rather than when isolated in laboratories; and that a full understanding of people comes through empathy and intuition rather than logical analysis and "dust bowl empiricism." Some contrasts between the logical positivist and humanistic epistemologies are summarized in Table 1-1.

An awareness of these differing epistemologies is important for several reasons. First, some of you are epistemological humanists (even though you may not have defined yourselves that way) and so believe that behavioral science research as conducted today can tell you little about people that is useful. Nonetheless, because logical positivism is the dominant epistemology, you should understand its strengths and weaknesses and be able to interpret the results of the research it generates. I personally believe that both approaches to research are useful and mutually reinforcing. As a result, this book goes beyond the laboratory experiment in describing how to do research.

The second reason an awareness of these two epistemologies is important is that your epistemology determines your opinions about which theories are valid, what kinds of research questions are important, the best way to carry out research, and the proper interpretation of data (see, for example, Diesing, 1991). Behavioral scientists vary greatly in epistemological viewpoints (Kimble, 1984; Krasner & Houts, 1984), thus providing

TABLE 1-1   Some Contrasts Between the Logical Positivist and Humanistic Views of Science

Logical Positivism	Humanism
Scientists' personal beliefs and values have no effect on science.	Personal beliefs and values strongly affect theory, choice of research topics and methods, and interpretation of results.
Knowledge is sought for its own sake; utility is irrelevant.	Research that does not generate directly applicable knowledge is wasteful.
Science aims to generate knowledge that applies to all people.	Science should aim to help people achieve self-determination.
Phenomena should be studied in isolation, free from the effects of "nuisance" variables.	Phenomena should be studied in their natural contexts. There are no such things as "nuisance" variables; all variables in the context are relevant.
Scientific inquiry must be carefully controlled, as in the traditional experiment.	Science should seek naturalism even at the cost of giving up control.
A brief, time-limited inquiry is sufficient to generate knowledge.	Research should be carried out in depth through the use of case studies.
The scientist should be emotionally distant from the people studied.	The scientist should be emotionally engaged with the people studied.
The scientist is the expert and is best able to design and interpret the results of research.	The research participants are the experts and should be full partners in research that touches their lives.
There is only one correct interpretation of scientific data.	The same data can be interpreted in many ways.
Scientific knowledge accurately represents the true state of the world.	Scientific knowledge represents the aspects and interpretations of the true state of the world that best serve the interests of the status quo.

ample opportunity to disagree about these issues. Such disagreements are not easily resolved. Personal epistemologies are closely related to culture, personality, and personal background (Mitroff & Kilmann, 1978; Riger, 1992), so individuals tend to see their own epistemologies as the only valid ones.

Finally, an awareness of the humanistic epistemology is important because it is playing a growing role in behavioral science research. Humanistic epistemology plays an important part in feminist critiques of the validity of behavioral science research (summarized by Riger, 1992), which are having an increasing impact on standards for the proper conduct of research (for example, see McHugh, Koeske, & Frieze, 1986). I will discuss issues raised by these critiques throughout this book.

THEORIES

The goals of behavioral science include the description, understanding, prediction, and control of behavior. A primary tool that behavioral scientists use to achieve these goals is theory. A **theory** is a set of statements about relationships between variables. Usually, these variables are abstract concepts (such as memory) rather than concrete objects or concrete attributes of objects (such as the length of a list to be memorized). In a scientific theory, most of the statements have either been verified by research or are potentially verifiable. There are four aspects of theories: their components, their characteristics, their purposes, and criteria for evaluating them.

Components of Theories

Chafetz (1978) notes that theories have three components: assumptions, hypothetical constructs and their definitions, and propositions. Let's examine each.

ASSUMPTIONS   Theoretical **assumptions** are beliefs that are taken as given and are usually not subject to empirical testing. Theorists make assumptions for two reasons: Either something cannot be subject to testing, such as assumptions about the nature of reality, or the present state of research technology does not allow something to be tested, such as assumptions about human nature. Assumptions that fall into this second category can, and should, be tested when advances in technology permit. To take an example from biology, Mendel's theory of heredity postulated the existence of genes, an assumption that technology has only recently allowed to be tested and verified. Theories include three types of assumptions: general scientific assumptions, paradigmatic assumptions, and domain assumptions.

General scientific assumptions deal with the nature of reality. Theorists and scientists in general must assume there is an objective reality that exists separately from individuals' subjective beliefs; if there were no reality, there would be nothing to study. Science must also assume people can know and understand that reality with reasonable accuracy; if people could not, science would be, by definition, impossible. The development of theory also assumes there is order to reality; that is, events do not happen randomly. A related assumption is that events have causes and it is possible to identify these causes and the processes by which they have their effects. These assumptions are not very esoteric. If you think about it, it would be impossible to conduct one's daily life without making these assumptions: We assume everyone experiences the same reality that we do and that most events in our lives have causes we can discover, understand, and often control.

Paradigmatic assumptions derive from **paradigms,** or general ways of conceptualizing and studying the subject matter of a particular scientific field. For example, logical positivism and humanism represent different paradigms for the study of human behavior, the former assuming that objective observation is the best route to valid knowledge, the latter assuming that subjective empathy and intuition represent the best route. Other paradigms in psychology make differing assumptions about human nature (Nye, 1999). Psychoanalytic theory, for example, assumes human nature (as represented by the id) is inherently bad and must be controlled by society; humanism assumes human nature is inherently good and should be free to express itself; and behaviorism assumes human nature is inherently neither good nor bad, that all behavior is shaped by environmental influences. Adherents of different paradigms are often at odds with one another because they are working from different assumptions; because assumptions are usually not testable, these differences cannot be resolved. Even when assumptions are testable, paradigmatic disagreements about how to test them and how to interpret the results of the tests can leave the issue unresolved (for example, see Pyke & Agnew, 1991).

Domain assumptions are specific to the domain, or subject, of a theory, such as psychopathology, memory, or work behavior. For example, Locke and Latham (1990) have developed a theory that focuses on the effects performance goals have on the quality of work performance, based on the general proposition that more difficult goals lead to better performance. Their theory makes several explicit assumptions, including the assumptions that most human activity is goal directed, that people are conscious of and think about their goals, and that people's goals influence how well they perform their work. Domain assumptions are not always explicit. In the domain of sex differences, for example, psychologists long implicitly assumed that male behavior was the pattern by which all human behavior should be judged; anything that did not fit the male pattern was "deviant" (Basow, 1992; Unger & Crawford, 1992). Domain assumptions, especially implicit domain assumptions, often reflect the cultural norms surrounding the subject of the theory and the personal beliefs of the theorist. Consequently they permeate a theory, shaping the content of the theory, the ways in which research on the theory is conducted, and how the results of the research are interpreted. As an example, consider these comments made by a researcher who studied an old-age community:

> As a person of a different age and social class, and as a sociologist, my perspective differed from [that of the community residents]. I thought that, as welfare recipients, they were poor; they thought they were "average." I initially felt that there was something sad about old people living together and that this was a social problem. They did not feel a bit sad about living together as old people, and although they felt that they *had* problems, they did not think that they *were* one. (Hochschild, 1973, p. 5)

Because of the problems engendered by implicit assumptions, it is important when reading about a theory to carefully separate aspects of the theory that are based on research, and therefore have evidence to support them, from those based on assumptions, and not to take assumptions as established fact.

HYPOTHETICAL CONSTRUCTS   Theories, as noted, consist of statements about the relationships between variables. The term **variable** refers to any thing or concept that can take on more than one value. Variables can be concrete in form, such as the size of an object, or they can be abstract concepts, such as personality. The abstract concepts are called **hypothetical constructs.** Hypothetical constructs are terms invented (that is, constructed) to refer to variables that cannot be directly observed (and may or may not really exist), but are useful because we can attribute observable behaviors to them. The personality trait of hostility, for example, is a hypothetical construct: It cannot be directly observed, but it does represent the concept that people can show consistent patterns of related behaviors. These behaviors—such as cutting remarks, use of physical and verbal coercion, expressed pleasure in the suffering of others, and so forth—can be directly observed. Psychologists therefore invented the term *hostility* to use in theories of personality to represent whatever inside the person (as opposed to situational factors) is causing these behaviors. However, because we cannot observe hostility directly— only the behaviors attributed to it—we hypothesize that hostility exists, but we cannot demonstrate its existence with certainty.

Kimble (1989) notes that scientists must be careful to avoid two pitfalls that can arise when they use hypothetical constructs. The first is reification: treating a hypothetical construct as something real rather than as a convenient term for an entity or process whose existence is merely hypothesized, not necessarily known with certainty. It is a fallacy to assume that

> if there is a word for [a concept] in the dictionary, a corresponding item of physical or psychological reality must exist, and the major task of science is to discover the a priori meanings of these linguistic givens. On the current psychological scene, this foolish assumption gives rise to ill-conceived attempts to decide what motives, intelligence, personality, and cognition "really are." (Kimble, 1989, p. 495)

The second pitfall is related to the first. Because hypothetical constructs might not really exist, they cannot be used as explanations for behavior:

> If someone says that a man has hallucinations, withdraws from society, lives in his own world, has extremely unusual associations, and reacts without emotion to imaginary catastrophes because he is schizophrenic, it is important to understand that the word *because* has been misused. The symptomatology defines (diagnoses) schizophrenia. The symptoms and the "cause" are identical. The "explanation" is circular and not an explanation at all. (Kimble, 1989, p. 495)

The continued use of a hypothetical construct depends on its usefulness. When a construct is no longer useful as it stands, it will be modified or will be discarded. For example, a popular topic of research in the 1970s was "fear of success," postulated to be a personality trait that prevented people from doing well because they were predisposed to see success as having negative consequences. Research, however, was unable to validate fear of success as a personality trait. As a result, it has gone out of use (see Basow, 1992, for a brief review of this topic).

The hypothetical constructs used in theories can be either simple or complex. Simple constructs are composed of only a single component and are referred to as being **unidimensional;** complex constructs are made up of two or more independent components and are called **multidimensional.** Let's examine this distinction by looking at the ways two theories treat the construct of leadership style. Fiedler's (1967) contingency theory views leadership style as a unidimensional construct: People's leadership styles vary along a single dimension—Figure 1-1(a). At one end of the dimension are leaders who are task oriented; their main concern is getting the job done. At the other end of the dimension are leaders who are relationship oriented; their main concern is maintaining good relationships among the group members. The unidimensional nature of Fiedler's conceptualization of the leadership style construct means that a person can score either high on task motivation or high on relationship motivation, but cannot score high on both simultaneously. To score high on one form of motivation, a person *must* score low on the other: The two styles are mutually exclusive.

The Ohio State theory of leadership (Stogdill & Coons, 1957), in contrast, views task motivation and relationship motivation as independent (uncorrelated) dimensions of leadership style—Figure 1-1(b). Because of this multidimensionality in the Ohio State theory, a person can score high on one dimension and low on the other (as in Fiedler's theory), but a person could also be conceptualized as being high on both dimensions simultaneously (that is, concerned with both the task and interpersonal relationships)

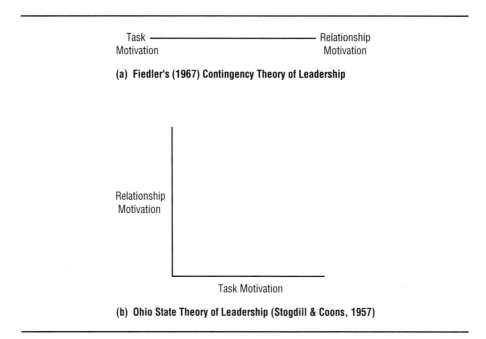

(a) Fiedler's (1967) Contingency Theory of Leadership

(b) Ohio State Theory of Leadership (Stogdill & Coons, 1957)

FIGURE 1-1   Unidimensional and Multidimensional Theories of Leadership Style
Fiedler's unidimensional contingency theory (a) holds that task motivation and relationship motivation are opposite ends of a single dimension: A person who is high on one must be low on the other. The multidimensional Ohio State theory (b) holds that task motivation and relationship motivation are independent: A person
can be high on both, low on both, or high on one and low on the other.

or low on both simultaneously. These differing views on the number of dimensions underlying the construct of leadership style affect how research on leadership is conducted
and how leadership training is carried out. For example, research on the Ohio State theory requires that leaders be placed into one of four categories, whereas Fiedler's theory
requires only two. When conducting leadership training, adherents of the two-dimen-
sional view of leadership style try to train leaders to score high on both dimensions; however, because adherents of the one-dimensional view believe it is impossible to score high
on both dimensions simultaneously, they train leaders to make the most effective use of
their existing styles (F. J. Landy, 1989).

Carver (1989) distinguishes a subcategory of multidimensional constructs that he
calls **multifaceted constructs.** Unlike the dimensions of a multidimensional construct,
which are considered independent, those of a multifaceted construct are considered
correlated. Because the facets of a multifaceted construct are correlated, the distinctions
among facets are sometimes ignored, and the construct is treated as unidimensional.
But treating such constructs as unidimensional can lead to mistakes in interpreting research results. For example, if only some facets of a multifaceted construct are related
to another variable, the importance of those facets will remain undiscovered. Consider
the Type A behavior pattern, which is related to heart disease. The Type A construct
includes competitiveness, hostility, impatience, and job involvement. An overall index

of Type A behavior composed of people's scores on these four facets has an average correlation of .14 with the onset of heart disease. However, scores on competitiveness and hostility have average correlations of .20 and .16, respectively, whereas scores on impatience and job involvement have average correlations of only .09 and .03 (Booth-Kewley & Friedman, 1987). The first two facets therefore determine the correlation found for the overall index, but if you just looked at the overall correlation, you would not know that. This situation is analogous to one in which four students work on a group project but only two people do most of the work. Because the outcome is treated as the group's product, the instructor doesn't know the relative contributions of the individual group members. I discuss problems related to research with multidimensional and multifaceted constructs in more detail in Chapters 5 and 8.

DEFINITIONS   An important component of a theory is the definition of its constructs. A theory must carefully define its constructs so that people who use the theory can completely understand the concepts involved. Theories use two types of definitions. The first, narrative definition, explains the meaning of the construct in words. Narrative definitions are similar to dictionary definitions of abstract concepts, but can be much more extensive. For example, Locke and Latham (1990) use almost three pages to explain what their construct of "goal" means and to distinguish it from related terms. Definitions can also take the form of classification systems for multidimensional constructs, laying out the dimensions and the distinctions between the types of behaviors defined by various combinations of dimensions. As an example of the kinds of distinctions that can be made, Buss (1971) identified eight forms of aggression, based on whether the aggression is physical or verbal, active or passive, direct or indirect (see Table 1-2). Such distinctions are important because different forms of a variable can have different causes, effects, and correlates. Boys, for example, are more likely to engage in active and physical aggression, and girls, in passive and verbal aggression (Hyde, 1984).

Because hypothetical constructs are abstract, they cannot be used in research, which is concrete. We therefore must develop concrete representations of hypothetical constructs to use in research; these concrete representations are called **operational definitions.** A hypothetical construct can have any number of operational definitions. As Table 1-2 shows, aggression can be divided into at least eight categories, each represented by a variety of behaviors. Direct active physical aggression, for example, can be operationalized as physical blows, bursts of unpleasant noise, or electric shocks, and each of these could be further operationalized in terms of number, intensity, or frequency, for a total of at least nine operational definitions. Table 1-2 shows examples of operational definitions of the other forms of aggression. Because operational definitions represent hypothetical constructs in research, they must accurately represent the constructs. The problems involved in developing accurate operational definitions, or measures, of hypothetical constructs are considered in Chapters 5, 7, and 11.

PROPOSITIONS   As noted, theories consist of statements about relationships among hypothetical constructs; these statements are called **propositions.** Figure 1-2 shows some of the constructs (rectangles) and propositions (arrows) included in Locke and Latham's (1990) goal-setting theory of work performance. This part of the theory holds that the more difficult a work goal is, the more value people place on achieving the goal

TABLE 1-2   Forms of Aggression

The general concept of aggression can be divided into more specific concepts based on whether the aggressive behavior is active or passive, physical or verbal, direct or indirect.

PHYSICAL AGGRESSION

	Active Aggression	*Passive Aggression*
Direct Aggression	Punching someone	Standing in someone's way
Indirect Aggression	Playing a practical joke	Refusing to do something important

VERBAL AGGRESSION

	Active Aggression	*Passive Aggression*
Direct Aggression	Saying something to hurt someone	Refusing to speak to someone
Indirect Aggression	Malicious gossip	Refusing to give consent

Note: From Buss, 1971, p. 8.

(arrow 1 in Figure 1-2), but (2) more difficult goals also lead people to have lower expectations of achieving the goals. More valued work goals and higher expectations of success at the goals lead to higher levels of goal acceptance (3 and 4). Higher acceptance leads to higher work motivation (5), which combines with ability at the task to affect work performance (6 and 7). Propositions can describe either causal or noncausal relationships. A causal proposition holds that one construct causes another; Figure 1-2, for example, contains the proposition that goal acceptance causes work motivation. Noncausal propositions, in contrast, say two constructs are correlated, but not that one causes the other. Most theoretical propositions are causal.

Just as research cannot deal with hypothetical constructs but uses operational definitions to represent them, research also cannot directly test theoretical propositions but, rather, tests hypotheses about relationships among operational definitions. For example, as Figure 1-3 shows, the proposition that differences in goal value cause differences in goal acceptance (arrow 3 in Figure 1-2) can be operationalized as the hypothesis that people offered $20 for successful completion of a task will be more likely to say that they will work hard to succeed at the task than will people offered $1.

Variables can play several roles in theory and research. An **independent variable** is one that a theory proposes as a cause of another variable. In Figure 1-2, for example, goal difficulty is an independent variable because the theory proposes it as a cause of goal value and expected level of success. A **dependent variable** is caused by another variable. In the example just given, goal value and expected level of success are dependent variables. Note that the labels "independent" and "dependent" are relative, not absolute: Whether we call a variable independent or dependent depends on its relationship to other variables. In Figure 1-2, work motivation is a dependent variable relative to goal acceptance and an independent variable relative to level of performance.

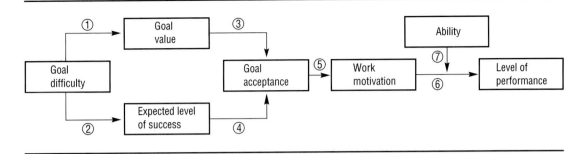

FIGURE 1-2 **Selected Variables From Locke and Latham's (1990) Goal-Setting Theory of Work Motivation**
More difficult goals lead to high goal value and lower success expectancies; higher goal value and high success expectancies lead to higher goal acceptance; higher goal acceptance leads to higher motivation; higher motivation combined with higher ability leads to better performance.

Theories may include **mediating variables,** which come between two other variables in a causal chain. In Figure 1-2, work motivation mediates the relationship between goal acceptance and work performance: The theory says goal acceptance causes work motivation, which then causes level of performance. Theories can also include **moderating variables,** which change or limit the relationship between an independent variable and a dependent variable. In Figure 1-2, ability moderates the effect of work motivation on performance; that is, the effect of work motivation on performance differs at different levels of ability. As shown in Table 1-3, the theory proposes that there is no effect of work motivation on performance when ability is low (no matter how hard people try, they cannot succeed unless they have a minimum level of ability), but when ability is high, high motivation leads to high performance and low motivation leads to low performance (even the most skilled people cannot succeed unless they try).

Characteristics of Theories

Theories can differ from one another on a variety of characteristics (Bordens & Abbott, 1999); two of them will concern us: how specific a theory is and its scope.

SPECIFICATION First, theories can differ on how well they are specified—that is, in how clearly they define their constructs and describe the proposed relationships between them. A well-specified theory can be stated as a list of propositions and corollaries (secondary relationships implied by the propositions), or it can be displayed in a diagram, as in Figure 1-2. A well-specified theory will also explicitly define all the hypothetical constructs included in it. In a poorly specified theory, there can be ambiguity about the meanings of constructs or about how the constructs are supposed to be related to one another. As we will see in later chapters, a poorly specified theory hinders the research process by making it difficult to construct valid measures of hypothetical constructs, derive hypotheses that test the theory, and interpret the results of research.

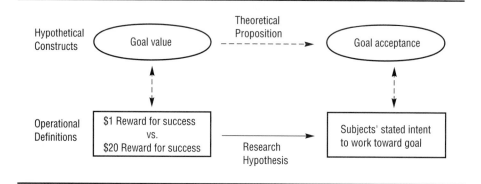

FIGURE 1-3   Relationship Between Theoretical Proposition and Research Hypothesis
The operational definitions are concrete representations of the theoretical propositions, and the research hypothesis is a concrete representation of the theoretical proposition.

SCOPE   A second way in which theories differ is in their scope: how much behavior they try to explain. Grand theories, such as psychoanalytic theory, try to explain all human behavior. However, most current psychological theories are narrower in scope, focusing on one aspect of behavior. Locke and Latham's (1990) theory, for example, deals solely with the determinants of work performance and, even more narrowly, with how work goals affect work performance. Narrow theories such as this do not attempt to deal with all the variables that could possibly affect the behavior they are concerned with; variables not directly involved in the theory are considered to be outside its scope. Figure 1-2, for example, includes only goal acceptance as a cause of work motivation. Many other factors affect work motivation; however, because these factors are not related to work goals, the focus of Locke and Latham's theory, they are considered to be outside the scope of the theory. These other factors do, however, fall within the scope of other theories.

A term sometimes used interchangeably with theory is **model.** However, the term *model* is also used more narrowly to describe the application of a general theoretical perspective to a more specific field of interest. For example, a theory in social psychology called *attribution theory* (Weiner, 1986) deals with how people interpret events they experience and how these interpretations affect behavior and emotion. The general principles of this theory have been used to develop more specific models of phenomena, such as helping behavior (Meyer & Mulherin, 1980), academic achievement (T. D. Wilson & Linville, 1982), and clinical depression (Abramson, Metalsky, & Alloy, 1989), that explain these phenomena in terms of the psychological processes the theory postulates.

Purposes of Theories

Theories serve three scientific purposes: organizing knowledge, extending knowledge, and guiding action. Let's examine these processes.

TABLE 1-3 Moderating Effect of Ability on the Relationship Between Work Motivation and Work Performance

Performance level is high only when *both* ability and motivation are high.

	High Ability	*Low Ability*
High Work Motivation	High work performance	Low work performance
Low Work Motivation	Low work performance	Low work performance

ORGANIZING KNOWLEDGE The process of organizing knowledge begins with two processes already examined. The first is specifying the scope of the theory—deciding what variables to include. As a theory develops, its scope may widen or narrow—usually the former. For example, Locke and Latham's (1990) theory began as a theory about the relationship of work goals to work performance, but was later expanded to include job satisfaction and job commitment. Once the scope of a theory is specified, its theorists must define and describe the variables it encompasses.

After theorists specify the scope of their theory and define its variables, they can develop general principles of behavior by identifying the common factors present in a set of observations. These common factors, such as the principle of reinforcement, are usually abstract concepts that represent the more concrete factors and relationships observed. For example, the abstract concept of reward represents such concrete factors as food, water, and praise. Theories then describe the relationships among the abstract concepts; these relationships are inferred, or deduced, from the relationships observed among the concrete behaviors. Thus, the abstract general principle that reward increases the likelihood of behavior is inferred from a set of observations of the relationships between specific concrete rewards and specific behaviors. Theories organize observations made in the course of everyday life as well as observations generated through research. Thus, many of the theories used in applied areas of psychology—such as counseling, clinical, industrial, and educational—originated in the experiences and observations of practitioners in the field.

EXTENDING KNOWLEDGE Once a theory is systematically laid out, it can be used to extend knowledge. Theories extend knowledge in three ways. The first is by using research results to modify the theory. When scientists test a theory, the results are seldom in complete accordance with its propositions. Sometimes the results completely contradict the theory; more often, they support some aspects of the theory but not others, or indicate that the theory works well under some conditions but not others. In any such case, the theory must be modified to reflect the research results, although sometimes modifications are not made until the results are verified. Modifications often require adding new variables to the theory to account for the research results.

Theories also extend knowledge by establishing linkages with other theories. As noted, most modern behavioral science theories are circumscribed in their scope: They focus on one aspect of human behavior. However, variables within the scope of one theory often overlap with variables in other theories, thus linking the theories. Such theories essentially comprise a theory of larger scope. For example, Figure 1-4 shows some linkages between the portion of Locke and Latham's (1990) theory shown in Figure 1-2 and other theories; some of these variables are also included in Locke and Latham's full theory. Linking theories in this way permits a better understanding of behavior.

Finally, theories can extend knowledge through the convergence of concepts: Theorists in one field borrow concepts developed from theories in other fields, thus linking knowledge across specialties. This process can be seen in the development of the attributional model of depression (Abramson, Seligman, & Teasdale, 1978), illustrated in Figure 1-5. One origin of the model was in animal research and classical conditioning: Dogs exposed to inescapable electrical shocks eventually gave up trying to escape the shocks, showing a lack of effort to escape (M. E. P. Seligman, 1975). These results were generalized to humans in experiments in verbal learning: Repeated failure at a task led to a lack of effort at the task, and participants reported that they felt little motivation to continue, felt helpless to control their levels of performance, and felt sad about their performance (M. E. P. Seligman, 1975). Seligman pointed out that these outcomes reflected, at a greatly reduced level, symptoms of clinical depression: Depressed people see themselves as failures, have low levels of motivation, and feel chronically sad. Seligman suggested one source of depression might be a feeling he called "learned helplessness," induced by a series of negative life events or failures.

The second origin of the model was in research on achievement motivation and social cognition. Research on achievement motivation found that people respond differently to failure at a task: Some people try harder to succeed at the task the next time they attempt it, whereas others give up. Social cognition researchers study, among other topics, how people understand cause-and-effect relationships in their lives. Their research suggested that differences in response to failure were a result of how people interpreted why they failed: People who see themselves as causing the failure and who see no likelihood of improvement show a lack of effort at the task, report low motivation to continue working at the task, and feel sad (Weiner, 1986). Abramson et al. (1978) suggested that learned helplessness resulted from the way people interpreted negative events in their lives. People who characteristically attribute the causes of negative life events to unchangeable factors within themselves (such as personality) are more likely to become depressed than people who attribute the events to factors outside themselves or who see a likelihood of change. This model therefore took concepts from five different areas of psychology—animal learning, human learning, clinical psychology, social cognition, and achievement motivation—and drew them together into a single model of depression (see Abramson et al., 1989, for a more recent version of the model).

These processes of knowledge extension point out an important characteristic of scientific knowledge: It is cumulative. Scientific knowledge normally grows slowly through the addition of new knowledge from research and theorizing that is grounded in and linked to existing knowledge. As Sir Isaac Newton is said to have remarked several centuries ago, "If I see farther than those who came before me, it is because I stand on the shoulders of giants." Although scientific knowledge normally grows slowly, sometimes a new theoretical perspective can radically and quickly change the way a field of knowledge conceptualizes its subject matter and the way it carries out research (Kuhn, 1970). For example, Newton and Albert Einstein radically changed the ways in which the scientists of their time viewed the structure and processes of the physical world.

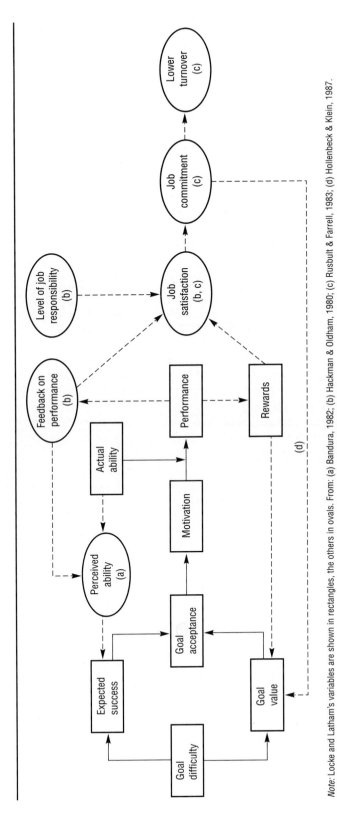

FIGURE 1-4 Connections Between Variables in Locke and Latham's (1990) Goal-Setting Theory and Variables in Other Theories
One can often broaden the scope of a theory by identifying how it overlaps with other theories.

Note: Locke and Latham's variables are shown in rectangles, the others in ovals. From: (a) Bandura, 1982; (b) Hackman & Oldham, 1980; (c) Rusbult & Farrell, 1983; (d) Hollenbeck & Klein, 1987.

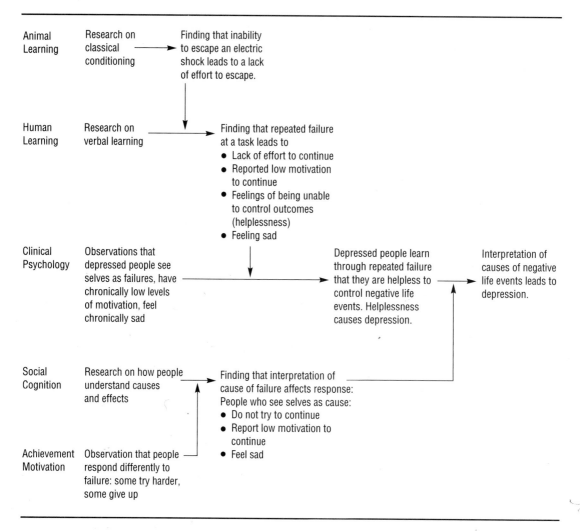

FIGURE 1-5   Convergence of Theories Into Abramson, Seligman, and Teasdale's (1978) Attributional Model of Depression

GUIDING ACTION   The third purpose of theories is to guide action. Thus, theories of work performance can be used to understand why productivity in a factory is low (perhaps the workers do not accept the work goals) and to devise ways of increasing productivity (perhaps by increasing goal value). The same theory can be used to predict how the level of productivity in a factory would change if changes were made in any of the variables within the scope of the theory, and these predictions could be used to anticipate the consequences of policy changes. However, before we apply theories, we want to be sure their propositions accurately describe the relationships among the variables. This is why we derive hypotheses from theories and test them: We want to ensure our theories are effective before we use them to change people's behavior or psychological states.

Notice how theories incorporate the four goals of science. Theories define variables and describe the relationships among them. These descriptions of relationships can be used to understand why behaviors occur, to predict what will happen given the degree to which the variables are active in a situation, and to control what happens in a situation by manipulating the levels of the relevant variables.

Criteria for Evaluating Theories

If you were to review the textbooks produced over the past, say, 30 years in any field of behavioral science, you would notice that some theories appear, are influential for a while, but then disappear, whereas others hold up over time. The latter theories are presumably better than the former. What makes a theory good? Shaw and Costanzo (1982) present eight criteria for a good theory, three they consider essential and five that are desirable.

The three essential criteria are logical consistency, falsifiability, and agreement with known data. *Logical consistency* simply means that the theory does not contradict itself. We would not, for example, want a theory of memory that says in one place that a particular set of conditions improves memory, and in another place says that the same conditions hurt memory. *Falsifiability* means you can derive hypotheses that can be examined in research to see if they are incorrect (Popper, 1959). Notice that we test theories to see if they are wrong, not to see if they are correct. It would be impossible to show unequivocally that a theory is true because you could always postulate a set of circumstances under which it might not be true. To prove that a theory is absolutely true, you would have to show that it works for all people under all possible circumstances; such a demonstration would be impossible to carry out. In contrast, one unequivocal demonstration that a hypothesis is incorrect means the theory from which it is derived is incorrect, at least under the conditions of that piece of research. *Agreement with known data* means the theory can explain data that already exist within the scope of the theory, even if the data weren't collected specifically to test the theory. No theory can perfectly account for all relevant data, but the more it does account for, the better it is.

Three desirable characteristics of a theory are clarity, parsimony, and consistency with related theories. A *clear* theory is well specified: Its definitions of constructs and its propositions are stated unambiguously, and the derivation of research hypotheses is straightforward. If a theory has clear propositions, it is also easy to evaluate against the necessary criteria of logical consistency, falsifiability, and agreement with known data. *Parsimony* means the theory is not unnecessarily complicated, that it uses no more constructs and propositions than are absolutely necessary to explain the behavior it encompasses. A parsimonious theory is also likely to be clear. Because most modern behavioral science theories tend to be limited in scope, they should be consistent with related theories. Although a theory that contradicts a related theory is not necessarily wrong (the problem might lie with the other theory), theories that can be easily integrated expand our overall knowledge and understanding of behavior.

It is also desirable for a theory to be useful in the following two ways. First, it should be applicable to the real world, helping us understand the processes involved in people's everyday lives. For example, psychological theories can help us understand how people acquire information and use it to make decisions (Gilovich, 1991) and they can help engineers design products that are more "user-friendly" (Norman, 1988). Second, a theory should stimulate research, not only basic research to test the theory, but also applied research to put the theory into use, and should inspire new discoveries. This inspiration can spring from dislike of as well as adherence to a theory; for example, much current knowledge of the psychology of women comes from research conducted because existing theories did not adequately deal with the realities of women's lives (Unger & Crawford, 1992).

RESEARCH

Having considered the nature of science and of theory, let us now take an overview of one way in which science and theory come together—in research. The term *research* can be used in two ways. The way I will use it most often in this book is to refer to empirical research, the process of collecting data by observing behavior. The second way in which *research* is used is to refer to theoretical or library research, the process of reviewing previous work on a topic in order to develop an empirical research project, draw conclusions from a body of empirical research, or formulate a theory. Chapter 16 discusses this form of research. The focus here will be on two topics that are explored in depth in this book: the empirical research process and criteria for evaluating empirical research.

The Research Process

The process of conducting research can be divided into five steps. The first step is developing an idea for research and refining it into a testable hypothesis. As we will see in Chapters 4 and 5, this step involves choosing a broad topic (such as the effect of television on children's behavior), narrowing the topic to a specific hypothesis (such as "Helpful TV characters promote helping behavior in children"), operationally defining hypothetical constructs ("helpful TV characters" and "helping behavior"), and, finally, making a specific prediction about the outcome of the study ("Children who watch a TV episode in which an adult character helps another adult character pick up books dropped by the second adult will be more likely to help a child pick up books dropped by another child than will a child who sees an adult TV character walk past the character who dropped books"). Chapter 4 discusses the process of and issues involved in formulating research questions, and Chapter 5 discusses operational definition as a measurement process.

The second step in the research process is choosing a research strategy. Chapter 2 previews the three main research strategies—case study research, correlational research, and experimental research—and Chapters 7 through 11 cover them in depth. The third step is data collection. The data collection process is covered in Chapter 12, and the crucial issue of collecting data ethically is discussed in Chapter 3. Once the data are in, the next step is data analysis and interpreting the results of the analysis. Because this is not a statistics book, I touch on data analysis only occasionally in the context of specific research strategies. However, Chapters 13 and 14 discuss some important issues in the meaningful interpretation of research results. Finally, the results of research must be communicated to other researchers and practitioners; Chapter 17 covers some aspects of this communication process.

Evaluating Research

What makes research good? T. D. Cook and Campbell (1979) present four criteria for evaluating how well behavioral science research is carried out—the validity of the research. **Construct validity** deals with the adequacy of operational definitions: Did the procedures used to concretely represent the hypothetical constructs studied in the research correctly represent those constructs? For example, does a score on a multiple-choice test really represent what we mean by the hypothetical construct of memory? If it doesn't, can we trust the results of a study of memory that operationally defined the construct in terms of the results of a multiple-choice test? Chapter 5 discusses construct validity in more detail.

    Internal validity deals with the degree to which the design of a piece of research ensures that the *only* possible explanation for the results is the effect of the independent variable. For example, young men tend to score better than young women on tests of advanced math skills. Although one might be tempted to explain this difference in biological terms, a number of other factors could explain the results, including the nature of the math test, the number of math courses taken in school, self-confidence in math ability, and expectations about how well one is supposed to do in math (see Unger & Crawford, 1992, for a summary of this research). To the extent that a study of sex differences allows these factors to influence its results, it lacks internal validity. Chapter 6 discusses internal validity, and Chapters 7 through 10 discuss its application to the research strategies.

    Statistical conclusion validity deals with the proper use and interpretation of statistics. Most statistical tests, for example, are based on assumptions about the nature of the data to which they are applied; one such assumption for some tests is that the distribution of the data follows a normal curve. If the assumptions underlying a statistical test are violated, conclusions drawn on the basis of the test could be invalid. Chapter 13 discusses some aspects of the interpretation of the outcome of statistical tests.

    External validity deals with the question of whether the results of a particular study would hold up under new conditions. For example, if you conducted a study using students at college A as subjects and repeated it exactly with students from college B, you would expect to get the same results. If you did, you would have demonstrated one aspect of the external validity of the study: The results hold across samples of college students. There are many aspects to external validity, and it is a controversial topic; Chapter 14 discusses it in detail.

Inference in Research

Let's pause for a moment to examine an issue that has been implicit in the discussion up to this point. That is the issue of the role of **inference** in psychological research. In conducting research, we observe the relationships between operational definitions of hypothetical constructs and then *infer*, or draw conclusions about, the nature of the unobservable relationship between the constructs based on the observed relationship between the operational definitions. For example, if you conducted the study on the effect of goal value on goal acceptance illustrated in Figure 1-3, the inferences you would make are shown by the broken lines. You would infer that the operational definitions represent the hypothetical constructs, and if you found that a higher reward led to a stronger stated intent to work toward the goal, you would infer that higher goal value leads to higher goal acceptance. Note that you cannot know with certainty that goal value leads to goal acceptance because you cannot directly observe that relationship; you can only draw the conclusion that goal value leads to goal acceptance because of what you know about the directly observed relationship between the operational definitions.

Scientific knowledge is tentative because it is based on inference; in any piece of research, your inferences might be faulty. In the study illustrated in Figure 1-3, for example, you might erroneously infer that the operational definitions correctly represented your hypothetical constructs when, in fact, they did not (a lack of construct validity). You might erroneously infer that a relationship exists between the two variables being studied when, in fact, there is none (a lack of statistical conclusion validity). You might erroneously infer that reward level was the only possible cause of goal acceptance in the study when, in fact, other possible causes were present (a lack of internal validity). Or, you might erroneously infer that the relationship you observed is true for all situations, not just the one in which you observed it (a lack of external validity). To the extent that you take steps to ensure the validity of your research and verify the results of research, you can have confidence in the conclusions that your theories represent. Nevertheless, you must keep the inferential and tentative nature of psychological knowledge constantly in mind. To do otherwise is to risk overlooking the need to revise theory and practice in the light of new knowledge, thereby perpetuating error.

THEORY, RESEARCH, AND APPLICATION

Also implicit in the discussion so far has been the idea that the scientific goals of describing, understanding, predicting, and controlling behavior induce an ineluctable relationship among theory, research, and application in the behavioral sciences. Let us conclude this chapter by summarizing that relationship.

The Interdependence of Theory, Research, and Application

The relationship between theory and research, as shown in Figure 1-6, has two aspects. The *deductive* aspect derives hypotheses from a theory to test the theory. The *inductive* aspect uses the results from tests of a theory and from other research to verify the propositions of the theory and modify it as necessary—failures to confirm a theory often suggest refinements and modifications to improve it. Figure 1-6 also shows that related theories can be used to revise, improve, and expand the theory that interests us, just as Locke and Latham's (1990) theory of work performance ties in with Hackman and Old-

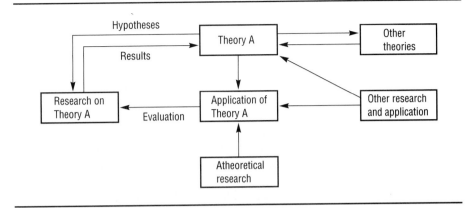

FIGURE 1-6 Interdependence of Theory, Research, and Application
Theory directs research and is modified as a result of research and of evaluations of applications of theory. Applications of a theory are also affected by atheoretical research and research based on other theories in the field of application. A theory may also be modified in light of other theories and the results of research on those theories.

ham's (1980) theory of work motivation and Rusbult and Farrell's (1983) theory of employee turnover (recall Figure 1-4).

The application of behavioral science takes tested theory and puts it to use. Research can evaluate the effectiveness of the application to test how well the theory works in the setting in which it is being applied. That information can also be used to improve the theory; an application failure would indicate that the theory's utility might be limited to certain situations. Research can also be used to gather useful data that are not based on theory. Architects and interior designers, for example, can use information about people's preferences for room lighting levels and for the size and placement of windows to provide more appealing indoor environments (Butler & Biner, 1987). Research can also test the validity of assumptions made by practitioners in behavioral science and other fields. The American legal system, for example, makes assumptions about eyewitnesses' perceptual processes and memory, about how jurors perceive and evaluate witnesses' testimony, about the efficacy of the persuasive tactics used by attorneys, and about jurors' individual and group decision-making processes. Research can test the validity of all these assumptions (Saks & Hastie, 1978).

The Uses of Behavioral Science
Theory and Research

Dooley (1995) suggests that behavioral science research and theory can be used in three ways: personally, professionally, and politically. The personal use of theory and research is in our own lives. We can, for example, use theory to understand the social world we inhabit: Theories of personality and social behavior can help us understand why people

TABLE 1-4   Examples of Applied Issues in Industrial Psychology That Are Related to Other Areas of Psychology

Issue	Area
How can equipment be designed to match human information-processing capabilities?	Cognitive
How do work groups influence work performance?	Social
How can people be motivated to work harder and perform better?	Motivation
What is the best way to teach job skills?	Learning
What kinds of warning signals are most effective?	Sensation and Perception
How can tests be designed to select the most qualified workers?	Psychometrics

act the way they do, and cognitive theories can help us understand why people make decisions we may think are foolish. We can use the scientific perspective to evaluate products and services that people try to persuade us to buy. For example, if a fitness center claims its programs improve psychological as well as physical well-being, the scientific perspective suggests questions we can ask to evaluate the claim of psychological benefit: What evidence supports the claim? How good is the evidence? Is it in the form of well-designed research, or does it consist solely of selected testimonials? Does the design of the research leave room for alternative explanations? If the research subjects exercised in groups, did the exercise improve their mental states or did the improvement come because they made new friends in their groups? Asking such questions makes us better consumers.

The professional use of theory and research is its application to behavioral science practice. For example, as shown in Table 1-4, industrial psychology draws on theory and research from a number of other areas of psychology, including cognition, social psychology, motivation, learning, sensation and perception, and psychometrics. Other traditional areas of psychological practice include clinical, counseling, and school psychology, and psychologists are moving into new areas, such as sports psychology, health education, and the legal system.

The political use of behavioral science involves the use of the results of research to influence public policy. Ever since the landmark 1954 *Brown v. Board of Education* school desegregation case, the results of behavioral science research have been used to influence court decisions that affect social policy (Tremper, 1987). Behavioral science research has also been presented to the U.S. Supreme Court in cases dealing with juror selection in death penalty trials (Bersoff, 1987), employee selection procedures (Bersoff, 1988), and sex discrimination in employment (S. T. Fiske, Bersoff, Borgida, Deaux, & Heilman, 1991). Research on the problems inherent in eyewitness identification of criminal defendants led the U.S. Department of Justice to issue specific guidelines for questioning eyewitnesses and for the procedures to be used when witnesses are asked to identify a suspect (Wells et al., 2000). In addition, Congress commissions the Office of

Technology Assessment to review psychological research on issues affecting legislation, such as the use of polygraph testing in employee selection (Saxe, Dougherty, & Cross, 1985). The social policies derived from such reviews of research can be no better than the quality of the research on which they are based, so behavioral research, good or poor, can affect the lives of everyone.

SUMMARY

The goals of science include (1) description, which involves defining phenomena, recording phenomena, and describing relationships between phenomena; (2) understanding, which consists of determining causality in relationships among phenomena; (3) prediction of events both in the real world and in research; and (4) control over phenomena. In determining if a relationship is causal, we look for three conditions: covariation of cause and effect, time precedence of the cause, and no alternative explanations. Science has four key values: (1) empiricism, or the use of objective evidence; (2) skepticism, or taking a critically evaluative viewpoint on evidence; (3) keeping conclusions tentative so that they can be changed on the basis of new evidence; and (4) making the processes and results of science public. There are two contrasting approaches to scientific knowledge: logical positivism and humanism.

Theories consist of assumptions, hypothetical constructs, and propositions. Assumptions are untestable beliefs that underlie theories. They deal with the nature of reality, ways of conceptualizing and studying behavior, and beliefs specific to the various topics studied by the behavioral sciences. Hypothetical constructs are abstract concepts that represent classes of observed behaviors. Theories must carefully define these constructs both conceptually and operationally. Propositions are a theory's statements about the relationships among the constructs it encompasses. Current theories are usually limited in scope, dealing with a narrow range of variables; they must be well specified, clearly laying out their definitions and propositions. Theories serve three purposes: organizing knowledge, extending knowledge, and guiding action. Three characteristics are necessary for a good theory (logical consistency, testability, and agreement with known data) and five more are desirable (clarity, parsimony, consistency with related theories, applicability to the real world, and stimulation of research).

The five steps in the research process are (1) developing an idea and refining it into a hypothesis, (2) choosing a research strategy, (3) collecting data, (4) analyzing and interpreting data, and (5) reporting results. Four general criteria for evaluating research are construct validity, internal validity, statistical conclusion validity, and external validity. The problem of inference in behavioral research and theory is that we cannot have direct knowledge about hypothetical constructs and the relationships among them. Rather, knowledge consists of conclusions drawn from imperfect concrete representations of constructs.

Theory, research, and application are interdependent. Theory organizes knowledge, research tests the validity of theories and of programs that apply behavioral science knowledge, and application can generate ideas for theory and research. Behavioral science research can be used in the personal, the professional, and the political spheres.

QUESTIONS AND EXERCISES FOR REVIEW

1. Describe the four goals of science. Do you feel one goal is more important than the others? If so, which one and why? What is it about the goals that leads you to your conclusion?

2. An important aspect of the descriptive goal of behavioral science is taxonomy—developing clearly defined categories of behavior. Describe ways in which a lack of clear definitions has confused discussions you've had. Give some examples of how conflicts in definitions have affected behavioral science theory, research, or application.

3. What are the three rules of causality? Can we use research that cannot show causality? Why or why not?

4. Can scientists be *too* empirical and *too* skeptical? That is, can these values hinder scientific progress? If so, how? What are some examples?

5. If scientific knowledge is tentative, can it be useful? That is, how can we confidently apply behavioral science if "the facts" change? How ethical is it to apply tentative knowledge?

6. Should *all* behavioral science knowledge be made public? That is, should some kinds of research results be kept secret because they might cause more harm than good? Who should make such decisions? What are some examples of such potentially harmful behavioral science research?

7. Do you consider yourself a positivist or a humanist, or some combination of the two? How has your philosophical orientation affected your view of behavioral science? For example, how did it affect your responses to the preceding questions?

8. What three kinds of assumptions do theories make? How can these assumptions bias theory and research and lead to disagreements among behavioral scientists?

9. Behavioral science is sometimes criticized because so much of it deals with hypothetical constructs rather than "real things." But other fields also use hypothetical constructs. What are some of these constructs?

10. How is the scientific goal of description related to specificity as a characteristic of theories? Has the lack of specificity in a theory ever hampered your understanding of the theory or any research in which you have been involved? Explain.

11. What are the three purposes for which theories are constructed?

12. Describe the eight criteria for evaluating theories. Using these criteria, evaluate a theory that you are familiar with.

13. What are the steps in the research process?

14. Describe the relationships among theory, research, and application. Which aspect appeals most to you? Why?

15. Describe the ways in which behavioral science knowledge can be used. What ethical considerations might apply to the use of behavioral science knowledge for political purposes?

2 RESEARCH STRATEGIES
An Overview

PURPOSES OF RESEARCH
Basic and Applied Research
Evaluation Research
Action Research

QUANTITATIVE AND
QUALITATIVE RESEARCH

RESEARCH STRATEGIES
The Experimental Strategy
   Experimentation and Causality
   Disadvantages of the Experi-
      mental Strategy
The Case Study Strategy
   Advantages of the Case Study
      Strategy
   Disadvantages of the Case
      Study Strategy
   Uses of the Case Study
      Strategy
The Correlational (Passive)
   Strategy
   Advantages of the
      Correlational Strategy
   Disadvantages of the
      Correlational Strategy

Uses of the Correlational
   Strategy
Comparing the Strategies

TIME PERSPECTIVES: SHORT
TERM VERSUS LONG TERM
Developmental Research
   Cross-Sectional Approach
   Longitudinal Approach
   Cohort-Sequential Approach
Prospective Research
Outcome Evaluation

RESEARCH SETTINGS:
LABORATORY VERSUS FIELD
Research Strategies and
   Research Settings
Research Settings and Research
   Participants

RESEARCH AS A SET OF
TRADEOFFS

SUMMARY

QUESTIONS AND EXERCISES
FOR REVIEW

The first chapter examined the nature of science and theory, and the relationships among theory, research, and application. This chapter begins to focus on research, examining some of the forms it can take. The form a particular piece of research takes can be classified along a number of dimensions. We can classify research in terms of which of three immediate purposes it fulfills — theory testing, applied problem solving, or evaluating the success of an intervention. Research can also be classified in terms of the type of data it produces, quantitative or qualitative. Researchers can collect data by using any of three research strategies — experimental, case study, or correlational. Research studies also differ in terms of time perspective (a short-term "snapshot" of behavior or a long-term, longitudinal approach) and where they are conducted (in the laboratory or in natural settings). This chapter reviews each of these topics to provide a context for the discussion of the foundations of research in Chapters 3 through 6. Many points reviewed here are covered in detail in Chapters 7 through 14.

PURPOSES OF RESEARCH

Research is usually classified into two general categories according to its immediate purpose: basic research, which tests theory in order to formulate general principles of behavior, and applied research, which seeks solutions to specific problems. Evaluation research, conducted to evaluate the success of psychological or social interventions, is becoming a field in its own right and so can be considered a third category of research. A fourth form, called *action research*, combines basic, applied, and evaluation research. Let's examine each of these, looking first at basic and applied research together, because they are so frequently contrasted with one another (Bickman, 1981).

Basic and Applied Research

Basic research is conducted to generate knowledge for the sake of knowledge, without being concerned with the immediate usefulness of the knowledge generated. It is usually guided by theories and models and focuses on testing theoretical propositions. In this process of theory testing, even relationships of small magnitude are considered important if they have a bearing on the validity of the theory. Some basic research is also conducted primarily to satisfy the researcher's curiosity about a phenomenon and may eventually lead to the development of a theory. The results of basic research are expected to be broad in scope and to be applicable, as general principles, to a variety of situations. Basic research tends to use the experimental strategy and to be conducted in laboratory settings, isolating the variables being studied from their natural contexts to gain greater control over them.

    Applied research is conducted to find a solution to a problem that is affecting some aspect of society, and its results are intended to be immediately useful in solving the problem, thereby improving the condition of society. Although applied research is frequently guided by theory, it need not be. Its goal is to identify variables that have large impacts on the problem of interest or variables that can be used to predict a particular behavior. As a result, applied research is sometimes narrower in scope than is basic research, focusing on behavior in only one or a few situations rather than on general principles of behavior that would apply to a variety of situations. Applied research tends to be conducted in natural settings and so studies variables in context, frequently using the correlational or case study strategies.

Although basic and applied research can be put into sharp contrast, as in the preceding two paragraphs, when you try to apply the labels to a particular piece of research the distinction is not always clear, and trying to make such distinctions might not be useful (Calder, Phillips, & Tybout, 1981). Basic research is often carried out in natural settings and, especially in personality and psychopathology research, makes use of non-experimental strategies. As noted in the previous chapter, theory can be used to develop solutions to problems, and the adequacy of the solution can test the adequacy of the theory. Through its link to theory, basic research can help improve society—usually considered a goal of applied research. These contributions take two forms (Lassiter & Dudley, 1991). First, and most commonly, basic research can develop a knowledge base for understanding an applied problem. For example, much basic research and theory on helping behavior was triggered by an incident in New York City in 1964 in which 38 witnesses to a murder did nothing, not even calling the police. The research inspired by this incident was designed to develop theories and models of helping behavior, not to immediately solve the problem of bystander apathy. However, those theories and models suggest a number of ways to increase the likelihood of people helping in both emergency and everyday situations (J. A. Piliavin, Dovidio, Gaertner, & Clark, 1981).

Second, basic research and related theory can be used to identify potential applied problems that might otherwise go unnoticed. Lassiter and Dudley (1991) provide an example in applying the principles of attribution theory to the use of videotaped confessions in criminal trials. Before members of a jury may consider a confession in coming to a verdict, they must feel convinced that the confession was completely voluntary—that is, it was not coerced or otherwise influenced by any factor other than the defendant's intention to confess. Videotaped confessions can be powerful evidence because they show the defendant's face as he or she is confessing, allowing the jurors to decide for themselves if the confession was coerced. However, a great deal of research stimulated by attribution theory has shown that the degree to which observers decide whether another person's behavior results from external influences (such as coercion) is, in part, determined by the observer's viewpoint. An observer who takes the other person's viewpoint, who sees what the other sees, is more likely to conclude that the other person's behavior was influenced by external circumstances than is an observer who merely watches the other person, focusing on the person's behavior rather than on situational factors that might be influencing that behavior (S. T. Fiske & Taylor, 1991).

Based on this research, Lassiter and Irvine (1986) hypothesized that the typical camera angle used in videotaping confessions, which focuses on the suspect's face, would lead observers to conclude that the confession was more voluntary than would other camera angles, such as one from the side showing both the suspect and the interrogating police officer, or one from the suspect's perspective looking at the police officer. Lassiter and Irvine videotaped a simulated confession from those three camera angles and found that as the camera's focus moved away from the suspect, observers' judgments of coercion increased. The importance of this research is that no one in the legal system had ever suggested that viewpoint might bias jurors' perceptions of how voluntary a videotaped confession was. Theory and basic research, therefore, had uncovered an applied problem that people involved in the applied setting had not suspected.

Evaluation Research

A great deal of applied behavioral science involves intervention—the use of behavioral science principles to change people's behavior. In addition, large amounts of public money are spent on social programs designed to enhance the lives of the programs' clients. Do these interventions and programs work as intended? **Evaluation research** addresses this question by using a variety of research strategies to assess the impact of interventions and programs on a set of success criteria (for example, see Weiss, 1998). Chapter 15 discusses evaluation research in more detail.

Action Research

Action research involves the systematic integration of theory, application, and evaluation (Susman & Evered, 1978). Action research starts when someone perceives that a problem exists in an applied setting; for example, a factory experiences an unacceptably high rate of absenteeism. In an action research program, plant managers would consult an industrial psychologist who would examine theories and models of absenteeism to compile a list of possible causes. She would then collect data in the organization (using observation, interviews, and surveys) to determine which cause or causes might be operating in that situation. Perhaps she finds that workers feel they are under too much stress and so take extra days off to compensate. The psychologist would then design an intervention, perhaps a stress reduction program, based on theory and research, and implement the intervention in such a way that its effects could be scientifically evaluated. Based on the results of the evaluation, the intervention might be continued, modified, or replaced by a program that might be more effective.

The action research model is diagrammed in Figure 2-1. Notice the integration of theory, application, and research. Theories of absenteeism and stress (based on basic and applied research) are used to define and develop a potential solution to the problem. The potential solution is applied to the problem, and research is conducted to evaluate its effectiveness. This research provides information about the validity of both the intervention itself and the theories underlying it. Action research is therefore perhaps the most complete form of science, encompassing all its aspects.

QUANTITATIVE AND QUALITATIVE RESEARCH

Behavioral science data can be classified as quantitative or qualitative. **Quantitative data** consist of numerical information, such as scores on a test or the frequency with which a behavior occurs. **Qualitative data** consist of nonnumerical information, such

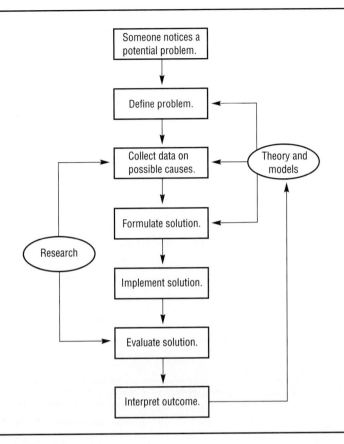

FIGURE 2-1   The Action Research Model

as descriptions of behavior or the content of people's responses to interview questions. Although any research method can provide quantitative data or qualitative data, or both, the perception exists that some research methods can provide only one type of data (Rabinowitz & Weseen, 1997). For example, experiments are commonly thought of as capable of providing only quantitative data, whereas other research methods, such as case studies, observational studies, and interviews, are inherently qualitative. This distinction has resulted in a status hierarchy, at least in the United States, in which research that produces quantitative data generally receives more respect than research that produces qualitative data (Marecek, Fine, & Kidder, 1997; Rabinowitz & Weseen, 1997).

A comparison of Table 2-1, which lists some of the characteristics that distinguish quantitative and qualitative research, with Table 1-1, which lists some of the characteristics that distinguish the logical positivist and humanistic views of science, indicates that the quantitative–qualitative distinction is one of philosophy rather than of method. Advocates of the quantitative approach to research tend to follow the logical positivist view of science, whereas advocates of the qualitative approach tend to follow the humanistic view. Adherents of both philosophies strive to understand human behavior but take different routes to achieving that understanding. As Marecek et al. (1997) note, "Many

TABLE 2-1   Some Contrasts Between the Quantitative and Qualitative Approaches to Research

QUANTITATIVE RESEARCH	QUALITATIVE RESEARCH
Focuses on identifying cause-and-effect relationships among variables	Focuses on understanding how people experience and interpret events in their lives
The variables to be studied and methods to be used are defined in advance by theories and hypotheses derived from theories and remain unchanged throughout the study	The variables to be studied and methods to be used emerge from the researcher's experiences in the research context and are modified as the research situation changes
To promote objectivity, the researcher keeps a psychological and emotional distance from the research	The researcher is an inseparable part of the research process; the researcher's experiences, not only those of the research participants, are valuable data
Frequently studies behavior divorced from its natural context (such as in laboratory research)	Studies behavior in its natural context and studies the interrelationship of behavior and context
Frequently studies behavior by manipulating it (as in experiments)	Studies behavior as it naturally occurs
Data are numerical—frequencies, means, and so forth	Data are open-ended—descriptions of behavior, narrative responses to interview questions, and so forth
Tries to maximize internal validity	Tries to maximize ecological validity
Focuses on the average behavior of people in a population	Focuses on both the similarities and differences in individual experiences and on both the similarities and differences in the ways in which people interpret their experiences

Note: From Banister, Burman, Parker, Taylor, & Tindall (1994); Marecek, Fine, & Kidder (1997); Stake (1995).

of the distinctions propped up between quantitative and qualitative methods are fictions. As we see it, *all* researchers—whether they work with numbers or words, in the laboratory, or in the field—must grapple with issues of generalizability, validity, replicability, ethics, audience, and their own subjectivity or bias" (p. 632). Consistent with the view, in this book I do not make a hard distinction between quantitative and qualitative research methods. Instead, I describe the methods most commonly used by qualitative researchers in the context of the research strategies they represent. Thus, case study research is covered in Chapter 9, which discusses the single-case research strategy. Observational methods, interviewing, and content analysis are covered in Chapter 10, which discusses conducting research in natural settings.

RESEARCH STRATEGIES

The ways in which research is conducted can be classified into three broad strategies: experimental, correlational, and case study. This section reviews the characteristics of these approaches and discusses some of their major advantages and disadvantages; Chapters 7 through 9 discuss the major issues involved in carrying out these strategies. As you will see, these strategies vary along a continuum that has a high degree of control over the research situation but a low degree of naturalism at one end, and low control but high naturalism at the other end. This review will first cover the strategies that fall at the ends of the continuum (experimental and case study) and contrast those with the middle strategy (correlational). In this chapter the description of these strategies is brief and, perhaps, somewhat oversimplified, to provide a broad overview. Chapters 7 through 11 address their complexities and the ways in which they overlap and can be combined.

The Experimental Strategy

From the logical positivist point of view, the **experiment** is the best way to conduct research because only experimentation can determine cause-and-effect relationships. This emphasis on the experiment carries over into the teaching of behavioral science. I informally surveyed nine undergraduate research methods textbooks and found that about three chapters per book were devoted to the experiment in its various forms, compared to half a chapter each for correlational and case study research. Let's therefore first consider some key characteristics of the experiment so that we can compare it to other research strategies.

EXPERIMENTATION AND CAUSALITY   Recall the three criteria for determining a cause-and-effect relationship: covariation of proposed cause and effect, time precedence of the proposed cause, and absence of alternative explanations for the effect. Although all three strategies let you assess the first two criteria to some degree, only in the classic or "true" experiment can you confidently conclude there are no alternative explanations for the results. The researcher can have this confidence because she or he has taken complete control of the research situation in order to ensure that there *can* be only one explanation for the results.

Let's consider a simple experiment, in which the researcher hypothesizes that caffeine consumption speeds up reaction time, to see how the researcher exerts this control. First, she controls the setting of the experiment—its physical characteristics (such as the location of the room in which the experiment is conducted, its size, its decor) and time at which it is conducted (such as morning or afternoon) to ensure these are the same for everyone who participates in the experiment. Second, she controls the independent variable, establishing two conditions, an **experimental condition** in which participants will take a pill containing a standard dose of caffeine and a **control condition** (or comparison condition) in which participants take a pill containing an inert substance. Both pills are identical in size, shape, color, and weight to ensure that the only difference between the conditions is the caffeine content of the pills. Third, the researcher controls the experimental procedure—what happens during the experiment—so that each participant has exactly the same experience except for the difference in the independent variable based on the condition the participant is in: All participants meet the same experimenter (who does not know which type of pill they will receive), receive the same greeting and instructions, take pills that are identical in appearance, wait the same amount of time after taking the pills, and have the dependent variable (reaction time) measured in the same way—how fast the participant can push a button in response to a signal light. Finally, she controls the characteristics of the participants to ensure that the people who take the caffeine pills and those who take the inert pill are as similar as possible—that their characteristics do not differ systematically across conditions.

Let's suppose our researcher finds the mean reaction time of the participants who took the caffeine pills was faster than the mean reaction time of the participants who took the inert pills. Can she correctly conclude that the caffeine caused the difference in mean reaction time? The difference itself shows covariation between caffeine consumption and reaction time. The researcher ensured that her participants took their pills before she measured their reaction times, so the potential cause came before the effect. Finally, caffeine was the only aspect of the experiment that differed between the experimental and control conditions, so there are no alternative explanations for the difference in mean reaction times between conditions. That is, nothing else covaried (the first criterion for causality) with reaction time. Because all three criteria for causality have been met, the researcher can correctly conclude that caffeine speeds up reaction time.

DISADVANTAGES OF THE EXPERIMENTAL STRATEGY   The great advantage of the experiment is that it allows us to determine causality; that determination is possible because of the high degree of control the researcher exerts over the research situation. However, that high degree of control also results in a high degree of artificiality so that some behavioral scientists question the extent to which laboratory findings apply to the "real world" (for example, see Argyris, 1980). Let's consider some of the types of artificiality induced by the controls in our caffeine experiment.

•   *The Setting*   Human caffeine consumption (except for that of researchers) rarely takes place in a laboratory in the presence of an experimenter. It is more likely to take place in homes, restaurants, and offices in the presence of family, friends, and coworkers, or alone.

•   *The Independent Variable*   People rarely consume caffeine in the form of pills. Although some over-the-counter stimulants contain high levels of caffeine, most people consume caffeine in the form of coffee, tea, or soft drinks.

•   *The Procedures*   Caffeine consumption rarely occurs under conditions as structured as those in the laboratory. In addition, people in natural settings must respond to visual signals that are frequently much more complex than signal lights, and signals can take other forms, such as sounds. People must also usually respond in ways much more complex than pushing a button.

•   *The Participants*   Not everyone drinks beverages containing caffeine, and those who do so do not get their caffeine in standard doses that are the same for everyone.

So, then, one might ask, what can this experiment tell us about the effect of drinking coffee alone in the home, on the ability of a heavy coffee drinker to safely stop a car in response to seeing a collision on the road ahead? Artificiality, as you can see, can be a very vexing problem—discussed in some detail in Chapter 14.

A second disadvantage of the experimental strategy is that it can be used only to study independent variables that can be manipulated, as our researcher manipulated (controlled) the dose of caffeine she administered to her participants. However, it is impossible to manipulate many variables of interest to behavioral scientists. Consider, for example, variables such as age, sex, personality, and personal history. Although we can compare the behavior of people who vary on such factors (as women and men vary as to sex), we cannot manipulate those factors in the sense of controlling which participant in our research will be female and which male. People come as male or female; we cannot assign people to sex as we can assign them to take a caffeine pill or an inert pill. The inability to manipulate some variables, such as biological sex, is a problem because such variables are often related to a variety of psychological and social variables. For example, men are somewhat better at mental rotation of objects and are more willing to express aggressive impulses physically (Basow, 1992). If we find differences between men and women on a dependent variable, such psychological and social variables can often provide plausible alternatives to biological sex as explanations for differences on the dependent variable. Similar problems exist for age, personality, and other such "person variables."

It might also be impossible or prohibitively difficult to study some variables under experimentally controlled conditions. For example, it is theoretically possible to design an experiment in which the size and complexity of an organization would be manipulated as independent variables to study their effects on behavior. However, it would be virtually impossible to carry out such an experiment. Similarly, it is possible to conceive of an experiment to determine the effects of an independent variable that would be unethical to manipulate. To take an extreme example, it would be physically possible to conduct an experimental study of brain damage in people—assigning some people to have a portion of their brain removed and others to undergo a mock operation—but it would certainly be unethical to do so. More realistically, how ethical would it be to experimentally study the effects of severe levels of stress? I discuss the ethical treatment of research participants in Chapter 3. As that chapter shows, in addition to putting limits on experimental manipulations the ethical requirements of research can, under some circumstances, bias the results of the research.

Because of these limitations of the experimental strategy, researchers frequently use the case study or correlational strategies instead of experiments. The next section examines the case study because of the contrast it offers to the experiment.

The Case Study Strategy

A **case study** is an in-depth, usually long-term, examination of a single instance of a phenomenon, for either descriptive or hypothesis-testing purposes (Yin, 1993, 1994). The scope of a case study can range from the anthropologist's description of an entire culture (Nance, 1975) to the sociologist's study of a neighborhood or a complex organization (Kanter, 1977; Liebow, 1967), to the psychologist's study of intergroup relations (Schofield, 1982), small-group decision making (Janis, 1972), or an individual's memory (Neisser, 1981). Although researchers often tend to think of the case study as a tool for description rather than hypothesis testing, Chapter 9 will show how case studies can also be used for testing hypotheses. The case study can therefore be a very valuable research tool, but it is underused and underappreciated by many behavioral scientists.

ADVANTAGES OF THE CASE STUDY STRATEGY A great advantage of the case study is its naturalism. Case studies commonly study people in their natural environments undergoing the natural experiences of their daily lives. Frequently, the researchers conceal their identities as data collectors, posing as just another person in the setting being studied, so that people's behavior in the situation is not biased by their knowledge that they are the subjects of research. Case studies are also usually carried out over long periods of time and encompass all the behaviors that occur in the setting, thus affording a great depth of understanding. The other research strategies, in contrast, often focus on one or a limited set of behaviors and use a more restricted time frame. As a result of this naturalism and depth, reports of case study research can give us a subjective "feel" for the situation under study that is frequently lacking in reports of research conducted using the other strategies.

The case study also allows us to investigate rarely occurring phenomena. Because the correlational and experimental strategies are based on the use of relatively large numbers of cases, they cannot be used to study phenomena that occur infrequently. The case study, in contrast, is designed for rare or one-of-a-kind phenomena, such as uncommon psychiatric disorders. Because of the depth at which they study phenomena, case studies can also lead to the discovery of overlooked behaviors. For example, Goodall (1978) observed a group of chimpanzees in the wild kill another group of chimps—a previously unrecorded and unsuspected aspect of chimpanzee behavior unlikely to have been found in other environments (such as zoos) or in short-term studies.

Finally, the case study can allow the scientist to gain a new point of view on a situation—that of the research participant. As noted in Chapter 1, scientists, at least in the logical positivist tradition, are supposed to be detached from their data and to use theory to interpret and to understand their data. A case study, in contrast, can incorporate the participants' viewpoints on and interpretations of the data, offering new insights. For example, Andersen (1981) revised her theory-based interpretation of data on the psychological well-being of the wives of corporate executives, based on her participants' comments on what they thought made them happy with their lives.

DISADVANTAGES OF THE CASE STUDY STRATEGY   The primary disadvantage of the case study strategy is the mirror image of that of the experimental strategy: The case study's high degree of naturalism means the researcher has very little or no control over the phenomenon being studied or the situation in which the study takes place. Consequently it is impossible to draw conclusions about causality. Let's say, for example, that you're interested in the effect of caffeine on hostility, so you decide to do a case study of a coworker (who happens to be male). Each day you note how much coffee he drinks in the morning, and throughout the day you keep a record of his verbal hostility—yelling, sarcastic comments, and so forth. If your data appear to show a relationship between your coworker's coffee consumption and his hostility, there are several alternative explanations for the behavior. For example, many things can happen during the workday that can anger a person, and maybe these factors, not the caffeine in the coffee, caused the aggression. Or perhaps it's a combination of the coffee and these other factors—maybe caffeine doesn't make him hostile unless something else upsets him.

Another disadvantage of the case study is that you have no way of knowing how typical your results are of other people or situations, or whether your results are unique to the case that you studied. For example, perhaps caffeine is related to hostility only in the person you observed, or only in people with a certain personality type, which happens to be that of your coworker. Or perhaps the relationship is limited to one setting: Your coworker's caffeine consumption is related to his aggression toward people in the office, but not toward family members or friends. However, because you observe your coworker only in the office, you have no data on the other situations.

A final disadvantage of case study research is that it is highly vulnerable to **researcher bias.** Chapter 6 discusses this problem in more detail, but let's note here that unless controls are imposed to prevent it, researchers' expectations about what will occur in a situation can affect the data collected (R. Rosenthal, 1976). For example, in your case study of caffeine and hostility your expectation that higher caffeine consumption leads to more hostility might lead you to pay closer attention to your coworker on days that he drank more coffee than usual or make you more likely to interpret his behavior as hostile on those days.

A striking example of the latter phenomenon comes from the field of anthropology (Critchfield, 1978). Two anthropologists studied the same village in Mexico 17 years apart. Robert Redfield, who conducted his study in the mid-1920s, found life in the village reasonably good and the people open and friendly to one another. Oscar Lewis, who studied the village in the early 1940s, found life there full of suffering and interpersonal strife. Interestingly, Lewis and Redfield agreed that the amount of time that had passed could not have brought about the large amount of change implied by the differences in the results of their studies. What, then, led to the conflicting findings? In Redfield's opinion,

> It must be recognized that the personal interests . . . of the investigator influence the content of a description of a village. . . . There are hidden questions behind the two books that have been written about [this village]. The hidden question behind my book is, "What do these people enjoy?" The hidden question behind Dr. Lewis's book is, "What do these people suffer from?" (quoted in Critchfield, 1978, p. 66)

USES OF THE CASE STUDY STRATEGY Despite its limitations, the case study, when properly conducted as described in Chapter 9, can be an extremely useful research tool. As we have already noted, the case study is the only research tool available for the study of rarely occurring phenomena, although the researcher must be careful about generalizing from a single case. Sometimes, however, a researcher is not interested in generalizing beyond the case studied. Allport (1961) distinguished between two approaches to the study of human behavior. The **nomothetic approach** attempts to formulate general principles of behavior that will apply to most people most of the time. This approach uses experimental and correlational research to study the average behavior of large groups of people. However, Allport wrote, any particular individual is only poorly represented by the group average, so the nomothetic approach must be accompanied by an **idiographic approach** that studies the behavior of individuals. The idiographic approach, of which the case study is an example, addresses the needs of the practitioner, who is not so much interested in how people in general behave as in how a particular client behaves. In meeting this need, Allport (1961) wrote, "Actuarial predictions [based on general principles of behavior] may sometimes help, universal and group norms are useful, but they do not go the whole distance" (p. 21). The idiographic approach goes the rest of the distance by revealing aspects of behavior that get lost in the compilation of group averages.

An important type of behavior that can "get lost in the average" is the single case that contradicts or disconfirms a general principle that is supposed to apply to all people. For example, in the 1930s, 1940s, and 1950s many psychologists who studied language subscribed to a "motor theory" of speech perception. Essentially, the theory held that people understand speech by matching the sounds they hear with the muscular movements they would use to produce the sounds themselves. Therefore, to understand a speech sound, people must have made the sound themselves (Neisser, 1967). The universality of this theory was disconfirmed by a case study of an 8-year-old child who had never spoken, but who understood what people said to him (Lenneberg, 1962).

Case study research is also a fruitful source of hypotheses for more controlled research. If an interesting behavior or relationship is observed in a case study, its generality can be studied in correlational and experimental research, and experimental research can be used to determine its causes and effects. For example, many influential theories of personality, psychopathology, psychotherapy, and organizational behavior were developed using the case study strategy (see, for example, Robbins, 1991; Rychlak, 1981).

The Correlational (Passive) Strategy

The **correlational strategy** looks for relationships between variables that are consistent across a large number of cases. In an expansion of the caffeine and hostility case study described in the preceding section, you might observe all the workers in an office to determine their levels of coffee consumption and verbal hostility, and compute the correlation coefficient between the variables. As you recall from your statistics classes, the correlation coefficient provides two pieces of information: the strength of the relationship between two variables, indexed from 0 to 1, and the direction of the relationship, positive (when the scores on one variable are high, so are the scores on the other variable) or negative (when the scores on one variable are high, the scores on the other variable are low). You can also determine the statistical significance of the relationship you observed in your sample of office workers—the probability that it occurred by chance.

Because researchers using the correlational strategy merely observe or measure the variables of interest without manipulating them as in the experimental strategy, the correlational strategy is also sometimes called the **passive research strategy** (for example, Wampold, 1996). The term *passive* also recognizes that researchers using this strategy will not always use correlation coefficients or related statistical procedures (such as multiple regression analysis) to analyze their data. For example, comparison of men's and women's scores on a variable will usually use the *t* test or *F* test because research participants are grouped by sex. Nonetheless, the study would be considered correlational or passive because the researchers could not assign participants to be male or female. Although the use of the term *passive research strategy* is growing, I will use the term *correlational research strategy* because it is still more commonly used to refer to this type of research.

ADVANTAGES OF THE CORRELATIONAL STRATEGY   The correlational strategy has advantages relative to both the case study and the experiment. The case study, as noted, can detect a relationship between two variables *within* a particular case—for example, a relationship between coffee consumption and hostility for one person. The correlational strategy lets us determine if such a relationship holds up *across* a number of cases—for example, the relationship between coffee consumption and hostility averaged across all the people working in an office. If the results of a case study and a correlational study are consistent, then we can conclude that the relationship observed in the single case could hold for people in general (although it might hold only for people in that office, as discussed in Chapter 14). If the results of the two studies are inconsistent, we might conclude that the relationship observed in the case study was unique to that individual. As already noted, the correlational strategy also allows for the statistical analysis of data, which the case study does not.

Relative to the experiment, the correlational strategy allows us to test hypotheses that are not amenable to the experimental strategy. Research on personality and psychopathology, for example, can be conducted only using the correlational strategy because it is impossible to manipulate those kinds of variables. Other research, such as that on the effects of brain damage or severe stress on humans, must use the correlational strategy because it would be unethical to manipulate some variables, due to their adverse effects on the research participants.

DISADVANTAGES OF THE CORRELATIONAL STRATEGY   The correlational strategy shares the major disadvantage of the case study strategy: Neither can determine causality. Although the correlational strategy can determine if a dependent variable covaries with an independent variable (as shown by the correlation coefficient), correlational studies are rarely conducted in a way that would establish time precedence of the independent variable and cannot rule out all alternative explanations. Let's examine these problems using the hypothesis that watching violent television programs causes children to become aggressive. Although this hypothesis can be (and has been) tested experimentally, there are potential ethical problems with such experiments. For example, if you really expect watching violent TV programs to cause children to hurt other people, is it ethical to risk making some children aggressive by assigning them to watch violent TV programs? However, in day-to-day life some children watch more violent TV programs than do other children, so we can use the correlational strategy to test the hypothesis that there is a positive relationship between watching violent TV programs and children's aggression.

In a typical study, a group of researchers might select a group of children to study, say, those attending a particular public school. The researchers could then ask the children's parents to list the TV shows that their children watch during a given week; these shows could be rated for their violence content, which would give each child a score on exposure to violent TV programming. Simultaneously, the researchers could have the children's teachers keep records of the children's aggressive behavior, providing each child with an aggression score. The researchers could then compute the correlation coefficient between the TV violence scores and the aggression scores; the typical correlation is around .20 (J. L. Freedman, 1984), which will be statistically significant given a sufficiently large sample.

Notice that the study has established covariation between the two variables, but not time precedence: Both variables were measured simultaneously. Consequently, as illustrated in panels (a) and (b) of Figure 2-2, two interpretations of causality are possible: first, that exposure to violent TV programming causes aggression and, second,

(a) **Watching televised violence causes aggressiveness.**

(b) **Being aggressive causes one to prefer violent TV programs.**

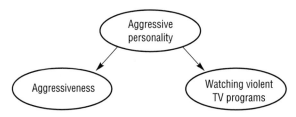

(c) **Having an aggressive personality causes one to *both* be aggressive *and* prefer violent TV programs.**

FIGURE 2-2   Alternative Explanations for a Correlation Between Watching Violent TV Programs and Aggressiveness

that children who are already aggressive due to other causes prefer to watch violent TV programs. Because we have no way of knowing which comes before the other—watching violent TV programs or being aggressive—there is no basis for choosing one as the cause and the other as the effect. This problem of not being able to distinguish which variable is the cause is sometimes referred to as **reverse causation:** The direction of causality might be the reverse of what we hypothesize.

This situation is further complicated by the possibility of a **reciprocal relationship** between viewing TV violence and aggression. That is, viewing TV violence might cause children to become aggressive, and this higher level of aggression might, in a circular fashion, induce a greater preference for violent TV programs, which leads to more aggression. Or, of course, it might go the other way: Aggression causes the watching of violent TV programs, which causes more aggression, and so forth. Reverse causation and reciprocal relationships also constitute possible alternatives to violent TV programs as a cause of aggression, so that the study also fails to meet the third criterion for causality.

Another alternative explanation that can never be ruled out in correlational research is known as the **third-variable problem.** As illustrated in panel (c) of Figure 2-2, some third variable, such as an aggressive personality, might be a cause of both aggression and watching violent TV programs. Because aggression and watching violent TV programs have a cause in common, they are correlated. Let's illustrate this problem with a concrete example. Assume that you're visiting the Florida coast during spring break and a storm comes in off the ocean. You notice something from your motel room window, which faces the sea: As the waves come higher and higher on to the beach, the palm trees bend further and further over. That is, the height of the waves and the angle of the palm trees are correlated. Now, are the waves causing the palm trees to bend, or are the bending palm trees pulling the waves higher on to the beach? Neither, of course: The rising waves and the bending trees have a common cause — the wind — that results in a correlation between wave height and tree angle even though neither is causing the other.

As Chapter 8 shows, there are ways of establishing time precedence of the independent variable in correlational research by taking a prospective approach. However, these methods do not eliminate the third-variable problem. Similarly, there are ways of ruling out some alternative explanations for correlational relationships, but to eliminate all the possible alternatives we must know them all and measure them all, which is almost never possible.

USES OF THE CORRELATIONAL STRATEGY   If the correlational strategy cannot determine causal relationships, of what use is it? One important use is the disconfirmation of causal hypotheses. Recall that causation requires that there be covariation between the independent and dependent variables; if there is no covariation, there can be no causality. Therefore, a zero correlation between two variables means that neither can be causing the other. This disconfirmational use of the correlational strategy is similar to that of the case study strategy. However, the correlational strategy shows that the disconfirmation holds across a number of people, whereas the case study can speak only to a single instance.

As already noted, the correlational strategy must be used when variables cannot be manipulated. It can also be used to study phenomena in their natural environments while imposing more control over the research situation than is usually done in a case study. For example, the effects of researcher bias can be reduced by collecting data through the use of standardized written questionnaires rather than by direct observation. Although completing the questionnaire intrudes on the research participants' normal activity, the questionnaire takes some of the subjectivity out of data collection. (The relative advantages and disadvantages of different modes of data collection are discussed in Chapter 5.)

Finally, the correlational research strategy provides an opportunity for the use of the **actuarial prediction** mentioned by Allport (1961) in his discussion of the idiographic and nomothetic approaches to research. As you may recall from statistics classes, the correlation coefficient not only shows the strength and direction of the relationship between two variables, but can also be used, through the development of a **regression equation,** to estimate people's scores on one variable from their scores on another variable. The equation takes the form $Y = a + bX$, where Y is the predicted score, a is a constant, X is the score being used to predict Y, and b is a multiplier representing how much weight X has in predicting Y. The equation can include more than one predictor variable. For example, at my university you could estimate a student's undergraduate grade point average (GPA) from the student's high school GPA and Scholastic Assessment Test (SAT) scores using this equation: College GPA = 1.272 + (.430 × high school GPA) + (.0007 × verbal SAT) + (.0004 × math SAT). Therefore, if you want to choose only those students who were likely to attain a GPA of 2.0, you could enter the applicable high school GPA and SAT scores into the equation and admit only those whose estimated college GPA equaled or exceeded 2.0. Such actuarial predictions are commonly used for employee selection (Cascio, 1998) and can be used in university admission decisions (Goldberg, 1977) and psychiatric diagnosis (Dawes, Faust, & Meehl, 1989). The predictions made by these actuarial methods are, of course, subject to error, but they are generally more accurate than subjective decisions made by individuals or committees working from the data used in the regression equation (Dawes, Faust, & Meehl, 1989).

Comparing the Strategies

Table 2-2 summarizes the three research strategies by comparing their main advantages, disadvantages, and uses. A key point is that there is no one best research strategy; rather, each is appropriate to different goals of research. For example, only the experiment can determine causality, only the case study allows the study of rare phenomena, and only the correlational strategy allows the systematic study of common phenomena that cannot be manipulated. Similarly, each strategy has its disadvantages. For example, the experiment tends to be artificial, neither the correlational strategy nor the case study allows us to determine causality, and the case study does not allow generalization across cases. This issue of competing advantages and disadvantages is discussed at the end of the chapter. First, however, let us look at two other aspects of research: whether or not it examines change over time and whether it is conducted in the laboratory or in a natural setting.

TIME PERSPECTIVES: SHORT TERM VERSUS LONG TERM

Much behavioral science research takes a short-term time perspective, focusing on what happens in a 30- to 60-minute research session. It is, however, often useful to take a longer-term approach, studying how phenomena change over time. Change over time is studied in three contexts: developmental research, prospective research, and the evaluation of intervention outcomes.

Developmental Research

The purpose of **developmental research** is to learn how people change as they move through the life span from birth, through childhood, adolescence, and adulthood, into old age. For example, one might want to know how cognitive processes develop in childhood and how they change over the life span. Three approaches to studying developmental questions are the cross-sectional, longitudinal, and cohort-sequential (Appelbaum & McCall, 1983; Baltes, Reese, & Nesselroade, 1977).

TABLE 2-2   Comparison of the Research Strategies

EXPERIMENTAL		
Advantages	*Disadvantages*	*Uses*
Can determine causality	Offers low naturalism	When knowing causality is essential
Offers quantitative indicators of impact of independent variable	Some variables cannot be studied	

CASE STUDY		
Advantages	*Disadvantages*	*Uses*
Offers high naturalism	Offers little control; cannot determine causality	When studying rare phenomena
Studies phenomena in depth	Allows low generalizability across cases	When taking an idiographic approach
Can study rare phenomena	Is most vulnerable to researcher bias	When a source of hypotheses for other strategies is needed
Can discover overlooked behavior		
Can reveal new points of view		
Can discover disconfirming cases		

CORRELATIONAL		
Advantages	*Disadvantages*	*Uses*
Can study variables that cannot be manipulated	Cannot determine causality	When variables cannot be manipulated
Offers quantitative indicator of relationship strength		When a balance between naturalism and control is desired
		When actuarial prediction is desired
		When it is unethical to manipulate a variable
		When discomfirmation of causal hypotheses is desired

CROSS-SECTIONAL APPROACH **Cross-sectional research** investigates age differences by comparing groups of people who are of different ages. As illustrated in Figure 2-3, a cross-sectional study conducted in 1990 (indicated by the vertical arrow) of age differences among women would compare groups of women who were 80 years old (born in 1910, Anne's group), 60 years old (born in 1930, Betty's group), 40 years old (born in 1950, Carla's group), and 20 years old (born in 1970, Denise's group). Relative to the other

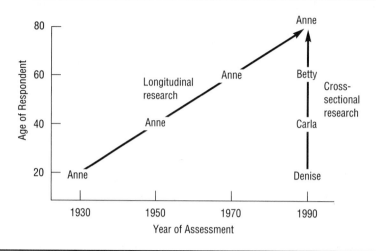

FIGURE 2-3
Longitudinal research (diagonal arrow) assesses the *same people* at *different ages* at *different times*. Cross-sectional research (vertical row) assesses *different people* at *different ages* at the *same time*.

approaches, which follow people across time, cross-sectional research is relatively quick and inexpensive: You find people in the age groups of interest, measure the characteristics of interest, and compare the members of the age groups on those characteristics.

Notice, however, that although you have assessed age differences, you have not been able to assess developmental trends—how characteristics change over time. You have examined your participants at only one point in their lives, so it is impossible to assess change. You may also have noticed another problem: There is no way to determine whether any differences found among the age groups are due to the chronological ages of the group members (for example, Anne is 80, Denise is 20) or to differences in life experiences (Anne was born in 1910, Denise in 1970). Consider, for example, Anne's life: She was a child during World War I, a teenager during the "Roaring Twenties," a young adult during the Great Depression of the 1930s, and she experienced World War II, the cold war, and the social and political upheavals of the Vietnam War era as a mature adult. Denise has experienced only the 1970s and 1980s, and then only as a child, adolescent, and young adult, not as a mature adult, as did Anne.

The effects of these differences in experience due to time of birth are called **cohort effects;** a cohort is the group of people born during the same period of time. This period of time may be a month of a particular year, a year, or a period of several years, depending on the focus of the research. Potential cohort effects can lead to a great deal of ambiguity in interpreting the results of cross-sectional research. Let's say you find differences in cognitive ability among Betty's, Carla's, and Denise's groups. These differences might be due to aging, but they could also be due to cohort-related factors. For example, childhood nutrition affects cognitive ability (Winick, 1979). Betty was a child during the Great Depression, when many children were malnourished; Carla was a child during the 1950s, when children were fed enough, but perhaps not well—there was little of today's concern with nutrition, and diets were often high in sugar and fats; Denise grew up at a time when parents were more concerned with proper nutrition. These nutritional differences provide a possible alternative to aging as an explanation for group differences in cognitive ability.

LONGITUDINAL APPROACH   **Longitudinal research** avoids cohort effects by studying the same group of people over time. As shown by the diagonal arrow in Figure 2-3, a researcher (or a research group) could have begun studying Anne's cohort in 1930, when they were 20 years old, and conducted an assessment every 20 years until 1990. Thus, the longitudinal approach makes it possible to study developmental trends.

The longitudinal approach, however, does have a number of disadvantages. It is, of course, time consuming. Whereas the cross-sectional approach allows you to collect all the data at once, using the longitudinal approach you must wait months, years, or even decades to collect all the data, depending on the number of assessments and the amount of time between them. Multiple assessments increase the costs of data collection, and as time goes by people will drop out of the study. This **attrition** can come about for many reasons; for example, participants may lose interest in the study and refuse to continue to provide data, or they may move and so cannot be located for later assessments. When dealing with older age groups, people die. Random attrition poses few problems, but if attrition is nonrandom, the sample will be biased. For example, in an 8-year study of adolescent drug use, Stein, Newcomb, and Bentler (1987) had a 55% attrition rate, due mainly to their inability to locate participants after the participants had left high school. However, by comparing the characteristics of their dropouts to those of the participants who completed the research, the researchers were able to conclude that their sample was probably not significantly biased. That is, the characteristics of the participants as assessed at the beginning of the study were not related to whether they dropped out. If, however, only the heaviest drug users when the study began had dropped out, Stein et al. could have applied their results only to a select subgroup of drug users. But Stein et al. could compare the dropouts to the full participants only on the variables they had measured at the outset; attrition could be associated with unmeasured variables and so result in biased findings. Attrition also raises research costs because you must plan for dropouts and start with a sample large enough to provide enough cases for proper data analysis at the end of the research.

Four other potential problems in longitudinal research, all related to the use of multiple assessments, are test sensitization, test reactivity, changes in measurement technology, and history effects. **Test sensitization** effects occur when participants' scores on a test are affected by their having taken the test earlier. For example, scores on achievement tests may increase simply because the test takers become more familiar with the questions each time they take the test. **Test reactivity** effects occur when being asked a question about a behavior affects that behavior. For example, Rubin and Mitchell (1976) found that almost half the college students who had participated in a questionnaire study of dating relationships said that participating had affected their relationships. The questions had started them thinking about aspects of their relationships they had not considered before, either bringing the couple closer together or breaking up the relationship.

Changes in measurement technology occur when research shows one measure is not as valid as originally thought, so it is replaced by a better one. If a longitudinal study used one measure at its outset and a different one later, the researchers face a dilemma: Continued use of the old measure could threaten the validity of their study, but the new measure's scores will not be comparable to the old measure's. One solution would be to continue to use the old measure but to add the new measure to the study, drawing what conclusions are possible from the old measure but giving more weight to conclusions based on the new measure during the period of its use.

History effects occur when events external to the research affect the behavior being studied so that you cannot tell whether changes in the behavior found from one assessment to another are due to age changes or to the events. Let's say, for example, that you are doing a longitudinal study of adolescent illegal drug use similar to Stein et al.'s (1987). As your participants get older, drug use declines. Is this a natural change due to aging, or is it due to some other factor? Perhaps during the course of the study drug enforcement became more effective, driving up the price of illegal drugs and making them less affordable. Over longer periods of time, historical factors that affect one generation (say, people born in 1920) but not another (say, those born in 1970) might limit the degree to which the results of research with one birth year cohort can be applied to another birth year cohort. One way to assess the degree of this **cross-generation problem** is the cohort-sequential approach to developmental research.

COHORT-SEQUENTIAL APPROACH   **Cohort-sequential research** combines cross-sectional and longitudinal approaches by starting a new longitudinal cohort each time an assessment is made. For example, as shown in Figure 2-4, Anne's cohort starts participating in the research in 1930, when they are 20 years old. In 1950, Anne's cohort (now 40 years old) is assessed for the second time and Betty's cohort (20 years old) joins the research and is assessed for the first time. This process of adding cohorts continues as the research progresses. As a result, the researcher can make both longitudinal comparisons (along the diagonals in Figure 2-4) and cross-sectional comparisons (along the columns in Figure 2-4). The researcher can also make **time-lagged comparisons** (along the rows in Figure 2-4) to see how the cohorts differ at the same age. For example, how similar is Anne's cohort at age 20 (in 1930) to Denise's cohort at age 20 (in 1990)? Let's look at an example of research using the cohort-sequential approach, which also shows some limitations of the cross-sectional and longitudinal approaches.

Hagenaars and Cobben (1978) used the cohort-sequential approach to analyze data from Dutch census records for the period 1899 to 1971. They used these data to compute the proportions of women in nine age groups reporting a religious affiliation on eight assessment occasions. We will look at their data for seven cohorts of women at four assessments. Each cohort was born in a different decade, and the data represent cross-sectional assessments made when the women were ages 20–30, 40–50, 60–70, and 80+, and longitudinal assessments at 20-year intervals (1909, 1929, 1949, and 1969). The design is shown in Table 2-3.

Figure 2-5 shows the results of two approaches to analyzing the data: the longitudinal results for cohort 4 and the cross-sectional results for cohorts 4 through 7 in 1969. Notice the inconsistency: The cross-sectional approach suggests that religious affiliation increases with age, whereas the longitudinal approach suggests that religious affiliation

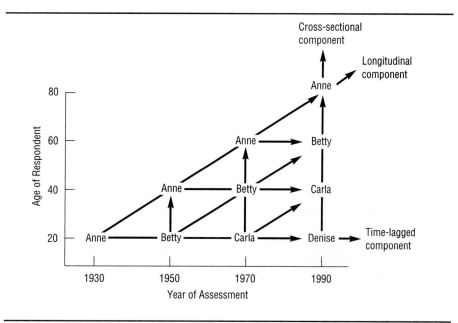

FIGURE 2-4
Cohort-sequential research includes both longitudinal and cross-sectional components. It also has a time-lagged component (horizontal arrow), assessing *different people* at the *same age* at *different times.*

decreases from ages 20–30 to ages 40–50 and thereafter remains stable. Which conclusion is correct? The time-lagged data for cohorts 4 through 7 at ages 20–30, shown in Figure 2-6, suggest an answer: The cohorts entered the research at different levels of religious affiliation, ranging from 95% for cohort 4 to 76% for cohort 7—a cohort effect. As a result, even if the religious affiliation rate of each cohort dropped over time, as suggested by the longitudinal analysis, the older cohorts would always show a higher level of religious affiliation if the amount of change was the same for each cohort.

As you can see, analyzing developmental trends is a complex task. You should undertake it only after a thorough study of the methodologies involved (see, for example, Appelbaum & McCall, 1983; Baltes et al., 1977). Yet you should be wary of substituting cross-sectional for longitudinal research, as this can lead to erroneous conclusions. Therefore, don't shy away from longitudinal research because of its complexity: If it is appropriate to answering your research question, learn how to use it and apply it to your question.

Prospective Research

Prospective research investigates the relationship between an independent variable at one time and a dependent variable at a later time. This approach can be especially important in correlational research when trying to establish time precedence of an

TABLE 2-3   Design of Hagenaars and Cobben's (1978) Cohort-Sequential Analysis of Dutch Census Data

Seven cohorts, or groups, of women were assessed at 20-year intervals, beginning when the members of each group were 20 years old.

Cohort Number	Decade of Birth	YEAR OF ASSESSMENT 1909	1929	1949	1969
1	1819–1829	x			
2	1839–1849	x	x		
3	1859–1869	x	x	x	
4	1879–1889	x	x	x	x
5	1899–1909		x	x	x
6	1919–1929			x	x
7	1939–1949				x

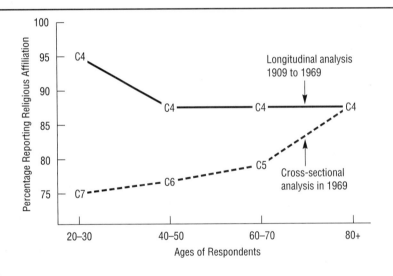

FIGURE 2-5   Results of Longitudinal and Cross-Sectional Analyses of Religious Affiliation Data
The cross-sectional analysis seems to show an increase of religious affiliation with age, but the longitudinal analysis shows an initial decline followed by a leveling off. (C4, C5, C6, and C7 refer to cohort numbers from Table 2-3.)

independent variable by showing that the level of the independent variable at time 1 covaries with the level of the dependent variable at time 2. For example, you could examine the correlation between the degree to which people exhibit the Type A behavior pattern (a hypothesized cause of heart disease) and whether they currently have heart disease, but this procedure leaves unanswered the question of whether the behavior came before the illness or the illness came before the behavior. In addition, the most serious cases of heart disease —those that had resulted in death—would not be included

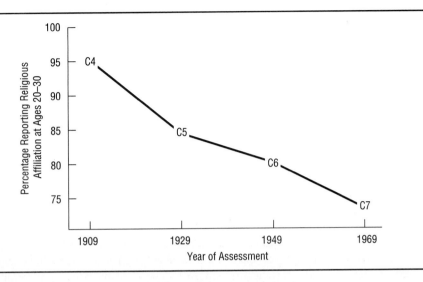

FIGURE 2-6   Results of Time-Lagged Analysis of Religious Affiliation Data
This analysis seems to show a linear decrease of religious affiliation with age, in contrast to the analyses in Figure 2-5. (C4, C5, C6, and C7 refer to cohort numbers from Table 2-3.)

in the study. However, if you were to measure Type A behavior in a group of healthy people now and examine their incidence of heart disease over, say, a 10-year period, then you could be certain that the presumed causal factor in the research, Type A behavior, came before the effect, heart disease. You could not, of course, rule out the influence of a third variable that might cause both Type A behavior and heart disease. Prospective research entails many problems of longitudinal developmental research, such as attrition, testing effects, and history effects, which must be taken into account in evaluating the meaning of the research results. Prospective research is discussed again in Chapter 8.

Outcome Evaluation

Outcome evaluation, as noted earlier, investigates the effectiveness of a treatment program, such as psychotherapy or an organizational intervention. Outcome evaluations assess participants on a minimum of three occasions: entering treatment, end of treatment, and a follow-up sometime after treatment ends. The entering-treatment versus end-of-treatment comparison assesses the effects of participating in the treatment, and the end-of-treatment versus follow-up comparison assesses the long-term effectiveness of the treatment, how well its effects hold up once treatment has ended. Outcome evaluation research shares the potential problems of attrition, testing effects, and history effects with longitudinal developmental and prospective research. Evaluation research is discussed in more detail in Chapter 15.

TABLE 2-4   Research Strategies and Research Settings

Any strategy can be used in any setting.

	RESEARCH STRATEGY		
	Single Case	*Correlational*	*Experimental*
Field Setting	Unconstrained case study	Use of hidden observers	Field experiment
Laboratory Setting	Single-case experiment	Questionnaire responses	Traditional experiment

RESEARCH SETTINGS: LABORATORY VERSUS FIELD

Research can be conducted in either the laboratory or a natural setting, often called a *field setting*. The laboratory setting offers the researcher a high degree of control over the research environment, the participants, and the independent and dependent variables, at the cost of being artificial. The field setting offers the researcher naturalism in environment, participants, the treatments participants experience (the independent variable), and the behaviors of participants in response to the treatments (the dependent variable). Let's briefly consider the relationship between the research strategies, settings, and participants.

Research Strategies and Research Settings

Although we tend to associate certain research strategies with certain settings—for example, the laboratory experiment and the naturalistic case study—any strategy can be used in either setting. Table 2-4 shows these combinations of settings and strategy.

It is easy to imagine a case study being conducted in a field setting, but how can one be done in the laboratory? Consider a situation in which a single individual comes to a psychological laboratory to participate in a study. The researcher systematically manipulates an independent variable and takes precise measurements of a dependent variable. Here we have a piece of research that has one of the primary characteristics of a case study—a focus on the behavior of a single individual—but is carried out under the highly controlled conditions of a laboratory setting. Such research is not usually called a case study, however, but a *single-case experiment*. Chapter 9 discusses both case studies and single-case experiments.

Experiments can be conducted in field settings as well as in laboratories. In such *field experiments*, the researcher manipulates an independent variable—a primary characteristic of the experiment—in a natural setting and observes its effect on people in the setting. For example, to see if a helpful model affects helping behavior, you might create a situation in which motorists drive by a disabled vehicle whose driver is or is not being helped by another motorist (the independent variable). Further down the road, they see another disabled vehicle; do they stop to help (the dependent variable)?

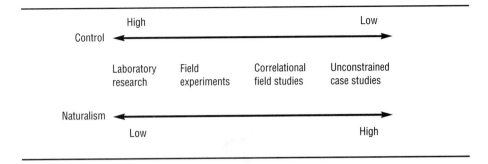

FIGURE 2-7   The Tradeoff Between Control and Naturalism in Research
Combinations of strategies and settings that are more naturalistic generally give the researcher less control over the research situation; combinations that are higher in control also tend to be less naturalistic.

Correlational research can be carried out in either setting, with varying degrees of control over what happens in the setting. At one extreme, a researcher could unobtrusively observe natural behaviors in a natural setting to determine the relationship between the behaviors. For example, you could observe natural conversations to see if men or women are more likely to interrupt the person with whom they are talking. The same study could be conducted in a laboratory setting in order to establish more control over the situation. For example, the researcher might want to control the topic of the conversation and eliminate distractions that might occur in a natural environment.

The combinations of settings and strategies allow for varying degrees of naturalism and control in research. However, as Figure 2-7 shows, these two desirable characteristics of research are, to a large extent, mutually exclusive: More control generally leads to less naturalism, and more naturalism generally leads to less control.

Research Settings and Research Participants

When we design research, we want our results to apply to some **target population** of people. This target population can be as broad as everyone in the world or as narrow as the workers in a particular job in a particular factory. When we conduct research, it is usually impossible to include everyone in the target population in the research, so we use a **participant sample** rather than the entire population, and want to apply the results found with the sample to the target population. This process of applying sample-based research results to a target population is one aspect of the problem of **generalization** in research. Let's briefly consider the relationship of research settings to participant samples.

Field research is generally carried out in a setting, such as a factory, where a sample of the target population, such as assembly workers, is naturally found. In laboratory research, however, one can either bring a sample of the target population into the laboratory or use a sample from another, perhaps more convenient, population. Much laboratory research is basic research, and most basic research in behavioral science is conducted in academic settings. As a result, most laboratory research in behavioral science that does not deal with special populations (such as psychiatric patients or children) is conducted using college students as participants (Sears, 1986). Compared to recruiting members of other populations for research, recruitment of college students is convenient (they can be required, within limits, to participate in research) and inexpensive (students participating for class credit are paid nothing, whereas nonstudent research participants usually must be paid for their time). However, the results of research conducted with college student participants may not generalize to other populations.

Most field research also uses such **convenience samples** of participants—whoever happens to be in the setting at the time the research is conducted. Therefore, the results of such research may not generalize across other natural settings or populations (Dipboye & Flanagan, 1979). The results of research conducted in one factory, for example, may not apply to another factory. The only way to ensure broad generalization across settings and populations is to systematically sample from every population and setting of interest, a difficult and expensive process. The nature of the research participants therefore represents another tradeoff in research: the use of college student samples versus convenient samples from specific settings versus participants systematically sampled from all settings and populations. Chapter 14 discusses the problems of generalization in more detail.

RESEARCH AS A SET OF TRADEOFFS

As you have noticed in the discussions of research strategies, time perspectives, and settings, the choice of any one strategy, time perspective, or setting over another results in a tradeoff: Increasing the level of one characteristic essential to good research (such as control) entails decreasing another (such as naturalism). McGrath (1981) notes that researchers would like to be able to maximize three essential characteristics simultaneously in a perfect study: generalizability across populations, precision in the control and measurement of variables, and naturalism. However, tradeoffs among these and other desirable characteristics are inherent in the selection of research strategies, time perspectives, settings, and other decisions that must be made in designing and conducting research. These unavoidable tradeoffs result in what McGrath (1981) considers a basic rule of research: that it is impossible to conduct a perfect study. No one study can provide a conclusive test of a hypothesis; the inherent limitations of the study, resulting from the loss of essential characteristics due to the tradeoffs involved, will always leave questions unanswered. For example, if an independent variable affects a dependent variable in one setting, you could always ask if it would have had the same effect in another setting or using different operational definitions.

What can we do, then, to maximize our confidence in the results of research? We must conduct multiple tests of a hypothesis using different strategies, time perspectives, settings, populations, and measures. The use of multiple studies and different methods serves three purposes. First, the strengths inherent in one method compensate for the inherent weaknesses of another. For example, an effect found under controlled laboratory conditions can be tested in field settings to see if it holds up there or if it is changed by the influence of variables present in the field setting that were controlled in the laboratory. The second purpose served by multiple studies is verification—the opportunity to learn if a hypothesis can stand up to repeated testing. Finally, using multiple methods allows us to assess the degree of convergence of the studies' results. The results of any one study might be due to the unique set of circumstances under which that study was conducted; to the extent that the results of multiple studies using different strategies, settings, populations, and so forth converge—are similar—the more confidence we can have that the hypothesis we are testing represents a general principle rather than one limited to a narrow set of circumstances.

SUMMARY

Basic research is conducted to establish general principles of behavior, is theory based, and is usually conducted in laboratory settings. Applied research is conducted to solve practical problems and is therefore problem based, and is usually conducted in field settings. Evaluation research is conducted to assess the effectiveness of an intervention, such as psychotherapy. Action research combines the purposes of the other three types. It uses theory to design an intervention to solve a problem defined via applied research; the evaluation of the intervention simultaneously tests the effectiveness of the intervention and the theory on which it is based.

The data produced by research can be either quantitative (numerical) or qualitative (nonnumerical). Although some research methods are thought of as being quantitative and others as being qualitative, any method can provide either, or both, kinds of data. Preference for quantitative or qualitative research reflects the researcher's philosophy of science.

Three broad strategies are used for conducting research. The experimental strategy emphasizes control and is the only one of the three that can determine causality; however, the high degree of control introduces artificiality into the research context. The case study strategy examines a single instance of a phenomenon in great detail and emphasizes naturalism; however, it cannot be used to determine causality and one cannot generalize across cases. The correlational strategy seeks general relationships across a large number of cases; although it cannot determine causality, it can show that a causal relationship does *not* exist between two variables and can be used to study variables that are not amenable to the experimental strategy.

Time perspectives affect research design. The longitudinal perspective looks at changes in behavior over time, whereas the cross-sectional perspective focuses on behavior at one point in time. The distinction between these perspectives is especially important in developmental research, which examines how behavior changes with age, because the cross-sectional and longitudinal approaches to data can lead to conflicting conclusions. The cohort-sequential approach allows the examination of possible reasons for those conflicts. The longitudinal perspective is also used in prospective research, which looks at the relationship of an independent variable at one point in time to a dependent variable at a later point in time, and in outcome evaluation.

The two research settings are laboratory and field. Each research strategy can be used in both settings, resulting in different combinations of control and naturalism in research. Different participant populations tend to be used in the two settings, which can limit the generalizability of the results.

Last, the selection of research strategies, time perspectives, settings, and populations can be seen as a tradeoff among three characteristics that are desirable in research: generalizability, control, and naturalism. Maximizing any one of these characteristics in a particular piece of research will minimize one or both of the other two. However, the use of multiple methods across a set of studies allows the strengths of one method to compensate for the weaknesses of others, providing a more solid database for formulating conclusions.

QUESTIONS AND EXERCISES FOR REVIEW

1. What are the similarities and differences among basic, applied, and evaluation research? How does action research combine the other three types?
2. What are some applications of the results of basic research to solving practical problems? What are some theory-testing applications of applied research?
3. Differentiate between quantitative and qualitative research. Do you think that this distinction is real or artificial? Why or why not? How did your personal philosophy of science influence your answer to these questions?
4. Compare and contrast the advantages and disadvantages of the experimental, correlational, and case study research strategies.
5. Artificiality is commonly considered a disadvantage of laboratory experiments. What are some ways in which artificiality could help you study behavior?
6. The capability of conducting research in natural settings is considered to be an advantage of case study and correlational research. What are some ways in which naturalism can *hinder* the research process?
7. What problems are involved in trying to infer causality from the results of case study and correlational research? If we cannot determine causality from the case study and correlational strategies, of what use are these strategies to research and the development of knowledge about behavior?
8. Differentiate between the cross-sectional and longitudinal time perspectives in research. What are their relative advantages and disadvantages? How does the cohort-sequential approach address those disadvantages?
9. How are research strategies and research settings related? Can you devise a hypothesis that can be tested using all six combinations of strategies and settings? Can you devise a hypothesis that can be tested in *only one* combination of strategy and setting?
10. How are research settings related to the characteristics of the participants in research? What problems do these characteristics present?
11. What is your personal preference for research type (basic, applied, and so on), strategy, time perspective, and setting? Why do you prefer these to their alternatives? How is your preference related to your epistemological perspective?
12. What are the relative advantages and disadvantages of multiple-method and single-method research?

3 THE ETHICAL TREATMENT OF RESEARCH PARTICIPANTS

RESPONSIBILITY FOR ETHICAL
RESEARCH
The Researcher
The Institutional Review Board
Membership of the IRB
Criteria for Approving
Research
Review Procedures

ETHICAL CONSIDERATIONS IN
PLANNING RESEARCH
Risk of Harm or Deprivation
Categories of Risk
Evaluating Risk
Deprivation as Risk
Benefits of Research
Risk-Benefit Analysis
Voluntary Participation
Overt Coercion
Subtle Coercion
Excessive Inducements

Informed Consent
Elements of Informed Consent
Public Behavior
Competence to Consent
Readability of Consent Forms
Informed Consent and
Internal Validity
Deception
Why Researchers Use
Deception
Ethical Objections to
Deception Research
Alternatives to Deception
Consent to Deception
Minimizing Harm in
Deception Research
How Harmful Is Deception
Research?

ETHICAL CONSIDERATIONS
DURING DATA COLLECTION
Avoidance of Harm
Screening for Risk Factors
Unanticipated Adverse Effects
Discovering Psychological
Problems

Withdrawal of Consent
Reluctance to Withdraw
The Right to Withdraw and
Internal Validity

ETHICAL CONSIDERATIONS
FOLLOWING DATA COLLECTION
Alleviating Adverse Effects
Debriefing
Components of Debriefing
Effective Debriefing
Can Debriefing Be Harmful?
Compensation of Control Groups
Confidentiality of Data
Protecting Confidentiality
Data Confidentiality and the
Law

SUMMARY

QUESTIONS AND EXERCISES
FOR REVIEW

Although the American Psychological Association (APA) was founded in 1892, its membership did not feel a need to establish a code of ethics for psychologists until 1952 and did not establish specific ethical guidelines for research with human participants until 1971 (APA, 1982). Until then, behavioral scientists believed that research participants were sufficiently protected by researchers' sensitivity to the participants' well-being (Grisso et al., 1991). However, several studies conducted in the 1960s and early 1970s led to debate about the ethics of invading research participants' privacy in order to collect data (Humphreys, 1975) and of causing harm, especially in the form of severe stress, to research participants (Milgram, 1974). These controversies led the APA to develop its first set of guidelines for research with human participants. Similar concerns over the ethics of biomedical, as well as social and behavioral science, research led to federal regulations concerning research with human participants (U.S. Public Health Service, 1971; U.S. Department of Health and Human Services [DHHS], 1992). In addition to the ethical guidelines set out in its code of ethics, the APA (1982) has published a book explaining the guidelines and discussing their implementation in research.

This chapter outlines the responsibilities and reviews the guidelines for conducting ethical research. I discuss the guidelines in terms of three phases of a research project: planning the research, collecting the data, and actions following data collection. The guidelines derive from three general ethical principles: respect for persons, beneficence, and justice (National Commission for Protection of Human Subjects of Biomedical and Behavioral Research, 1978). The term *respect* refers to protecting people's privacy and freedom of choice in deciding whether to participate in research, and it is reflected in the ethical guidelines for voluntary participation in research, informed consent, freedom to withdraw from research, and confidentiality of data. The term *beneficence* refers to protecting research participants from harm and is reflected in the ethical guidelines for risk-benefit analysis, avoidance of harm during research, and confidentiality of data. And *justice* refers to ensuring that the burdens of research participation and the benefits of research are shared by all members of society so that the burdens do not fall unduly on some groups (such as the poor and others with little power) while the benefits accrue only to members of other groups. This principle is reflected in the ethical guidelines for voluntary participation and informed consent.

Before beginning this discussion of research ethics, it is important to note that the ethical principles laid out by the APA and other professional organizations are guidelines, not rules. That is, they set out broadly defined parameters for behavior covering a wide range of research topics, settings, methods, and participants, not a rigid set of do's and don'ts. Consequently, people will have honest disagreements about the ethical propriety of particular studies. These disagreements are based on personal values, such as those discussed in Chapter 1, and the effects that those values have on judgments about the potential risks to participants posed by the research and about the benefits to be gained from the research by the participants, science, and society.

These differences of opinion surrounded the three studies cited earlier that aroused behavioral scientists' concern about the ethics of research, and they still surround discussion of those studies today. Research continues to stimulate ethical debate. For example, a study of alcoholics (Jacob, Krahn, & Leonard, 1991) raised the question of the ethical propriety of, among other issues, providing alcoholic beverages to alcoholics (Koocher, 1991; Stricker, 1991), leading to further discussion of these issues by the researchers (Jacob & Leonard, 1991) and the editors of the journal that published the research report (Kendall & Beutler, 1991). Because answers to ethical questions are matters of values and judgment, they will never, except in the most extreme cases, be completely resolved. However, these disagreements are beneficial to science because they help keep the importance of conducting ethically sound research in the forefront of researchers' minds.

RESPONSIBILITY FOR ETHICAL RESEARCH

Responsibility for the ethical conduct of research is vested in the researcher (by the APA's 1992 code of ethics) and in the institution sponsoring the research (by federal regulations; DHHS, 1992). Let's examine each of these responsibilities.

The Researcher

"Psychologists are responsible for the ethical conduct of research conducted by them or others under their supervision or control" (APA, 1992, p. 1608). The ultimate responsibility for the ethical treatment of research participants lies with the person in charge of the research project. As the APA code states, researchers are responsible not only for their own actions, but also for the actions of those who work for them on the research project. These responsibilities place two obligations on researchers. The first is to carefully consider the ethical aspects of the research they design and conduct. The next three sections of this chapter review the ethical guidelines for research. The second obligation is to train students and research assistants in the ethical conduct of research and to monitor their research to ensure it is conducted ethically.

An important aspect of ethical decision making in research is weighing the expected risks of harm presented by participation in the research against the potential benefits of the research to the participants, science, and society. However, researchers can face a conflict of interest in making this risk-benefit analysis. On the one hand, they want to conduct ethical research; on the other, successful completion of the research could enhance their prestige, status within the profession, and sometimes incomes. So, researchers, like all people under these circumstances, might inadvertently underestimate the risks of the research and overestimate its benefits. In addition, the researcher might not notice all the potential risks to participants in the research. For these reasons, federal regulations (DHHS, 1992) require institutions that sponsor research with human participants to establish boards to review all research before it is conducted to ensure that the research meets ethical standards.

The Institutional Review Board

The purpose of the **institutional review board (IRB)** is to examine proposed research to ensure that it will be carried out ethically. Although federal regulations exempt some types of research from review, most IRBs require proposed research that falls into those categories to be reviewed to ensure that it meets the criteria for exemption (Sieber, 1992).

MEMBERSHIP OF THE IRB   An IRB consists of at least five members who have varied backgrounds that allow them to review proposed research from diverse viewpoints. They must also be familiar with applicable laws, regulations, and institutional policies. When the research includes members of a population defined by federal regulations as vulnerable to exploitation (such as children and psychiatric patients), the board should also include a member knowledgeable of issues relevant to that population. In addition to its members meeting these knowledge requirements, each IRB must have at least one member who is a scientist, one member who is not a scientist, and one member who is otherwise not affiliated with the institution. Because of these requirements, IRBs often have many more than five members. Interestingly, except when the research being reviewed includes prisoners as participants, IRBs are not required to include a representative of the population with which the research will be conducted. However, researchers often find it useful to consult with members of the research population to determine their views of the ethicality of proposed research and their opinions of any potential risks not noticed by the researcher (Sieber, 1992).

CRITERIA FOR APPROVING RESEARCH   Federal regulations establish specific criteria that IRBs must use in deciding whether to approve proposed research. These criteria are shown in Box 3-1 and reflect the ethical guidelines reviewed in this chapter. These are also the only criteria an IRB can use in evaluating the ethical propriety of proposed research. IRBs are, for example, forbidden to consider the ethics of the uses to which the results of the research can be put (DHHS, 1992, sec. 46.111a2). The ethical use of research results is, of course, an important question, addressed in Chapter 18. In addition to their authority to approve or disapprove the initiation of a research project, IRBs are authorized to stop a project if it deviates from the procedures they approved or if it results in unanticipated severe harm to participants.

REVIEW PROCEDURES   The review process begins when a researcher submits a **research protocol** to the IRB. The protocol provides the IRB with the information it needs to make its decision and consists of the elements shown in Box 3-2. Depending on the nature of the research and the amount of explanation and description required, the protocol might be very brief or quite long. Once the IRB receives the protocol, its members review it. The IRB may contact the researcher for clarifications during the review process, and the board may call in nonvoting technical experts to evaluate the scientific

BOX 3-1 Criteria for Approval of Research by IRBs

1. Risks to participants are minimized.

2. Risks to participants are reasonable in relation to anticipated benefits to participants and the importance of the knowledge that can reasonably be expected from the research.

3. Selection of participants is equitable in that members of some populations, such as minority groups, do not bear an inordinate proportion of the risks of the research or receive an inordinately small proportion of expected benefits.

4. Each participant gives informed consent to participate in the research.

5. Informed consent is appropriately documented.

6. The research plan makes adequate provision for monitoring data collection to ensure the safety of participants.

7. There are adequate provisions to protect the privacy of participants and to maintain the confidentiality of data.

8. When some or all of the participants are likely to be vulnerable to coercion or undue influence, safeguards have been included in the study to protect the rights and welfare of the participants.

Source: Adapted from DHHS, 1992, sec. 46.111.

BOX 3-2 Elements of a Research Protocol

1. The rationale for the research: Why is it being conducted?

2. The procedures to be used in the research, including

   a. The reasons for choosing the participant population to be used and the procedures to be used to recruit participants.

   b. A detailed description of any research apparatus, and its purpose and effects on participants.

   c. Copies of any questionnaires that participants are to complete.

   d. A detailed description of the participants' experiences in the research and in the various experimental conditions.

   e. Summaries of instructions that participants will receive, or transcripts of the instructions if they are used to manipulate the independent variable.

   f. If any adverse effects of participation are anticipated, a detailed description of how these effects will be removed or alleviated.

   g. If participants are deceived in any way, a detailed description of the procedures to be used to explain the deception to participants and relieve any uneasiness that they feel about it, to include summaries of oral explanations and copies of handouts.

3. A description of the benefits expected to accrue from the research to participants, science, and society.

4. A description of any anticipated risks to participants, a description of how anticipated risks will be minimized, and a description of the procedures to be followed if participants suffer harm from the research. If there are any alternative procedures that would present less risk to participants, they must be described and the reasons for not using them explained.

5. A risk-benefit analysis showing that the anticipated benefits of the research outweigh its expected risks.

6. A description of the procedures for obtaining informed consent, including a copy of the consent form.

merit of the proposed research. The board then meets to make its decision. The decision may be to (1) approve the proposal as it is, (2) approve the protocol contingent on specified changes, (3) require that the protocol be amended and submitted for further review, or (4) disapprove the research. Outright disapproval is extremely rare; the board is more likely to require changes to questionable procedures. When contingent approval is given, the researcher must submit the changes to the IRB and await final approval before beginning the research. However, the board usually delegates such approval authority to one member, so the process proceeds quickly. Once the IRB approves a protocol, the research must be carried out exactly as described, *with no changes, no matter how minor.* Any changes must be approved by the IRB; however, minor changes, such as rewording nonessential instructions, usually receive swift approval.

When developing an IRB protocol, it is useful to discuss it with people who have done similar research to anticipate problems and deal with them in advance. Other experts can also be helpful. For example, a campus physician can give advice about how to effectively screen potential participants for possible health risks involved in the research, such as a history of cardiovascular disease when the research procedures call for strenuous exercise. Finally, members of the IRB can provide advice on how the board as a whole is likely to view a particular research procedure, and many IRBs will give advisory opinions when a researcher is uncertain about the acceptability of a procedure. However, because the vast majority of behavioral research poses little risk to its participants, most protocols face little difficulty in gaining approval.

ETHICAL CONSIDERATIONS IN PLANNING RESEARCH

Four ethical issues must be considered when planning research: the risk of harm or deprivation to participants, voluntary participation in the research, informed consent to participate in the research, and deceiving participants as part of the research.

Risk of Harm or Deprivation

The design of ethical research requires you to consider several categories of risk, to evaluate the severity and likelihood of the possible risk, the risk of deprivation of benefit as well as risk of direct harm, and the likely benefits of the research to the participants, science, and society. After evaluating these factors, you must weigh the expected benefits of the research against its anticipated risks. For research to be ethical, the expected benefits must outweigh the anticipated risks.

CATEGORIES OF RISK   When we think about the risk of harm in research, we typically think in terms of physical harm, such as receiving an electrical shock or a side effect of taking a drug. However, as Sieber (1992) points out, there are other types of harm that participants in behavioral research could be exposed to. Perhaps the most common, especially among college students who participate in research, is inconvenience stemming from taking time away from more preferred activities or boredom with the research procedure. Other nonphysical risks might be more severe. Psychological harm might result, for example, if a participant is subjected to psychological stress, such as apparently having severely injured another research participant. Although researchers are obligated to remove any such negative effects if they occur, the occurrence itself can have an adverse impact on the participant.

Social harm can result from the disruption of social relationships. For example, Rubin and Mitchell (1976) found that joint participation in a survey on dating relationships by members of dating couples led some of the couples to become less close than they had been before participating in the research, principally through discussing issues included in the survey. Finally, some forms of research might carry risk of economic or legal harm to participants. For example, an employee who, as part of an organizational research project, expresses criticism of the company might be fired if he or she is identified, or in some forms of research, such as on drug abuse, participants might disclose illegal behavior that could result in their arrest if identified. For these reasons, as discussed later, confidentiality is an important part of the researcher-participant relationship.

EVALUATING RISK   Because harm can accrue to research participants, researchers have the obligation to assess the potential risks to participants in their research and to minimize the risk or not conduct the research if the degree of risk is not justified by the potential benefits of the research. Any research that entails more than **minimal risk** to participants must be carefully evaluated. As defined by federal regulations, "*Minimal risk* means that the probability and magnitude of harm or discomfort anticipated in the research are not greater . . . than those ordinarily encountered in daily life" (DHHS, 1992, sec. 46.102i). Levine (cited in Diener & Crandall, 1978) suggests that the degree of risk to research participants is a <u>function of five factors</u>:

1. Likelihood of occurrence. The less probable the harm, the more justifiable is the study.
2. Severity. Minor harm is more justifiable than possible major injuries.
3. Duration after the research. The investigator should determine whether harm, if it does occur, will be short-lived or long-lasting.
4. Reversibility. An important factor is whether the harm can be reversed.
5. Measures for early detection. If incipient damage is recognized early it is less likely that people will be exposed to severe harm. (p. 27)

Each of the risk categories identified by Sieber (1992) should be assessed along each of these dimensions, as shown schematically in Figure 3-1.

One step that can minimize risk to participants is screening potential participants for risk factors and allowing only those people who are at low risk for harm to participate. For example, Jacob et al. (1991), in their study of the effects of alcohol consumption, took health histories from all their potential participants to eliminate those who might suffer adverse physical reactions to alcohol. When Zimbardo (1973) conducted a study that he anticipated would be stressful, he used psychological screening to weed out potential participants who might be unusually sensitive to stress. As noted later, such precautions cannot absolutely guarantee that no harm will come to participants; however, they do reduce the likelihood of harm.

Evaluation of risks involved in research with children requires special consideration because the nature and degree of risk posed by a procedure can change with the

Dimension of Risk

Category of Risk	Likelihood	Severity	Duration	Reversibility	Detection
Inconvenience					
Physical					
Psychological					
Social					
Economic					
Legal					

FIGURE 3-1   Risk Assessment Matrix
For each category of risk, the researcher should evaluate the likelihood of harm; the probable severity, duration, and reversibility of the harm; and the ease of detecting that the harm is occurring.

ages of the children involved (Thompson, 1990). For example, vulnerability to coercion and manipulation decreases with age, while threats to self-esteem increase with age. It is therefore essential to carefully consider the ages of child research participants when assessing risk. Thompson (1990) and Koocher and Keith-Spiegel (1990) provide excellent guides to this process.

DEPRIVATION AS RISK   Research that tests the efficacy of a treatment, such as a psychotherapeutic, organizational, or educational intervention, needs a baseline or control condition against which to compare the effects of the treatment. Typically, participants in this control condition receive no treatment, or a placebo treatment that should have no effect on the problem being treated, or a treatment believed to be less effective than the one being tested (Kazdin, 1997). Consequently, the members of the control group are deprived of the benefits the researchers expect to accrue from the treatment being tested. This situation presents a true ethical dilemma because such controls are necessary to accurately assess the effectiveness of the treatment and it would be unethical to put treatments of unknown effectiveness into general use. In effect, members of control conditions in treatment effectiveness research must suffer some deprivation to ensure that only safe and effective treatments are offered to the public.

The degree of risk that members of a control group face depends on the severity of the problem being treated. The risk may be especially high in psychotherapy research, in which participants may be suffering from conditions that hamper their ability to carry on their lives and whose condition may deteriorate or at least not improve if left untreated. One solution makes use of the fact that, in many locations, treatment services cannot meet the client demand so that people must be placed on waiting lists for treatment. People on the waiting list are recruited for control groups. Members of such waiting-list control groups are deprived of treatment, but it is a deprivation they would have to endure even if no study were being conducted because treatment resources are unavailable. In addition, as discussed later, people in a waiting-list control group have the option of not participating in the research or of withdrawing from it. In conducting such studies, researchers must ensure that clients with the most severe problems receive priority for treatment. However, the data from these people should not be used in the research because doing so would lead to a lack of comparability between treatment and control groups. The ethical issues involved in conducting well-controlled treatment effectiveness research are discussed in more detail by Imber et al. (1986) and Kazdin (1997).

BENEFITS OF RESEARCH   Although participants in behavioral research face risk, they can also benefit from participation. Some research participants receive monetary benefits. These benefits can be direct payments to compensate participants for their time and inconvenience or, in the case of participants in psychotherapy research, reduction or elimination of fees that would otherwise be charged for treatment. Psychological benefits can also accrue. For example, many research participants have reported they had learned something of value about themselves from their experiences (for example, see Milgram, 1974; Zimbardo, 1973). Finally, a study can be designed to provide educational benefits to participants when their firsthand experience with research procedures is accompanied by an explanation of how and why the research was conducted.

Research can benefit not only its participants but also science and society. As discussed in Chapter 2, basic researchers are motivated by a desire to advance knowledge and applied researchers by a desire to improve society. Only rarely is either type of researcher primarily interested in providing direct, immediate benefits to the participants in research (Kimmel, 1996; Sieber, 1992). However, researchers do expect participants to benefit indirectly, along with the rest of society, through application of the knowledge gained from basic research and social policy formulated as a result of applied research.

RISK-BENEFIT ANALYSIS   Because research entails both potential risks to participants and potential benefits to participants, science, and society, researchers must carefully consider whether the anticipated benefits of their research justify the anticipated risks to participants. Only when anticipated benefits outweigh anticipated risks is research ethically justified. In much behavioral science research this **risk-benefit analysis** is not problematic because participants face only minimal risk in the form of short-term inconvenience, even if they can be expected to receive only a small benefit. Sometimes, however, the ethical questions are more difficult. For example, how much harm, say, in the form of severe stress, is justified by the potential to gain scientific or practical knowledge, however great? Remember, before a study is conducted, the value of the knowledge that it will produce is only potential; there is no guarantee it will produce valuable results. Related questions include: Can monetary reimbursement compensate for stress? If so, how many dollars is a particular amount of stress worth?

The resolution of such questions is difficult for a number of reasons (Diener & Crandall, 1978; Sieber, 1992). First, risk-benefit analyses are necessarily subjective. Ethical judgments are value judgments, so perceptions of risk and benefit can vary greatly from person to person. Thus, there is no way to objectively quantify the amount or probability of either the potential risks to participants or the potential benefits of the research. It is therefore impossible to conclusively demonstrate that the anticipated benefits of any piece of proposed research outweigh its anticipated risks. Second, a risk-benefit analysis can deal only with anticipated risks and benefits; *un*anticipated risks and benefits are always possible. Because of this possibility of unanticipated risk, researchers are obligated to carefully monitor participants during the research to detect and avert any developing risks; this obligation is discussed later in this chapter. In addition, as Rubin and Mitchell (1976) found, a study can benefit some participants and harm others. Finally, as noted earlier, risk-benefit analyses can be problematic because the analysis is initially made by the researcher, who may have a conflict of interest in its outcome. Perhaps the best guideline for weighing the risks and benefits of research is one suggested by S. W. Cook (1976): "The conditions of the research should be such that investigators would be willing for members of their own families to take part" (p. 239).

Voluntary Participation

The risk-benefit analysis is designed to protect research participants from harm. The principle of **voluntary participation** in research is designed to protect potential participants' autonomy by giving them the choice of whether or not to participate. This freedom of choice has two aspects: the freedom to decide about participation free from any coercion or excessive inducement and the freedom to withdraw from the research without penalty once it has begun. This section discusses people's initial decisions to participate in research; freedom to withdraw is discussed later.

OVERT COERCION With one exception, people today are rarely dragooned into research participation against their will. The only current situation in which people are given little choice about participating in research resides in the "subject pools" found at many colleges and universities, in which students enrolled in behavioral science courses are required to participate in research as the "subjects" of studies. However, abuses have occurred in the not-so-distant past, especially with prisoners and the mentally ill (Dworkin, 1992; Sieber, 1992), leading to very specific ethical guidelines and regulations governing research with populations who may have limited power to refuse research participation (APA, 1982; DHHS, 1992).

Subject pools are quite common. Sieber and Saks (1989) reported that about 75% of psychology departments with graduate programs have subject pools and that about 95% recruit from introductory courses. The primary justification given for requiring students to participate in research is that research participation, like homework assignments, has educational value: Students get firsthand experience with behavioral science research. Critics of the subject pool system charge that most pools are run solely for the convenience of researchers and that, if educational benefits accrue, they are minimal. As a result, the critics say, the coercive aspects of participation and the resultant limitation of the students' freedom of choice outweigh the educational benefits (for example, see Diener & Crandall, 1978). Because of these concerns, the APA (1982) has issued specific ethical guidelines for subject pools that include a requirement for alternatives to research participation that provide the same benefits to students as does participation. Requiring students to participate in research does limit their freedom of choice, so researchers who use subject pools have a strong ethical obligation to make participation as educational as possible. At a minimum, researchers should explain the purpose of the research and how the procedures used will fulfill that purpose, and they should answer participants' questions about the research.

Discussions of the coerciveness of subject pools are usually based on the opinions of faculty members. What do the students who are required to participate in research think about the process? Surprisingly little research has been conducted on this question. Leak (1981) found that only 2% of the subject pool members he surveyed felt coerced into participating. However, 47% did think that being offered extra credit toward the final course grade was coercive, although only 3% objected to extra credit being given. Leak interpreted these findings as indicating that "some [students] find extra credit a temptation somewhat hard to refuse" (p. 148). Overall, students appear to find research participation a positive and educational experience (Brody, Gluck, & Aragon, 2000). However, because many do not, alternatives must be offered.

SUBTLE COERCION   Alternative assignments must be carefully designed, because if students perceive them to be more aversive than research participation, they represent a subtle form of coercion—research participation becomes the lesser of two evils. Psychological manipulation is another form of subtle coercion that must be avoided. Participants who have completed a study might be reluctant to refuse when asked to "stay a little while longer" and participate in another study, about which they did not know. "Strong encouragement" by an instructor to participate in research might make some students reluctant to use alternative assignments for fear it will adversely impact their grades (Koocher & Keith-Spiegel, 1998). Researchers and teachers are not the only sources of subtle coercion. Reluctant participants may give in to peer pressure to participate (Lidz et al., 1984), and employers may "encourage" employees to participate in research that they favor (Mirvis & Seashore, 1979). Because researchers do not directly control these sources of influence, before collecting data they must ensure that potential participants understand their right to refuse participation.

EXCESSIVE INDUCEMENTS   It is quite common and usually ethical to offer people inducements to participate in research—for example, to offer participants money to compensate them for their time and inconvenience. Inducements can become ethically problematic, however, when they are so large that potential research participants feel unable to turn them down and so are effectively coerced into participating. For example, Koocher (1991) and Stricker (1991) thought that Jacob et al.'s (1991) payment of $400 to the families participating in their research might have constituted an offer impossible to refuse. Jacob and Leonard (1991) defended their procedure by pointing out that money was the only inducement they *could* offer their participants and that the participants gave 75 hours of their time to the research—working out to $5.33 per hour per family, which did not constitute an excessive amount.

The point at which an inducement becomes sufficiently large as to constitute coercion depends on the people to whom it is offered. As noted, Leak (1981) found that college students thought that extra credit for research participation was a coercive inducement. Koocher and Keith-Spiegel (1998) note that $3 per day is a lot of money to prisoners and so might constitute an excessive inducement. The impropriety of large inducements depends largely on the extent to which people feel compelled by their need for the inducement to participate in research that they would otherwise avoid. That is, a large inducement for a study involving severe risk is ethically more questionable than the same inducement for a study presenting minimal risk, and people with a strong need for the inducement, such as unemployed people with a need for money, feel the greatest compulsion to participate. It is therefore ethically least proper to offer large inducements to people with great need when the research involves more than minimal risk. However, a large inducement offered to someone not in need might constitute appropriate compensation for the risk. Note that benefits other than money can constitute excessive inducements—for example, a costly service such as psychotherapy or medical care (Koocher & Keith-Spiegel, 1998).

Informed Consent

For participation in research to be truly voluntary, potential participants must understand what will happen to them during the research and the risks and benefits of participation. The principle of **informed consent** requires that potential participants receive this information before data about them are collected so that they can make an informed decision about participation.

ELEMENTS OF INFORMED CONSENT   Federal regulations specify eight basic elements of informed consent, shown in Box 3-3. These regulations also require that, with a few exceptions, researchers obtain the participants' written consent to participate in the form of an informed consent form. This form must include the information shown in Box 3-3 unless the IRB grants a waiver. The form must be signed by the participant, who has the right to receive a copy of the form. The format of the informed consent form varies from institution to institution; contact your IRB for its format.

An IRB can waive the requirement for written informed consent under limited circumstances. One circumstance is when people can give what Sieber (1992) calls *behavioral consent*, such as hanging up on a telephone interviewer or not returning a mail survey. Under these circumstances, an oral or written statement of the purpose of the research is sufficient to give potential participants the opportunity to indicate consent or refusal behaviorally. A second circumstance is when a signed consent form is the only record linking participants to the research and the participants could be harmed if their participation were revealed. Sieber (1992) cites research on criminal behavior as one example of this circumstance. Under these conditions, the elements of informed consent must still be provided to potential participants, but they would give oral consent to participate rather than signing a consent form.

PUBLIC BEHAVIOR   A major and somewhat controversial exception to the requirement for obtaining informed consent is research consisting solely of observations of public behavior when the identities of the participants are not recorded. There is a presumption

BOX 3-3 Elements of Informed Consent

1. A statement that the study involves research, an explanation of the purposes of the research and the expected duration of the participant's participation, a description of the procedures to be used, and identification of any procedures that are not standard

2. A description of any reasonably foreseeable risks or discomforts to the participant

3. A description of any benefits to the participant or to others which may reasonably be expected from the research

4. A disclosure of appropriate alternative procedures or courses of treatment, if any, that might be advantageous to the participant

5. A statement describing the extent, if any, to which confidentiality of records identifying the participant will be maintained

6. For research involving more than minimal risk, an explanation as to whether any compensation will be given and an explanation as to whether any medical treatments are available if injury occurs and, if so, what they consist of

7. An explanation of whom to contact for answers to pertinent questions about the research and research participants' rights, and whom to contact in the event of a research-related injury to the participant

8. A statement that participation is voluntary, that refusal to participate will involve no penalty or loss of benefits to which the participant is otherwise entitled, and that the participant may discontinue participation at any time without penalty or loss of benefits to which the participant is otherwise entitled

Source: Adapted from DHHS, 1992, sec. 46.116.

that people understand that what they do in public can be observed; consequently, people give implicit consent for others to observe what they do by the fact of doing it publicly. Although this presumption of implicit consent is generally accepted, as shown by its inclusion in federal regulations, not everyone agrees with it. Steininger, Newell, and Garcia (1984), for example, argue that scientific observation of public behavior requires the informed consent of participants because it differs in purpose from casual observation. They take the position that although people do implicitly consent to the *observation* of their public behavior, they do not implicitly consent to have it *recorded*, a process that separates scientific observation from casual observation. Steininger et al. hold that recording of behavior without informed consent is an invasion of privacy. Note, however, that federal regulations waive the requirement for informed consent only when no information concerning the identity of the participants is recorded. General descriptive information, such as sex, apparent age, and so forth, is acceptable because it cannot be used to identify a specific individual; the recording of any identifying information, such as an automobile license plate number, requires informed consent.

The ethical issues involved in observing public behavior are complicated by the question of what constitutes a public venue for observation. For example, take Middlemist, Knowles, and Matter's (1976) study of the effects of personal space invasion on somatic arousal. They conducted their research in public men's lavatories on a university campus. In one part of their research, they had an observer note which urinals were chosen by users of a lavatory and how far those urinals were from others already in use. The observer also noted how long it took the men to begin urinating (using sound as the indicator) after stepping up to the urinal. Middlemist et al. used the amount of time before urination began as a measure of arousal; somatic arousal tightens the muscles that control urination so that more arousal could lead to longer delays in urination. They hypothesized that closer physical distances between the men at the urinals would lead to greater arousal and so to longer delays in urination. The ethical question this study raises is whether a public lavatory is a sufficiently public place to allow observation of behavior. Koocher (1977) expressed the problem this way: "Though one could claim that a college lavatory is a public place, it is a non sequitur to suggest that one does not expect a degree of privacy there" (p. 121). Middlemist, Knowles, and Matter (1977) replied that "the behavior studied was naturally occurring and would have happened in the same way without the observer. The information gathered was available to everyone in the lavatory: the only unusual feature was that the information was recorded" (p. 122). The last point brings us back to Steininger et al.'s (1984) question: Without informed consent, is recording public behavior less ethical than observing it?

Most field research takes place in settings that are unambiguously public and thus rarely raises questions on that score. However, much field research also involves experimentation, in which the researcher manipulates the natural situation in order to observe people's responses to the manipulation. How ethical is it to intervene in a natural setting rather than simply to observe it? Consider another part of Middlemist et al.'s (1976) research, in which they manipulated the distance between an actual user of the urinals in a public men's room and someone working for them who pretended to use another urinal. This confederate used either the urinal directly adjacent to the user's or one farther away. Again, an observer recorded the amount of time that passed before the user began to urinate. Was it ethical to manipulate personal space in this context, and to observe and record the resulting behavior? Middlemist et al. (1977) gave two reasons for concluding that it was. First, they had interviewed half the men whom they had observed in the first study, telling them what had happened. None reported being bothered by being observed and having their behavior recorded. Second, "The men felt that an invasion of personal space at a urinal was not unusual, had been encountered many times, and was not an experience that caused them any great pain or embarrassment" (p. 122). The second point reflects a belief held by many researchers that a manipulation that mimics an everyday event presents no ethical problems because it presents minimal risk to participants (Aronson, Ellsworth, Carlsmith, & Gonzales, 1990; Diener & Crandall, 1978).

But what about manipulations that go beyond the scope of everyday experiences? For example, is it ethical to present passersby with a man lying on the floor with what appears to be blood spurting from a realistic wound, as did Shotland and Heinold (1985)? Before conducting such studies, you must carefully consider their potential emotional impact on participants and the degree to which any adverse effects can be alleviated after participation. At a minimum, you should anticipate such problems by having your research proposal reviewed by colleagues before the IRB review. It might also be useful to interview people in the population in which the participants will be drawn to determine their opinions about the study's impact on participants (Sieber, 1992). If the study is carried out, the researcher has a strong ethical obligation to monitor participants' reactions to the situation and to terminate the study if reactions are more extreme than anticipated.

COMPETENCE TO CONSENT   To provide informed consent to participate in research, people must be capable of understanding the risks and benefits involved and capable of realistically evaluating them. However, not all people are capable of understanding these issues, and therefore they are not competent to give consent. These groups include children, the mentally ill, the mentally retarded, and people suffering from intellectually incapacitating illness such as Alzheimer's disease (APA, 1982). It is important to note that the law defines *child* rather broadly in terms of ability to give consent to participation in research: Most states set 18 as the age of consent for this purpose (Annas, Glantz, & Katz, 1977). This legal position has an important implication for researchers who recruit participants from college or university subject pools: Some first-year students might not yet be 18 years old and may therefore not be legally competent to give informed consent.

Meeting the consent requirement for people considered incompetent to give consent is a two-part process. First, the potential participant's parent or legal guardian must provide informed consent to allow the person to participate. When gaining the permission of the parent or guardian may not adequately protect the participant, IRBs may waive this requirement provided that other mechanisms are in place for ensuring the participant's welfare (DHHS, 1992). The federal regulation cites neglected or abused children as examples of such a circumstance. The second process is obtaining the **affirmative assent** of the potential participant. That is, the person must specifically agree to participate; the only exceptions to this rule are when the participant is incapable of giving assent (as with infants) or when the research provides a direct benefit to the participant in terms of health or well-being. The participants' assent must be affirmative in that they must specifically agree to participate; "mere failure to object should not . . . be construed as assent" (DHHS, 1992, sec. 46.402b).

Consent of a parent or guardian and assent of the participant do not relieve researchers of their responsibility for the welfare of participants in their research. In some instances, parents or guardians might not act in the best interest of the participant (Dworkin, 1992; Thompson, 1990). Although probably rare, such problems are most likely to arise when the parent or guardian receives more direct benefit from the research (such as a monetary payment) than does the participant (Koocher & Keith-Spiegel, 1990). Researchers must be sensitive to this possibility when designing and conducting their research.

READABILITY OF CONSENT FORMS   Even when potential participants have the cognitive capacity to give informed consent, researchers do not always provide the required information in a form that lets them understand the research procedures to be used and the attendant risks and benefits. Ogloff and Otto (1991), for example, found that the average consent form used in psychological research was written at the college senior level; even those intended to be used with high school students were written at the college sophomore level. Ogloff and Otto (1991) noted that their findings imply that "to the extent that participants [rely] on consent forms that they . . . have . . . difficulty reading and comprehending, informed consent [is] not obtained" (p. 249). Researchers have an absolute responsibility to ensure that participants in their research fully understand the procedures, risks, and benefits involved. They must therefore design their consent forms carefully.

Researchers can take a number of steps to increase understanding of their consent forms. First, they can write the forms at an appropriate reading level; some commentators suggest a seventh- or eighth-grade level, even for college students (Young, Hooker, & Freeberg, 1990). Second, researchers can have members of the population from which they will recruit participants read the consent form and comment on its clarity (Ogloff & Otto, 1991). When the research involves greater-than-minimal risk, researchers can supplement the written consent form with an oral explanation and have potential participants explain the contents of the consent form in their own words to ensure understanding (Ogloff & Otto, 1991).

INFORMED CONSENT AND INTERNAL VALIDITY   Although fully informing potential participants about the purpose and procedures of the research allows them to make reasoned decisions about participation, the information they receive can affect how they respond to the research situation. For example, Taffel (1955) found people could be conditioned to use words more frequently in an interview if the interviewer reinforced the words by saying "good" each time the speaker used the words as part of a reply to a question. Resnick and Schwartz (1973) attempted to replicate these results under two conditions, one in which participants were told as little as possible about the rationale and procedures of the research and a second condition in which participants were fully informed on these points. In the minimal-information condition, Resnick and Schwartz replicated Taffel's results: Use of the reinforced words increased over time. In the full-information condition, the opposite occurred: Use of the reinforced words decreased over time. Full knowledge of the purpose of the study — that "good" was intended to increase the use of certain words — apparently aroused a state called *psychological reactance* in the participants (Brehm & Brehm, 1981): They did the opposite of what someone was trying to get them to do. Because participants' knowledge of the purpose of research can affect their responses, researchers sometimes find it useful either to withhold information from participants or to deceive them about the nature of the research. These practices have resulted in ethical controversy.

Deception

Deception is used quite frequently in some areas of behaviorial science research; for example, Nicks, Korn, and Mainieri (1997) found that about one third of the studies published during 1994 in social psychology journals used some form of deception. Deception can take two forms (Arellano-Goldamos, cited in Schuler, 1982). With *active deception*, the researcher provides participants with false information. Some of the more common forms of active deception are

- Providing false information about the purpose of the research, such as telling participants that an experiment deals with aversive conditioning rather than aggression.
- Providing false information about the nature of the research task, such as telling participants that a personality inventory is an opinion survey.

- Using confederates who pose either as other participants in the research or as people who happen to be in the research setting. Not only are the identities of the confederates misrepresented to the participants, but the ways in which they interact with the participants are deceptive in that they are following a script rather than acting naturally.
- Providing participants with false information about their performance, such as by giving them an impossible task in order to induce failure.
- Leading participants to think that they are interacting with another person, who actually does not exist. Communications from the "other person" are actually materials the researcher prepared.

With *passive deception,* the researcher either withholds information from the participants or observes or records their behavior without their knowledge. This section addresses the issues of why researchers use deception, the ethical objections to deception, alternatives to deception in research, minimizing harm if deception is used, and whether deception is actually harmful to research participants.

WHY RESEARCHERS USE DECEPTION   There are five reasons why researchers might include deceptive elements in their studies (Diener & Crandall, 1978; Sieber, 1992). First, as shown by Resnick and Schwartz's (1973) study, participants' knowledge of the purposes of the research or the procedures that are used could lead them to give artificial responses. Consequently, researchers might withhold the true purpose of the research from participants or give them a false explanation for it. A second reason for using deception, related to the first, is to obtain information participants would be reluctant to give, due to defensiveness or embarrassment, if they knew the true purpose of the research. Use of disguised personality or attitude measures falls into this category.

The third reason for the use of deception is to allow manipulation of an independent variable. For example, if a researcher is interested in whether support from another person helps people resist group pressure to change their opinions, at least two deceptions are required to manipulate the independent variable. First, a fictitious group must be constructed that will pressure participants to change their opinions. Second, in the experimental condition a member of the group must pretend to agree with the participants' positions and take their side against the group. The researcher will also probably deceive the participants about the purpose of the research, presenting it as studying group interaction rather than response to group pressure. If participants knew the true purpose, it could affect their responses to the situation.

A fourth reason for deception, related to the third, is to study events that occur only rarely in the natural environment and so are difficult to study outside the laboratory. For example, emergencies, by definition, are rare events, but psychologists are interested in how people respond to them and the factors affecting their responses. It is far more efficient to create a simulated emergency in the laboratory than to hope that a researcher is on the scene and ready to collect data when one occurs naturally. However, as noted in Chapter 2, naturalistic research has advantages over laboratory research. Therefore, do not avoid field research in favor of laboratory research merely for the sake of convenience.

Finally, deception can be used to minimize the risk of harm to research participants. In studies on conflict and aggression, for example, researchers employ confederates who pose as participants and instigate the conflict or aggression being studied. The confederates behave in ways that limit the conflict to nonharmful levels, and they can stop the experiment if the situation appears to be getting out of hand. Such controls would be difficult with two antagonistic real participants.

ETHICAL OBJECTIONS TO DECEPTION RESEARCH   Advocates of nondeceptive research hold that deception is in itself unethical and that the expected methodological advantages of deception research are outweighed by its potential harm (see, for example, Baumrind, 1985). The fundamental position of the advocates of nondeceptive research is that deception is lying and that lying is unethical under most circumstances. They also point to adverse effects that can result from deception. One such effect is that misrepresenting the purposes or procedures of the research limits or eliminates potential participants' ability to give informed consent: Fully informed consent can come only with full information. All responsible researchers would agree with Sieber (1992) that it is morally indefensible to use deception to trick people into participating in research that they would avoid if they fully understood its purpose and procedures. One role of the IRB in reviewing deception research is to safeguard against this possibility.

Deception may also harm research participants by making them feel foolish for being taken in by it. The use of deception in research might also reduce public trust in behavioral science by making it appear to be one great deception. Furthermore, the use of deception might threaten the validity of research. If research participants believe that deception is commonplace in behavioral science research, they might spend their time trying to deduce the deception (even if there isn't one) rather than attending to the research task. There is some evidence that such suspiciousness exists, but studies of its effects show no clear pattern of effects on research results (J. Greenberg & Folger, 1988). Finally, public awareness of deception research might lead people to interpret real events as behavioral science experiments. J. Greenberg and Folger (1988) and Mac-Coun and Kerr (1987) describe real emergencies on college campuses that some bystanders interpreted as experimental manipulations.

ALTERNATIVES TO DECEPTION   In addition to this ethical critique of deception research, the advocates of nondeceptive research point out that alternative forms of research are available (see, for example, Sieber, 1992). Research using naturally occurring behaviors in natural settings is one alternative. Simulation research is another alternative. In **simulation research** (also called *active role playing*), the researcher designs a laboratory situation that evokes the psychological processes present in a real-life situation (Crano & Brewer, 1986). A classic example from research on bargaining and negotiation is the Acme-Bolt Trucking Game (Deutsch & Krauss, 1960). Participants take the roles of trucking company operators who must maximize profits by making as many deliveries as possible in a given amount of time. They can take either a long or short route to their destinations; however, both participants control gates that can block the other's short route. Profits are maximized for both participants when they cooperate on access to the short route. Researchers can vary aspects of the situation, such as the amount and type of communication between the participants, to determine their effects on cooperative behavior. Crano and Brewer (1986) and Jones (1985) describe this and other simulations in more detail.

A third, and more controversial, proposed alternative to deception research is passive role playing (J. Greenberg & Folger, 1988). In **passive role playing** the researcher gives participants a detailed description of a situation, such as a condition of an experiment, and asks them to imagine themselves in the situation and respond as though they were in the situation. With this procedure, participants can be asked to respond to any kind of situation without risk of harm. Two major criticisms have been leveled against this approach. First, unless the participants have actually experienced the situation, their responses are hypothetical, and research has shown that hypothetical responses bear little relation to people's responses in the actual situation. The second criticism is that role playing cannot consistently replicate the results of deception experiments: Sometimes it does and sometimes it doesn't. As discussed in Chapter 4, these failures to replicate don't invalidate either methodology, but raise the as yet unanswered question of which methodology provides the more valid data.

Despite the controversy over whether passive role playing can substitute for deception in research, it does have two important uses. First, it can be used to assess the ways in which participants will interpret an experimental situation (Crano & Brewer, 1986; J. Greenberg & Folger, 1988). Researchers can give participants a detailed description of a situation and ask them to comment on its realism and believability. Second, participants can role-play a situation and comment on its ethical components, such as any aspects they would find disturbing (Sieber, 1992).

CONSENT TO DECEPTION   Some commentators have suggested that one way to resolve the conflict between informed consent and deception is to obtain potential participants' consent to be deceived. Several approaches to this process have been suggested. When participants are recruited from a subject pool, a general announcement can be made that some experiments will include deception and that signing up for an experiment gives permission for deception to be used. Anyone not willing to participate under these conditions would be allowed to do alternate assignments (D. T. Campbell, 1969a). One drawback to this approach is that it denies students the opportunity to participate in nondeceptive research if they wish to. Alternatively, students could be asked to sign up for various categories of research, one of which is studies including deception; participants for deception research would be recruited only from this roster (Milgram, 1977). In any research situation, the consent form can inform potential participants that the research might entail deception. In this case, participants would give consent to be deceived (Sieber, 1992). In any of these cases, researchers have a special obligation that any deception used entail the minimum possible risk to participants.

MINIMIZING HARM IN DECEPTION RESEARCH   The APA (1992) has the following policy regarding the use of deception in research:

   a. Psychologists do not conduct a study involving deception unless they have determined that the use of deceptive techniques is justified by the study's prospective . . . value and that equally effective alternative procedures that do not use deception are not feasible.

b. Psychologists never deceive research participants about significant aspects that would affect their willingness to participate, such as physical risks, discomfort, or unpleasant emotional experiences.

c. Any other deception that is any integral feature of the design and conduct of an experiment must be explained to participants as early as is feasible, preferably at the conclusion of their participation. (p. 1609)

This policy implies that researchers who are considering using deception in research should ask themselves six questions (Diener & Crandall, 1978; Sieber, 1992):

1. Is deception really necessary, or can equally valid data be obtained through an alternative approach? If appropriate alternatives are available, they must be used.

2. How much deception is necessary? Many forms of deception are possible; use only those that are absolutely necessary.

3. How much harm is the deception likely to cause participants? Consider all the categories of intent listed in Figure 3-1. When the research involves children, give careful consideration to the highly impressionable nature of young children and the effects deception can have on them. Koocher and Keith-Spiegel (1990, pp. 133–142) present an excellent outline of this issue. There are three key sources of information about the kinds and degree of harm likely to come to participants: published discussion of the ethics of deception, other researchers who have conducted similar studies, and members of the participant population who realistically role-play the study.

4. Is it feasible to obtain participants' consent to be deceived? If so, it should be obtained.

5. Is it possible to inform participants about the deception after they have completed participation and to remove any adverse effects? How effective are the procedures for doing so? Researchers employing deception have an absolute obligation to remove the effects of deception.

6. All things considered, do the expected benefits of the research outweigh the anticipated risks to participants? Only if the answer to this question is an absolute yes should the research go beyond the planning stage.

 How Harmful Is Deception Research?   One ethical criticism of deception research is that it harms participants by attacking their self-esteem and by making them feel used and foolish. However, research conducted with former participants in deception research does not provide much support for this position (Christensen, 1988). Former participants generally don't think they have been harmed and say that although deception is undesirable, they understand and accept its necessity once it has been explained. On the whole, college students (who are the majority of participants in behavioral science research that uses deception) see deception research as being less ethically problematic than do researchers. Nonetheless, it is important to bear in mind that the results of the research reviewed by Christensen reflect the average response of groups of people; specific individuals may still have very strong feelings about being deceived. Also, some forms of deception are seen as more reprehensible than others. For example, people always want to be informed if they are going to be asked about aspects of their lives they consider to be private, such as sexual behavior.

ETHICAL CONSIDERATIONS DURING DATA COLLECTION

The researcher's ethical obligations continue when participants agree to take part in the study. Our most basic obligation as researchers is to treat participants with courtesy and respect. We must never lose sight of the fact that the vast majority of research participants receive no monetary compensation and so are doing us a favor by participating in our research. Their kindness should be reciprocated by kindness on our part. Let's examine two other, more complex, ethical obligations in detail: avoidance of harm and honoring retractions of consent.

Avoidance of Harm

In some research, the design of the study poses risks to participants that must be monitored to ensure that they do not become excessive, but even research designed to pose minimal risk can have unexpected adverse effects. Researchers therefore have an obligation to screen potential participants for known risk factors, allowing only those at low risk to participate. They must also monitor participants during the research for signs of unanticipated negative effects. A more difficult problem arises when participation in the research reveals evidence of a psychological or emotional problem in a participant.

SCREENING FOR RISK FACTORS Some individuals can be especially vulnerable to the risks posed by participation in a study. For example, people with histories of cardiovascular disease would be especially vulnerable to the physical risks posed by strenuous exercise, and people with certain personality characteristics would be especially vulnerable to high levels of psychological stress. Researchers must establish screening procedures to ensure that people at special risk do not participate in the research. Some professional associations have established standardized screening procedures, such as the American College of Sports Medicine's (1995) guidelines for exercise testing. When standardized guidelines are not available, researchers must consult with knowledgeable professionals to establish appropriate screening procedures and participation criteria.

UNANTICIPATED ADVERSE EFFECTS Even the best planned research can have unanticipated adverse effects on participants. These effects and the possible responses to them are illustrated by two of the studies that aroused behavioral scientists' concern with the ethics of research. In the early 1960s, Milgram (1974), thinking about the guards at Nazi concentration camps in the 1930s and 1940s, became interested in why people would obey supervisors' orders to harm others. He designed a series of laboratory experiments to test some of the factors he thought might affect this behavior. He recruited participants for these experiments from the general population through newspaper advertisements and paid them $4.50 in advance for an hour's participation (about $25 today, after correcting for inflation). When participants came to the lab, an experimenter greeted them and introduced them to another "participant," actually a confederate playing the part of a participant. The experimenter explained that the study investigated the effect of punishment on learning: A teacher (always the participant) would attempt to teach a learner (always the confederate) a list of words by giving the learner a painful electric shock every time the learner made a mistake. With each mistake, the teacher would have to increase the shock level, starting at 15 volts and going up to 450 volts in 15-volt increments. The 450-volt level was described as being extremely dangerous. During the "teaching" process, the confederate was in a separate room from the participant; he made a preset series of errors but received no shocks. He had an indicator so that he could give predetermined responses to different levels of shock, ranging from slight moans at low levels to apparent physical collapse at higher levels. Milgram's research question was whether participants would continue to give shocks after it became apparent that the learner was in extreme pain. Almost two thirds did but exhibited severe stress symptoms while doing so. This degree of stress had not been anticipated by Milgram or by a group of clinical psychologists and psychiatrists who had reviewed a detailed description of the study before it began.

About a decade later, Zimbardo (1973) became interested in how social roles affect behavior. He and his colleagues designed a simulation in which paid college students were randomly assigned to play the roles of guards and prisoners in a simulated prison. Concerned about the possible effects of stress on the participants, who would be living their roles 24 hours a day in a realistic prison environment, the researchers used standardized psychiatric screening instruments to identify potential participants who might be especially vulnerable to stress. These individuals were not recruited for the study. Despite this precaution, one "prisoner" developed severe stress symptoms a few days into the study and was removed from the study for treatment. A few days later, a second "prisoner" developed similar symptoms.

What should researchers do if faced with unanticipated severe negative effects of their research, as were Milgram and Zimbardo? Zimbardo's and Milgram's responses illustrate the alternatives available. Zimbardo and his colleagues called off their study. After considering the issues, they decided the knowledge they expected to gain from the research was not worth the harm accruing to participants. Milgram made the same kind of risk-benefit analysis but came to the opposite conclusion: The importance of knowing why people would continue to follow orders to hurt others despite the stress they experienced outweighed the harm caused by the stress. When faced with unexpected harm to participants, researchers must suspend the study and conduct a new risk-benefit analysis based on what occurred in the study. They must now also report the unexpected harm and the actions they have taken to their IRB. If the researchers believe the expected benefits of the research justify the harm to participants and want to continue the research, the IRB must re-review the research based on the new risk-benefit considerations. The research must be held in abeyance until the IRB gives approval to continue; the research may not be continued without approval.

Sometimes even minimal-risk studies result in idiosyncratic adverse reactions in participants. Koocher and Keith-Spiegel (1998), for example, relate the case of a young woman who broke down in tears while listening to a piece of popular music as part of an experiment. It turned out that the song had sentimental associations with a former boyfriend who had recently dropped the participant for another woman. When such reactions occur, the researcher should stop the experimental session and provide appropriate assistance to the participant. A more difficult issue is determining whether a participant's response indicates a general risk that could affect all participants in the research or whether the response is unique to that person. No general rules can be established, but three indicators are the severity of the response, the participant's explanation for the response, and the researcher's experience with the research procedure that elicited the response. A severe response is more problematic than a mild response; a cause unique to the individual (as in the case just described) is less problematic than a general or unknown cause; and if the first adverse response occurs only after many participants have undergone the procedure, there is less problem than if it occurs early in data collection. In any case, when faced with an unanticipated adverse response, it is wise to suspend the study and discuss the situation with more experienced colleagues before making a decision on how to proceed.

DISCOVERING PSYCHOLOGICAL PROBLEMS   Some psychological research focuses on factors related to psychological disorders, such as depression. Frequently this research is conducted by having samples of participants from nonclinical populations complete self-report psychological screening instruments and other measures. The researcher then correlates the scores on the screening instrument with the scores on the other measures, or selects people for participation in research on the basis of their scores on the screening instrument. What should you do if a participant's score on a screening instrument or behavior in a research setting suggests the presence of a severe disorder? Should you intervene by attempting to persuade the participant to seek treatment?

Stanton and New (1988) note that both costs and benefits are involved in referring participants for treatment:

> Possible benefits . . . include amelioration of . . . distress and promotion of a positive perception of psychological researchers as caring professionals. . . . A possible cost . . . is the potentially iatrogenic labeling . . . of subjects. A label of "depression" given by an authority may translate as "abnormal" in the view of the subject. (p. 283)

In surveys of depression researchers, Burbach, Farha, and Thorpe (1986) and Stanton and New (1988) found a wide range of opinions on how to resolve this dilemma, ranging from " 'it is very much a responsibility of researchers to give attention to the special needs of depressed subjects' " to " 'any follow-up of depressed subjects represents an unwarranted invasion of privacy' " (Stanton & New, 1988, p. 283). However, Stanton and New also found a general consensus that something should be done and suggested some guidelines. They suggest that, as a minimum, all participants in studies of psychological or emotional problems be given information about available treatment resources, such as student counseling centers. Researchers could also offer to discuss participants' responses with them; this discussion could be a vehicle for referral. Whether researchers should take the initiative and contact participants is more problematic (Burbach et al., 1986; Stanton & New, 1988). If researchers are contemplating this option, they should include the possibility of follow-up contact in their consent forms in order to avoid invasion of privacy. The follow-up should be conducted by someone with sufficient training and experience to determine if referral to treatment is warranted; screening instrument scores alone are not a sufficient basis for referral. Stanton and New found that over 40% of depression researchers who worked with nonclinical populations made no provisions for dealing with the potential problems of distressed participants; such provisions must be made.

Withdrawal of Consent

The principles of voluntary participation and informed consent give research participants the **right to withdraw consent** from research after it has begun. This right is absolute; researchers are not permitted to use any form of coercion or inducement in an attempt to persuade withdrawing participants to continue. Specifically, participants may not be threatened with the loss of any benefits promised to them for participation. If participants are paid, whenever possible the payment should be made before data are collected to avoid the perception that the payment might be withheld if the participant withdraws from the research. Although the ethical requirement is clear, there are two problematic aspects to the right to withdraw from participation: participants' possible reluctance to exercise the right and the right's potential effects on the internal validity of research.

RELUCTANCE TO WITHDRAW   Even though participants are informed of their right to withdraw from the research, they may be reluctant to exercise that right. Milgram (1974) noted that many participants in his obedience studies seemed to feel they had entered into an implicit contract with the researcher: Having agreed to participate, they felt morally bound to continue to the end despite the distress they experienced. Milgram also suggested that this perceived contract might be seen as especially binding when people are paid for their participation. In research with children, the problem of reluctance to withdraw stems from children's difficulty in saying no to an adult. Rather than asking that an experimental session be terminated, children will show behavioral indicators of unwillingness to continue, such as passivity or fidgetiness, or verbal indicators, such as frequently asking, "When will we be done?" (Keith-Spiegel, 1983). Researchers must be sensitive to these problems and ask participants if they wish to continue if they exhibit indicators of unwillingness, reminding them of their right to withdraw.

THE RIGHT TO WITHDRAW AND INTERNAL VALIDITY   Researchers inform potential research participants about their rights to refuse participation in research and to withdraw from research in order to validate their autonomy and freedom to control events that affect them (Sieber, 1992). However, when feelings of control can affect the variable or process being studied in the research, informed consent and the right to withdraw could affect the results of the research. Take, for example, the effects of stress. A great deal of research has shown that stress has adverse cognitive, emotional, and behavioral effects, but that these effects are reduced or disappear when people believe they can control the stressful situation (J. S. Greenberg, 1983). Because informed participants in stress research have control over whether to participate and whether to continue participation once the research has begun, the stressors they experience may have no adverse effects. Research that has manipulated the presence of informed consent in stress research has found exactly that: Participants who are fully informed about the nature of the research and their right to withdraw from it do not show the adverse effects of stress found with uninformed participants (Dill, Gilden, Hill, & Hanselka, 1982).

These findings, along with those of Resnick and Schwartz (1973) discussed earlier, have two implications. The first is that whenever informed consent and the right to withdraw could affect the outcome of research, either the research must be conducted in ways that do not require informed consent (such as observation of public behavior) or the researcher must deceive the participants about the true purpose or procedures of the research. The second implication is that failures to replicate studies conducted before informed consent was required could be due to the presence of informed consent if participants' awareness of the nature of the research or their right to withdraw from the research could affect their behavior (Christensen, 2001).

ETHICAL CONSIDERATIONS FOLLOWING DATA COLLECTION

After researchers have collected data from a participant, a number of ethical obligations remain. These obligations include alleviating any adverse effects produced by the research procedures, educating participants about the study, explaining any deception that was used, compensating members of control groups who were deprived of a benefit during the research, and maintaining the confidentiality of participants' data.

Alleviating Adverse Effects

Sometimes the procedures used in research induce predictable adverse effects in the participants. For example, research on the effects of alcohol consumption induces at least mild intoxication and research on the effects of stress subjects participants to stress. Before participants leave the laboratory, researchers must ensure that any such effects are removed and take any other precautions that might be necessary to protect the participants' welfare. For example, a complete and sensitive debriefing should be conducted so that the participants understand the necessity of the procedure that caused the unpleasant effects, even when fully informed consent was obtained beforehand. Zimbardo (1973) and his colleagues held group discussions with their participants to let them air their feelings and help them resolve their anxieties about their experiences in the simulated prison. If the procedures leave the participants temporarily physically impaired, as with alcohol consumption, they should stay in the laboratory until the effects wear off. If they live some distance from the research site, it is wise to provide transportation to and from the site, such as by providing taxi fare. In some cases, long-term follow-ups might be advisable to ensure that all the negative effects of participation have been removed. Both Milgram (1974) and Zimbardo (1973) conducted such follow-ups. However, if follow-ups are contemplated, they must be included in the informed consent form.

Debriefing

After a person completes participation in research, the researcher conducts a post-experimental interview. This interview has three functions (J. Greenberg & Folger, 1988): educating the participants about the research, explaining any deception that was used, and eliciting the participants' aid in improving the research. The first two functions are ethical obligations and are part of a process called **debriefing,** which is discussed here; Chapter 12 discusses the third function. This section examines three issues concerning debriefing: the components of a debriefing, constructing an effective debriefing, and potential harm that might come from debriefing.

COMPONENTS OF DEBRIEFING   A debriefing can have as many as five components (J. Greenberg & Folger, 1988; J. Mills, 1976; Sieber, 1992). The first component, which is part of all debriefings, is educational. Researchers have an ethical obligation to educate participants about the research (APA, 1992). Such education often comprises the primary benefit derived by participants recruited from subject pools and so is especially important in those cases (APA, 1982). If possible, provide this information at the end of the participant's research session, but no later than the conclusion of the research (APA, 1992). Explain the purpose of the research, including the dependent and independent variables, hypotheses, the procedures used, and the rationale underlying the hypotheses and procedures. Also explain the short- and long-term scientific and social benefits expected from the research. Participants should have an opportunity to have their questions answered and should be given the name and telephone number of a person to contact if they have questions later. In short, participants should leave the research understanding that they have made a contribution to science.

Not all research participants want to wait for a debriefing (Brody et al., 2000). This trait is perhaps especially characteristic of participants drafted from subject pools. However, researchers can take steps to alleviate this problem. The first is to include enough time for the debriefing in the time period scheduled for the research—do not hold participants overtime for it. Second, at the beginning of the research session, let participants know there will be a discussion at the end. That way, they will not be expecting to leave immediately on completion of the research task. Finally, if the research is of minimal risk and does not involve deception, the educational information can be provided in the form of a handout that participants can read at their leisure. If a handout is used, offer to stay and discuss the research with any interested participants.

When deception is used in the research, the educational component of debriefing is usually integrated with two other components, dehoaxing and desensitization. **Dehoaxing** consists of explaining the nature of the deception to the participants and the reasons why deception was necessary (Holmes, 1976a). J. Mills (1976) suggests that dehoaxing be done in two stages, first explaining why deception in general is sometimes necessary to research and then explaining the particular deception used in the study. Needless to say, dehoaxing must be done tactfully so that participants don't feel foolish about being taken in. Participants do not always believe a researcher who tells them that deception was involved in the research, especially when the deception involved false information about themselves (Ross, Lepper, & Hubbard, 1975). It can therefore be useful to provide participants with concrete proof of the deception. Milgram (1974), for example, reintroduced participants to the confederate to demonstrate that the confederate had sustained no injury and bore the participant no ill will.

Desensitization consists of removing any anxiety or other adverse effects that participants may feel as a result of being deceived (Holmes, 1976b). Dehoaxing is part of this process, as is a tactful and sensitive discussion of the participant's feelings and concerns. Milgram (1974), for example, explained to the participants in his research that their obedience to the experimenter's instructions to shock the learner was a normal response to the situation, that most people responded as they did, and that their actions did not reflect on them personally. J. Mills (1976) recommends that the person who designs the experiment should conduct the debriefing. Not only does this procedure demonstrate the project director's concern for the well-being of the participants, but it also serves as a check on the ethical propriety of the research: "If the experimenter cannot face the [participants] afterwards and truthfully describe the purpose of the experiment to them, he probably shouldn't have conducted the experiment in the first place" (p. 12).

When participants have been deceived, they should be offered an opportunity to withdraw their data from use in the research (Sieber, 1992). This offers protects participants' autonomy and privacy by allowing them to consent to the use of their data once they have been fully informed of the nature of the research. Finally, it is common during debriefings to request participants not to discuss the true nature of the research with anyone. This request is designed to ensure the effectiveness of the deception with future participants. Although the results of the research on the effectiveness of such requests are mixed, it appears that the more convinced participants are of the scientific value of the research and of the necessity of deception in the research, the more likely they are to comply with a request for confidentiality (J. Greenberg & Folger, 1988).

EFFECTIVE DEBRIEFING   Research on the effectiveness of debriefings for the dehoaxing and desensitization of deceived research participants has found they generally work as intended. There are, however, several necessary components to an effective debriefing (J. Greenberg & Folger, 1988). First, the debriefing should take place immediately after participation in the research. Although there can be valid reasons for delaying a debriefing and although delayed debriefings can be effective, they also prolong any harm that has accrued to participants as a result of the deception. Second, the dehoaxing must be unambiguous and the participants must receive an explanation for the deception that they perceive to be valid. Participants must also be warned that they might continue to have doubts about the dehoaxing after they leave the laboratory. Ross et al. (1975) found that such perseverance effects can occur, but that they have little adverse effect if the participants are expecting them. Third, the desensitization must be conducted completely and tactfully. Finally, participants who are convinced of the scientific value of the research react more positively to dehoaxing than those who are not, so the educational component of the debriefing is very important.

Constructing an effective debriefing can be difficult, but help is available. Aronson et al. (1990) provide a detailed outline for a debriefing, and J. Mills (1976) presents a sample debriefing script; colleagues experienced in debriefing can help you adapt these models to your needs. Effective debriefings are essential. Not only do they fulfill an ethical obligation, but they can also leave participants interested in and enthusiastic about psychological research (S. S. Smith & Richardson, 1983).

CAN DEBRIEFING BE HARMFUL?   One purpose of debriefing is to fulfill the ethical obligation of providing full information to participants and of relieving their anxieties over any negative behaviors the research may have induced, such as aggression. However, some commentators (D. T. Campbell, 1969a; Diener & Crandall, 1978; Sieber, 1992) have suggested that in a few circumstances providing full information might actually harm participants by causing them additional anxiety or inconvenience. For example, if the information has been withheld from participants that they were selected for participation because they had a socially undesirable characteristic, such as low self-esteem, being told that by a researcher might have an adverse impact. Recall Stanton and New's (1988) observation that participants might interpret what a researcher intends to be a neutral descriptor as a negative trait. Much concern over proper debriefing centers around desensitizing participants who have been deceived into performing a negative behavior. But what if they are deceived into performing a positive behavior, such as helping someone? Participants in experimental groups who have been deceived in that way usually feel better about themselves than participants in control groups who, while not deceived, have also not been induced to do anything positive (Blanchard & Cook, 1976). Should researchers attack this feeling of satisfaction by telling participants that they were deceived into being nice, implying that otherwise they would not have been? In field experiments, people who are unaware of having been in an experiment might be annoyed by being stopped by a researcher for an explanation in which they have no interest.

Such circumstances represent ethical dilemmas because the harm of debriefing must be weighed against the harm of not debriefing. APA (1992) ethical guidelines recognize that debriefing might not always be desirable and enjoin researchers to "take reasonable measures to reduce the risk of harm" (p. 1609) if participants are not given full information at the completion of the research. This injunction implies that if omission of a debriefing appears to be the lesser of two evils, it should occur only in research that poses minimal risk or in which participants' experience was positive. When the debriefing itself might cause harm, special care must be taken when it is conducted (for example, Blanchard & Cook, 1976). Omission of a debriefing must be made explicit and be completely justified in the research protocol submitted to the IRB.

Compensation of Control Groups

The discussion of research risks earlier in the chapter noted that in some forms of research, such as psychotherapy research, members of some control groups are deprived of a benefit given to participants in the experimental condition. As soon as possible after members of deprived control groups complete their participation, they should be given appropriate compensation. In the case of psychotherapy research, this compensation usually consists of the psychotherapeutic service that was withheld as part of the research. Also consider compensating members of control groups when other participants are given a reward as part of an experimental manipulation, such as when the research tests the effects of monetary or other rewards on performance. Even though the members of the control group were not deprived of anything they needed, it seems only fair that all participants in a study receive the same benefits.

Confidentiality of Data

Research participants have a right to privacy that researchers must safeguard by keeping the information provided by each individual participant in strict confidence. The need for confidence is especially important when participants have provided information that is personal or that could embarrass them if it were revealed. Two aspects of the confidentiality requirement will be examined: means of protecting confidentiality and the legal status of research data.

PROTECTING CONFIDENTIALITY   The simplest and most effective way of protecting the confidentiality of participants' data is not to record their identities. If researchers don't know the identity of the person who provided a particular piece of information, they cannot even inadvertently embarrass someone by letting the information slip. Similarly, if the data records were lost or stolen, no one could use the information to embarrass a participant. Sometimes, however, the nature of the research requires that participants be identified in some way. In longitudinal research, one must be able to link the data provided by each participant at different times. Even in this case, however, names or other unique identifiers, such as Social Security numbers, are not always necessary. You could, for example, ask participants to provide aliases that they would use each time data were collected. Because you would record only the aliases, success of this strategy depends on participants' ability to remember the aliases they used. Unique identifiers are required when participants give the researcher permission to use data collected about them by others, such as academic records. Whenever unique identifiers must be used, only a code number should appear on the data sheet for each participant and the record of participants' names and code numbers should be stored separately to prevent compromise. Destroy the identification lists as soon as they are no longer needed. Identities can also be protected by encryption. Kinsey, for example, had his interviewers record sexual histories in a code consisting of symbols, numbers, and random combinations of letters. Interview records were identified only by serial numbers, and the list linking identities to serial numbers was kept in a different code (Pomeroy, 1972).

Modern technology has led to the storage of research data in computer files. It is extremely important to remember that these files are not totally secure. Passwords can be compromised and, in most computer centers, at least a few systems operation personnel can gain access to any file on the system. Although data security programs are available, not all are effective. Security programs for desktop computers may be especially vulnerable: One expert was able to bypass or defeat 23 of the 24 programs he tested (Schneier, 1993).

Case study research can present special confidentiality problems when it is prepared for publication (for example, C. G. Johnson, 1982). Because such research deals with a single individual, researchers typically use aliases to protect participants' identities. However, even when aliases are used, combinations of other information, such as sex, age, race, and occupation, might be enough to identify someone. Johnson suggests that researchers have other people, including participants if possible, read their manuscripts to determine if identities can be deduced from the information given.

Research with children also raises special confidentiality issues (Koocher & Keith-Spiegel, 1990). Parents have an interest in their children's welfare and might want to know how their children performed on an experimental task or the information they provided in an interview. However, researchers have an ethical obligation to protect the confidentiality of the data provided by their participants, in this case the children. Researchers can avoid conflicts with parents over this issue by taking two steps. First, clearly explain to parents as part of the informed consent process the principle of confidentiality and the limits that it places on disclosure of information about their children. If parents do not find these limits acceptable, they can refuse permission for their children's participation. Second, if the researcher agrees to provide any information to parents, the nature of this information should be clearly explained to the children as part of the assent process. If the children do not want such information disclosed, they can refuse to participate. In such a case, explain the child's refusal to the parents tactfully, so that the parents do not try to coerce the child into participation.

DATA CONFIDENTIALITY AND THE LAW   The law grants certain professionals, such as attorneys, medical personnel, psychotherapists, and clergy, the right of privileged communication with their clients. Although not absolute, the right means that, except under very unusual circumstances, the law cannot compel these professionals to disclose information provided by their clients as part of the professional relationship. *In general, researchers do not enjoy the right of privileged communication with the participants in their research* (Knerr, 1982). This lack of protection means that researchers can be subpoenaed to testify about information provided by specific participants and that research records can be subpoenaed as evidence. There are two ways (short of defying a subpoena) in which a researcher can protect participants who might provide information that could make the participant liable to criminal or civil prosecution. The first is provision of complete anonymity; if there is no record of identities, there is nothing to subpoena. Second, Congress has authorized DHHS to grant certificates of confidentiality that protect researchers from being compelled to identify research participants or disclose information provided by them (see, for example, Ross & Allgeier, 1996). Researchers must apply for these certificates through the National Institutes of Mental Health's (NIMH) Division of Extramural Activities. Approval is not automatic; the researcher must demonstrate a bona fide need to protect participants' confidentiality. More information is available from NIMH.

SUMMARY

Research in behavioral science is guided by three general ethical principles: respect for persons, beneficence, and justice. These principles are reflected in the APA's ethical guidelines for the conduct of research and in federal regulations governing the conduct of research with human participants. Primary responsibility for the ethical conduct of research lies with the researcher, who must design and carry out research in ways that do not abridge the rights of participants. The institution sponsoring the research must review proposed research to ensure compliance with ethical standards. No research involving human participants may be conducted without the approval of the IRB.

Researchers have four ethical issues to consider in the course of planning research. First, they must carefully evaluate the risks that the research poses for participants. These risks include not only active risks, such as physical injury or psychological stress, but also passive risks, such as deprivation of benefits. Along with the risks, the researcher must consider the potential benefits of the research for the participants, science, and society. Only when the anticipated benefits outweigh the predicted risks should the research be carried out. The second issue is ensuring that participation in the research is voluntary and that the participants are free from coercion or excessive inducements. Third, the researcher must obtain the informed consent of participants to collect data about them, except in the case of observation of public behavior. Researchers must ensure that all participants are competent to give consent and that they fully understand the potential risks and benefits of participation. Finally, if researchers are considering using deception, they must ensure that equally valid alternative procedures are not available, that the deception causes the least possible harm, and that they can effectively dehoax and desensitize participants.

While collecting data, researchers must monitor participants both to prevent undue levels of anticipated harm and to detect unanticipated harm. If either situation arises, they must take prompt action to ensure the participants' welfare. If the unanticipated adverse effects affect participants generally, rather than being the idiosyncratic reaction of one participant, the researcher must suspend data collection, conduct a new risk-benefit analysis, and resubmit the research to the IRB for approval to continue the research. Researchers who use psychiatric screening instruments must also consider what actions to take if they detect participants who appear to exhibit severe distress. Finally, researchers must respect participants' right to withdraw from the research and remind them of this right if necessary.

After participants have completed their part in the research, the researcher must debrief them. In all research, debriefing consists of educating the participants about the purpose and procedures of the research and ensuring that any negative effects induced by the procedures are alleviated. If the research includes deception, the researcher must explain the deception and alleviate any of its negative effects. Debriefings must be carefully designed and carried out with sensitivity to ensure that participants do not suffer further harm by being made to feel foolish. If members of a control group have been deprived of a benefit, the benefit must be provided to them. Finally, researchers must ensure the confidentiality of the information that participants provide.

QUESTIONS AND EXERCISES FOR REVIEW

1. What are the three basic principles of ethical research?
2. What is the purpose of the institutional review board (IRB)? What criteria does it use in deciding whether to approve research?
3. What information should be included in a research protocol submitted to an IRB?
4. Describe the categories of risks that could face participants in psychological research. What factors affect the degree of risk to research participants?
5. Describe the ethical issues involved in withholding a benefit from a control group. Include factors to consider both when designing the research and after the data have been collected.
6. What benefits can accrue from research?
7. What factors make risk-benefit analyses problematic? Do you think the IRB is a sufficient safeguard against these problems? Why or why not?
8. Do you think subject pools are coercive? Why or why not? If they are, what can be done to make them less coercive?
9. Given your experience, how widespread a problem do you think subtle coercion to participate in research is? What examples do you know of?

10. Why can offering inducements to participate in research be problematic?
11. What are the elements of informed consent? When is written consent not necessary? Describe the problems of competence and understanding that affect informed consent.
12. What ethical issues are involved in observing public behavior? What is your position on the issue? Why do you hold that position?
13. How can full information about research and the right to withdraw from research affect the results of research? What are the implications of these effects for replication research?
14. What types of deception are used in research? Why do researchers use deception?
15. What ethical objections are raised against the use of deception in research? What evidence supports these objections? Describe the procedures that have been proposed as alternatives to deception. What are their advantages and disadvantages? What is your position on the use of deception in research? What are your reasons for holding that position?
16. What factors should researchers who are thinking about using deception consider in making their decisions?
17. Describe the steps that researchers should take to avoid harm to participants during data collection. What should you do if unanticipated severe adverse effects develop?
18. What should a researcher do if a participant appears to be having psychological problems?
19. Explain participants' right to withdraw from research. What factors can affect a research participant's willingness to exercise the right to withdraw from research?
20. Describe the components of a debriefing. What makes a debriefing effective? Under what circumstances might a complete debriefing be unwise?
21. Describe the problems involved in maintaining confidentiality of research data. What steps can be taken to ensure confidentiality?
22. Besides debriefing and confidentiality, what other ethical obligations does the researcher have to participants following data collection?
23. What special ethical problems can arise when research participants are children?

4 FORMULATING A RESEARCH QUESTION

FORMULATING RESEARCH
HYPOTHESES
Establishing a Background
Choosing a Topic
  Interest
  Feasibility
Formulating the Question
  Refining a Topic Into a
    Question
  Characteristics of a Good
    Research Question
  Sources of Ideas
Reviewing the Literature
  Purposes of the Literature
    Review
  Types of Information
  Primary Versus Secondary
    Sources
  Where to Find Information
  LIbrary Research Tools
  Evaluating Information

Formulating Hypotheses
  Research Hypotheses
  Statistical Hypotheses
Designing the Study
Writing the Research Proposal

REPLICATION RESEARCH
Forms of Replication
Implications of Replication
  Research
Considerations in Conducting
  Replication Research
  Importance of the Hypothesis
  Avoiding Overduplication

DESIGNING RESEARCH
FOR UTILIZATION
Knowledge Utilization
Design Considerations
  Independent and Dependent
    Variables
  Research Population
  Research Setting

BIAS IN THE FORMULATION OF
RESEARCH QUESTIONS
Biased Assumptions
Biased Theory
Avoiding Bias

SUMMARY

QUESTIONS AND EXERCISES
FOR REVIEW

Scientists conduct research to answer questions. As noted in Chapter 1, these questions can be posed by theory, by practical problems, by the need to evaluate an intervention, or by the investigator's curiosity. This chapter examines four issues related to research questions: formulating research hypotheses, the role of replication research in behavioral science, designing research for utilization, and bias in hypothesis formulation.

FORMULATING RESEARCH HYPOTHESES

The first problem any researcher faces is that of coming up with a research question and refining that question into a testable hypothesis. Solving that problem involves a process made up of the elements shown in Figure 4-1. Although this presentation will treat these elements as separate steps in a sequential process, in practice a researcher may work on two or more elements simultaneously.

Establishing a Background

Background for research consists of everything a researcher knows about a potential research topic. This knowledge can take two forms. Informal background consists of your personal experience, what you learn from your family life, work, recreation, and so forth. Life experiences generate interest in aspects of human behavior that can evolve into research topics and can provide the bases for specific hypotheses. Formal background consists of the sum of your education and training in behavioral science. Knowledge of theory, research results, and the methods available for conducting research provide the scientific basis for carrying out research.

Note the reciprocal relationship between background and the next element shown in Figure 4-1, choosing a topic. As you think about doing research on a topic, you may realize you don't know enough about theory, prior research on the topic, or research methods to continue the process of hypothesis formulation, and so have to go back and develop more formal background before continuing. Developing a formal background involves the process of literature reviewing, which is described later in this chapter. The need to improve your formal background can sometimes feel frustrating because it appears to interrupt the flow of the research project—just as you're getting started, you have to stop and back up. This backing up can be especially frustrating when working under a deadline, such as for developing a thesis or dissertation project. However, an inadequate background inevitably leads to other problems farther down the line, such as poor research design or data analysis, or the inability to rule out alternative explanations for your results. The time you invest improving your formal background near the start of a project therefore pays dividends at its end.

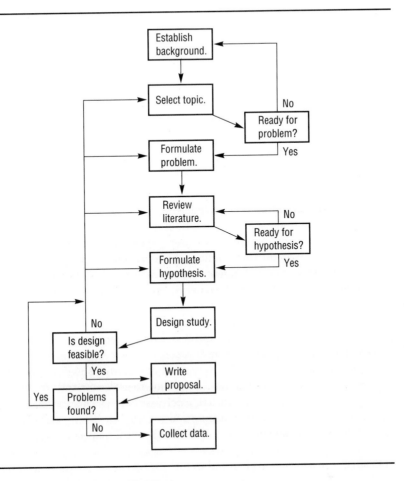

FIGURE 4-1   The Process of Formulating a Hypothesis

Choosing a Topic

Two factors influence the choice of a research topic: the researcher's interest in the topic and the feasibility of carrying out research on the topic.

INTEREST   Choice of a topic for research grows naturally from the researcher's background: Different people conduct research on different topics because their personal and professional backgrounds give rise to different interests. Interest in a topic is important because interest leads to commitment to the research; this commitment carries the researcher through times of problem and frustration during the project. A strong interest in a topic also usually produces a strong formal background—the interest leads you to read up on what is already known about the topic. Choosing a topic of personal interest to you therefore usually leads to better-quality research than does a less personally interesting topic.

However, sometimes you may feel pushed toward a research topic that you don't find particularly interesting. For example, a student might be assigned to be a professor's research assistant and feel compelled to do his or her own research on the professor's topic. This feeling of being pushed in an uninteresting direction might arise because the student believes that such behavior is expected or because it seems to be convenient to be able to make use of the professor's laboratory and equipment. In other cases, researchers might feel that their personal interests are not valued by other psychologists and so they start researching a topic that is less interesting to them but more prestigious. However, because low interest often leads to low commitment, the costs of doing research you find uninteresting, such as low motivation and easy distraction, should be carefully weighed against any expected benefits.

As a student, it can also be useful to investigate the validity of your beliefs about the requirement to tailor your own research interests to those of the professor with whom you work. A student who believes he is expected to do his own research only in his professor's area of interest might find on discussing his interests with the professor that she is very supportive of what the student wants to do. However, if she does not feel sufficiently knowledgeable in the student's area of interest to provide advice on research, she will probably refer him to someone better able to help him. There are two points to bear in mind about this question of whose interests to follow, yours or your professor's. First, sometimes students *are* expected to follow directly in their professors' footsteps; it depends on the intellectual traditions of the university, department, and professor. Investigate these traditions by talking to professors and advanced students in the department. Second, if you are a research assistant, you may be expected to work on the professor's research while pursuing your own interests in your "spare time," even with the professor's support. You must clarify these role expectations.

FEASIBILITY   In addition to choosing an interesting research topic, you must be sure it is feasible to conduct research on the topic. All research requires resources, and if the resources required to conduct research on a particular topic are not readily available, it might not be feasible to conduct this research. Some topics, such as psychopathology or learning disabilities, require access to special populations; are these research populations available? Other topics, such as the physiological bases of behavior, require special equipment; if the equipment is not on hand, the research cannot be conducted. It may also be difficult to gain access to certain settings, such as schools or factories, and the time required for longitudinal or prospective research may not be available. When choosing a research topic, then, it is extremely important to ask yourself not only "Do I *want* to do research on this topic?" but also "*Can* I do research on this topic?"

Formulating the Question

One of the more difficult tasks that novice researchers face is coming up with a research question once they have chosen a topic. This section discusses three aspects of question

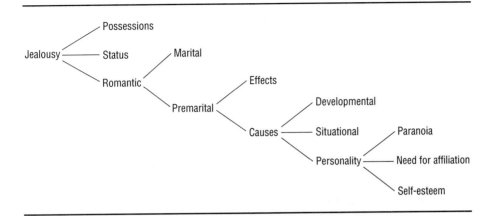

FIGURE 4-2 Refining the Topic of Jealousy Into a Research Question
You subdivide broad concepts until you reach a specific concept you can address in a study.

formulation: refining a broad topic into a specific, researchable question, the characteristics of a good research question, and sources of ideas for research questions.

REFINING A TOPIC INTO A QUESTION   Once a topic is selected, the researcher must narrow
the topic down to a more specific research question on which data can be collected.
Let's say you choose the topic of jealousy, which is, of course, an aspect of the broader
topic of interpersonal relations. As shown in Figure 4-2, the first question you might ask
yourself is "What *aspect* of jealousy interests me: jealousy over possessions, jealousy over
social position, romantic jealousy, or some other aspect?" If you choose romantic jealousy, you can narrow it still further; for example, are you interested in jealousy in marriage or in premarital relationships? If you choose premarital jealousy, are you interested
in its causes or its effects? If you are interested in causes, what kind of cause—developmental, situational, personality, or some other type of cause? If you're interested in personality variables as a cause of jealousy, what aspect of personality interests you—for
example, paranoia, need for affiliation, or self-esteem? You've refined your topic into a
researchable question when you can phrase the question in terms of the relationship between two operationally definable variables, such as "Is self-esteem related to jealousy
in premarital relationships?"

CHARACTERISTICS OF A GOOD RESEARCH QUESTION   While going through this refining process, keep one question always in mind: Is this going to be a good research question? In
the broadest sense, a good research question is one that has the potential to expand our
knowledge base. Three characteristics of a research question affect its potential for increasing knowledge. The first characteristic is how well grounded the question is in the
current knowledge base. The problem must have a basis in theory, prior research, or
practice; unless the question is anchored in what is already known, we cannot judge how
much it can add to the knowledge base. At this point the researcher's background comes

into play—identifying the ways in which the research question will expand our knowledge of human behavior.

The second characteristic of a good research question is how researchable it is—that is, how easy it is to formulate clear operational definitions of the variables involved and clear hypotheses about the relationships between the variables. Consider the hypothetical construct of *codependency* (see Lyon & Greenberg, 1991). As Lyon and Greenberg point out, because there is no theory underlying the construct, there are no criteria for determining whether any particular person is codependent; that is, there is no way to develop a clear operational definition for codependency. This problem is aggravated because the symptoms usually used to describe codependency overlap considerably with those of other psychiatric diagnoses, making it almost impossible to say whether a person who presents these symptoms exhibits "codependency" or one of the more traditional personality disorders. This problem of overlapping categories represents poor discriminant validity in measuring the construct, an issue discussed in the next chapter. If codependency cannot be operationally defined, it cannot be the subject of research.

The third characteristic of a good research question is its importance. The more information that the answer to a research question can provide, the more important it is. Research can add information to the scientific knowledge base in many ways. For example, practitioners' experiences may lead them to suspect that two variables, such as psychological stress and physical health, are related. Research can provide empirical evidence that supports or refutes the existence of the relationship. If no relationship is found, practitioners' and researchers' efforts can go in other directions. Once the existence of a phenomenon is established, determining why a phenomenon occurs is more informative than additional demonstrations that it does occur. Consider the common finding that women are absent from work more often than are men (Steers & Rhodes, 1978). This descriptive finding provides information that is nice to know, but research that tells us why the difference occurs allows us to understand, predict, and perhaps design interventions to alleviate the problem.

When testing theories, a research question that simultaneously tests several competing theories provides more information than research that tests a single theory. If different theories predict different outcomes under the same set of conditions, then a research question phrased as a comparison of the theories—which theory correctly predicts the outcome—can tell us which is more valid. For example, psychoanalytic theory postulates that the venting of aggressive impulses (catharsis) provides for a release of anger and so reduces the likelihood of future aggression; learning theory, in contrast, postulates that the pleasant feeling brought about by expressing aggression will reinforce aggressive impulse and increase the likelihood of future aggression. A study comparing the two theories found that venting verbal aggression increased future verbal aggression, thereby supporting the learning theory view of aggression and simultaneously disconfirming the psychoanalytic view, at least for that form of aggression (Ebbesen, Duncan, & Konecni, 1975).

If you test only one theory, test a hypothesis derived from a proposition that is important to the theory. Some propositions are crucial to a theory—if the proposition is wrong, the entire theory is wrong. Other propositions are more peripheral to a theory—if they are correct, that's good, but if they are wrong, the theory will still survive. For example, a central proposition of Locke and Latham's (1990) goal-setting theory of work performance is that more difficult goals are valued more highly than less difficult goals; if hypotheses based on this proposition are not supported, then the theory is not valid. Other possible hypotheses related to goal setting, such as the hypothesis that goals set by a supervisor lead to lower goal commitment than goals selected by the workers themselves, are less central to the theory. Therefore, the ambiguous results of research on this hypothesis do not affect the theory, even though the hypothesis does address an important practical question (Locke & Latham, 1990).

SOURCES OF IDEAS   Where do ideas for good research questions come from? There are, of course, as many answers to this question as there are researchers. However, some suggestions for getting started, drawn from several sources (Evans, 1985; McGuire, 1973; Tesser, 1990; Wicker, 1985) are listed in Box 4-1 and outlined next. These categories are not intended to be mutually exclusive: Any one idea could fall into more than one category, such as when theory is applied to solve a practical problem.

Chapter 1 noted that theory is central to research; basic research is conducted to test hypotheses derived from theories. Researchers can, however, have different motives for testing theories: They can be attempting to find evidence to support a theory they favor, to find evidence to refute a theory they don't like, or to compare competing theories. Chapter 1 also showed how existing theories can be creatively merged to form new theories that need testing, as Abramson, Seligman, and Teasdale (1978) merged the theory of learned helplessness and attribution theory into a new theory of depression. It is interesting to note that Abramson et al. took two theories that were based primarily on laboratory research and combined them in a way that addressed a practical problem. M. E. P. Seligman (1975) originally discovered the learned helplessness phenomenon in research with dogs, and most research on attribution theory has been conducted in the laboratory (Weiner, 1986).

Practical problems themselves also provide ideas for research. One aspect of problem-oriented research is problem definition: determining the precise nature of a suspected problem. For example, if one suspects that violent television programs cause children to be aggressive, then applied research can answer questions such as Is there, in fact, a relationship between watching televised violence and aggression? If so, to what forms of aggression is it related? Is the relationship the same for girls and boys, and for children of different ages? Is the relationship causal? If so, what about violent television programs causes aggression; for example, is it the violence itself or the exciting nature of the program as a whole? Once a problem has been defined, potential solutions can be developed and tested through applied research. Problem-oriented research can also test the validity of psychological assumptions made by practitioners in behavioral science and other fields. The legal system, for example, makes a number of assumptions about eyewitness perception and memory and about the validity of aspects of witnesses' behavior, such as their apparent degree of confidence while testifying, as indicators of the accuracy of their testimony. Research has shown many of these assumptions to be incorrect (Wells et al., 2000).

Prior research can also be a valuable source of ideas for empirical investigation. Case studies can provide hypotheses for investigation using the correlational and experimental strategies, and the hypotheses about the causality of relationships found in

BOX 4-1   Some Sources of Ideas for Research

Theory	**Prior Research**
Confirmation	Case studies
Refutation	Conflicting findings
Comparison	Overlooked variables
Merger	Setting and expanding boundaries
	Testing alternative explanations
Practical Problems	
Problem definition	**Logical Analysis**
Solution seeking	Analogy
Validating practitioners' assumptions	Looking at things backward
	Everyday Experience

correlational research can be tested experimentally. The results of different research studies on a hypothesis can be inconsistent, with some supporting the hypothesis and others not, and research that shows why the inconsistencies exist can be very informative. For example, a study I conducted as a graduate student (Whitley, 1982) showed that two earlier studies obtained conflicting results because of differences in their operational definitions of the independent variable. Sometimes while reading through the research that has been done on a topic, you come to realize that an important variable has been overlooked and needs to be included in research on the topic. For example, Phares (1992) pointed out that the role of fathers has been virtually ignored in research on child and adolescent psychopathology. Research is also necessary to establish the boundary conditions of effects found in earlier research — the conditions under which the effect operates. For example, do effects found in the laboratory hold up in natural settings? Consider the case of research on televised violence and aggression, which finds consistently strong effects in laboratory experiments but very inconsistent effects in field experiments (J. L. Freedman, 1984). Research can also be conducted to extend the results of prior research to new technologies. For example, research on the effects of violent television programs on aggression has led to research on the effects of violent video games on aggression (for example, see J. Cooper & Mackie, 1986). Finally, perusal of the research literature can also suggest possible alternative explanations for research results that can be tested in new research. Chapter 1 noted how Eagly and Carli (1981) showed that what appeared to be sex differences in opinion conformity were really due to differences in knowledge about the topics of the opinions.

Logical analysis can lead to ideas for research in several ways. Reasoning by analogy looks for potential similarities between psychological processes and physical or biological processes. McGuire (1964), for example, was interested in the problem of how to prevent people from being influenced by attempts at persuasion and hit on the analogy of inoculation: If injecting a person with a weakened version of an infectious agent can prevent infection by the agent, can presentation of weakened versions of persuasive arguments prevent persuasion when the full-strength arguments are presented? (It can.) One can also take accepted principles and look at them in reverse. For example, although the evidence is mixed, many psychologists accept the principle that people who are satisfied with their jobs will work harder and do better at them; that is, high job satisfaction results in high job performance. But what if it works the other way? Podsakoff and Farh (1989), among others, have shown that research participants who are told that they have done well on a task are more satisfied than are those who are told that they have done poorly, even though the actual outcome of the task was experimentally controlled to be the same for both groups of participants. Lastly, one can look at the "mirror image" of prior research. For example, if watching violent TV programs leads to aggression in children, will TV programs that depict positive behavior lead to positive behavior by children? Research suggests that they do, and that such positive TV programs have a stronger effect on positive behavior than violent programs have on aggressive behavior (Hearold, 1986).

Finally, don't overlook your everyday experience as a source of research ideas. Every time you ask yourself, "Why do people act that way?" you have a potential research question: Why *do* people act that way? Singer and Glass (1975), for example, got started on their research on the relationship between perceptions of personal control and stress because they were struck by what seemed to them to be a curious phenomenon: People who experienced the same urban environment (New York City) reacted in very different ways—some developed stress symptoms and hated the city, whereas others found the city exciting and loved it.

Reviewing the Literature

Once you have formulated your research question on the basis of your general background on the topic, it is time to collect more specific background information on the question. This process is called the literature review. The term *literature review* requires a little clarification because it is used in three ways. First, it is used to refer to the focus of this discussion, the process of collecting theoretical, empirical, and methodological information on a topic. The term is also used to refer to two products of that process: to the part of the introduction section of a research report that presents the background of the study, discussed in Chapter 17, and to a comprehensive summary and analysis of theory and research on a topic, discussed in Chapter 16.

PURPOSES OF THE LITERATURE REVIEW   When used to develop the background for a study, the **literature review** has three purposes. The first is to provide a scientific context for the research and to validate it against the three criteria for a good research question. You want your research to be well grounded in the body of existing scientific knowledge so that it both ties in with and extends what is already there. The literature review helps you generate this context by bringing to light the theory and research relevant to your question. The literature review also lets you determine the important theoretical, practical, and methodological issues that surround your research question. When you report on your research, you will begin by showing the reader why your research was important to the scientific understanding of your topic; this aspect of the literature review gives you that information. Although your formal background in the topic will be helpful, the information in that background might not be specific or current enough to provide an appropriate context for your research question.

The second purpose of the literature review is to avoid duplication of effort. If you find your research question has been addressed a number of times using a variety of methods and has a reasonably firm answer, further research may not be productive. Although replication is important in establishing the reliability and validity of research results, eventually we have enough information to draw firm conclusions, at which point further research may be a waste of effort. However, new perspectives on old questions, such as applications to new settings or populations, can provide new information and so should be pursued. The issue of replication is discussed in detail later in this chapter.

The third purpose of the literature review is to identify potential problems in conducting the research. Research reports contain information on the effectiveness of operational definitions, potential alternative explanations that must be controlled, and appropriate ways to analyze the data. Knowing in advance the problems that can arise in your research will help you avoid them.

TYPES OF INFORMATION   The purposes of the literature review imply that you should be looking for four types of information. First, you should be looking for relevant theories. Although your background in the topic will make you aware of some of the theories relevant to your question, make sure you know about all the relevant theories. This knowledge can help you in two ways. First, it may let you reformulate your research question into a comparison of theories, thereby providing more information than if you simply set out to test a single theory. Second, if your results are not consistent with the particular theory you favor, they may be consistent with another theory, which will provide your results with a niche in the knowledge base.

The second type of information to look for is on what has been done in previous research on your question. This information lets you know three things. First, you will know what has been done, allowing you to avoid unproductive duplication. Second, you will know what has *not* been done; to the extent that your research question— or your approach to answering that question—is novel, your research increases in importance. Third, you will know what still needs to be done to answer the question fully. The results of research studies often leave parts of their questions unanswered or raise new questions; to the extent that your research addresses such questions, it increases in importance.

The third type of information to look for concerns method: how prior research was carried out. This information includes settings, characteristics of participants, operational definitions, and procedures. This knowledge lets you anticipate and avoid problems reported by your predecessors. It can also save you work: If you find operational definitions and procedures that have worked well in the past, you might want to adopt them. There is nothing wrong with borrowing methods used by other researchers; in fact, it is considered a compliment, as long as you give credit to the people who developed them. In addition, using the same or similar methods in studying a phenomenon makes it easier to compare the results of the studies and to draw conclusions from a set of studies.

The fourth type of information to look for concerns data analysis. Research design and data analysis go hand in hand. It is both frustrating and embarrassing to collect data on a question and then realize you have no idea about how to analyze the data to find the answer to your question. Whether your analysis is statistical or qualitative, you must plan it in advance so that your analytic technique matches the type of data you collect (the next chapter touches on this issue again). Clearly, seeing how other researchers have analyzed their data can help you decide how to analyze yours. If you don't understand the statistical techniques used in a study, consult a textbook or someone who has experience using the techniques. Huck, Cormier, and Bounds (1974) have written a very useful book about how to interpret the statistics used in research reports.

PRIMARY VERSUS SECONDARY SOURCES   Information about research can be found in either primary sources or secondary sources. A **primary source** is an original research report or presentation of a theory written by the people who conducted the research or developed the theory. A primary source will include detailed information about the research or theory laid out in complete detail. Research reports published in professional journals are examples of primary research sources. They provide complete explanations of why the research was conducted, detailed descriptions of how the data were collected and analyzed, and the researchers' interpretations of the meaning of the results. Original presentations of theories can be found in books, as Locke and Lathams (1990) did with their goal-setting theory of work performance, or in professional journals, as Abramson, Metalsky, and Alloy (1989) did with their attributional theory of depression.

A **secondary source** summarizes information from primary sources. Examples of secondary sources include the introduction and discussion sections of research reports, journal articles and book chapters that review what is known about a topic, and textbooks. Secondary sources can also include nonprofessional publications such as newspapers, magazines, and television programs. Secondary sources are useful because they provide information from primary sources in concise form, compare and contrast the strengths and weaknesses of studies and theories, and point out gaps in the research literature and topics for future research. Because secondary sources are summaries, they necessarily omit information from the primary sources. As a result, secondary sources sometimes provide inaccurate descriptions of the results of the research and the meaning of those results. Friend, Rafferty, and Bramel (1990) and Treadway and McCloskey (1987) describe the ways in which the results of two classic social psychology experiments have been incorrectly described in secondary sources. Therefore, when you find an interesting study described in a secondary source, you should go back to the original research report to see what it actually says.

WHERE TO FIND INFORMATION   Sources of information for literature reviews can also be classified as published or unpublished. Published sources consist of professional journals and books, and receive wide distribution to academic libraries. Most research and much theoretical work in behavioral science is published in professional journals. An important characteristic of most articles published in professional journals is that they have undergone peer review. Peer review is a process in which an article is evaluated prior to publication by experts on its topic and, in the case of research reports, the methodology it uses. If the article does not meet the standards of quality set by the journal editor and evaluated by the reviewers, the report will not be published. Chapter 17 describes the review process in more detail; for now, let's view it as a quality check.

Books are used to publish research reports in many areas of behavioral science, such as sociology and anthropology, especially reports of long-term field studies. In other areas, such as psychology, professional books are used primarily for literature reviews, the presentation of theories, and methodological issues, usually on a single topic or set of related topics. Books can be classified as either monographs or edited books. Monographs are written by one author or a team of authors; in edited books, each chapter is written by an author or a team of authors, with an editor or a team of editors contributing opening and closing chapters that provide a context for the other chapters. Textbooks, of course, provide overviews of topics at various levels of detail and sophistication. Introductory-level texts provide only broad and often highly selective pictures of a field, designed for students with little background on the topic. Specialized graduate-level texts, in contrast, go deeply into a topic, analyzing the theories and research methods used. Professional books and textbooks are usually, although not always, peer reviewed, but the review criteria are often less stringent than those for journal articles.

Unlike published research, unpublished research reports receive only limited distribution. For example, master's theses and doctoral dissertations are normally held only at the library of the university where the work is done. Reports of research given at conventions and other professional meetings are typically distributed only at the meeting and to people who write to the author to ask for a copy. Unlike journals, books, and theses and dissertations, convention papers have no comprehensive archive in the form of libraries; however, the Educational Resources Information Center (ERIC) distributes copies of selected convention papers to academic libraries. Technical reports are reports of research done under contract to a business or government agency. They are usually distributed only to the agency for whom they were done, but some technical reports done for the federal government are published by the U.S. Government Printing Office; those done for private industry are rarely distributed to the public.

The Internet is a constantly expanding source of information about research. Research organizations and individual researchers often have Web pages describing recent and ongoing research projects. You can access these pages directly if you know the Web address (URL), or you can locate them through Web directories such as Yahoo! that categorize Web sites by topic or search engines such as Alta Vista, Excite, and Lycos that search the Web for pages containing key words the user enters. Also, the Web sites of professional organizations frequently include links to Web pages that index research sites. Peer-reviewed electronic journals, which publish studies on their Web sites, are also being established. *Links to Psychological Journals* (http://www.psychwww.com/resource/journals.htm) indexes a large number of electronic journals in psychology and the social sciences by title, topic, and key words.

You can also get information directly from the authors of published studies. The first page of most journal articles includes a footnote giving the postal and electronic mail addresses of one of the authors (usually the first author). You can write to the author to get information about the research that was not included in the research report, such as a copy of a measure or a set of stimuli. The author may also be able to provide you with information on the topic of the article that has not yet been published and with advice on other sources of information that are available.

LIBRARY RESEARCH TOOLS   Your library contains a number of tools to help you find information on the topic. One such tool is the library's catalog, which indexes the library's holdings in the form of books, periodicals, government documents, dissertations and theses written at the institution, audio and visual records, and other materials. The catalog can be searched by authors' names, titles, subjects, and key words. On-line (Internet-linked) catalogs also usually include pages of links to Internet-based indexes (such as the ERIC index) and search engines, and often include pages of links to the on-line catalogs of nearby and regional libraries. If you cannot find what you are looking for in your library, a neighboring college or university might have it. Materials from libraries other than the one at your college and university can usually be obtained through interlibrary loan (see Reed & Baxter, 1992, chap. 11).

Journal articles (and in some cases, books) are indexed in publications such as *Psyc-INFO* (the on-line version of *Psychological Abstracts*), *Sociological Abstracts*, and ERIC, which also provide abstracts, or summaries, of the materials they index. There are also indexes to some unpublished sources. *Dissertation Abstracts International* indexes doctoral dissertations. Dissertations from universities other than your own can sometimes be borrowed on interlibrary loan, and microfiche or paper copies can be purchased from University Microfilms, the company that publishes the index. In addition to journals, the ERIC database indexes selected convention papers and technical reports in education and related fields. Finally, the *Catalog of U.S. Government Publications* lists and indexes publications, including research reports, published by the U.S. Government Printing Office.

Because research reports, theoretical articles, and literature review articles cite the studies on which they are based, a second source of studies is the bibliographies of these publications. If one or a few articles are central to the topic under review, you can conduct a citation search. *Social Sciences Citation Index* (SSCI) indexes all the sources cited in articles published in major journals in the social and behavioral sciences. Therefore, if Smith and Jones have written a particularly important article on a subject, you can look up all the subsequent journal articles that cited Smith and Jones's work; these articles probably deal with the same topic and so are probably relevant to your literature review. Reed and Baxter (1992, chap. 6) explain how to use SSCI.

These indexes may be found on Web sites linked to your library's Web site, on a local area computer network in the library, or both. The mechanics of searching a computerized index vary depending on the particular software a library uses; see your reference librarian for information on how to use your library's system. Regardless of the software used, conducting an effective search depends on constructing the right search strategy, which is the list of terms that you tell the program to look for in the index. Constructing a good search strategy requires a knowledge both of the topic you are researching and of the way the search software operates. See Joswick (1994) and Reed and Baxter (1992, chap. 8) for suggestions on constructing effective search strategies.

What should you do if you conduct a literature search and cannot find information relevant to your topic? Your first step should be to think about the search you conducted. If you conducted a computer search, did you use the correct search terms? Each index has a thesaurus that lists the terms the index uses to categorize articles; if you don't use these "official" terms, you might not find what you're looking for. The thesaurus might also suggest synonyms, related terms, or broader terms to search under. If a revised search doesn't turn anything up, consider two possibilities. First, think about how researchable your topic is. If no one has ever conducted research on your question before, it might be because no one has been able to find a way to do so; alternatively, you might be breaking new ground and therefore be dealing with an especially important question. Second, journals are reluctant to publish the results of studies that do not support the hypotheses

BOX 4-2   Criteria for Evaluating Research Reports

General Guidelines

When evaluating a research report, ask the following questions. These questions are phrased primarily in terms of experimental research, but the same principles apply to other research strategies.

1. *Internal validity:* Might differences between groups be accounted for by something other than the different conditions of the independent variable?

    a. Were research participants randomly assigned to groups so that there was no systematic bias in favor of one group over another? Could bias have been introduced after assignment of participants because of different dropout rates in the conditions?

    b. Were all the necessary control groups used, including special control groups in addition to the baseline group to account for possible alternative explanations? Were participants in all groups treated identically except for administration of the independent variable?

    c. Were measures taken to prevent the intrusion of experimenter bias?

    d. Were measures taken to control for possible confounds, such as history, statistical regression, order effects, and so forth?

2. *Construct validity:* Did the researchers use appropriate operational definitions of their independent and dependent variables?

    a. Is there evidence for the validity of the operational definitions?

    b. How good is that evidence?

3. *Statistical validity:* Were the data analyzed properly?

    a. Was the statistic used appropriate to the data?

    b. Were the proper comparisons made between groups? For example, were follow-up tests used in multigroup and factorial designs to determine which differences in means were significant?

    c. Were the results statistically significant? If not, was there adequate statistical power?

Source: Adapted from Leavitt (1991) and Henninger (1997).

tested (Greenwald, 1975); consequently, other people may have done research on a topic and have been unable to find support for their hypotheses, but their research has not been published. One way to check on this possibility is by using the so-called invisible college: informal networks of people who conduct research on a topic. These people may be able to provide you information about research that hasn't made it into print.

Let me conclude this brief discussion of literature searching with a cautionary note. Computer technology makes literature searching seductively easy: sit down at the terminal, type in your search terms, and the computer lists your sources. However, a computer search is not always the most effective way to locate information: It will both turn up a large number of studies irrelevant to your literature review that happen to be indexed under your search terms and overlook a large number of relevant studies that happen not to be indexed under those terms. As Durlak and Lipsey (1991) described their experience, "We discovered . . . that only one of every three entries appearing in our computer-generated study lists was relevant [to the literature review] and approximately two thirds of the relevant studies were not picked up via the computer search" (p. 301). Supplementing a computer search with other means, such as reviewing the reference

BOX 4-2 *(continued)*

4. *Generalization:* Did the research have adequate external and ecological validity?

    a. *Research participants:* From what population was the participant sample drawn? Is it appropriate to the generalizations the authors want to make?

    b. *Experimental procedures:* Did the operational definitions and research setting have adequate realism?

    c. Did the researchers use enough levels of the independent variable to determine if there was a meaningful relationship with the dependent variable?

    d. Are the necessary independent variables included to detect any moderator variables?

5. *Going from data to conclusions:*

    a. If the study was designed to test a theory, does the theory clearly predict one experimental outcome over another? Do the researchers state an explicit hypothesis? If not, is one easily identifiable?

    b. Can all the steps and all the assumptions from theory to prediction be clearly stated?

    c. Can all the steps and assumptions from data to conclusions be clearly stated? Are all the conclusions supported by data?

    d. Are the conclusions consistent with the research strategy used? For example, are causal conclusions drawn only when a true experiment is conducted?

6. *Of what value is the research?* (No attempt has been made to order the following list in terms of importance.)

    a. Is the size of the relationship found large enough to have practical significance in terms of the goals of the research?

    b. Does it provide an answer to a practical problem?

    c. Does it have theoretical significance?

    d. Does it suggest directions for future research?

    e. Does it demonstrate previously unnoticed behavioral phenomena?

    f. Does it explore the conditions under which a phenomenon occurs?

    g. Does it represent a methodological or technical advance?

(continued)

lists of relevant research reports, is slower, but in the long run more productive, than relying on the computer alone.

EVALUATING INFORMATION   Much of the information you will review will be from research reports. Novice researchers often tend to accept the information in these reports, especially those published in professional journals, rather uncritically. Because these reports appear in peer-reviewed journals, the reasoning goes, they must be correct; who am I to question the judgments of experienced researchers, reviewers, and editors? However, as noted in the previous chapter, no study is perfect. Therefore, read research reports critically, keeping alert for factors, such as alternative explanations of results, that might lessen the validity of the conclusions. Take these validity judgments into consideration when formulating your hypotheses, giving the most weight to the information that you judge to be most valid. The factors that contribute to the validity of research are discussed throughout this book, and Box 4-2 lists some questions you should bear in mind while reading research reports. To give you practice in applying such questions to research reports, Huck and Sandler (1979) have compiled summaries of problematic studies.

BOX 4-2   *(continued)*

Information From the Internet

Because there are no controls, such as peer review, over the quality of the information posted on most Web pages, there are some additional factors to consider when evaluating research reports posted on the Internet.

1. *How credible is the source of the information?*

   a. Who is the author of the page, and what are his or her credentials or level of expertise regarding the topic of the page? For example, is the author a well-known, respected researcher on the topic?

   b. Who is sponsoring the Web page? For example, is it a well-known college, university, research institute, or public service organization? Note that a tilde (~) as part of a Web address usually indicates a personal Web page, not one officially sponsored by the organization hosting the page. For example, a college or university Web site may contain both official pages and unofficial personal pages for which it

provides space as a service for the institution's students, staff, and faculty.

2. *What is the purpose of the Web page?* Is it designed to provide objective information, or is it designed to sell a product or service or to advocate a particular position on a political or social issue? Commercial sites have vested interests in selling their products or services and so might emphasize research results supporting the efficacy of the products or services and downplay or omit information on their shortcomings. Similarly, an advocacy organization might emphasize research results that support its position on issues and downplay or omit contradictory information. It can be useful to compare the information from the Web sites or organizations on all sides of an issue.

3. *How current is the information on the page?* When was the page first produced and when was it last updated? Some Web pages are posted but never updated.

Working through their book will help you develop the critical sense you need to evaluate research reports.

In closing this section on literature reviewing, let me note that although Figure 4-1 shows literature reviewing and the next element in the hypothesis formulation process, formulating hypotheses, as separate elements, they are actually concurrent, interdependent processes. You will use the information from the literature review to help you refine your general research question into a specific hypothesis. Simultaneously, as your hypothesis becomes more specific you will find yourself in need of more specific information from the literature review, such as the advantages and disadvantages of different operational definitions and variables that you must control in order to rule out alternative explanations for your results. You may also need to continue your literature review after you have analyzed your data as you search for possible explanations of unexpected findings and look for the ways in which those findings fit in with what is already known about your topic.

Formulating Hypotheses

Once you have formulated your research question and refined it based on the information derived from your literature review, you must formulate one or more specific hypotheses to test in your research. Each hypothesis you formulate will take two forms: a narrative research hypothesis and a statistical hypothesis.

RESEARCH HYPOTHESES   The **research hypothesis** states an expectation about the relationship between two variables; this expectation derives from and answers the research question, and so is grounded in prior theory and research on the question. For example, for the research question "Is self-esteem related to premarital romantic jealousy?" the research hypothesis (based on a thorough literature review) could be stated as "Unmarried members of romantic relationships who have low self-esteem will exhibit more romantic jealousy than will unmarried members of romantic relationships who have high self-esteem."

Notice that the hypothesis specifies that a negative relationship exists between self-esteem and jealousy—low self-esteem is associated with high jealousy—not just that some unspecified type of relationship exists. Because of this specificity, the results of a study can unambiguously support or refute the hypothesis: Any outcome other than one in which low self-esteem is related to high jealousy means the hypothesis is wrong. An ambiguous research hypothesis, in contrast, can render the results of the research ambiguous. Consider the hypothesis "There is a relationship between self-esteem and jealousy" and this empirical outcome: High self-esteem is related to high jealousy. In one sense, these results support the hypothesis: There *is* a relationship between the variables. Yet the results directly contradict the relationship suggested by the results of the literature review. What are we to conclude? In this example of a single simple hypothesis, we can, of course, conclude that the research hypothesis "that we *really* meant to test"—the unambiguous hypothesis—was not supported. However, in research that tests multiple complex hypotheses, the conclusions may not be so clear-cut (for an example, see Wampold, Davis, & Good, 1990, p. 363). It is therefore always best to state research hypotheses in terms of specific relationships.

STATISTICAL HYPOTHESES   The **statistical hypothesis** transforms the research hypothesis into a statement about the expected result of a statistical test. The research hypothesis "People low in self-esteem exhibit more romantic jealousy than people high in self-esteem" can be stated as either of two equivalent statistical hypotheses: (1) "There will be a significant negative correlation between scores on a measure of self-esteem and scores on a measure of romantic jealousy" or (2) "People classified as low on self-esteem will have significantly higher mean scores on a measure of romantic jealousy than will people classified as high on self-esteem." The results of the appropriate statistical test can be compared to the statistical hypothesis to determine its validity.

The statistical hypothesis must accurately represent the research hypothesis. If the statistical hypothesis is not congruent with the research hypothesis, then the results of the statistical test will not provide accurate information to use in drawing conclusions about the validity of the research hypothesis. Consider the following example from Huck and Sandler (1979): Two educational researchers were interested in whether giving students classroom instruction on material covered by a textbook in addition to having them read the textbook would improve their scores on a test of the textbook material. Students were divided into three groups: Group 1 read the textbook and received classroom instruction on the material covered by the book, Group 2 just read the book, and Group 3 received classroom instruction unrelated to the topic of the book. At the

TABLE 4-1   Mean Scores Illustrating a Test of the Wrong Statistical Hypothesis

The research hypothesis called for a comparison of Groups 1 and 2, but the tested hypothesis was Group 1 versus the combination of Groups 2 and 3.

GROUP		
1 *Textbook and Instruction*	*2* *Textbook Only*	*3* *No Textbook and No Instruction*
25.06	21.66	13.41

end of the experiment, all the students took a 30-point test on the material the book covered; the groups' mean scores are shown in Table 4-1. The researchers statistically tested their hypothesis that additional instruction would improve learning by comparing the mean score of Group 1 to the combined means of the other two groups. Notice the following:

1. The research hypothesis was that students who both received classroom instruction and read the textbook (Group 1) would do better than students who only read the textbook (Group 2).

2. The research hypothesis transforms into the statistical hypothesis that the mean score of Group 1 would be greater than the mean score of Group 2. Group 3 is irrelevant to the research hypothesis, which does not say anything about students who have had no instruction (although the other groups could be compared to Group 3 to see if instruction had any effect at all on students' knowledge of the topic).

3. *The researchers tested a different statistical hypothesis*: that the mean of Group 1 was greater than the average of the means of Groups 2 and 3. Consequently, the results of the statistical test told the researchers nothing about the validity of their research hypothesis.

Figure 4-3 illustrates the way in which the process of hypothesis formulation affects the conclusions drawn about the validity of theories (or other bases for research questions). The solid line shows that a theory leads to the formulation of a research question. The question is stated as a research hypothesis, which is transformed into a statistical hypothesis. The statistical hypothesis is compared to the results of the appropriate statistical test. The broken line indicates the chain of conclusions drawn from the results of research. Conclusions about the status of the research hypothesis (confirmed or disconfirmed) are based on the match between the statistical hypothesis and the results of the statistical test. The conclusions drawn about the research hypothesis are correct *if and only if* the statistical hypothesis is congruent with the research hypothesis. Similarly, the correctness of the answer to the research question depends on the validity of the conclusions drawn about the research hypothesis, and the validity of the conclusions drawn about the theory depend on the correctness of the answer to the research question. In essence, then, the validity of all tests of theory (and of other types of research) depends on congruence between the research hypothesis and the statistical hy-

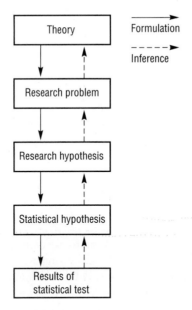

Note: Adapted from Wampold, Davis, & Good, 1990, p. 362.

FIGURE 4-3   Hypothesis Formulation and Inference in Research
In problem formulation, research hypotheses are derived from research problems, which are themselves de-rived from theory; the statistical hypothesis phrases the research hypothesis in terms of what the results of the statistical test would look like if the hypotheses were correct. The results of the statistical test are com-pared to the statistical hypothesis. In inference, use the statistical hypothesis to determine the implications of the results of the statistical test for the research hypothesis, and then determine the implications of the out-come of the research—whether or not the hypothesis was supported—for answering the research problem and for the theory.

pothesis. This congruence, in turn, is partly a function of the specificity of the research hypothesis: The more specific the research hypothesis, the easier it is to formulate a congruent statistical hypothesis. The specificity of the research hypothesis depends strongly on the clarity and specificity of the theory being tested.

Designing the Study

Once you have formulated your hypotheses, you can design your study. In designing a study you must answer five questions:

1. "*How* will I conduct the study?" The answer to this question includes choosing a research strategy and a specific design within the chosen strategy. A research design is the specific way in which a strategy is carried out; for example, as shown in Chap-ter 7, there are a number of ways of carrying out the experimental strategy.

2. *"What* will I study?" This question is answered by your choice of operational definitions for the hypothetical constructs you are studying.

3. *"Where* will I conduct the study?" Will you use a laboratory or field setting? What specific laboratory set-up or field location will you use?

4. *"Whom* will I study?" What population will you sample for your research participants and what sampling technique will you use? If you collect data from members of minority groups, you must design your research to take the groups' cultures into account. See the guidelines formulated by the Council of National Psychological Associations for the Advancement of Ethnic Minority Interests (2000) for factors to consider when conducting research with members of specific groups.

5. *"When* will I conduct the study?" Will time factors such as hour of the day or season of the year affect the phenomenon you will study? Do you want to take a cross-sectional or longitudinal approach to your study?

Answers to these questions are discussed in Chapters 7 through 12; however, the process of answering these questions is related to the process of hypothesis formulation in two ways. First, if you have difficulty in answering any of these questions, you will want to expand your literature review or seek advice from others to find the answers. Second, you must check the feasibility of your answer to each question; that is, ask yourself, "Are the resources needed to carry out the study in this way available to me?" If the answer is no, you might have to reformulate your hypothesis, reformulate your research question, or even select a new topic.

Writing the Research Proposal

After you have decided on a research design, you should write a research proposal; you will be required to do so for a thesis or dissertation. The proposal should lay out the theoretical and empirical bases for your research question and hypotheses (that is, their scientific context) and the research design you intend to use. The proposal serves two functions. First, the process of writing down the background for and design of your study helps you identify any missing elements. In presenting the reasoning behind your hypotheses, for example, you might find a gap in the logic underlying your derivation of the hypotheses from the theory that they are intended to test. Second, you can have other people read the proposal so that they can find any problems in background or design you might have overlooked. A fresh eye, unbiased by the researcher's intense study of a topic, can bring a new, useful perspective to the research question, hypotheses, and design. How detailed you make the proposal depends on its purpose. A thesis or dissertation proposal (called a *prospectus*) will be highly detailed; one that you prepare for your own use will contain less detail. In either case, any problems found in the research proposal must be dealt with by backing up in the process shown in Figure 4-1 until a resolution can be found.

Once you have validated your research proposal by ensuring that it is as problem free as possible, you can begin that process. For now, let's move on to some other issues surrounding research questions: replication research, designing research for utilization, and sources of bias in the hypothesis formulation process.

REPLICATION RESEARCH

Replication—the repeating of experiments to determine if equivalent results can be obtained a second time—has an ambiguous status in science. On the one hand, scientists and philosophers of science extol the virtues of and necessity for replication; on the other hand, replication research that is actually conducted is held in low esteem and is rarely published (Neuliep & Crandall, 1990, 1993b). This section explains the two forms that replication research can take and their relation to replication's ambiguous status in science, the implication of successful and unsuccessful replication research, and some issues to weigh when planning replication research.

Forms of Replication

Replication research can take two forms. **Exact replication** seeks to reproduce the conditions of the original research as precisely as possible, to determine if the results can be repeated. Exact replication is the less valued form of replication, being seen as lacking in creativity and importance and as adding little to the scientific knowledge base because it duplicates someone else's work (Mulkay & Gilbert, 1986; Neuliep & Crandall, 1990). This bad reputation exists despite the fact that duplication performs an important function—it protects against error. Any research result that confirms a hypothesis has a specifiable probability of being wrong due to random error—the Type I error. However, the more often an effect is duplicated, the more confidence we can have in the validity of the results: It is unlikely that random error would cause the hypothesis to be confirmed *every* time the experiment was conducted. Flaws in research designs and procedures can also lead to incorrect results that should not hold up in a properly conducted replication. The importance of this error detection function is emphasized by the facts that researchers are eager to conduct exact replications when they suspect that there is a problem in the original research (Mulkay & Gilbert, 1986) and that replication studies *are* published when they demonstrate error (Neuliep & Crandall, 1990). Amir and Sharon (1990) present several examples of influential pieces of psychological research that subsequent researchers were unable to replicate.

The second form of replication research, **conceptual replication,** tests the same hypothesis (concept) as the original research, but uses a different setting, set of operational definitions, or participant population. The purpose of conceptual replication is to test the generalizability of research results, to see how well they hold up under new test conditions. For example, a principle that holds up well when a variety of operational definitions is used has a higher probability of being correct than one that can be demonstrated only under one set of operational definitions. The latter circumstance leads to the suspicion that the effect found in the original research was caused by some unique characteristic of the operational definitions rather than by the hypothetical constructs that the operational definitions were intended to represent. In addition, a principle that can be replicated in a variety of settings and with a variety of populations has a higher probability of being a general principle than does a principle limited to a limited set of conditions. Chapter 14 discusses the issue of generalizability.

Implications of Replication Research

As shown in Table 4-2, replication research can have important implications for the principle being tested. These implications are functions of the type of replication conducted and whether or not the replication was successful in terms of obtaining results equivalent to those of the original research. A successful exact replication supports the principle being tested. Although the replication increases confidence that the principle is correct under the original test conditions, we don't know how well the principle will perform under other circumstances. A successful conceptual replication both increases confidence that the principle is correct and extends knowledge of the principle's applicability beyond the original test conditions. The greater the variety of conditions among a set of successful conceptual replications, the more widely applicable the principle.

Unsuccessful replications are less easy to interpret. The crux of the problem is that there is no way, given one study and one replication, of knowing where the error lies. Perhaps, as implied by the unsuccessful replication, the original study was flawed or suffered from a Type I error. However, it is also possible that the replication was flawed or suffered from a Type II error—incorrectly accepting the null hypothesis (Neuliep & Crandall, 1990). Therefore, failed replications should themselves be replicated before we draw firm conclusions from them. With this caveat in mind, we can say that a failed exact replication damages the principle it tests, suggesting that the principle is not valid. A failed conceptual replication limits the principle's generalizability. It shows that the principle doesn't work under the conditions of the replication, but says nothing about the validity of the principle under the original research conditions or under any conditions in which it has *not* been tested.

Considerations in Conducting Replication Research

Given the relatively low status of replication research among scientists and the possible difficulty of fitting the results of such research into the body of scientific knowledge, is it worth doing? Replications *are* worth doing and are quite frequently conducted, although conceptual replications are much more common than exact replications and replications are frequently conducted in conjunction with tests of new hypotheses, called *replications and extensions* (Neuliep & Crandall, 1993a). The greater frequency of conceptual replications and of replications and extensions is probably due to their ability to produce new information through generalization of the replicated principle and the testing of new hypotheses. The question, then, is not should you do replication research, but under what conditions should you do replication research? Two factors must be considered in answering this question: the importance of the hypothesis tested in the study you're considering replicating and the amount of research already conducted on the hypothesis.

IMPORTANCE OF THE HYPOTHESIS   The first consideration is the importance of the information you expect to gain from a replication. Replications are important to the extent

TABLE 4-2   Implications for the Principle Being Tested of the Success of the Replication and the Type of Replication

| | RESULT OF REPLICATION | |
Type of Replication	Successful	Unsuccessful
Exact	Supports the principle	Damages the principle
Conceptual	Supports and extends the principle	Limits the principle

Note: Adapted from Rosenthal, 1990b, p. 5.

that they test important hypotheses and can add new information about those hypotheses. As noted in the discussion of the characteristics of a good research question, the importance of a hypothesis is proportional to its importance to the theory from which it derives. Important hypotheses should be replicated when either of two conditions apply. The first condition is when there is reason to suspect a problem with the original research; a replication can be conducted to investigate. Two circumstances could lead to such a suspicion. First, someone could notice a possible alternative explanation for the results of the research. A replication can test the validity of that alternative explanation. For example, small-group researchers were once excited about a phenomenon called the "risky shift": Decisions made about the best solution to a problem after a group discussion appeared to be riskier (that is, to involve a higher probability of incurring a loss) than individual decisions by group members prior to the discussion. However, because of the nature of the problems used in the research, most group members made initial choices that were slightly risky. Other researchers therefore decided to see what would happen with problems that led to relatively conservative (nonrisky) individual initial decisions. These researchers hypothesized that group decisions went in the same direction as the individual initial decisions but were more extreme; that is, slightly risky individual initial decisions led to riskier group decisions, but slightly conservative individual initial decisions would lead to group decisions that were even more conservative. This alternative hypothesis was confirmed, and the "risky shift" was shown to be a special case of the more general principle expressed in the alternative hypothesis.

The second circumstance that could lead to suspicion of a problem with the original research is that its results contradict or don't fit in well with an established theory or principle. Although the logical positivist epistemology says that the validity of theories should be judged by the results of research, rather than judging the validity of research by its consistency with theory, the epistemology also says that theories should be judged by the weight of the evidence that bears on them. Therefore, if many studies support a theory and one does not, the inconsistent study is suspect. That study still deserves replication, however, because its nonconforming results might be due to some special feature of its design. If further research confirms the validity of the unsuccessful replication and shows that the failure to replicate was due to a specific aspect of the replication's design, then that aspect represents a limitation of the theory. For example, a theory might do well in explaining some forms of aggression but not others.

The second condition for replicating an important hypothesis is to test its generalizability. This kind of replication is important because it helps define the **boundary conditions** of a theory — the circumstances under which it does and does not work. Research on cognitive dissonance theory, a classic theory in social behavioral science, provides an example of this process. As originally formulated (Festinger, 1957), the theory was relatively simple: If people perform actions that contradict their beliefs, they experience an unpleasant state called *cognitive dissonance*. People are motivated to reduce this unpleasantness; one way in which they can do so is by changing their beliefs to fit their behaviors. Replication research, however, has shown that this kind of belief change occurs only under a very narrow set of conditions (J. Cooper & Fazio, 1984). The effect of cognitive dissonance on belief change is limited by these boundary conditions.

AVOIDING OVERDUPLICATION   The second consideration in planning a replication study is the amount of replication already done. Although replication research is valuable, one must avoid overduplication of well-established effects. That is, after a certain point, principles become well enough established that replication wastes resources. For example, discussing research on the use of tests of cognitive and perceptual abilities to predict job performance, Schmidt (1992) wrote that

> as of 1980, 882 studies based on a total sample of 70,935 subjects had been conducted relating measures of perceptual speed to the job performance of clerical workers. . . . For other abilities, there were often 200–300 cumulative studies. Clearly, further research on these relationships is not the best use of available resources. (p. 1179)

Well-established effects should be replicated only if there is some strong reason to do so, such as the testing of alternative explanations or an important aspect of generalization. When is a principle well enough established not to require further replication? Unfortunately, there is no agreed-on answer to this question (Lamal, 1990), although journal editors do agree that a principle can reach the point of needing no further replication (Neuliep & Crandall, 1990). In the absence of objective criteria for determining how well established an effect is, perhaps the best indicator is consensus: If psychologists familiar with a topic believe that no further replication of an effect is needed, replication would probably not be useful.

DESIGNING RESEARCH FOR UTILIZATION

Application is one of the three aspects of behavioral science, yet the results of behavioral science research are often not used in applied settings. In psychology, for example, the modal number of psychotherapy research reports read by practicing psychotherapists in a year is zero (Morrow-Bradley & Elliott, 1986), and commentators in other areas of behavioral science also report low rates of use of research results (for example, Dempster, 1988; Ruback & Innes, 1988). This section examines two issues: the factors affecting knowledge utilization and the design of research for utilization.

Knowledge Utilization

When the topic of a research report is relevant to the work of practitioners or policy makers in applied settings, they use two criteria to determine if the results of the research are usable: a truth test and a utility test (Weiss & Bucuvalas, 1980). The **truth test** determines the practitioner's perception of the validity of the research and has two aspects, research quality (was the research conducted by proper scientific methods?) and conformity to user expectations (are the results compatible with the practitioner's experience, knowledge, and values?). The **utility test** determines the practitioner's perception of the usefulness of the research results for guiding action, either through direct intervention or by providing alternative approaches to problems. It also has two aspects, action orientation (does the research show how to make a feasible change in things that can be feasibly changed?) and challenge to the status quo (does the research challenge current philosophy, program, or practice? does it offer new perspectives?). The results of research are likely to be used only if they pass both tests. In addition, if the practitioner or policy maker is a member of an organization, the results of the research must also fit the organization's goals, official policy, and image (Weiss, 1984). For example, even the results of good research that contradict a policy on which an organization or its influential members stake their public image or personal power are likely to be ignored or dismissed as irrelevant (Archer, Pettigrew, & Aronson, 1992).

In formulating a research question, the researcher has reasonably direct control over three of these four aspects. A thorough background in the field of application provides a basis for formulating research questions that can challenge the status quo and have an action orientation, and research competence will result in valid research. Background must be gained through experience and course work in the area of application, and the design of valid research is the concern of the remaining chapters of this book. Therefore, the rest of this discussion will concern factors to consider in designing action-oriented research.

Design Considerations

Three components of research affect its action orientation as perceived by policy makers: the independent and dependent variables, the research participants, and the research setting (Calder, Phillips, & Tybout, 1981; Ruback & Innes, 1988; Wells, 1978).

INDEPENDENT AND DEPENDENT VARIABLES Independent variables studied in applied research can be divided into two categories (Ruback & Innes, 1988; Wells, 1978). **Policy variables** are those over which practitioners or decision makers in the applied setting have some degree of control and can manipulate by changing policies or procedures to bring about changes in the behaviors they affect. **Estimator variables** are those that affect behavior in the applied setting but that practitioners and policy makers cannot or do not control and so cannot manipulate. Estimator variables can, however, be useful in understanding and predicting (estimating the level of) the behaviors they affect. Consider, for example, Figure 4-4, which reproduces the portion of Locke and Latham's (1990) goal-setting theory of work performance described in Chapter 1. The figure

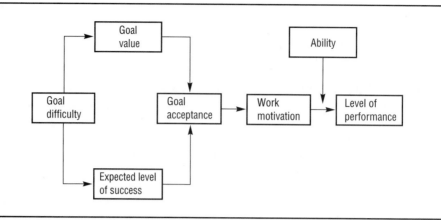

FIGURE 4-4   Selected Variables From the Goal-Setting Theory of Work Motivation (Locke & Latham, 1990)
People place more value on a more difficult goal but have lower expectations of success for it. The higher the goal value and level of expected success, the more likely people are to accept the goal. Greater goal acceptance leads to higher work motivation, which, in combination with ability at the task, affects level of work performance.

includes six variables that affect work performance. Only two of these variables—goal difficulty and worker ability—are under the control of managers in a work setting: Managers can set difficult goals and select the most able applicants as employees or train current employees to high levels of ability. These variables are therefore policy variables. The other four variables—goal value, expected level of success, goal acceptance, and work motivation—are beliefs and psychological states of the workers that managers cannot directly control. Practitioners and policy makers are more likely to see research that uses policy variables as independent variables as usable because policy variables are action oriented—they can be controlled.

Estimator variables can be useful in understanding how policy variables work. For example, if a program instituted to use difficult goals to improve work performance is not sufficiently effective, knowledge of the estimator variables involved in the process can suggest possible sources of the problem. One possibility is that the difficult goals led to such low expectations of success that goal acceptance and therefore work motivation were low. Additional programs could then be instituted to increase the levels of these variables, based on theories that include policy variables that can affect them. Also note that although the estimator variables used in this example were beliefs and psychological states, situational factors can also be estimator variables. For example, employers want to minimize the turnover of good employees, but a major factor affecting an employee's likelihood of quitting is the availability of other jobs (F. J. Landy, 1989), a factor not under the employer's control and therefore an estimator variable.

Dependent variables studied in applied research can vary in their utility to practitioners and policy makers. A high-utility dependent variable is one that practitioners and policy makers consider to be important. Some problems and the variables associated with them are more important to practitioners and policy makers than are other problems, and they consider research on more important problems to be more useful. For example, psychologists who do research in prisons have studied factors that affect, among other things, the health and happiness of prisoners. However, prison administrators consider the health of their prisoners to be more important than their happiness, and so see health research as more relevant, more important, and—if studied in relation to policy variables—more useful (Ruback & Innes, 1988). The relative importance of problems to practitioners can be determined by needs assessments that ask practitioners about their perceptions of problem importance (Elliott, 1983). The dependent variable should also be measured in a way that practitioners can clearly understand and relate to their experience. For example, when reading reports of psychotherapy outcome studies, practicing therapists are more interested in the percentage of people in the treatment group who improved to a clinically significant degree compared to the percentage who improved in the control group, than in the groups' mean scores on psychological tests, the most common measure used in research reports (Morrow-Bradley & Elliott, 1986).

Table 4-3 shows how the type of independent variable and the type of dependent variable combine to affect practitioners' and policy makers' perceptions of the relevance, importance, and usefulness of research. Research on the effects of policy variables on high-utility dependent variables is most likely to be perceived as relevant and to be used, whereas research on the effects of estimator variables on low-utility dependent variables is least likely to be perceived as relevant and to be used. Results of research on the effects of estimator variables on high-utility dependent variables can be useful in understanding and predicting phenomena in applied settings, but cannot be used to control the phenomena. As a result, practitioners and policy makers are likely to see this kind of research as intellectually interesting but not very useful. Finally, research on the effects of policy variables on low-utility dependent variables can be helpful to researchers in designing research using the policy variables—for example, by identifying problems in measuring or manipulating the variables—but is not of interest to practitioners and policy makers because it does not help them control a problem that concerns them.

RESEARCH POPULATION The second factor that affects practitioners' and policy makers' perceptions of the usefulness of research is the population from which the research participants were sampled. Practitioners and policy makers are more likely to perceive as useful research that is conducted using a representative sample of people who would normally be found in the applied setting of interest to them. From the practitioner's point of view, research whose results the researcher intends to be applied in schools should be conducted with schoolchildren; psychotherapy research should be conducted with clients in psychotherapy; industrial research should be conducted with workers; and so forth. However, as noted in Chapter 14, up to three quarters of psychological research has college students as participants, which lowers its perceived (but not necessarily its actual) relevance to applied settings.

RESEARCH SETTING Finally, the setting in which research is conducted affects its perceived usefulness. Practitioners and policy makers generally see research conducted in the setting to which it is to be applied as more useful than research conducted in other

TABLE 4-3   Effects of Type of Independent and Dependent Variables on Relevance of Research to Practitioners

	TYPE OF INDEPENDENT VARIABLE	
Type of Dependent Variable	Policy	Estimator
High utility	Relevant and potentially useful to practitioners	No direct relevance; can be helpful in understanding the phenomenon
Low utility	Irrelevant, but can provide potentially useful information about research methods	Irrelevant and unlikely to be useful to practitioners

Note: Adapted from Ruback & Innes, 1988, p. 684.

settings. Dempster (1988), for example, suggests that research on the spacing effect—the principle that in a set amount of study time, information presented a little bit at a time is learned better than information presented in one massed session (that is, studying an assignment a section at a time is more effective than cramming)—is not used in classroom instruction because so little of the research has been conducted in classroom environments using actual classroom materials. Even though the spacing effect has been consistently found in a large number of laboratory experiments using a wide range of materials, because little research has used classroom materials in the classroom, teachers see the research as irrelevant to their needs. When conducting applied research in natural settings, however, it is important not to disrupt the natural flow of events in the setting. Consequently, research procedures must be as unobtrusive as possible, which will usually entail using the case study and correlational research strategies rather than the experimental strategy (Calder et al., 1981). Chapter 10 discusses research in natural settings.

In summary, then, if you want to design research that has a high probability of being used by practitioners and policy makers, you should

1. Develop a strong background in the applied area.
2. Study the effects of policy variables rather than the effects of estimator variables.
3. Study high-utility dependent variables.
4. Conduct the research using a representative sample of people from the setting of interest.
5. Conduct the research in that setting, disrupting it as little as possible.

BIAS IN THE FORMULATION OF RESEARCH QUESTIONS

Despite the logical positivist assertion that the scientist is an unbiased observer of nature, there is ample evidence that the ways in which individual scientists formulate research questions, seek evidence to answer those questions, and interpret the evidence that they find are influenced by their intellectual values and personal epistemologies (Leavitt, 1991; Pyke & Agnew, 1991). These influences lead to bias in research in the sense that scientists tend to conceptualize the research process in ways that are congruent with their assumptions about human nature and with the theories that guide their research; competing viewpoints are given less weight than one's own (Diesing, 1991). This bias stems from basic human cognitive processes (Gilovich, 1991) and is therefore unavoidable to some degree. As scientists we can, however, be aware of the possibility of bias in our work and take steps to minimize its effects. I discuss aspects of bias in research throughout this book. Most of the examples I use deal with sex bias in research; I chose these examples not because sex bias is more important than other forms of bias, but because it has been the subject of most of the more recent discussions of bias in psychological research (see, for example, Gannon, Luchetta, Rhodes, Pardie, & Segrist, 1992).

Bias can enter into the formulation of research questions in two ways: through biased assumptions and through biased theory. Let's examine a few examples of each; further examples are provided by Eichler (1988) and McHugh, Koeske, and Frieze (1986).

Biased Assumptions

As noted in Chapter 1, an assumption is a belief that is so basic we take it for granted. Frequently, we are not aware of the assumptions we are making when we design research. For example, we may do research in a certain way because everyone has always done it that way, thereby implicitly incorporating other people's assumptions into our work. If any of these assumptions are biased, our research becomes biased without our intending it to be, and these biases are passed on to other researchers who model their work on ours. Therefore, we should examine the ways in which we do research so that we identify and eliminate any biased assumptions.

A basic form of biased assumption is assuming that research on one group is more important than research on other groups, or assuming that a problem is more important and therefore more in need of research when found in one group than when found in other groups. Historically, participants in psychological research have been White, male, and middle class (Gannon et al., 1992; Graham, 1992), implying that research on other groups was unnecessary or less important. For example, some psychologists see the fact that alcoholism among men has received much more research attention than alcoholism among women as reflecting the assumption that it is less important to find the causes of and effective treatments for alcoholism among women (McHugh et al., 1986).

A second form of biased assumption is assuming that what is actually a general problem is applicable to only one group. For example, almost two thirds of the research on adolescent contraceptive use has been conducted using only female participants (Whitley & Schofield, 1986), and almost all research on parental effects on child and adolescent psychopathology has examined only the role of the mother (Phares, 1992). Such research assumes that men have no role in these processes; this assumption retards progress in solving the problems of low contraceptive use and poor parenting because only half the available data are being considered.

Finally, a biased research question can result from conceptualizing a general topic in terms associated more with one group than another. For example, research on social power might examine leadership, which is a stereotypically masculine concept, rather than motherhood, even though both mothers and leaders exert social power (McHugh et al., 1986). Research based on such biased assumptions can overlook variables relevant to the general topic that operate only in aspects of the topic that are ignored.

Biased Theory

The theory from which a research question is derived can be biased in two ways. First, the theory itself might be biased. For example, early psychoanalytically based research on battered women tried unsuccessfully to explain the women's wanting to remain with the men who abused them in terms of masochism, which the theory assumes is more characteristic of women than of men. Better understanding of abused women's behavior emerged only when other theoretical frameworks were used (Denmark, Russo, Frieze, & Sechzer, 1988). A biased theory can therefore focus research attention in the wrong direction, delaying the answers to research questions and the resolution of practical problems. Second, the research used to validate a theory might be biased. It might, for example, use only participants from one group but assume that the results apply to members of all groups. The procedures used in the research might also lead to the appearance of group differences that don't actually exist; recall Eagly and Carli's (1981) finding that apparent sex differences in conformity were actually caused by the nature of the research procedures. If a theory is modified to conform with biased research results, then the theory itself can become biased.

Avoiding Bias

What can you do to avoid bias during the process of formulating a research question? First, be aware that the problem of bias exists; at each stage of the process, ask yourself if some form of bias might have slipped into the research question. When you have other people review your research proposal, ask them to be alert for bias—it is usually difficult for people to spot their own biases. Second, when reviewing research literature, look for indicators of possible bias such as generalizing from a limited sample to all people without evidence to support the generalization or the use of procedures that might produce biased results. See Eichler (1988) and McHugh et al. (1986) for more complete lists of indicators of potential bias.

Finally, examine your final research design. If you find you've limited yourself to participants from only one group, ask yourself if the limitation derives naturally from the nature of the research question or if the question also applies to members of other groups. For example, research on the psychological correlates of pregnancy can be conducted only with women, but research on expectant parenthood can include both sexes. Also, ask yourself if the particular example of a larger topic you chose to study is group stereotyped. For example, is parenting being studied in terms of motherhood rather than fatherhood? In contrast, it is sometimes necessary to limit research participation to members of a group—for example, to avoid an overly complex research design. In such cases, however, consider the limitations imposed by the use of a single group when interpreting the results of your study.

Biased research produces invalid results: It leads to the inaccurate description of behavior and of relationships between variables, and to a poor understanding of behavioral phenomena. Poorly understood phenomena cannot be predicted or controlled. Bias in the research process is therefore antithetical to the goals of science and must be avoided.

SUMMARY

Any research hypothesis is rooted in the researcher's background, which consists of both formal education and everyday experience. The researcher's background leads to the choice of a research topic that is of interest to the researcher and on which it is feasible for the researcher to conduct research. The general topic must be refined into a more narrow research question, which must be well grounded theoretically and empirically, researchable, and important. Sources of research ideas include theory, practical problems, prior research, logical analysis, and everyday experience. After formulating the question, the researcher reviews the literature on the question to put the question into a scientific context, avoid duplication of research effort, and identify problems that might arise in planning and conducting the research. These goals are accomplished by gathering information on theories relevant to the question, on the content of prior research, on methods that have been used to study the question, and on methods of data analysis. On the basis of this literature review, the researcher formulates the research hypothesis that will be the focus of the project and the statistical hypothesis that will be used in data analysis. The researcher then designs the study and writes a research proposal that can be used to identify issues or problems overlooked in formulating the hypothesis.

Replication research is the process of repeating the test of a hypothesis to verify or extend the results of the original research. Exact replication consists of a precise duplication of the original research; conceptual replication varies one or more aspects of the research, such as operational definitions, participant population, or setting. Depending on the type of replication and the outcomes of the original and replication studies, replication research can support, extend, limit, or damage the principle being tested. Because replication research can lead to ambiguous outcomes, you should conduct it only on important hypotheses when you have reason to suspect a problem with the original research or when it is useful to test its generality. Before conducting a replication, conduct a thorough review of the literature to avoid unnecessary duplication of effort.

Practitioners and policy makers are most likely to use research when they perceive it to be valid and useful. Researchers can increase perceptions of validity by conducting well-designed and well-executed research. They can increase perceived utility by studying independent variables the practitioner can control and dependent variables of direct interest to the practitioner. Practitioners perceive research conducted in natural settings of interest to them that uses the people in those settings as participants, as more useful than research conducted in other settings or with other participants.

Avoid bias in formulating research questions. Biased questions can result from biased assumptions about the importance of topics or about the people to which topics apply, or from conceptualizing topics in terms more relevant to one group. Biased questions can also arise from biased theories and prior research that was biased. Researchers must carefully examine their theories, research questions, and background literature to detect and avoid bias in their research.

QUESTIONS AND EXERCISES FOR REVIEW

1. Describe your formal and informal background in your area of behavioral science. What areas of research would your background best support? What areas would it support least well? How would you go about developing a background in an area of research that interests you?
2. What factors might limit the feasibility of your conducting research on a topic that interests you?
3. Describe the process of refining a research topic into a research question.
4. What are the characteristics of a good research question?
5. Describe the sources of ideas for research questions.
6. What are the purposes of the literature review? What kinds of information should you look for?
7. What is the difference between primary and secondary sources of information? What are the advantages and disadvantages of using secondary sources?
8. Where can published and unpublished research reports be found? What tools does the library provide to help you locate research reports? What considerations should you keep in mind when searching a computer database? How would you go about conducting a literature review on the topic you used for Question 2?
9. What constitutes a good research hypothesis? Give examples of bad hypotheses and show how they can be improved. Describe the relationship between the research hypothesis and the statistical hypothesis.
10. How is the hypothesis tested in a piece of research related to the theory from which it is derived? What processes intervene between theory and hypothesis?
11. What questions must be answered when designing a study? How does the literature review help in answering these questions?
12. What does a research proposal contain? What are the purposes of the proposal?
13. What are the purposes of replication research? Under what conditions should replication research be conducted? What kinds of information can the different forms of replication provide?
14. What factors affect practitioners' and policy makers' use of research results? How can research be designed to maximize the likelihood of utilization?
15. Describe the sources of bias in formulating research questions. Identify some biased research questions. In what ways are they biased, and how could you "unbias" them?

5 DEVELOPING A MEASUREMENT STRATEGY

RELIABILITY AND VALIDITY
Manifest Variables and
    Hypothetical Constructs
Reliability, Validity, and
    Measurement Error
    Reliability and Validity
    Measurement Error
Assessing Reliability
    Forms of Reliability
    Choosing Among the Forms
    of Reliability
    Standards for Reliability
Assessing Validity
    Categories of Validity
    Evidence
    Discriminant Validity
    Relationships Among the
    Categories of Validity
    Evidence
    Determining a Measure's
    Degree of Validity
    Differential Validity

MODALITIES OF MEASUREMENT
Self-Report Measures
    Advantages of Self-Report
    Measures
    Limitations of Self-Report
    Measures
Behavioral Measures
    Advantages of Behavioral
    Measures
    Limitations of Behavioral
    Measures
Physiological Measures
    Advantages of Physiological
    Measures
    Limitations of Physiological
    Measures
Choosing a Measurement
    Modality

LOCATING AND EVALUATING
MEASURES
Categories of Measures
Locating Measures
Evaluating Measures
    Theoretical Background
    Quality of Development
    Reliability and Validity
    Freedom From Response Bias
    Comparing Measures

SUMMARY

QUESTIONS AND EXERCISES
FOR REVIEW

A basic tenet of behavioral science is that people differ from one another, and one goal of behavioral science is to determine the causes and effects of these differences. To study why people differ, you must first be able to state the ways in which people differ (identify the important variables) and state the degree to which they differ on these variables. To study variables, you must first observe them (detect their presence) and then measure them (assign numbers to them that represent the degree to which they are present). Measurement consists of the sets of procedures we use to assign numbers to (to quantify) variables.

The process of quantification assists the research process in several ways. First, it lets you classify individuals and things into meaningful categories based on important characteristics, such as gender. For the sake of convenience, I refer to these characteristics as *traits*, although the term encompasses more than personality traits. Second, for some variables you can systematically arrange people or things on the basis of how much of the variable characterizes them. These processes of classification and arrangement let you find relationships between variables—to find, for example, whether Variable B is present most of the time that Variable A is present. Finally, using numbers lets you apply arithmetic processes to derive descriptive statistics, such as means and standard deviations that summarize the characteristics of groups of subjects and correlation coefficients that describe relationships between variables, and inferential statis-

tics, such as the *t* test and analysis of variance that assist in decision making.

Because of these contributions to the research process, one of the most important aspects of a research project is developing a measurement strategy, that is, deciding how to measure the variables of interest. When the variables are hypothetical constructs, the procedures used to measure them constitute their operational definitions, so the validity of the entire project hinges on the validity of the measurement strategy. This process of measurement consists of four steps:

1. Decide what to measure. This decision is made by your hypothesis: You want to measure the variables you are studying.

2. Develop a measurement strategy by identifying ways of measuring each variable. You may be able to use self-report, behavioral, or physiological measures, or a combination of them. There may be several possibilities within each of these modalities of measurement, and you may be able to choose between measures at the nominal, ordinal, interval, or ratio levels.

3. Evaluate the measures, and choose those that best fit your needs.

4. Apply the measures.

This chapter deals with the second step. To help you develop a measurement strategy, I discuss three topics: reliability and validity in measurement, modalities of measurement, and the evaluation of measures.

RELIABILITY AND VALIDITY

Reliability and validity are two of the most basic and most important aspects of measurement. This section begins by explaining the distinction between manifest variables and hypothetical constructs, then explains how the degree of reliability and validity of measures of hypothetical constructs are affected by measurement error, and concludes with discussions of how to assess the reliability and validity of measures.

Manifest Variables and Hypothetical Constructs

We can measure only what we can observe. We can, however, observe many things: the physical characteristics of people and objects, behavior, physiological responses, answers to questions, and so forth. Such variables, which we can directly observe, can be called **manifest variables** to distinguish them from hypothetical constructs, which we cannot directly observe. The problem, of course, is that behavioral scientists are frequently interested in measuring hypothetical constructs because many variables that behavioral science deals with are hypothetical constructs. As noted in Chapter 1, we use operational definitions, which consist of manifest variables, to represent hypothetical constructs in research. In doing so, we assume that the hypothetical construct is causing the presence and strength of the manifest variable used as its operational definition. For example, we assume that a certain personality characteristic, such as hostility, causes people to behave in certain ways. We therefore assume that the presence and strength of the manifest variable reflects, albeit imperfectly, the presence and strength of the hypothetical construct. Consequently, we infer the strength of the hypothetical construct (such as a person's level of hostility) from the strength of the manifest variable (such as the way the person acts or how the person answers questions about hostile behavior). By measuring the manifest variable, we measure the hypothetical construct; we therefore consider the manifest variable to be a measure of the hypothetical construct.

These inferences present a problem for measurement: How much confidence can you have that your inference about the relationship between the operational definition and the hypothetical construct is correct? Measurement theorists developed the concepts of reliability and validity as means of checking the adequacy of measures as indicators of hypothetical constructs. Those concepts are the principal topics of this section.

However, we are not always interested in manifest variables as measures of hypothetical constructs; sometimes we are interested in manifest variables for their own sake. We might be interested, for example, in whether men and women express different opinions on a political issue. We can directly observe people's sex and their answers to questions on the political issue, which constitute their opinions. We can then examine sex differences in response to the questionnaire items to answer our question. At no point do we make inferences about hypothetical constructs. Problems can arise, however, because manifest variables *can* be used as measures of constructs. We might be tempted, for example, to assume that certain opinions represent conservative political attitudes and that other opinions represent liberal political attitudes, and conclude that members of one sex are more politically liberal than members of the other sex because their opinions differ. However, unless evidence shows that these opinions accurately represent the hypothetical construct of political orientation, we have no way of knowing whether our conclusion about sex differences on this construct is correct. It is therefore essential to maintain an awareness of the distinction between the use of manifest variables in research for their own sakes and their use as operational definitions of hypothetical constructs, and to draw the proper conclusions based on how they are used.

Reliability, Validity, and Measurement Error

The concepts of reliability and validity are distinct but closely related. This section defines reliability and validity and shows how they are related through the concept of measurement error.

RELIABILITY AND VALIDITY   The **reliability** of a measure is its degree of consistency: A perfectly reliable measure gives the same result every time it is applied to the same person or thing, barring changes in the variable being measured. We want measures to be reliable—to show little change over time—because we generally assume that the traits we measure are stable—that is, that they show little change over time. For example, if you measure someone's IQ as 130 today, you expect to get the same result tomorrow, next week, and next month: IQ is assumed to be stable over time. As a result, an IQ measure that gave radically different results each time it was used would be suspect: You would have no way of knowing which score was correct.

The **validity** of a measure is its degree of accuracy: A perfectly valid measure assesses the trait it is supposed to assess, assesses all aspects of the trait, and assesses only that trait. Bear in mind that the validity of a measure is relative to a purpose; that is, a measure can be valid for one purpose but not for another. The polygraph, for example, does an excellent job at its intended purpose of measuring physiological response but cannot accurately detect when a person is telling the truth, a purpose for which it was not designed but is sometimes used (Lykken, 1981). Although reliability and validity are distinct concepts, they are closely related. An unreliable measure—one that gives very different results every time it is applied to the same person or thing—is unlikely to be seen as accurate (valid). This inference of low validity would be correct, although, as shown later, high reliability is no guarantee of validity. The link between reliability and validity is measurement error.

MEASUREMENT ERROR   When we measure a variable, we obtain an **observed score**—the score we can see. The observed score is composed of two components: the **true score** (the actual degree of the trait that characterizes the person being assessed) and **measurement error** (other things that we did not want to measure, but did anyway because of the imperfections of our measuring instrument). There are two kinds of measurement error. **Random error** fluctuates each time a measurement is made; sometimes it's high and sometimes it's low. As a result, the observed score fluctuates; sometimes the observed score will be higher than the true score, and sometimes it will be lower. Therefore, random error leads to instability of measurement and lower reliability estimates. Random error can result from sources such as a person's being distracted during the measurement process; mental or physical states of the person, such as mood or fatigue; or equipment failures, such as a timer going out of calibration. **Systematic** (nonrandom) **error** is present every time a measurement is made. As a result, the observed score is stable, but inaccurate as an indicator of the true score. Systematic error can result from sources such as poorly worded questions that consistently elicit a different kind of response from the one intended, or an instrument's measuring traits in addition to the one it is intended to measure.

The effects of random and systematic error on reliability and validity are illustrated in Figure 5-1, with the bars representing observed scores. Figure 5-1(a) represents a valid, reliable measure: It has a very high proportion of true score and relatively little error of either kind. Figure 5-1(b) represents an unreliable measure: It is mostly random error. Note that as a result of its large proportion of random error, the measure has relatively little true score; it is therefore of low validity. Figure 5-1(c) represents a measure that is reliable but is of low validity. Its reliability stems from its being composed mostly of systematic (stable) error and very little random (unstable) error. However, it also has very little true score, and so is of low validity. Figure 5-1 carries an important implication: An unreliable measure always has low validity, but *high reliability does not guarantee high validity*. It is therefore not enough to know that a measure is reliable before using it; you must also have evidence for its validity.

Assessing Reliability

When you judge a measure's degree of reliability, you must first decide which of several forms of reliability estimates is appropriate for the measure and then decide whether the measure has adequate reliability. This section describes the forms that reliability estimates can take, discusses the factors to weigh in choosing an appropriate form of reliability assessment for a measure, and explains the standards used to judge the adequacy of a measure's reliability.

FORMS OF RELIABILITY   The term *reliability* refers to consistency, which can be assessed in three ways: across time, across different forms of a measure, and, for multi-item measures, across items.

Consistency across time is an indicator of reliability because we assume that the traits we want to measure are relatively stable across time; therefore, measures that have a high degree of true score should also be stable across time. Consequently, one way of assessing reliability, referred to as **test-retest reliability,** is to assess people's scores on a measure on one occasion, assess the same people's scores on the same measure on a later occasion, and compute the correlation coefficient for the two assessments; that correlation coefficient represents the degree of reliability shown by the measure. Note that the concept of reliability does not require that people's scores be exactly the same on both occasions; random error makes this outcome unlikely. All that is required is that people's scores fall in generally the same rank order: that people who score high the first

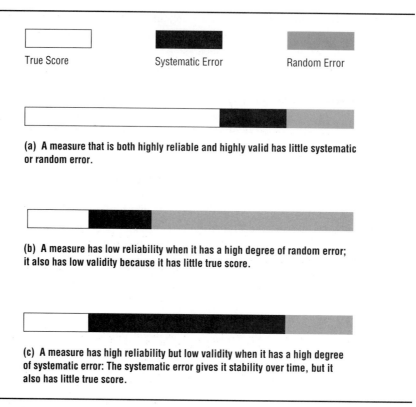

(a) A measure that is both highly reliable and highly valid has little systematic or random error.

(b) A measure has low reliability when it has a high degree of random error; it also has low validity because it has little true score.

(c) A measure has high reliability but low validity when it has a high degree of systematic error: The systematic error gives it stability over time, but it also has little true score.

FIGURE 5-1   Reliability, Validity, and Measurement Error

time also score high the second time and that people who score low the first time also score low the second time. How much time should elapse between the two assessments? The answer depends on the trait being assessed. Some traits, such as mood, are assumed to be highly changeable, whereas others, such as adult IQ, are assumed to be relatively stable for most of a lifetime. The assumed stability of most traits falls somewhere between these two. One should therefore use a time period over which it is reasonable to assume that the trait will be relatively stable. This time period can be derived from the theory that defines the trait or from research on the trait.

Consistency across forms can be used as an indicator of reliability when a measure has two or more forms designed to be equivalent (referred to as alternate forms); that is, each form is designed to give approximately the same score for any person. Measures having several forms can be useful when you want to assess people at short intervals but don't want to bias their responses by using the same questions each time. Because each form is designed to measure the same trait in the same manner, **alternate forms reliability** can be assessed as the correlation between scores on the two forms. Sometimes the measuring instruments used are people; for example, two observers watch children at play and rate how aggressive each child is on a 7-point scale. In this case, the reliability of this measure of aggression can be assessed by correlating the ratings of the two raters to obtain an **interrater reliability.**

Interrater reliability can also be assessed when the rater puts behavior into categories (such as aggressive or nonaggressive) rather than rating the behavior on a quantitative scale. In such cases, you can assess reliability in terms of the percentage of times the raters agree on the category in which each observed behavior goes. However, be careful to consider the likelihood of agreements occurring by chance when evaluating reliability in this way. For example, if only two categories are used, raters would agree 50% of the time if they categorized behaviors by flipping a coin, with heads meaning one category and tails the other. A statistic called *Cohen's kappa* provides an index of agreement that is corrected for chance (Bakeman & Gottman, 1989) and that can be interpreted in the same way as a correlation coefficient.

Consistency among items can be used as an indicator of reliability when a measuring instrument uses multiple items or questions to assess a trait, with the sum of a person's scores on the items being the total score for the measure. Most standardized tests and many research measures are constructed in this manner. Because each item is designed to assess the same trait, the reliability of the measure can be assessed in terms of the correlations among the items. A simple way to accomplish this is to split the items into two parts and compute the correlation between the respondents' total scores on the two parts; this is referred to as **split-half reliability.** More generally, one could look at the pattern of correlations among all the items. The most common example of this approach is called *Cronbach's alpha.* Alpha is a function of the mean correlation of all the items with one another and can be interpreted as a correlation coefficient. Because they assess the degree to which responses to the items on a measure are similar, split-half correlations and Cronbach's alpha are considered indicators of the **internal consistency** of measures.

CHOOSING AMONG THE FORMS OF RELIABILITY Which form of reliability assessment is the best? As for most questions in behavioral science, there is no single answer. Sometimes the decision is driven by the choice of measure; for example, measurement by raters requires the use of some form of interrater reliability. Because we're trying to assess the stability of measurement, test-retest is probably the ideal form of reliability assessment. However, some traits, such as mood, are not stable across time; internal consistency might provide a better estimate of reliability in such a case. In other cases, it might not be possible to test people more than once, again leading to the use of internal consistency reliability. Fortunately, the internal consistency of a measure is reasonably well related to its stability across time (Schuerger, Zarella, & Hotz, 1989).

STANDARDS FOR RELIABILITY How large should a reliability coefficient be to be considered good? There are no absolute rules, but J. P. Robinson, Shaver, and Wrightsman (1991a) suggest a minimum internal consistency coefficient of .70 and a minimum test-retest correlation of .50 across at least a 3-month period, and Bakeman and Gottman (1989) suggest a minimum kappa of .70 for interrater reliability. Higher reliability coefficients and high test-retest correlations across longer intervals indicate better reliability. However, when comparing the relative reliabilities of several measures when the reliability of each is assessed in a separate study, it is important to remember that several factors can affect the magnitude of the reliability coefficient found for any one measure in any one study. For example, test-retest correlations tend to decrease as the test-retest interval increases, and the scores of older respondents tend to show greater temporal stability than do those of younger respondents (Schuerger et al., 1989). There-fore, the evaluation of a measure's reliability must consider the effects of the charac-teristics of the reliability study. Two measures that would have the same reliability coefficient when assessed under the same circumstances might have different coeffi-cients when assessed under different circumstances. Just as a person's observed score on a measure is an imprecise indicator of his or her true score on the trait, the reliability coefficient found in any one study is an imprecise indicator of the measure's true relia-bility; true reliability is better indicated by a measure's mean reliability coefficient across a number of studies. In addition, the test-retest coefficient of any measure is going to reflect the natural degree of (in)stability of the trait so that measures of more labile traits, such as mood, will have lower coefficients than measures of more stable traits. Therefore, what constitutes a good stability coefficient for a labile trait, such as mood, might be a poor coefficient for a more stable trait, such as IQ.

Assessing Validity

The term *validity* refers to the accuracy of measurement; that is, it addresses the ques-tion of how confident we can be that a measure actually indicates a person's true score on a trait. The concept of validity has six important aspects (Gronlund, 1988, p. 136):

1. "Validity is *inferred* from available evidence (not measured)." That is, we cannot produce direct evidence that a measure is valid, we can only infer its degree of validity from indirect evidence. This situation contrasts with that of reliability, for which we can gather direct, quantitative evidence of temporal stability and internal consistency.

2. "Validity depends on *many different types* of evidence." These types are tradi-tionally referred to as "content related," "criterion related," and "construct related." These three terms represent a wide variety of techniques for gathering validity evi-dence, and some techniques could be placed in more than one category. Bear in mind that these categories are merely labels used when discussing validity evidence and that no one category necessarily represents better evidence of validity than does any other category.

3. "Validity is expressed by *degree* (high, moderate, low)." That is, a measure can-not be categorized as valid or invalid in absolute terms, but only as a matter of degree.

4. "Validity is *specific* to a particular use." That is, a measure is usually more valid for one trait than for any other. As already noted, the polygraph exhibits a high degree of validity as a measure of physiological states, but a low degree of validity as a measure of whether someone is telling the truth.

5. "Validity refers to the *inferences drawn*, not the [measure] itself." It is imprecise (although convenient) to say that a measure is of high or low validity. When we talk about the validity of a measure, we are not referring to a characteristic of the measure itself, but to a characteristic of the conclusions that we draw about people based on their responses to the measure. That is, a measure does not possess high or low validity; rather, the conclusions we draw from it have high or low validity. As F. J. Landy (1986) notes in the context of psychological tests,

Researchers are not really interested in the properties of tests. Instead, they are interested in the attributes of people who take those tests. Thus, validation processes are not so much directed toward the integrity of tests as they are directed toward the inferences that can be made about the attributes of the people who have produced the test scores. (p. 1186)

However, as a matter of tradition and convenience, we usually refer to the validity of a measure rather than to the validity of the conclusions drawn from it.

6. "Validity is a *unitary* construct." Earlier conceptions of validity considered the three categories of validity evidence—content related, criterion related, and construct related—to be distinct forms of validity. The current view of validity, in contrast, is that validity is one concept, not three, but one concept that has three categories into which we can place evidence for or against a measure's validity. Let's examine each of these three categories of validity evidence. A breakdown of the categories is shown in Figure 5-2.

CATEGORIES OF VALIDITY EVIDENCE **Content-related evidence of validity** consists of demonstrating that the content of a measure of a trait—for example, the items on a questionnaire—adequately assesses all aspects of the trait. Adequate assessment has two characteristics: The content of the measure must be *relevant* to the trait and *representative* of the trait. Relevance and representativeness are judgments based on the nature of the trait as defined by the theory of the trait. A relevant measure assesses only the trait it is attempting to assess, and little else. If a trait has more than one aspect, a representative measure includes all aspects. The clearest examples of these concepts come from academic tests. Relevant test items ask only about the material the test is supposed to cover, not about other material. For example, a question about how to compute a *t* test would not be relevant to students' knowledge of social psychology, although it would be relevant to their knowledge of statistics. Representative test items sample all the topics that the test is supposed to cover. For example, if a test covers three chapters of a textbook, each of which received equal emphasis in the course, the principle of representativeness requires that the test contain questions on each chapter, not just one or two, and that each chapter have equal weight in determining the overall test score.

The assessment of self-esteem provides an example from the realm of psychological assessment. If we define self-esteem as self-evaluation, an item such as "I'm less competent than most people" would be more relevant than an item such as "I prefer Chevrolets to Fords." In terms of representativeness, we might divide self-esteem into global self-evaluation, self-evaluation relative to achievement situations, and self-evaluation relative to social situations (Wylie, 1989), and include items that assess each aspect. We would also want to determine, on the basis of the theory of self-esteem we were using, how much importance each component should have in forming an overall self-esteem score. For example, should each component contribute equally to the overall score, or should some components be given more weight than others? The degree to which a measure provides content-related evidence of validity can be represented quantitatively as a function of the proportion of a set of expert judges who, given a definition of a trait, agree that each item on a measure is relevant to the trait and that the measure represents all aspects of the trait (Lawshe, 1975).

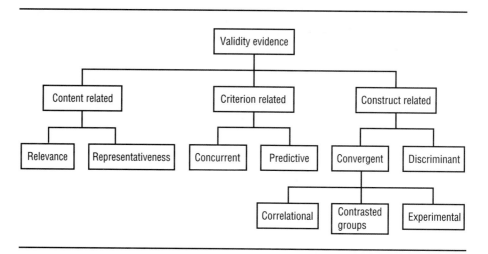

FIGURE 5-2   Categories of Validity Evidence

In the most general sense, **criterion-related evidence of validity** is the degree to which scores on one measure predict (that is, are correlated with) scores on another measure, called the *criterion* (Cronbach, 1990). However, the term is more commonly used to refer to the degree to which a measure can predict performance on some criterion task (Cascio, 1998). Criterion-related evidence is most commonly used to evaluate the validity of measures used to determine a person's potential for doing well at a particular task; aptitude tests and employment selection tests are examples of such measures. Thus, the correlation coefficient for the relationship between Scholastic Assessment Test (SAT) scores and college grade point average (GPA), which is about .44 at the university where I teach, represents criterion-related evidence of the SAT's validity as a predictor of academic performance in college. In general, criterion-related evidence of validity is expressed as the degree of correlation of the test score with the score on the criterion.

Research to assess the criterion-related evidence for the validity of a measure can take two forms. In predictive designs, people are assessed using the measure, their performance on the relevant task is assessed at a later point in time, and their scores on the measure are correlated with their performance scores. In concurrent designs, people are assessed using the measure, their level of performance at the time of the assessment is measured, and the two sets of scores are correlated. The choice of a predictive or concurrent design for a validity study should reflect the purpose of the measure being validated (Anastasi & Urbani, 1997). If the purpose is to predict future outcomes (such as selecting people who will later become high performers), then the predictive design is preferred; if the purpose is to assess people's current status on the criterion (such as a psychiatric screening instrument), then the concurrent design is preferred. Another way of looking at it is that predictive designs are better for measures used to assess potential for future performance, whereas concurrent designs are better for measures intended to assess current levels of performance.

The criteria used in studies of the criterion-related validity of a measure can take two forms (Binning & Barrett, 1989). Frequently, criteria take the form of manifest variables. For example, you could correlate salespeople's scores on a sales aptitude test with the dollar value of the amount of products they sell. If the test is valid, you would expect to find a reasonably high correlation. Sometimes, however, the criterion is a hypothetical construct and scores on the measure being validated are correlated with scores on an operational definition of the criterion construct. In this case, we are not primarily interested in the measure's relationship with the operational definition but, rather, in the measure's relationship with the hypothetical construct; we use its relationship with the operational definition to infer its relationship with the construct. For example, the SAT is designed to measure high school students' readiness to do college-level academic work—a hypothetical construct. Validation studies of the SAT typically use a predictive design, correlating test-takers' SAT scores with their first-year college GPAs, with GPA being used as an operational definition of college-level academic achievement.

Whenever the criterion is a hypothetical construct, the accuracy with which the correlation between the scores on the measure being validated and scores on the operational definition of the construct indicates the degree of validity of the measure, depends on the accuracy of the operational definition as a representation of the hypothetical construct. That is, because our true interest lies in the relationship between scores on the measure and the hypothetical construct, the correlation between scores on the measure and scores on the operational definition indicates the measure's degree of validity if and only if the operational definition is itself a valid measure of the construct.

Consider Figure 5-3, which uses the validation of the SAT as an example. Rectangles represent the manifest variables of SAT scores and GPAs, and the solid line between them represents their observed correlation. The broken line between SAT scores and the hypothetical construct (represented by an oval) of academic achievement represents the inference we want to make. However, to make that inference, we must, as it were, go through GPA as an operational definition of academic achievement; therefore, the link between SAT scores and academic achievement (the SAT's criterion-related validity) is no stronger than the link between GPAs and academic achievement (GPA's construct-related validity).

More generally, whenever the criterion used in a study of the criterion-related validity of a measure is a hypothetical construct, we must consider the construct-related validity of the operational definitions of the hypothetical construct when drawing conclusions about the validity of the measure. The less evidence there is for the construct-related validity of the operational definitions, the less confidence we can have that the correlations between scores on the measure and scores on the operational definitions provide information about the validity of the measure. Without evidence for the construct-related validity of the operational definition, a high correlation does not provide evidence for the validity of the measure; conversely, a low correlation does not provide evidence against the validity of the measure.

Construct-related evidence of validity is the degree to which people's scores on a measure reflect their true scores on a hypothetical construct. The basis for construct-related evidence of validity is the theory underlying the construct. The theory should

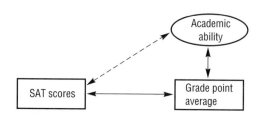

FIGURE 5-3   Criterion-Related Validity When the Criterion Is an Operational Definition of a Hypothetical Construct
The conclusion drawn about the criterion-related validity of the measure (SAT scores) is dependent on the construct-related validity of the operational definition (grade point average) as a representation of the hypothetical construct (academic ability).

specify the ways in which the construct being measured is related to other constructs and the ways in which people who differ on the construct should behave. To the extent that people who score differently on a measure of a construct show traits and behaviors consistent with the theory, construct-related evidence for the validity of the measure exists. Therefore, there are three steps to the process of collecting construct-related evidence of validity (Zeller & Carmines, 1980): (1) formulating hypotheses that represent the links between the construct being measured and other constructs and behaviors specified by the theory of the trait; (2) conducting a study to determine the empirical relationships between the measure being evaluated and measures of the other constructs and behaviors; and (3) interpreting the empirical evidence in terms of the degree to which it provides evidence of construct-related validity.

Many different types of relationships can be used to assess construct-related evidence of validity (Cascio, 1998; Ghiselli, Campbell, & Zedeck, 1981); only a few are briefly described here. One means of gathering evidence that a measure is assessing the correct construct is the correlational approach, which examines the degree to which a measure correlates with other well-validated measures of the same construct. Correlations with different constructs can also provide evidence of validity if the theory of the trait postulates those relationships. For example, we might expect people who score high on measures of self-esteem also to score high in feelings of control over their lives and in trust of other people, and to score low in feelings of alienation from others. If the theory of the construct predicts that people who score high on the trait should behave differently from people who score low on it, we can also examine the correlation between scores on the measure of the construct and the behaviors the theory predicts. For example, people who score high and low on a measure of shyness should exhibit different patterns of behavior in social situations. Another form of evidence comes from the contrasted groups approach: The theory might predict that certain kinds of people should score differently on a measure of the construct. For example, we would expect people in the helping professions to score higher on a measure of empathy than people in other professions.

The experimental approach can be used when the theory of the construct predicts that people who score high and low on the trait will respond differently to some experimental manipulation. For example, people who exhibit a trait known as "depressogenic attributional style" are hypothesized to have different cognitive, emotional, and behavioral reactions to failure from other people (Abramson, Metalsky, & Alloy, 1989). We could therefore construct an experiment in which success or failure on a task is the independent variable, and observe if people who do and who do not exhibit the trait react in the ways predicted by the theory. Finally, scores on a measure should change in response to treatments designed to bring about changes in the level of the construct. For example, people exposed to an anxiety-arousing situation should score higher on a measure of state anxiety than people exposed to a control condition.

In sum, one line of evidence for the construct-related validity of a measure is the degree to which the measure supports predictions based on the theory of the construct. What should we conclude if a particular validation study does *not* find such evidence? One possible conclusion is that the measure is not valid. There are, however, three alternative explanations (Cronbach & Meehl, 1955). The first, and easiest to check, is that an inappropriate or inadequate method was used to test the hypotheses that were intended to provide evidence of validity. The methodology can be reviewed for flaws. A second alternative explanation is that the theory of the construct is wrong, predicting a relationship that is nonexistent. The tenability of this explanation depends on the state of the theory: It is less likely to be true of a well-tested theory than of a new theory. Finally, it is possible that the measure of the trait with which the new measure was expected to correlate lacks validity; for example, a failure to find a correlation between a new measure of self-esteem and a measure of feelings of control might be due to an invalid measure of feelings of control rather than to an invalid measure of self-esteem. The tenability of this explanation depends on the state of the evidence for the validity of the other measure. We should therefore not be too quick to reject the construct-related validity of a measure on the basis of a single test; conclusions of both low and high evidence for validity should be drawn only on the basis of a body of research.

DISCRIMINANT VALIDITY   So far, this discussion of validity has focused on what D. T. Campbell and Fiske (1959) refer to as **convergent validity,** the extent to which evidence comes together, or converges, to indicate the degree of validity of a measure: in other words, evidence that lets us conclude the measure is assessing what it is designed to assess. An equally important aspect of validity is what Campbell and Fiske named **discriminant validity,** evidence that a measure is *not* assessing something it is *not* supposed to assess. For example, a measure designed to assess shyness, but that also assesses anxiety, lacks discriminant validity relative to anxiety. The measure's lack of discrimination between shyness and anxiety makes it difficult to conclude whether high scores on the measure represent high shyness, high anxiety, or both high anxiety and high shyness. Although most discussions of discriminant validity tend to focus, as does this shyness and anxiety example, on construct-related evidence of validity, the concept is also related to content-related evidence of validity. As already seen, the content of a measure should reflect the trait to be assessed and *only* the trait to be assessed; to the extent that a measure is high in relevance, it will show high discriminant validity.

As an aspect of construct-related evidence of validity, discrimination is evaluated by considering the measure's correlation with variables that the theory of a construct postulates to be irrelevant to that construct. A low correlation with an irrelevant variable is evidence for discriminant validity. Irrelevant variables can be of two forms. Substantive variables are other constructs that might be measured along with the construct of interest. For example, because a paper-and-pencil IQ test might measure reading ability along with IQ, it would be desirable to show that reading ability scores were uncorrelated with scores on the IQ measure. Method variables concern the manner by which a construct is assessed, for example, by self-report or behavioral observation. A person's score on a measure is partially a function of the assessment method used, which is one form of systematic measurement error (D. T. Campbell & Fiske, 1959). For example, scores on self-report measures of two traits could be correlated because people have an extremity response bias—a tendency to use only the high or low end of a self-report scale—rather than because the traits are related to one another.

A common method for assessing discriminant validity is the multitrait-multimethod matrix, or MTMMM (D.T. Campbell & Fiske, 1959). The MTMMM consists of the correlations between several constructs that are unrelated in theory (usually at least three), each measured by several different methods, with the number of methods usually equaling the number of constructs. Let's say that you wanted to do a validation study of a new self-esteem measure. Your theory says self-esteem should not be correlated with loneliness and shyness. You could measure each of the three traits in three different ways—self-report, ratings by friends, and behavioral observation—and calculate the MTMMM, which consists of the correlations among the nine variables. The MTMMM provides three types of information:

1. *High correlations* among measures of the *same construct* using *different methods* provide evidence for the convergent validity of the measures. Because of the different methods, none of the correlations are due to the type of measure being used.

2. *Low correlations* among measures of *different constructs* using the *same method* indicate good discriminant validity on the basis of method. Even when the same measurement method is used (which should increase correlations), the correlations are low, indicating that the measures are assessing different traits.

3. *High correlations* among measures of *different constructs* using *different methods* indicate a lack of distinctiveness among the constructs. Even when different methods are used (which should minimize correlations) the correlations are high, indicating that the constructs are similar. That is, even though the theory says that the constructs (say, shyness and self-esteem) are different, the evidence says they are essentially similar: One concept may have been given different names. R. J. Cohen, Swerdlik, and Phillips (1996) present a detailed explanation of the MTMMM. The MTMMM itself provides no statistical test of the degree of either convergence or discrimination; however, the matrix can be analyzed using additional statistical techniques that provide such tests (Cole, 1987).

RELATIONSHIPS AMONG THE CATEGORIES OF VALIDITY EVIDENCE   Now that we have examined the categories of validity evidence separately, it is time to reemphasize that all three categories represent one concept: validity. As a result, the different categories are related to and reinforce one another. For example, measures that have a high degree of relevant and representative content should also do well at predicting performance and should show good convergence and discrimination relative to measures of other

TABLE 5-1 Validation of Empathy Measures

Examples of construct-related and content-related evidence.

Construct-Related Evidence	
Contrasting groups	Child abusers score lower than nonabusers.
	Social workers score higher than clerical workers.
	Prisoners who volunteer to help disadvantaged people score higher than prisoners who don't volunteer.
	Delinquents have lower scores than nondelinquents.
Behavioral differences	High scorers are more likely to help people than low scorers.
	Therapists with high scores tend to have better success rates.
	High scorers tend to become more anxious when watching a speaker make a fool of him- or herself.
	Groups with low empathy scores have intense internal feuding.
	High scorers are better at conveying ideas while playing charades.
	Higher scoring salespeople have better sales records.
	Higher scorers are less aggressive.
Convergence with related traits	Medical students who score higher have more humanistic reasons for choosing medicine as a career.
	High scorers tend to have greater knowledge of leadership.
	Higher scorers are more extraverted and self-disclosing.
	Higher scorers have more affiliative urges.
	Higher scorers are more anxious.
Convergence with other empathy measures	Empathy measures correlate well with each other.
Discrimination	Empathy scores are not correlated with intelligence.

Content-Related Evidence
Experts have analyzed measures to see if their items tap basic aspects of empathy.

Note: Adapted from M. Mitchell & Jolley, 1992, p. 119.

constructs. Evidence that a measure accurately predicts performance on a task is also construct-related evidence when the theory of the construct predicts the behavior being assessed. The criteria used to collect criterion-related evidence are sometimes themselves measures of constructs and so require construct-related evidence of their validity to support their use as criteria (Cronbach, 1997). Table 5-1 presents an example of how all categories of evidence can be brought together to support measures of the empathy construct.

DETERMINING A MEASURE'S DEGREE OF VALIDITY   Let me summarize this discussion of reliability and validity by taking a brief look at the process of determining a measure's

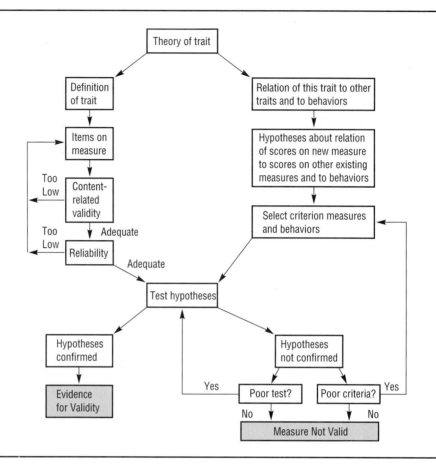

FIGURE 5-4   The Measure Validation Process
Items are selected and validated, reliability is assessed, construct-relevant hypotheses are formulated, and the hypotheses are tested.

degree of validity; more detailed discussions appear in DeVellis (1991) and Spector (1992). As Figure 5-4 illustrates, the development of a measure starts with the theory of a trait. The theory defines the trait and states the ways in which the trait should be related to other traits and behaviors; ideally, the theory also states the traits and behaviors that its trait should not be related to. A well-specified theory clearly spells out these definitions and relationships.

Given the definition of the trait, the developers of the measure select items they think will measure the trait. These items can be statements that respondents can use to rate themselves, criteria that observers can use to rate or describe behaviors they observe, or physiological responses. For example, a theory of self-esteem might define self-esteem in terms of self-evaluation. A self-rating item might therefore be something like "I am at least as smart as most people"; observers might be asked to record the number of positive and negative statements a person makes about him- or herself during a given period of time. In either case, the developers of the measure will ensure that the items are relevant to the trait and represent all aspects of the trait as defined by the theory (content-related validity). The items in the set are then rated on their relevance and representativeness by outside experts as a check on the measure's content-related validity. If this evidence suggests that the measure's degree of content-related validity is too low, the item set must be revised until the measure attains adequate content-related validity. The measure's reliability can then be checked for both internal consistency and stability over time. If these checks indicate that the degree of reliability is not adequate, the developers must revise the item set until it attains an adequate degree of reliability.

Concurrently with these processes, the developers analyze the theory of the trait to determine the relationships to other traits and behaviors that the theory proposes for the trait. These propositions are turned into hypotheses, such as "Our new measure of self-esteem will have large positive correlations with other valid measures of self-esteem, small to moderate negative correlations with valid measures of anxiety and depression, and zero to small correlations with measures of shyness. In addition, when people who score low on our measure of self-esteem experience failure on an experimental task, they will be more likely to blame themselves for the failure than will people who score high on the measure." With the hypotheses set, the developers can select appropriate criterion measures and experimental procedures to test the hypotheses.

The developers then test the hypotheses and evaluate the results of the tests. If the hypotheses are confirmed, the developers have evidence for the validity of their measure. If the hypotheses are not confirmed, the developers must reexamine the adequacy of their research procedures and criterion measures. If both are good, the evidence suggests that the measure has low validity for assessing the trait. If one or both are weak, then the developers must improve them and retest their hypotheses.

DIFFERENTIAL VALIDITY   **Differential validity** exists when a measure is more valid for assessing a trait for members of one group than for members of another group; that is, it assesses more of the true score for members of one group than for members of another group. For example, an IQ test might be highly valid for one cultural group but less valid for a different cultural group. When a measure exhibits differential validity, research based on the measure is more valid for the group for which the measure is more valid; conclusions drawn about members of the other group on the basis of the measure are less valid and therefore biased. Differential validity has two sources. One source is differential content validity. If the content of a measure is more relevant to members of one group than to members of another group, the measure will be more valid for the first group. For example, many questions used in mathematics achievement tests during the 1970s based their problems on situations more familiar to boys than to girls (Dwyer, 1979), such as the computation of baseball batting averages. This differential content validity might be one reason why boys scored higher than girls on these tests even though girls received higher math grades in school. Differential validity can also occur when the trait being assessed takes different forms in different groups, but the measure assesses only one form of the trait. Gilligan (1982), for example, suggests that women and men use different bases for moral reasoning. Therefore, measures designed to assess the construct of moral reasoning that are based only on the masculine form would be less valid for women.

There are four ways in which validation research can indicate that a measure might be differentially valid. First, group means on the measure might differ when the theory of the trait predicts no such differences. Using the measure under these circumstances could lead to the erroneous conclusion that one group is superior to another on the trait. A second indicator of possible differential validity is different convergent validity correlations for different groups. For example, a new measure of self-esteem that had a correlation of .60 with another well-validated measure of self-esteem for men but a correlation of .01 for women is probably valid only for men. Its use with women would lead to erroneous conclusions. Third, a similar situation could arise for criterion-related validity: a high correlation with the criterion for one group, but a low correlation for another. Finally, experimental validity studies that find different outcomes for different groups when those differences are not predicted by the theory could indicate differential validity.

How big a problem is differential validity? This question has been explored most extensively for ethnic group differences in the criterion-related validity of employment selection tests. A systematic review of those studies indicated that differential validity was not a problem in that context (Hunter, Schmidt, & Hunter, 1979). However, this research says nothing about other aspects of validity for those measures or the possible differential validity of other types of measures. A well-conducted program of validation research will include tests for differential validity, and it is wise to avoid using measures that have not been validated for the groups one plans to use in research.

MODALITIES OF MEASUREMENT

The term *modality of measurement* refers to the manner in which one measures a person's traits. I will discuss the three most commonly used modalities: self-report, behavioral, and physiological.

Self-Report Measures

As the name implies, **self-report measures** have people report on some aspect of themselves. People can be asked to make four kinds of self-reports. Cognitive self-reports deal with what people think; for example, you might be interested in people's stereotypes of members of social groups. Affective self-reports deal with how people feel; for example, you might be interested in people's mood states or in their emotional reaction to a stimulus, such as their liking or disliking for it. Behavioral self-reports deal with how people act, in terms of what they have done in the past (called *retrospective* reports), what they are currently doing (called *concurrent* reports), or what they would do if they were in a certain situation (called *hypothetical* reports). Finally, kinesthetic self-reports deal with people's perceptions of their bodily states, such as degree of hunger or sexual arousal.

ADVANTAGES OF SELF-REPORT MEASURES   Self-reports have two principal advantages relative to the other measurement modalities. First, self-report is often the most direct way to obtain some kinds of information. For example, information about a person's inner states (such as mood), beliefs (such as those concerning social groups), interpretations (such as whether another person's behavior is perceived as friendly or unfriendly), and thought processes (such as how a decision was reached) can be obtained most directly through self-report. Behaviors that cannot be directly observed due to privacy concerns (such as sexual behavior) can also be measured by self-report. Second, self-report data can be easy to collect. Questionnaires can be administered to people in groups, whereas other measurement modalities usually require people to participate individually in the research. In addition, the equipment used for measuring self-reports (paper and pencils) is inexpensive compared to the cost of physiological recording equipment. Finally, questionnaires can be administered by people who require relatively little training compared to that needed by observers in behavioral research or by the operators of physiological recording equipment.

LIMITATIONS OF SELF-REPORT MEASURES A basic issue concerning self-report measures is people's ability to make accurate self-reports. Retrospective reports of behavior and events are problematic not only because memory decays over time, but also because memory is reconstructive (Penrod, Loftus, & Winkler, 1982); that is, events that occur between the time something happens and the time it is recalled affect the accuracy of the memory. For example, the more often people recount an event, the more confident they become of the correctness of their account, even if their beliefs about what happened are actually incorrect. In addition, when people cannot remember exactly what transpired during an event, they report what they believe should have happened under the circumstances—a report that is often inaccurate (Shweder & D'Andrade, 1980). Finally, Nisbett and Wilson (1977) have suggested that people do not actually know the factors that influence their behavior or their cognitive processes and so cannot accurately report on these factors.

A second limitation of self-reports is that people might not be willing to make totally accurate reports. When asked about socially undesirable behaviors or beliefs, for example, people may edit their responses to make themselves look good. Even when the behavior of interest is neutral, people who feel a high degree of evaluation apprehension, either as a personality trait or as a result of the research situation, might alter their responses to make a positive self-presentation (S. J. Weber & Cook, 1972).

Finally, self-reports depend on the verbal skills of the respondents. That is, respondents must be able to understand the question, formulate a response, and express the response in the manner required by the researcher (for example, on a 7-point scale). To a large extent, this problem can be addressed by using a vocabulary appropriate to the respondent population. For some categories of people—such as children, the developmentally disabled, people with some forms of mental disorder—there might be a question of their ability to make valid self-reports or to use rating scales. In some cases, however, it might be possible to test respondents' ability to make an appropriate response and one might therefore have confidence that the report was made properly (Butzin & Anderson, 1973).

Despite these shortcomings, self-report may be the best available measurement modality for a study. When you use self-report measurement, you can take several steps to alleviate its limitations. When asking people about their behaviors, ask about things they have actually done, not about what they would or might do under a set of circumstances: People are poor predictors of how they would behave in situations they have not encountered. Also, ask only about recent behaviors to reduce the influence of memory decay. Phrase the questions you use clearly and precisely; Chapter 11 discusses question wording. Structure the research situation to reduce the influence of factors that might motivate people to edit their responses; Chapter 6 discusses these techniques. Finally, whenever possible, check the validity of self-reports with other kinds of evidence. For example, self-reports of levels of anxiety or nervousness might be checked against observers' ratings of behaviors associated with these states or against measures of physiological arousal.

Behavioral Measures

In behavioral measurement the researcher watches and records what people actually do, as opposed to self-reports, which focus on what people say they do. **Behavioral measures** are used in research for any of three reasons. The first reason is because the behavior itself is under study; for example, the effectiveness of the treatment of a child for disruptive behavior might be assessed by having the child's parents and teachers keep records of his or her behavior. Second, the behavior may be used as an operational definition of a hypothetical construct; for example, level of aggression might be assessed as the frequency with which a research participant delivers a supposed electric shock to a confederate of the experimenter who is posing as another participant. Finally, behaviors may be used as nonverbal cues to psychological states; for example, speech disfluencies, such as stuttering, might be used as indicators of nervousness.

Aronson, Ellsworth, Carlsmith, and Gonzales (1990) also describe what they call *behavioroid* measures, which they define as "an approximation of a behavioral measure [that] may be achieved by measuring subjects' *commitment* to perform a behavior, without actually making them carry it out" (p. 271). For example, people's helpfulness might be assessed by asking them to sign up to conduct a time-consuming tutoring session. Although this commitment is a type of self-report, Aronson et al. suggest that "the crucial difference between a simple questionnaire item and a behavioroid measure is that the latter has consequences. From the subjects' point of view, they cannot just check a scale and forget it, they are committing themselves to future behavior" (p. 272).

A technique similar to self-report is self-observation, in which people use diaries to record behaviors as they are performed or soon thereafter. This technique differs from self-report in that the recording and reporting of the behavior are concurrent with it (or almost so) rather than retrospective. Researchers can control the time sampling of the behaviors by using electronic "beepers" to cue participants to record their current behavior (Csikszentmihalyi & Larson, 1987).

Many aspects of behavior can be measured. Some of these aspects are the frequency, rate (frequency per unit time), and speed with which a behavior is performed; the latency (time between stimulus and response), duration, and intensity of a behavior; the total amount of different (but perhaps related) behaviors that are performed; the accuracy with which a behavior is performed (for example, number of errors); and persistence at the behavior (continued attempts in the face of failure).

ADVANTAGES OF BEHAVIORAL MEASURES   A major advantage of behavioral measures is that they can be used without people's being aware that they are under observation. As a re-

Although physiological variables have frequently been used as indicators of psychological states, such use is inadvisable because, in most cases, there is no evidence for the construct validity of a particular physiological variable as a measure of a particular psychological state (Cacioppo & Tassinary, 1990). To establish construct validity, one must be able to show (1) that a particular psychological state results in a particular physiological response (convergent validity) *and* (2) that the physiological factor varies *only* in response to changes in the psychological state (discriminant validity). The first condition has been met for many psychological-physiological relationships, the second for none: Any one physiological factor varies in response to many psychological states (Tomarken, 1995). For example, does an elevated pulse rate indicate anxiety (a negative emotion) or excitement (a positive emotion)? As a result, Aronson et al. (1990) recommend that physiological measures be used only as indicators of general somatic arousal, not as indicators of specific psychological states.

Even as indicators of generalized arousal, physiological measures have their limitations. They can be very sensitive to the effects of participant variables irrelevant to arousal, such as bodily movement (including speech) and changes in direction of attention, and to environmental variables, such as changes in room temperature and lighting level (Cacioppo & Tassinary, 1990). Physiological measures should therefore be used only in closely controlled environments in which the influence of factors such as these can be minimized.

Choosing a Measurement Modality

Having considered the advantages and limitations of the different measurement modalities, the question arises of which to use. There are three approaches to answering this question. Some authorities give primacy to behavioral measures, holding that they should be used whenever possible. For example, Aronson et al. (1990) state that "the greater the commitment demanded of the subject by the [measure], the more confidence we can place in the experimental results" (p. 277). Another view holds that giving behavioral measures primacy ignores the fact that behavior is not always the primary focus of research. If the focus is on variables best measured through self-report or physiological response, then that modality should be used.

A third position holds that one should use multiple modalities to measure variables, especially to measure hypothetical constructs (for example, see Judd, Smith, & Kidder, 1991; Kazdin, 1997). There are two reasons for following this path of **multiple operationism.** The first is that many variables have multiple components, some best measured through self-report, some behaviorally, and some physiologically. Including all the components of a variable as part of the measurement strategy will improve the content validity of the measurement process. Kazdin (1997) uses the measurement of depression as an example:

> Some components of depression are based on *self-report*. Individuals *report* that they feel sad, worthless, and no longer are interested in activities that were previously pleasurable. In addition, there are *overt behavioral components* such as reduced social interaction, changes in eating (more or less eating) and reduced activity. Similarly, *psychophysiological components* include changes in sleep electroencephalogram activity. (p. 292)

TABLE 5-2 Relative Advantages and Limitations of Three Measurement Modalities

	MODALITY		
	Self-Report	*Behavioral*	*Physiological*
Ability to assess psychological states	High	Low	Low
Ability to assess private behavior	High	Low	Low
Ability to assess behavior in multiple situations	High	Varies	Low
Ability to assess past behavior	High	Low	Low
Obtrusiveness	High	Varies	High
Potential for accurate measurement	Varies	Varies[a]	Varies[a]
Potential for editing by research participant	High	Varies	Low
Dependence on participants' verbal skills	High	Low	Low
Participants' psychological involvement in process	Varies	High	Low
Ease of use	High	Varies	Low
Requirement for researcher training	Low	High	High
Expense	Low	Low	High

Note: These are general characteristics that may vary somewhat with the research situation. "Varies" indicates that the characteristic is highly situation dependent.

[a] Probably high if used to assess something that is directly observed; probably low if used to infer psychological states or processes.

The second reason to use multiple operations derives from the earlier discussion of the modalities' advantages and limitations, summarized in Table 5-2. As can be seen from Table 5-2, each modality has its own set of advantages and limitations so that, in choosing a single modality, one trades off its limitations for its advantages. When multiple measurement modalities are used, the advantages of one can compensate for the limitations of another, thereby improving the overall quality of measurement in the research. As Figure 5-5 illustrates, each modality measures some true score and some error. Although there is some overlap in the true score they measure, each modality measures some true score missed by the others. As a result, using multiple modalities leads to a more accurate assessment of the trait. For the same reason, you might want to use multiple measures of a construct within a modality. As Figure 5-6 illustrates, you could assess depression using two self-report measures, two behavioral measures, and two physiological measures. Within each modality, any one measure assesses only part of its aspect of the construct. When multiple measures are used, what one measure misses another can pick up, just as one modality can pick up what another modality misses (Figure 5-5). Finally, when choosing a measure within a modality you must attend to the issues of reliability and validity. Your goal should be to develop the best possible measurement strategy consistent with the purposes of your research.

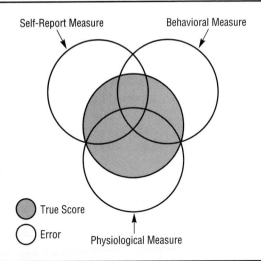

FIGURE 5-5   Use of Multiple Measurement Modalities to Triangulate on a Construct
Each measure assesses its own "piece" of the construct so that the measures as a group provide a more accurate assessment of the construct than does any one measure.

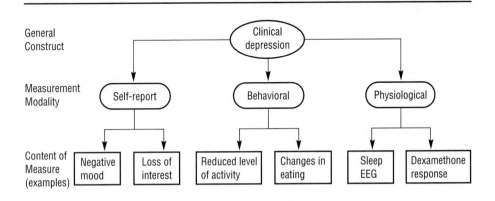

FIGURE 5-6   An Example of the Use of Multiple Measurement Modalities and Multiple Measures Within Modality
Clinical depression can be assessed via the self-report, behavioral, and physiological modalities, and there can be several specific measures within each modality.

LOCATING AND EVALUATING MEASURES

As noted in Chapter 4, one purpose of the literature review is to assist in finding ways to carry out the research. Measurement is part of research, so one goal of your literature review will be the identification of measures that you can use in your research. Once you have identified a set of potential measures, you must select the ones you will use. This section addresses the issues of locating and evaluating measures. First, however, it discusses one way in which measures can be categorized.

Categories of Measures

This discussion will use the system for categorizing measures shown in Figure 5-7. The first distinction made is between measures that assess manifest variables and measures that assess hypothetical constructs. There are two categories of measures that assess hypothetical constructs: psychometric tests and research measures. These categories are distinguished by the purposes to which their measures are put. **Psychometric tests** are used to provide information about a particular individual's score on a construct in order to determine where that individual stands on the construct relative to other people. For example, a score on an IQ test represents an individual's IQ relative to that of other people: the same as most people, higher than most people, or lower than most people. **Research measures** are used to provide information about the mean scores of groups of people in order to determine relationships between constructs or to compare groups of people on a construct. Measurement instruments designed as psychometric tests can be used as research measures, but instruments designed as research measures generally cannot be used as psychometric tests. This difference exists because psychometric tests are **normed;** that is, they are administered to large, diverse groups of people in order to estimate precisely the population mean and standard deviation of the test. Knowledge of these norms and norms for subgroups within the overall population allows the determination of where an individual stands on the construct relative to the population as a whole. Because researchers are not usually interested in individual scores on their measures, research measures are rarely normed.

The discussion in this chapter focuses primarily on research measures, which can be divided into two categories: developed measures and ad hoc measures. **Developed research measures** have undergone the validation process described earlier in this chapter, and so information is available on their reliability, validity, and other characteristics. **Ad hoc research measures** are created for use in a particular study. Little or no effort is made to assess their reliability or validity; at best, internal consistency is reported for multi-item measures. Ad hoc measures are virtually useless for the assessment of hypothetical constructs. Because no evidence exists for the validity of an ad hoc measure, we have no way of determining how accurately it assesses the construct it is supposed to assess, or even if it assesses the construct at all. Consequently, research that deals with a hypothetical construct and uses an ad hoc measure to assess that construct is a waste of resources: Because we don't know if the measure accurately assesses the construct, the research can tell us nothing about the construct. Consider, for example, a study that finds a negative correlation between an ad hoc measure of self-esteem and an

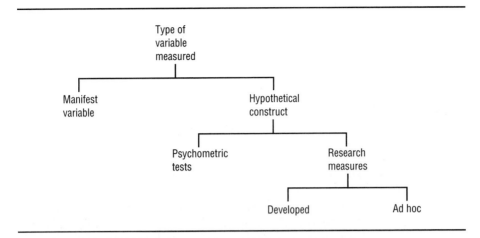

FIGURE 5-7   Categories of Measures

ad hoc measure of jealousy. Can we conclude on that basis that there is a relationship between the hypothetical constructs of self-esteem and jealousy? No. Because there is no evidence that the measures accurately assess the constructs, there is no basis for concluding that the relationship between the measures accurately reflects the relationship between the constructs. For this reason, eschew ad hoc measures in your research and be aware of the problems they pose as you read research reports.

LOCATING MEASURES

Having decided to use measures developed by someone else, how do you find those appropriate for your constructs and information on their reliability, validity, and so forth? A good way to locate information on psychometric tests is with reference books such as the *Mental Measurements Yearbook* (Plake & Impara, 1999) and *Tests in Print* (Murphey & Impara, 1999). These books present reviews of tests, similar to book reviews, that comment on the background, development, reliability, validity, and usefulness of the tests. Reed and Baxter (1992) describe the use of these and related reference books. In addition, every published test has a user's manual that describes in detail the development of the test and the procedures used to assess its reliability and validity.

An efficient way to locate research measures is with directories and compendiums. The *Directory of Unpublished Experimental Measures*, now in its seventh volume (B. A. Goldman & Saunders, 1997), lists measures that have been used in research reported in major journals. It classifies measures by type, such as achievement and personality; provides very brief summaries of the measure's purpose and the data available on the measure's reliability and validity; and gives the citation for the article in which it was first reported. A compendium, such as *Measures of Personality and Social Psychological Attitudes* (J. P. Robinson, Shaver, & Wrightsman, 1991b), is a compilation of measures used in a specific field of research. Compendiums provide information on the development, reliability, and validity of each measure that they include. This information is usually more extensive than that given in directories, and compendiums frequently compare different measures of a construct on their strengths and limitations. Compendiums also reproduce all or part of a measure when the copyright holder gives permission.

Published reviews of the research literature on a topic often include discussions of measurement issues, although details of development, reliability, and validity are rarely provided for specific measures. If a measure is extensively used in research, there may be published reviews of the research on its reliability and validity (see, for example, Beck, Steer, & Garbin, 1988). Finally, every research report describes how its constructs were measured and should report reliability and validity data on the measures or cite sources of such information. As you conduct your literature review for your research, you can keep track of every relevant measure you find, noting the construct measured, a description of the measure, the source of the measure, and the information needed to evaluate measures, which is discussed next. You can use this database to choose the measures best suited to your needs.

Evaluating Measures

Any hypothetical construct can be measured in many ways, using multiple measurement modalities and multiple measures within modalities. When faced with a choice among several measures of a construct, which should a researcher use? J. P. Robinson et al. (1991a) have suggested a set of criteria (shown in Table 5-3) that one can use for evaluating and comparing measures. This discussion groups these criteria under four headings: theoretical background, quality of development, reliability and validity, and freedom from response bias.

THEORETICAL BACKGROUND   Measurement is based on theory. The developers of a measure must therefore completely review the theories dealing with the construct they want to measure. The purpose of the review is to define the construct completely so that the content of the measure is relevant to and representative of the construct. When developing a measure of a construct that has more than one aspect, as with the earlier example of depression, developers can take either of two approaches. In the first approach, they can attempt to develop a comprehensive measure that covers as many aspects of the construct as possible within the modality they plan to use. For example, a self-report measure of depression could include items related to mood, interest in life, activity level, eating patterns, and some physical symptoms, but it could not include physiological indicators that require special equipment to measure, such as EEG patterns. The second approach is to focus on a specific aspect of the construct, such as depressed mood.

As a researcher looking for a measure, your first task is to define the content of the construct you want to measure. If the construct has multiple components, then you must decide the focus of your research: Will it be on the construct as a whole, on all the individual components, or on one or some of the components? Finally, you must choose

TABLE 5-3   Some General Rating Criteria for Evaluating Measures

Criterion Rating	Exemplary	Extensive	Moderate	Minimal	None
Theoretical background	Reflects several important works in the field plus extensive content validity check	Either reviews several works or extensive content validity	Reviews more than one source	Reviews one (no sources)	Ad hoc
Available norms	Means and SDs for several sub-samples and total sample	Means and SDs for total and some groups	Means for some subgroups	Means for total group only	None
Samples of respondents	Random sample of nation/community with response rate over 60%	Cross-sectional sample of nation/community; random national sample of college students	Some represen-tation on non-college groups; random sample of college students in same departments or colleges	Two or more college classes (some hetero-geneity)	One classroom group only (no heterogeneity)
Coefficient α	.80 or better	.70–.79	.60–.69	<.60	Not reported
Test-retest	Scale scores correlate more than .50 across at least a 1-year period	Scale scores correlate more than .50 across a 3–12-month period	Scale scores correlate more than .50 across a 1–3-month period	Scale scores correlate more than .50 across less than a 1-month period	No data reported
Known groups validity	Discriminate between known groups highly significantly; groups also diverse	Discriminate between known groups highly significantly	Discriminate between known groups significantly	Discriminate between known groups	No known groups data
Convergent validity	Highly significant correlations with more than two related measures	Significant cor-relations with more than two related measures	Significant cor-relations with two related measures	Significant cor-relation with one related measure	No significant correlations reported
Discriminant validity	Significantly different from four or more unrelated measures	Significantly different from two or three unrelated measures	Significantly different from one unrelated measure	Different from one correlated measure	No difference or no data
Freedom from response bias	Three or more studies show independence	Two studies show independence	One study shows independence	Some show independence, others do not	No tests of independence

Note: From J. P. Robinson, Shaver, & Wrightsman, 1991a, pp. 12–13.

appropriate measures. If your interest is in the construct as a whole, you will want measures that cover all components of the construct and provide a single global score for the construct. If your interest is in the components, you will want a separate measure for each component or a general measure that also provides a score for each component. As a general rule, it is better to use a measurement strategy that provides a separate score for each component. This strategy is preferred because it is possible for an independent variable to have different effects on or different relationships to different components of a construct (Carver, 1989). As a hypothetical example, a particular event in a person's life might lead to mildly depressed mood (one component of depression), but have no effect on eating patterns (another component of depression). If your research shows that your independent variable has the same effect on or relationship to each of the components of the construct being studied, then the component scores can be combined into a global score. However, if you look only at the global score, you have no way of detecting any differences among the components in relation to the independent variable.

Your first concern in choosing a measure, then, is in its degree of content-related validity. Generally speaking, the more thorough the theoretical background work done by the developers and the more thorough the content validity checks they make, the greater is the resultant content-related validity of the measure. However, you, as the potential user of the measure, are the ultimate judge of its content-related validity. Because the validity of a measure is related to its purpose, you must review the content of the measure to ensure that it gives the construct the meaning that you want the construct to have; does the content of the measure reflect the meaning of the construct as *you* understand it? Some measures will meet this test better than others; the final decision is yours.

QUALITY OF DEVELOPMENT   The quality of the development of a measure has two aspects. One aspect is the nature of the participant samples used in the developmental research on the measure, that is, in testing its reliability and validity. To determine if differential validity is a problem, the samples must be as heterogeneous as possible; a national random sample is ideal, though usually impractical. Most research measures are developed using college student samples so that their reliability and validity for other populations is either unknown or less well tested. When you review the reliability and validity data for a measure that you are considering, focus on the data generated with populations similar to the one you will use in your research. If there are no data for your population, regard the measure as being of no better than moderate quality despite the conclusions about reliability and validity that can be drawn on the basis of data from other populations.

The second aspect of quality of development is the availability of norms. Norms are essential for psychometric tests and very useful for research measures. Norms let you compare your sample's mean score and standard deviation with those of the larger norming sample. If these descriptive data for your sample are very different from the norms, you may have a skewed sample, so interpret the results of your research cautiously. Norms should be provided for as many groups of people as possible—such as sex, ethnicity, and age—so that you can compare the results in your sample to the norms for the appropriate groups.

RELIABILITY AND VALIDITY   Three points concerning reliability and validity are especially important in the context of evaluating and comparing measures. The first point is that test-retest coefficients vary as a function of the nature of the construct being measured and the test-retest interval. Labile constructs (such as mood) will have lower co-efficients across the same test-retest interval than more stable constructs (such as IQ); these lower coefficients derive from the nature of the construct and so do not necessar-ily reflect a lower degree of reliability of the measure. Longer test-retest intervals lead to lower coefficients because longer intervals allow more opportunity for change in true scores on the construct; because these lower coefficients could reflect real change rather than random error, they do not necessarily reflect a lower degree of reliability. The best indicator of the true reliability of a measure is its average reliability across a number of studies. However, the reliability of a scale can vary from respondent sample to respon-dent sample and over time. Therefore, it is always wise to check their reliability, at least in terms of internal consistency, for your sample.

The second point is that the validity of a measure is relative to its purpose, not only in terms of content-related validity, but also in terms of its construct-related validity. That is, in reviewing validity studies of a measure, you must consider as evidence of va-lidity only those studies that used the measure for the same purpose that you intend to use it. For example, if you intend to use the polygraph as a measure of anxiety, then you need to review studies of its validity as a measure of anxiety, not just as a measure of physiological response.

The third point is the importance of discriminant validity. Just because a measure has good convergent validity does not mean it measures only the construct it was de-signed to measure; it could be measuring other constructs as well. For example, many self-report research measures of depression that have good convergent validity show poor discriminant validity relative to anxiety (Dobson, 1985). If you want a relatively "pure" measure of depression, you would have to find one with low correlations with measures of anxiety.

FREEDOM FROM RESPONSE BIAS   Measures can be evaluated for the extent that they are likely to elicit response biases. A **response bias** is a tendency for a person to respond to a measure for reasons other than the response's being a reflection of the construct being assessed by the content of the measure. Two common response biases are **social desir-ability response bias,** a tendency to respond in ways that make the person look good (socially desirable) to others, and **acquiescence response bias,** a tendency to either agree or disagree with items on self-report measures regardless of the content of the item. Chapter 11 discusses these and other forms of response bias in more detail; for now, just consider them to be undesirable characteristics of a measure.

The degree to which a measure elicits socially desirable responses is usually assessed by correlating scores on the measure with scores on a measure of social desirability response bias. The lower the correlation, the freer the measure is of social desirability re-sponse bias. However, there are two forms of social desirability response bias and mea-sures of social desirability response bias differ in the degree to which they assess the two forms: Some assess mostly one or the other, whereas other measures assess both simul-taneously (Paulhus, 1991). Therefore, when research on a measure reveals a high correlation with a measure of social desirability response bias, one needs to ask two questions. First, what measure of social desirability response bias was used? The answer to this question will indicate the type of social desirability response bias being assessed. Second, is that type of social desirability response bias relevant to the construct? If it is relevant, then the response bias is not a problem. However, you should ensure that a measure has been checked for both forms of social desirability response bias: Even if one form of social desirability response bias is not a problem for the measure, the other might be.

The susceptibility of a measure to acquiescence response bias can be assessed by examining its content. If the items are constructed so that only agreement or disagreement leads to a high score, then acquiescence could be a problem. In contrast, a balanced measure, in which half the items require agreement for a high score and half require disagreement, is less susceptible: To get a high score, respondents must both agree and disagree with items; only agreeing or only disagreeing will lead to a mid-range score. Therefore, measures with balanced content are preferred to measures with unbalanced content.

COMPARING MEASURES   As we have seen, an ideal measure will exhibit a high degree of a rather large number of characteristics (Table 5-3). However, no measure is likely to be high on all these characteristics simultaneously. In choosing a measure, it is therefore necessary to decide which characteristics are most essential to your research and give them more weight in making your choice. For example, you might decide that internal consistency is more important than test-retest reliability and that reliability and validity are more important than the availability of norms. Edwards and Newman (1982) present a system for making choices based on differentially weighted criteria, and you might consider using it. However, because ad hoc measures generally have no history of reliability and validity research, they should not be used: Without evidence of validity, you have no way of knowing whether you are measuring the construct you set out to measure.

SUMMARY

Reliability is the consistency of measurement; validity is the accuracy of measurement. Random measurement error reduces both the reliability and validity of a measure; systematic measurement error can result in a measure that is reliable but of low validity. Reliability can be assessed in three ways: as stability across time, as consistency across forms of a measure, and as consistency among the items comprising a measure. The most appropriate form of reliability assessment for a measure depends on the characteristics of the trait the measure is designed to assess. There are three categories of evidence of convergent validity. Content-related evidence concerns the degree to which the items on a measure are relevant to and representative of the trait being assessed. Criterion-related evidence concerns the degree to which scores on the measure can predict performance on a relevant task. Construct-related evidence concerns the degree to which people who score high and low on the measure behave in ways predicted by the theory of the trait. In addition to exhibiting convergent validity, a measure should exhibit discriminant validity: Scores on the measure should be unrelated to variables that the theory of the trait says are not related to the trait. Finally, a potential source of bias in measurement is differential validity, in which a measure is more valid for members of one group than for members of another group.

There are three modalities of measurement. Self-report measures have people answer questions about their emotions, behaviors, and thoughts. Behavioral measures assess what people do, the actions they perform. Physiological measures assess people's biological responses to stimuli. Each modality has both advantages and disadvantages relative to the others. Because many psychological variables have multiple components, some of which may be better measured through one modality than another, multiple measurement modalities should be used when appropriate. In addition to ensuring representativeness in measurement, this multiple operationism allows the advantages of one modality to compensate for the limitations of others. The use of multiple measures within modalities allows for similar compensation: Aspects of the trait not assessed by one measure can be assessed by another.

Evaluating and selecting measures requires distinguishing among various tpes of measures used in research; ad hoc measures of hypothetical constructs are virtually useless. Four criteria for evaluating measures are theoretical background, quality of development, reliability and validity, and freedom from response bias.

QUESTIONS AND EXERCISES FOR REVIEW

1. What is the difference between hypothetical constructs and manifest variables? Describe some examples you know of in which manifest variables have been improperly interpreted in terms of hypothetical constructs.
2. Describe the relationship between reliability and validity in measurement. Why is a reliable measure not necessarily a valid measure? Is a valid measure necessarily reliable? Why or why not?
3. Read the Method sections of several research articles that use measures of hypothetical constructs. How well do the authors describe the reliability and validity of those measures? How does this information, or the lack of it, influence your interpretation of the results of those studies?
4. What factors affect the decision about the best form of reliability to use with a measure? What level of reliability can be considered adequate? What factors must we consider in deciding whether a measure exhibits a sufficient degree of reliability?
5. Explain the following aspects of the concept of validity:
   a. Validity is an inference. What kinds of inferences are involved?
   b. Validity is a matter of degree.
   c. Validity is specific to a purpose.
   d. Validity is a unitary concept.
6. Name, define, and explain the two aspects of content-related evidence of validity.
7. Name, define, and explain the two aspects of criterion-related evidence of validity. What issue affects the validity of the measure of the criterion?
8. Explain the three ways of collecting construct-related evidence of validity. What interpretations can be made if a validity study fails to find the hypothesized relationships that would provide construct-related evidence of validity?

9. In what ways can we assess the discriminant validity of a measure? What does evidence indicating a lack of discriminant validity for a measure imply for interpreting the research results based on that measure?

10. Describe the process of validating a new measure.

11. What are the sources and indicators of differential validity?

12. What are the relative advantages and disadvantages of self-report, behavioral, and physiological measures?

13. Describe the advantages of multiple operationism. What limitations might it have?

14. What resources exist for locating published measures?

15. In what ways are psychometric tests and research measures similar, and in what ways do they differ?

16. Why do ad hoc measures of hypothetical constructs threaten the validity of research results? In what aspects of validity are such measures deficient?

17. Describe the criteria for evaluating measures. Choose two measures of a hypothetical construct that interests you. Compare and contrast those measures using the criteria for evaluating measures.

6 THE INTERNAL VALIDITY OF RESEARCH

CONFOUNDS
Natural Confounds
Treatment Confounds
Measurement Confounds

THREATS TO INTERNAL
VALIDITY
Time-Related Threats
    History
    Maturation
    Testing
    Instrumentation Change
    Statistical Regression
Control Groups in
    Pretest-Posttest Research
Selection Threats
    Nonrandom Assignment
    Preexisting Groups
    Mortality

REACTIVITY
Sources of Reactivity
    Evaluation Apprehension
    Novelty Effects

Controlling Reactivity
    General Control Measures
    Controls With Behavioral
        Measures
    Controls With Self-Report
        Measures
    Noting Instances of Reactivity

DEMAND CHARACTERISTICS
Sources of Demand
    Characteristics
Participant Roles
    The Good Participant
    The Negative Participant
    The Apathetic Participant
    Impact of Participant Roles
Controlling Demand
    Characteristics
    Cue Reduction
    Motivation
    Role-Play Control Groups
    Separating the Dependent
        Variable From the Study

EXPERIMENTER EXPECTANCIES
Types of Expectancy Effects
    Biased Observation
    Influencing Participants'
        Responses
Techniques of Control
    Rehearsal and Monitoring
    Minimizing the Experimenter's
        Role
    Condition Blindness
    Avoidance of Data Snooping

SUMMARY

QUESTIONS AND EXERCISES
FOR REVIEW

Chapter 1 pointed out that a major objective of research design is ensuring that any effects found are caused only by the independent variable and not by other factors in the research situation. These other factors are **extraneous variables.** Extraneous variables provide alternative explanations for the observed effect; if they are present, the researcher cannot conclude that the independent variable caused the effect. For example, Chapter 2 noted that in cross-sectional developmental research it is difficult to separate the effects of age, the independent variable in the research, from cohort effects, which provide a possible alternative explanation for any differences found between age groups. To the extent that there are plausible alternative explanations for the effect of an independent variable, we say that a study exhibits low **internal validity;** conversely, to the extent that we can have confidence that the results of a study are due only to the effects of the independent variable, we can conclude that a study exhibits high internal validity.

The presence of plausible alternative explanations for an effect can be ruled out on either of two grounds. Sometimes logic can show that it is unlikely that an extraneous variable had an effect. For example, in cross-sectional developmental research, if the difference in ages between the groups being compared is not large—say, 2-year-olds being compared to 3-year-olds—then cohort effects are unlikely. Cohort effects result from differences in age groups' social environments, and in many cases a small age difference reflects a small difference in social environments. There are, of course, exceptions. For example, a child's transition from preschooler to kindergartner represents both a 1-year age difference and a major change in the social environment.

The second way of ruling out alternative explanations is either to institute control measures that limit the effects of extraneous variables or to use research designs that estimate their effects as well as the effect of the independent variable. In the latter case, one could show that even if extraneous variables did have effects on the dependent variable, the independent variable also had an effect and so was a cause of the dependent variable. These control measures will be included in the discussions of possible sources of alternative explanations.

Alternative explanations can be classified into two broad categories, confounds and artifacts. A **confound** exists when two variables are combined so that the effect of one cannot be separated from the effect of the other. For example, if you conducted a study in which the experimental group contained only men and the control group contained only women, sex of participant would be confounded with the independent variable. An **artifact** exists when some aspect of the research situation other than the independent variable affects the dependent variable. For example, if a study is conducted by a researcher who the participants think is cold and unfriendly, these characteristics could affect their performance in the study. Perhaps they don't try as hard to do well as they would have for a friendly researcher. If the results of the study cannot be replicated, then it is possible that the original results were an artifact of the researcher's demeanor, not the effect of the independent variable. The distinction between confound and artifact is not rigid; if an extraneous variable causes an artifact in only one condition of an experiment, it also constitutes a confound. This chapter discusses the nature of confounds, a set of factors identified by D. T. Campbell and Stanley (1963) as possible sources of artifacts and confounds, and three other possible sources of artifacts and confounds: reactivity, demand characteristics, and experimenter expectancies.

CONFOUNDS

Researchers can easily avoid obvious confounds, such as the example just given in which sex of participant was confounded with the independent variable. However, more subtle confounds can creep into research and sometimes remain undetected until later researchers look at the topic of the research from a new perspective. The research on sex differences in persuasion discussed in Chapter 1 provides an example of a subtle confound. Recall that research on this topic typically found that women were more likely to change their expressed opinions in response to a persuasive message than were men. Eagly and Carli (1981) showed, however, that these findings resulted from a confound between sex of research participant and interest in the topic of the opinions used in the research. The research frequently used topics, such as professional sports, that men found more interesting than did women. As illustrated in panel (a) of Figure 6-1, the combination of being male and having greater interest in the topic led to less opinion change than did the combination of being female and having less interest. Because the variables of sex and level of interest were confounded, there was no way of knowing which variable was related to attitude change. One way in which to disentangle the effects of confounded variables is to "unconfound" them by treating each as an independent variable in the same study. This procedure results in what is called a *factorial research design*, discussed in the next chapter. Such a design is illustrated in panel (b) of Figure 6-1 and lets the researcher determine the separate effects of two previously confounded variables on a dependent variable.

Natural Confounds

The combination of the variables of sex and interest in certain topics is an example of what might be called a "natural confound": In nature, some variables tend to be associated with certain other variables. For example, people who share demographic characteristics such as age, sex, and ethnicity have undergone a common set of experiences associated with those variables, leading them to have some common attitudes, values, and other characteristics. Because of such natural confounds, when demographic variables are used as independent variables in research, one can almost never be sure whether group differences found on the dependent variable are due to the demographic variable, such as biological sex, or to a confounded variable, such as the results of sex role socialization.

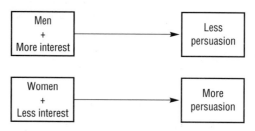

(a) **Confounding sex of research participant and interest in the topic in persuasion research — there is no way of knowing which variable — sex or interest — is inhibiting persuasion.**

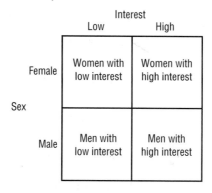

(b) **Unconfounding sex of research participant and interest in topic by making each an independent variable — the researcher can now assess the separate relationships of sex and interest to persuasion.**

FIGURE 6-1   Confounding and Unconfounding of Independent Variables

Treatment Confounds

Treatment confounds occur when the manipulated independent variable (or treatment) in an experiment is confounded with another variable or treatment. For example, having a female experimenter conduct all the experimental sessions and a male experimenter conduct all the control sessions would result in a treatment confound. Although participants in each condition should have been exposed to only one treatment—the conditions of the independent variable—they actually received two combined treatments, condition of the independent variable and sex of the experimenter.

Because researchers are aware of the dangers of treatment confounds, they are careful to avoid them when they design research. However, confounds sometimes slip in when the study is conducted. For example, if the experimental condition requires equipment that is in short supply and the control condition does not, the researcher might have people participate individually in the experimental condition and in groups in the control condition. Although this procedure makes data collection easier and faster than having people in the control condition participate individually, it also confounds treatment with the social context of research participation. If differences between the experimental and control conditions are found, are they due to the independent variable or to working alone versus working in a group? A confound can also develop when data collection extends over a period of time, such as a semester, and all the research sessions for the control condition are run early in the term and all the experimental condition sessions later in the term. Such a procedure might be convenient if the experimental condition requires an elaborate lab set-up that would have to be frequently dismantled if experimental and control sessions were alternated. However, you would not know if any effects found were due to the independent variable or to the time period during which the sessions were conducted.

You must be very careful to avoid treatment confounds when designing and conducting research. The critical question to ask is, Do the participants in the experimental and control conditions have *exactly* the same experiences in *exactly* the same physical, social, and temporal environment except for the manipulation of the independent variable? If the answer is no, then a treatment confound exists and must be eliminated.

Measurement Confounds

Confounds can occur in the measures used to assess dependent variables as well as in independent variables. A *measurement confound* occurs when a measure assesses more than one hypothetical construct. For example, many self-report measures that are designed to assess depression also assess anxiety (Dobson, 1985). Consequently, one does not know if a high score on such a measure represents high depression, high anxiety, or both. Measurement confounds, which are shown by the lack of discriminant validity in a measure, often result from natural confounds between the constructs being assessed. For example, a high degree of anxiety might be a natural concomitant of depression. However, because measurement confounds, even natural confounds, obscure the relationship between an independent variable and the dependent variable that one is interested in, only measures high in discriminant validity should be used in research. When measurement confounds cannot be avoided, statistical techniques, such as partial correlation analysis (described in Chapter 8), can sometimes be used to separate the effects of the confounded variables.

THREATS TO INTERNAL VALIDITY

In 1963, D. T. Campbell and Stanley published the first, and now classic, analysis of the concept of internal validity in research. They identified a number of potential threats to internal validity, of which eight will be discussed here. Five of these threats are problems that can arise when research is conducted over a period of time, and the last three are related to the assignment of participants to experimental and control conditions.

Time-Related Threats

D. T. Campbell and Stanley (1963) initially wrote their analysis of internal validity for educational researchers, especially those interested in the effectiveness of new educational programs. These researchers frequently conduct longitudinal studies, examining the impact of a program on students' test scores by testing the students before the program is implemented (a pretest) and again after the program has had an opportunity to have an effect (a posttest). Campbell and Stanley's analysis therefore focused largely on problems that can arise in these pretest-posttest designs. Some of these problems were examined in the discussion of longitudinal research in Chapter 2. This discussion focuses on their potential impact on studies in which data are collected over a period of time and on the role of control group as a way of assessing the impact of these problems on a study.

HISTORY   The term **history** refers to events occurring outside the research situation while the research is being conducted that affect participants' responses on the dependent measure. For example, Greene and Loftus (1984) conducted a study in which university students read a story about a trial that included eyewitness testimony and gave their opinions about whether the defendant was guilty or not guilty. They collected their data over the course of a semester, and partway through the semester an incident in which a man was mistakenly identified as a criminal received wide publicity in the city where the university was located. Greene and Loftus found that fewer participants made "guilty" judgments during the time the incident was publicized compared to students who participated before and after the publicity. A follow-up experiment provided evidence that the publicity caused the drop in "guilty" judgments. Because events outside the research situation can affect participants' responses, researchers must be aware of events that could affect their data and check to see if such an effect is present.

MATURATION   The term **maturation** refers to natural change over time. The change can be related either to age, as the term implies, or to the cumulative effects of various experiences over a period of time—what might be considered as getting wiser in addition to getting older. For example, Bouchard (1972) examined the relative effectiveness of two problem-solving strategies with college students as research participants. Students who were instructed to use the control strategy participated early in the semester, and those instructed to use the experimental strategy participated later in the semester. The participants in the experimental condition performed better on the problem-solving task than those in the control condition. Although this difference could reflect a difference in the effectiveness of the strategies, it could also be due to maturation: Because of their classroom experiences, students could have become better problem solvers over the course of the semester. Such maturation problems can be controlled by distributing experimental and control sessions of a study evenly across the time period over which the study is conducted. Maturation effects will then be about equal in both conditions, so they will cancel out when the conditions are compared.

TESTING Much behavioral science research is directed at testing the effectiveness of an intervention for changing a personal characteristic, such as mental health, behavior, or attitudes. One way to conduct such research is to pretest participants on the dependent variable (the characteristic to be changed), conduct the intervention, posttest participants on the dependent variable, and examine the amount of change from pretest to posttest. A **testing confound** occurs when taking the pretest affects scores on the posttest independently of the effect of the intervention. For example, people might try to keep their responses consistent across different administrations of a measure or try to "do better" on the posttest than they did on the pretest. The simplest way to deal with testing confounds is not to give a pretest; as noted later, pretesting is not necessary in many forms of research.

If a pretest is necessary or desirable, the presence and degree of testing effects can be tested by using what is known as a *Solomon four-group experimental design* (Braver & Braver, 1988). As its name says, the Solomon four-group design requires four sets of research participants (see Figure 6-2): two control conditions, one with a pretest and one without, and two experimental conditions, one with a pretest and one without. If a simple testing confound exists, the posttest means of Groups 1 and 3 in Figure 6-2 will differ: Because the only way in which these groups differ is in whether or not they received a pretest, a difference in the posttest means indicates that the pretest affected performance on the posttest. The presence of a more complex testing confound can be detected by comparing the differences in the posttest means of Groups 1 and 3 (the control conditions of the experiment) with the difference in posttest means of Groups 2 and 4 (the experimental conditions). If these differences are not equal, then pretesting is combining with the effect of the experimental manipulation to affect posttest scores: The pretest has different effects on the posttest performance of the experimental and control groups. Either form of testing confound calls the internal validity of the research into question.

INSTRUMENTATION CHANGE **Instrumentation change** occurs when the measure used to assess the dependent variable changes over time, leading to artificial differences in scores at different points in time. Instrumentation change can take several forms. Mechanical and electrical measuring devices can go out of calibration as they are used, resulting in cumulative inaccuracies. For example, a timer may begin to run faster or slower with use. Although this problem is probably less severe with modern solid-state electronic devices than in the days of electromechanical instrumentation, battery-powered instruments can go out of calibration when their batteries weaken. The solution to this form of instrumentation change is to periodically test any apparatus that might be subject to it. Another form of instrumentation change occurs when observers classify participants' behavior into categories such as aggressive or nonaggressive: As they gain experience, observers may change the classification they give a behavior. This problem can be reduced by careful construction of classification systems and carefully training observers.

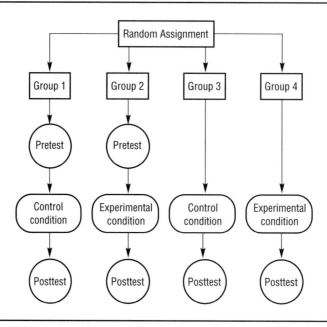

FIGURE 6-2   The Solomon Four-Group Design
A difference in the posttest means of Groups 1 and 3 indicates a simple testing confound: Responses on the posttest differ because of a pretest. Unequal differences in the posttest means of Groups 1 and 3 versus Groups 2 and 4 indicate a complex testing confound: The effect of the pretest is different in the experimental and control conditions.

STATISTICAL REGRESSION   Statistical regression can occur when people are selected for participation in research based on their having extreme scores on what will be the dependent variable. For example, treatment outcome research is conducted with participants who have extreme scores on measures of the problem being treated: To test the effectiveness of a treatment program designed to alleviate a problem such as test anxiety, you need participants who score high on a measure of test anxiety. Now recall the discussion of random measurement error in Chapter 5. One reason why a person might get an extremely high score on a measure is because random error raised the score beyond the person's already high true score; conversely, random error could make a low true score extremely low. When extreme scorers are measured a second time, random error can have little influence in raising extremely high scores or lowering extremely low scores: Those scores are already about as high or low as they can go. However, random error can move the scores in the other direction, where there is room for change. Consequently, people who get extreme scores on the first administration of a measure will, on the average, get less extreme scores on the second administration of the measure: Scores for high initial scorers decrease and scores for low initial scorers increase. This increase and decrease of initial extreme scores is called **statistical regression;** because the scores

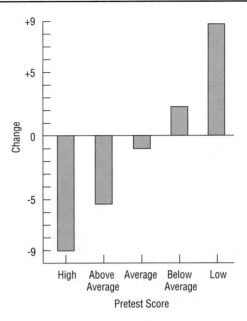

Note: Adapted from Huck & Sandler, 1979, p. 20.

FIGURE 6-3   Changes in Scores From Pretest to Posttest Grouped by Pretest Scores
Extreme scores on the pretest are partially due to random measurement error; these errors tend to be in the other direction at the posttest, causing extreme scores to change more than moderate scores, a process called *regression toward the mean.*

change in the direction of the population mean score on the measure, this phenomenon is also called "regression toward the mean."

Huck and Sandler (1979) describe an excellent example of statistical regression. Cadets in an Air Force officer training program took a personality test near the beginning of their training and were divided into five groups based on their scores: high, above average, average, below average, and low. They took the same test near the end of their training. Figure 6-3 shows the average amount of change in each group's scores. Notice that the cadets who had the most extreme scores on the initial administration of the test showed the greatest change and that the change was in the direction of the mean: Initially high scorers went down and initially low scorers went up. The best solution to the problem of statistical regression is not to select research participants on the basis of extreme scores on the dependent variable. However, this procedure is impossible in some forms of research, such as that on treatment effectiveness. In those cases, the solution to this problem, and to other time-related problems in pretest-posttest research, is use of a control group.

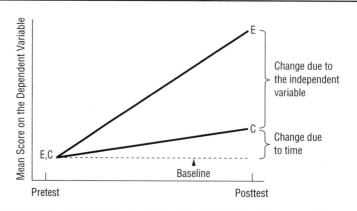

FIGURE 6-4   Use of a Control Group to Separate Treatment-Related and Time-Related Change
The pretest-posttest change for the experimental group includes both treatment and time effects, whereas the change for the control group includes only time effects; therefore, the difference between the two shows the true treatment effect.

Control Groups in Pretest-Posttest Research

You can separate the effects of time-related threats to internal validity from the effects of the independent variable in pretest-posttest research by using a control group. For this procedure to be effective, the members of the control group must be as similar as possible to the members of the experimental group. In most research, this equivalence is attained by randomly assigning participants to groups. When participants are selected on the basis of extreme scores on the dependent variable, randomly assign the people selected to groups. As discussed in the next chapter, random assignment does not guarantee equivalence between groups, but it produces equivalence most of the time. As shown in the "Pretest" section of Figure 6-4, this procedure results in the members of the experimental and control groups having the same mean pretest score on the dependent variable. The "Posttest" section of Figure 6-4 shows mean posttest scores for the two groups; the dashed line indicates the baseline score—the pretest mean. The pretest-posttest change in mean scores for the control group represents the collective effects of time-related threats to internal validity—the amount of change that would have occurred if no experimental treatment had taken place. The posttest difference between the mean scores of the experimental and control groups represents the effect the experimental treatment has over and above the effects of time-related threats to internal validity.

The last sentence has two important implications. The first is that pretest-posttest research must always include a control group. Without a control group, there is no way to determine whether any changes found are due to the effect of the independent variable or the effects of one or more of the time-related threats to internal validity. The second implication is that a pretest is not needed in most research. If the experimental and control groups have the same mean score on the dependent variable before the manipulation of the independent variable, the effect of the independent variable will always be shown in the difference in the mean scores of the groups when the effect of the independent variable is measured. Not conducting a pretest has two advantages: It saves the time and other resources that would be expended on pretesting, and it avoids the possibility of testing confounds and the need to use the complex Solomon four-group design.

Although pretesting has these disadvantages, I don't want to leave the impression that it should never be used. Pretesting serves several valuable purposes in research, such as verifying the preexperimental equivalence of experimental and control groups on the dependent variable and allowing researchers to compare the characteristics of people who drop out from research with the characteristics of those who complete it. In planning research in which pretesting might be used, carefully consider its advantages and disadvantages for that piece of research to determine if the value of the information that it will produce will compensate for the difficulties it entails.

Selection Threats

A **selection bias** occurs when research participants in the control condition differ in some way from those in the experimental condition. This section briefly considers three forms of selection bias: nonrandom assignment of research participants to the conditions of an experiment, the use of preexisting groups in research, and mortality.

NONRANDOM ASSIGNMENT   The example given earlier of a confound—only men in the experimental condition and only women in the control condition—is an example of a selection bias due to nonrandom assignment. Researchers are careful to avoid such obvious selection confounds, but they can slip in unnoticed in other ways. For example, a selection bias occurs when researchers let participants volunteer for the experimental condition of a study or when they use people who volunteer for research as the experimental group and use data from nonvolunteers as the control condition. These procedures can result in a selection bias because, as shown in Box 6-1, people who volunteer for research differ on a number of characteristics from those who do not volunteer. To the extent that these characteristics are related to the dependent variable in the research, you cannot be sure that any differences found between the experimental and control groups are due to the independent variable rather than to differences in participant characteristics. Data collection procedures can also lead to selection confounds. For example, collecting all the data for one condition of an experiment before collecting the data for the other condition can cause a selection confound as well as leave the door open for a history confound if people who volunteer early in the data collection period differ from those who volunteer later in the period.

PREEXISTING GROUPS   Selection biases can also arise in research conducted in natural settings when researchers must assign preexisting natural groups, rather than individuals, to experimental and control conditions. For example, in educational research the students in one classroom might be designated the experimental group and those in

BOX 6-1   Differences Between People Who Do and Do Not Volunteer for Psychological Research

- People who volunteer for psychological research tend to be

    Better educated

    Of higher socioeconomic status

    Higher scorers on IQ tests

    Higher in need for social approval

    More sociable

    More excitement-seeking

    More unconventional

    Less authoritarian

    Less conforming

    From smaller towns

    More interested in religion

    More altruistic

    More self-disclosing

    More maladjusted, especially when the research appears to deal with unusual situations or with treatment for a psychological disorder

    Younger

- Women are more likely to volunteer than are men for most research, but men are more likely to volunteer for stressful research.

- Jews are more likely to volunteer than are Protestants, and Protestants are more likely to volunteer than are Catholics.

Source: Based on Rosenthal & Rosnow, 1975, pp. 88–89.

another classroom, the control group; in organizational research, one department of a company might become the experimental group and another department, the control group. Selection bias is a problem in these situations because people are not randomly assigned to natural groups. Sometimes people choose to join a group, sometimes the group chooses them, and sometimes they are assigned to a group by a decision maker, such as a school administrator or personnel director. In any of these cases, the choices and assignments are probably not random, but are based on the characteristics of the people involved. For example, people prefer to join groups whose members are similar to them and groups select as new members people who are similar to the old members (Forsyth, 1998). Therefore, people in preexisting groups have common characteristics that can be confounded with treatment conditions when the groups are used as experimental and control groups in research. Chapter 10, which deals with research in natural settings, discusses this problem in more detail.

MORTALITY   **Mortality** refers to people's dropping out of a study as it is conducted. In longitudinal research, if only people with certain characteristics drop out, such as the heaviest drug users in a study of drug abuse, the results of the study can be applied only to those people whose characteristics match those of the "survivors." In experimental research, **differential mortality** occurs when people in one condition of the experiment are more likely to withdraw from the research than are people in other conditions. For example, Huck and Sandler (1979) describe a study that tested the effect of isolation on attention over a 7-day period. Participants in the experimental condition were put in isolation chambers that were dark and soundproof, providing little sensory stimulation; participants in the control condition were put in similar chambers that were well lit and each of which contained a television and a radio that the participant could use when testing was not in progress. Testing consisted of 90-minute periods in which participants were required to pull a lever as soon as they heard a "beep"; 60 beeps were sounded at random intervals during each test period. Five percent of the control participants withdrew from the research, compared to 48 percent of the experimental participants. The researchers found that the experimental participants made more correct responses to the beeps than did the control participants. However, because the experimental participants who finished the research were people who could put up with 7 days of isolation, they were probably very different from the control participants in their psychological makeup. Consequently, there was probably a confound between participants' characteristics and the condition in which they participated.

There is no real solution to the problem of differential mortality. When faced with the problem, researchers can try to determine if survivors and dropouts in the high-dropout condition differ on any demographic characteristics or on variables assessed during a pretest. If they do, these differences can be taken into account when interpreting the results of the research by comparing the survivors with the members of the other group who have similar characteristics. If differences appear between the groups on the dependent variable, then the independent variable probably caused them. However, the results of the study would apply only to people with characteristics similar to those of the survivors in the high-dropout condition. Also, if differential mortality does not occur until after some time into the data collection period, analysis of the data collected before mortality became a problem would not be affected by selection. For example, if none of the experimental participants in the isolation study just described dropped out until the 5th day, the data from the first 4 days would present no selection problem.

REACTIVITY

Whenever the process of measuring a variable rather than the content of the measure affects scores on the measure, the process is said to be *reactive*. **Reactivity** threatens the internal validity of research because participants' scores on measures result from the reactive situation rather than from the effects of the independent variable. This section examines the sources of reactivity in measurement and some steps the researcher can take to control reactivity.

Sources of Reactivity

Reactivity can stem from two sources: evaluation apprehension and novelty effects. These factors can elicit social desirability response biases, distract people from the research task, and affect physiological response.

EVALUATION APPREHENSION   **Evaluation apprehension** is the nervousness people feel when they believe someone is judging their behavior. High levels of evaluation apprehension motivate people to avoid the adverse judgments of others by behaving in ways they believe will lead to positive judgments. Consequently, people review their behavioral options in the situation and choose the one they think will put them in the best light with anyone observing their behavior. In this context, "behavior" includes both directly observable actions and responses to self-report measures; "behavior" also includes the lack of an active response, such as remaining passive in the face of a stimulus or omitting an item on a questionnaire. Evaluation apprehension is especially likely to be aroused in the presence of authority figures and people who are perceived to have special abilities to analyze human behavior. Researchers are viewed this way by most research participants (even though we may not view ourselves that way), so evaluation apprehension is likely to be high among participants in research (Haynes & Horn, 1982; S. J. Weber & Cook, 1972).

Evaluation apprehension is also likely to make a research participant more aware of other people present in the research setting, such as the researcher and other participants, and so lead the participant to pay attention to those people and their reactions to her or his behavior. Consequently, the participant can become distracted from the research task, leading to deficits in task performance, such as an increased number of errors. If error rate or evaluation of the participants' performance is a dependent variable in the research, then the validity of the research could be reduced even if there is no social desirability response bias.

The nature of the behavior being studied can increase participants' levels of evaluation apprehension. When people believe they are being observed, they are likely to try to avoid acting in ways that contravene social norms, such as acting aggressively or expressing prejudicial attitudes, or performing behaviors that they believe would embarrass them. They are also likely to underreport such attitudes and behaviors in self-report measures. It is important to remember that the social desirability and embarrassment potential of behaviors are in the eyes of the research participant, not necessarily those of the researcher. What the researcher considers an innocuous behavior or question might be quite sensitive for the research participant. Consider a hypothetical study that tests the prediction that high levels of anxiety lead people to eat more than they would if they were not feeling anxious. The researcher manipulates participants' anxiety levels and has them fill out a questionnaire. There is a bowl of peanuts on the table at which the participants sit, and the researcher tells the participants they can snack on the peanuts while completing the questionnaire. Although eating peanuts is a relatively innocuous behavior, an obese person might avoid eating while under observation, no matter how strong the desire to eat, to avoid making a bad impression on the researcher. Other behaviors assessed by self-report, such as sexual behavior or aspects of personal history, might be considered private by people and so might not be reported accurately.

NOVELTY EFFECTS   Any aspects of the research situation that are new (or novel) to the participants can induce reactivity. These **novelty effects** stem from participants' apprehensions about dealing with the unfamiliar and their paying attention to the novel features of the situation rather than the task at hand. For example, people are more likely to experience a novelty effect when they are brought into a new environment, such as a laboratory, to participate in the research than they are in a more familiar setting. However, adding a new feature, such as an observer or a piece of research equipment, to a familiar environment can also cause a novelty effect; this problem may be especially severe when children are studied. Finally, people are often apprehensive about being attached to physiological recording equipment because they are unsure of the effects it will have, and this apprehensiveness will be reflected in the levels of physiological arousal the equipment records.

Controlling Reactivity

There are a number of steps you can take to limit reactivity. Some of these control measures can be used with more than one measurement modality, and others are better suited to self-report or behavioral measurement. In addition, it can be useful to keep track of apparently reactive behavior.

GENERAL CONTROL MEASURES   Because evaluation apprehension is a major factor in reactivity, research procedures directed at reducing this form of anxiety can limit reactivity (Harris & Lahey, 1982; Shrauger & Osberg, 1981; S. J. Weber & Cook, 1972). Labeling experimenters as *psychologists* or implying they have special expertise in evaluating abilities or personality tend to increase evaluation apprehension and so should be avoided. Experimenters should also avoid giving participants negative feedback to responses, such as by frowning or other nonverbal or paralinguistic cues. In contrast, putting participants at ease, such as by greeting them in a friendly manner and explaining the experiment to them, tends to reduce evaluation anxiety. Aronson, Ellsworth, Carlsmith, and Gonzales (1990) suggest that research situations and tasks that participants find interesting and psychologically involving can get them so wrapped up in what they are doing that they are distracted from their anxiety and focus on the research task rather than on the researcher and the research environment.

Novelty effects can be controlled by giving participants time to adjust to the new situation. For example, once people become used to the feel of physiological recording devices, pulse rate and other physiological variables return to their normal ranges. Similarly, people can become so used to having outside observers present in their natural environments that they forget to "edit" their behavior for social desirability or are no longer motivated to do so (Harris & Lahey, 1982; Haynes & Horn, 1982). Schofield (1982) gives an example of the latter response in this quotation from her field notes from an observational study of a middle school:

> Today as I entered the sixth grade house as classes were changing, I saw Richard and another black male whom I don't know tussling. After glancing at me, Richard's companion drew away from him and leaned over as if to pick up his books on the floor. Richard said, "Aw, come on, she just writes. She never does anything." He then gave his companion a light shove and they were at it again. (p. 33)

Finally, when studying behaviors that might be influenced by social desirability concerns, one could deceive the research participants about the true nature of the research, leading them to believe that the study is concerned with some innocuous behavior. For example, Milgram (1974) told the participants in his studies of destructive obedience that the research dealt with the use of punishment in learning. Milgram believed that if he told his participants that the purpose of the research was to see if they would follow instructions that would result in severe pain for a fellow participant, then his dependent variable of whether the participants gave or refused to give the severe shock would be impossible to interpret. Because hurting someone is socially undesirable, Milgram would have no way of knowing whether a participant's refusal to continue was the participant's true response to the situation or simply a case of social desirability response bias. However, before using deception to reduce reactivity, you should carefully consider its ethical implications.

CONTROLS WITH BEHAVIORAL MEASURES   Because some reactivity stems from research participants' knowledge that they are under observation, one way to limit reactivity is to prevent participants from realizing they are being observed. One way to accomplish such covert observation is to keep the observers hidden or have them play a role that allows them to blend into the environment. In an example of the latter strategy, Piliavin, Rodin, and Piliavin (1969) studied subway riders' responses to a staged emergency by having an observer play the role of a passenger. Modern technology has facilitated covert observation through the development of small television cameras and other devices that can be easily concealed and record behavior without the presence of an observer. There is also what Aronson et al. (1990) call the *waiting room ploy*, in which people come to participate in an experiment, but the experimental manipulation occurs while they are waiting for what they think will be the experiment to begin. Latané and Darley (1968), for example, had a receptionist greet college students who had come to participate in an experiment and direct them to a waiting room. As they waited, either alone or with other students waiting for experiments (actually confederates of the experimenters), the room began to fill with what appeared to be smoke. The researchers wanted to see if the participants' responses would be affected by the presence of the actors, who ignored the smoke. Finally, case study research in natural environments can use participant observation, in which the researcher pretends to be just another person in the situation that he or she observes. For example, a researcher studied the coping strategies used by medical students to deal with the stress of dissecting human cadavers by enrolling in their human anatomy class and observing their reactions (A. C. Smith & Kleinman, 1989). Although these methods are effective in preventing reactivity, they raise the ethical issue of collecting data without people's knowledge and consent.

As an alternative to covert observation, you could have observations made by people, such as parents or teachers, who form a natural part of the observation setting. Unfortunately, unless such observers are well trained, two problems can arise. First, the observers' data might be biased because of their knowledge of and prior beliefs about the people being observed. Second, the observers' behavior can change as a result of making and recording observations, which, in turn, can affect the behavior of the people being observed (Hay, Nelson, & Hay, 1980).

CONTROLS WITH SELF-REPORT MEASURES   When collecting self-report data, it is impossible to prevent people from knowing that they are, in a sense, under observation. However, allowing people to respond anonymously helps to reduce evaluation apprehension and so can lessen reactivity. Anonymity is easily gained through the use of written questionnaires. When questionnaires are administered in a group setting, research procedures can be established that make it impossible for the responses of any participant to be identified as coming from that person. As a result, evaluation apprehension is minimized. Paulhus (1991) suggests three procedures for enhancing and reinforcing participants' perceptions of anonymity: (1) Physically separate people (for example, leave an empty chair between two people), especially people who are acquainted; (2) remind people several times to leave their names and other identifying information off the questionnaire and response sheet; and (3) have participants turn their questionnaires in by sealing them in envelopes and dropping them in a box on the way out and tell them about this procedure before they begin to fill out the questionnaire. Interestingly, computer-administered questionnaires are more reactive than written questionnaires, perhaps because respondents are uncertain about anonymity. However, administration of a questionnaire in an interview format is most reactive because anonymity is impossible (Paulhus, 1991).

Another way to reduce socially desirable responding in self-reports is to convince people that you know when they are not being completely truthful. Most people would rather admit to a socially undesirable truth than be caught lying. The *bogus pipeline* technique, for example, has people answer questions while attached to what they think is a lie detector; various deceptions are used to convince research participants of its accuracy (Roese & Jamieson, 1993). However, with this procedure you face the ethical dilemmas of (1) lying to research participants so that they will be truthful and of (2) falsely convincing them of the effectiveness of an invalid lie-detecting device.

NOTING INSTANCES OF REACTIVITY   Although reactivity should be avoided to the greatest extent possible, it sometimes becomes obvious, especially early in observational research, that people's awareness of being under observation is affecting their behavior. Schofield (1982) recommends that researchers carefully note instances of apparent reactivity because these occurrences can be helpful in several ways. First, knowledge of the circumstances that lead to reactive behavior can provide clues for finding ways to avoid it. For example, an observer might be able to locate a less conspicuous spot from which to make observations. Second, people are likely to be most reactive in situations that raise sensitive issues; these issues might become an additional focus of the research. Schofield, for example, noted that during faculty meetings she observed teachers glancing at her when they discussed certain topics; she then incorporated these topics into her interview and observation plans. Finally, noting which responses appear to result from reactivity prevents them from being confused with natural responses during data analysis.

DEMAND CHARACTERISTICS

Orne (1962) postulated that participants in behavioral science research are curious about what is happening to them and want to understand their experience and its meaning. He suggested that to achieve this understanding, participants look for information about the nature of the research and form their own hypotheses about the goals of the research. They can then act on these hypotheses, purposively behaving in ways that affect the outcome of the research. Orne gave the name **demand characteristics** to the information present in the research situation that allows participants to form their own hypotheses. He used the term *demand* because holding a hypothesis could place a demand on participants to act in certain ways. When demand characteristics affect participants' behavior in ways that lead them to give artificial responses, they constitute a form of reactivity.

Sources of Demand Characteristics

Research participants have two sources of information available to them that allow them to formulate hypotheses. One is the information that the researcher provides them as part of the informed consent procedure. For example, AuBuchon and Calhoun (1985) wanted to know if women would report more negative menstrual symptoms when they knew that those symptoms were the research topic. They told half the women in a study that the study was examining the physical and psychological changes women experience during menstruation; the other participants were told that the study was examining such changes over time, with no mention of menstruation. The researchers found that the women who were told the study was about menstrual symptoms reported high levels of negative mood and more physical symptoms than did the women who did not know the study was about menstruation. The latter group of women reported the same average mood state and number of symptoms as did a comparison group of men. AuBuchon and Calhoun (1985) concluded that "the report of stereotypic menstrual cycle symptomatology is influenced by social expectancy [that such symptoms will occur] and experimental demand characteristics" (p. 35).

The second source of information is clues to the research hypothesis that are part of the research procedures. For example, Velten (1968) developed a procedure for inducing mildly depressed and happy mood states in research participants. Participants read aloud a set of 60 mood-related statements; in the depressed condition, one such statement might be "Right now, I am feeling sadder than I have in a very long time." Velten found that people who underwent the mood induction reported happier or sadder moods, as appropriate, than people who read a set of 60 neutral statements. However, as Polivy and Doyle (1980) have pointed out, the Velten mood statements provide research participants with very strong cues about how the researcher expects them to feel. Consequently, participants who are unaffected by the mood induction statements might simulate the appropriate mood, acting as though they were happy or sad in order to help the researcher get "good" data.

The following sections examine aspects of demand characteristics: the motivations that research participation can arouse and the behavioral consequences of those motivations, and means of controlling demand characteristics in research.

Participant Roles

Participation in psychological research can lead to three types of motivation: evaluation apprehension, reactance, and apathy. When demand characteristics allow participants to deduce a hypothesis for the research, these motivations can lead participants to play one of three corresponding **participant roles:** the good participant, the negative participant, and the apathetic participant (J. Greenberg & Folger, 1988).

THE GOOD PARTICIPANT   The discussion of reactivity noted that it is not unusual for research participants to feel anxious about how the researcher will evaluate their behavior. A possible result of this evaluation apprehension is a social desirability response bias, which could lead the participant to want to "help" the researcher by responding in the "right" way—a way that will support the hypothesis the participant thinks is under investigation. To the extent that these "good" behaviors fail to reflect participants' true responses to the independent variable, they reduce the internal validity of the research: The outcome is determined by the participant's response bias, not by the independent variable.

THE NEGATIVE PARTICIPANT   At the other end of the behavioral spectrum from the good participant is the negative participant. This role can be activated when people feel they are being coerced into doing something they don't want to do, such as doing what the researcher is telling them to do. This perceived infringement on participants' freedom of choice arouses a state called *psychological reactance* (Brehm & Brehm, 1981) that motivates them to show the researcher they cannot be pushed around. They demonstrate their independence by doing the opposite of what they think the researcher wants them to do. In contrast to good participants who try to confirm what they believe is the researcher's hypothesis, negative participants try to disconfirm the hypothesis. As with good participants, to the extent that these behaviors do not reflect the negative participants' normal responses, they reduce the internal validity of the research.

THE APATHETIC PARTICIPANT   Both good participants and negative participants feel a high level of motivation to affect the results of research, albeit in opposite directions. Apathetic participants feel no motivation; they simply don't want to be there. Consequently, they pay little attention to the research task, responding in essentially a random fashion to the independent variable and rushing through the research task as quickly as possible in order to get it over with. The apathetic role is probably most likely to be engendered in participants recruited from subject pools who really want neither to participate in research nor to do the alternative assignments and who see rushing through research participation as the most convenient way to meet the course requirement. Children may also be apathetic participants if they are participating simply because they are reluctant to say no to an adult's request for their help. Of course, both adults and children who are initially interested in participation may become apathetic if they find the research task boring. Because apathetic responses are essentially random, they too reduce the internal validity of research.

IMPACT OF PARTICIPANT ROLES   Orne's (1962) article launched a decade of research on the impact of participant roles on the results of research, focusing on the good role and the negative role. The results of such research have, however, been inconclusive: Some studies have found evidence for the impact of participant roles, but others have not (J. Greenberg & Folger, 1988). For example, Christensen (1977) found he could elicit the negative role in participants only when the researcher acted in an extremely manipulative and controlling manner. These results suggest that the vast bulk of research, in which the researcher politely solicits the cooperation of participants, would be unlikely to evoke role-related behavior. This difficulty in activating participant roles might also relate to what Fillenbaum (1966) called the "faithful" role: Most research participants try to enact the role of neutral research participant, which involves following the researcher's instructions and responding as normally as the circumstances of the research allow. This role might induce its own behavioral biases, such as trying too hard to "act naturally," but may also be the closest to realistic responding that we can expect of participants when they know they are under observation.

There appears to be no research on the prevalence of apathy among research participants. It is, however, a phenomenon that almost everyone who has collected data has encountered. As noted earlier, it can have obvious behavioral indicators, and people who appear apathetic about participating in research should be offered the opportunity to withdraw.

Controlling Demand Characteristics

The lack of strong research evidence to support the effects of demand characteristics on research results might lead one to decide, as did Kruglanski (1975), to ignore the issue. However, the procedures most commonly recommended as controls for demand characteristics (for example, Aronson et al., 1990; R. Rosenthal & Rosnow, 1991) are easy to implement and may also help to reduce reactivity in general. Let's briefly examine a few.

CUE REDUCTION   Because demand characteristics consist of cues to the research hypothesis that are contained in the research procedures, reducing those cues should reduce the likelihood of artifactual results. For example, avoid using very obvious manipulations such as the Velten (1968) mood induction technique described earlier. Also, ask colleagues to look out for possible demand characteristics when they review your research proposal. Pilot studies and postexperimental interviews, described in Chapter 12, provide the opportunity to get the research participants' viewpoint on your procedures and their perceptions of demand characteristics, if any. Because fully informed consent could reveal the research hypothesis and induce demand, researchers sometimes deceive participants by withholding the hypothesis or by giving them a false hypothesis. However, because of the potential ethical problems involved in deception, undertake such procedures only when absolutely necessary and, if possible, obtain participants' consent to deception. In addition, a thorough debriefing is essential.

MOTIVATION   Because the good-participant role is a function of evaluation apprehension, the steps (discussed earlier) to reduce evaluation apprehension can also reduce the impact of demand characteristics. Current ethical requirements for reminding potential research participants of their freedom to decline participation and to withdraw from research might also reduce the likelihood of their taking the negative role. Psychological reactance—the motivation underlying the negative role—is aroused when people believe their freedom of choice is threatened. Reminding participants of the principle of voluntary participation should reduce any threat to freedom of choice and so reduce reactivity and the likelihood of negative responding. S. S. Smith and Richardson (1983) found that providing participants with information about the importance of a study increased their enthusiasm for it. If such information can be provided to participants as part of their introduction to a study without inducing other biases, it may help motivate potentially apathetic participants.

ROLE-PLAY CONTROL GROUPS   The concept of the good-participant role includes the supposition that "good" participants will tailor their responses so as to give researchers the data that participants think the researchers want. In essence, they try to "fake good," with a good response being one that confirms the hypothesis as the participant understands it. Therefore, one way of determining if demand characteristics are affecting data is to describe the potentially demand-characteristic-laden manipulation to a group of participants and ask them to respond as if they had experienced it. Their responses would represent the effects of demand characteristics. For example, Alloy, Abramson, and Viscusi (1981) used this method in conjunction with the Velten (1968) mood induction technique: They described the Velten procedure to some participants, giving them a few mood statements as samples, and asked the participants to respond to the dependent measures in the way they thought people who had undergone the procedure would respond; that is, they were to "fake good." Alloy et al. found that the role-playing participants responded differently from the participants who had actually undergone the Velten procedure; they were therefore able to eliminate demand characteristics as an explanation for their results. If the role-playing and real participants had responded similarly, there would have been no way for Alloy et al. to tell whether the differences between the mood induction group and a neutral mood control group were due to the induced mood or to demand characteristics.

SEPARATING THE DEPENDENT MEASURE FROM THE STUDY   Demand characteristics are tied to the hypothesis of a study as perceived by the participants. Thus, if people believe their participation in a study has ended, demand characteristics are unlikely to affect their behavior. Therefore, if a dependent variable is measured outside the context of a study, any demand characteristics induced by the study should have no effect. Take, for example, a classic study in social psychology conducted by Festinger and Carlsmith (1959). After the researcher told college student participants their session of the study had ended, he sent them to a secretary who gave them a questionnaire to complete. The questionnaire asked the participants about their reactions to the study, such as how interesting they had found it. Their evaluation of the study was its dependent variable. However, because every participant in every psychology study conducted at the college completed the same questionnaire, it was unlikely that the participants would think the questionnaire was part of the study; consequently, their responses were unlikely to be influenced by any demand characteristics of the study. However, because this procedure involves deception—people are led to believe that their participation in the study is over and that their responses to the questionnaire are not part of the study—it should be used only when the study meets the criteria for permissible deception.

EXPERIMENTER EXPECTANCIES

In the early 1900s, Germany was amazed by the phenomenon of a horse named Clever Hans, who could do arithmetic as well as other amazing feats. Hans's owner would select members of an audience to pose simple arithmetic problems to Hans, who would then correctly answer them by stomping his hoof the proper number of times. How could a horse do arithmetic? Pfungst (1904/1965) provided an answer by conducting an experiment in which Hans had to do arithmetic when neither Hans's owner nor anyone in the audience knew the answer to the problem. Under these conditions, Hans's mathematical ability disappeared. Apparently, Hans's owner and the person posing the question (who, of course, knew the answer) would change their postures, such as by leaning forward, when Hans reached the correct number of hoof taps. Because Hans could perceive these changes and was rewarded for each correct answer, he had learned to stop tapping when people's postures changed. In essence, the questioners' expectation that Hans would stop tapping when he reached the correct answer affected their behavior, which in turn affected Hans's behavior so that he appeared to give the correct answer.

Types of Expectancy Effects

R. Rosenthal (1976) noted that the same phenomenon could occur in the laboratory and named them **experimenter expectancy effects.** Experimenters' expectancies about how participants should perform on the research task could affect the way they behaved toward research participants; their behavior could then affect the participants' responses to the research task, biasing the data. There are two possible sources of experimenter expectancies. One is the research hypothesis: Experimenters generally expect to find data that support it. The second source of expectancies is the data collected early in a research project: If a pattern is apparent in early data, experimenters generally expect later data to be consistent with that pattern. Rosenthal proposed two mechanisms by which experimenter expectancies could affect the data they collect: biased observation and influencing participant behavior.

BIASED OBSERVATION   As noted in the discussion of case study research in Chapter 2, observer expectations about what they would find could affect their interpretation of what they observe. These interpretations are in the direction of the expectation. Rosenthal (1976) noted that the same phenomenon can occur in laboratory research when experimenters collect data by recording their observations of participant behavior. For example, in one study researchers observed the behavior of flatworms. Half the observers were told that the worms came from a high-response genetic strain and would show a great deal of movement; the other observers were told that their worms came from a low-response strain and would show little movement. Although all the worms came from the same genetic strain, the observers who expected a high degree of response reported more movement than those expecting a low degree of response.

INFLUENCING PARTICIPANTS' RESPONSES   Rosenthal (1976) noted that experimenters' expectancies could also influence participants' responses. In one set of studies, experimenters were asked to elicit participants' ratings of the physical attractiveness of the people shown in ten photographs. Half the experimenters were told to expect high ratings; the others were told to expect low ratings. In fact, the photographs had been selected because a previous group of research participants had rated the people in them as being average in physical attractiveness. The participants whose experimenters expected high ratings gave higher ratings than those whose experimenters expected low ratings.

There are three possible mechanisms by which experimenter expectancies could affect participants' responses (Barber, 1976; R. Rosenthal, 1976). First, experimenters might introduce variations into the research procedures, treating experimental and control participants differently, and so inducing differences in response. Second, experimenters might give nonverbal feedback to participants about "right" and "wrong" responses. Like Clever Hans's questioners, they might change their postures or facial expressions, perhaps rewarding "correct" responses with a smile and "incorrect" responses with a frown. Participants high in evaluation apprehension might be especially sensitive to such cues. Finally, experimenters might give verbal feedback, muttering "good" or "uh-huh" when they get the response they expect. This feedback could let participants know what responses were expected of them. It is important to note that the general presumption is that when experimenters do these things, they do them without being aware of their behavior. These are unconscious behaviors, not attempts at intentional bias. Researchers can, of course, intentionally bias their data to get the results they want; Chapter 18 discusses this issue.

Techniques of Control

Aronson et al. (1990) and R. Rosenthal and Rosnow (1991) discuss a number of steps one can take to control the effects of experimenter expectancies. Four of the most common are rehearsal and monitoring of experimenters, minimizing the experimenter's role, condition blindness, and avoidance of data snooping.

REHEARSAL AND MONITORING   Because variations in experimenter behavior between the experimental and control conditions can affect participant response, precautions should be taken to minimize these variations. It is therefore very important to provide experimenters with a detailed script for their interactions with participants and to rehearse experimenters until they can follow the script flawlessly and consistently. If possible, also monitor experimenters' behavior while they are collecting data to ensure that their responses don't change over time.

MINIMIZING THE EXPERIMENTER'S ROLE   Experimenters' expectancies can affect data only to the extent that the experimenter is involved in data collection or interacts with participants. Therefore, the less experimenters do in an experiment, the less effect their expectancies can have. For example, if the dependent variable is measured by self-report or an automated device rather than by experimenter observation, the experimenter's expectancies cannot bias data recording.

The effects of experimenter expectancies on participant behavior can be minimized by minimizing the experimenter's contact with participants. As Aronson et al. (1990) note, some researchers have removed the experimenter entirely from the experiment. The experimenter brings participants to a room and leaves them alone with a tape recorder, computer terminal, or instruction booklet. The machine or booklet then instructs participants on the research task. Although this procedure may seem at first glance overly sterile and perhaps dehumanizing to participants, Aronson et al. report that participants are quite accepting of the procedure once its purpose is explained. However, they also note an important drawback:

> By shutting the subject in a room with a tape recorder, a booklet, or a microcomputer, the experimenter too is shut off from information that could be of the utmost importance in interpreting the outcome of the experiment. For example, in attempting to convey a set of

instructions to a subject in a face-to-face interaction, the experimenter may come to realize that these instructions are not viable: there is nothing quite like a yawn in the face to convince the experimenter that the instructions are dull and unmotivating. If the instructions are presented on a tape recording, the experimenter might never see the yawn and might run the whole experiment without realizing that the subjects are totally indifferent to the treatment. (Aronson et al., 1990, p. 238)

CONDITION BLINDNESS   Perhaps the most widely used control for experimenter expectancy effects is **condition blindness:** The experimenter does not know whether any particular participant is in the experimental or control condition when data are collected. Because the experimenter does not know which condition participants are in, his or her expectancies about how participants should behave in the different conditions cannot affect their responses. Carrying out research that uses this technique can be procedurally complex, often requiring two experimenters. One experimenter works with participants through the manipulation of the independent variable. The other experimenter, who does not know whether the participant is in the experimental or control condition, then takes over and measures the dependent variable. Despite this complexity, there is consensus that condition blindness is the best available control for experimenter expectancy effects (J. Greenberg & Folger, 1988).

AVOIDANCE OF DATA SNOOPING   The term *data snooping* refers to analyzing data collected before a study is completed "to see what's happening." If these analyses show a particular pattern of results, such as support for the research hypothesis, then this pattern could establish an experimenter expectancy for the data still to be collected. Researchers should therefore resist the temptation to data-snoop. However, as discussed in Chapter 12, it is a good and often necessary practice to conduct pilot studies to test experimental procedures. The results of pilot studies can also establish expectancies about the outcome of the main study, so the experimenters who collect the data for the main study should be kept unaware of pilot results until they have finished collecting their data.

SUMMARY

Many factors can influence the internal validity of research. Internal validity represents the degree of confidence we can have that the independent variable, rather than some other factor in the research situation, affected the dependent variable. Five categories of factors can threaten the internal validity of research: confounding, time-related and selection threats, reactivity, demand characteristics, and experimenter expectancies.

A confound exists when two variables are combined so that the effect of one cannot be separated from the effect of the other. A treatment confound occurs when the operational definition of the independent variable manipulates two hypothetical constructs simultaneously. A measurement confound occurs when a measure assesses two constructs simultaneously. Some confounds are considered natural because they reflect naturally occurring combinations of variables.

D. T. Campbell and Stanley (1963) identified several potential threats to the internal validity of research. A history threat occurs when an event outside the research affects the dependent variable. The term *maturation* refers to natural change over time.

A testing confound occurs when taking a pretest affects scores on the posttest. Instrumentation change occurs when a measuring instrument changes over time, resulting in artificial changes in what it measures. Statistical regression can occur when participants are selected for research because they have extreme scores on the dependent variable; the random error that contributed to the initial extreme score makes it likely that the score will be closer to the mean at a second assessment. The presence and magnitude of these effects can be assessed in pretest-posttest research through the use of a control group. A selection confound occurs when participants assigned to the experimental and control groups of a study have different characteristics. Selection confounds can result from nonrandom assignment of participants to conditions, from the use of preexisting groups, and from mortality.

Reactivity occurs when the act of measuring a variable affects the score on the measure. Reactivity can result from evaluation apprehension or novelty effects. The effects of reactivity can be reduced by alleviating evaluation apprehension—such as by putting participants at ease—by providing participants with an engaging task, by covert measurement of the dependent variable, and by having participants respond anonymously to questionnaires. Novelty effects can be reduced by allowing people time to adjust to the novel aspects of the situation and by covert observation.

Demand characteristics are factors in the research situation that provide participants with cues to the hypothesis being tested. Once aware of the hypothesis, a participant might take on any of three roles. The good participant tries to "help" the researcher by providing data that will confirm the hypothesis, the negative participant tries to provide data that will disconfirm the hypothesis, and the apathetic participant responds in essentially a random manner. The effects of demand characteristics can be minimized by reducing cues to the hypothesis, motivating participants to avoid enacting roles that threaten internal validity, establishing role-play control groups to estimate the effects of demand characteristics, and separating the dependent variable from the study.

Experimenters' expectancies about the outcome of a study can threaten the internal validity of the study. Experimenter expectancies can lead to biased observations and can influence participants' behavior. The effects of experimenter expectancies can be reduced by rehearsing experimenters and monitoring their performance, minimizing experimenter contact with participants, keeping experimenters blind to whether a participant is a member of the experimental or control group, and resisting the temptation to data-snoop.

Despite the fairly large number of potential threats to the internal validity of research, there are a number of steps you can take to control or reduce these threats. These steps are shown in Box 6-2.

QUESTIONS AND EXERCISES FOR REVIEW

1. How can you rule out alternative explanations for the effect of an independent variable?
2. How are treatment and measurement confounds similar? In what ways are they different? What is a natural confound? What implications do measurement confounds and natural confounds have for the design and interpretation of research?

BOX 6-2   Enhancing Internal Validity

Avoid treatment confounds by ensuring that all participants have exactly the same experience in exactly the same environment except for differences that are part of the independent variable.

Avoid measurement confounds by using only measures that are high in discriminant validity.

Always use a control group in pretest-posttest research.

Be alert for history effects in cross-sectional research.

Be alert for mortality effects. Always check experimental and control groups for differential mortality.

Measure variables under conditions that minimize reactivity.

When collecting data with questionnaires, conduct a pilot study to determine if context effects could be a problem.

Be alert for demand characteristics in your procedures. Use role-play control groups when you cannot avoid high-demand procedures.

When observers code behaviors, use low-inference coding systems to minimize expectancy effects.

Thoroughly train and rehearse experimenters for their interactions with participants. Monitor their performance throughout data collection.

Whenever possible, keep experimenters blind to the condition that participants are in when the experimenters measure the dependent variable.

Avoid data snooping, and whenever possible keep experimenters blind to the results of pilot studies.

3. Describe the time-related threats to internal validity, including the effects they have on pretest-posttest research and on cross-sectional research in which data are collected over a period of time. How does a control group control for these effects in pretest-posttest research?

4. Describe the types of selection biases. How can these biases be controlled? What are the advantages and disadvantages of these procedures? What implications does the problem of selection biases have for interpreting longitudinal research and research that uses preexisting groups for its experimental and control conditions?

5. Describe the effects of evaluation apprehension and novelty on research participants. What steps can you take to control those effects? What are advantages and disadvantages of those steps?

6. Describe the sources of demand characteristics in research. What roles can participants take in research? What motivational factor is associated with each role? Describe the means for controlling demand characteristics. What are the advantages and disadvantages of those means?

7. How can experimenters' expectancies about the outcome of research affect the data collected in the research? How can experimenter expectancy effects be controlled? Describe the advantages and disadvantages of these control measures.

8. Huck and Sandler (1979) present summaries of studies that illustrate the various kinds of internal validity problems. Get a copy of their book from your library, and practice your ability to identify internal validity problems by working through some of their examples.

9. This chapter has focused on the problems involved in designing internally valid research. Given these problems, do you think it is possible for behavioral science to generate valid knowledge about human behavior? Why or why not?

7 THE EXPERIMENTAL RESEARCH STRATEGY

A NOTE ON STATISTICS

MANIPULATING THE
INDEPENDENT VARIABLE
Conditions of the Independent
   Variable
   *Experimental and Control
      Conditions*
   Comparison Conditions
Additional Control and
   Comparison Conditions
   Hypothesis Testing
   *Ruling Out Specific
      Alternative Explanations*
Characteristics of a Good
   Manipulation
   Construct Validity
   Reliability
   Strength
   Salience
Using Multiple Stimuli

CONTROLLING EXTRANEOUS
VARIANCE
Holding Extraneous Variables
   Constant

Between-Subjects Designs
   Simple Random Assignment
   *Matched Random
      Assignment*
Within-Subjects Designs
   *Advantages Relative to
      Between-Subjects Designs*
   The Problem of Order Effects
   Controlling Order Effects
   When Order Effects Are Good

MULTIPLE-GROUP DESIGNS
Quantitative Independent
   Variables
Qualitative Independent Variables
Interpreting the Results of
   Multiple-Group Experiments

FACTORIAL DESIGNS
The Nature of Factorial Designs
   Describing Factorial Designs
   *Information Provided by
      Factorial Designs*
   *Outcomes of Factorial
      Designs*

Interaction Effects
   Displaying Interactions
   Interpreting Interactions
Forms of Factorial Designs
   *Between- and Within-Subjects
      Designs*
   *Manipulated and Measured
      Independent Variables*
   Design Complexity
Uses for Factorial Designs
   *Testing Moderator
      Hypotheses*
   Detecting Order Effects
   *Blocking on Extraneous
      Variables*

SUMMARY

QUESTIONS AND EXERCISES
FOR REVIEW

Chapter 2 noted that from the logical positivist point of view the experiment is the ideal research strategy. The positivists take this position because in the experiment, the experimenter takes complete control of the research situation, determining the independent variable and how it will be manipulated, the dependent variable and how it will be measured, the setting, the participants, and the course of events during the experiment. Experimenters thus create their own artificial universes in which to test their hypotheses. This high degree of control over the research situation allows experimenters to establish the conditions that allow them to determine causality: covariation of proposed cause and effect, time precedence of the cause, and lack of alternatives to the independent variable as explanations for any effects found on the dependent measure. These conditions are reflected in the three defining characteristics of the experiment:

1. *Manipulation of the independent variable.* The experimenter creates the conditions to be studied. For example, in an experiment on the effects of stress, the experimenter creates a high-stress condition and a low-stress condition, and assesses the effects of these conditions on a dependent variable. Manipulation of the independent variable in experimentation stands in contrast to research in which the researcher identifies natural situations that differ in their stress levels, measures the level of stress in each situation, and correlates stress scores with scores on the dependent variable. If the independent variable in a study is measured rather than manipulated, the study is not an experiment.

2. *Holding all other variables in the research situation constant.* Participants in the experimental and control conditions undergo experiences that are as similar as possible except for the manipulation of the independent variable. In the hypothetical stress experiment, all participants have exactly the same experiences before and after their exposure to high or low stress. As noted in the previous chapter, deviation from this procedure can open the door to alternative explanations for any effects found.

3. *Participants in the experimental and control conditions having equivalent personal characteristics and being equivalent with respect to the dependent variable before they take part in the experiment.* This equivalence can be attained by holding the characteristics constant across conditions, randomly assigning participants to conditions, matching experimental and control participants on selected characteristics, or having the same people participate in both the experimental and control conditions. These procedures reduce the likelihood of a selection bias.

This chapter discusses three aspects of experimental research. First I examine the manipulation of the independent variable, considering the roles of experimental and control conditions and the characteristics of a good manipulation. Then I discuss controlling extraneous variance in experiments by holding potential sources of variance constant and by using variance methods of assigning research participants to conditions of the independent variable. The chapter concludes with a discussion of experiments that use more than two conditions of the independent variable and those that use more than one independent variable. However, before getting into these issues, we must take a brief side trip into the realm of statistics.

A NOTE ON STATISTICS

Statistics and research design are closely related: Proper research design allows us to collect valid data, and statistics help us to interpret those data. Descriptive statistics, such as the difference between the mean scores of an experimental group and a control group on a dependent variable and the standard deviations of those means, let us know how much effect our independent variable had. Inferential statistics or statistical tests, such as the *t* test, analysis of variance (ANOVA), and chi-square tell us how likely it is that the observed effect is real rather than being due to chance differences between the groups. Many of the statistical tests most commonly used in experimental research, such as the *t* test and ANOVA, are called *parametric statistics* and operate by dividing (or partitioning) the variance in the dependent variable scores into two pieces: variance caused by the independent variable and variance caused by everything else in the research situation. Because this concept of partitioning of variance will be important in the discussion of experiments, let's look at it more closely.

Consider experiments on the effects of stress, in which a common dependent variable is the number of mistakes participants make on a task, such as proofreading a document. Looking at all the participants in the research, both experimental and control, the number of mistakes they make will vary: Some people will make many mistakes, some will make a few, and some will make a moderate number. If stress does affect performance, some of this variance will be due to the independent variable: Some people in the high-stress condition will make more mistakes than people in the low-stress condition. This variance in the dependent variable that results from the independent variable is called **treatment variance.** However, not all the variance in the number of mistakes will be due to the independent variable. Some variance will be due to differences among participants: Some people will be more skilled at the task and so make fewer mistakes than low-skill people regardless of whether they experience high or low stress. Some people will be more vulnerable to stress and so make more mistakes in the high-stress condition than their counterparts in the low-stress condition. Variance in the dependent variable can also result from random measurement error (as noted in Chapter 5) and slight unintentional variations in how the experimenter treats each participant. For example, an experimenter who is having a "bad day" might be less patient with that day's research participants, perhaps speaking abruptly and appearing to be irritated, thereby making that day's participants more nervous than the participants with whom the experimenter interacts on "good days." This increased nervousness could cause the participants to make more errors.

From a statistical point of view, all variance in the dependent variable that is not caused by the independent variable is **error variance.** The value of a parametric statistical test, such as the *F* value in ANOVA, represents the ratio of treatment variance to error variance—that is, treatment variance divided by error variance. Consequently, the value of a statistical test increases as the treatment variance increases and as the error variance decreases. The larger the value, the less likely it is that the results of the experiment were due to chance factors (the errors represented by the error variance) and the more likely it is that they were due to the effect of the independent variable; in other words, the results are more likely to be "statistically significant." Therefore, two goals of research design are to increase the effect of the independent variable (and so increase the treatment variance) and to reduce the error variance (and so increase the ratio of treatment to error variance).

MANIPULATING THE INDEPENDENT VARIABLE

The experimenter manipulates the independent variable to establish conditions that will test the research hypothesis. In its simplest form, the experiment has two conditions, an experimental condition and a control or comparison condition; more complex experiments have additional control or comparison conditions. This section examines the functions of the conditions of an experiment, discusses the characteristics of a good manipulation, and considers situations in which you might want to use multiple stimuli in each condition of the independent variable.

Conditions of the Independent Variable

Experiments can take two forms. Sometimes experimenters want to examine how people behave in the presence of treatment versus its absence; in such situations, the experiment consists of an experimental condition and a control condition. In other cases, experimenters want to compare the effects of two treatments, such as two methods of studying; in such situations, the experiment has two comparison conditions rather than experimental and control conditions.

EXPERIMENTAL AND CONTROL CONDITIONS   In the experimental condition of an experiment, the research participants undergo an experience or treatment that the researcher thinks will affect their behavior. For example, you might hypothesize that knowing the topic of an ambiguous paragraph helps people remember the information presented in it (as did Bransford & Johnson, 1972). In the experimental condition of a study testing this hypothesis, you could tell participants the topic of the paragraph, read the paragraph to them, and then measure their recall of the content of the paragraph. The control condition of the experiment establishes a baseline against which you can assess the effect of the treatment. This baseline consists of an experience that is as similar as possible to that of the experimental condition, except that the treatment is absent. In the example, you would read the paragraph to the research participants and measure their recall without telling them the topic of the paragraph.

This equivalence in experience between the experimental and control conditions lets you rule out what Kazdin (1997) calls **nonspecific treatment effects** as the cause of any differences between the conditions. Nonspecific treatment effects are changes brought about in participants by all their experiences in the research that do not include the treatment, such as contact with the experimenter, being given a rationale for the research, and so forth. Nonspecific treatment effects are similar to **placebo effects,** in which people taking part in drug or psychotherapy research improve because they think they are receiving a treatment even if they are being given an inert substance or are not actually undergoing therapy. For example, let's say you wanted to determine if exercise improves psychological well-being. You obtain a sample of mildly depressed individuals, measure their levels of depression, and assign half to an exercise group and half to a control group. The people in the treatment condition meet for 1 hour 3 days a week for 6 weeks, taking part in an exercise program that you direct. You tell the people in the control condition that you will contact them again in 6 weeks. You assess the participants' levels of depression at the end of the 6-week period. Under these conditions, it would be impossible to tell if any difference found between the experimental and control groups were due to the effects of the independent variable or to differences in the way in which the two sets of participants were treated. For example, if the people in the experimental condition improved relative to those in the control condition, was the improvement due to the exercise, to their meeting and interacting with each other 3 days a week, or to the attention you gave them? The only way to rule out these alternative explanations would be to have the control participants meet in your presence on the same schedule as the experimental participants, but to perform a task other than exercising, such as a crafts project.

COMPARISON CONDITIONS   Not all experiments include conditions in which the participants experience an absence of or substitute for the experimental treatment. Instead, an experiment might compare the effects of two treatments. For example, you might want to compare the relative efficacy of two ways of studying for a test, such as cramming versus long-term study. Other experiments compare responses to high versus low levels of a treatment. For example, a study of the effect of stress on memory would have a high-stress condition and a low-stress condition. It would be impossible to create a no-stress condition because the requirement for research participants to try to learn and remember material would create some degree of stress even in the absence of an experimental stressor.

Because all experiments compare the effects of different conditions of the independent variable on the dependent variable, some people prefer the term *comparison condition* to describe what I have called the *control condition*. Although the term *comparison condition* is perhaps more descriptive of the true nature of experimental research, I've retained the term *control condition* because it has been used for so long.

Additional Control and Comparison Conditions

Although the archetypical experiment has only two conditions, experimental and control, some experiments have more than one control condition. Two situations that call for multiple control or comparison conditions are when they are required for a complete test of the hypotheses under study and to control for specific alternative explanations for the effect of the independent variable.

HYPOTHESIS TESTING   Sometimes the hypothesis one is testing has more than one component to it. A complete test of the hypothesis would require the presence of control conditions that would let one test all the components of the hypothesis. Consider an experiment conducted by Bransford and Johnson (1972). They hypothesized that people understand an ambiguous message better and remember its contents better if they have a context in which to put the information, and that comprehension and re-call are improved only when people are given the context before they receive the in-formation. Here is one of the paragraphs they used as a message:

> The procedure is actually quite simple. First you arrange things into different groups de-pending on their makeup. Of course, one pile may be sufficient depending on how much there is to do. If you have to go somewhere else due to lack of facilities that is the next step, otherwise you are pretty well set. It is important not to overdo any particular endeavor. That is, it is better to do too few things at once than too many. In the short run this may not seem important, but complications from doing too many can easily arise. A mistake can be expensive as well. The manipulation of the appropriate mechanisms should be self-explanatory, and we need not dwell on it here. At first, the whole procedure will seem com-plicated. Soon, however, it will become just another facet of life. It is difficult to foresee any end to the necessity for this task in the immediate future, but then one never can tell. (Bransford & Johnson, 1972, p. 722)

Bransford and Johnson's hypothesis had two parts: first, that context improves un-derstanding of and memory for information, and second, that the context must come before the information. Their experiment therefore required three groups of partici-pants: one that received the context before the information, one that received the con-text after the information, and one that received no context. They tested the first part of their hypothesis by comparing the understanding and recall of the context-before group with those of the no-context group, and they tested the second part of their hy-pothesis by comparing the context-before group to the context-after group. Their hy-pothesis would be completely confirmed only if the context-before group performed better than both of the other groups. By the way, the paragraph was about washing clothes, and people who were told the context before hearing the paragraph did under-stand it and remember its contents better than the people in the other conditions.

RULING OUT SPECIFIC ALTERNATIVE EXPLANATIONS   The baseline control condition allows researchers to rule out nonspecific treatment effects as alternatives to the effect of the independent variable as a cause of experimental and control group differences on the dependent variable. Sometimes, however, there are also specific alternative explana-tions that the experimenter must be able to rule out. In such cases, the experimenter adds control conditions to determine the validity of these alternative explanations. For example, recall Alloy, Abramson, and Viscusi's (1981) study mentioned in the previous chapter. Alloy et al. saw that the procedure they used to induce temporary mood states in their research participants could elicit strong demand characteristics. They added a role-play control condition to their experiment to determine the magnitude of any de-mand characteristic effects. In addition to their induced mood experimental condition, they therefore had two control conditions: a neutral mood condition for baseline com-parisons and the role-play condition.

Researchers can also use additional control conditions to untangle the effects of natural confounds. Let's say you conducted an experiment to see if having music play-ing while studying leads to less learning than not having music playing. If you found that people who studied with music playing learned less than those who studied in si-lence, you could not definitely attribute the effect to music; after all, *any* background noise could have detracted from learning. You would therefore need an additional control group who studied to random background noise. Comparing the music condition to the noise condition would tell you if it was music per se that detracted from learning or if it was merely sound that had the effect.

Determining the appropriate control or comparison conditions to use is an important aspect of experimental design. Thoroughly analyze your hypothesis to ensure that you test it completely, and carefully examine your research design to ensure that you have accounted for all alternative explanations.

Characteristics of a Good Manipulation

Chapter 5 stated that two characteristics of a good measure are construct validity and reliability. The procedures used to manipulate an independent variable should also be characterized by construct validity and reliability. In addition, a manipulation must be strong and salient to participants.

CONSTRUCT VALIDITY   Whenever a manipulation is intended to operationally define a hypothetical construct, make sure the manipulation accurately represents the construct. For example, if you have research participants write essays to manipulate their moods, how do you know their moods actually changed in the ways you wanted them to change? Just as you want to ensure the construct validity of your measures, you also want to ensure the construct validity of your manipulations. The construct validity of a manipulation is tested by means of a **manipulation check.** The manipulation check tests the convergent validity of the manipulation by checking it against measures of the construct and by ensuring that participants in different conditions of the experiment are experiencing different levels or conditions of the independent variable. For example, participants in a high-stress condition should report more stress symptoms than participants in a low-stress condition. A manipulation check should also test the discriminant validity of the manipulation by ensuring that it manipulates only the construct it is supposed to manipulate.

Manipulation checks can take two forms that can be used either separately or together. One way to conduct a manipulation check is to interview research participants after data have been collected, asking them questions that determine if the manipulation had the intended effect. For example, if you were trying to manipulate the degree to which participants perceived a confederate as friendly or unfriendly, as part of your postexperimental interview with participants you could ask them about their perceptions of the confederate. If the manipulation was successful, participants should describe the confederate in ways that are consistent with the manipulation. The other way to conduct a manipulation check is to include dependent variables that assess the construct being manipulated. For example, Schwarz and Clore (1983) assessed the effectiveness of their mood manipulation by having participants complete a mood measure. Statistical analysis of participants' mood scores showed that participants in the sad-mood condition reported moods that were more negative than those of participants in a neutral-mood condition and that participants in the happy-mood condition reported moods that were more positive than those of the participants in the neutral condition, indicating that the manipulation worked as intended.

Manipulation checks can be made at two points in the research project. The first point is during pilot testing, when the bugs are being worked out of the research procedures. One potential bug is the effectiveness of the manipulation. It is not unusual to have to tinker with the manipulation to ensure that it has the intended effect and only the intended effect. Manipulation checks can also be made during data collection to ensure that all participants experience the independent variable as intended. However, if manipulation checks are made only concurrently with data collection, it is too late to fix the manipulation if problems are discovered unless you are willing to stop data collection and start the research all over again. Researchers are sometimes tempted to omit manipulation checks because someone else has used a manipulation successfully. However, it is always wise to include a manipulation check because the validity of manipulations, like that of measures, can vary from participant population to participant population.

In the best case, manipulation checks support the validity of the manipulation. But what does the check mean if it fails—that is, if it does not support the manipulation? It is, of course, possible that the manipulation is not valid as an operational definition of the construct. There are, however, other possibilities to consider before abandoning the manipulation. One possibility is that the manipulation is valid but is not strong enough to have the desired impact; manipulation strength is discussed shortly. Another possibility is that the research participants didn't notice the manipulation in the context of everything that was happening; this issue of salience is also discussed later. A third possibility is that the measure being used to assess the construct in the manipulation check is not valid or is not sensitive to the effect of the manipulation. It is therefore wise to use multiple measures in manipulation checks as well as multiple measures of the dependent variable in the research. Finally, it is possible the participants are not paying attention to the manipulation. Sometimes, participants are inattentive because they are bored or otherwise unmotivated. In other cases, some aspect of the research environment might distract participants from the manipulation. Inattention can be a special problem when the independent variable is manipulated by giving different information to participants experiencing the different conditions of the independent variable. For example, a group of students with whom I was once working tried to replicate the Bransford and Johnson (1972) study described earlier. The participants' context information was contained on a sheet of paper that also included their instructions for the experiment. Participants were instructed to read the information on the sheet, after which the experimenter read the ambiguous passage to them. We were unable to get any differences between groups. We then decided to have the experimenter read the instructions aloud to participants, who read along on their instruction sheets. Suddenly we started getting the same results as Bransford and Johnson. Apparently the participants hadn't been paying attention to the context information when they read it. It is therefore essential to construct a research situation that encourages participants to attend to the manipulation.

RELIABILITY   Chapter 5 noted that a reliable measure is a consistent measure, one that gives essentially the same results every time it is used. Similarly, reliability of manipulation consists of consistency of manipulation: Every time a manipulation is applied, it is applied in the same way. If a manipulation is applied reliably, every participant in the experiment experiences it in essentially the same way. High reliability can be attained by automating the experiment, but as pointed out in the previous chapter, automation has severe drawbacks. High reliability can also be attained by preparing detailed scripts for experimenters to follow and by rehearsing experimenters until they can conduct every condition of the experiment correctly and consistently. Remember that low reliability entails low validity; no matter how valid a manipulation is in principle, if it is not applied reliably, it is useless.

STRENGTH   A **strong manipulation** is one in which the conditions of the independent variable are different enough to differentially affect behavior. Let's say, for example, that you're interested in the effects of lighting level on work performance. You hypothesize that brighter light improves performance on an assembly task; the dependent variables will be speed of assembly and the number of errors made. You test the hypothesis by having half the participants in your experiment work under a 60-watt light and the others under a 75-watt light. It would not be surprising to find no difference in performance between the groups: The difference in lighting level is not large enough to have an effect on performance.

Strong manipulations are achieved by using extreme levels of the independent variable. The lighting and work performance study, for example, might use 15-watt and 100-watt lights to have more impact on behavior and so increase the amount of treatment variance in the dependent variable. Although it is desirable to have a strong manipulation, there are two factors to consider in choosing the strength of a manipulation. One consideration is realism: An overly extreme manipulation might be unrealistic. For example, it would be unrealistic to use total darkness and a 1,000-watt light as the conditions in the lighting experiment: People almost never do assembly tasks under those conditions. A lack of realism has two disadvantages. First, participants might not take the research seriously and so provide data of unknown validity. Second, even if there were no internal validity problems, it is unlikely that the results would generalize to any real-life situations to which the research was intended to apply. The second consideration is ethical: An extreme manipulation might unduly harm research participants. There are, for example, ethical limits on the amount of stress to which a researcher can subject participants.

There is an exception to the general rule that stronger manipulations are better for obtaining differences between conditions on the dependent variable. As I will discuss shortly, sometimes the relationship between the independent and dependent variables is U-shaped. Under such conditions, the largest differences in behavior will show up not when the two extreme conditions are compared but, rather, when the extremes are compared to a moderate level of the independent variable.

SALIENCE   For a manipulation to affect research participants, they have to notice it in the context of everything else that is happening in the experiment. This characteristic of "noticeability" is called *salience*. A **salient manipulation** stands out from the background, and it is sometimes necessary to put a lot of effort into establishing the salience of a manipulation. For example, D. Landy and Aronson (1968) conducted a study to determine if people react more strongly to evaluations of them made by another person if they think that person is especially discerning, that is, especially skilled in deducing the personality characteristics of other people. The researchers manipulated how discerning the other person appeared by having him perform a task, in the presence of the participant, designed to show either the presence (experimental condition) or absence (control condition) of discernment. But how could the researchers be sure the participants noticed how discerning the other person was? They

> told the subject that "degree of discernment" was an aspect of the confederate's behavior that was of particular interest to them; asked the subject to rate the confederate's discernment; [and] informed the subject exactly how the confederate's behavior might reflect either high or low discernment. (Aronson, Ellsworth, Carlsmith, & Gonzales, 1990, pp. 223–224)

Not all manipulations require this degree of emphasis, but experimenters do need to ensure that the participants in their research notice the manipulation.

Using Multiple Stimuli

The **stimulus** is the person, object, or event that represents the operational definition of a condition of the independent variable and to which research participants respond. For example, in a study on the effects of the physical attractiveness of a person on how that person is evaluated by other people, the independent variable is physical attractiveness, its operational definition might be pictures of a person made up to appear attractive or unattractive, and a stimulus would be the particular picture to which a research participant responds with an evaluation. When the independent variable is a manifest variable, only one stimulus can represent one of its conditions. For example, in a study of the effects of caffeine on physiological arousal, a condition in which participants ingest 100 mg of caffeine can be represented only by a stimulus that consists of 100 mg of caffeine. However, when the independent variable is a hypothetical construct, it can very often be represented by any number of stimuli. In the physical attractiveness study, for example, the concept of physical attractiveness could be represented by pictures of any of thousands of people.

Although many constructs can be represented by multiple stimuli, most research dealing with such constructs uses only one stimulus to represent any one condition of the independent variable, such as one picture of an attractive person and one picture of an unattractive person. If the research finds a difference between the conditions, a problem arises in interpreting the results: Although the outcome could be due to the effects of the independent variable, it could also be due to the unique features of the stimulus or to an interaction between the independent variable and the unique features of the stimulus (Wells & Windschitl, 1999). Let's say, for example, that the stimuli used in our hypothetical attractiveness study were pictures of a model made up to portray an attractive person in one picture and an unattractive person in the other picture. In making their evaluations, were the participants responding to the general construct of physical attractiveness — the intended independent variable — or to the unique characteristics of the particular model who posed for the pictures, such as the shape of her face, the size of her mouth, and the distance between her eyes? That is, were the research participants responding to the *general* characteristic of physical attractiveness or to the *unique* characteristics of that particular person? There is no way to answer this question if only a single, unique stimulus is used to represent each condition of the independent variable.

The question would have an answer, however, if each research participant had responded to a set of stimuli that provided a sample of the possible stimuli that could represent the conditions of the independent variable. For example, you could have participants in each condition of the experiment rate four people rather than just one. With multiple stimuli per condition, it becomes possible to apply a special form of ANOVA, called the *random effects model*, that separates the variance in the dependent variable due to specific stimuli, such as the models used to portray the attractive people, from the variance due to the hypothesized construct represented by the stimuli, such as the concept of "attractive person." This form of ANOVA is extremely complex (Richter & Seay, 1987), but because it separates irrelevant stimulus variance from the relevant variance due to the hypothetical construct, it provides a much more valid test of the effects of the independent variable than would the use of a single stimulus per condition.

CONTROLLING EXTRANEOUS VARIANCE

The experiment is characterized not only by manipulation of the independent variable but also by procedures used to control factors that cause extraneous variance in the dependent variable. As noted earlier, any variance in the dependent variable that is not caused by the independent variable is considered error variance. Some of this variance is due to random factors, such as slight variations in the way the experimenter treats research participants. Other variance is due to factors that are systematically related to the dependent variable but are not of interest to the researcher. For example, there are sex differences on many variables that behavioral scientists study (Basow, 1992), but these differences are not of interest to all researchers. Variables that are related to or can influence the dependent variable in a study but are not a focus of the research are called **extraneous variables.** When extraneous variables are not treated as independent variables in the research, their effects form part of the error variance in the statistical analysis of the data. Experimenters therefore take steps to control extraneous variance.

Holding Extraneous Variables Constant

Extraneous variables that are part of the research situation, such as the characteristics of the room in which the research takes place, are fairly easy to control: The experimenter holds these variables constant across conditions of the independent variable. Because these factors do not vary as part of the experiment, they cannot cause systematic variance in the dependent variable — their effects are reasonably constant for each participant in the research. Individual differences in participants' responses to these controlled variables form part of the error variance in the experiment.

Extraneous variables that are characteristics of the research participants, such as personality and background, are more difficult to control: Differences among people, unlike differences among rooms, cannot always be eliminated by the actions of the experimenter. Nevertheless, it is sometimes possible to hold participant variables constant. For example, if a researcher uses only men or only women as participants in an experiment, sex of participant can have no systematic effect on the dependent variable. However, as pointed out in Chapter 4, this strategy can bias the results of research and limit their generalizability if participants with only one characteristic of the extraneous variable—for example, only men—are used in all research on a topic. As discussed in more detail later, you can avoid this problem by treating participant characteristics as independent variables in experiments.

Experimenters most commonly control the effects of variance in research participants' personal characteristics by the ways in which they assign participants to conditions of the independent variable. In **between-subjects designs** (also called **independent groups designs**), a participant takes part in either the experimental or control condition, but not both. The researcher distributes the effects of extraneous participant variables evenly across the experimental and control groups by either randomly assigning participants to conditions or matching the participants in each condition on key extraneous variables. In **within-subjects designs** (also called **repeated measures designs**), each participant takes part in both the experimental and control conditions so that the effects of participant variables are perfectly balanced across conditions.

Between-Subjects Designs

Between-subjects designs are more commonly used in behavioral research than are within-subjects designs. Some reasons for this preference will be discussed later in comparing the advantages and disadvantages of these types of designs. Because between-subjects designs have different people in the experimental and control groups, a major consideration in using them is ensuring that participants in the two groups are equivalent in their personal characteristics. Experimenters can use two strategies to attain equivalence: simple random assignment of participants to conditions and matched random assignment.

SIMPLE RANDOM ASSIGNMENT   The strategy most often used to assign participants to groups is **simple random assignment.** When a participant arrives to take part in the experiment, the experimenter uses a random procedure, such as a table of random numbers or flipping a coin, to determine if the participant will be in the experimental or control condition. For example, an even number or "heads" could mean the control condition, and an odd number or "tails" the experimental condition. When you use random assignment, you assume that, because group assignments are random, members of the two groups will, on the average, have the same personal characteristics. For example, if some participants are unusually skilled at the research task and others unusually unskilled, then randomly assigning people to groups should put about half the skilled and half the unskilled people in each group. Consequently, the effects of their skill should cancel out when the groups' mean scores on the task are compared.

Consider an experiment that tests the effects of practice on memory (Kidd & Greenwald, 1988). Participants listen as the experimenter reads a 9-digit number to them; they then must correctly recall it. They do this 96 times. Participants in the ex-

TABLE 7-1   Effect of Simple Random Assignment

Simple random assignment evenly distributes people with different skill levels among the conditions of an experiment so that individual differences in skill do not affect the difference in the mean scores found in the conditions.

Experimental Condition	NINE-DIGIT NUMBERS RECALLED CORRECTLY		
	Effect of Skill	*Effect of Practice*	*Total Score*
Person A	70%	+20%	90%
Person B	60	+20	80
Person C	50	+20	70
Mean	60	+20	80
Control Condition			
Person D	70	0	70
Person E	60	0	60
Person F	50	0	50
Mean	60	0	60

perimental condition are given four task-relevant practice sessions before being tested "for record," whereas the participants in the control condition practice a different memory task. Without practice on the actual task, participants can correctly recall an average of 60% of the numbers. Let's assume that an unusually skilled person can correctly recall 70% of the numbers without practice and that an unusually unskilled person can recall 50%. Let's say you do an experiment such as this with six participants: two who happen to be highly skilled, two with average skill, and two with unusually low skill. Simple random assignment puts one person from each skill level into each condition of the experiment. The first column in Table 7-1 shows the effect of random assignment: The average skill level of each group is the same. Let's say that, as Kidd and Greenwald found, four task-relevant practice sessions added 20 percentage points to a person's score and that irrelevant practice neither helps nor hinders memory. The second column in Table 7-1 shows the effect of practice, and the third column shows the participants' total scores (skill plus practice effects). Because the different levels of skill are equally distributed between the two experimental conditions, the difference in the groups' mean total scores is the same as the effect of the independent variable: 20 percentage points. Random assignment therefore controls the effects of participant characteristics by balancing them out across groups. In research in which the independent variable is manipulated using material in a questionnaire, participants can also be randomly assigned to conditions by randomizing the experimental and control versions of the questionnaire before distributing them.

　　As an alternative to true random assignment, researchers sometimes use what might be called "quasi-random" assignment. Under this procedure, the researcher assigns participants alternately to the experimental and control conditions as they come to the laboratory: The first person to arrive goes into the experimental condition, the second to the control condition, the third to the experimental condition, and so forth. This procedure assumes that the order in which people arrive for the experiment is random so that the even-numbered people are, on the average, equivalent to the odd-numbered people. However, the validity of this assumption is open to question: People who are more motivated to participate in the study might arrive earlier, thereby inducing a self-selection bias into the experiment. Therefore, never use such quasi-random procedures.

Random assignment of participants to conditions does not guarantee that the members of the experimental and control group will be equivalent. Although equivalence or near-equivalence will be the most common outcome of randomization (Strube, 1991), there is a real, albeit small, possibility of the groups' being very different. For example, if you had a participant pool composed of 10 men and 10 women and randomly assigned them to experimental and control groups, there is about a 1 in 2,400 chance of getting a group with 8 or more men in it. These odds are probably good enough for most research, but researchers who want to can exercise more control over the characteristics of the members of the experimental and control group by matching the members of the groups on important personal characteristics.

MATCHED RANDOM ASSIGNMENT   With **matched random assignment** of participants to conditions, the researcher attempts to ensure that the members of the experimental and control groups are equivalent on one or more characteristics. The researcher does this by first measuring the characteristic and then balancing group membership on the characteristic. To continue with the example of participant sex, the researcher could guarantee that the groups were equivalent on this characteristic by randomly assigning half the men to the experimental group and half to the control group and doing the same for the women. Each group would then be composed of 5 men and 5 women.

Matching on physical characteristics of participants, such as sex, is fairly easy; for other characteristics, such as IQ and personality, it is more difficult. For these kinds of characteristics, you must first pretest all potential participants to determine their scores on the variable. You must then rank order the people by their scores and then divide them into pairs from the top down. The first member of each pair is randomly assigned to either the experimental or control group; the other member of the pair is assigned to the other group. Figure 7-1 illustrates this process for 10 people ranging in IQ score from 125 to 110. The mean IQ scores of the experimental and control groups are 116.8 and 116.0, a trivial difference. Nonrandom assignment, such as putting the odd-numbered people (those ranked first, third, and so on) in the experimental group and the even-numbered people in the control group, results in a larger difference in mean IQ scores: 117.4 for the experimental group and 116.0 for the control group. A major drawback of matched random assignment for psychological characteristics is the cost, in time, money, and resources, of pretesting. In addition, as discussed in Chapter 6, pretesting may cause internal validity problems. Matched random assignment is therefore normally used only when the control variable is known to have a strong effect on the dependent variable and the researcher wants stronger control over it than simple random assignment affords.

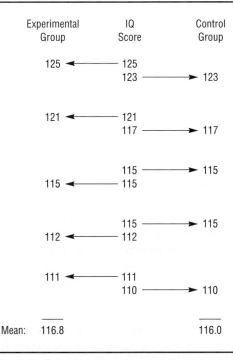

Experimental Group	IQ Score	Control Group
125 ←	125	
	123 →	123
121 ←	121	
	117 →	117
	115 →	115
115 ←	115	
	115 →	115
112 ←	112	
111 ←	111	
	110 →	110
Mean: 116.8		116.0

FIGURE 7-1   Matched Random Assignment
The researcher first measures the participants' scores on the matching variable (in this case IQ), rank orders participants by score, divides them into pairs, and randomly assigns the members of the pairs to the experimental and control conditions.

Within-Subjects Designs

In within-subjects (or repeated measures) designs, each research participant experiences both the experimental and control conditions of the independent variable. Consider, for example, the study of the effect of practice on memory for 9-digit numbers, discussed earlier. In a between-subjects design, each participant would be tested once, either after a task-relevant practice session or after a task-irrelevant practice session. In a within-subjects design, each participant would be tested twice, once after a task-relevant practice session and once after a task-irrelevant practice session. Let's look at some of the advantages and limitations of within-subjects designs.

ADVANTAGES RELATIVE TO BETWEEN-SUBJECTS DESIGNS Because participants in within-subjects designs take part in both the experimental and control conditions, these designs result in perfect equivalence of participants in both conditions. Because the same people are in each condition, the personal characteristics of the participants match perfectly. This perfect matching results in one of the primary advantages that within-subjects designs have over between-subjects designs: reduced error variance. This reduction in error variance means that within-subjects experiments are more likely than equivalent between-subjects experiments to produce statistically significant results. This advantage will be stronger to the extent that participant characteristics affect scores on the dependent variable. A second advantage of within-subjects designs is that because the same people participate in both the experimental and control conditions, a two-condition within-subjects design requires only half the participants required by the equivalent between-subjects design. This advantage can be especially useful when people are selected for participation in research on the basis of a rarely occurring characteristic, such as an unusual psychiatric disorder.

THE PROBLEM OF ORDER EFFECTS   Despite these advantages, researchers use within-subjects designs much less frequently than between-subjects designs. This less frequent use results from a set of disadvantages inherent in within-subjects designs referred to collectively as **order effects.** An order effect occurs when participants' scores on the dependent variable are affected by the order in which they experience the conditions of the independent variable. For example, participants might do better on whichever condition they experience second, regardless of whether it is the experimental or control condition. There are four general categories of order effects: practice effects, fatigue effects, carryover effects, and sensitization effects (Greenwald, 1976).

Practice effects are differences on the dependent variable that result from repeatedly performing the experimental task. For example, when people are faced with an unfamiliar task, they often do poorly the first time they try it but improve with practice. The more often the experiment requires them to engage in a task, the better participants become at it. Another kind of practice effect relates to the independent variable. Let's say you are conducting a study on the effects of stress, using background noise as the stressor. Over time, participants might habituate to, or become used to, the noise so that it has less effect on their performance. **Fatigue effects,** in contrast, result when participants become tired or bored from repeatedly performing the same task. Unlike practice effects, fatigue effects lead to decrements in performance.

Carryover effects occur when the effect of one condition of the experiment carries over to and affects participants' performance in another condition. Let's say you are conducting a study of the effects of caffeine consumption on reaction time. In the experimental condition you give participants a standardized dose of caffeine, and in the control condition you give them an inert substance. If participants take part in the caffeine condition first, the effects of the drug might still be present in their bodies when they take part in the control condition. The effects of the caffeine can then "carry over" and affect performance in the control condition. However, you wouldn't want to give all participants the inert substance first, because practice effects would be confounded with the effects of the caffeine in the experimental condition.

Sensitization effects are a form of reactivity: Experiencing one condition of the experiment affects their performance in the other condition. For example, Wexley, Yukl, Kovacs, and Sanders (1972) studied the effect of raters' exposure to very highly qualified and very poorly qualified job applicants on ratings of average applicants. Participants watched videotapes of three job interviews. In one condition, they saw the interviews of two highly qualified applicants prior to the interview of an average applicant; in another condition, participants saw the interviews of two poorly qualified applicants followed by that of an average applicant. When seen in isolation, the average applicant received a mean rating of 5.5 on a 9-point scale; when seen following the highly qualified applicants, the average applicant's mean rating was 2.5, whereas following the poorly qualified applicants the mean rating was 8.1.

Sensitization can also induce demand characteristics when exposure to more than one condition of the independent variable allows research participants to form hypotheses about the purpose of the research or calls forth a social desirability response bias. Let's say you're conducting a study on the effects of physical attractiveness on how likable a person is perceived to be. In one condition, you show participants a picture of a physically attractive person and in the other condition, a picture of a less attractive person. You ask participants to rate the person in the picture on the degree to which they thought they would like the person if they met him or her. Participants will probably respond naturally to the first picture, giving their true estimate of likability, but when they see the second picture, problems could arise. Because it is socially undesirable to evaluate people solely on the basis of appearance, participants might deliberately manipulate their responses giving the same rating to the person in the second picture that they gave to the person in the first picture, even if their true responses are different.

CONTROLLING ORDER EFFECTS   In some cases, the researcher can design a within-subjects experiment in ways that control for order effects. Practice effects can be controlled by **counterbalancing** the order in which participants experience the experimental and control conditions. Half the participants undergo the experimental condition first, and the other half undergo the control condition first. This procedure is designed to spread practice effects evenly across the conditions so that they cancel out when the conditions are compared. Counterbalancing is easy to carry out when an experiment has only two conditions. For example, the left side of Table 7-2 illustrates counterbalanced orders of conditions for a two-condition (Conditions A and B) experiment. As you see, there are only two orders in which participants can experience the conditions: A before B and B before A. However, as discussed later in this chapter, experiments frequently have three or more conditions; under these circumstances, counterbalancing becomes much more difficult because all possible orderings of conditions must be used: Each condition must appear in each position in the ordering sequence an equal number of times to balance the order in which participants experience the conditions, and each condition must follow every other condition an equal number of times to balance the sequencing of conditions. These rules are met for the three-condition (A, B, and C) experiment illustrated on the right side of Table 7-2. Condition A, for example, appears in each position in the order (first in rows 1 and 2, second in rows 3 and 5, and third in rows 4 and 6) and precedes Condition B twice (in rows 1 and 5) and follows Condition B twice (in rows 3 and 6). Notice that the three-condition experiment requires that participants be divided into six groups in order to completely counterbalance the order of conditions. The number of orders increases dramatically with the number of conditions: Four conditions would require 24 orders of conditions, and five conditions, 120 orders.

TABLE 7-2   Counterbalancing in Two- and Three-Condition Within-Subjects Experiments

Each condition appears in each order of the sequence, and each condition appears before and after every other condition.

Two Conditions		Three Conditions		
A	B	A	B	C
B	A	A	C	B
		B	A	C
		B	C	A
		C	A	B
		C	B	A

TABLE 7-3   Basic and Balanced Latin Squares Designs

	ORDER OF CONDITIONS								
	Basic Design					Balanced Design			
1	A	B	C	D	1	A	B	C	D
2	B	C	D	A	2	B	D	A	C
3	C	D	A	B	3	C	A	D	B
4	D	A	B	C	4	D	C	B	A

Because the number of condition orders required by complete counterbalancing can quickly become enormous as the number of conditions increases, partial counterbalancing is frequently used for more than three conditions. One way to partially counterbalance is to randomly assign a different order of conditions to each participant. A more systematic technique is to use a **Latin square design.** In this design the number of orders is equal to the number of conditions, with each condition appearing in each place in the order. The left side of Table 7-3 shows the basic Latin square design for a four-condition experiment. As you can see, each of the conditions comes in each of the possible places in the four orders. For example, Condition A comes first in row 1, fourth in row 2, third in row 3, and second in row 4. The basic Latin square design therefore balances the order of conditions, but not their sequencing. For example, except when it comes first in a row, Condition B always follows Condition A and precedes Condition C. Sequencing can be partially controlled by using a balanced Latin square design: each condition is preceded once by every other condition. For example, in the balanced design on the right side of Table 7-3, Condition B is preceded by Condition A in row 1, by Condition D in row 3, and by Condition C in row 4. Although the balanced Latin square design controls the sequencing of pairs of conditions, it does not control

TABLE 7-4 Differential Order Effects

Order of participation in the conditions has a greater effect when the experimental condition is experienced after the control condition.

	CONDITION		
	Experimental (E)	Control (C)	Difference
True performance level	40	30	10
Order effect for E → C	0	10	
Order effect for C → E	20	0	
Observed Score	60	40	20

higher order sequences; for example, the sequence ABC precedes, but does not follow, Condition D.

Counterbalancing can also be used to distribute carryover effects across conditions. However, it is better to also insert a **washout period** between conditions. A washout period is a period of time over which the effects of a condition dissipate. For example, in the hypothetical caffeine study described earlier, you might have participants undergo one condition one day and have them come back for the other condition the next day without consuming any caffeine in the meanwhile. The purpose of this procedure is to allow the caffeine to "wash out" of the bodies of those participants who experienced the experimental condition first so that it does not affect their performance in the control condition. The washout period might be minutes, hours, or days, depending on how long the effects of a condition can be expected to last.

Sensitization effects are harder to control than practice or carryover effects. Although counterbalancing will spread these effects across conditions, it will not eliminate the effects of any demand characteristics produced. Therefore, it is best not to use a within-subjects design when sensitization effects are likely to produce demand characteristics, as in the physical attractiveness example given earlier.

The use of counterbalancing assumes that order effects are equal regardless of the sequence in which participants experience the conditions. For example, in a two-condition experiment, counterbalancing assumes that the order effect for participating in the experimental condition (E) first is the same as the order effect for participating in the control condition (C) first. Table 7-4 illustrates this **differential order effect.** The true effect of the independent variable is to increase participants' scores on the dependent variable by 10 points in the experimental condition compared to the control condition. Experiencing the experimental condition first adds another 10 points to their scores in the control condition. However, experiencing the control condition first adds 20 points to the scores in the experimental condition. This differential order effect (C before E greater than E before C) artificially increases the observed difference between the conditions by 10 points, resulting in an overestimation of the effect of the independent variable. Order effects can be detected by using a factorial experimental design, discussed later in the chapter.

WHEN ORDER EFFECTS ARE GOOD   Before leaving the topic of order effects, it is important to note that order effects are not always bad; sometimes, researchers want an order effect because it is the variable being studied. For example, an educational researcher might be interested in the effects of practice on learning, a psychopharmacologist might be interested in carryover effects of drugs, or a person studying achievement motivation might be interested in sensitization effects, such as the effect on motivation of success followed by failure compared to the effect of failure followed by success. In none of these cases would it be appropriate to control order effects.

MULTIPLE-GROUP DESIGNS

As noted, experiments often consist of more than the traditional two groups, experimental and control. Experiments with more than two groups can be referred to as **multiple-group designs.** Multiple-group experiments (as well as two-group experiments) can involve either quantitative independent variables or qualitative independent variables. Quantitative independent variables vary by degree; the conditions of the independent variable—called *levels* in these cases—represent more or less of the independent variable. Drug dosage and the amount of time that person is allowed to study material before being tested on it are examples of quantitative independent variables. Qualitative independent variables vary by quality; the conditions of the independent variable represent different types or aspects of the independent variable. Different brands of drugs and the conditions under which a person studies are examples of qualitative independent variables. Let's look at examples of research using each type of independent variable. Although these examples each use three levels or conditions of the independent variable, multiple-group designs can have as many groups as are needed to test the hypotheses being studied.

Quantitative Independent Variables

When studying the effects of quantitative independent variables, researchers are usually interested in determining the effects on the dependent variable of adding more of the independent variable. These effects can be classified in terms of two general categories of relationships that can exist between an independent variable and a dependent variable. In **linear relationships,** scores on the dependent variable increase or decrease constantly as the level of the independent variable increases or decreases; the relationship can be graphed as a straight line. Panels (a) and (b) of Figure 7-2 illustrate the two types of linear relations. In a **positive relationship,** panel (a), scores on the dependent variable increase as the level of the independent variable increases; in a **negative relationship,** panel (b), scores on the dependent variable decrease as the level of the independent variable increases. In the second category of relationships, **curvilinear relationships,** the relationship between the independent variable and the dependent variable takes a form other than a straight line. Panel (c) of Figure 7-2 illustrates some curvilinear relationships.

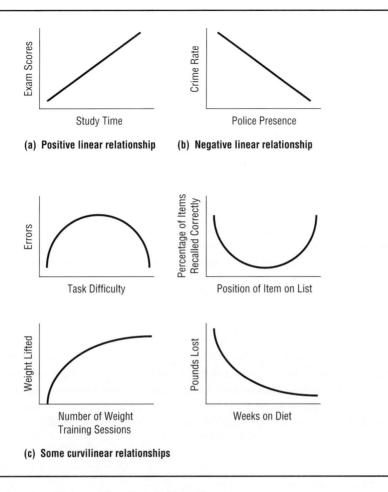

(a) Positive linear relationship   (b) Negative linear relationship

(c) Some curvilinear relationships

FIGURE 7-2 Examples of Linear and Curvilinear Relationships

When you study the effects of a quantitative variable, it is important to use at least three levels of the variable. If there is a curvilinear relationship between the independent variable and the dependent variable, it can be found *only* if there are more than two levels of the independent variable. Why? If you have only two points on a graph, you can draw only a straight line between the two points, which represents a linear relationship. If you have more than two points, you can draw a curved line if that's what the points represent. This idea is illustrated by three studies on the effect of a person's degree of responsibility for a crime on how much punishment people think is appropriate.

DeJong, Morris, and Hastorf (1976) conducted an experiment in which people read a summary of an armed robbery trial; the defendant was one of two men who took part in the crime. In one version of the summary, the defendant had a high degree of

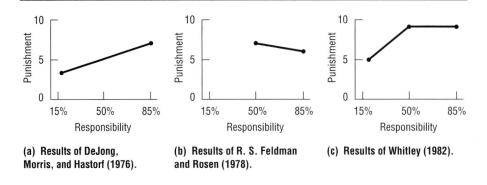

(a) Results of DeJong, Morris, and Hastorf (1976).

(b) Results of R. S. Feldman and Rosen (1978).

(c) Results of Whitley (1982).

FIGURE 7-3   Using Three Levels of a Quantitative Independent Variable
Only when all three levels are used does the true curvilinear relationship between the variables become apparent.

responsibility for planning and executing the crime; in another version, he had a lesser degree of responsibility. At the trial, the defendant pleaded guilty to the charge of robbery. DeJong et al. asked the research participants to assign a prison sentence, with a maximum of 10 years, to the defendant. People who had read the summary in which the defendant had a greater responsibility for the crime assigned longer sentences than people who had read the less-responsibility summary. Feldman and Rosen (1978) tried to replicate the study but found no relationship between degree of responsibility for the crime and the punishment assigned by research participants: Both criminals were assigned sentences of about the same length. When I read the reports of these studies, I noticed a feature that could, perhaps, account for the contradictory results. Although both studies operationally defined high responsibility in similar terms (about 85% responsible), they defined lesser responsibility differently: DeJong et al. used a low level of responsibility (about 15%) whereas Feldman and Rosen's defendant had equal responsibility with his accomplice (about 50%). Panels (a) and (b) of Figure 7-3 illustrate the results of these studies. I therefore conducted a replication of the studies using a three-group design in which the defendant had 15%, or 50%, or 85% responsibility for the crime (Whitley, 1982). The results of my study, illustrated in panel (c) of Figure 7-3, showed a curvilinear relationship between responsibility and punishment: punishment rose as responsibility increased up to 50% and then leveled off. These results replicated those of both DeJong et al. (1976) and Feldman and Rosen (1978).

As these studies show, it is extremely important to look for curvilinear effects when studying quantitative independent variables. It would be appropriate to use just two groups only if there is a substantial body of research using multiple-group designs that showed that only a linear relationship existed between the independent and dependent variables that you are studying. However, when using multiple levels of an independent variable you should ensure that the levels represent the entire range of the variable. For example, DeJong et al. (1976) could have used three levels of responsibility—say, 15%, 33%, and 50%—and still not have detected the curvilinear relationship because the curve begins beyond that range of values. Similarly, Feldman and Rosen (1978) would still have concluded that no relationship existed if they had used 50%, 67%, and 85% as their levels of responsibility.

Qualitative Independent Variables

Multiple-group designs that use qualitative independent variables compare conditions that differ in characteristics rather than amount. For example, a researcher might be interested in how research participants react to people who are depressed compared to people who are schizophrenic and to people having no psychiatric diagnosis. Qualitative independent variables are also involved when a study requires more than one control group. For example, in the study described earlier, Bransford and Johnson (1972) had one experimental group, those who were given the context before the information, and two control groups, no context and context after the information. One can also have one control group and more than one experimental group. Kremer and Stephens (1983), for example, wanted to see whether information about the state of mind of a rude person affected how victims of the rudeness evaluated the person and how the timing of the information affected evaluations. Research participants were annoyed by a confederate of the researchers who was acting as an experimenter for the study. They were then put into one of three conditions. In one experimental condition, another person posing as a colleague of the experimenter told the participants immediately after they had been rudely treated that the confederate had been having a bad day and did not usually act like that. Participants in the second experimental condition received the same information, but only after a delay of several minutes. Participants in the baseline condition received no information about the experimenter's state of mind. All participants were given an opportunity to evaluate the experimenter by recommending, using a 7-point scale, whether he should continue to receive research funding, with a rating of 1 meaning "Give the funds to someone else" and a rating of 7 meaning "Give the funds to the experimenter." The results of the study are illustrated in Figure 7-4: Information about the confederate's state of mind led to more positive evaluations, but only if the participants received the information immediately after being annoyed.

Interpreting the Results of Multiple-Group Experiments

Multiple-group designs are very useful to the research psychologist, potentially providing a wealth of information unavailable from two-group designs and providing additional controls for threats to the internal validity of the research. However, a potential pitfall exists in the interpretation of the results of the statistical analysis of these designs. The data from multiple-group designs are analyzed using what is known as a one-way ANOVA, which was designed for this purpose. The statistical test in ANOVA is the F test, which is analogous to the t test in two-group designs. A statistically significant F value means that out of all the possible two-group comparisons among the group means, at least one comparison is statistically significant; however, it does not tell you *which* comparison is significant. For example, Kremer and Stephens's (1983) data

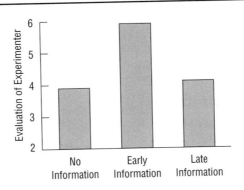

Note: Results of Kremer & Stephens, 1983.

FIGURE 7-4   Two Experimental Conditions Compare the Timing of Information to a No-Information Control Condition
The difference between the early and late information conditions shows the importance of the timing of presentation of the information.

analysis found a significant F value, but it did not tell them which of the three comparisons among group means was significant (Figure 7-4): no information versus early information, no information versus late information, or early information versus late information.

To determine the significant difference or differences, you must conduct a **post hoc** (or after-the-fact) **analysis,** which directly compares the group means. When you have specific hypotheses about differences in means, the comparisons among those means are made with **a priori** (or preplanned) **contrasts.** Similar comparisons must be made when a quantitative independent variable is used to determine where the significant differences among groups lie. There are also specific a priori contrasts that help you determine if the effect found is linear or curvilinear. Kremer and Stephens's (1983) a priori contrast analysis found that the differences between the means of the early-information and no-information groups and between the early-information and late-information groups were significant, but that the difference between the no-information and late-information groups was not. These results showed that both the information and the timing of the information affected evaluations of the confederate.

Never interpret the results of a multiple-group experiment solely on the basis of the F test; the appropriate post hoc or a priori analyses should always be conducted. Most statistics textbooks describe how to conduct these analyses.

FACTORIAL DESIGNS

Up to this point, the discussion of research has assumed that any one study uses only one independent variable. However, much, if not most, research in behavioral science uses two or more independent variables. Designs with multiple independent variables are called **factorial designs;** each independent variable is a factor in the design. This section looks at the nature of factorial designs, discusses the interpretation of interaction effects, considers some of the uses of factorial designs, and examines some of the forms that factorial designs can take.

The Nature of Factorial Designs

Factorial designs can be very complex, so this section introduces the topic by discussing the shorthand that researchers use to describe factorial designs, the kinds of information that factorial designs provide, and the various outcomes that can result when factorial designs are used.

DESCRIBING FACTORIAL DESIGNS   By convention, a factorial design is described in terms of the number of independent variables it uses and the number of conditions or levels of each independent variable. A 2 × 2 (read as "2 by 2") design, for example, has two independent variables, each with two conditions. The number of numbers (in this case the two 2s) indicates the number of independent variables; the numbers themselves indicate the number of conditions of each independent variable. A 3 × 2 design has two independent variables, one with three conditions (indicated by the 3) and the other with two conditions (indicated by the 2); a 3 × 2 × 2 design has three independent variables, one with three conditions and the others with two conditions each. For the sake of simplicity, most of this discussion of factorial designs deals only with 2 × 2 designs. Bear in mind, however, that the same principles apply to all factorial designs regardless of complexity.

INFORMATION PROVIDED BY FACTORIAL DESIGNS   Factorial designs provide two types of information about the effects of the independent variables. A **main effect** is the effect that one independent variable has independently of the effect of the other independent variable. The main effect of an independent variable represents what you would have found if you conducted the experiment using only that independent variable and ignored the possible effects of the other independent variable. For example, if you studied the effects of frustration on aggression in men and women, the main effect for frustration is the difference in mean aggression scores between the frustrated group and the nonfrustrated group ignoring the fact that both groups were composed of both men and women. An **interaction effect** (or simply "interaction") occurs when two or more independent variables combine to produce an effect over and above their main effects. Interactions can be seen only when the effects of two or more independent variables are considered simultaneously; consequently, interaction effects can be found only when a factorial design is used.

Let's look at a study conducted by Platz and Hosch (1988) as an example of a factorial design. Platz and Hosch were interested in the accuracy of cross-racial identifications, specifically in whether people are able to identify members of their own races more accurately than members of other races. Although Platz and Hosch used a 3 × 3 design, for now let's consider only two conditions of each of the independent variables. They had Black confederates and White confederates buy something in a convenience

TABLE 7-5   Partial Results of Platz and Hosch's (1988) Study of Cross-Racial Identification: Percentage of Correct Identifications

Black and White clerks were equally accurate in identifying White customers, but Black clerks were more accurate in identifying Black customers.

	CUSTOMER		
	White	Black	Clerk Average
White clerk	53%	40%	47%
Black clerk	55	64	59
Customer average	54	52	

Note: Percentages are rounded to nearest whole number.

store staffed by Black clerks or White clerks. Two hours later, the clerks were asked to pick the customers out from sets of facial photographs. The researchers found that identification accuracy depended on both the race of the clerk and the race of the customer; the percentage of correct choices made by the clerks, arranged by race of clerk and race of customer, are shown in Table 7-5 and Figure 7-5. The row in Table 7-5 labeled "Customer Average" shows the main effect for customer race: 54% of the clerks (ignoring race of clerk) correctly identified the White customer, and 52% of the clerks correctly identified the Black customer. If this were a two-group experiment with race of customer as the independent variable, one would conclude that race of customer had no influence on accuracy of identification. The column labeled "Clerk Average" shows the main effect for race of clerk (ignoring race of customer): 47% of the White clerks made correct identifications, and 59% of the Black clerks made correct identifications. Because this difference was not statistically significant, if this were a two-group study with race of clerk as the independent variable, one would conclude that race of clerk is unrelated to accuracy of identification.

However, as you can see from the percentages in Table 7-5 and the graphs in Figure 7-5, both of these conclusions would be wrong. In actuality, both race of clerk and race of customer were related to accuracy of identification: Clerks were more accurate in identifying members of their own race than members of the other race. However, White customers were identified with equal accuracy by White and Black clerks. Accuracy was determined neither by race of clerk alone nor by race of customer alone but, rather, by the unique combined effect, or interaction, of the variables.

The data from factorial experiments are analyzed using a form of ANOVA designed for this purpose. The ANOVA provides a test of the statistical significance of each main effect and interaction. If the interaction effect is not significant, the results of the experiment can be interpreted as if two experiments were conducted, one with each of the independent variables. If the interaction effect is significant, the interpretation of the results becomes more complex.

OUTCOMES OF FACTORIAL DESIGNS   There are eight possible outcomes of a 2 × 2 factorial design: There may or may not be an effect for the first independent variable, there may

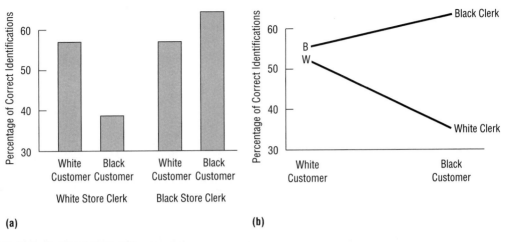

(a)   (b)

Note: Partial results of Platz & Hosch, 1988.

FIGURE 7-5
Black and White clerks were equally accurate in identifying White customers, but Black clerks were more accurate in identifying Black customers. Whenever the lines on a line graph are not parallel there is an interaction effect.

or may not be an effect for the second independent variable, and the independent variables may or may not interact. Examples of these outcomes are illustrated in Figure 7-6, which uses a hypothetical experiment with aggression as the dependent variable, and sex of participant and whether or not the participants have a frustrating experience as the independent variables. These results are completely fictitious; they do not illustrate the results of any real experiments. However, they do provide good concrete illustrations of the possible outcomes of a 2 × 2 experiment.

Each panel in Figure 7-6 on pages 208–209 has two parts: a table of means and a graph of those means. The first four panels illustrate situations in which there is no interaction. In panel (a), neither independent variable has an effect, in panels (b) and (c), only one independent variable has an effect, and in panel (d), both independent variables have effects. Panels (e), (f), and (g) illustrate outcomes that include both main effects and interactions. Panel (h) illustrates a situation in which there is an interaction but no main effects. Note that whenever there is an interaction, the lines in the graph are not parallel.

Interaction Effects

Factorial designs are quite common in behavioral science research, and they frequently find interaction effects. These effects can be difficult to interpret. Let's look first at the ways of displaying interaction effects in research reports and then at how to go about interpreting them.

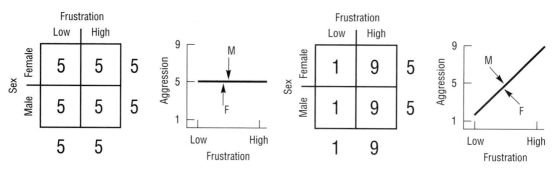

(a) No main effects and no interaction

(b) Main effect for frustration, no main effect for sex, no interaction

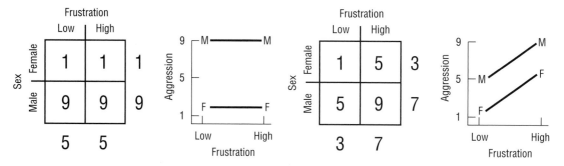

(c) No main effect for frustration, main effect for sex, no interaction

(d) Main effect for frustration, main effect for sex, no interaction

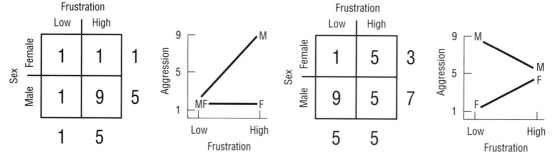

(e) Main effect for frustration, main effect for sex, sex by frustration interaction

(f) No main effect for frustration, main effect for sex, sex by frustration interaction

FIGURE 7-6   Possible Outcomes of a 2 × 2 Factorial Design

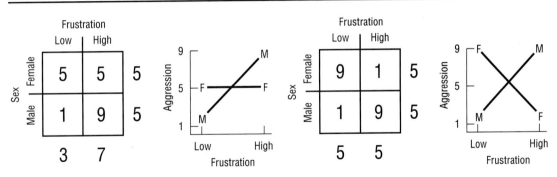

(g) Main effect for frustration, no main effect for sex, sex by frustration interaction

(h) No main effects, sex by frustration interaction

FIGURE 7-6   *(continued)*

DISPLAYING INTERACTIONS   The results of a factorial experiment can be displayed either in the form of a table, as in Table 7-5 and Figure 7-6, or in the form of a graph, as in the examples in Figures 7-5 and 7-6. A tabular display typically takes the form of a matrix, with each cell in the matrix representing one combination of the independent variables. For example, the upper left-hand cell in Table 7-5 represents what happened when White clerks were asked to identify a White customer. The decision about which independent variable goes across the top of the matrix and which goes along the side is essentially arbitrary; the placement that most clearly illustrates the results is normally used. The main effects—the means of the conditions of one independent variable averaged across the conditions of the other independent variable—can be displayed at the bottom and right edge of the table as shown in Table 7-5.

When the independent variables are qualitative variables, as in the Platz and Hosch (1988) experiment, the results can be graphed in the form of a histogram, as in panel (a) of Figure 7-5. For quantitative independent variables and qualitative variables in simpler factorial designs, a line graph can be used, as in panel (b) of Figure 7-5 and in Figure 7-6. In the line graph format, the conditions of one independent variable are arranged along the horizontal (X) axis—race of customer in Figure 7-5(b) and frustration level in Figure 7-6—and the means for each combination of conditions of the independent variables are plotted using the vertical (Y) axis for the dependent variable. Lines connect the points within conditions of the second independent variable.

INTERPRETING INTERACTIONS   When interpreting interaction effects, it can be useful to think of a piece of research as a question. The question is "Does the independent variable have an effect on the dependent variable?" When the outcome is one or more main effects without an interaction, the answer is a simple yes. When the outcome is an interaction, with or without main effects, the answer is "It depends": The answer for one independent variable depends on the condition of the other independent variable. For example, in the Platz and Hosch (1988) study, one question was "Is a person's race

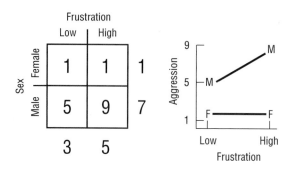

FIGURE 7-7   Hypothetical Experimental Results Illustrating the Presence of Both an Interaction and a True Main Effect
The effect of frustration is different for men and women, but men score higher than women regardless of frustration level.

related to the accuracy with which the person can identify another person?" The answer, as we saw in Table 7-5 and Figure 7-5, is not a simple yes or no; it depends on the race of the other person. Black participants were more accurate in identifying Black people, and White participants were more accurate in identifying White people. The other question asked by Platz and Hosch study was "Does a person's race affect how accurately that person is identified by someone else?" Again, the answer is "It depends," this time on the race of the person making the identification. White people were identified with equal accuracy by Black and White participants, but Black people were more accurately identified by Black participants than by White participants.

The "it depends" nature of interactions has an important implication for understanding the results of research: If the research produces an interaction, any main effects found may be deceptive, representing statistical artifact rather than a true main effect of the independent variable. Consequently, if the statistical analysis finds both a main effect and an interaction, the main effect for one independent variable may apply only to one condition of the other independent variable, not to both conditions. For example, Figure 7-6(e) illustrates a situation in which there are two main effects—the average aggression score for men is higher than that for women and higher for participants in the high-frustration condition than for those in the low-frustration condition—and an interaction—men who experienced high frustration were more aggressive than the participants in any of the other conditions. Notice, however, that sex of participant is related to aggression only in the high-frustration condition; there is no sex difference in the low-frustration condition. Similarly, differences in frustration lead to differences in aggression only for men; women respond to both high and low frustration with the same level of aggression.

However, sometimes there can be both an interaction and a true main effect. Figure 7-7 illustrates this situation. In this hypothetical outcome of a frustration-aggression experiment, women's aggression is, as in the last example, still unaffected by level of

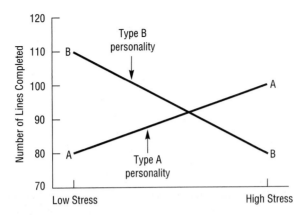

Note: Results of Fazio, Cooper, Dayson, & Johnson, 1981.

FIGURE 7-8   Quality of Task Performance Was an Interactive Function of Stress and Personality Type

frustration and men's aggression increases with level of frustration. However, unlike Figure 7-6(e), men are more aggressive than women in both the high- and low-frustration conditions. Thus, men are more aggressive overall than are women and men's aggression is influenced by level of frustration whereas women's aggression is not.

When there is an interaction but no main effects, the effect of one independent variable in one condition of the second independent variable is reversed in the other condition of the second independent variable. This phenomenon can be seen in the results of a study conducted by Fazio, Cooper, Dayson, and Johnson (1981). One independent variable in their study was the personality type of their participants, Type A or Type B. One characteristic of Type A people is that they find it easier to ignore stress than do Type B people. The other independent variable was the degree of stress that the participants underwent while they performed a proofreading task. The dependent variable was the number of lines the participants could proof in a given amount of time. The results of the study are shown in Figure 7-8. Type A people performed better under high stress than under low stress, whereas Type B people performed better under low stress than under high stress: Stress had opposite effects on performance depending on personality type.

When you face a significant interaction effect in a factorial design, you are in a position much like that which occurs when you find a significant F value in a multiple group design: There is a significant difference somewhere among the means, but you do not yet know where the difference or differences lie. Again the solution is to conduct post hoc comparisons if the hypothesis did not predict a particular form of interaction. If the hypothesis did specify a particular outcome, then a priori contrasts should be used. For example, a replication of the Platz and Hosch (1988) study would hypothesize that people would make more accurate identifications of members of their own races. This hypothesis would be tested statistically by grouping research participants by race and comparing their accuracy in identifying members of their own and other races. Most statistics textbooks discuss the use of both a priori and post hoc contrasts in factorial designs.

Forms of Factorial Designs

Factorial designs can take a number of forms, depending on whether the independent variables are manipulated in a between-subjects or within-subjects format, whether the independent variables are manipulated or measured, the number of independent variables, and the number of conditions of the independent variables.

BETWEEN- AND WITHIN-SUBJECTS DESIGNS   The independent variables in a factorial design can be between-subjects variables, or within-subjects variables, or a combination of the two. The two most common designs are probably completely between-subjects designs and mixed between-within designs. Platz and Hosch (1988), for example, used a mixed between-within design. Race of store clerk was the between-subjects variable. Race of customer was manipulated as a within-subjects variable by having both a White customer and a Black customer interact with each clerk, and each clerk was asked to identify the Black customer from a set of photographs of Black men and the White customer from a set of photographs of White men. Platz and Hosch counterbalanced the order in which the customers dealt with the clerk and the order in which the clerks saw the sets of photographs. The between-within procedure allowed Platz and Hosch to use fewer store clerks as research participants than a completely between-subjects design would have required. This economy was necessary because the stores that gave their permission to be used for the research employed only one quarter as many Black clerks as White clerks. The within-subjects aspect of the design also allowed the researchers to control for possible individual differences in the clerks' abilities to remember faces. Because each clerk interacted with both a Black customer and a White customer, differences in memory ability could not be accidentally confounded with race of customer.

Special forms of ANOVA are required for the analysis of data from mixed between-within designs. If you plan to conduct such a study, consult a statistics text to ensure that you understand those procedures.

MANIPULATED AND MEASURED INDEPENDENT VARIABLES   The independent variable in a true experiment is manipulated by the experimenter. However, researchers are often interested in variables, such as personality traits, that cannot be manipulated but can only be measured, and in the interactions between measured and manipulated variables. Consequently, one frequently sees research using factorial designs in which at least one of the independent variables is measured rather than manipulated. For example, Fazio et al. (1981) manipulated level of stress but measured personality type; Platz and Hosch (1988) manipulated race of customer but measured race of clerk. As noted in Chapter 2, measured independent variables result in correlational rather than experimental research. Mixed experimental-correlational designs such as those used by Fazio et al. and by Platz and Hosch can be quite useful, but be careful in interpreting their results.

Remember that correlational research can never determine whether changes in the level or condition of an independent variable cause changes in a dependent variable; it can determine only if a relationship exists between the variables. Therefore, be careful never to interpret the results of the correlational part of a mixed correlational-experimental study as indicating causality. For example, Fazio et al. could not correctly say that personality type caused differences in performance on the research task, only that it was related to those differences. However, because they manipulated level of stress, they could legitimately say that stress caused differences in performance.

It is also possible to have factorial designs in which all the independent variables are correlational. For example, McFatter (1994) examined the relationships of two personality characteristics—introversion-extraversion and neuroticism—to mood. He noted that most previous research had examined the separate relationship of each variable to mood but that little research had considered both in the same study. McFatter found an interaction between introversion-extraversion and neuroticism: Neurotic introverts reported less positive mood and more negative mood than did people with other combinations of the traits. In this case, of course, McFatter could not interpret his findings in causal terms. The next chapter discusses correlational research in detail.

DESIGN COMPLEXITY   The examples of factorial designs used so far in this discussion have all been 2×2 designs. However, in principle there is no limit on the number of independent variables one can have or on the number of levels or conditions per independent variable. For example, although we have looked at the Platz and Hosch study as a 2×2 design, they actually used a 3×3 design: They included Hispanic customers and clerks as well as Black and White customers and clerks. Sprecher, McKinney, and Orbuch (1987) used a $2 \times 2 \times 2 \times 2$ design to investigate the factors that influence people's evaluation of other people whom they learn are sexually active. The independent variables were the sex of the person being evaluated, the age of the person (16 or 21), the type of relationship in which the sexual behavior took place (casual or close), and sex of the research participant.

Although there is no theoretical limit on the number of independent variables or number of conditions, studies rarely use more than three independent variables or three conditions per independent variable. The reason for this limitation is practical: The total number of conditions in the study increases quickly as the number of independent variables and number of conditions per independent variable increase. For example, as shown in Figure 7-6, a 2×2 design has a total of four conditions: all the possible combinations of the two conditions of each of the two independent variables. A 3×3 design, such as Platz and Hosch's (1988), has 9 conditions, and a $2 \times 2 \times 2 \times 2$ design, such as Sprecher et al.'s (1987), has 16 conditions. Note that the total number of conditions is the product of the number of conditions of the independent variables: $2 \times 2 = 4$, $3 \times 3 = 9$, $2 \times 2 \times 2 \times 2 = 16$, and so forth. As the total number of conditions increases, the number of research participants needed in a between-subjects design increases: With 10 participants per condition, a 2×2 design requires 40 participants but a $2 \times 2 \times 2 \times 2$ design requires 160. In addition, the complexity of the data analysis and of the interpretation of the results of that analysis increases. Consequently, most researchers limit themselves to relatively simple designs.

Uses for Factorial Designs

Factorial designs are fairly complex, requiring two or more independent variables and multiple groups of participants, one group for each combination of the independent variables. Why should you bother with this complexity when you can determine the effect of an independent variable with a simpler design? Factorial designs can be used to test hypotheses about moderator variables, to detect order effects in counterbalanced within-subjects designs, and to control extraneous variance by a technique called *blocking*.

TESTING MODERATOR HYPOTHESES   The discussion of the "it depends" nature of interactions probably reminded you of the discussion of moderator variables in Chapter 1. As you recall, a **moderator variable** changes the effect of an independent variable: the effect of the independent variable is different under different conditions of the moderator variable. Thus, in the Platz and Hosch (1988) study, you could say that race of store clerk moderated the effect that race of customer had on accuracy of identification. You could also look at it the other way and say that race of customer moderated the relationship between race of clerk and accuracy of identification. The variable you consider the moderator variable depends on your frame of reference — that is, on which variable you conceptualize as the independent variable being studied and which as the moderator variable influencing the effect of the independent variable. If you are testing a theory, the theory often provides the frame of reference, designating which variables are independent variables and which are moderator variables. Note, however, that because the effect of a moderator variable takes the form of an interaction, the hypothesis that one variable moderates the effect of another can be tested only with a factorial design and will be supported only if the predicted interaction is found.

DETECTING ORDER EFFECTS   Order effects present a potential threat to the validity of the conclusions that can be drawn from the research using within-subjects designs. When the order of conditions is counterbalanced, researchers can detect the presence and size of order effects by using a between-within factorial design, with the independent variable being tested as the within-subjects factor and order of conditions (experimental before control and control before experimental) as the between-subjects factor. Some possible outcomes of this procedure are shown in Table 7-6. The top panel shows an outcome in which the independent variable had an effect and there was no order effect. In this case, there will be a main effect for the independent variable (the mean for the experimental condition is 10 points greater than the mean for the control condition), no main effect for the order factor (the two order means are equal), and no interaction effect. The middle panel shows the outcome for the same experiment when there is an order effect that is the same for both orders. There is a main effect for the independent variable and no order effect, but there is an interaction between the conditions of the independent variable and the order in which participants experienced the conditions. In this case, experiencing a condition as the second condition added 10 points to the participants' scores. Because the order effect happens to be the same as the effect of the independent variable, there is no difference between the means in the experimental and control conditions for participants who experienced the experimental condition

TABLE 7-6   Use of Between-Within Designs to Detect Order Effects

No Order Effect
There is a main effect for condition, no main effect for order, and no interaction.

| | CONDITION | | |
	Experimental (E)	Control (C)	Order Mean
Order E → C	40	30	35
Order C → E	40	30	35
Condition Mean	40	30	

Equal Order Effects
There is a main effect for condition, no main effect for order, and an interaction.

| | CONDITION | | |
	Experimental (E)	Control (C)	Order Mean
Order E → C	40	40	40
Order C → E	50	30	40
Condition Mean	45	35	

Differential Order Effects
There are main effects for condition and order, and an interaction.

| | CONDITION | | |
	Experimental (E)	Control (C)	Order Mean
Order E → C	40	40	40
Order C → E	60	30	45
Condition Mean	50	35	

first, and an exaggerated difference for those who experienced the control condition first. Note, however, that because the order effect was the same for both orders, the difference between the means for the experimental and control conditions reflects the true difference between the means. The bottom panel of Table 7-6 shows the outcome with a differential order effect, in which experiencing the control condition second added 10 points to a person's score, whereas experiencing the experimental condition second added 20 points. In this case, there are main effects for both the independent variable and order, as well as an interaction between the two. Note also that the difference in means in the experimental and control conditions is greater than the true difference shown in the top panel.

Although order effects contaminate one's data, all is not lost. Note that order effects do not affect the scores in the condition that participants experience first. Consequently, one can analyze the experimental and control data from the experimental-first and control-first participants as a between-subjects design and still test the hypothesis. The cost of this procedure is the loss of the advantages of a within-subjects design, but

TABLE 7-7   Effect of Blocking on an Extraneous Variable on Statistical Analysis

Blocking increases the sensitivity of the statistical test by reducing the error variance.

Scores

Experimental Group		Control Group	
M1	13	M7	15
M2	21	M8	13
M3	17	M9	9
M4	14	M10	9
M5	15	M11	8
M6	11	M12	11
F1	16	F7	19
F2	16	F8	16
F3	22	F9	18
F4	20	F10	23
F5	21	F11	14
F6	19	F12	15

Analysis of Two-Group Design

Source of Variance	Degrees of Freedom	Mean Square	F	p
Conditions	1	45.37	2.71	ns
Error	22	16.75		

Analysis of 2 (Condition) × 2 (Sex) Design

Source of Variance	Degrees of Freedom	Mean Square	F	p
Conditions	1	45.37	4.57	< .05
Sex	1	155.04	15.63	< .001
Interaction	1	15.05	1.52	ns
Error	20	9.92		

Note: M = male participants, F = female participants.

the benefit is the ability to draw valid conclusions from the data. Order effects are always potential threats to the validity of within-subjects designs, so researchers should always test to see if these effects are contaminating their data.

BLOCKING ON EXTRANEOUS VARIABLES   Recall that from a statistical point of view any variance not attributable to an independent variable is error variance and that extraneous variables are one source of such variance. One way in which researchers can deal with the effects of extraneous variables is to include them as independent variables in a factorial design. A factorial ANOVA will remove the variance due to the extraneous variable and its interaction with the independent variable from the error variance and treat

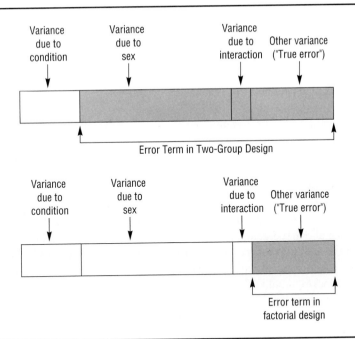

FIGURE 7-9   Blocking Reduces the Error Term for the Statistical Analysis
When the variance due to sex and the sex by condition interaction is "pulled out" of the error term by block-ing on sex, then the size of the error term is reduced, increasing the likelihood of statistical significance for the *F* test.

it as variance due to an independent variable and to the interaction of two independent variables. This procedure can reduce the error variance and so increase the sensitivity of the statistical test of the effect of the independent variable. Consider the data pre-sented in the top panel of Table 7-7, which come from a hypothetical experiment in which the researcher ensured that equal numbers of men and women participated in the experimental and control conditions. The experimental group had a mean score of 16.9 and the control group a mean score of 14.2; however, as shown by the statistical analysis in the middle panel of the table, this difference was not statistically significant. The statistical analysis shown in the bottom panel of the table shows what happens when the participants are blocked on sex. **Blocking** means that the participants are grouped according to an extraneous variable and that variable is added as a factor in the design. The new analysis finds significant effects for both the independent variable and for participant sex, with women, who had a mean score of 18.1, performing better than men, who had a mean score of 13.0.

The numbers in the "Mean Square" columns in the middle and bottom panels of Table 7-7 represent the amount of variance in the dependent variable attributable to each factor in the design, including error. The bottom panel shows that participant sex accounted for much more variance in the dependent variable than did the indepen-dent variable. As illustrated in Figure 7-9, this variance, along with the nonsignificant variance accounted for by the interaction, was treated as part of the error variance in the analysis shown in the middle panel, increasing the size of that error variance. The variance attributable to the independent variable is the same in both analyses. Because the F test is the ratio of the variance due to an independent variable to the error variance, the F value in the middle panel is smaller than that in the bottom panel. An experimenter who ignored the effect of participant sex as an extraneous variable would incorrectly conclude that the independent variable had no effect on the dependent variable.

When conducting your literature review for a research project, it is extremely important to identify extraneous variables so that you can take steps to control them. A major advantage of the use of an extraneous variable as a factor in a factorial design is that it becomes possible to determine if the extraneous variable interacts with the independent variable. The alternative methods of control, such as holding the extraneous variable constant across conditions of the independent variable, ignore its possible moderating effects and, as discussed in Chapter 14, they also limit the interpretations you can make about the generalizability of the results of the research. However, use blocking with care: It operates to reduce error variance only when the blocking variable has a strong effect on or is highly correlated with the dependent variable. Under other conditions, blocking could actually increase the error variance by decreasing the degrees of freedom associated with the error term.

SUMMARY

Five aspects of experimental research are considerations in manipulating the independent variable, ways of controlling unwanted variance in the dependent variable, the functions of control groups, and the use of multiple-group and factorial experiments. Inferential statistics assist the research process by partitioning participants' scores on the dependent variable into treatment variance caused by the independent variable and error variance caused by extraneous variables. Two goals of research design are increasing treatment variance and reducing error variance.

Every experiment has at least one experimental condition and at least one control or comparison condition. The most basic function of a control condition is to provide a baseline against which to assess the effects of the independent variable. However, additional control conditions might be needed to fully test the hypothesis being studied or to rule out alternative explanations for the predicted effects of the independent variable.

Manipulations of independent variables must be valid, reliable, strong, and salient. Manipulation checks are used to test the construct validity of a manipulation. Reliable manipulations are consistently applied to all participants. Strong manipulations serve to increase treatment variance. Salient manipulations are noticeable by participants. When the stimuli used for a manipulation are samples from a population of possible stimuli, multiple stimuli should be used in each condition of the experiment. This procedure allows one to separate the effects of the construct being measured from the effects of the unique properties of the stimuli.

Extraneous variables are characteristics of the research situation and participants that add unwanted (error) variance to the dependent variable. Experimenters control the effects of situational extraneous variables by holding those variables constant for all participants, thereby spreading their effects evenly across the conditions of the experiment. Extraneous variables that are characteristics of the research participants can be dealt with in five ways. Some characteristics, such as sex of participant, can be held constant. Researchers can balance the effects of other characteristics across conditions by randomly assigning participants to conditions, matching participants on key characteristics and randomly assigning the members of matched pairs to conditions, or by using a within-subjects design. Finally, participants can be blocked on a characteristic and the characteristic can be treated as an independent variable in a factorial design.

Simple random assignment and matched random assignment of participants to conditions are used in between-subjects designs, in which a participant experiences only one condition of the independent variable. In within-subjects designs, each participant experiences each condition of the independent variable, thereby providing a perfect "match" between the participants in the conditions. This procedure reduces error variance and requires fewer participants than an equivalent between-subjects design. However, order effects—practice, carryover, and sensitization—can threaten the internal validity of a within-subjects experiment. Counterbalancing the order of conditions can spread these effects across conditions, and using a washout period can control carryover effects. When order is counterbalanced, a factorial design that includes order as a factor can detect order effects and determine if they are equal across orders.

Experiments can include more than one level of a quantitative independent variable or more than one category of a qualitative independent variable. Such a multiple-group design is the only way to determine if a quantitative independent variable has a curvilinear relationship to the dependent variable. Be careful, however, to conduct the appropriate follow-up statistical tests to determine which of the several possible differences among the means are statistically significant.

A factorial design has more than one independent variable. Factorial designs provide information about main effects (the separate effects of each independent variable) and interactions (the joint effect that two or more independent variables have over and above their main effects). Researchers must take care when interpreting the results of factorial experiments that find interaction effects because such effects indicate that the effect of one independent variable is different under different conditions of the other independent variable. Factorial designs can be within-subjects, or between-subjects, or a combination of the two. One or more factors can also be measured variables, but the results found for these variables cannot be interpreted in causal terms. Factorial designs can be used to test the effects of hypothesized moderator variables, to detect order effects in within-subjects designs, and to control the effects of extraneous variables.

QUESTIONS AND EXERCISES FOR REVIEW

1. What are the three defining characteristics of the experiment? How do correlational studies and case studies differ from experiments? (Review Chapter 2.)
2. Describe the purposes of control and comparison conditions in an experiment.
3. What are the characteristics of a good manipulation? What problems do you think might arise in attempting to maximize these characteristics?

4. Choose three recently published experiments on topics that interest you. How did each group of researchers manipulate their independent variables? Based on the criteria discussed in the chapter, how good do you think these manipulations were? What are your reasons for your evaluations?

5. How can manipulation checks be conducted? What do you see as the advantages and disadvantages of each approach? Describe the factors that can result in a failed manipulation check.

6. Describe the advantages of using multiple stimuli in research. Describe some research situations in which the use of multiple stimuli would be appropriate. How would the failure to use multiple stimuli when appropriate limit the conclusions that could be drawn from a study?

7. Describe the ways in which an experimenter can control extraneous variance. What do you see as the advantages and disadvantages of each?

8. How do within-subjects designs and between-subjects designs differ? Describe the advantages and disadvantages of within-subjects designs relative to between-subjects designs. Describe the steps an experimenter can take to overcome these disadvantages.

9. Look again at the three studies that you chose for Question 4. Did each use a between-subjects design, a within-subjects design, or a mixed design? For each study, describe how the between-subjects factors could be manipulated as within-subjects factors and how the within-subjects factors could be manipulated as between-subjects factors. What benefits would accrue and what problems would arise from the changes in each case?

10. What advantages do multiple-group experiments have over two-group experiments? Describe the problems in interpreting the results of multiple-group experiments.

11. For each of these factorial designs, what are the number of independent variables, the number of conditions of each independent variable, and the total number of conditions?
    a. 2×2
    b. 3×2
    c. $3 \times 2 \times 2$
    d. $4 \times 3 \times 2 \times 2$

12. Describe the possible outcomes of a 2×2 factorial design. If the results of a factorial experiment show both an interaction and a main effect, how should the main effect be interpreted?

13. What advantages do factorial designs have over designs that include only one independent variable? What can factorial designs do that the other designs cannot?

14. Choose three recently published experiments on topics that interest you that used factorial designs. In each case, were the factors all between-subjects, all within-subjects, mixed between and within, or mixed experimental and correlational? In your opinion, did the researchers properly interpret the results of their studies? What are your reasons for your answer?

8 THE CORRELATIONAL (PASSIVE) RESEARCH STRATEGY

THE NATURE OF
CORRELATIONAL RESEARCH
Assumptions of Linearity and
   Additivity
   Linearity
   Additivity
Factors Affecting the Correlation
   Coefficient
   Reliability of the Measures
   Restriction in Range
   Outliers
   Subgroup Differences
Multifaceted Constructs
   Keeping Facets Separate
   Combining Facets
Some Recommendations

SIMPLE AND PARTIAL
CORRELATION ANALYSIS
Simple Correlational Analysis
   The Correlation Coefficient
   Differences in Correlations
Partial Correlation Analysis

MULTIPLE REGRESSION
ANALYSIS (MRA)
Forms of MRA
   Simultaneous MRA
   Hierarchical MRA

Information Provided by MRA
   The Multiple Correlation
      Coefficient
   The Regression Coefficient
   Change in R^2
The Problem of Multicollinearity
   Effects of Multicollinearity
   Causes of Multicollinearity
   Detecting Multicollinearity
   Dealing With Multicollinearity
MRA as an Alternative to ANOVA
   Continuous Independent
      Variables
   Correlated Independent
      Variables

SOME OTHER CORRELATIONAL
TECHNIQUES
Logistic Regression Analysis
Multiway Frequency Analysis
Data Types and Data Analysis

TESTING MEDIATIONAL
HYPOTHESES
Simple Mediation: Three Variables
Complex Models
   Path Analysis
   Latent Variables Analysis
   Prospective Research

Limits on Interpretation
   Completeness of the Model
   Alternative Models

FACTOR ANALYSIS
Uses of Factor Analysis
   Data Reduction
   Scale Development
Considerations in Factor Analysis
   Number of Research
      Participants
   Quality of the Data
   Methods of Factor Extraction
      and Rotation
   Determining the Number of
      Factors
   Interpreting the Factors
   Factor Scores

SUMMARY

QUESTIONS AND EXERCISES
FOR REVIEW

Although the experiment is the only research strategy that can determine if one variable causes another, not all phenomena of interest to behavioral scientists can be studied experimentally. For example, it is impossible to manipulate some factors, such as personality, that behavioral scientists would like to study as independent variables. If manipulation is not possible, neither is experimentation. In other cases, it might be unethical to manipulate a variable. For example, researchers might want to conduct an experimental study of the effects of long-term exposure to severe stress. Although such an experiment would be possible, it would raise ethical concerns about harm to the participants.

Most variables that cannot be studied experimentally can be studied correlationally. Even though personality traits cannot be manipulated, they can be measured and the degree to which they are related to other variables, such as behaviors, can be determined. Even though it is not ethical to intentionally subject people to long-term, severe stress, it is possible to locate people who experience different degrees of stress, some of it severe, as part of their everyday lives and to correlate degree of stress with outcome variables such as frequency of illness.

As noted in Chapter 2, the major drawback to the correlational (passive) research strategy is that it cannot determine if one variable causes another. Although correlational research can determine if two variables covary—the first requirement for causality—it cannot always establish time precedence of the presumed cause and cannot rule out all alternative explanations for any relationships found. Yet correlational research can show that one variable does *not* cause another: Because the covariance of two variables is an absolute requirement for causality, lack of a correlation can demonstrate a lack of causality.

This chapter provides an overview of correlational research. It first notes some assumptions underlying correlational research methods and some factors that can have unwanted effects on correlation coefficients, and then outlines the principal methods of correlational research, followed by a discussion of the role of correlational research in testing mediational hypotheses. The chapter concludes with a discussion of factor analysis, a technique for examining patterns of correlations among variables.

First, a note on terminology: Throughout this chapter I use the term *independent variable* to refer to the variable or variables in a correlational study that the theory being tested presumes is the causal variable or variables. This term is, to some degree, misleading because *independent variable* is frequently used to refer only to the manipulated variables in experiments. However, researchers conducting correlational studies usually assume that one variable or a set of variables causes another, which I call the *dependent variable*. I use these terms as a matter of convenience and do not intend to imply that correlational research can determine causality.

THE NATURE OF CORRELATIONAL RESEARCH

Correlational research can be carried out in a number of ways. However, several issues are involved in all forms of correlational research. This section discusses three of those issues: the assumptions of linearity and additivity, factors that affect the size of a correlation coefficient found in a study, and the multifaceted nature of some constructs.

Assumptions of Linearity and Additivity

As noted in the previous chapter, all statistical tests are based on assumptions. Two of the assumptions underlying correlational statistics are that the relationship between the variables is linear and that there are no interactions present when multiple independent variables are studied.

LINEARITY   Generally, the use of correlational research methods assumes that the relationship between the independent and dependent variables is linear—that is, that the relationship can be graphed as a straight line. Curvilinear relationships cannot be detected by simple correlational methods. For example, the correlation coefficient for the relationship illustrated in panel (a) of Figure 8-1 would be zero, even though the scores on the two variables are clearly related. A more subtle problem is illustrated in panel (b) of Figure 8-1, which shows a relationship between two variables that is initially linear and positive but eventually becomes zero. In this case the correlation coefficient for the two sets of scores will be positive. However, because the relationship is not completely linear, the coefficient will be misleading; that is, it will not reflect the true relationship between the variables. As a general rule, one should plot the relationship between the scores on two variables before conducting a correlational analysis in order to ensure that the relationship is linear. If there is reason to suspect a curvilinear relationship between the independent and dependent variables in a study, simple correlational analysis is not appropriate.

ADDITIVITY   Correlational analyses involving more than one independent variable also generally assume that the relationship between the independent and dependent variable is **additive.** That is, people's scores on the dependent variable can be predicted by an equation that sums their weighted scores on the independent variables. For example, Schuman, Walsh, Olson, and Etheridge (1985) used total Scholastic Assessment Test (SAT) scores, self-reported average number of hours of study per day (HOURS), and self-reported percentage of classes attended (ATTEND) to predict grade point average (GPA) for college students. They found that the formula GPA = 1.99 + .0003 × SAT + .009 × HOURS + .008 × ATTEND predicted 13.5% of the variance in GPA. Another way of looking at the assumption of additivity is that it presumes there are no interactions among the independent variables. This means that Schuman et al. assumed that, for example, class attendance had the same relationship to GPA regardless of SAT scores; that is, they assumed that cutting class had the same effect on the grades of students with high SAT scores as it did on the grades of students with low SAT scores.

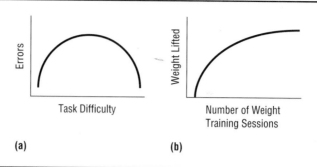

FIGURE 8-1   Examples of Curvilinear Relationships

Although interaction effects cannot be tested using simple correlation analysis, they can be tested using multiple regression analysis, which is discussed later in this chapter.

Factors Affecting the Correlation Coefficient

Even given a linear relationship between two variables, several aspects of the instruments used to measure the variables, the distributions of scores on the variables, and the participant sample can affect the observed correlation. Low reliability and restriction in range lead to underestimates of the population value of a correlation, and outliers and differences in subgroup correlations can dramatically affect the size of the correlation coefficient.

RELIABILITY OF THE MEASURES   The relationship between the true scores of two variables is called their *true score correlation;* the relationship a study finds is called their *observed correlation.* The observed correlation is an estimate of the true score correlation; its value is not necessarily equal to that of the true score correlation. All else being equal, the more reliable the measures of the two variables (the less random error they contain), the closer the observed correlation will be to the true score correlation. As the measures become less reliable, the observed correlation will underestimate the true score correlation. The relationship between reliability and the size of the observed correlation is $r_{xy} = r_{XY} \sqrt{r_{xx} r_{yy}}$, where r_{xy} is the observed correlation, r_{XY} is the true score correlation, and r_{xx} and r_{yy} are the reliabilities of the measures. For example, with a true score correlation of .55 and two measures with reliabilities of .80, the maximum possible observed correlation is .44. This shrinkage of the observed correlation relative to the true score correlation is called **attenuation.** Thus, it is imperative to use the most reliable available measures when conducting correlational research. The same principle applies, of course, to experimental research. However, because the reliability of a carefully manipulated independent variable should approach 1.00, the attenuation of the observed relationship relative to the true score relationship is greatly reduced. Nonetheless, an unreliable measure of the dependent variable can lead to underestimates of the size of its relationship to the independent variable.

TABLE 8-1   Hypothetical Data for Correlation of Years Since Doctorate With Number of Publications

Case	Years	Publications	Case	Years	Publications
1	1	2	9	4	8
2	2	4	10	16	12
3	5	5	11	15	9
4	7	12	12	19	4
5	10	5	13	8	8
6	4	9	14	14	i1
7	3	3	15	28	21
8	8	1			

Note: Adapted from J. Cohen & Cohen, 1983, p. 35.

RESTRICTION IN RANGE   Restriction in range occurs when the scores of one or both variables in a sample have a range of values that is less than the range of scores in the population. Restriction in range reduces the correlation found in a sample relative to the correlation that exists in the population. This reduction occurs because as a variable's range narrows, the variable comes closer to being a constant. Because the correlation between a constant and a variable is zero, as a variable's sampled range becomes smaller, its maximum possible correlation with another variable will approach zero, that is, become smaller. Consider the data in Table 8-1, which show the number of years since the award of the doctoral degree and total number of publications for 15 hypothetical professors, and Figure 8-2, which shows a scatterplot of those data. The correlation between the two variables is .68; however, if only those professors with less than 10 years experience are considered (shown by the dashed line in Figure 8-2), the correlation is reduced to .34.

Restriction in range is especially likely to be a problem when research participants are selected on the basis of extreme scores on one of the variables or if the participant sample is drawn from a subgroup of the population that has a natural restriction in range on a variable. For example, studies of the concurrent validity of employment selection tests correlate the test scores of people already on the job with measures of job performance. Because only good performers are likely to be hired and remain on the job, their job performance scores, and possibly their test scores, are restricted to the high end of the range. College students provide an example of a subpopulation with a natural restriction in age range, with most being 18 to 22 years old. Correlations between age and other variables may therefore be deceptively low when college students serve as research participants.

OUTLIERS   Outliers are extreme scores, usually defined as being scores more than three standard deviations above or below the mean (Tabachnick & Fidell, 1996). The influence of outliers can be seen in the data in Table 8-1 and Figure 8-2. Notice that Case 15 (shown in a square in Figure 8-2) has unusually high values for both variables—28 years since doctorate and 21 publications—and so lies well outside the

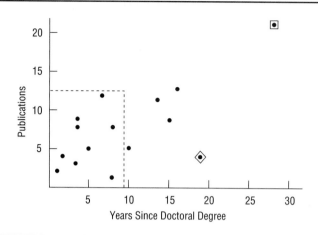

FIGURE 8-2   Scatterplot of Data From Table 8-1

scatterplot of cases. If Case 15 is removed from the data set, the correlation between years since doctorate and publications becomes .38; Case 15's unusually high values on both variables inflated the correlation. Outliers can also artificially lower a correlation. Consider Case 12 (shown in a diamond in Figure 8-2), which has an unusually low number of publications (4) given the number of years since doctorate (19) compared to the rest of the cases. If Case 12 is removed from the data set along with Case 15, the correlation becomes .60.

The example just used illustrates the detection of outliers by inspection; that is, by looking at the distribution of scores on a variable or at a scatterplot of the relationship between two sets of scores. However, if a study includes more than two variables, inspection might not be sufficient to detect outliers because they might be the result of a combination of three or more variables. Tabachnick and Fidell (1996) describe statistical procedures that can be used in these situations to detect outliers.

What should you do about outliers? Tabachnick and Fidell (1996) suggest transforming the data mathematically, such as using the logarithms of the scores, to remove the effects of outliers. However, in such a case the results of the statistical analysis relate to the transformed rather than to the original data, so that their meaning may be unclear. J. Cohen and Cohen (1983) suggest omitting the outliers from the data analysis, especially if there are only a few. In this case some data are lost. Ultimately the decision about outliers rests with the researcher and must be based on the probable meaning of the outlying scores. For example, you might want to discard scores that most likely represent coding or other errors. Data sets with outliers that represent accurate data could be transformed to remove the effects of the outliers, or the outliers could be excluded from the data analysis but studied separately as special cases.

SUBGROUP DIFFERENCES   The participant sample on which a correlation is based might contain two or more subgroups, such as women and men. Unless the correlations between the variables being studied are the same for all groups and all groups have the

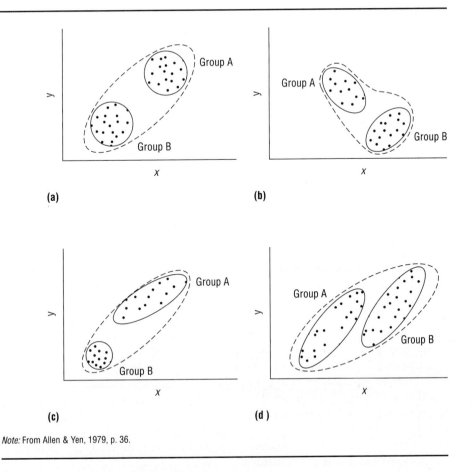

Note: From Allen & Yen, 1979, p. 36.

FIGURE 8-3 Examples of Problems Created by Combining Groups

same mean scores on the variables, the correlation in the combined group will not accurately reflect the subgroup correlations. Some examples of this problem are shown in
Figure 8-3. In panel (a), the correlation between the variables is zero for each group.
However, because Group A scores higher on both variables than does Group B, the correlation in the combined groups is positive. In panel (b), the correlation for Group A is
negative, but that for Group B is positive. However, because Group A scores higher on
Variable y and lower on Variable x than does Group B, the correlation in the combined
groups is negative. In panel (c), there is a positive correlation for Group A and no correlation for Group B. However, because Group A scores higher on both variables, the
correlation in the combined groups is positive. Finally, panel (d) presents an interesting situation: The correlation is positive in both groups, but Group B scores higher on
Variable x than does Group A. This difference in mean scores reduces the correlation
in the combined groups. Because of these potential problems, it is always wise to examine subgroup means and correlations before analyzing the data for the combined group.
One could also plot the subgroup's scores on the variables on a single scatterplot as in

Figure 8-3, but unless the groups' scores are plotted in different symbols or different colors, differences in the groups' scatterplots may be difficult to pick out.

Subgroup scores should also be examined for within-groups outliers that might appear to be normal cases when the groups are combined. For example, in Panel (d) of Figure 8-3, a member of Group A who scored in the range of scores represented by Group B would be an outlier relative to the scores in Group A, but not to the scores on the combined groups.

Multifaceted Constructs

As noted in Chapter 1, Carver (1989) defined multifaceted constructs as constructs "that are composed of two or more subordinate concepts, each of which can be distinguished from the others and measured separately, despite their being related to each other both logically and empirically" (p. 577). An example of a multifaceted construct is attributional style (Abramson, Metalsky, & Alloy, 1989), which is composed of three facets: internality, stability, and globality. These facets are interrelated in that the theory holds that a person who attributes negative life events to causes that are internal, stable, and global is, under certain circumstances, more prone to depression and low self-esteem than a person who does not exhibit this attributional pattern. Not all multidimensional constructs are multifaceted in the sense used here. For example, the two components of the Ohio State leadership model (Stogdill & Coons, 1956), initiating structure and consideration, are assumed to have independent effects on different aspects of leadership behavior. A test of whether a construct is multifaceted as opposed to one that is simply multidimensional is whether you (or other researchers) are tempted to combine the scores on the facets into an overall index, as internality, stability, and globality are often combined into an overall attributional style score (Peterson & Seligman, 1984). A major issue in research using multifaceted constructs is that of when facets should and should not be combined.

KEEPING FACETS SEPARATE   There are three circumstances in which facets should not be combined. The first is when the facets are theoretically or empirically related to different dependent variables or to different facets of a dependent variable. For example, the attributional theory of depression holds that internality attributions are (under specific circumstances) related to self-esteem, stability attributions to the duration of depression, and globality attributions to the generality of depressive symptoms (Abramson et al., 1989). For the theory to be adequately tested, one must separately test the relationships of the facets of attributional style to their appropriate dependent variables (Carver, 1989). In addition, specific relationships between the facets of a construct and different dependent variables can be discovered empirically (see, for example, Snyder, 1986).

When the facets of a multifaceted construct are combined into a general index, useful information can be lost. For example, Crandall (1994) developed a scale to measure people's attitudes toward fatness in other people, which he named the Antifat Attitudes Questionnaire. The questionnaire measures three facets of antifat attitudes: dislike of fat people, degree of belief that fatness is due to lack of willpower, and fear of

TABLE 8-2 Correlations Between an Overall Measure and the Three Facets of Antifat Attitudes and Three Other Variables

A different pattern of correlations exists for the overall measure and its facets.

	Belief in a Just World	Modern Racism	Authoritarianism
Overall antifat attitudes	.50[*]	.23[*]	.09
Dislike of fat people	.47[*]	.23[*]	.29[*]
Lack of willpower	.48[*]	.28[*]	.16
Fear of getting fat	.09	−.08	−.31[*]

[*]$p < .05$.

Note: Facet correlations from Crandall, 1994, p. 886; overall correlations courtesy of Professor Crandall.

becoming fat. Table 8-2 shows the correlations between total scores on the Antifat Attitudes Questionnaire, its three facets, and three other variables: the degree to which a person believes that people deserve whatever happens to them (belief in a just world), racist attitudes (modern racism), and the degree to which a person defers to authority figures (authoritarianism). As you can see, belief in a just world and racist attitudes have positive correlations with the total antifat attitude score and the dislike and willpower facets, but have no correlation with the fear-of-fat facet. In contrast, authoritarianism is uncorrelated with both the total score and with the willpower facet, but has a positive correlation with the dislike facet and a negative correlation with the fear-of-fat facet. Focusing solely on the relationships of the total antifat attitude score with the scores on the other variables would give an inaccurate picture of the true pattern of relationships, which are shown by the correlations involving the facet scores. Therefore, unless you are certain that the combined score on a construct and the scores on all the facets have the same relation to a dependent variable, test both the combined score and the facet scores to derive the most accurate information from your research.

The second circumstance in which you should avoid combined scores is when the theory of the construct predicts an interaction among the facets. Carver (1989) points out that the attributional theory of depression can be interpreted as predicting an interaction among the facets: A person becomes at risk for depression when negative events are consistently attributed to causes that are internal *and* stable *and* global. That is, all three conditions must be simultaneously present for the effect to occur, which represents an interaction among the facets. If facets are combined into a single score, it is impossible to test for their interaction. Finally, facets should not be combined simply as a convenience. Although dealing with one overall construct is simpler than dealing with each of its components, the potential loss of useful information described earlier far outweighs the gain in simplicity.

COMBINING FACETS When, then, can researchers combine scores across facets? One circumstance is when a researcher is interested in the latent variable represented by the combination of facets rather than in the particular aspects of the variable represented by the facets. A **latent variable** is an unmeasured variable represented by the combination of several operational definitions of a construct. For example, the latent variable of depression has at least three facets: mood, symptoms, and surface syndrome (Boyle, 1985). A research question, such as whether depression (as a hypothetical construct rather than as measured in any one manifestation) is related to a dependent variable such as aggression, could be tested by correlating a depression index made up of scores on the three facets of depression with a measure of aggression, which could also be an index made up of scores from measures of several facets of aggression. Although interest in the latent variable is a justification for combining across facets, bear two cautions in mind. First, if the latent variable is more important in relation to the dependent variable than any of its facets, it should be a better predictor of the dependent variable; this possibility should be tested. Second, using statistical methods specifically designed to deal with latent variables might be a better approach than combining across facets.

A second justification for combining across facets is when, from a theoretical perspective, the latent variable is more important, more interesting, or represents a more appropriate level of abstraction than do the facets. Thus, Eysenck (1972), while acknowledging that his construct of introversion-extraversion is composed of several facets, regards the general construct as more important than the facets. Note, however, that what constitutes the appropriate level of abstraction of a construct can be a matter of opinion and disagreement among theorists and researchers. Facets can also be combined if you are trying to predict a multiple-act criterion rather than a single behavior. A multiple-act criterion consists of an index based on many related behaviors (Fishbein & Ajzen, 1975); for example, a multiple-act criterion of religious behavior might consist of an index composed of frequency of church attendance, frequency of praying, active membership in religious organizations, and so forth. If each facet of the general construct is related somewhat to each behavior, the combination of the facets should relate well to the combination of the behaviors. Finally, you can combine facets if they correlate highly, but in such cases the facets probably represent the same construct rather than different facets of a construct. Metalsky, Halberstadt, and Abramson (1987), for example, recommend combining the stability and globality facets of attributional style into a single "generality" facet because researchers consistently find them to be highly correlated.

Some Recommendations

The linearity assumption, the variety of factors that can have undesirable effects on the correlation coefficient, and the use of multifaceted constructs suggest these guidelines for correlational research:

1. Use only the most reliable measures of the variables.
2. Whenever possible, check the ranges of the scores on the variables in your sample against published norms or other data to determine if the ranges are restricted in the sample.
3. Plot the scores for the subgroups and the combined group on graphs (as in Figures 8-2 and 8-3) before computing the correlation coefficient. Use different sym-

bols, or better, different colors, for each subgroup. Examine the plots for deviations from linearity and for outliers.

4. Compute subgroup correlations and means. Check to ensure that they do not have an adverse effect on the combined correlation.

5. When dealing with multifaceted constructs, avoid combining facets unless there is a compelling reason to do so.

The next three sections examine some ways of conducting correlational studies. First considered is simple and partial correlation analysis, then multiple regression analysis, and finally logistic regression analysis and multiway frequency analysis.

SIMPLE AND PARTIAL CORRELATION ANALYSIS

Simple correlation analysis investigates the correlation between two variables and the difference in correlations found in two groups. Partial correlation analysis is a way of examining the correlation between two variables while controlling for their relationships with a third variable.

Simple Correlational Analysis

Researchers use simple correlations to determine the relationship between two variables and to develop equations to predict the value of one variable from the value of the other. Researchers are also sometimes interested in differences in correlations, which address the question of whether two variables have the same relationship in different groups of people, such as men and women.

THE CORRELATION COEFFICIENT   The correlation coefficient, r, is an index of the degree of relationship between two variables—that is, an index of the accuracy with which scores on one variable can predict scores on another variable. For example, the correlation between people's heights and their weights is about .70, indicating that weight can be predicted from height (and vice versa) with some, but not perfect, accuracy. The square of the correlation coefficient (r^2) represents the proportion of the variance on one variable that can be accounted for by the other variable. For example, if the correlation of height with weight is .70, then 49% of the differences in weights among people can be attributed to the differences in their heights; 51% of the variance in weights is due to other factors, such as individual differences in muscle mass, metabolic rate, and eating habits.

The prediction function of correlation is carried out through **bivariate regression:** an equation is developed to predict one variable (Y) from the other (X). The equation is of the form $Y = a + bX$, where a is referred to as the **intercept** (the value of Y when $X = 0$) and b as the **slope** (amount of change in Y for each unit change in X). For the data in Table 8-1, the regression equation is publications = 3.11 + .47 × years. Note that unless $r = 1$, the prediction will be less than perfect. For example, the predicted value for Case 9 in Table 8-1 is 4.99, an underestimate of three publications, and the

TABLE 8-3   Hypothetical Data Illustrating Equal Correlation But Different Slope

X	Y	
	Group 1	Group 2
1	1	1
2	1	1
3	2	3
4	2	3
5	3	5
6	3	5
7	4	7
8	4	7
9	5	9
10	5	9

predicted value for Case 8 is 7.1, an overestimate of six publications. However, the under- and overestimates will cancel out across the sample, thus providing an accurate picture of the relationship "on the average."

DIFFERENCES IN CORRELATIONS   Although it can be useful to know the strength of the relationship between two variables, it can be more interesting to know if the relationship is the same in different groups in the population. For example, is the relationship between scores on an aptitude test and ratings of job performance (the criterion validity of the test) the same for African-American and European-American job applicants? You can test the equality of the correlation coefficients found in two groups by using Fisher's z' transformation; you can also test the null hypothesis that more than two correlations are all equal to one another (J. Cohen & Cohen, 1983).

Be careful when testing differences in correlation coefficients, however, because a lack of difference in correlation coefficients does not necessarily mean that the relationship between the variables is the same. This problem is illustrated in Table 8-3. The correlation between Variable X and Variable Y is .98 for each group, indicating that one could predict Y scores equally well from X scores in both groups. However, as shown in Figure 8-4, scores on Y increase twice as fast for each increment in X in Group 2 (slope = .97) than they do in Group 1 (slope = .48). For example, if Y represented salary and X represented years of experience, with Group 1 being women and Group 2 being men, then the salary difference between men and women increases as experience increases: Although men and women start at the same salary, men's salaries increase faster than women's (the slopes are different). Nonetheless, men's and women's salaries can be predicted from years of experience with equal accuracy using the within-groups regression equation (the correlations are the same).

The apparent contradiction between the conclusions drawn from r and slope arises because r is a standardized index: X and Y scores are transformed to have a mean of

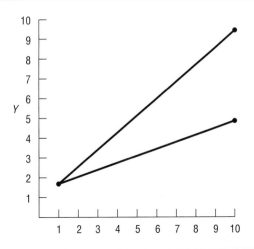

FIGURE 8-4   Plot of Regression Lines for Data in Table 8-3

0 and a standard deviation of 1. Slope, in contrast, is an unstandardized index based on the raw (unstandardized) standard deviations of X and Y. Slope and r are related through the standard deviations (sd) of X and Y: $b = r (sd_x \div sd_y)$. For the data in Table 8-3, the standard deviation of Y is larger in Group 2 (2.98) than in Group 1 (1.49), whereas the standard deviation of X is constant for the two groups. Consequently, the value of b in Group 2 is twice that in Group 1. It is also possible for r to be different in two groups, but for b to have the same value in the two groups. Therefore, whenever you compare correlations between two groups, check to ensure that their standard deviations are similar. If they are, there is no problem. If they are different, calculate the regression equations for each group and test the equality of slopes (see J. Cohen & Cohen, 1983, for the formula). A difference in the slopes for a relationship in two groups represents an interaction between the grouping variable and variable X: The relationship between X and Y differs in the two groups. The results of the study should be interpreted accordingly: Because the relationship between the variables is different in the two groups, the grouping variable moderates their relationship.

Partial Correlation Analysis

As noted in the previous chapter, researchers often encounter the problem of an extraneous variable—a variable other than the independent variable that affects the dependent variable—which must be controlled. In an experiment, this control can be achieved through holding the variable constant, matched random assignment of research participants to conditions, or blocking on the extraneous variable. In correlational research, researchers cannot assign people to conditions of the independent variable because they are dealing solely with measured variables. Therefore, when

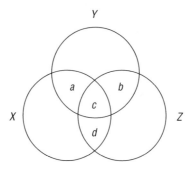

(a) Intercorrelation of variables *X*, *Y*, and *Z*

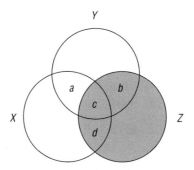

(b) Variable *Z* partialed out (shaded area)
from the correlation between *X* and *Y*

FIGURE 8-5   Correlations Among Three Variables
The relationship between *X* and *Y* with *Z* controlled is represented by Area *a*.

investigating the relationship between one variable, X, and another, Y, there may be
some extraneous third variable, Z, that is correlated with both X and Y, raising the
question of what the correlation of X with Y would be if Z were not also correlated
with them.

This problem is illustrated in Figure 8-5, in which variables are represented by
circles and correlations are represented by overlapping areas of the circles. In panel (a),
the correlation of X with Y is represented by Area $a + c$, the correlation of Z with Y by
Area $b + c$, and the correlation of X with Z by Area $c + d$. The research question is
"What would be the correlation of X with Y if Z were not there?" By removing the circle
representing Z from the diagram as shown in panel (b) of Figure 8-5, the answer is seen
to be Area *a*. This process controls for the effects of Z because the resulting **partial
correlation** shows what the relationship between X and Y would be if all the research
participants had the same score on Z, just as random assignment of participants to

TABLE 8-4   Results of Feather's (1985) Study

The correlation between masculinity and depression becomes nonsignificant when self-esteem is controlled, but the correlation between self-esteem and depression is virtually unaffected when masculinity is controlled.

Zero-Order Correlations

	Masculinity	*Self-Esteem*
Depression	−.26*	−.52*
Self-esteem	.67*	
Partial correlations		

Correlation of	*Controlling for*	
Masculinity and depression	Self-esteem	.14
Masculinity and self-esteem	Depression	.64*
Depression and self-esteem	Masculinity	−.48*

*$p < .001$.

conditions in an experiment assumes that group means on extraneous variables are equal.

The partial correlation coefficient (*pr*) is interpreted in the same way as the simple (or **zero-order**) correlation coefficient, *r*: Just as *r* represents the strength of the relationship between two variables, *pr* represents the strength of that relationship when the effect of a third variable is removed or held constant. As illustrated in Figure 8-5, *pr* (Area *a*) will usually be smaller than *r* (Area *a* + *c*). As an example of partial correlation analysis, consider a study by Feather (1985). Feather noted that positive correlations are frequently found between self-esteem and a personality characteristic called *psychological masculinity*, and that negative correlations are frequently found between masculinity and depression. However, he went on to note, self-esteem is also negatively correlated with depression. Because some theories hold that masculinity should be related to depression independently of other factors, Feather investigated the question of what the correlation between masculinity and depression would be if self-esteem were controlled; that is, what is the partial correlation of masculinity with depression controlling for self-esteem? Table 8-4 shows the results of Feather's study. The correlation between masculinity and depression controlling for self-esteem was substantially reduced from its zero-order level. However, the correlation between self-esteem and depression controlling for masculinity was essentially unchanged. Feather therefore concluded that the relationship between masculinity and depression could be almost completely accounted for by masculinity's correlation with self-esteem. That is, he concluded that the masculinity-depression relationship was spurious, or false, because masculinity and self-esteem were confounded—the real relationship was between self-esteem and depression.

MULTIPLE REGRESSION ANALYSIS (MRA)

Multiple regression analysis (MRA) is an extension of simple and partial correlation to situations in which there are more than two independent variables. MRA can be used for two purposes. The first purpose is to derive an equation that predicts scores on some **criterion** (dependent) **variable** from a set of **predictor** (independent) **variables.** For example, the equation $Y = a + b_1X_1 + b_2X_2$ estimates the value of a variable, Y, from two predictors, X_1 and X_2; a is the intercept, as in bivariate regression, and b_1 and b_2 are the weights given to variables X_1 and X_2, respectively. The Schuman et al. (1985) study cited earlier used MRA to determine the degree to which college GPA could be predicted from three variables: SAT scores, hours of study, and class attendance. Their prediction equation could be written as $Y = 1.99 + .0003X_1 + .009X_2 + .008X_3$, where Y represents GPA, X_1 represents SAT score, X_2 represents hours of study, and X_3 represents class attendance. Therefore, a student with a combined SAT score of 1,000 who spent 2 hours a day studying and attended 90% of all class meetings could expect a GPA of 3.03.

MRA can also be used to explain variation in a dependent variable in terms of its degree of association with members of a set of measured independent variables, similarly to the way in which factorial analysis of variance explains variation in a dependent variable in terms of the effect caused by a set of manipulated independent variables. However, because MRA is carried out through a series of partial correlation analyses, MRA, in contrast to analysis of variance, does not assume that the independent variables are uncorrelated.

This section examines a number of issues involved in the use of MRA. It begins with a look at the ways in which MRA can be conducted and the information that MRA can provide. Then multicollinearity is discussed, a major potential threat to the validity of MRA. Finally, two situations are examined in which MRA might be preferred to analysis of variance as a means of data analysis.

Forms of MRA

MRA can take three forms—simultaneous, hierarchical and stepwise. Of these, only simultaneous and hierarchical analysis should be used because the results of stepwise regression can frequently be erroneous (see Thompson, 1995, for an overview of the issues involved). Consequently, this discussion covers only simultaneous and hierarchical analysis.

SIMULTANEOUS MRA   The purpose of **simultaneous MRA** is to derive the equation that most accurately predicts a criterion variable from a set of predictor variables, using all the predictors in the set. Note that simultaneous MRA is not designed to determine which predictor does the best job of predicting the criterion, which is second best, and so forth, but only to derive the best predictive equation using an entire set of predictors. For example, one might use a number of variables—such as SAT scores, high school GPA, and so forth—to try to predict college GPA. When the predictor variables are relatively uncorrelated with one another, the use of multiple predictors will lead to greater predictive accuracy than does the use of any one of the predictors by itself. This increase in the predictive utility of the regression equation occurs because most criterion variables have multiple predictors, and the more predictors that are used in estimating the criterion, the more accurate the estimation will be.

HIERARCHICAL **MRA**   Hierarchical **MRA** is similar to partial correlation analysis. In the example given earlier, Feather (1985) asked the question of whether there a relationship between masculinity and depression after self-esteem is partialed out. In this case, he chose to partial self-esteem in order to answer his research question. Although Feather partialed only one variable (self-esteem) before considering the relationship between masculinity and depression, hierarchical MRA allows as many variables to be partialed as the investigator needs, in the order he or she wants to use. The researcher therefore creates the regression equation by adding, or entering, variables to the equation. This control by the investigator over the order of partialing makes hierarchical MRA appropriate for testing hypotheses about relationships between predictor variables and a criterion variable with other variables controlled.

Whitley's (1990b) study on the relationship of people's beliefs about the causes of homosexuality to their attitudes toward lesbians and gay men provides an example of the use of hierarchical MRA to test a hypothesis. Drawing on attribution theory (Weiner, 1986), which deals with how one's interpretations of the causes of other people's actions affect one's reactions to those people, Whitley hypothesized that the greater the degree to which people perceived the causes of homosexuality to be under a person's control, the more negative their attitudes toward lesbians and gay men would be. Whitley also collected data on two sets of extraneous variables. First, prior research indicated that attitudes toward gay people were related to at least three other variables (Herek, 1988): the sex of the research participant, whether the gay person was of the same sex as the research participant, and whether the participant knew a lesbian or a gay man. Second, attribution theory also includes two constructs in addition to controllability that are *not* supposed to be related to attitudes: the extent to which a cause is perceived to be a function of the person rather than of the environment (internality) and the perceived stability of the cause over time. The research question therefore was whether controllability attributions were related to attitudes toward lesbians and gay men with the effects of the other variables controlled.

The results of the MRA are shown in Table 8-5. Consistent with previous research, sex of the gay person toward whom participants were expressing their attitudes, similarity of sex of participant and gay person, and acquaintance with a lesbian or gay man were all related to attitudes toward gay people. In addition, controllability attributions were significantly related to these attitudes, but the other attributions were not. Whitley (1990b) therefore concluded that controllability attributions were related to attitudes toward lesbians and gay men even when other important variables were controlled.

Information Provided by MRA

MRA can provide three types of information about the relationship between the independent variables and the dependent variable: the multiple correlation coefficient, the

TABLE 8-5   Results of Whitley's (1990b) Study

As hypothesized, controllability attributions had a significant relationship to attitudes toward homosexuality with the other variables controlled.

Variable	β
Sex of respondent (R)[a]	−.082
Sex of target person (T)[a]	−.126[*]
Similarity of sex of R and T[b]	−.318[**]
Acquaintance with gay person	.276[**]
Stability attribution	−.002
Internality attribution	−.066
Controllability attribution	−.201[**]

Note: A high attitude score indicates a favorable attitude. β is an index of the strength of the relationship (see next section).

[a]Scored female = 1, male = 2.

[b]Scored same = 1, different = 2.

[*]$p < .05$. [**]$p < .001$.

regression coefficient, and change in the squared multiple regression coefficient. Each of these statistics can be tested to determine if its value is different from zero.

THE MULTIPLE CORRELATION COEFFICIENT   The **multiple correlation coefficient** (R) is an index of the degree of association between the predictor variables *as a set* and the criterion variable, just as r is an index of the degree of association between a single predictor variable and a criterion variable. Note that R provides no information about the relationship of any one predictor variable to the criterion variable. The squared multiple correlation coefficient (R^2) represents the proportion of variance in the criterion variable accounted for by its relationship with the total set of predictor variables. For a given set of variables R^2 will always be the same regardless of the form of MRA used.

THE REGRESSION COEFFICIENT   The **regression coefficient** is the value by which the score on a predictor variable is multiplied to predict the score on the criterion variable. That is, in the predictive equation $Y = a + bX$, b is the regression coefficient, representing the slope of the relationship between X and Y. Regression coefficients can be either standardized (β, the Greek letter beta) or unstandardized (B). In either case, the coefficient represents the amount of change in Y brought about by a unit change in X. For β, the units are standard deviations, and for B, the units are the natural units of X, such as dollars or IQ scores. Because the βs for all the independent variables in an analysis are on the same scale (a mean of 0 and a standard deviation of 1), researchers can use these coefficients to compare the degree to which the different independent variables used in the same regression analysis are predictive of the dependent variable. That is, an independent variable with a β of .679 better predicts (has a larger partial correlation with) the dependent variable than an independent variable with a β of .152, even

TABLE 8-6 Hypothetical Data Illustrating the Effects of Entering a Variable Into an MRA in Different Orders

Zero-Order Correlations

	Motivation	Qualifications	GPA
Qualifications	.396		
GPA	.506	.703	
Exam score	.508	.673	.750

Using Motivation to Predict Exam Scores

	Change in R^2
Motivation entered first	.258
Entered second after qualifications	.069
Entered second after GPA	.022
Entered last	.018

Note: Correlations adapted from Tabachnick & Fidell, 1996, p. 143.

though both may be statistically significant. In contrast, because the Bs have the same units regardless of the sample, these coefficients can be used to compare the predictive utility of independent variables across samples, such as for women compared to men. The statistical significance of the difference between the Bs for the same variable in two samples can be determined using a form of the *t* test (J. Cohen & Cohen, 1983).

CHANGE IN R^2   Change in R^2 is used in hierarchical MRA and represents the increase in the proportion of variance in the dependent variable that is accounted for by adding another independent variable to the regression equation. That is, it addresses the question of whether adding X_2 to the equation helps to predict Y any better than does X_1 alone. Change in R^2 is a ratio level variable; that is, it is legitimate to state that an independent variable that results in a change in R^2 of .262 predicts twice as much variance in the dependent variable than one that results in a change in R^2 of .131.

However, the change in R^2 associated with an independent variable can fluctuate as a function of the order in which the variable is entered into the equation. A variable entered earlier will generally result in a larger change in R^2 than if entered later, especially if it has a high correlation with the other predictor variables. Consider, for example, the hypothetical situation shown in Table 8-6. The zero-order correlations represent graduate students' scores on a measure of motivation to succeed in graduate school, ratings of their qualifications for admission to graduate school, their graduate school GPAs, and their scores on their predoctoral comprehensive examinations. The second part of the table shows the change in R^2 for motivation in predicting exam scores when it is entered into the regression equation in different sequences. As you can see, change in R^2 ranges from .258 to .018 depending on the order of entry. It is therefore essential to think carefully about the order in which you enter variables in MRA.

The Problem of Multicollinearity

Multicollinearity is a condition that arises when two or more predictor variables are highly correlated with each other. Multicollinearity can have several adverse effects on the results of MRA, so researchers must be aware of the problem, check to see if it is affecting their data, and take steps to deal with it if it is found.

EFFECTS OF MULTICOLLINEARITY   One effect of multicollinearity is inflation of the standard errors of regression coefficients. Artificially large standard errors can lead to a nonsignificant statistical test and the erroneous conclusion that there is no relationship between the predictor variables and the criterion variable. Multicollinearity can also lead to misleading conclusions about changes in R^2. If two predictor variables are highly correlated, when the relationship of one predictor variable is partialed out from the criterion variable the second predictor variable is left with only a small partial correlation with the criterion variable. For these reasons, multicollinearity poses a grave threat to the validity of conclusions drawn from MRA.

CAUSES OF MULTICOLLINEARITY   Multicollinearity can arise from several causes. One cause is the inclusion of multiple measures of one construct in the set of predictor variables. Because measures of the same construct will be highly correlated, they will lead to multicollinearity. If multiple measures of constructs are to be used — generally a good practice — a latent variables approach (described later in this chapter) should be taken to the data analysis. Some variables, such as height and weight, are naturally correlated and so can lead to multicollinearity. In other cases, measures of conceptually different constructs have highly correlated scores; scores on depression and anxiety measures, for example, are often highly correlated (Dobson, 1985). Finally, sampling error can lead to artificially high correlations between variables in a data set: Two variables with a moderate correlation in the population might be highly correlated in a sample because people who scored high on both variables or low on both variables were accidentally oversampled relative to their incidence in the population. For example, sex and IQ scores are uncorrelated in the population, but a sample might contain an unrepresentatively high number of high-scoring women and low-scoring men, thereby producing a correlation between sex and IQ score in the sample.

DETECTING MULTICOLLINEARITY   Because of its adverse effects, it is very important to test the correlation matrix of predictor variables for multicollinearity before conducting MRA. Statisticians have developed a number of guidelines for detecting the presence of multicollinearity; unfortunately, because multicollinearity is a characteristic of a sample rather than of a population, there is no statistical test for it (Pedhazur, 1997). The simplest test for multicollinearity is inspection of the correlation matrix; correlations equal to or greater than .80 are generally taken as being indicative of multicollinearity (Gunst & Mason, 1980). Inspection, however, can determine only if there is a high correlation between two variables; multicollinearity is also a function of the pattern of correlations among several predictors, none of which might exceed .80, so multicollinearity might not be detectable through inspection. R. H. Myers (1986) therefore suggests another method of testing for multicollinearity: Compute a series of multiple regression equations using each predictor variable as the dependent variable and the remaining variables as the independent variables. If R for an equation exceeds .9, the predicted variable is multicollinear with at least one of the other variables. The multiple regression module of many statistical software packages gives the option of computing the variance inflation factor (VIF). A VIF greater than 10 indicates the presence of multicollinearity.

DEALING WITH MULTICOLLINEARITY   One solution to the problem of multicollinearity is preventive: Avoid including redundant variables, such as multiple measures of a construct and natural confounds, in the set of predictor variables. Instead, combine them into indexes, such as the mean standard score on a set of depression measures or a weight-height ratio. If some measures of conceptually different constructs tend to be highly correlated, use the measures that show the least correlation. If multicollinearity is still present after these steps have been taken, you can try other solutions. If sampling error could be the source of an artificial confound, collecting more data to reduce the sampling error might reduce the problem. Another solution is to delete independent variables that might be the cause of the problem. In that case, however, you might also be deleting valuable information. Finally, you might conduct a factor analysis (described later in this chapter) to empirically determine which variables to combine into an index. However, the theoretical or practical meaning of a variable constructed in this way and the meaning of its relationship to the dependent variable might be unclear.

MRA as an Alternative to ANOVA

As noted earlier, correlational analyses assume that the relationships of the independent variables to the dependent variable are linear and additive. That is, the use of correlational analyses assumes there are no curvilinear relationships between the independent and dependent variables and no interactions among the independent variables. There are, however, mathematical ways around these assumptions. The arithmetic-square of the score on an independent variable can be used to represent the curvilinear effect of the variable; that is, you can use a variable that is equal to X^2 to represent the curvilinear effect of X. The arithmetic product of the scores for two independent variables can be used to represent their interaction; for example, you can use a variable that is equal to X times Z to represent the interaction of X and Z. However, MRA using nonlinear and interaction terms must be carried out very carefully, with the predictor variables entered into the regression equation in a specific hierarchical order. For example, the predictor representing a variable's linear effect must be entered before the predictor representing its curvilinear effect, and main effects must be entered before interactions. See Pedhazur (1997) and West, Aiken, and Krull (1996) for more information about these kinds of analyses. One implication of this ability to include nonlinear and interaction terms in MRA is that you can use it in place of a factorial ANOVA. There are two conditions when MRA would be preferred to ANOVA: when one or more of the independent variables is measured on a continuous scale, and when independent variables are correlated.

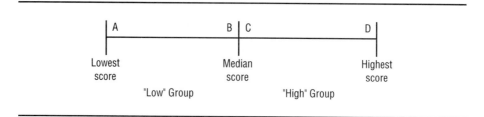

FIGURE 8-6   Use of Median Split to Classify Research Participants Into Groups on a Continuous Variable

CONTINUOUS INDEPENDENT VARIABLES   In ANOVA, when an independent variable is measured as a continuous variable, such as a personality trait, it must be transformed into a categorical variable so that research participants can be placed into the discrete groups required by ANOVA. This transformation is often accomplished using a **median split:** that is, the median score for the sample being used is determined, with people scoring above the median being classified as "high" on the variable and those scoring below the median being classified as "low." This procedure raises conceptual, empirical, and statistical problems. The conceptual problem is illustrated in Figure 8-6, which presents the scores of four research participants—A, B, C, and D—on a continuous variable. As you can see, use of a median split to classify participants on this scale makes the implicit assumptions that Participant A is very similar to Participant B, that Participant C is very similar to Participant D, and that Participants B and C are very different from each other. The problem is whether these assumptions are tenable for the hypothesis being tested; often they will not be.

The empirical problem brought about by the use of median splits is that of the reliability of the resulting classification of research participants. Because classification cutoff scores are relative (changing from sample to sample as the median changes) rather than absolute, participants who are in different samples but who have the same scores might be classified differently. This problem is especially likely to occur in small samples, in which the sample median might be a poor estimate of the population median. Comparability of results across studies is therefore reduced. Comparability can be further reduced when different studies use median splits on different measures of the same construct. For example, although scores on S. L. Bem's (1974) Sex Role Inventory and Spence, Helmreich, and Stapp's (1975) Personal Attributes Questionnaire (two measures of the personality variable of sex role self-concept) are highly correlated, agreement between category classification based on median splits is only about 60%, which is reduced to about 40% when agreements due to chance are taken into account (Kelly, Furman, & Young, 1978).

Median splits engender two statistical problems. The first is that of power—the ability of a sample correlation to accurately estimate the population correlation. Bollen and Barb (1981) have shown that given a population correlation of .30—the conventionally accepted level of a moderate correlation (J. Cohen, 1988)—the estimated r in large samples is .303, whereas a median split gives an estimate of .190, much less than the true size of the correlation. Although increasing the number of categories improves the sample correlation relative to its population value (for example, three categories gives an estimate of .226), there is always some loss of power. The second statistical problem is that the use of median splits with two or more correlated independent variables in a factorial design can lead to false statistical significance: A main effect or interaction appears statistically significant when, in fact, it is not (Maxwell & Delaney, 1993). This can happen because dichotomizing two correlated independent variables confounds their effects on a dependent variable so that in an ANOVA the "effect" for one independent variable represents not only its true relationship with the dependent variable but also some of the other independent variable's relationship with the dependent variable. Consequently, the apparent effect of the first independent variable is inflated. The more highly correlated the predictor variables, the more likely false significant effects become.

These problems all have the same solution: Treat the independent variable as continuous rather than as a set of categories and analyze the data using MRA. One might argue, however, that sometimes a researcher wants to investigate both an experimentally manipulated (thus, categorical) variable and a continuous variable in one study. For example, Rosenblatt and Greenberg (1988) investigated the relationships of research participants' level of depression (a personality variable) and the characteristics of another person (a manipulated variable) to the participants' liking for the person. Because the manipulated variable in such studies is categorical, one might think it necessary to categorize the personality variable and use ANOVA to analyze the data. However, MRA can accommodate categorical variables such as the conditions of an experiment as well as continuous variables by assigning values, such as 1 and 0, to the experimental and control conditions of the manipulated variable. The situation becomes more complex if the manipulated variable has more than two conditions; see Pedhazur (1997) or West et al. (1996) for information on how to handle such situations.

CORRELATED INDEPENDENT VARIABLES   Because ANOVA assumes that the independent variables are uncorrelated and MRA does not, the second condition under which MRA is to be preferred to ANOVA is when independent variables are correlated. Correlations between categorical independent variables can occur when there are unequal numbers of subjects in each group. The 2-to-1 female-to-male ratio in psychiatric diagnoses of depression (Nolen-Hoeksema, 1987), for example, means that gender and receiving a diagnosis of depression are correlated. If these variables were to be used as factors in an ANOVA, the assumption of uncorrelated independent variables would be violated and the validity of the analysis could be open to question. Therefore, if you conduct a factorial study with unequal group sizes, test to see if the factors are correlated. If they are, use MRA rather than ANOVA.

SOME OTHER CORRELATIONAL TECHNIQUES

Simple and partial correlation analysis and MRA are probably the most commonly used correlational techniques. However, all three approaches assume that the dependent variable in the research is continuous, although some forms of the correlation coefficient, such as the point biserial correlation, can be used when one of the variables is dichotomous. This section briefly looks at two correlational techniques designed for categorical dependent variables—logistic regression analysis and multiway frequency analysis—and concludes with a note on the relation between data types and data analysis.

Logistic Regression Analysis

MRA uses a set of continuous independent variables to predict scores on a continuous dependent variable. What is to be done if the dependent variable is categorical? The answer to this question is a technique called **logistic regression analysis.** Logistic regression analysis can be used for most of the same purposes as MRA, has the same caveats, such as the use of the proper type (simultaneous and hierarchical) and the assumptions of linearity and additivity, and is similarly vulnerable to the problem of multicollinearity. However, because the criterion variable is categorical rather than continuous, interpretation of the results is more complex. To give one example, unlike the regression coefficient the odds ratio used in logistic regression does not represent the amount of change in the dependent variable associated with a unit change in the independent variable; it describes the likelihood that a research participant is a member of one category of the dependent variable rather than a member of the other categories.

Griffin, Botvin, Doyle, Diaz, and Epstein (1999), for example, used logistic regression to investigate factors that predict adolescent cigarette smoking. They used scores on variables measured when the research participants were in the 7th grade to predict which participants would be heavy smokers in the 12th grade. Griffin et al. found that in the 7th grade, 12th-grade heavy smokers, compared to light smokers and nonsmokers, had had lower grades in school, had been more likely to have used alcohol and marijuana, had had mothers who smoked (fathers' smoking was not related to that of their children), had had more friends who were smokers, and had been more likely to engage in a variety of risky behaviors. See Tabachnick and Fidell (1996) and Wright (1995) for relatively nontechnical introductions to logistic regression analysis.

Multiway Frequency Analysis

Multiway frequency analysis allows a researcher to examine the pattern of relationships among a set of nominal level variables. The most familiar example of multiway frequency analysis is the chi-square (χ^2) test for association, which examines the degree of relationship between two nominal level variables. For example, one theory of self-concept holds that people tend to define themselves in terms of characteristics that set them apart from most other people with whom they associate (McGuire & McGuire, 1982). Kite (1992) tested this proposition in the college context, hypothesizing that "nontraditional" college students, being older than most college students, would be more likely to define themselves in terms of age than would college students in the traditional age range or faculty members who, although older than traditional college students, are in the same age range as the majority of their peers. Research participants were asked to write a paragraph in response to the instruction to "Tell us about yourself"; the dependent variable was whether the participants referred to their ages in their

TABLE 8-7 Two-Way (3 × 2) Frequency Table Showing Percentages of People in Three Categories Who Mentioned Their Ages in Describing Themselves

	GROUP		
	Traditional Students	*"Nontraditional" Students*	*Faculty Members*
Mention of age	16.3	57.1	35.7
No mention of age	83.7	42.9	64.3

Note: Adapted from Kite, 1992, p. 1830.

responses. Table 8-7 shows the distribution of responses: "Nontraditional" students were more likely to mention their ages than were members of the other groups, $\chi^2 (2, N = 140) = 17.62, p < .001$.

Loglinear analysis extends the principles of chi-square analysis to situations in which there are more than two variables. For example, Tabachnick and Fidell (1996) analyzed data from a survey that asked psychotherapists about being sexually attracted to clients (Pope, Keith-Spiegel, & Tabachnick, 1986). Tabachnick and Fidell examined the pattern of relationships among five dichotomous variables: whether the therapist thought that the client was aware of the therapist's being sexually attracted to him or her, whether the therapist thought that the attraction was beneficial to the therapy, whether the therapist thought that it was harmful to therapy, whether the therapist had sought the advice of another professional about being sexually attracted to a client, and whether the therapist felt uncomfortable about being sexually attracted to a client. Tabachnick and Fidell found that 58% of the therapists who had felt attracted to a client had sought advice (the researchers use the term *consultation*) about the attraction. Seeking advice was also related to other variables in the study:

> Those who sought consultation were . . . more likely to see the attraction as beneficial. Of those seeking consultation, 78% judged the attraction to be beneficial. Of those not seeking consultation, 53% judged it beneficial. . . . Seeking consultation was also related to client awareness and therapist discomfort. Therapists who thought clients were aware of the attraction were more likely to seek consultation (80%) than those who thought the client unaware (43%). Those who felt discomfort were more likely to seek consultation (69%) than those who felt no such discomfort (39%). (Tabachnick & Fidell, 1996, pp. 316–317)

When one of the variables in a loglinear analysis is considered to be the dependent variable and the others are considered to be independent variables, the procedure is sometimes called **logit analysis.** Logit analysis is analogous to ANOVA for nominal level dependent variables, allowing the assessment of main effects and interactions for the independent variables. For example, Epperson, Bushway, and Warman (1983) conducted a study to examine the relationship of three counselor variables to their clients' propensity to drop out of counseling after only one session. The variables were sex of counselor, counselor's experience level (trainee or staff counselor), and whether or not the counselor accepted clients' definitions of their problems, a variable that Epperson et al. called *problem recognition*. Epperson et al. found two main effects: female counselors

TABLE 8-8   Data Types and Data Analysis

Dependent Variable	INDEPENDENT VARIABLE	
	Categorical	Continuous
Categorical	Chi-square analysis	Logistic regression analysis
	Loglinear analysis	
	Logit analysis[a]	
Continuous	Analysis of variance	Multiple regression analysis

[a]If the distribution of scores on the dependent variable meets certain assumptions, dichotomous dependent variables can be analyzed by ANOVA or the *t* test. See Lunney, 1970, and J. L. Myers, DiCecco, White, & Borden, 1982.

had higher client dropout rates (33%) than did male counselors (20%), and counselors who did not accept clients' problem definitions had higher dropout rates (55%) than counselors who did accept clients' problem definitions (19%). Epperson et al. also found an interaction between counselor experience and problem recognition: Trainees had similar client dropout rates regardless of whether they accepted clients' problem definitions (27%) or not (32%), whereas experienced counselors who did not accept clients' problem definitions had a much higher dropout rate (59%) than those who did (17%).

Although loglinear and logit analysis are useful tools for data analysis, they are complex to carry out and the results must be carefully interpreted. Marascuilo and Busk (1987) and Tabachnick and Fidell (1996) present good introductions to these techniques.

Data Types and Data Analysis

Let's make a brief digression to tie together a set of concepts from this chapter and the previous chapter. Think of variables as providing two types of data—categorical (nominal level) and continuous (interval and ratio level)—and as being either the independent or dependent variables in a study. The two types of data and two roles for variables result in the four combinations shown in Table 8-8. Each combination of categorical or continuous independent variable and categorical or continuous dependent variable has an appropriate statistical procedure for data analysis. Be sure to use the right form of statistical analysis for the combination of data types that you have in your research.

TESTING MEDIATIONAL HYPOTHESES

As described in the discussion of the role of theory in research in Chapter 1, theories do not always postulate direct relationships between variables. Theories sometimes postulate that an independent variable (I) affects a mediating variable (M), which in turn affects the dependent variable (D); that is, $I \rightarrow M \rightarrow D$. For example, Condon and Crano (1988) postulated that the well-established relationship between attitude similarity and liking—the more similar someone's attitudes are to our own, the more we like the person—is mediated by a third variable, the assumption that the other person likes us. That is, similarity → assumed reciprocity of liking → attraction. This section discusses some ways in which such mediational models can be tested.

Simple Mediation: Three Variables

Condon and Crano's (1988) model is an example of the simplest form of mediation, one involving only three variables. R. M. Baron and Kenny (1986) state that a mediational situation potentially exists when I is correlated with both D and M and when M is correlated with D. The existence of mediation can be tested by taking the partial correlation of I with D controlling for M: If the partial correlation is substantially smaller than the zero-order correlation between I and D, then M mediates the relationship between I and D. For example, Condon and Crano found that the zero-order correlation between similarity and attraction of .64 was reduced to .18 when assumed reciprocity of liking was controlled. MRA can also be used to test for mediation and provides a test for determining whether the mediation effect is statistically significant (see Kenny, Kashy, & Bolger, 1998, pp. 258–261).

Complex Models

Mediational models only sometimes take the form of the simple three-variable case. Consider the model shown in Figure 8-7, in which arrows lead from hypothesized causes to their effects. Drawing on Weiner's (1986) attribution theory, Meyer and Mulherin (1980) postulated that how Person A responds to a request for help from Person B depends on the degree to which Person A perceives the cause of Person B's need for help to be under Person B's control: the greater the perceived controllability, the less likely Person A is to help. However, the theory also holds that the relationship between perceived controllability and helping is mediated by Person A's emotional responses of anger and sympathy.

PATH ANALYSIS   Models of this form can be tested by **path analysis,** also called *structural equation modeling*. The terms *causal analysis* or *causal modeling* are also sometimes used; however, these terms are inaccurate because, although the models do hypothesize causal relationships, they are tested using correlational methods; therefore, one cannot draw causal conclusions from them. Path analysis uses sets of multiple regression analyses to estimate the strength of the relationship between an independent variable and a dependent variable controlling for the hypothesized mediating variables. This method is called *path analysis* because the lines indicating the hypothesized relationships in diagrams such as Figure 8-7 are referred to as *paths*, and the regression coefficients for the relationships as *path coefficients*. The model is tested statistically in two ways. First, the significance of each hypothesized path (indicated by solid lines in Figure 8-7) is tested, and any possible paths that are hypothesized not to exist, such as the path from controllability directly to helping in Meyer and Mulherin's (1980) model (indicated by the

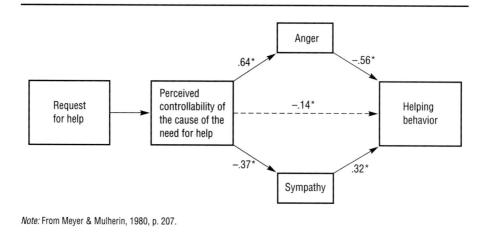

Note: From Meyer & Mulherin, 1980, p. 207.

FIGURE 8-7   Attributional Model of Response to a Request for Help
Causes perceived as controllable lead to more anger and less sympathy, which lessen the likelihood of helping.

broken line in Figure 8-7), should also be tested to ensure that they are not significant. Second, equations can be developed to reconstruct the correlation matrix for the variables from the path coefficients. This reconstructed matrix can be tested to determine how well it matches the original matrix; this test is referred to as a *goodness-of-fit test*. The better the goodness of fit, the more consistent the proposed model is with the data. See Pedhazur (1997) or Knoke and Bohrnstedt (1994) for the mechanics of this technique.

LATENT VARIABLES ANALYSIS   Meyer and Mulherin (1980) tested their model using manifest variables: They used one measure of each construct and tested the relationships among these measures. You can also use multiple measures of each construct and conduct a **latent variables analysis** (also called *covariance structure analysis* and *LISREL analysis*). This technique uses the multiple measures of each construct to estimate a latent variable score representing the construct for each research participant. For example, each participant in a study might complete three depression inventories (manifest variables), which jointly represent the latent variable of depression. Latent variables are assumed to be measured with less error than are any of the individual observed variables—the rationale is that true score variance on the latent variable that is missed by one manifest variable will be picked up by another. The technique then estimates the path coefficients for the relationships among the latent variables. This technique is being increasingly used to study relationships between hypothetical constructs such as personality, attitudes, and perceptions (Breckler, 1990), so a general understanding of it is useful. Relatively nontechnical introductions are provided by Coovert, Penner, and MacCallum (1990) and Fassinger (1987). For a latent variables analysis of Meyer and Mulherin's (1980) model, see Reisenzein (1986).

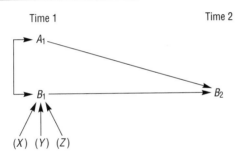

(a) Schematic diagram of a prospective correlational study

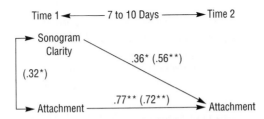

(b) Results of Lydon and Dunkel-Schetter's (1994) study of the effect of sonogram clarity on pregnant women's attachment to their fetuses

FIGURE 8-8   Prospective Correlation Analysis
A significant path coefficient from A_1 to B_2 indicates that Variable *A* may have time precedence over Variable *B*.

PROSPECTIVE RESEARCH   The use of prospective correlations—examining the correlation of a hypothesized cause at Time 1 with its hypothesized effect at Time 2—is one way of investigating the time precedence of a possible causal variable (P. A. Barnett & Gotlib, 1988). As shown in panel (a) of Figure 8-8, this kind of analysis takes the form of a path model. Variable B at Time 2 (B_2) has at least two possible causes, Variables A_1 and B_1 (the double-headed arrow represents their correlation). Variable B_1 is included as a cause of B_2 for two reasons. First, B_1 is an extraneous variable relative to A_1 and an alternative explanation to A_1 as a cause of scores on B_2: People who score high on B at Time 1 are likely to score high on B at Time 2, regardless of the effects of A. Second, B_1 represents other, unmeasured, causes of Variable B—Variables X, Y, and Z in Figure 8-8. It would be best, of course, to include Variables X, Y, and Z directly in the model as extraneous variables, but they might be either unknown or too difficult to measure. The question, then, is whether if, with B_1 controlled, A_1 has a significant relationship to B_2; in other terms, is the partial correlation of A_1 with B_2 controlling for B_1 greater than zero?

For example, panel (b) of Figure 8-8 shows the results of a study conducted by Lydon and Dunkel-Schetter (1994). They wanted to know if the clarity of a sonogram increased pregnant women's feelings of attachment to their fetuses. They measured the women's feelings of attachment immediately prior to the mothers' undergoing an ultrasound examination and immediately afterward measured the clarity of the sonogram (which the mothers saw in real time) by asking the mothers to list the parts of the fetus's body that they had seen. Clarity was operationally defined as the number of body parts listed. Attachment was again measured 7 to 10 days after the examination. As shown in panel (b) of Figure 8-8, Time 1 level of attachment was correlated with sonogram clarity ($r = .32$), indicating that women with higher initial attachment levels reported having seen more body parts; attachment at Time 1 was also highly correlated with attachment at Time 2 ($r = .77$). Sonogram clarity had a zero-order correlation of .56 with attachment at Time 2, and the significant path coefficient of .36 indicated that clarity could explain 12% of the variance in Time 2 attachment in addition to the variance explainable by presonogram attachment. Thus, mothers who saw more fetal body parts during their ultrasound examinations had higher levels of attachment to their fetuses at Time 2 than did mothers who saw fewer body parts even when initial level of attachment was controlled. By the way, initial level of attachment was high for all mothers, averaging 3.7 on a 5-point scale.

Although prospective correlational research can be useful in identifying the potential time precedence of one variable over another, draw conclusions cautiously: Some unmeasured third variable may be causing Variable A and thus be the ultimate, hidden, cause of Variable B (T. D. Cook & Campbell, 1979). In addition, as discussed next, path analysis has a number of limitations that you must always take into account.

Limits on Interpretation

Although path analysis can be an extremely useful data analysis tool, there are a number of limitations on the interpretation of its results (Cliff, 1983), two of which are emphasized here.

COMPLETENESS OF THE MODEL   The first limitation deals with the completeness of the model being tested. The issue of completeness includes two questions: (1) Are all relevant variables included? (2) Are there any curvilinear or nonadditive relationships? Because path analysis examines the patterns of partial correlations among variables, addition or deletion of a variable, or omission of an important variable, can radically change the pattern of results. Scarr (1985) provides an example of this situation. She first shows that a model predicting children's IQ scores at age 48 months from maternal positive discipline and positive control (for example, use of reasoning rather than physical punishment) adequately fits data collected from 125 families—panel (a) in Figure 8-9. However, if maternal IQ scores and educational level are added to the model as hypothesized causes of discipline and control, then the only significant predictor of child IQ score is maternal IQ score—panel (b) in Figure 8-9. Maternal IQ score is correlated with both discipline and control, and it is more highly correlated with child IQ score than are the other two variables. Therefore, with maternal IQ score partialed out, discipline and control have no relationships to child IQ score. You should therefore be certain that all relevant variables are included in a path model before conducting the

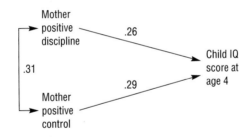

(a) Three-variable model

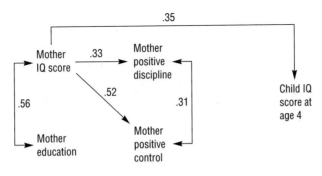

(b) Five-variable model

Note: Based on Scarr, 1985, pp. 504, 505.

FIGURE 8-9   Effect of Adding Variables to a Path Model
Adding mother IQ score and mother education to the model makes the paths from mother positive discipline and mother positive control to child IQ score at age 4 nonsignificant. Nonsignificant paths have been omitted for clarity.

analysis. Note that including variables that are not relevant (but might be) will not change the conclusions drawn from the analysis. For example, Scarr (1985) goes on to show that the ability of maternal positive discipline to predict child's social adjustment is not substantially reduced by adding maternal IQ score and educational level to the model.

Most path models assume strict linearity and additivity; that is, they do not consider the possibility of curvilinear relationships or interactions. In theory, it is possible to include such factors in path models, but they are difficult to compute and interpret (J. Cohen & Cohen, 1983). If different models are hypothesized for different participant groups or experimental conditions, separate path models can be tested for each group or condition (for example, see Elliot & Harackiewicz, 1994).

ALTERNATIVE MODELS   The second limitation on the interpretation of path analyses concerns the fit of a model to the data: It is entirely possible that more than one model will

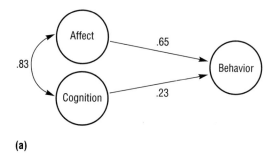

(a)

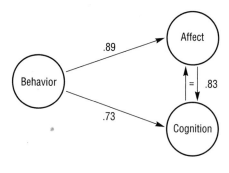

(b)

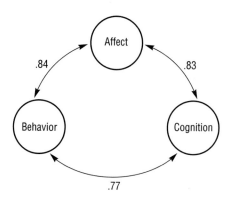

(c)

Note: From Breckler, 1990, p. 266.

FIGURE 8-10   Three Theoretical Models Relating Affect, Behavior, and Cognition

fit the data equally well (Breckler, 1990). For example, Fishbein and Ajzen (1975) proposed a model of attitude structure in which the affective and cognitive components of attitudes are causes of behavior toward the attitude object—panel (a) of Figure 8-10. However, Breckler showed that two other models fit available data equally well: Panel (b) of Figure 8-10 illustrates a model drawn from D. J. Bem's (1972) self-perception theory in which behavior toward an object is held to cause affect and cognition related to the object, and panel (c) illustrates classic theories of attitude structure that hold that affect, behavior, and cognition are interrelated but do not cause one another (McGuire, 1985). The implication of this example is that when doing a path analysis you should test not only your preferred model but also any plausible alternative models. These alternatives include different arrangements of possible causal sequences, including reverse causation and reciprocal causation.

Bear in mind that some alternative models might be ruled out by logic (for example, weight cannot cause height) or prospective correlations (for example, if Variable A does not predict Variable B across time, Variable A does not have time precedence over Variable B). In addition, sometimes experiments can be designed to eliminate specific causal possibilities or to demonstrate causality. In fact, it is not uncommon for the independent variable in a path model to be a manipulated variable. For example, Condon and Crano (1988) manipulated the apparent similarity in attitudes between the participants in their research and the person the participants were evaluating, and Meyer and Mulherin (1980) manipulated the reason why the person about whom the participants in their research read, needed help. Under these conditions, one can conclude that the independent variable causes the mediating and dependent variables. What one cannot conclude with certainty is that the mediating variable causes the dependent variable, only that the mediating variable is correlated with the dependent variable. However, other research that manipulates the mediating variable as an independent variable could reveal a causal relationship.

FACTOR ANALYSIS

Factor analysis is a statistical technique that can be applied to a set of variables to identify subsets of variables that are correlated with each other but that are relatively uncorrelated with the variables in the other subsets. These subsets of variables are called **factors.** At a conceptual level, factors represent the processes that created the correlations among the variables. For example, a factor might represent a hypothetical construct, such as attitudes toward computers. Computer attitudes could be assessed by a set of items, such as those shown in Box 8-1. People who have similar attitudes toward computers should respond to the items in the same way, leading to correlations among the items. Factor analysis can examine the correlations among the items to determine the extent to which the items are interrelated; the more strongly the items in a set are interrelated, the more likely it is that they represent one construct. If a factor analysis finds more than one factor in a set of variables, the factors might represent different constructs or different facets of a single multifaceted construct. For example, as discussed later, the 20 items in Box 8-1, all of which deal with attitudes toward computers, represent four factors: feelings of anxiety related to using computers, perceived positive effects of computers on society, perceived negative effects of computers on society, and the personal usefulness of computers.

This section briefly examines the uses of factor analysis in research and the issues to consider when conducting or reading about a factor analysis. For more detailed but still relatively nontechnical discussions of these issues, see Fabrigar, Wegener, Mac-Callum, and Strahan (1999) and Tabachnick and Fidell (1996).

Uses of Factor Analysis

At the most general level, factor analysis is used to summarize the pattern of correlations among a set of variables. For example, the 190 correlations among the scores on the 20 items in Box 8-1 can be summarized in terms of the four factors underlying those correlations. In practice, factor analysis can serve several purposes (Fabrigar et al., 1999), two of which tend to predominate.

DATA REDUCTION   One use of factor analysis is to condense a large number of variables into a few to simplify data analysis. If you have a large number of correlated dependent variables in a study, it can be easier to understand the results if they are presented in terms of a few factors rather than many individual variables. Consider, for example, the question of whether there are sex differences in attitudes toward computers. You could administer a questionnaire composed of the items in Box 8-1 to men and women and test to see if there are sex differences on each item, but it could be difficult to draw over-all conclusions from the results of 20 statistical tests. However, it would be easier to draw conclusions from tests for sex differences on the four factors those items represent.

SCALE DEVELOPMENT   The second major use of factor analysis is in the development of scales for measuring hypothetical constructs. As noted in Chapter 5, a scale should represent only one construct or be composed of subscales, each of which represents a construct or facet of a construct. After a set of items have been chosen for use on a scale, the scale developers administer the items to groups of people. They then use factor analysis to determine if the items intercorrelate in the way they should. For example, if a scale is supposed to measure just one construct, a factor analysis should find just one factor, which would represent that construct. If it finds more than one factor, the scale developers can discard the items that are not related to the factor that represents their construct. Similarly, if a scale is designed to measure more than one facet of a construct, there should be a factor for each facet.

Considerations in Factor Analysis

Factor analysis is a very heterogeneous technique: There are at least seven approaches to determining the number of factors underlying a set of correlations and nine ways of simplifying those factors so that they can be easily interpreted (Tabachnick & Fidell, 1996). Consequently, there are a large number of opinions about the "right" way to con-duct a factor analysis. The following discussion focuses on the more common questions

BOX 8-1   Items for an "Attitudes Toward Computers" Scale

1. I look forward to using a computer in my work.
2. I'm afraid of computers.
3. I feel more competent working with computers than do most people.
4. I dislike computers.
5. I could create a simple database on a computer.
6. People are becoming slaves to computers.
7. Soon our lives will be controlled by computers.
8. I feel intimidated by computers.
9. Computers are dehumanizing to society.
10. Computers can eliminate a lot of tedious work for people.
11. The use of computers is enhancing our standard of living.
12. Computers are a fast and efficient means of gaining information.
13. I avoid computers as much as possible.
14. Computers will replace the need for working people.
15. Computers are bringing us into a bright new era.
16. Soon our world will be completely run by computers.
17. Life is easier because of computers.
18. I feel that having a computer would help me in my work.
19. I prefer not to learn how to use a computer.
20. I would like to own, or do own, a computer.

Sources: Items adapted from Heinssen, Glass, & Knight, 1987; Meier, 1988; Nickell & Pinto, 1986; and Popovich, Hyde, Zakrajsek, & Blumer, 1987.

that arise in factor analysis and on the most common answers to these questions. These points are illustrated with a factor analysis of responses to the 20 items shown in Box 8-1.

NUMBER OF RESEARCH PARTICIPANTS   A major concern in factor analysis is the stability of the factors found—that is, the likelihood that a factor analysis of scores on the same items from another sample of people will produce the same results. One factor that influences stability is the number of respondents on which a factor analysis is based. There are no hard and fast rules for determining an adequate sample size, but most authorities recommend a minimum of 200 to 300 participants (Tabachnick & Fidell, 1996), although little improvement in stability may be found when sample sizes exceed 300, as long as there are more respondents than items (Tinsley & Tinsley, 1987). There were 314 respondents to the items in Box 8-1, which is adequate.

QUALITY OF THE DATA   The quality of the data also affects factor stability. Because factor analysis is based on correlations, all the factors noted earlier as threats to the validity of correlational research—outliers, restriction in range, and so forth—also threaten the validity of a factor analysis. Multicollinearity is also a problem in factor analysis because a large number of extremely high correlations leads to problems in the mathematics underlying the technique.

The correlation matrix of the scores on the items to be factor analyzed should include at least several large correlations, indicating that sets of items are interrelated. Tabachnick and Fidell (1996) recommend not conducting a factor analysis if there are no correlations larger than .30. Because examining the correlations in a large matrix can be cumbersome, you can also examine the determinant of the correlation matrix, a statistic available in most factor analysis computer programs. The closer the determinant is to zero, the higher the correlations among the variables, and the more likely you are to find stable factors.

Examination of the distributions of scores for the sample factor analysis found no outliers. The correlation matrix contained many high correlations but did not exhibit multicollinearity when each variable was regressed on the others: There were no Rs in excess of .9. The determinant of the matrix was .0002. These results indicated that the matrix was highly "factorable."

METHODS OF FACTOR EXTRACTION AND ROTATION   The term *extraction* refers to the method used to determine the number of factors underlying a set of correlations. Factors are extracted in order of importance, which is defined as the percentage of variance in the variables being analyzed that a factor can account for. The first factor accounts for the most variance, the second factor for the next largest percentage of variance, and so forth. A factor analysis will initially extract as many factors as there are variables, each accounting for a decreasing percentage of variance. Tabachnick and Fidell (1996) list seven extraction methods but point out that all give very similar results with high-quality data and a reasonable sample size.

The term *rotation* refers to the method used to clarify the factors once they are extracted. With unrotated factors it can be difficult to see which variables are associated with, or "load on," which factor, because any variable can appear to be associated with more than one factor. Rotation minimizes these multiple loadings. There are two general categories of rotation. Orthogonal rotation forces factors to be uncorrelated with one another; oblique rotation allows factors to be correlated. There are several specific types of rotation in each category; however, like the different methods of extraction, different methods of rotation within the same category provide equivalent results with high-quality data and an adequate sample size (Tabachnick & Fidell, 1996). As a practical matter, Tabachnick and Fidell recommend principal components extraction and varimax rotation (a type of orthogonal rotation) for most purposes. These are the default methods in most factor analysis computer programs and were used for the sample factor analysis.

DETERMINING THE NUMBER OF FACTORS   In a perfect world, a factor analysis would be able to tell you, "There are X number of factors underlying this correlation matrix, and that's all." Unfortunately, it's not always easy to decide how many factors there "really" are underlying a set of correlations. The decision is a matter of judgment rather than statistics—which can lead to different interpretations of factor analyses of the same data—although there are some guidelines. Two of the most commonly used rules are based on the **eigenvalues** associated with the factors. A factor's eigenvalue represents the percentage of variance in the variables being analyzed that can be accounted for by

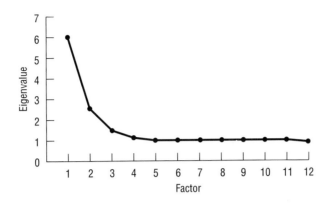

FIGURE 8-11 Plot of Eigenvalues for Factor Analysis of Items in Box 8-1
There are four eigenvalues greater than 1 and the plot levels off after Factor 4, indicating that four factors should be rotated.

that factor; the larger a factor's eigenvalue, the more variance it accounts for. Generally, factors with eigenvalues of less than 1 are considered unimportant, and the default procedure for most computer programs is to rotate only those factors with eigenvalues greater than 1. The initial results of the sample factor analysis showed four factors with eigenvalues greater than 1.

Sometimes, however, a factor analysis results in a large number of factors with eigenvalues greater than 1. For example, I once conducted a factor analysis on 61 variables that found 13 factors with eigenvalues greater than 1. Because the goal of factor analysis is to reduce a large number of variables to the smallest reasonable number, researchers often use the **scree test** to reduce the number of factors when many have eigenvalues greater than 1. The scree test is conducted by plotting the eigenvalue of each factor against its order of extraction. Figure 8-11 shows the scree plot for the first 12 factors found in the sample analysis. Generally, the scree plot will decline sharply, then level off. For example, the scree in Figure 8-11 levels off after the fourth factor. The point at which the scree levels off indicates the optimal number of factors in the data. After conducting the scree test, the researcher reruns the factor analysis, constraining the number of factors to be rotated to the number indicated by the scree test. Both the eigenvalues-greater-than-1 rule and the scree test indicated that there were four factors in the sample data of Box 8-1.

INTERPRETING THE FACTORS   The result of a factor analysis is a matrix of **factor loadings** such as that shown in Table 8-9 for the sample factor analysis. The loadings represent the correlation of each item with the underlying factor; therefore, higher factor loadings show stronger associations with a factor. Most authorities hold that an item should have a loading of at least .30 to be considered part of a factor. As a practical matter, the cutoff for factor loadings can be set relative to the size of the loadings: A large number

TABLE 8-9   Results of a Factor Analysis of the Items in Box 8-1

Item		Factor 1	Factor 2	Factor 3	Factor 4
8	Intimidated by computers	**.82**	.22	.02	−.14
13	Avoid computers	**.81**	.18	−.09	**−.33**
2	Afraid of computers	**.78**	.25	−.09	−.13
4	Dislike computers	**.68**	.22	−.11	**−.41**
3	Feel competent	**−.67**	.01	.01	.27
5	Could create a database	**−.66**	.01	.08	−.02
1	Look forward to using	**−.58**	−.02	.09	**.53**
16	World controlled by computers	.05	**.79**	−.06	−.02
7	Lives controlled by computers	.20	**.75**	−.04	.09
14	Computers will replace people	.06	**.75**	−.01	−.10
9	Computers dehumanize society	.06	**.61**	−.22	−.19
6	People are slaves to computers	.16	**.59**	−.12	−.19
11	Computers enhance life	.00	−.12	**.74**	.08
12	Efficient for gaining information	−.11	.04	**.71**	.09
17	Computers make life easier	−.07	−.08	**.70**	.10
15	Computers bring bright new era	−.16	−.14	**.65**	.21
10	Eliminate tedious work	.04	−.09	**.59**	.03
18	Computer would help me	−.19	−.10	.19	**.77**
20	Computer ownership	−.20	−.08	.18	**.72**
19	Prefer not to learn how to use	**.32**	.17	−.10	**−.71**

of high loadings justifies a higher cutoff. For example, 88% of the factor loadings greater than .30 in Table 8-9 are also greater than .50, so it would be reasonable to use .50 as a cutoff for this analysis. Therefore, we can say that Factor 1 consists of Items 1, 2, 3, 4, 5, 8, and 13, that Factor 2 consists of Items 6, 7, 9, 14, and 16, that Factor 3 consists of Items 10, 11, 12, 15, and 17, and that Factor 4 consists of Items 1, 18, 19, and 20.

Having decided which variables load on which factors, you must decide what the factors mean—that is, what construct underlies the variables—and name the factors. Factor interpretation and naming are completely judgmental processes: You examine the items that load on a factor and try to determine the concept common to them, giving more weight to items that have factor loadings with higher absolute values (that is, ignoring the factor loadings' plus or minus signs). For example, Factor 1 appears to represent anxiety about using computers, Factor 2 appears to represent perceptions of computers' negative impact on society, Factor 3 appears to represent perceptions of computers' positive impact on society, and Factor 4 appears to represent the perceived personal utility of computers.

Note two characteristics of the factor loadings shown in Table 8-9. First, a loading can be either positive or negative; positive loadings indicate positive correlations with the factor, negative loadings indicate negative correlations. Typically, items with negative loadings are worded in the opposite direction of items with positive loadings. Consider, for example, Item 8, which loaded positively on Factor 1, and Item 3, which loaded negatively. A high score on Item 8 ("I feel intimidated by computers") indicates a high degree of anxiety, whereas a high score on Item 3 ("I feel more competent working with computers than do most people") indicates a low degree of anxiety.

The second notable characteristic of the factor loadings in Table 8-9 is that an item can load on more than one factor: Items 1, 4, 13, and 19 have loadings greater than .30 on both Factor 1 and Factor 4. A large number of items loading on two factors indicates that the factors are correlated and suggests that an oblique rotation might be appropriate for the data.

FACTOR SCORES At the outset of this discussion of factor analysis, I noted that one purpose of factor analysis is to reduce a large number of variables to a smaller number. One does this by computing **factor scores,** respondents' combined scores for each factor. Factor scores can be computed in two ways. The first is to have the factor analysis computer program generate factor score coefficients for the items. These coefficients are standardized regression coefficients that predict the factor score from Z scores on the items: Multiply each participant's Z score on each item by its factor score coefficient for a factor, and sum the resulting products to obtain the participant's factor score for that factor. Typically, one uses only the items that one considers to have loaded on the factor—that is, items with factor loadings above the cutoff. When all the items use the same rating scale (such as a 1-to-7 scale), you can use a simpler process: Reverse score items with negative loadings and sum participants' scores on the items that load on each factor, just as one sums the scores on the items of a multi-item scale. You can then use factor scores as the dependent variables in other analyses of the data.

Factor analysis can be a very powerful tool for data reduction and for understanding the patterns of relationships among variables. However, it is also a very complex tool, and so you should undertake a factor analysis only after becoming familiar with the complexities of the technique and under the guidance of someone well-versed in its use.

SUMMARY

Correlational, or passive, research methods can be used to test hypotheses that are not amenable to experimental investigation, either because the constructs used as independent variables cannot be manipulated or because manipulation of the independent variables would be unethical. This chapter reviewed four aspects of correlational research: the nature of correlational research, the principal methods of correlational research, the use of correlational research to test mediational hypotheses, and factor analysis.

Except for special forms of multiple regression analysis, correlational research methods assume that the relationships between the independent and dependent variables are linear and additive. Be careful when interpreting the results of correlational research, because a number of factors can have adverse effects on the sizes of correlation coefficients. The reliability of measures puts a ceiling on the size of the correlation between their scores, and restriction in the range of scores attenuates the correlation. Outliers can either artificially inflate or deflate the correlation depending on their relation to the bulk of the scores. Differences in subgroups in the participant sample can result in a correlation for the entire sample that misrepresents the relationship between the variables in the subgroups. When conducting research with multifaceted constructs, generally treat the facets of the construct as separate variables rather than combine them into a general index of the construct. Using a general index can obscure the unique relationships of the facets to the dependent variable and make it impossible to detect interactions among the facets.

Although simple correlation is the basis for all correlational research, most studies use more complex techniques. A difference in the slope of the relationship between two variables in different groups represents an interaction between the grouping variable and the variables being tested. Partial correlation determines the relationship between two variables when the effects of a third variable are controlled.

Multiple regression analysis (MRA) examines the relationships among the members of a set of predictor variables to a criterion variable. Simultaneous MRA provides an equation that most accurately predicts the criterion variable using all the predictor variables. Hierarchical MRA allows the researcher to partial out multiple predictors from the relationship between another predictor and the criterion. Because it controls the effects of the partialed predictors, hierarchical MRA is best suited for hypothesis testing. Stepwise MRA has a number of statistical flaws and should not be used. MRA provides three types of information on the relationship between the predictor variables and the criterion variable. The multiple correlation coefficient (R) is an index of the size of the relationship between the predictor variables as a set and the criterion. A predictor's regression coefficient is an index of the size of its relationship with the criterion. Change in R^2 indicates the amount of variance in the criterion that is accounted for by adding a predictor variable to hierarchical regression. Multicollinearity is a potential problem in MRA that stems from high correlations among the predictor variables. Multicollinearity can result from having multiple measures of a construct in the set of predictor variables, from natural confounds, or from sampling error, and it can be overcome by deleting redundant variables from the predictor set or by combining multicollinear predictors into a single variable. MRA is useful as an alternative to ANOVA when the independent variables are correlated or when the independent variables are continuous rather than categorical. Although continuous variables can be transformed into categories, this procedure can have an adverse impact on the research.

Logistic regression analysis is analogous to MRA but is used with a nominal level dependent variable. It shares the assumptions of linearity and additivity and the problem of multicollinearity with MRA. Multiway frequency analysis can be used when both the independent and dependent variables are measured at the nominal level. Types of multiway frequency analysis include chi-square analysis, loglinear analysis, and logit analysis.

Mediational hypotheses are tested by correlational analysis. Simple, three variable hypotheses can be tested using either partial correlation analysis or MRA; more complex hypotheses are tested using MRA. Latent variables analysis is used when hypothetical constructs are assessed using multiple measures. Path models can also be used to test the time precedence of a proposed causal variable. When interpreting the results of path analyses, be sure that the model being tested is complete and that no alternative models fit the data.

Factor analysis examines the pattern of correlations in a set of variables to find subsets of variables whose members are related to one another and are independent of the other subsets. It is used to reduce a larger number of variables to a smaller number for data analysis and to determine if the items on a scale represent one or more than one construct. Important considerations in factor analysis include having an adequate sample size, having a set of variables that are strongly intercorrelated but not multicollinear, choice of factor extraction and rotation methods, determining the number of factors to interpret, and the interpretation of those factors.

QUESTIONS AND EXERCISES FOR REVIEW

1. Describe the circumstances in which the correlational research strategy would be preferable to the experimental strategy. What can correlational research tell us about causality?
2. Describe the effects of each of these factors on the size of a correlation coefficient:
   a. Low reliability of the measures
   b. Restriction in range
   c. Outliers
   d. Subgroup differences in the correlation between the variables
3. For the factors listed in Question 2, describe how you can determine if a problem exists and describe what can be done to rectify the problem.
4. Find three journal articles on a topic that interests you that used correlational research. Did the researchers report whether they checked for the potential problems listed in Question 2? If they found any, did they take the appropriate steps? If they did not check, how would the presence of each potential problem affect the interpretation of their results?
5. If you find a significant difference between groups, such as men and women, in the size of the correlation between two variables, how should you interpret the finding?
6. Explain why it is generally undesirable to combine the facets of a multifaceted construct into an overall index. Describe the circumstances under which it might be useful to combine facets.
7. Describe the purpose of partial correlation analysis.
8. Describe the forms of multiple regression analysis (MRA) and the purpose for which each is best suited.
9. Describe the type of information that each of the following provide about the relationship between the predictor variables and the criterion variable in MRA:
   a. The multiple correlation coefficient (R)
   b. The standardized regression coefficient (β)
   c. The unstandardized regression coefficient (B)
   d. Change in R^2
10. Describe the effects of multicollinearity. How can you detect and deal with this problem?
11. Describe the circumstances under which MRA is preferable to ANOVA.
12. Why is it undesirable to use a median split to transform a continuous variable into a categorical variable?

13. How is logistic regression analysis similar to MRA, and how is it different?

14. When should a researcher use multiway frequency analysis?

15. How does the nature of the independent and dependent variables affect the form of data analysis you should use?

16. Describe how mediational hypotheses are tested. Explain the limits on the interpretation of research that tests mediational hypotheses.

17. What is factor analysis? Describe the major issues to consider in conducting and understanding the results of a factor analysis.

9 THE SINGLE-CASE RESEARCH STRATEGY

THE ROLE OF SINGLE-CASE
RESEARCH IN PSYCHOLOGY
Some History
Current Status of Single-Case
   Research
   Objections to Single-Case
     Research
   Uses of Single-Case Research

VALIDITY CRITERIA IN SINGLE-
CASE RESEARCH
Measurement Criteria
   Objectivity
   Multiple Dependent Variables
   Multiple Sources of
     Information
   Frequent Assessment
Replication Criteria
Control Criteria
Impact Criteria
Treatment Criteria

CASE STUDY RESEARCH
Choosing Cases to Study
   Select for Validity
   Units of Analysis
Data Collection
   Plan Carefully
   Search for Disconfirming
     Evidence
   Maintain a Chain of Evidence

SINGLE-CASE EXPERIMENTS
Designs for Single-Case
   Experiments
   The A-B-A Design
   The A-B Design
   The A-B-C-B Design
   Multiple-Baseline Designs
   The Simultaneous Treatments
     Design
   The Changing Criterion
     Design
The Importance of a Stable
   Baseline
   Trends
   Variability
   What Constitutes a Stable
     Baseline?

DATA ANALYSIS IN SINGLE-
CASE RESEARCH
Qualitative Data
   Pattern Matching
   Explanation Building
   Cautions
Quantitative Data
   Visual Analysis
   Statistical Analysis

SUMMARY

QUESTIONS AND EXERCISES
FOR REVIEW

As discussed in Chapter 2, the single-case research strategy makes an intensive study of a single person, group, organization, or culture. Single-case research can take the form of either a case study or a single-case experiment. Both forms of research focus on a single instance of the phenomenon under study. However, case study research usually focuses on an event in an unconstrained natural context, whereas the single-case experiment is usually carried out in a more controlled environment with the researcher manipulating the independent variable. This chapter takes a brief look at the role of single-case research in psychology, examines the factors that affect the validity of the conclusions that one can draw from single-case research, discusses some of the factors that influence the design of case studies and single-subject experiments, and concludes with a look at the issue of data analysis in single-case research.

THE ROLE OF SINGLE-CASE RESEARCH IN PSYCHOLOGY

Although many areas of behavioral science, such as sociology, anthropology, educational research, and organizational research, have made considerable use of the single-case research strategy, it has long been out of favor in most areas of psychology. As a prelude to a general discussion of single-case research, this section provides a brief history of single-case research in psychology, lists some of the objections made to its use by many experimental psychologists, and discusses the ways in which single-case research can be useful to psychologists.

Some History

Psychological research today is dominated by the group comparison approach exemplified by experimental and correlational research strategies. This approach defines psychological knowledge in terms of the average behavior of groups of people (the nomothetic perspective) rather than on patterns of individual behavior (the idiographic approach). In sharp contrast, the founders of psychological research in the last half of the 19th century, such as Ebbinghaus, Hall, and Wundt, studied individual behavior (Barlow & Hersen, 1984; Danziger, 1990). Reports of psychological research published at that time listed the data for individual research participants rather than the mean scores that one finds today, and it often identified the participants by name. In addition, the research frequently included repeated measurement of the phenomena of interest in order to document individual change over time.

In their history of trends in psychological research, Barlow and Hersen (1984) note that in the early 20th century researchers began to change their focus to the average behavior of groups of people. This change came as a result of the emergence of the field of mental measurement, which required the determination of population average scores on measures so that people could be assessed relative to that average. The psychological testing movement spurred the development of descriptive statistics, including correlational methods, in the first quarter of the 20th century. The group focus became the norm with the development of modern inferential statistics in the 1920s and 1930s. These statistics allowed researchers to compare the average scores of groups of people — both natural groups and those formed for experiments — and provided a relatively objective tool for deciding if differences found between groups were real or due to chance: the statistical significance criterion.

While these changes were taking place, some psychologists retained their focus on the individual. Many researchers conducting experiments on sensory and perceptual processes continued to analyze data from individual research participants, and clinical psychologists conducted treatment research by means of uncontrolled case studies. However, unlike experimental research that focused on individual behavior, these case studies did not specify the operational definition of variables and took no steps to avoid the confounding of variables. These problems, coupled with a tendency for case study researchers to make exaggerated claims on the basis of limited evidence, brought the case study methodology into disrepute.

By the 1940s and 1950s, however, clinical psychologists' training began to include more background in research methodology, leading to greater emphasis on control in clinical research. Because the group comparison approach was the model for well-controlled psychological research, clinical research shifted to that model. However, by the 1960s, disenchantment with the approach began to set in. Three major objections developed to the group comparison approach to clinical research (Barlow & Hersen, 1984). First, questions were raised about the ethics of withholding or delaying treatment for members of no-treatment control groups. Second, for some diagnoses it was often impossible to find the relatively large number of patients required for group comparison research. Finally, the individual became lost in the group average. Clinical practice focuses on the individual, so practitioners began to ignore group-based clinical research, which they saw as irrelevant to their needs. In addition, clinicians are interested in patterns of change over time, and the group comparison research rarely takes a longitudinal approach.

This disenchantment led, in the 1960s and 1970s, to a renewed interest in single-case research and in the development of criteria for well-controlled case studies and single-case experiments (Barlow & Hersen, 1984; Kazdin, 1982); this development process continues currently (Kratochwill & Levin, 1992). To a large extent, these developments have taken place in the context of the behaviorist school of psychology, especially in the fields of behavior therapy and behavior modification. Consequently, most single-case experiments deal with the behavioral treatment of clinical disorders and emphasize behavioral observation as a measurement modality. However, as noted in Chapter 2, the single-case research strategy can be applied to other areas of psychology, such as cognition, human development, and group processes, and it can be used with other measurement modalities, such as self-report and physiological measures (see, for example, Barlow & Hersen, 1984; Yin, 1993, 1994).

Current Status of Single-Case Research

Use of the single-case research strategy is on the rise, especially in evaluation research (Yin, 1993, 1994). Nonetheless, the validity of the strategy is still being debated, with opponents of the strategy emphasizing its weaknesses and supporters of the strategy emphasizing its strengths. Before discussing the conduct of single-case research, let's review some of these points, which were discussed in more detail in Chapter 2.

OBJECTIONS TO SINGLE-CASE RESEARCH   The relative unpopularity of single-case research in psychology is probably due to three problems commonly attributed to the strategy by researchers trained in the group comparison tradition (Yin, 1994). Both case study research and single-case experiments are perceived as exhibiting a lack of generalizability. The argument is that it is impossible to generalize from a single case to people in general. However, as Barlow and Hersen (1984) and Yin (1994) point out, and as discussed in Chapter 14, use of the experimental or correlational strategy provides no guarantee of generalizability. Generalizability comes from replication, and the generalizability of single-case research can be tested through replication just as can the generalizability of research based on other strategies. Two other criticisms are leveled specifically at case study research. The first is that case study research lacks rigor, that it is too uncontrolled. Although many published case studies have been poorly controlled, leaving room for alternative explanations for their findings, controls can be instituted that enhance the internal validity of case study research (Kratochwill, Mott, & Dodson, 1984). The second criticism of case study research is that it takes too long to conduct. Although anthropological studies of whole cultures can take years, other case study research is not necessarily so time consuming. In addition, one advantage of the case study is its ability to provide a longitudinal, in-depth analysis of a phenomenon.

USES OF SINGLE-CASE RESEARCH   Single-case research can play an important role in the development of psychological knowledge. As noted, the single-case research strategy is a necessity for idiographic research and is often the only tool available for studying rare phenomena. It can also provide great depth of understanding through its longitudinal approach to data collection. Case studies are especially useful in providing in-depth information because they frequently take into account the environmental, social, and historical contexts of the behavior being studied and make use of data sources, such as records, documents, and interviews, not usually included in other types of research. Single cases can also show the limitations of theories by bringing to light cases that contradict general theoretical propositions. Finally, even relatively uncontrolled case studies can provide hypotheses for testing in more controlled research strategies and can bring to light previously undiscovered phenomena.

VALIDITY CRITERIA IN SINGLE-CASE RESEARCH

As noted in the historical overview, case study research has long been perceived to be sloppy and lacking in control, and so to be of minimal value as a source of useful infor-

TABLE 9-1 Validity Criteria for Single-Case Research

	Criterion	*Lower Validity*	*Higher Validity*
Measurement Criteria	Objectivity	Subjective	Objective[a]
	Dependent variables	One	Multiple
	Sources of information	One	Multiple
	Assessments	Two	Frequent[a]
Replication Criteria	Number	None	Multiple
	Cases	Homogeneous	Heterogeneous
Control Criteria	Baseline case or observation	None	Multiple
	Control for specific alternative explanations	None	Multiple
Impact Criteria	Problem type	Acute	Chronic
	Magnitude	Small	Large
	Timing	Delayed	Immediate
	Follow-ups	None	Multiple
Treatment Criteria	Degree of control	None/observed	Manipulated[a]
	Standardization	Low	High[a]
	Implementation	No monitoring	Frequent monitoring

[a]Present in all single-case experiments.

Note: Adapted from Kratochwill, Mott, & Dodson, 1984, p. 62.

mation about human behavior and psychological processes. In addition, Kazdin (1997) points out that single-case research is especially vulnerable to the internal validity threats of history and maturation because of its longitudinal nature and its usual lack of a control condition to assess these types of changes. Clinical research is also vulnerable to statistical regression because it often deals with extreme cases. However, many problems associated with single-case research can be rectified if researchers plan their studies carefully. Fifteen criteria, which can be divided into the five categories shown in Table 9-1, can be used to evaluate the internal validity of case studies and single-case experiments (Kratochwill, 1992; Kratochwill et al., 1984; Yin, 1994). As noted in the table, several of these criteria are present in all single-case experiments. The criteria emphasize the impact and breadth of the effect of an intervention as means of ruling out chance effects and confounds as explanations for changes in the dependent variables.

Measurement Criteria

As in all forms of research, proper measurement is essential to the validity of single-case research. Four measurement criteria for validity are objectivity of measurement, use of multiple dependent variables, use of multiple sources of information for the dependent variables, and frequent assessment of the dependent variables.

OBJECTIVITY   Kratochwill et al. (1984) and Yin (1994) note that a major shortcoming of much case study research is the use of informal, subjective data, such as the researcher's impressions of the effect of an independent variable, rather than more formal, objective measures of the dependent variable. As noted in Chapter 5, formal measures help researchers avoid the problem of observer bias and can be tested for reliability and validity. Measurement validity can be enhanced by the use of multiple dependent variables, multiple measures of each variable, and frequent assessment of the variables.

MULTIPLE DEPENDENT VARIABLES   One indicator of the breadth of an effect is the number of dependent variables affected by it. If the researcher measures only one outcome and finds an apparent effect, that effect could be the result of chance factors or a confound. However, if a number of dependent variables all change in the manner predicted by the theory on which the research is based, then it becomes less likely all the changes were due to chance or confounds. Most theories predict relatively broad effects for their independent variables. Hackman and Oldham's (1980) theory of work design, for example, holds that the more skills a job requires, the extent to which a worker does a complete task rather than just part of it, the more important the task, the more independence the worker has, and the more feedback the worker has on the quality of the work, the higher will be work motivation, job satisfaction, and work effectiveness. A case study test of an implementation of the theory could therefore assess three dependent variables, two of which are psychological states and the third of which is behavioral.

MULTIPLE SOURCES OF INFORMATION   The single-case researcher should try to use as many sources of information as possible for each dependent variable (Yin, 1994). A. C. Smith and Kleinman (1989), for example, used both observations and interviews as sources of information for their case study of medical students' strategies for coping with stress. It is also sometimes possible to get information about an individual from several people who have opportunities to observe the person. Ollendick (1981), for example, studied the effectiveness of a treatment for reducing the occurrence of a child's tics by having both the child's mother and teacher keep records of occurrences. Official records can also be a source of information. For example, businesses keep records of costs, productivity, and rates of employee turnover and absences; the first two provide direct indicators of work effectiveness, and the last two can be used as indirect indicators of job satisfaction and motivation. Artifacts—things that people produce either intentionally or unintentionally—can provide physical evidence of the effect of an independent variable. For example, wastage of raw materials is a negative indicator of work effectiveness in manufacturing: the more waste, the less effective the work. Finally, documents other than official records, such as letters, news reports, even graffiti, can be a source of information. Graffiti, for example, could be used as an indicator of the level of morale in a factory. As noted in Chapter 5 in the discussion of multiple operationism, the more sources of evidence that are available about the effect of an independent variable and the greater the extent to which the different sources of evidence lead to the same conclusion, the more confidence we can have in the conclusions drawn from the research.

FREQUENT ASSESSMENT   Finally, the more often the dependent variable is assessed during the research, the easier it is to rule out some alternative explanations. For example, if assessments are made only at the beginning and end of a study, then history or maturation could account for any changes observed over the course of the study. However, if the study concerns an intervention, then assessments can be made before the intervention, during the course of the intervention, and following the intervention. Such continuous data collection allows you to determine if change is associated with the onset of the intervention, thus reducing the likelihood of a history confound. The data also allow assessment of the impact criteria described next, helping to rule out maturation as an alternative explanation. The use of continuous assessment requires careful selection of sources of information. Highly intrusive measures, such as questionnaires and physiological measures, might induce reactivity that could threaten the validity of the study. Consequently, observations and records might be better suited as sources of information for more frequent assessments.

Replication Criteria

Chapter 4 showed that replication is an important tool in research, helping to determine the generalizability and limits of research findings. Replication cases should be as different from each other as possible (heterogeneous) rather than similar to each other (homogeneous) (Kratochwill et al., 1984). Successful replication across a diverse set of cases demonstrates the robustness of a phenomenon, and failures to replicate can be compared to successful replications to determine the boundary conditions of a phenomenon. Research on the success of an educational innovation, for example, might include urban, suburban, and rural schools to determine if the innovation is effective for different populations of children. Clinical research would seek heterogeneity on both patient variables, such as sex, ethnicity, and socioeconomic status, and therapist variables, such as level of experience. To the extent that the hypothesis is supported across these variations in case characteristics, the results are more generalizable.

Yin (1994) has developed a model for replicated case study research, shown in Figure 9-1, that can also be applied to single-case experiments. Following the model discussed in Chapter 4, researchers use theory to develop a set of hypotheses. These hypotheses provide a basis for selecting cases that can provide data to test them and a basis for determining the dependent variables to use and the best sources of information for each dependent variable. The researchers then conduct the case studies and write up the results for each study. Finally, the researchers compare the results across the cases to draw conclusions about the hypothesis and to determine the implications of those conclusions for theory and application.

Control Criteria

A major objection to case study research is that it is impossible to assess the impact of an independent variable because there is no control or comparison condition to use as

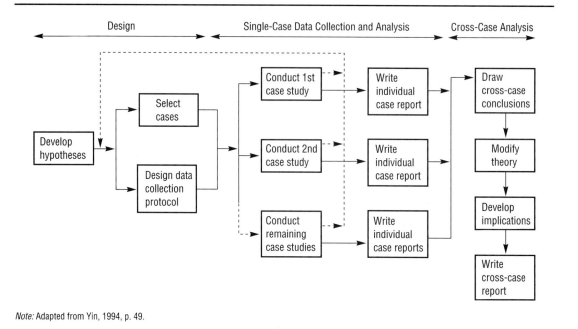

Note: Adapted from Yin, 1994, p. 49.

FIGURE 9-1   Replicated Case Study Research
Cases are selected to test the generalizability of findings.

a baseline. However, as Yin (1994) points out, a situation analogous to the experimental and control conditions of experimental research can be achieved by including both **test cases** and **control cases** in case study research. A test case, like the experimental condition in an experiment, allows the researcher to observe what happens when the independent variable is present and so could have an effect on the dependent variable. A control case, like the control condition in an experiment, allows the researcher to observe what happens in the absence of the independent variable. A comparison of the two types of cases helps rule out many threats to internal validity, as does the comparison of the experimental to the control condition in an experiment. Just as a complete test of a hypothesis in experimental research might require more than one control group, so might case study research require more than one control case.

Yin (1994) gives the example of a case study test of the hypothesis that when computers are used in school districts for both administrative and instructional purposes, then the overall rate of computer usage will increase, but that the use of computers for either purpose alone will have no effect. As shown in Table 9-2, a complete test of this hypothesis requires at least three cases: one in which computers are used for both administrative and instructional purposes, one in which computers are used for administration only, and one in which computers are used for instruction only. Only if all three predictions shown in Table 9-2 are borne out will the hypothesis be fully supported.

Control cases can also help the researcher discriminate among possible explanations for a phenomenon. For example, Szanton (1981) studied attempts by university

TABLE 9-2 Use of Replication in Case Study Research to Test a Hypothesis

Hypothesis: Joint instructional and administrative use of computers in a school district leads to increasing use of computers over time.

Case	*Prediction*
Joint use	Increase in use
Administrative use only	No increase in use
Instructional use only	No increase in use

Note: Based on Yin, 1994.

and research groups to help cities deal with urban problems. One set of studies demonstrated that university groups were unable to help cities solve a variety of problems. A second set of studies showed that nonuniversity groups also failed to help cities, demonstrating that the failures in the first group of cases were probably not due to the academic basis of the advisers. A third set of studies showed that university groups had been successful in helping private enterprise, demonstrating that university-based advisers could be successful. A final group of studies dealt with university groups that had been successful in advising cities, comparing these cases to the failure cases to identify boundary conditions that limit the success of university-based advice to city governments.

It is important to bear in mind that the use of control cases is not always desirable. For example, the use of control cases in clinical research raises the same ethical concerns as the use of no-treatment control groups, discussed in Chapter 3. In both situations, the researcher must carefully weigh the value of the knowledge to be gained from a control condition or case against the potential harm that could arise from leaving a problem untreated.

Impact Criteria

In treatment-outcome research, the magnitude of the impact that a treatment has is an indicator of the degree to which history, maturation, and statistical regression might be threats to the validity of the research (Kazdin, 1997): The greater the impact of a treatment, the less likely the change is due to these factors. Kratochwill et al. (1984) list three indicators of impact. A treatment is more likely to be the cause of a change in a chronic problem than an acute problem. Chronicity is itself an indicator that maturation is not affecting the problem, because the problem has not ameliorated over time without intervention. A large impact is more indicative of possible causality than is a small impact because statistical regression is more likely to bring about a small apparent change than a large apparent change. A treatment that has an immediate impact is more likely to be valid than one that has a delayed impact because it is unlikely that a historical event was coincident with the treatment (a possibility that can be further checked through replication), and maturation effects tend to appear in the form of gradual change over time rather than immediate change.

The impact of a treatment can also be tested through follow-up assessments. The effects of many treatments are expected to endure after the treatment itself has been terminated. The longer the effects of the treatment remain and the greater the long-term effects of the treatment, the more effective the treatment is.

Treatment Criteria

Three aspects of the treatment can affect the validity of intervention research (Kratochwill et al., 1984). The first aspect is the degree of control that the researcher has over the treatment. In the ideal case, the researcher can manipulate the treatment as the independent variable in a single-case experiment; in other cases, the researcher can only observe what happens when a treatment occurs naturally. For example, clinical researchers might be able to decide exactly when treatment will start for a patient and, in a complex treatment program, exactly when each phase of the program will begin. Controlling the onset of treatment allows researchers to establish a pretreatment baseline against which to compare changes in the dependent variable.

Second, treatments should be standardized as much as possible. That is, a specific treatment plan should be developed that adheres exactly to the theory whose propositions are being tested. For example, an organizational intervention based on Hackman and Oldham's (1980) theory of job design must be carefully planned so that all the elements the theory holds to be essential for success are included. Such detailed plans (also called *protocols*) also allow other researchers to replicate the research exactly.

Finally, researchers must ensure that the treatment is implemented exactly as described in the protocol. Implementation failures are special risks when the treatment is carried out by people other than the researchers. Therapists implementing a test protocol in a clinic, for example, might deviate from the protocol without realizing it if the protocol requires them to do things that they are not used to doing. In organizations, people might resist the implementation of programs that they do not agree with or perceive as threats to their positions in the organization. Researchers must therefore carefully monitor the implementation of the treatment plan to ensure that the treatments given match the treatment plan and are therefore in accordance with the theory being tested. Treatments that deviate from the protocol do not provide a valid test of the theory being investigated.

When researchers are careful to meet these measurement, control, replication, impact, and treatment criteria, high-validity single-case research is an achievable objective. Let's now see how these criteria can be operationalized in case studies and single-case experiments.

CASE STUDY RESEARCH

Yin (1994) notes that the case study is, perhaps, the most difficult type of research to define. This difficulty arises because case studies can be used for a number of purposes.

One purpose is descriptive, providing a narrative, detailed description of the events that take place in a situation. For example, Kidder (1981) described how a group of engineers invented and developed a new computer. A major focus of Kidder's work was on the interpersonal dynamics of the design team and how pressures from other parts of the organization, such as the marketing department, affected the design process. Other case studies are explanatory, testing the effectiveness of theories and models as explanations of events. Janis (1972), for example, compared the group processes involved in good and bad political decisions as a means of testing a theory of decision making. Finally, evaluation case studies, perhaps the type most commonly used in psychology, assess the effectiveness of a clinical or other intervention. This section reviews factors to consider in choosing the cases to include in a case study research project and some issues to consider in collecting case study data. Yin (1994) provides a detailed outline of how to conduct case study research.

Choosing Cases to Study

With the validity criteria just described in mind, the researcher can evaluate potential cases to include in a case study research project.

SELECT FOR VALIDITY   As discussed in Chapter 4, it is impossible to conduct a perfect piece of research because it is impossible to meet all the criteria necessary for perfection simultaneously; one must make tradeoffs among the criteria. Let's examine a few of the issues that can arise in trying to balance the demands of the validity criteria of case study research.

Ideally, the researcher wants to manipulate the independent variable, even in case study research. One criterion for choosing cases, then, is to look for situations in which it is possible to manipulate the independent variable. For example, in a clinical or organizational intervention, the intervention is the manipulated independent variable. If the nature of the research makes manipulation impossible, then test cases must be chosen that represent the presence of the independent variable as you would have operationally defined it if you had been able to manipulate it. That is, you decide on your operational definition of the independent variable before choosing cases and use only those cases that match the operational definition. If no cases can be found that represent an exact match with the operational definition of the independent variable, then you must decide if any cases are reasonably close to the ideal operational definition. You can then choose the best-fitting cases from among those, but you must also take into account any effects of not having an exact operational definition of the independent variable. For example, the operational definition you end up using might not completely fit the operational definition implied by the theory that you are testing. In that case, you must take the difference in operational definitions into account when deciding what implications your results have for the theory.

As noted, heterogeneity of cases helps in determining the generalizability of the results of case study research and so should be a criterion for choosing replication cases. However, when the research includes control cases, be careful to ensure that each test case has a control case as similar to it as possible. The less well the test and control cases match on extraneous variables, the more plausible extraneous variables become as alternative explanations for any differences between cases. Therefore, seek heterogeneity among test cases, but match each test case with a similar control case.

A final consideration in selecting cases is access, the opportunity to collect data. Cases selected for research should allow the opportunity for continuous assessment, the use of multiple sources of information, and appropriate follow-ups. Regardless of how ideal a case seems to be on other characteristics, one that does not allow for proper data collection is of minimum usefulness.

UNITS OF ANALYSIS   It is frequently possible to view behavior as being carried on at more than one level of aggregation. For example, in studying group decision making you can focus either on the decisions made by the group as a unit or on the decisions made by the individual group members who contributed to the group decision. Consider a jury's verdict, which is a single group-level decision based on 12 individual decisions. When studying behavior that can be viewed in terms of more than one level of aggregation, the researcher must decide on the level or levels at which to collect data. For example, should one study the collective decision of a jury or the individual decisions of its members? The answer to this question, which is based on the goals of the research, indicates the **unit of analysis** for the study: the level of aggregation at which data are to be collected.

In experimental and correlational research, the individual research participant is usually the unit of analysis. When a case study focuses on a single person, that person is the unit of analysis. However, if the research is conducted in a group or organizational context, there may be many possible units of analysis. For example, a case study of a labor union could focus on the union as a whole, on one of its locals, on the workers in a company represented by the local, on work groups within the company, or on individuals within work groups (Yin, 1994). Choice of the unit of analysis should be driven by the research question or hypothesis: What unit does the question deal with? For example, A. C. Smith and Kleinman (1989) wanted to determine the strategies that medical students used to deal with forms of stress peculiar to their studies: having to handle cadavers in their human anatomy lab and to violate the social norm that prohibits us from touching the unclothed bodies of strangers. They conducted their research with members of medical school classes. However, their unit of analysis was not the class as a group but, rather, the individual students in the class about whom and from whom they collected data.

In addition to focusing on a single unit of analysis, it is sometimes possible to conduct an **embedded case study,** which deals with the same question or hypothesis for different units of analysis, comparing results across units. For example, one could study the processes by which individual jurors make guilty-or-not-guilty decisions and the processes by which those individual decisions lead to a verdict by the jury as a whole. However, it might not be feasible to conduct an embedded case study even when it might be desirable. For example, A. C. Smith and Kleinman (1989) found it was not possible to study group processes that help people to deal with stress—such as social support—among the medical students they studied because a social norm existed that forbade students and faculty from discussing the students' emotional responses to their medical school experiences.

TABLE 9-3   Excerpt From a Hypothetical Data Collection Plan

	DEPENDENT VARIABLE: JOB SATISFACTION	
Operational Definition:	*Expressed Attitudes*	*Absenteeism*
Sources	Questionnaire completed by all workers	Records kept by personnel office
	Observation of work behavior and workers' on-the-job remarks	Observation in work areas
	Interviews with selected workers	Interviews with selected workers (to ensure that dissatisfaction is a cause of absenteeism in this factory)
	Interviews with supervisors	Interviews with supervisors (same goal)
	Interviews with selected workers' spouses	Interviews with selected workers' spouses (same goal)

Data Collection

Regardless of the research strategy you use, you must take great care in collecting your data to ensure its validity. This principle is especially true for case study research. If you have access to large numbers of research participants, as is often true of experimental and correlational research, it is fairly easy to restart data collection if a problem develops. In case study research, however, you may have only one opportunity to collect data and so must make the most of it. You must therefore plan the research carefully, actively search for data that might disconfirm your hypotheses, and maintain a chain of empirical evidence to support the conclusions you draw.

PLAN CAREFULLY   To maximize the validity of your data, you must formulate a data collection plan well before data collection begins. This plan should include the dependent variables that will be used, the operational definitions for each variable, and the sources of information for each operational definition. Table 9-3 shows an excerpt from a hypothetical collection plan for a study using job satisfaction as a dependent variable.

The plan should also specify when data will be collected from each source. Although data collection as an overall process should take place throughout the course of the study, the timing of collection from each source should be designed so as to disrupt the natural course of events in the situation as little as possible. For example, if the study in Table 9-3 were scheduled to last 6 months, questionnaires might be used at the beginning, in the middle, and at the end to minimize demands on the research participants, and interviews might be conducted throughout the study, but with no source being interviewed more than three times. Observations could be made on a daily basis, and records could be checked weekly. When planning data collection, whenever possible the researcher should consult with people at the case study site to get their input on the optimal timing for each type of data collection. For example, although a researcher might want to consult absenteeism records weekly, the personnel office might collate those data only on a biweekly basis.

Although a carefully planned case study is the ideal, detailed planning is not always possible. For example, a clinician might unexpectedly encounter an unusual case or discover a novel but effective form of therapy during a course of treatment. In such situations, the information uncovered would be of great value to other psychologists, so the people involved write up their findings in the form of a case study. In such situations, even though preplanning is not possible, adhere to the validity criteria listed in Table 9-1 as closely as possible. For example, perhaps you could initiate a set of objective measures during the course of treatment and make assessments at frequent intervals thereafter. You could also carefully record problem type, magnitude, and timing of effects, and carry the measurements through a follow-up period. Novel treatments may not be standardized, but careful records of what was done will let others implement the treatment and further test it. Such case studies can make important contributions to the scientific knowledge base, but the reports of such studies should clearly indicate which portions of the research were ad hoc and which were planned so that readers can judge the validity of the conclusions drawn by the researchers.

SEARCH FOR DISCONFIRMING EVIDENCE As the Lewis–Redfield debate described in Chapter 2 illustrated, researchers tend to interpret their data as supporting the theories they favor. Consequently, it is important in conducting case study research to search actively for data that might disconfirm hypotheses as well as for supporting data (Yin, 1994). For example, in studying the relation of job dissatisfaction to absenteeism, you might design a set of interview questions that focus only on the role of dissatisfaction in absenteeism. A better approach would also ask about other possible causes of absenteeism, such as the need to care for sick children, and the perceived importance of the different factors. In drawing conclusions from the data, you would weigh the supporting evidence against the disconfirming evidence to determine the validity of the hypotheses.

MAINTAIN A CHAIN OF EVIDENCE Recordkeeping is an important aspect of any form of research. However, it is especially important in case study research because the source of a piece of information is an essential clue to the validity of the information. For example, if your records simply state that, in an organization being studied, job dissatisfaction is a cause of absenteeism, how do you judge the validity of that conclusion? If your records show where that information came from, such as a series of interviews with employees who have records of absenteeism, then you can judge the validity of the information. Yin (1994) refers to the function of recordkeeping as "maintaining a chain of evidence" that allows a person, especially someone not connected to the research project, to trace the source of every conclusion drawn from the research and to link every conclusion to a hypothesis.

There are four essential links in this chain (Yin, 1994): First, the research report written about the study should clearly indicate the data on which each conclusion is based. For example, case studies frequently quote excerpts from interviews and documents or provide detailed descriptions of observations in support of a conclusion (see, for example, Simon, Eder, & Evans, 1992; A. C. Smith & Kleinman, 1989). Second, the case study records should include complete transcripts of interviews and copies of documents and observation records so that the quotations and examples used in the report can be read in context. Each record should also clearly indicate the circumstances under which the data were collected, such as the date and place of an interview and, to the extent that confidentiality allows, the identity of the person interviewed. Third, the record should indicate how the circumstances under which each set of data (such as an interview) was collected fit the requirements of the data collection plan. This procedure ensures that the data were collected as specified in the plan; for example, it ensures that the correct person was interviewed on the correct topic at the correct point in the research project. Finally, the data collection plan should indicate how the data collected relate to the study questions by showing which data are intended to answer which questions.

A chain of evidence such as this supports the validity of a case study in two ways. First, it allows you to work forward, tracing the links from a study question to the data collection plan to ensure that plans were made to answer each question completely. You can then go from the data collection plan to the records to make sure that all the relevant data were collected. Finally, you can go from the records to the report to ensure that all relevant data were reported. The second way to check validity is to work backward from the conclusions drawn in the report, examining the evidence in the records supporting the conclusions, checking the validity of the data by determining if the data were collected according to plan, and seeing if the plan made adequate provisions to answer all the study questions completely.

SINGLE-CASE EXPERIMENTS

Like case studies, single-case experiments focus on the behavior of a single person or case rather than on the average behavior of the members of a group of people or cases. However, the single-case experimenter exerts more control over the research situation than does the case study researcher. The principal differences are that the single-case experimenter manipulates the independent variable in the research, obtains baseline data against which to compare the effects of the independent variable, controls the research context to reduce the effects of extraneous variables, and assesses the dependent variable continuously over a period of time. In essence, the single-case experimenter trades off some of the case study researcher's naturalism in order to gain more control while maintaining a focus on individual behavior. There is no hard and fast line dividing case studies from single-case experiments: As the researcher exerts more control over the research situation, the research becomes more like a single-case experiment than a case study. This section looks at some of the basic designs that are used for single-case experimentation and then discusses the importance of the baseline period for assessing the validity of single-case experiments.

Designs for Single-Case Experiments

The single-case experiment is a very flexible research strategy that can be implemented in a wide variety of ways (Barlow & Hersen, 1984). Its essence, however, is quite straightforward: The researcher assesses the dependent variable for a case (usually a be-havior) over a period of time in order to determine the baseline frequency of the be-havior in the absence of the independent variable. This baseline period, designated "A" in descriptions of single-case experiments, is equivalent to the control condition in a within-subjects experiment. The researcher then exposes the case to the independent variable and assesses the dependent variable again. This experimental condition is des-ignated "B," and if additional conditions are used, they are designated with ascending letters of the alphabet: "C," etc. The effect of the independent variable is determined by comparing the case's rate of behavior in the experimental condition with the rate in the baseline condition. This section discusses six of the most basic single-case experi-mental designs: A-B-A, A-B, A-B-C-B, multiple baseline, simultaneous treatment, and changing criterion.

THE A-B-A DESIGN   The **A-B-A design** is the most basic of the single-case experimen-tal designs: The researcher assesses the case's behavior over a baseline period, introduces the independent variable, and then removes the independent variable. The logic of the design is that the independent variable should bring about a change in behavior from Period A to Period B. Furthermore, if the independent variable is the true cause of the change, the behavior should revert to the baseline level if the independent variable is removed. That is, there should be a reversal of behavior from Period B to the second A period; for this reason, these designs are also called **reversal designs.**

Walker and Buckley (1968) used an A-B-A design to test the effectiveness of a con-ditioning procedure as a way of increasing the amount of time children pay attention to a classroom task. The participant in the experiment was a 9-year-old boy who was eas-ily distracted in class. The conditioning procedure consisted of having the boy sit at a table and work on a school task. During the time he was there, the experimenter would make slight noises; each time the boy ignored the distraction, he was rewarded with a point. After the experiment was over, he was allowed to trade his points for a prize. The results of the experiment are shown in Figure 9-2. As you can see, the reward had a dra-matic effect on the boy's "attending behavior." He spent a much larger proportion of his time on task during the reward period than during the baseline period, and his time on task decreased markedly and rapidly when the reward was withdrawn. After completion of the experiment, the boy was enrolled in a program designed to bring about lasting improvement in his attention span through the use of reinforcement by his teachers.

THE A-B DESIGN   Use of the A-B-A or other reversal design implies that the continued presence of the independent variable is necessary for maintaining the behavior change and that the removal of the treatment is ethically feasible. If the independent variable is expected to bring about a change that should continue even after exposure to the in-dependent variable is terminated—if, for example, the independent variable was a smoking cessation program — or if removal of the treatment might result in harm, then an A-B design is used. As its name indicates, the A-B design does not include a rever-sal period to allow a return to baseline levels of behavior; consequently, the researcher must use criteria other than return to baseline to assess the effect of the independent variable. These criteria include the magnitude and immediacy of the effect, and the continuation of the effect during long-term follow-up assessments.

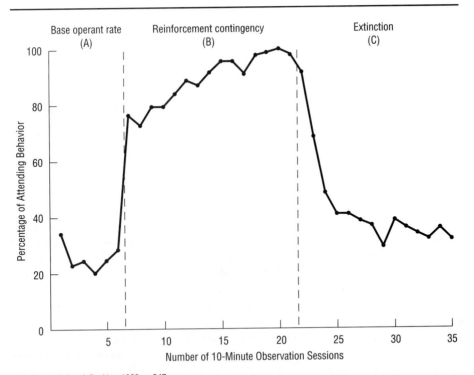

Note: From Walker & Buckley, 1968, p. 247.

FIGURE 9-2   An A-B-A Design
Walker and Buckley (1968) first collected baseline data on the amount of time a child paid attention in class (first A period), then rewarded the child for paying attention (B period), then removed the reward (second A period). Attention increased with reward and decreased when reward was removed, indicating that the reward caused the increase in attention.

THE A-B-C-B DESIGN   Chapter 7 noted that research hypotheses sometimes require special control groups to fully test a hypothesis or to rule out alternative explanations for the effect of the independent variable. The **A-B-C-B design** introduces an additional control condition — the C condition — to single-case experimentation. Miller, Hersen, Eisler, and Watts (1974) wanted to determine if reward could be used to help alcoholics reduce their drinking. The researchers hypothesized that rewarding an alcoholic each time he showed a zero blood alcohol concentration (BAC) would result in his stopping drinking in order to obtain the reward. Their hypothesis specified that the change in behavior would be contingent on the reward. That is, they expected the procedure to work only if the alcoholic was rewarded when he had a zero BAC; a reward when he had an elevated BAC was hypothesized to be ineffective. Miller et al. tested their hypotheses by having an alcoholic take a surprise blood-alcohol test twice a week for 3 weeks as a baseline condition. He was then told he would be given $3 every time he had a zero BAC on a test. For the next 3 weeks, he was rewarded with $3 for a zero BAC (the B experimental condition). During the following 3-week period, the alcoholic

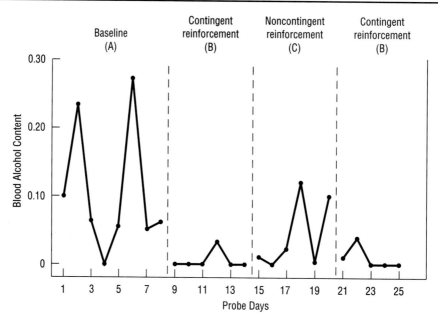

Note: From Miller et al., 1974, p. 262.

FIGURE 9-3   An A-B-C-B Design
Miller, Hersen, Eisler, and Watts (1974) first took baseline blood alcohol content (BAC) measures from an alcoholic (A period), provided reward contingent on his having a zero BAC (first B period), provided a non-contingent reward (C period), and reinstated the contingent reward (second B period). BAC decreased under contingent reward, increased under noncontingent reward, and decreased again under contingent reward, indicating that contingent reward, not just any reward, was necessary to bring the behavior change about.

received noncontingent reward: He was given $3 regardless of his BAC (the C experimental condition). Finally, the B condition was reinstated for 3 weeks.

Figure 9-3 shows the results of the experiment. The alcoholic's BAC was high during the A period, with a mean of 0.11% and a high of 0.27%. The BAC dropped to zero during the first B period, increased during the C period, and returned to zero during the second B period. The increase from the first B period to the C period and the reversal in the second B period supported the researchers' hypothesis that the reward had to be contingent on a zero BAC in order to maintain a low level of drinking. Note that Miller et al. could have added a second A period to the end of the experimental sequence to try to show a reversal from the B condition to the A condition. However, such a A-B-C-B-A design would not have been ethical in this case because it probably would have resulted in the alcoholic's returning to a high level of drinking.

MULTIPLE-BASELINE DESIGNS   History is a threat to the internal validity of single-case experiments because it is possible that some outside event may coincide with the institution of the independent variable and will therefore be the true cause of change in the

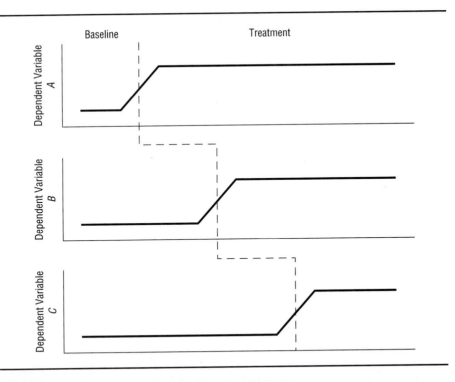

FIGURE 9-4   Schematic Representation of a Multiple Baseline Design
Different behaviors are targeted for treatment at different times. If each targeted behavior changes only when its treatment is instituted, it is unlikely that a history confound occurred because it is unlikely that a history confound would be coincident with the institution of *each* treatment.

dependent variable. One technique that researchers can use to reduce the likelihood of a history confound as an explanation for the results of the study is the **multiple-baseline design.** In one type of multiple-baseline design, the researcher identifies several dependent variables. All the dependent variables are observed for a baseline period, then the independent variable is applied to one of them. After a predetermined period of time, the treatment is applied to the second dependent variable. After another predetermined period of time, the treatment is applied to the third dependent variable, and so forth. Each dependent variable has a longer baseline than the one before it; for example, the second dependent variable has a baseline period that totals the original baseline plus the predetermined wait after the treatment is applied to the first dependent variable. Figure 9-4 illustrates this process. If the treatment has the predicted effect on each dependent variable in sequence, it becomes unlikely that history could be an explanation each time. In addition to multiple baselines across dependent variables, they can also be used across settings and research participants. Multiple-baseline designs therefore also test the generalizability of the effect being studied. Let's look at examples of each of these types of multiple-baseline applications.

Bornstein, Bellack, and Hersen (1977) conducted an A-B multiple-baseline study across behaviors to test the effectiveness of social skills training for children. They

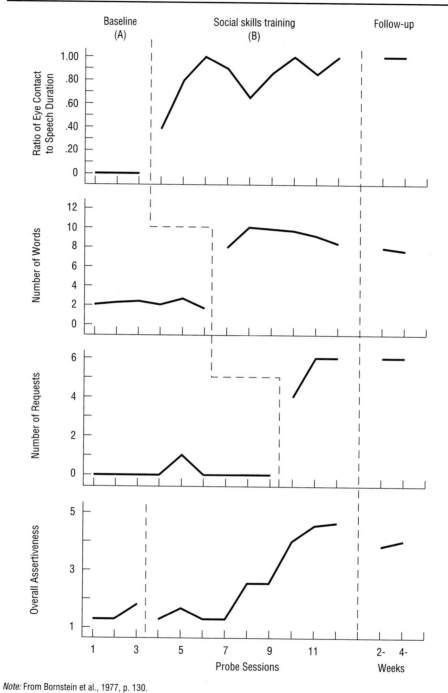

Baseline (A) · Social skills training (B) · Follow-up

Note: From Bornstein et al., 1977, p. 130.

FIGURE 9-5 An A-B Multiple-Baseline Design Across Behaviors

Bornstein, Bellack, and Hersen (1977) studied the effect of social skills training on three behaviors related to assertiveness. Each behavior changed only when it was targeted for treatment.

focused on three behavioral indicators of assertiveness: the proportion of time that the child maintained eye contact while speaking, the loudness of the child's speech, and the number of requests the child made. Reinforcement of the first behavior followed a 1-week baseline, reinforcement of the second behavior began a week later (providing a 2-week baseline for it), and reinforcement of the third behavior began a week following the beginning of treatment for the second behavior (providing a 3-week baseline for it). The results for one of the participants in the research are shown in Figure 9-5; the study was replicated across several children, including both boys and girls. The first three panels of the figure clearly show the effect of the treatment for each behavior; the bottom panel shows the cumulative effect across behaviors. Notice that each behavior shows a change only after the treatment for it is instituted. If all three behaviors had changed when the treatment for the first had been instituted, then a history confound could have occurred. Because simultaneous changes would also occur for behaviors that are naturally correlated, only uncorrelated behaviors should be used in designs in which the baseline changes across variables (Barlow & Hersen, 1984). A difficulty in implementing this design is that it may not be possible to find several uncorrelated behaviors that will respond to the same independent variable.

Ollendick (1981) conducted a study with an A-B design of a behavioral treatment for a child's facial tics using baselines across two settings, school and home. He taught the child techniques for controlling the tics and had the child keep track of his tics as a way of reinforcing the success of the treatment: The child would have a rewarding feeling of success when he saw the frequency of tics decline. Ollendick referred to the recordkeeping procedure as "self-monitoring." The results of the study are shown in Figure 9-6. The school and home settings had a common 5-day baseline, after which the child kept track of his tics in school; 5 days later, he began to keep track at home. Notice that the tics in school showed a more dramatic change because they started at a higher level and that the treatment at school did not affect the behavior at home. Notice also that Ollendick checked the reliability of the child's recordkeeping by having his teacher keep track of tics at school and his mother keep track at home; they also recorded the baseline data.

Dyer, Christian, and Luce (1982) conducted a study with an A-B-A-B design in which the baseline changed across research participants to test the effectiveness of a treatment for improving the performance of autistic children on certain tasks. The treatment consisted of making the children wait briefly before responding to questions. The treatment was used because teachers of autistic children had noticed that the children seemed to start making responses to stimuli before actually paying attention to them. The study included three children—two girls and a boy—each of whom was tested on a different task; these procedures helped demonstrate the generalizability of the results. Each child had a baseline period of different length before the treatment was instituted. The results of the study are shown in Figure 9-7. The treatment was effective for each child. The A-B-A-B design showed that it was the treatment that was changing the children's behavior, and the multiple-baseline approach helped to improve generalizability and rule out a history confound as an explanation of the effect.

THE SIMULTANEOUS TREATMENTS DESIGN   The **simultaneous treatments design,** also called the *alternating treatments design,* can be used to test the relative effectiveness of several

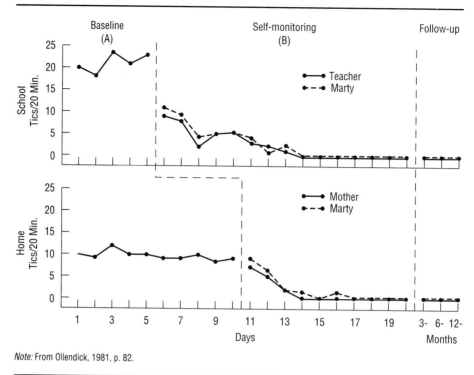

Note: From Ollendick, 1981, p. 82.

FIGURE 9-6 A Multiple-Baseline Design Across Settings
Ollendick (1981) studied the effectiveness of self-monitoring for reducing tics in both a school and home setting.

treatments in one experiment. A no-treatment condition can also be included. In a simultaneous treatments experiment, each research session is divided into several equal time periods, one for each treatment. Each treatment is used during its time period, and the order of treatments is counterbalanced across research sessions. Ollendick, Shapiro, and Barrett (1981) used a simultaneous treatments design to compare the effectiveness of two treatments for controlling stereotypic hand movements made by mentally retarded children. Stereotypic movements are motions that follow the same pattern time after time and interfere with the proper movement required by a stimulus. The treatments were physical restraint of the stereotypic movements and "positive practice," in which the experimenter assisted the child in making the proper movement. In addition, the researchers included a no-treatment control condition. Each 15-minute research session was divided into three 5-minute periods, one for each treatment. The results for one of the research participants are shown in Figure 9-8. Stereotypic behaviors tended to increase during the baseline period and continued at a high level when no intervention was used. However, physical restraint brought about a gradual decline in the movements, and positive practice led to a rapid and greater decline.

Unlike other single-case experimental designs, the simultaneous treatments design

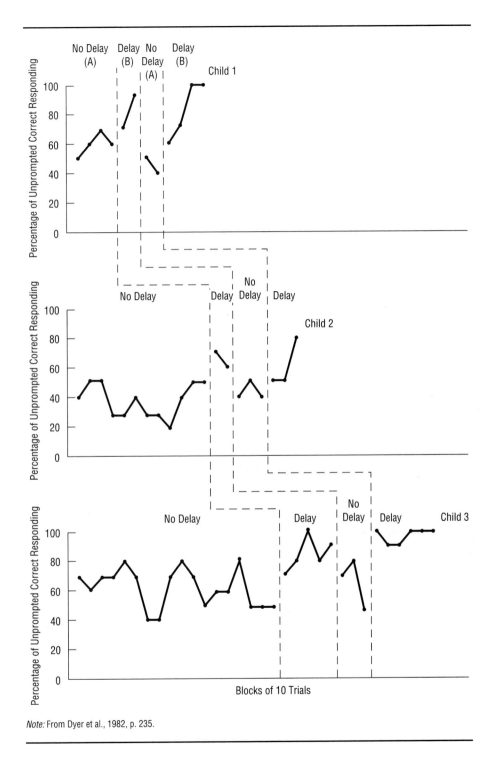

Note: From Dyer et al., 1982, p. 235.

FIGURE 9-7   A Multiple-Baseline Design Across Participants

Dyer, Christian, and Luce (1982) tested the effectiveness of an intervention for improving the task performance of autistic children.

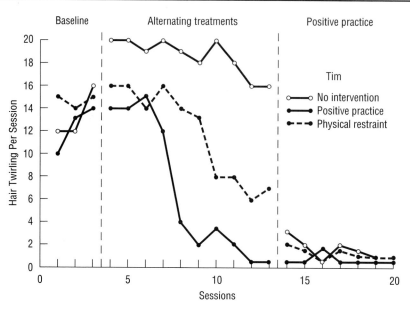

Note: From Ollendick et al., 1981, p. 574.

FIGURE 9-8   A Simultaneous Treatments Design
Ollendick, Shapiro, and Barrett (1981) compared two treatments for controlling stereotypic hand movements made by a mentally retarded child to a no-treatment control condition. Each treatment session was divided into three periods, one for each condition of the experiment. During the baseline phase of the experiment, each treatment was assigned a period within each session for data collection purposes, but no treatment took place; this procedure provided a baseline for each treatment implemented in the next phase of the study. The treatments were implemented during the alternating treatments phase; both treatments reduced the behavior relative to no treatment, but positive practice was more effective than restraint. In the positive practice phase, as in the baseline phase, each condition was allocated a period within each session, but only positive practice was given.

allows the direct comparison of two treatments. It also allows the inclusion of a control condition. As in the Ollendick et al. (1981) experiment, this control condition helps to rule out history and maturation as threats to the internal validity of the research, just as a control condition does in group comparison experimental designs. However, two factors limit the use of this design. First, the treatments must not have carryover effects; otherwise, it becomes impossible to tell just which treatment is having an effect. Second, the participants must not be aware of the changes in treatment, or else reactivity might become a problem. Awareness of change can be lessened by using treatments that differ only slightly. For example, the experimenters in Ollendick et al.'s research held the children's hands in both treatment conditions, but restrained the hands in one condition and guided them in another.

THE CHANGING CRITERION DESIGN   As noted in the discussion of the validity criteria for single-case research, an immediate large change in the dependent variable in response

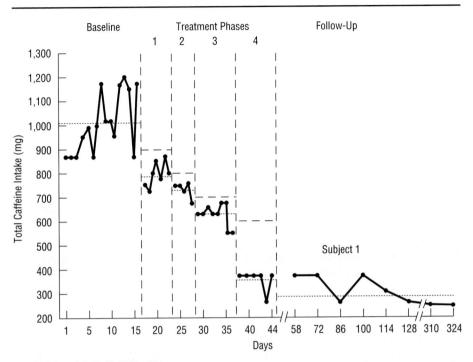

Baseline   Treatment Phases   Follow-Up
                1   2   3   4

Note: From Foxx & Rubinoff, 1979, p. 339.

FIGURE 9-9   A Changing Criterion Design
Because small changes were expected, Foxx and Rubinoff (1979) established a set of incremental criteria for evaluating the effectiveness of a treatment designed to reduce caffeine consumption.

to treatment was an indicator of the effectiveness of the treatment. But what if the nature of the treatment or the dependent variable leads one to expect a gradual change? In a **changing criterion design,** the researcher sets specific criteria for the dependent variable to reach as indicators of treatment effectiveness. If the treatment leads to the expected change across an increasingly difficult criterion, then it is considered to be effective. To the extent that the dependent variable meets the changing criterion, history confounds can be eliminated because it is unlikely that an external event would affect the dependent variable coincident with every change in the criterion.

Foxx and Rubinoff (1979) used a changing criterion design to assess the effectiveness of a behavioral treatment for excessive coffee drinking. Research participants had an average daily caffeine intake exceeding 1,000 milligrams (mg), equivalent to about 10 cups of coffee; the goal was to reduce intake below 600 mg. As shown in Figure 9-9, the treatment protocol required participants to reduce their caffeine intake in increments of 102 mg; once the first 102-mg criterion was met (such as from 1,000 mg to 898 mg), the treatment aimed at reducing intake by another 102 mg, continuing until the final goal was met and sustained during a follow-up evaluation. Kazdin (1997) notes that the changing criterion design is weaker than the other single-case experimental designs because it brings change gradually, making it more difficult to rule out confounds as an explanation for the change. However, it is the best design to use when change is expected to be slow.

The Importance of a Stable Baseline

Having looked at some single-case experiments, let's now pause to consider one of the most essential elements of these designs—the baseline period. The baseline period serves as the control condition of a single-subject experiment and, as such, serves as the basis for deciding if the independent variable had an effect. For the researcher to draw valid conclusions, the baseline data in single-case experiments must be stable; that is, they should exhibit no upward or downward trend and should have low variability (Kazdin, 1997).

TRENDS   Baseline data show a **trend** if their values increase or decrease over time; a no-trend baseline is essentially flat, exhibiting random variations around a mean value. Consider the hypothetical baselines shown in Figure 9-10; the solid lines connect the data points for disruptive behavior of a hyperactive child, and the broken lines indicate the trend. Panel (a) shows a no-trend baseline; the data points vary randomly around a mean of 37.5. Panel (b) shows an increasing baseline, with the rate of disruptive behavior rising from 25 to 100. Panel (c) shows a decreasing baseline, with the rate of disruptive behavior falling from 75 to 25. A trend in baseline data causes the greatest problem for research when the trend is in the direction of the change that the treatment is intended to produce. For example, if an experiment were conducted to test the effectiveness of a treatment designed to reduce disruptive behavior and the rate of disruptive behavior declined after the treatment was introduced, a decreasing baseline could make it impossible to decide whether the independent variable affected the behavior or if the natural downward trend were continuing.

If baseline data show a trend in the expected direction of the effect of the treatment, consider replacing the research participant with a person who shows a flat baseline. Or you could implement the treatment and see if the rate of behavior change is affected. For example, if both the baseline trend and the expected treatment effect are toward a decrease in the occurrence of a behavior, does the behavior decrease more quickly after implementation of the treatment? Figure 9-11 illustrates such a situation: The baseline shows a decreasing trend, but the rate of change increases during the treatment phase of the research.

If a study does not include baseline data, it becomes impossible to determine the effect of the independent variable. Consider the data in Figure 9-12, which are based on data from a single-case experiment on the effectiveness of a behavioral weight loss treatment (J. E. Martin & Sachs, 1973). Panel (a) shows the data as reported in the study. The data pertain only to the treatment period because the researchers collected no baseline data; nonetheless, they concluded that the treatment had been effective. However, consider panel (b), which adds a hypothetical decreasing baseline. Under these conditions, one would conclude that there was no evidence for the effectiveness of the treatment: During the treatment period, the person being treated merely contin-

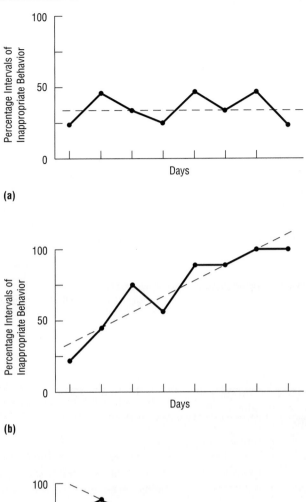

(a)

(b)

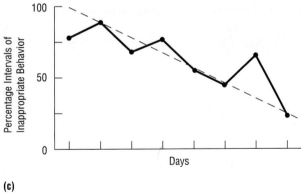

(c)

Note: Adapted from Kazdin, 1997, p. 211.

FIGURE 9-10 Hypothetical Baseline Trends for a Child's Disruptive Behavior
A stable baseline with no systematic trend over time; a trend with behavior becoming worse over time; a trend with behavior improving over time. The trend shown in panel (c) is most likely to make data interpretation difficult because it is in the direction of the expected effect.

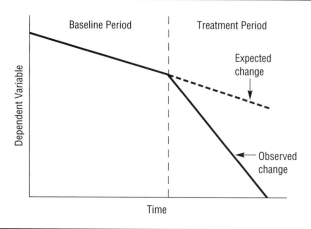

FIGURE 9-11   An Effective Treatment With a Decreasing Baseline
The behavior during treatment changes faster than expected on the basis of the baseline data (broken line).

ued a weight loss that had already begun. Panel (c) adds a hypothetical no-trend base-line; under these conditions, the treatment appears to have had an effect.

VARIABILITY   In addition to showing no trend, a stable baseline shows little variabil-ity around the mean value of the data. For example, Panel (a) of Figure 9-13 shows a high-variability baseline: Although the trend is flat, the data have a standard devia-tion of about 41. In contrast, the low-variability baseline shown in panel (b) is also flat but has a standard deviation of about 12. The more variability there is in the base-line data, the harder it becomes to tell if any changes that occur after the institution of the independent variable are due to the independent variable or to natural fluctua-tions in the dependent variable. Turn back for a moment to Figure 9-3 and notice the high variability in Miller et al.'s (1974) baseline data. If the alcoholic's BACs during treatment had fallen into the range of baseline variability, it would not have been possible to say with any degree of certainty that the independent variable had had an effect. However, the near-zero BAC levels during treatment and the reversal during the "C" phase indicate that the treatment was having the desired effect. Kazdin (1982) discusses in detail the interpretation of single-case experiments with high-variability baselines.

WHAT CONSTITUTES A STABLE BASELINE?   Unfortunately, there are no absolute criteria for determining the stability of baseline data. Because reactivity is one factor that can lead to instability (Bordens & Abbott, 1999), stability might be achieved only after a rela-tive lengthy period of observation during which novelty effects can wear off. In addi-tion, different variables show different levels of natural variability, from the high variability shown by BACs in Figure 9-3 to the almost zero variability shown by the as-sertiveness behaviors in Figure 9-5. A behavior can also differ in variability across set-

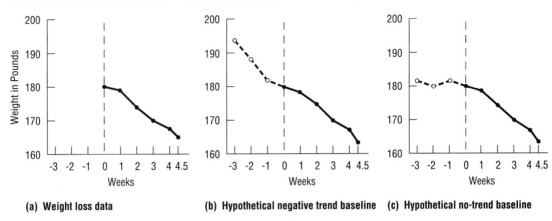

(a) Weight loss data   (b) Hypothetical negative trend baseline   (c) Hypothetical no-trend baseline

Note: (a) and treatment data in (b) and (c) are from Martin & Sachs, 1973, p. 157.

FIGURE 9-12   Effect of Different Baselines on Interpretation of the Results of a Single-Case Experiment
With no baseline there is no way to evaluate the effectiveness of the treatment. A decreasing baseline suggests that the treatment has no effect. A flat baseline suggests that the treatment is effective.

tings, as shown by the data for facial tics shown in Figure 9-6. Consequently, deciding whether a baseline is sufficiently stable to allow institution of the independent variable depends greatly on one's knowledge of the dependent variable. Researchers who are relatively inexperienced with a particular variable should seek the advice of more experienced colleagues.

DATA ANALYSIS IN SINGLE-CASE RESEARCH

Data analysis in group comparison research is relatively straightforward: The data are numerical, and there is a well-developed set of statistical techniques designed to help the researcher draw conclusions from them. The situation is relatively more complex for single-case research. Case study data are frequently qualitative, consisting of notes made during observations, transcripts of interviews, and so forth, and so are not always amenable to statistical analysis. In addition, many researchers who use the case study method eschew statistical analysis on philosophical grounds; recall the discussion in Chapter 1 of differing approaches to scientific knowledge. Single-case experiments and some case studies do produce quantitative, or numerical, data. However, statisticians have only recently taken an interest in the analysis of single-case data, so quantitative data from single-case research are often analyzed by visual inspection—graphing the results and deciding whether the pattern of data indicates that the independent variable had an effect. This section provides a brief overview of some of the issues in the qualitative and quantitative analysis of single-case data.

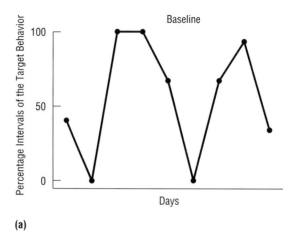

(a)

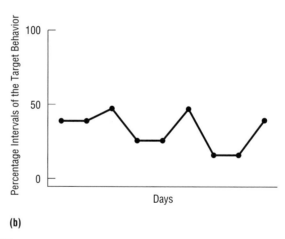

(b)

Note: Kazdin, 1997, p. 213.

FIGURE 9-13   Hypothetical Baseline Data Illustrating High (a) and Low (b) Variability
Treatment effects are more easily evaluated with little variability in the data.

Qualitative Data

Yin (1994) suggests two strategies for analyzing qualitative data. With **pattern matching,** the researcher starts with a theory and examines the data to see if they support predictions made by the theory. With **explanation building,** the researcher examines the data in order to find patterns that emerge from them; these patterns then suggest hypotheses that explain the process being studied.

TABLE 9-4 Pattern Matching in Kerckhoff and Back (1968)

Theoretical Prediction	Observation
Hysteria results from stress.	Workers were in a new plant. There was a high degree of ambiguity about work procedures and expectations. Such ambiguity tends to be stressful.
	There was pressure for increased production just before the outbreak.
	Workers had to work long overtime shifts on short notice.
Victims should show specific vulnerability factors.	These factors were more common among affected workers than with unaffected workers.
Group hysteria is transmitted through the social network.	98% of affected workers were on the same shift.
	Affected workers were closer friends with other affected workers than with unaffected workers.
Group hysteria spreads quickly.	80% of cases occurred in 2 days.

Note: Adapted from Evans, 1985, pp. 219–220.

PATTERN MATCHING The pattern-matching approach starts with a theory from which the researcher derives hypotheses before collecting data. These hypotheses drive the data collection process by providing a framework for the data collection plan. The plan is devised so that it is possible to collect both data that support the hypotheses and data that could contradict the hypotheses. After the data have been collected, the researcher can list the hypotheses along with their supporting and disconfirming data. For example, Kerckhoff and Back (1968) conducted a case study of the spread of a mysterious illness through one department of a clothing factory. Because medical investigators could find no physical cause for the symptoms presented by the affected employees, Kerckhoff and Back hypothesized that the illness was psychosomatic and spread through "hysterical contagion." They developed a set of hypotheses based on clinical theories of hysterical disorders and group hysteria, some of which are shown in the left-hand column of Table 9-4; data relevant to the hypotheses are summarized in the right-hand column. Once the hypotheses and data are displayed in this format, the researcher can judge how well the data fit the hypotheses. Based on their observations, Kerckhoff and Back concluded that their hypotheses were supported.

EXPLANATION BUILDING The explanation-building approach to qualitative data analysis requires the researcher to search for patterns in the data. The goal is to devise hypotheses and theories that explain the process under study (Lofland & Lofland, 1995). There are four aspects to the process of explanation building (Marshall & Rossman, 1989): organizing the data, generating categories, themes, and patterns, testing emergent hypotheses, and searching for alternative explanations. These aspects are not discrete steps, but go on simultaneously and continuously throughout the data analysis

BOX 9-1   Examples of Patterns That Might Be Found in Qualitative Data

1. Types: Does a behavior take only one or more than one form? For example, aggression can be physical or verbal, direct or indirect, active or passive (recall Table 1-2).

2. Frequency: How often does a behavior occur? How many people (or what proportion of a group of people) perform the behavior?

3. Magnitude: How strong or weak is the behavior? For example, aggressive behaviors can vary in the degree of injury they inflict.

4. Structure: How are aspects of the behavior related to one another? For example, are certain categories of people more likely to use some forms of aggression and not others?

5. Processes: Is there a progression in the way things happen? For example, do events happen in sequence with one form of aggression leading to another? Is there a cycle to events, with a behavior occurring periodically or a sequence repeating itself?

6. Causality: What are the apparent causes of a behavior? Does there appear to be only one cause or multiple causes? Do the causes appear to be cumulative, such that a certain number must be present for the behavior to occur? Does the cause appear to be a characteristic of the situation or of the people in the situation?

7. Consequences: What are the apparent effects of a behavior? What functions does a behavior appear to serve? For example, does being aggressive appear to allow one person to control another? Always bear in mind, however, that the observed effect might not be the intended effect. For example, a behavior might cause an unintended injury.

8. Agency: What strategies do people use to cope with situational demands? For example, a victim of aggression might try to minimize contact with the aggressor.

Source: Adapted from Lofland & Lofland, 1995.

process. Organization consists of examining the data for what appear to be key items of information around which the entire data set can be organized. These key items form the basis for determining patterns in the data, such as consistencies in behavior and in responses to questions. Box 9-1 shows some examples of the types of patterns that might be found in qualitative data. The patterns form the basis for hypotheses that are used to explain the phenomenon being studied, and the validity of the hypotheses can be checked against other data. Finally, the researcher must examine data for possible alternatives to the initial hypotheses. Miles and Huberman (1984) and Patton (1990) provide detailed descriptions of methods for qualitative data analysis, including data from replicated case studies.

A. C. Smith and Kleinman (1989) took the explanation-building approach to the data from their study of the strategies that medical students use to cope with stress. Their observations and interviews revealed five coping strategies that the students used separately and in combination: treating the experience as intellectual rather than emotional, focusing on positive aspects of the experience, blaming the patient for the student's discomfort, making jokes to relieve tension, and avoiding stressful situations. Similarly, Simon et al. (1992) looked for patterns in their interview and observation data of adolescent girls in order to derive the norms or rules that they had concerning how the emotion of love should be experienced. They identified five such "feeling norms": (1) "Romantic relationships should be important, but not everything in life" (p. 33); (2) "One should have romantic feelings only for someone of the opposite sex" (p. 34); (3) "One should not have romantic feelings for a boy who is already attached" (p. 36); (4) "One should have romantic feelings for only one boy at a time" (p. 39); and (5) "One should always be in love" (p. 41).

CAUTIONS   The analysis of qualitative data is necessarily subjective, and its practitioners consider this subjectivity to be a major strength of qualitative research (see, for example, Stake, 1995). However, even the most ardent advocates of the qualitative approach warn that data analysis must be conducted with two cautions in mind. The first is the possibility of bias, such as we saw in the Lewis-Redfield debate in Chapter 2: It's always easier to notice and pay attention to data that fit our theories than to data that contradict them. Researchers can minimize this problem by developing a data collection plan that actively searches for contradictory data and following the plan closely. The second, related, potential problem is overlooking alternative explanations for data, especially in explanation building. This problem can be reduced by having colleagues review the research with the purpose of noticing issues you have overlooked. The process will be even more effective if some of the colleagues have different theoretical perspectives on the issues from yours. This, by the way, is a good practice for all research, not just qualitative research.

Quantitative Data

Single-case experiments produce quantitative data, which have traditionally been analyzed through visual inspection of graphic presentations of the data. However, statistical techniques have also recently been developed for the analysis of single-case data.

VISUAL ANALYSIS   In **visual data analysis,** the researcher plots a graph of the results of the experiment and examines the data to determine if the independent variable had an effect on the dependent variable. The researchers who conducted the experiments described in the section on single-case experiments all used visual analysis to draw conclusions from their data. Visual analysis is necessarily subjective, so not surprisingly there can be disagreements among researchers about the conclusions drawn from a study (Parsonson & Baer, 1992). In contrast, reports of single-case experiments always present the graphs of their data, allowing everyone who reads the report to draw his or her own conclusions. This situation contrasts with the presentation of results in reports of group comparison experiments, in which means rather than raw data are presented.

In the absence of statistical analysis, impact is the primary indicator used to determine if the independent variable had an effect (Kazdin, 1997). The larger the change following the introduction of the independent variable and the faster the change, the more likely it is that the independent variable caused the change. In reversal designs, a return of the dependent variable to near-pretreatment levels during reversal phases also indicates the causality of the dependent variable. When the treatment brings about a permanent change or when a reversal would be undesirable, the effectiveness of the independent variable can be assessed by the dependent variable's staying below a criterion level during a long-term follow-up. For example, Figure 9-9 shows that the research participant had a long-term caffeine intake level well below the treatment goal of 600 mg per day.

STATISTICAL ANALYSIS   Although statisticians have begun to develop inferential statistics for single-case experiments (Krishef, 1991), these techniques are quite complex and so are beyond the scope of this book. In general, however, they compare the level, variability, and trend of the baseline data to the same characteristics of the treatment data, and determine the probability of a change having occurred by chance after the introduction of the independent variable. The major advantage of statistical analysis of single-case data is that it is more sensitive than visual analysis. That is, researchers using visual analysis sometimes conclude that the independent variable had no effect when statistical analysis shows that it did. This problem is most severe when the independent variable has a small effect or when there is a high degree of variability in the data (Parsonson & Baer, 1992). The major drawback of statistical analysis is that the primary statistical tool, called *time series analysis*, requires 25 to 50 data points both before and after the introduction of the independent variable in order to provide accurate results. Few single-case experiments collect data over that length of time.

SUMMARY

The single-case approach was psychology's original research strategy, but it was largely superseded by the group comparison approach during the first quarter of the 20th century. However, the inability of the group comparison approach to fully meet the needs of clinical research led to the development of modern single-case research techniques. Four issues in single-case research are validity criteria, case study research, single-case experiments, and data analysis.

    High-validity single-case research uses objective measurement techniques, multiple dependent variables, multiple sources of information for each variable, and frequent assessment of the variables throughout the course of the research. High-validity research also includes multiple replications using heterogeneous participants. Case studies include control cases that test both convergent and discriminant hypotheses. The possibility of history and maturation confounds is minimized when the independent variable has an immediate large impact on a chronic problem and the impact is maintained during long-term follow-ups. Finally, validity is maximized when the independent variable is manipulated and highly standardized and its implementation is carefully monitored.

    The researcher must carefully choose the cases for case study research. Ideally, you want to be able to manipulate the independent variable; if implementation is not possible, you must choose cases that exactly represent the independent variable. You must also have sufficient access to the cases to implement the validity criteria for single-case research. Further, you must carefully consider the appropriate unit of analysis for the study, such as a group as a whole versus the individual members of the group. A multi-level embedded case study could also be appropriate. Careful planning of data collection is essential. A data collection plan lists the dependent variables in the study, the operational definitions of each, the sources of information for each dependent variable, and the schedule for collecting data from each source. Throughout the data collection process, carefully maintain a chain of evidence linking the conclusions you draw from the data to the sources of those data, and linking the data sources to the data collection plan and the collection plan to the study questions.

There are five basic single-case experimental designs. In the A-B-A design, the researcher measures behavior during a baseline period, introduces an independent variable to see if it changes the behavior, and then withdraws the independent variable to see if the behavior returns to baseline. In the A-B-C-B design, the effects of two independent variables are compared by introducing them sequentially. The multiple-baseline design examines the effect of an independent variable on different behaviors, in different settings, and on different people, using an increasingly long baseline for each behavior, setting, or person. The simultaneous treatments design compares the effects of different independent variables by using each during every experimental session. Finally, the changing criterion design sets increasingly difficult targets for changes in behavior.

A stable baseline in a single-case experiment exhibits a minimal trend and low variability. A trend in the direction of the treatment effect calls the effectiveness of the independent variable into question, as does a treatment effect that falls into the range of variation of the baseline data. Unfortunately, there are no absolute criteria for baseline stability; it is a matter of professional judgment and experience.

Single-case data can be either qualitative or quantitative. When the research has a specific set of hypotheses, qualitative data can be analyzed by pattern-matching: examining the data for consistencies with and discrepancies from the predictions derived from the hypotheses. Explanation building is used with qualitative data from exploratory studies: The researcher examines the data for patterns that can explain the phenomenon being studied. When conducting qualitative data analyses, be careful to avoid theoretical biases and to be alert for alternative explanations for results. Quantitative data from single-case research are most often analyzed through visual inspection: The data are graphed and the impact of the independent variable is assessed. One drawback of visual analysis is that people often cannot detect small effects. More recently, statistical techniques have been developed for the analysis of quantitative single-case data.

QUESTIONS AND EXERCISES FOR REVIEW

1. Describe the objections commonly raised to single-case research. How do the advocates of single-case research answer these objections? How valid do you think these objections and answers are? What are your reasons for your position on this issue?
2. What criteria are used for judging the validity of single-case research? Read three case studies and single-case experiments that deal with a topic that interests you. How well does each meet the validity criteria?
3. Describe the use of control cases in case study research. What are the criteria for choosing control cases?
4. Describe Yin's model for replicated single-case research.

5. How do the impact criteria for single-case research help rule out history and maturation as alternative explanations of the independent variable?

6. How do characteristics of the independent variable or treatment affect the validity of single-case research?

7. What criteria are used for selecting cases in case study research? Explain the importance of carefully considering the unit of analysis for a case study.

8. Describe the structure of a case study data collection plan, and explain the importance of maintaining a chain of evidence during data collection. What are the links in this chain?

9. Describe the basic outline of a single-case experiment. How are single-case experiments related to case studies and to within-subjects experimental designs?

10. What procedures are used in each of the following single-case research designs, and what is the purpose of each design?
    a. A-B-A
    b. A-B-C-B
    c. Multiple baseline
    d. Simultaneous treatments
    e. Changing criterion

11. The experiments illustrated in Figures 9-5 and 9-6 used A-B designs. What do you think were the researchers' reasons for using this design rather than an A-B-A design?

12. Explain the importance of a stable baseline in single-case experimentation; how do the trend and variability of the baseline data affect the interpretation of the data collected during the treatment period? What constitutes a stable baseline?

13. What are the pattern-matching and explanation-building approaches to qualitative data analysis? What cautions must the researcher observe during qualitative data analysis? Is one of these forms of analysis more scientific than the other? Explain your conclusion.

14. What criteria are used in visual data analysis for deciding if the independent variable had an effect? What do you see as the major shortcomings of visual data analysis?

15. Choose a hypothesis that interests you and outline how you would test it using each of the three research strategies used in behavioral science. Describe the relative advantages and disadvantages of each strategy for testing the hypothesis, and show how the advantages of one strategy compensate for some of the disadvantages of one or both of the other strategies. Describe any uncompensated disadvantages.

10 RESEARCH IN NATURAL SETTINGS

THE PROBLEM OF CONTROL IN
FIELD SETTINGS
Control Over Variables
Control Over Research
  Populations

FIELD EXPERIMENTS
Choosing a Research Setting
  Settings and Samples
  *Characteristics of a Good
    Setting*
Implementing the Independent
  Variable
  The Street Theater Strategy
  The Accosting Strategy
Problems in Field
  Experimentation
  Construct Validity
  *Control Over Extraneous
    Variables*
  *Vulnerability to Outside
    Interference*

NATURAL EXPERIMENTS AND
QUASI-EXPERIMENTS
The Group Comparison Approach
  *The Nonequivalent Control
    Group Design*
  *The Problem of Preexisting
    Differences*
  *The Problem of Biased
    Selection*
  *How Severe Are These
    Problems?*

The Time Series Approach
  *The Interrupted Time Series
    Design*
  The Control Series Design

NATURALISTIC OBSERVATION
Categories of Naturalistic
  Observation
  Complete Participant
  Participant as Observer
  Observer as Participant
  Nonparticipant Observation
Problems in Naturalistic
  Observation
  Cognitive Biases
  Recordkeeping
  Reactivity
  Influencing Events
  Effects on the Observer

INTERVIEWS
Types of Interviews
  Unstructured Interviews
  Semistructured Interviews
  Structured Interviews
Standardizing Interview
  Procedures
Elements of an Interview
  Establishing Rapport
  Listening Analytically
  Probing
  Motivating
  Maintaining Control
Group Interviews

ARCHIVAL DATA
Types of Archives
Advantages of Using Archival
  Data
Limitations of Archival Research
  Access
  Validity
  Alternative Explanations
  The Ecological Fallacy

ANALYZING OPEN-ENDED DATA
Characteristics of Coding
  Systems
  *Theory-Based Versus Ad Hoc
    Development*
  Broad Versus Narrow Focus
  Number of Coding Categories
  Degree of Inference Required
  Unit of Behavior
  *Concurrent Versus After-the-
    Fact Coding*
Developing Coding Systems
  *Rules for Developing Coding
    Systems*
  Reliability in Coding
Content Analysis

SUMMARY

QUESTIONS AND EXERCISES
FOR REVIEW

As noted in Chapter 2, the laboratory experiment has been the model for much research in the behavioral sciences. However, the laboratory experiment has a number of shortcomings, especially its artificiality. Compared to people's normal life experiences — to which we frequently want the results of our research to apply — laboratory research takes place in an artificial setting, uses artificial operational definitions of variables, has participants perform artificial tasks, and uses as research participants people who may not constitute a reasonable sample of the population. In addition, as discussed in Chapter 6, laboratory research can be reactive because research participants know they are being studied. Not surprisingly, then, many researchers, especially those with applied interests, have expressed concerns over the potential lack of naturalism of laboratory research (see, for example, J. Greenberg & Folger, 1988). These critics of laboratory research hold that the validity of the conclusions one can draw from a study is closely related to its **ecological validity,** the degree to which the research situation mimics a natural situation. Chapter 14 discusses this issue.

This chapter examines some issues related to research in natural settings, also called **field research.** It first briefly discusses the problem of control in field research. Then it looks at five field research methods: field experiments, natural experiments, quasi-experiments, naturalistic observation, and interviews. The chapter concludes with a discussion of archival data and the analysis of open-ended data.

THE PROBLEM OF CONTROL IN FIELD SETTINGS

As discussed in Chapter 2, the decision to use a laboratory or field setting for research involves making a tradeoff between control and naturalism. This section briefly reviews the ways in which the use of field settings limits the degree of control that the researcher has over the research (Aronson, Brewer, & Carlsmith, 1985). These factors also limit the degree to which causal conclusions can be drawn from field research.

Control Over Variables

First, the researcher may have limited control over the independent variable. Although he or she can manipulate the independent variable in some forms of field research, the "manipulation" is often natural and therefore uncontrolled in terms of intensity, duration, and when and where it occurs. The researcher may also have only a limited choice of operational definitions for the dependent variable. The dependent variable in field research is usually behavioral and usually measured by means of observation, resulting in the limitations discussed in Chapter 5. For example, you can learn what people do in a situation, but not their reasons for doing it. In addition, as discussed later in this chapter, some forms of field research, such as participant observation, can make the accurate recording of observations especially difficult. The third limit placed on control by field research is control over extraneous variables. The complexity of field research situations means that any number of uncontrolled factors could serve as alternative explanations for any effects that one wants to attribute to the independent variable. However, as Bouchard (1976) notes, replication across heterogeneous settings can provide evidence against setting factors as causes of the dependent variable: The more often an effect is replicated across different settings, the less likely it is that some aspect of the setting, rather than the independent variable, was the cause of the dependent variable.

Control Over Research Populations

In laboratory research, the researcher can choose the population from which participants are drawn. Consequently, laboratory researchers can test for interactions between the independent variable and characteristics of the participants, such as personality traits. In field settings, screening potential participants for certain characteristics and choosing some, but not all, people for the research often disrupts the naturalism of the research environment. Therefore, to gain naturalism, a field researcher might lose the ability to test certain kinds of hypotheses. Field settings may also make it impossible to randomly assign participants to conditions of the independent variable. For example, field research testing the effectiveness of an educational intervention might use the students in one school as the experimental group and those in another school as the control group. Although the schools can be randomly assigned to the experimental or control condition, children are not randomly assigned to schools. As a result, participant characteristics may not be balanced across conditions, leaving them as possible alternative explanations for any effects found in the research.

The next three sections of this chapter examine four research methods that vary in the degree of naturalism they employ. In field experiments and quasi-experiments, the researcher intervenes in the natural setting by manipulating independent variables, whereas the researcher takes a more passive role in natural experiments and naturalistic observation.

FIELD EXPERIMENTS

Field experiments attempt to achieve a balance between control and naturalism in research by studying people's natural behavioral responses to manipulated independent variables in natural settings. The field experimenter tries to establish conditions that are as close as possible to those of a true laboratory experiment by manipulating the independent variable and exposing participants to conditions of the independent variable in a reasonably random fashion. The goal is to allow causal conclusions to be drawn from research conducted in natural settings. For example, Piliavin, Rodin, and Piliavin (1969) studied how the manipulated characteristics of a person, such as appearing to be either drunk or ill, who collapsed on a New York subway train affected the responses of bystanders. C. Seligman, Finegan, Hazlewood, and Wilkinson (1985) studied how the manipulated reasons for a pizza deliveryman's being early or late—whether it was a factor associated with the deliveryman or something beyond his control—affected the size of the tip he received.

Although field experiments and laboratory experiments may appear on the surface to be very different because of the difference in settings, Aronson et al. (1985) point out that there is no simple distinction between them. Rather, experiments fall along a laboratory-field continuum defined by three characteristics of the research. The first characteristic is the way in which the participants in the research perceive their experience: "One of the most important differences involves the actual phenomenology of the subjects—what subjects think is going on. Are they aware that they are in an experiment, or does this event appear to be part of their normal life?" (Aronson et al., 1985, p. 444). In field experiments, participants are unaware they are in an experiment. Consequently, field experiments usually involve deception and a lack of informed consent, and the attendant ethical issues discussed in Chapter 3. The second characteristic defining the laboratory-field distinction is the ease with which the experimenter can assign participants to conditions of the independent variable; the experimenter has much more control over assignment in the laboratory. Finally, in the laboratory the experimenter has a much higher degree of control over extraneous variables and how the dependent variable is measured. The field experimenter must be content with a research environment that contains a host of uncontrolled factors in addition to the independent variable and with observing behavior as the dependent variable. This reliance on behavioral measures entails the advantages and disadvantages discussed in Chapter 5.

This section looks at three issues relevant to field experimentation: choosing the research setting, ways in which the independent variable can be implemented, and problems inherent in field experimentation.

Choosing a Research Setting

In the laboratory, experimenters have the ability to manufacture the research settings that they need to test their hypotheses. In the field, however, researchers must carefully choose settings that permit a valid test of the hypothesis. In choosing a setting, the field experimenter must consider the extent to which the setting restricts the sample of people available as research participants and the amenability of the setting to the manipulation of the independent variable.

SETTINGS AND SAMPLES   Bochner (1979) notes that natural research settings vary along a dimension of "publicness," in that some settings are more likely to have a wider variety of people in them than are other settings. At the high end of the dimension are settings in which the researcher could, in principle, find any member of the public. Such settings include public parks, streets, and highways. In the middle of the dimension are reasonably public settings in which the people are likely to similar on one or more characteristics. Such settings include public meetings, racetracks, residential households, and college campuses. At the low end of the dimension are settings that are less public and more institutionalized, where people are linked by some common characteristic. Such settings include student dormitories, public lavatories, subway trains, restaurants, stores, and libraries.

The choice of one type of research setting over another should be governed by the hypothesis to be tested. "The correct sequence is for investigators to have an idea which they wish to explore, and then find a suitable place where that idea can be translated into a psychological experiment" (Bochner, 1979, p. 34). It is also useful to try to conduct the experiment in a variety of settings to determine the extent to which the setting affects the results. Like the multiple operationism discussed in Chapter 5, multiple research settings enhance the generalizability of the research.

CHARACTERISTICS OF A GOOD SETTING   There are two important characteristics of a good setting for a field experiment (Aronson, Ellsworth, Carlsmith, & Gonzales, 1990; Bochner, 1979). The first is the ability to manipulate the independent variable in the setting. At a minimum, the researchers must have sufficient control over events in the setting to permit them to expose people in the setting to the independent variable in a reasonably random way. That is, random assignment of participants in field experiments consists of randomly deciding which condition of the independent variable will be conducted at any one time. For example, Piliavin et al. (1969) could use a table of random numbers to determine whether a particular subway trip would have a drunk or ill victim. Although C. Seligman et al. (1985) could not randomly determine whether a customer's pizza was early or late (that was determined by how busy the cook was), they randomly decided whether to blame the deliveryman or the situation when they called customers to inform them that their pizzas would be early or late. The capability to randomly assign participants to conditions is important because if you cannot use random assignment, then the study is not a true experiment, and you must be very cautious in drawing causal conclusions about the effects of the independent variable.

The second important characteristic of a field experimental setting is that the events used to manipulate the independent variable should be occurrences that could reasonably be expected to take place in that setting. For example, people who are drunk or ill do ride subways and sometimes they collapse (Piliavin et al., 1969); pizzas are sometimes delivered earlier than expected and sometimes later (C. Seligman et al., 1985). Even events that are a little unusual can sometimes be tailored to fit the situation. For example, pizzerias rarely call customers to inform them that their food will arrive early or late. C. Seligman et al. (1985) made the call plausible by telling customers that the pizzeria was making the call "in an effort to offer better service to our customers" (p. 316). To the extent that research participants perceive the situation to be abnormal, their responses will be abnormal, obviating one of the advantages of field research.

In addition to allowing random assignment of research participants to conditions and being a plausible setting for manipulation of the independent variable, the research setting must be one the researchers have permission to use. This requirement is perhaps obvious if the setting is privately owned, such as a restaurant or store, but it can also apply to public property. For example, police might look with suspicion on someone loitering in a public park closely observing a group of children. If the implementation of an independent variable consisted of a simulated emergency, someone could call the police. It is therefore a good procedure to coordinate field experiments with people who have custody of or are responsible for public safety in a proposed research setting. Not only will this procedure avoid false alarms that are likely to incur the displeasure of public officials and consequently of the institution sponsoring the research, but it also will help keep the people in the setting unaware that research is being conducted: As Bochner (1979) remarked, nothing draws attention to field researchers like the police sweeping in to arrest them.

Implementing the Independent Variable

The implementation of the independent variable is the manner in which it is "delivered," so to speak, to the research participants. Bochner (1979) identified two implementation strategies: street theater and accosting. As with the choice of a setting, the choice of how to implement the independent variable should be governed by how well the strategy assists in achieving a valid test of the hypothesis.

THE STREET THEATER STRATEGY   "The principle of the street theater strategy . . . is to stage an incident or introduce an event that will be witnessed by virtually every person in the surrounding area" (Bochner, 1979, p. 38). Piliavin et al. (1969) employed this strategy,

> using the express trains of the New York 8th Avenue Independent Subway as a laboratory on wheels. Four teams of students, each one made up of a victim, model [who would assist the victim], and two observers, staged standard collapses in which type of victim (drunk or ill), race of victim (black or white) and the presence or absence of a model were varied. . . . As the train passed the first station [after the one at which the researchers boarded] . . . the victim staggered forward and collapsed. Until receiving help, the victim remained supine on the floor looking at the ceiling. . . . On 38 trials the victim smelled of liquor and carried a liquor bottle wrapped tightly in a brown bag (drunk condition), while on the remaining 65 trials they appeared sober and carried a black cane (cane condition). In all other respects, victims dressed and behaved identically in the two conditions. (pp. 289, 291)

Using this procedure, Piliavin et al. found that subway riders were more likely to go to the assistance of someone who appeared ill than someone who appeared drunk.

THE ACCOSTING STRATEGY   "The principle of the accosting strategy is to select a specific subject who then becomes the target for the experimental intervention" (Bochner, 1979, p. 39). C. Seligman et al. (1985) employed this strategy in their study of the effect of the reason given to customers for an early or late pizza delivery on the tip received by the deliveryman. The theory that the researchers were testing predicted that customers who thought that the deliveryman was responsible for an early delivery would tip more than if they thought him to be responsible for a late delivery, but that if situational factors, such as heavy traffic, affected delivery time, there would be no difference in tips for early and late delivery. Research participants were customers of a pizzeria who called for a pizza; all were told that it would be delivered in 45 minutes. If the workload at the pizzeria resulted in the pizza being ready early, customers were called back and informed of the early delivery; half were told that the early delivery was early because the deliveryman was doing a good job, and half were told that it would be early because traffic was lighter than normal. Similarly, if the workload resulted in a delay, customers were called back and told that the pizza would be late; half were told that the late delivery was the deliveryman's fault, half that it was due to heavy traffic. The deliveryman recorded the amount of the tip he received for each delivery. He received the largest average tip when he was credited for an early delivery and the smallest when he was blamed for late delivery. When early or late delivery was attributed to situational factors, the average tips did not differ.

Problems in Field Experimentation

Transferring the experiment from the laboratory to the field creates a number of potential problems that the researcher must take into consideration. This section briefly considers three: construct validity, control over extraneous variables, and vulnerability to outside interference.

CONSTRUCT VALIDITY   Field experiments frequently avoid problems of construct validity by using manifest variables rather than hypothetical constructs as independent and dependent variables. Piliavin et al. (1969), for example, manipulated directly observable characteristics of the victim (race and ill or drunk) and measured speed of response. However, sometimes researchers want to manipulate hypothetical constructs; C. Seligman et al. (1985), for example, wanted to manipulate people's beliefs about why the deliveryman was early or late. To ensure that the reasons they gave in the telephone calls to customers created the desired beliefs, the researchers conducted a pilot study in which they asked people in their university library to fill out a questionnaire about pizza delivery services. The questionnaire included items about reasons for deliveries being early and late—including the reasons used as the operational definition of the independent variable—and asked people to indicate whether the reason reflected a characteristic of the driver or of the situation (the hypothetical construct they wanted to manipulate). The results of this manipulation check supported the validity of their operational definition.

Bochner (1979) points out that although the dependent variables in field experiments are almost always behavioral measures and therefore represent manifest variables, discriminant validity can be a problem. He specifically points to the possibility that a research participant's response might be influenced by other people and therefore not be an accurate representation of the person's natural behavior. For example, the customer who gave the tip in C. Seligman et al.'s (1985) study might have been influenced by recommendations about the appropriate size of the tip made by other people who were present when it was delivered.

CONTROL OVER EXTRANEOUS VARIABLES   Conducting an experiment outside the laboratory means that the researcher is trading control over extraneous variables for naturalism in behavior and setting. Consequently, the researcher must be careful to ensure that the conditions of the independent variable are not confounded with some aspect of the environment. Piliavin et al. (1969), for example, used both northbound and southbound subway trains for their research, and so had to ensure that all the conditions of the independent variables were represented in both categories of trains. It is, of course, unlikely that direction of travel itself would affect people's responses, but it is possible that the characteristics of people who are traveling north and south at the same time of day might differ. For example, those traveling south might be on their way to work and those traveling north, going home from a night shift. Consequently the northbound travelers could be more fatigued and less alert, characteristics that could affect speed of response.

This situation represents a general problem in field research: People select themselves into field settings so that characteristics of research participants might be confounded with setting. It is therefore a good idea to use multiple settings for field experiments. If you get the same results across settings, it is unlikely that some characteristic of one of the settings or of the people who inhabit it is an alternative explanation to the independent variable as a cause of the dependent variable.

VULNERABILITY TO OUTSIDE INTERFERENCE   Finally, field experiments can be disrupted by events beyond the researcher's control. Weather problems in outdoor research is the most obvious example, but there can be human interference as well. Gonzalez, Ellsworth, and Pembroke (1993), for example, staged a theft in front of a class as part of an eyewitness identification experiment; at the time, the class did not know the theft was staged. One of the students began to chase the thief, an eventuality not anticipated by the experimenters. Political events can also be problematic. Piliavin et al.'s (1969) researchers were all students at Columbia University. While the research was going on, the students at Columbia organized a strike to protest some of the university's policies; "the teams disbanded, and the study was of necessity over" before all the intended data had been collected (p. 291).

NATURAL EXPERIMENTS AND QUASI-EXPERIMENTS

The **natural experiment** attempts to achieve naturalism in treatment and setting by taking advantage of events outside the experimenter's control that, in effect, manipulate an independent variable. Natural experiments can come about in several ways. One form of natural experiment takes advantage of naturally occurring events. For example, researchers can investigate brain functions by studying head injury victims. Morrow, Urtunski, Kim, and Boller (1981) provided evidence that emotional responses originate in the right side of the brain by comparing the responses of people with right-brain lesions to those of people with left-brain lesions. In situations such as this, a natural experiment allows researchers to study independent variables that could not be manipulated for ethical reasons. Natural experiments can also take advantage of human errors. Sommer (1991), for example, was able to determine that people often interpret questionnaire response options metaphorically rather than literally by comparing college students' responses to two versions of a course evaluation questionnaire. In one version, a typographical error had resulted in response options that were unrelated to the question, such as having the options "Excellent, Very Good, Good, Poor, Terrible" for responses to the statement "I always come to class." Sommer found that responses to both the correct and the incorrect versions of the questionnaire were virtually identical. A third form of natural experiment results from intentional human behavior. Schofield and Pavelchak (1989), for example, examined the effects of people's watching a controversial television program on their social attitudes. The natural experiment is, of course, actually a correlational study because the researcher does not manipulate the independent variable, cannot randomly assign research participants to conditions, and has little control over extraneous variables. Nonetheless, the term *natural experiment* is commonly used for this type of research.

The **quasi-experiment** attempts to achieve naturalism in settings by manipulating an independent variable in a natural setting using existing groups of people as the experimental and control groups. For example, J. Greenberg (1990) studied the effects of an organizational intervention by conducting the intervention in one factory operated by a corporation and using two other, geographically separate, factories as control groups. He then compared the behavior of the workers in the factories. Individual participants in quasi-experiments cannot be randomly assigned to the experimental and control conditions, although the groups to which they belong can be. The researcher is also not likely to have much control over extraneous variables in the natural setting used for the research. However, D. T. Campbell and Stanley (1963) called this kind of research a *quasi-* (the Latin word for "as if") *experiment* because the researchers do manipulate the independent variable "as if" they were conducting a true experiment.

The natural experiment and the quasi-experiment differ in that the researcher manipulates the independent variable and can do a limited form of random assignment in the quasi-experiment, but must take advantage of an uncontrollable event in the natural experiment. However, the two are similar and are discussed together because they use the same two approaches to collecting and analyzing data: the group comparison approach and the time series approach.

The Group Comparison Approach

In the group comparison approach, the researcher establishes an experimental group that experiences the treatment condition of the independent variable and a no-treatment control group. As in any other experiment, the hypothesis may require that multiple experimental groups and multiple control groups be used to rule out alternative explanations for the effect of the independent variable. The most common group comparison design for natural and quasi-experiments is the nonequivalent control group design (T. D. Cook & Campbell, 1979).

THE NONEQUIVALENT CONTROL GROUP DESIGN   In the **nonequivalent control group design,** the researcher studies two (or more) groups of people. The members of one group experience the treatment condition of the independent variable; the members of the other group, chosen to be as similar as possible to the experimental group, serve as the control group. This control group is not considered equivalent to the experimental group because participants are not randomly assigned to conditions. Only the use of random assignment can give researchers reasonable confidence that person-related extraneous variables, such as personal experiences, personality, and so forth, are not confounded with conditions of the independent variable—that is, that the groups are equivalent on these variables. Let's briefly look at how researchers use the nonequivalent control group design in natural and quasi-experimental research.

Schofield and Pavelchak (1989) used a natural experiment to study the effects of television on people's attitudes toward social issues. In 1983 the ABC television network showed a movie titled *The Day After*, which graphically portrayed the probable effects of nuclear war on an American town. Schofield and Pavelchak wanted to see if watching a realistic portrayal of the effects of nuclear war would affect people's attitudes toward nuclear war and U.S. nuclear policy. Two weeks before the show, they sent pretest questionnaires to 1,000 residents of Pittsburgh, Pennsylvania; 261 people returned the questionnaires. These 261 people were sent a posttest questionnaire after the movie had been broadcast. Of the 179 people who returned this questionnaire, 109 reported that they had watched the movie and so became the experimental group; the others became the control group. Schofield and Pavelchak determined that the members of two groups were reasonably similar by comparing their pretest responses, which did not differ significantly. Their study found similar changes in the opinions of both groups—including less optimism about surviving a nuclear war, a decreased desire to survive such a war, and less optimism about being able to influence major political events—which Schofield and Pavelchak attributed to the widespread publicity about the program. However, they found that people who had watched the program reported that they were more likely to take part in antinuclear activities following the broadcast.

J. Greenberg (1990) used a quasi-experiment to test the effect of explaining the reasons for a temporary pay cut to the affected workers. He hypothesized that workers who received a full explanation would be less dissatisfied than those who received no explanation. The research took place at three plants operated by a company that unexpectedly lost a major contract; two of the plants lost work because of the contract cancelation, whereas the other plant was unaffected. Workers at one affected plant were given a full and accurate explanation of the situation. They were told about the canceled contract, that the pay cut was being implemented as an alternative to laying workers off, and that managerial pay was being cut by the same percentage as workers' pay. Workers at the other affected plant were simply told that the pay cut was taking place. Workers at the unaffected plant served as a baseline control group. The workers at all three plants made the same product, were of the same average age and educational level, and had the same average tenure with the company. Greenberg used employee turnover and theft rates before, during, and after the pay cut period as indicators of dissatisfaction. Turnover and theft increased during the pay cut period at the plant where the cut was announced without an explanation, but they remained unchanged at the other two plants.

The nonequivalent control group design is a useful tool in situations in which it is impractical to randomly assign research participants to conditions. However, using the design poses two problems that limit the degree to which one can draw causal conclusions from the research: the possibility of preexisting differences between groups on the dependent variable and biased selection of people into the experimental and control groups.

THE PROBLEM OF PREEXISTING DIFFERENCES   You will have noticed that both Schofield and Pavelchak (1989) and J. Greenberg (1990) included a pretest in their research designs. Such pretesting is conducted whenever possible to ensure that the experimental and control groups are similar on the dependent variable before the independent vari-

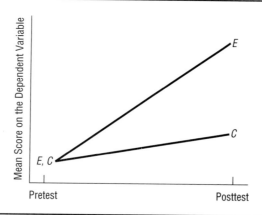

FIGURE 10-1   Design of a Pretest-Posttest Nonequivalent Control Group Design Quasi-Experiment
The pretest shows that the experimental (E) and control (C) group means on the dependent variables are
statistically equal at the pretest but differ significantly at the posttest.

able is introduced. Pretests are rarely used in true experiments because random assignment of participants to conditions results in experimental and control groups that have
a high probability of being equivalent on the dependent variable prior to implementation of the independent variable.

Consider a study in which an independent variable is supposed to increase the
reading scores of sixth graders and the researchers do not conduct a pretest. At the end
of the study, the experimental group has higher reading scores than the control group.
This difference might be due to the effect of the independent variable, but it could also
result if the experimental group started out with higher scores and the independent
variable had no effect. If the researchers conduct a pretest, they can determine if the
groups initially differ on the dependent variable. If the groups do not differ, the researchers can proceed with the study and assess the effect of the independent variable
with a posttest. The desired outcome is little change in the scores of the control group,
coupled with a significant change in the scores of the experimental group. Of course,
history, maturation, and other time-related effects will frequently lead to some change
in the control group's scores. The simplest nonequivalent control group design with a
pretest is therefore a 2 × 2 factorial design with one between-subjects factor (the conditions of the independent variable) and one within-subjects factor (time). As shown
in Figure 10-1, the desired outcome is an interaction in which the groups are the same
at the pretest but differ at the posttest.

If the experimental and control groups do differ on the pretest, the researchers have
a problem: There is no way to directly determine the effect of the independent variable
above and beyond any effects resulting from the preexisting difference between the
groups. One approach to dealing with this problem is the statistical technique known
as **analysis of covariance (ANCOVA;** Porter & Raudenbush, 1987; Tabachnick &
Fidell, 1996). ANCOVA provides a test of the effect of the independent variable that
is adjusted for group differences in pretest scores based on a regression analysis of the

relation between the pretest and posttest scores. In essence, ANCOVA asks the question "What would the posttest means look like if the experimental and control groups had not differed on the pretest?" Although ANCOVA can be a powerful statistical tool, it requires that the slopes of the relationship between pretest and posttest scores be equal in both groups, a requirement that the researcher must test before conducting the analysis. In addition, ANCOVA does not always provide a precise answer to the research question being asked (Porter & Raudenbush, 1987).

"But," you might say, "there is a simpler solution to the problem of group differences on the pretest. Remember the matching strategy for assigning participants to conditions? Why not use that?" Achieving equivalence by matching people in the experimental and control groups on their pretest scores is tempting, but it can result in invalid results. Recall that the type of matching discussed in Chapter 7 was matched *random* assignment to groups: Members of matched pairs were randomly assigned to the experimental and control conditions. Random assignment of individual participants to conditions is not possible when a natural or quasi-experiment is being conducted.

Judd, Smith, and Kidder (1991) provide an example of the problem posed by trying to match participants when they cannot be randomly assigned to conditions, based on critiques of evaluations of early childhood intervention programs (D. T. Campbell & Erlebacher, 1970). Let's say you're trying to assess the effect of an educational intervention on the achievement scores of disadvantaged children, and your control group consists of (for want of a better term) advantaged children. A pretest shows that the average achievement scores of the advantaged children are higher than those of the disadvantaged children. You therefore conduct your research using children from the two groups who have similar pretest scores; as shown in Figure 10-2, you would be taking the highest scorers from the disadvantaged group and the lowest scorers from the advantaged group. What happens to extreme test scores over time? They regress toward the group mean. Consequently, the scores of the disadvantaged children chosen for the research will be lower at the posttest than at the pretest because their pretest scores were extremely high relative to their group's average score, and the scores of the advantaged children chosen for the research will be higher at the posttest than at the pretest because their pretest scores were extremely low relative to their group's average score. Therefore, it will appear that the intervention improved the scores of the advantaged children and hurt the scores of the disadvantaged children. Trying to match members of nonequivalent groups that differ on the pretest will always lead to the possibility of a regression confound and so should not be done.

THE PROBLEM OF BIASED SELECTION   As discussed in Chapter 7, participants in true experiments are randomly assigned to conditions of the independent variable to avoid any bias that would result from confounding personal characteristics of the participants with conditions of the independent variable. However, participants in nonequivalent control group designs are not randomly assigned to conditions; it is therefore possible that the personal characteristics of the members of the experimental group differ from those of the control group. This problem is especially severe when participants select themselves into what will become the experimental and control groups. For example, Schofield and Pavelchak's (1989) participants essentially chose to be in the experimental or control group by deciding to watch or not to watch the movie. To the extent

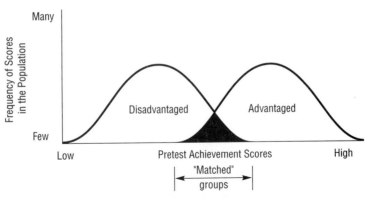

Note: From Judd et al., 1991, p. 122.

FIGURE 10-2   Effect of "Matching" Members on Nonequivalent Groups That Differ on a Pretest
Students from hypothetical advantaged and disadvantaged student populations are "matched" on pretest academic achievement scores. Because the "matched" students come from the higher end of the disadvantaged distribution and the lower end of the advantaged distribution, regression toward the mean will lead to the disadvantaged students appearing to do worse and the advantaged students appearing to do better on the posttest.

that the "watchers" were similar to each other and different from the "nonwatchers," a confound exists. For example, the movie had many gruesome scenes that were well publicized in advance; perhaps the nonwatchers were more squeamish than the watchers. In J. Greenberg's (1990) study, two kinds of biased selection could have been present. First, the participants applied to work at particular locations that appealed to them, one of which became the experimental site and the other of which became the control site. To the extent that different types of people preferred to work in the different locations, a confound was possible. Second, the factories decided whom to hire from among the applicants. To the extent that one personnel office hired people of a different type than another personnel office, a confound was possible.

The nature of research that uses the nonequivalent control group design therefore makes it impossible to rule out differences in the characteristics of the experimental and control participants as an alternative explanation to the effect of the independent variable for differences between the conditions. Consequently, this design cannot determine causality with certainty. However, we can take two steps to increase our confidence that the independent variable was the cause of the difference. The first is replication: The more often an effect is replicated under different circumstance, the more likely it is that the independent variable was the causal agent. Second, in quasi-experimental research, it is sometimes possible to have multiple naturally occurring groups randomly assigned to experimental and control conditions. For example, in educational research, the schools in a school district might be randomly assigned as experimental and control sites for an educational intervention. This design is illustrated in Figure 10-3: Students (that is, research participants) are not randomly assigned to

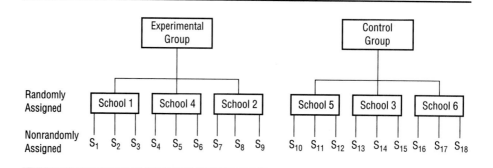

FIGURE 10-3 Nested Assignment in a Nonequivalent Control Group Quasi-Experiment
Schools are randomly assigned to the experimental or control condition, but the students are not randomly assigned to the schools they attend.

schools, but schools are randomly assigned to conditions of the independent variable. Even though students were not randomly assigned to schools, randomly assigning schools to conditions provides a limited degree of equivalence between the experimental and control groups. The data from such a study can then be analyzed using a **nested analysis of variance design,** which can separate the variance in the dependent variable due to the effect of the independent variable and from that due to the effect of attending a particular school (Hopkins, 1982).

HOW SEVERE ARE THESE PROBLEMS?   To examine the degree to which the results of true experiments and nonequivalent control group quasi-experiments might differ, Heinsman and Shadish (1996) compared the findings of 51 true experiments with those of 47 quasi-experiments that tested the same four hypotheses. They found that the results of the quasi-experiments were very similar to those of true experiments when the quasi-experiments were characterized by small differences between the experimental and controls on the pretests, low attrition rates, and low levels of participant self-selection into conditions. Therefore, well-designed nonequivalent control group quasi-experiments are likely to provide results similar to those of true experiments and to lead to the same conclusion regarding the hypotheses being tested.

The Time Series Approach

In the time series approach to quasi-experimentation, the researchers make a number of observations of the dependent variable, manipulate the independent variable, and make further observations of the dependent variable. The researchers then compare the level of the dependent variable before and after the manipulation of the independent variable. In a time series natural experiment, the researchers observe the dependent variable before and after the occurrence of an independent variable that they do not control. The time series approach is therefore essentially a single-case research technique and shares the advantages and limitations of that type of research. However, as

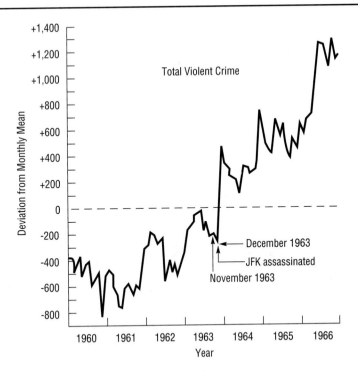

Note: From Berkowitz, 1970, p. 101.

FIGURE 10-4   Application of an Interrupted Time Series Design to a Natural Experiment
Berkowitz (1970) examined the violent crime rate in the United States before and after John F. Kennedy's assassination. The crime rate showed a marked increase after the assassination.

our examples will illustrate, the problems studied using the time series approach generally preclude the use of a reversal period. The time series approach can take two forms: the interrupted time series design and the control series design.

THE INTERRUPTED TIME SERIES DESIGN   The **interrupted time series design** consists of the basic single-case approach in which a baseline period is followed by a treatment that "interrupts" the baseline, followed by a period of posttreatment observations. Berkowitz (1970; Berkowitz & Macauley, 1971) used this approach in a natural experiment on aggression. As shown in Figure 10-4, using FBI crime statistics he plotted the monthly frequency of violent crime from January 1960, to November 1963. President John F. Kennedy was assassinated in November 1963; this event constituted the independent variable. Berkowitz then plotted the monthly violent crime statistics from December 1963 to December 1966. Given the sudden large increase in the crime rate, Berkowitz concluded that Kennedy's assassination was a possible cause of the increase. However, as with other forms of nonexperimental research, one must also consider the possibility of alternative explanations for the results of natural experiments such as this one. For

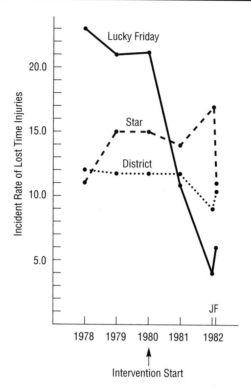

Note: From Fiedler, Bell, Chemers, & Patrick, 1984, p. 13.

FIGURE 10-5   A Control Series Experiment
Time lost to injuries was recorded in three mines from 1978 to 1982, with a safety intervention being implemented in the Lucky Friday mine in 1980. The sharp decrease in time lost to injuries in the Lucky Friday mine and the lack of change in the control mines indicate that the intervention was the cause of the improved safety.

example, social changes coinciding with the assassination, suggested by the upward trend in the baseline data for 1961 to 1963, might also have led to an increase in the violent crime rate.

THE CONTROL SERIES DESIGN   The **control series design** consists of an interrupted time series design with the addition of one or more control cases. Fiedler, Bell, Chemers, and Patrick (1984) used a control series quasi-experiment to evaluate the effectiveness of an intervention designed to improve mine safety. As shown in Figure 10-5, Fiedler et al. plotted the safety records for three mines for the years 1978 to 1980. In 1980, they conducted their safety intervention in the Lucky Friday mine. They then plotted the safety records of the mines for 1981 and 1982. The safety record of the Lucky Friday mine showed a sudden large improvement while that of the District mine stayed essentially the same and the record of the Star mine deteriorated. Fiedler et al. therefore concluded that the intervention was a success. Note that the Lucky Friday's safety record at the beginning of the study was much worse than those of the other two mines (that's why the mining company chose the Lucky Friday for the intervention). Regression toward the mean is therefore a possible alternative explanation for the improvement in safety. However, because the Lucky Friday's injury rate fell to well below the mean, it is unlikely that regression was the cause of the change.

NATURALISTIC OBSERVATION

The goal of naturalistic observation is to study human behavior as it occurs in natural settings in response to natural events, uninfluenced by the researcher. As such, naturalistic observation tries to maximize the ecological validity of research but incurs the cost of minimizing control. Naturalistic observation is not a single method of research but, rather, a set of methods that vary along two dimensions (Bouchard, 1976). One dimension is that of participation, the degree to which the researcher-observer takes part in the events being observed. Participation can range from complete participation, in which the observer becomes an active member of the research setting, to complete nonparticipation, in which the observer remains apart from the situation and simply observes what occurs and records those observations. Level of researcher participation is also related to research strategy used. Generally speaking, the higher the level of researcher participation, the more likely a study is to use the case study strategy and involve qualitative data; the lower the level of researcher participation, the more likely a study is to involve group comparison strategies and quantitative data.

The second dimension is deception, the degree to which the observer conceals his or her identity as a researcher. In complete deception, the other occupants of the research setting are not aware of the observer's role as researcher; the researcher is, in effect, an undercover agent collecting data on the other people in the setting without their knowledge or consent. In the absence of deception, the other members of the research setting are completely informed of the observer's role as researcher. As noted in Chapter 3, the use of deceptive research methods places special obligations on researchers to protect the research participants.

This section examines four categories of naturalistic observation derived from these dimensions and discusses some of the problems that can arise in research involving high levels of participation.

Categories of Naturalistic Observation

The dimensions of naturalistic observation research are illustrated in Figure 10-6, along with four prototypical categories of naturalistic observation research. Gold (1969) developed these categories as a means of distinguishing among various meanings of the way in which the term **participant observation** was being used in sociological research. In participant observation, the observer participates in the research setting. For example, Alfred (1976) joined a satanic church to study its members' motivations for joining a satanic group, but did not tell any of the group members that he was a researcher. Thorne (1988) was already a member of the draft resistance movement of the 1960s

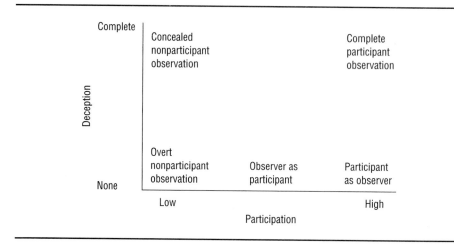

FIGURE 10-6   Dimensions and Categories of Naturalistic Observation
Types of naturalistic observation vary by the degree of deception and the degree of participation involved.

when she decided to study it as a sociologist, telling everyone with whom she had contact of her role as researcher. Black and Reiss (1967) had observers ride with police officers as they conducted their patrols in three large cities to study police-community interactions, informing the officers, but not the citizens with whom they dealt, of the observers' roles as researchers.

Based on such differences in levels of participation and degree of deception, Gold distinguished three categories of participant observation (see Figure 10-6): complete participation, participant as observer, and observer as participant. A fourth category, nonparticipant observation, includes observational research in which the researcher overtly or covertly records behavior without taking part in the research setting. Let's take a brief look at each of these categories.

COMPLETE PARTICIPANT   In research in which the observer is a complete participant, the observer becomes a full member of the research setting (usually a group or community) without the other members of the setting being aware of the observer's role as researcher. The researcher interacts as intimately as possible with the other members of the setting in as many ways as possible. As Alfred (1976) describes his research on Satanism:

> I approached the group in April 1968 as an outsider and indicated an immediate interest in joining. My feigned conversion to Satanism was accepted as genuine and I made rapid progress in the group, as measured by my advancement in ritual rank, my being given administrative as well as magical responsibilities, and my appointment to the "ruling" body of the church.
>
> . . . I attended fifty-two of the group's weekly rituals, participating in all but eight of these early on. I was also present at twelve meetings of the ruling council, at twelve classes on various aspects of Satanism, and at six parties. All these occasions included much discussion and conversation. (pp. 183–184)

Levels of involvement such as these give the complete participant observer unique insight into the operations of a group and access to information about other members of the group that they would not reveal to nonmembers. However, it does raise the ethical issue of deception, and can lead to other problems, discussed shortly.

PARTICIPANT AS OBSERVER   The participant as observer, like the complete participant, participates fully in the research setting but avoids the ethical problem of deception by fully informing the other people in the setting of her or his role as researcher. Thorne (1988) describes her approach to research:

> I initially ventured into the draft resistance movement . . . because I was strongly opposed to the Vietnam war and wanted to be part of organized protest. . . . At the same period of time, I was looking around for a thesis topic, and after about a month of [participating in activities of the movement], I decided to become a sociological observer, as well as a participant committed to the goals of the movement. . . .
>
> As a point of principle, I wanted to avoid disguised research. From the start, I explained my research intentions to those I saw on a regular basis, as well as reassuring them that I shared their political commitments; their responses to my research activity ranged from hostility to mild tolerance. Overall, I was allowed to hang (often . . . under a specter of suspicion) because I did movement work and professed commitment to the goals of ending the war and the draft. (p. 134)

The participant as observer can avoid the problem of deception but, as Thorne's experience illustrates, may induce reactivity among the other members of the research setting. Hostility and suspicion lead people to control the amount and type of information they give the researcher. Thorne also notes that even the best attempts to avoid deception are not always successful:

> I discovered that people I had told tended to forget about my sociologist's role. . . . Furthermore, in the course of [participating in movement activities], I encountered many people whom I had no chance to tell about my research intentions. In these situations I was, in effect, a disguised researcher. (p. 134)

OBSERVER AS PARTICIPANT   When the researcher takes the observer as participant role, he or she enters into the research setting but interacts with the other members of the setting no more than is necessary to collect data. To use Jones's (1985) phrase, the researcher is "only *in*, but not *of*, the setting" (p. 61). The observer's role as researcher may or may not be known to the other members of the setting. For example, Black and Reiss (1967) had observers dressed in civilian clothes ride in patrol cars with uniformed police officers in Boston, Chicago, and Washington, D.C., to observe police-citizen interactions. The police officers knew that the observers were researchers, but the citizens who interacted with the officers were told nothing at all about the observers. If asked, the officers told the citizens that the observers were detectives. This research therefore had both deceptive and nondeceptive elements.

NONPARTICIPANT OBSERVATION   In nonparticipant observation, the observer avoids taking part in the research setting, merely watching what happens and recording the observations. The observations may be conducted overtly so that the people being observed are aware that they are under observation, or covertly so that the people are unaware of the observer. Schofield (1982), for example, conducted overt nonparticipant observation in a newly opened integrated school to study the ways in which race affected the patterns of interactions among students and between students and teachers. The observers stood in hallways, playgrounds, and the backs of classrooms, and the students and teachers knew that they were there. J. C. Baxter (1970), in contrast, used covert observation to study the relationships of ethnicity, sex, and age to interpersonal distance. He sat near several exhibits at a zoo and recorded the sex, age (in terms of adult or child), and apparent ethnic group membership of pairs of people and estimated the distance between them. Note that, as in Baxter's case, covert observers do not need to be physically concealed from the people whom they are observing; Baxter sat on a bench in plain view. Rather, the people under observation are not aware that an observer is watching and recording their behavior; most people pay little attention to someone who is apparently resting on a bench, as Baxter was.

Problems in Naturalistic Observation

Naturalistic observation methods allow the researcher to study natural behavior in its natural context, but they also involve some costs arising from the low degree of control that the researcher has over the research environment. Let's briefly examine four categories of problems that can arise in naturalistic research: cognitive biases that can limit the validity of the data, limitations on recordkeeping, reactivity, and adverse effects on the researcher.

COGNITIVE BIASES   Human beings are the data collection mechanisms in naturalistic observation research; consequently, the normal human cognitive processes that lead to bias in everyday perceptual processes can bias the results of observations (Jones, 1985). One such bias is **selective attention:** People do not pay equal attention to everything that goes on around them; they selectively attend to stimuli that are salient to them, that is, those that attract their attention (S. T. Fiske & Taylor, 1991). For example, observers are more likely to attend to people who stand out from the background, such as those who are dressed differently from others in the setting, or those who constitute a minority in the setting, such as the only woman in a group of men. Point of view also affects attention: We are more likely to pay attention to people at whom we are looking face to face, rather than from behind or from one side. To the extent that people or events that are salient in a setting distract the observer's attention from other, perhaps more important, people or events, the data from those observations will be biased.

As discussed in Chapter 2, the Redfield-Lewis debate over interpretations of the quality of life in a Mexican village showed that people's expectations about what they will see affect their interpretations of those events. People tend to interpret events to conform with what they already believe about the situation (S. T. Fiske & Taylor, 1991). Recall Redfield's comment that "the hidden question behind my book is, 'What do these people enjoy?' The hidden question behind Dr. Lewis's book is, 'What do these people suffer from?'" (quoted in Critchfield, 1978, p. 66). Even when people have no strong preset expectations, their first impressions of a person or situation establish expectations that color their interpretations of later events (S. T. Fiske & Taylor, 1991).

Finally, when people cannot take notes on events as they happen, as is normally the case in complete participation, they tend to remember what they think should have happened in a situation rather than what did happen (S. T. Fiske & Taylor, 1991). This kind of reconstructive memory occurs because people have mental scripts that tell them how events should unfold; for example, you can probably very easily describe the sequence of events in a job interview. These mental scripts provide people with a framework for understanding and remembering things, so that memory tends to follow the script even when the actual event departs from it. Shweder (1975), for example, found that observers at a boys' camp tended to recall the boys' behavior as more closely fitting their stereotypes of how boys should behave at camp than how the boys actually behaved.

These kinds of cognitive biases are normal aspects of human information processing and so are likely to affect any observational study. However, as discussed later in this chapter, researchers can enhance the reliability and validity of behavioral observations by training observers, using behavioral ratings rather than observers' interpretations of behavior as data, and, whenever possible, recording the behavior as it occurs.

RECORDKEEPING   Unfortunately, concurrent recording of behavior is not always possible. Complete participant observers are normally unable to take notes as events occur because note taking would inhibit their full participation in events and reveal their roles as researchers. Note taking is not always possible even in overt observation. The participant as observer must take full part in the events being studied, and Black and Reiss (1967) found that their observers as participants could not take complete notes while watching police-citizen interactions and that it was difficult to write notes afterward in a moving patrol car, especially at night. Observers must therefore frequently write down their observations after the event, some times several hours later. Under these conditions, both the cognitive biases described earlier and normal memory lapses can lead to inaccurate recall. However, as Bogdan (1972) points out, experience has taught field researchers a number of techniques for recording observations with reasonable accuracy; some of these techniques are shown in Box 10-1.

REACTIVITY   As noted in Chapter 6, when people are aware that they are part of a research study, they may change their behavior to show themselves in a favorable light. Reactivity may be a special problem when the phenomenon under study includes behavior that is illegal or disapproved of by a powerful segment of society. Recall Thorne's (1988) comment that her research activities were sometimes viewed with suspicion even though she was a committed member of the draft resistance movement. The possibility of reactivity leads some researchers to use covert methods in both participant and nonparticipant research.

INFLUENCING EVENTS   In trying to reduce reactivity by concealing their status as researchers, covert participant observers can run the risk of contaminating the naturalism

BOX 10-1   Hints for Recalling Observations

Record observations as soon after the event as possible.

Don't talk to anyone about your observation session until after you have recorded the observations. Talking about observations can have two adverse effects: What you talk about becomes more salient, and the other person's comments might distort your memory.

Record your observations in complete privacy to eliminate distractions.

Record observations in the order that the events happened; recording salient events first can distort memory for other events.

Draw a diagram of the physical layout of the observation setting, and as you record your notes attempt to trace your steps in the sequence that they occurred during the observation period.

Outline the topics covered in particularly long periods of observation before attempting to record those periods; then record one topic at a time.

Make observations in time periods of manageable size and record the observations for one period before starting another. You can increase the lengths of the periods as you gain experience.

When recording dialog, don't worry about whether your quotations are flawless verbatim reproductions of what was said.

Pick up pieces of lost data after your initial recording session. If after a recording session you recall something that you omitted, go back and put it in.

Source: Adapted from Bogdan, 1972, pp. 41–42.

of what they observe by unintentionally influencing the people and events that they are observing. Alfred (1976) described his experience this way:

> Throughout the research, I tried to minimize . . . my own effect on the group I was studying. I was generally nondirective in my comments and conversation, demurred in first requests for suggestions or ideas, answered subsequent requests with suggestions made previously in similar situations by others, and even selected at random pages from books out of which I was asked to read something of my choice. Even in the group's ruling council I was able to avoid undue influence, since it was an advisory rather than a legislative body. . . . Such efforts and devices, however, did not completely solve the problem . . . ; I often had to choose what ideas to second, since I was generally perceived as a high-status member and since my behavior was interpreted by others as flowing from genuine satanic conviction and devotion to the church rather than as random acts or simple yesmanship. (p. 184)

The more complete an observer's participation in the research setting, the more likely such forms of reactivity are to occur and the more likely they are to be unavoidable. The only solutions to this problem are, as illustrated by Alfred's comments, to attempt to minimize one's influences on the research setting and to be aware of the possibility of such influences when interpreting data.

EFFECTS ON THE OBSERVER   The role of participant observer can be very stressful, especially when the observer is concealing his or her identity as a researcher. In such cases, the researcher must work simultaneously at playing the role of a real member of the research setting—dressing, speaking, behaving, and interacting according to the norms of the setting, which may differ significantly from the observer's own norms—and making careful, complete observations. In addition, covert observers often feel anxious or guilty over the deception they are carrying out and feel they are invading the privacy of the people they are observing. Not surprisingly, then, covert participant observers often feel overwhelmed by their roles (Lofland & Lofland, 1995).

Sometimes, covert participant observers act to relieve some of the stress by "confessing" their researcher roles to the people they are observing or to leaders among the people. Alfred (1976), for example, told the leader of the Satanic church he was studying about his role as researcher and asked the leader's permission to publish the results of the research. He got a surprising response. Although Alfred had developed ethical qualms over his deceptive role, the church leader not only saw it as ethical, but commendable: As a proper Satanist, Alfred was supposed to deceive people and manipulate them for his own ends! Even overt participant observation is not without its stresses. Thorne (1988) reports that throughout her research she experienced conflicts between her dual roles of researcher and activist; for example, she wanted to experience as many different resistance activities as possible in order to get a reasonably representative sample of experiences, but she felt that this lack of total commitment to any one activity limited her effectiveness in any of them. Thorne notes that although conflicts such as these are inevitable, their particular forms are not predictable in advance of the research. They are personal issues that each researcher must resolve in his or her own way.

Because participant observers live the roles they play, they can become socialized into those roles; that is, they can change to become the types of people whom they are studying. Reiss (1968) found this happening to the observers in his study of police-citizen interactions. Over the course of their experiences, the observers tended to become more pro-police in their attitudes, albeit each in his own way. Sociologists among the observers, for example, initially tended to attribute police officers' behavior to their personal characteristics, seeing them as bigoted and basically disinterested in the welfare of the citizenry. As they experienced police work, however, they tended to come to attribute police behavior to the stresses of the environment in which they worked, facing dangers unappreciated by "civilians." The extreme of socialization is what Reiss calls "going native": completely adopting the value system, attitudes, and behaviors of the people being studied. He cites the example of an observer he refers to as "Mr. M—" who worked in a high-crime African-American neighborhood:

> . . . on the last evening he was in the [police] station, one of the officers said, "Mr. M—, what did you learn while you were here this summer?" And Mr. M—, to the shock of a fellow observer, replied, "I learned to hate niggers." I suspect he even shocked many of the officers with that. He had become a kind of mockery of what they were. (pp. 365–366)

As Reiss (1968) notes, "Participant observation can be socialization with a sociological vengeance" (p. 365).

INTERVIEWS

In an interview the researcher asks questions of a research participant, who then responds. Interviews can fulfill several purposes in research. One purpose, of course, is

BOX 10-2   Types of Data That Interviews Can Provide

1. *Developing detailed descriptions of experiences, places, events, and so forth.* For example, what is life like for people who have been laid off from work and cannot find a job comparable to the one they had held? How do they use their time each day? What psychological and social effects (such as changes in friendships) has the layoff had on them? What effects has it had on their families and their relationships with their family members?

2. *Describing processes.* For example, what strategies do laid-off workers use to find new jobs? How do the strategies change over time if a job search is unsuccessful?

3. *Learning how events are interpreted.* For example, how do people make sense of being laid off? To what causes do they attribute the layoff? Whom do they blame and why?

4. *Integrating multiple perspectives.* For example, how are layoff experiences, processes, and interpretations similar and different for people at different levels of an organization (such as executives and laborers) or for people from different types of organizations?

Source: Adapted from R. S. Weiss (1994).

data collection; Box 10-2 describes some of the types of data that can be collected using interviews. A second role for interviews is exploratory: When planning research that will be conducted in an unfamiliar setting, researchers can use interviews to collect information about the setting, such as access and opportunities for collecting different types of data. As noted in Chapter 3, researchers can also interview members of populations from which they want to collect data to determine the acceptability of the research to potential participants. Finally, as discussed in Chapter 12, debriefing interviews can be used to obtain research participants' perspectives on studies in which they have taken part.

Interviewing is a complex topic; I can present only a broad overview here. More detailed information is available in Fowler and Mangione (1990), Rubin and Rubin (1995), and R. S. Weiss (1994).

Types of Interviews

Interviews can be categorized as unstructured, semistructured, or structured based on the extent to which the questions and the order in which they are asked are planned in advance of data collection. Although all three types of interviews can be used in research, field researchers tend to prefer unstructured and semistructured interviews because of the less formal atmosphere surrounding them.

UNSTRUCTURED INTERVIEWS   An **unstructured interview** proceeds much like a normal conversation: Questions emerge from the context of the situation and follow a normal conversational flow. Although the researcher has a general purpose in mind, there is no preset group of questions that are posed to every respondent. This format allows the researcher to tailor the questions to each respondent and the circumstances of the interview, but the lack of standardization—not every respondent answers every question—can make it difficult to organize and analyze the data. Stratton (1997) also cautions that because of the conversational nature of unstructured interviews the interviewer can fall into several traps that threaten the validity of the interview data, such as "feeding the answer you want [to the interviewees], negotiating agreement about what is the truth, and arguing with the respondents to try to persuade them to adapt a more sensible position" (p. 123).

SEMISTRUCTURED INTERVIEWS   A **semistructured interview** follows an interview guide that specifies the topics and issues to be covered and may include some specific questions, but there is no specified order in which the topics must be covered. This format makes data collection more systematic than in the unstructured interview while allowing the interview to be flexible and somewhat conversational. However, some topics may be skipped and the use of unstandardized questions reduces the comparability of responses. The loose structure of the semistructured interview also makes it vulnerable to the traps that unstructured interviews can fall into.

STRUCTURED INTERVIEWS   A **structured interview** uses specific questions that are asked in a specific order. All respondents therefore answer the same questions, providing a consistent database across people. However, the interviewer has no freedom to adapt the questions or their order to specific respondents, which may limit the naturalness of response, although the interviewer is allowed to clarify questions, such as by defining terms. Structured interviews can use either open- or closed-ended questions. Open-ended questions let respondents answer in their own words, whereas closed-ended questions require respondents to choose from a given set of alternatives. A particular drawback of closed-ended questions is that respondents may find it difficult to answer in terms of the preset categories if they think the categories don't correctly represent their responses. Nonetheless, closed-ended questions can be useful as a means of ensuring standardization when multiple interviewers are used to collect the data.

Standardizing Interview Procedures

To the greatest extent possible, interview procedures, especially those of structured interviews, should be standardized. That is, interviewers must do everything completely and in exactly the same way for each interview. Although standardization reduces interviewers' freedom to adapt the interview to respondents and to circumstances, it ensures consistency of data collection. Consistency, in turn, enhances reliability, which contributes to validity. Standardization has four aspects (Fowler & Mangione, 1990). First, in structured interviews, the interviewer must read each question to the respondent exactly as written; even apparently minor variations in question wording can lead to large variations in response. Fowler and Mangione (1990) report that 20–40% of interviewers deviate from the written questions they are given and that more experienced interviewers are more likely to deviate. When using multiple interviewers, it is therefore essential to write interview questions that the interviewers can read easily, to train interviewers to read questions exactly, and to monitor interviewers' behavior as closely as possible.

Second, as discussed in more detail shortly, when a respondent gives an inadequate response to a question, the interviewer must probe for more information. When doing so, the interviewer must be careful to probe nondirectively, that is, not to suggest an answer to the respondent. To the greatest extent possible, standard probes should be used. Pilot testing of the questionnaire used in the interview is a useful means of identifying situations that might require probes and for developing standard probes for each problematic question.

Third, the interviewer must record each respondent's answers to the same question in the same way, the only variance being due to differences in answers between respondents. As Fowler and Mangione (1990) note, "The key to standardized recording is to have no interviewer judgment, no interviewer summaries, no interviewer effects on what is written down" (p. 46). Interpretation should take place during data analysis, not during data collection. Chapter 6 discussed the ways in which researchers' expectations can influence the results they obtain; the face-to-face interaction between interviewer and respondent maximizes the potential for such researcher effects. Just as interviewers must be trained and monitored on questioning, they must be trained and monitored on recording.

Finally, the interviewer must be what Fowler and Mangione (1990) call "interpersonally neutral" when interacting with respondents. Interpersonal neutrality has two aspects. First, interviewers should not volunteer personal information about themselves, their opinions, or their values. Such information might lead respondents to tailor their answers to fit their expectations of what would please the interviewer. Second, interviewers must be careful that any feedback they give respondents about their answers does not imply any evaluation or judgment. An apparently negative reaction from the interviewer will lead the respondent to avoid answering further questions on the topic. An apparently approving reaction might lead the respondent to think the interviewer wants a certain type of answer, such as one that inaccurately emphasizes the positive or negative aspects of a situation.

Elements of an Interview

To collect data successfully, as an interviewer you must continuously perform a number of interpersonal tasks (Downs, Smeyak, & Martin, 1980). These tasks include establishing rapport with respondents, listening analytically, probing for additional information, motivating respondents, and maintaining control of the interview.

ESTABLISHING RAPPORT   You must establish a productive climate for the interview by putting the respondent at ease and working into the topic of the interview gradually. The respondent is probably in a novel situation and therefore feeling some anxiety about both the interview process and content. You can help the respondent adjust to the situation by acting in a relaxed and friendly manner. A full explanation of the topics to be covered in the interview and of the interview process will also help the respondent adjust, as well as help the respondent provide the desired information. Throughout the interview, respond nonevaluatively to whatever the respondent says, not reacting with shock, dismay, or disapproval to the respondents' self-reports. Of course, respond with sympathy and support when appropriate.

LISTENING ANALYTICALLY   You must listen analytically to the respondent's answers in order to identify inadequate responses to questions. Inadequate responses include no response to the question, incomplete responses, irrelevant responses, inaccurate responses, poorly organized responses that are difficult to follow, and responses that include terms that are unfamiliar to you. To be able to identify inadequate responses, pay close attention to what the respondent says. You must also be well prepared for the interview to be able to identify inaccurate responses and to link information from different parts of the interview to identify contradictions among responses.

PROBING   When you identify an inadequate response, tactfully probe for additional information. Two common probes are requests for elaboration (such as "Could you tell me some more about that?") and clarification (such as "I'm not familiar with that term; would you explain it to me?"). An expectant silence is often a useful probe, conveying the message that more is expected. When probing, be sensitive to the respondent's state of mind; if the respondent has no more information or feels threatened by the probe, move on to the next question. If the respondent appears not to have understood the question, perhaps by giving an irrelevant response, you could probe by repeating the question, perhaps with clarifications suggested by the content of the inadequate response. If the respondent provides inaccurate or contradictory information, tactfully point out the inaccuracy or contradiction and ask for clarification. For example, in an interview conducted in 2001, you might say something along the lines of "I think that I may have made a mistake in writing down something you said. Earlier, I wrote down that you were born in 1946, but just now you mentioned that you are 50 years old. Did I get your year of birth wrong?" Finally, when concluding a topic or asking a complex question, summarize what the respondent has said and ask if he or she has anything to add.

MOTIVATING   As Cannell and Kahn (1968) point out, respondents are subject to forces that act to increase motivation, such as liking for the interviewer and a desire to be helpful, and other forces that act to decrease motivation, such as dislike of the topic of the interview or embarrassment at not knowing much about the topic. Reinforce the factors that increase motivation, and reduce the impact of forces that inhibit motivation. Motivation can be increased by a complete orientation to the purposes and process of interview, emphasizing the importance of the research and the importance of the respondent's information. You can reinforce the respondent's talkativeness by inserting conversational phrases that indicate attention, such as "I see," "Uh huh," and so forth. Also, be careful not to punish the respondent for answering by reacting with disapproval; an interviewer must therefore be especially skilled in controlling nonverbal responses.

MAINTAINING CONTROL   Finally, you must always maintain control of the interview, especially in semistructured and structured interviews. That is, you must ensure that the questions are asked in the prescribed order and that all questions are asked or topics covered. It is very easy to let a respondent get off on a digression that, while interesting, is irrelevant to the purpose of the interview, using up time and distracting the respondent's attention from the research.

Group Interviews

In a group interview, the researcher interviews several people simultaneously using a semistructured format (A. E. Goldman & McDonald, 1987). The interviewer asks a question or introduces a topic and then lets the group members discuss it. The goal is to develop a free-flowing discussion in which the participants talk freely and interact with one another, building on each others' comments. In a successful group interview, then, the group process produces information and insights that would not have occurred to the group members had they been interviewed individually.

However, the group context also has its drawbacks. For example, the interviewer may not be able to explore any one person's comments in depth as would happen in an individual interview, and people may be reluctant to discuss certain topics in a group setting. In addition, there can be problems of group dynamics, such as people trying to dominate the discussion and people who ramble on without contributing anything of substance. It is therefore essential that researchers who conduct group interviews be well trained in group dynamics and have supervised experience in conducting group interviews before working on their own.

ARCHIVAL DATA

So far the discussion of research in natural settings has focused primarily on behavioral measures of dependent variables. Natural settings provide an additional data source not available to laboratory researchers: archives. **Archives** are records or documents that describe the characteristics of individuals, groups, or organizations. The data in these records are usually collected and maintained for purposes other than research. The original purpose of the U.S. census, for example, was to determine the population of the states so that representatives could be apportioned among them, and the data are now also used for administrative purposes, such as the distribution of federal monetary subsidies to the states. However, census data can also be used for research on the variables included in the census survey, such as the relationship between educational level and income. This section describes the types of archives from which one can draw data and briefly discusses some of the advantages and disadvantages of archival research. Lee and Peterson (1997) and Kellehear (1993) provide more detailed descriptions of the ways in which researchers can use archival data.

Types of Archives

Judd et al. (1991) identify three types of archives. Statistical archives commonly store data in summary form, such as means, proportions, and rates. In the public domain, statistical archives include those of the census; FBI crime statistics; Department of Labor statistics on wages, hours worked, and productivity; local government birth, death, and public health records; and so forth. In the private domain, organizations keep records of variables such as the sex and ethnic composition of their membership, and businesses also keep records on variables such as absenteeism, tardiness, and turnover. The Berkowitz (1970) study on the effect of President Kennedy's assassination on societal violence described earlier is an example of research conducted using data from statistical archives, in this case crime statistics compiled by the FBI. As discussed earlier, Fiedler et al. (1984) used mine safety statistics maintained by the company to evaluate the effectiveness of their intervention.

Another type of archival data consists of written and electronic records. The speeches and writings of public figures are usually preserved, and diaries and letters can reflect the writers' beliefs, attitudes, and motivations. Tetlock (1979), for example, analyzed government officials' public speeches concerning what turned out to be good and poor policy decisions. He found that speeches concerning poor decisions were more simplistic and biased than those about good decisions. Communications media can also provide data, both in the form of news reports and entertainment. For example, Lau and Russell (1980) and Peterson (1980) studied newspaper reports of professional athletes' and coaches' expressed reasons for winning and losing to test a theory about how people react to success and failure. They found that the players and coaches almost always took credit for winning and blamed circumstantial factors for losing, which supported both the theory and the results of laboratory research. In the realm of entertainment, Weigel, Loomis, and Soja (1980) used prime-time television programs to study the depiction of racial minorities and race relations. Among their findings was that interactions between African and European Americans were more likely to be shown as taking place in work settings than in social settings. In the clinical domain, psychotherapy researchers may have access to projective test protocols and other therapy records (Lee & Peterson, 1997).

Finally, survey archives are records of people's responses to national surveys of public opinion. This type of archive will be part of the next chapter's discussion of survey research.

Advantages of Using Archival Data

Archival data have a number of advantages for researchers (Kellehear, 1993; Lee & Peterson, 1997). In addition to being naturalistic, archival data are nonreactive. Because the records from which the data come are not made for research purposes, there are no reactivity problems associated with people knowing that they are participating in research. The use of archival data also allows the researcher to expand the research population to include participants not usually available to the researcher such as people from other cultures, people whose social roles and positions isolate them from researchers, and historical figures. For example, Lee, Hallahan, and Herzog (1996) investigated cultural differences in how people explain significant life events by examining newspaper articles from different countries, Gruenfeld and Preston (2000) investigated the relationship between the complexity of U.S. Supreme Court justices' reasoning about cases involving legal precedents and whether they voted to overturn those precedents, and Simonton (1994) has studied the nature of genius by examining the lives of writers, artists, and scientists. Archival data also permit researchers to conduct what might be termed *retrospective longitudinal research*, in which data collected from records made by people at one point are used to predict later life outcomes. For example, Peterson, Seligman, and Valliant (1988) examined the relationship between the ways people interpret significant life events and long-term health outcomes by using data from essays written by World War II veterans soon after their return to the United States to predict their health status 35 years later.

In addition to providing researchers access to various kinds of data, the use of archival data confers some practical advantages on the research. First, archival research is usually less expensive than the collection of original data, especially for longitudinal and cross-cultural research. Second, most archival research raises few ethical issues unless deception is used to gain access to records or individuals' privacy is invaded by revealing the names of people included in the records. Finally, archival research can easily be restarted if mistakes are made. For example, if researchers realize in the midst of a study that they have overlooked an important variable, they can modify the records to include the variable. Researchers collecting data from participants would have to start data collection from scratch with a new participant sample.

Limitations of Archival Research

Although archival data provide some advantages, they also present some problems that researchers must take into consideration when using them as data sources. Let's examine some of these problems.

ACCESS   The first problem is that of access. Individuals might not want to release private documents, such as diaries and letters, to archival researchers, and organizations are often wary about opening their records to outsiders. Even government records that are supposed to be open to the public might be restricted in practice. Maris (1969), for example, wanted to study the relationship between suicide and sex, age, and marital status, using death certificates from Cook County, Illinois. The county clerk refused to allow him to see the records even though state law said that they were supposed to be open to the public. Access is less of a problem for printed media, which are stored in public libraries. Researchers can record radio and television programs as they are broadcast but might have trouble gaining access to recordings in company archives.

VALIDITY   The second problem is that of the validity of archival records as operational definitions. The information available in statistical archives might not provide good operational definitions of hypothetical constructs; after all, they were intended only to assess manifest variables. Archived data can also suffer from what Webb, Campbell, Schwartz, Sechrist, and Grove (1981) called *selective deposit* and *selective survival*. In selective deposit, the people who control the data limit what the archive includes. For example, even though the *Congressional Record* is supposed to be a verbatim record of what is said on the floors of the U.S. Senate and House of Representatives, legislators can edit their remarks before the *Record* goes to press. In selective survival, the people who control the archive limit the data stored there. For example, Schoeneman and Rubanowitz (1985) analyzed the contents of newspaper advice columns but noted that the columnists chose the letters printed from the thousands of letters they received. Finally, when archives include data on hypothetical constructs, the operational definitions might change over time. For example, Judd et al. (1991) noted that in the 1970 U.S. census, 90% of the people who classified themselves as "Hispanic" also classified themselves as "White," but that in the 1980 census, only 58% of self-described Hispanics classified themselves as "White," while 38% used the "Other" racial category.

ALTERNATIVE EXPLANATIONS   The third problem derives from the correlational nature of archival research. As with all correlational studies, those using archival data might uncover spurious correlations caused by unmeasured third variables. For example, a large number of studies have found a relationship between outdoor air temperature and the incidence of a variety of violent crimes (Anderson, 1989), suggesting that heat causes aggression. However, it is also possible that people drink more alcoholic beverages during hot periods and that alcohol, not the heat, causes the aggression; other explanations are also possible (P. A. Bell, 1992).

THE ECOLOGICAL FALLACY   The fourth problem can arise from the use of **aggregate data** from statistical archives. Data are said to be aggregated when each data point represents many people rather than one. For example, W. S. Robinson (1950) examined the relationship between race and illiteracy by using U.S. census data for 1930 to correlate the proportion of African Americans living in each state with the states' illiteracy rates. He found that states with a higher proportion of African-American residents had higher illiteracy rates, $r = .77$. From these data, one might conclude that there was a strong relationship between race and literacy in 1930. However, Robinson then showed that when data collected on the race and literacy status of individuals were correlated, the relationship was actually quite small, $r = .20$. The term **ecological fallacy** is used to describe the errors that can result from drawing individual level conclusions from aggregate level data. Robinson suggested that a confounded third variable—region of the country—accounted for the difference between his aggregate level and individual level results. Illiteracy was higher overall in southern states than in northern states, and the illiteracy rate was higher among African Americans in the South than among those in the North. When Firebaugh (1978) controlled these regional differences statistically, the aggregate level correlation was similar to the individual level correlation. The lesson from these studies is that one should never apply the results of aggregate level research to individuals unless one is certain that all the relevant variables have been taken into consideration. See Dooley (1995) for a more detailed discussion of the ecological fallacy problem.

ANALYZING OPEN-ENDED DATA

Much of the data generated in natural setting research is open-ended; that is, it consists of behavioral observations, narrative responses to interview questions, the contents of archival records, and so forth, rather than closed-ended responses on rating scales. To be useful, these data must be classified into meaningful categories, or **coded**. The researcher can then use those categories as the basis for qualitative analysis by searching the data for theoretically relevant patterns or emergent patterns (see Chapter 9) or as the basis for quantitative analysis. This section discusses the development and reliability of coding systems and gives an example of a quantitative content analysis of open-ended data.

Characteristics of Coding Systems

Coding systems can be characterized along six dimensions (Crano & Brewer, 1986): theory-based versus ad hoc development, broad versus narrow focus, number of coding categories used, degree of inference required, unit of behavior, and concurrent versus after-the-fact coding. Each of these characteristics entails advantages and disadvantages, and each is related to how reliably data can be coded.

THEORY-BASED VERSUS AD HOC DEVELOPMENT   Theory-based coding systems, as the term implies, organize data into categories derived from theories dealing with the behavior under study. Bales's (1950) Interaction Process Analysis system, shown in Figure 10-7, is an example of a theory-based system. Using Interaction Process Analysis, verbal and nonverbal communications in small groups can be placed into 1 of 12 categories derived from Bales's theory of group process. Each of the 12 categories is a member of two other categories that can be used to describe the nature of group interaction: types of problems that can inhibit group effectiveness, and whether the tone of the interaction is positive, negative, or neutral. An extension of this system (Bales & Cohen, 1979) allows individual behavior in the group to be coded in terms of three dimensions: friendly versus unfriendly, instrumentally controlled versus emotionally expressive, and dominant versus submissive. Because theory-based coding systems are tied to a theory, they permit easy comparison of research results with the propositions of the theory. However, unless the system has been well tested, the theory-based categories might not fit actual behavior very well. There might be observed behaviors that don't fit any category or behaviors that can be put into more than one category.

Ad hoc coding systems emerge from the data. The researcher examines the data and creates categories into which responses can be coded. For example, Straits (1967) studied the reasons people gave for quitting smoking. He asked people who had quit, "Why did you want to stop smoking?" and asked people who still smoked, "What reasons might you have for giving up smoking?" Given reasons offered by 200 respondents, Straits developed the coding system shown in Box 10-3: 21 types of reasons grouped into four higher level categories. Higher level categories such as these are useful because although they ignore the detailed information available in the lower level categories, they ease data analysis by giving fewer categories to handle. Straits used logical analysis of the lower level categories to create the higher levels; there are also statistical techniques that can be used in some circumstances (see, for example, L. A. Baxter, 1992). Ad hoc systems have the advantage of creating categories that represent all the observed behavior, including categories that might be absent in theory-based systems. This advantage is balanced by two disadvantages. First, the categories created might not fit the theory being tested and so make interpretation of results difficult. Second, the categories might be unique to the sample of research participants used in the study and

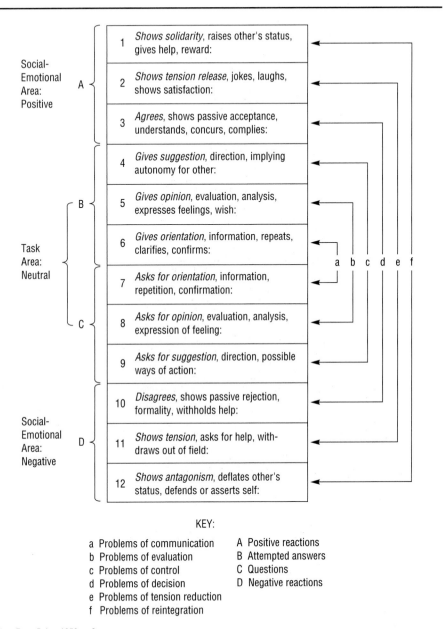

KEY:

a Problems of communication   A Positive reactions
b Problems of evaluation   B Attempted answers
c Problems of control   C Questions
d Problems of decision   D Negative reactions
e Problems of tension reduction
f Problems of reintegration

Note: From Bales, 1950, p. 9.

FIGURE 10-7   Categories for Coding Group Interactions

BOX 10-3   Coding Categories for Straits's (1967) Study of Reasons for Quitting Smoking

Current Health Reasons

1. Didn't feel well (unspecified illness)

2. Nasal congestion (bad cold, sinus, etc.)

3. Cough, sore throat (smoker's cough, dry throat, etc.)

4. Shortness of breath (cutting down on wind, etc.)

5. Poor appetite, loss of weight

6. Other ailments (headaches, nervous condition, nausea, dizziness, etc.)

Advised by Doctor

7. Unspecified (ordered by doctor, etc.)

8. Because of specific ailment (heart trouble, palsy, etc.)

9. Doctor said smoking harmful

Source: Adapted from Singleton & Straits, 1999, p. 459.

Future Health Reasons

10. Smoking is harmful (unspecified)

11. Live longer

12. Fear of cancer (lung cancer, etc.)

Other

13. Sensory dislike (bad taste in mouth, smell, dirty house, etc.)

14. Pressure from close associates (wife, co-worker, etc.)

15. Financial reason (waste of money, etc.)

16. Test of willpower (to see if could, control life, etc.)

17. Work requirement (smoking not allowed)

18. Quit temporarily (because of operation, illness, Lent, etc., and didn't return to smoking)

19. Other reasons

20. Don't know

21. No answer

so do not generalize to other samples. The second problem can, of course, be checked through replication research.

BROAD VERSUS NARROW FOCUS   A broadly focused coding system attempts to categorize all the behaviors found in a situation being studied by using relatively high-level categories and ignoring fine distinctions between similar behaviors. For example, a study of small-group interaction might code the types of places the group meets, the roles taken by group members, the content of their interactions (what is discussed), and the tone of the interaction. Because so many types of behavior must be coded, there is not enough time to make fine distinctions between behaviors; detail is traded off for comprehensiveness. Narrowly focused coding systems use larger number of categories in order to get a more detailed picture of a more restricted set of behaviors. For example, Benjamin's (1979) Structural Analysis of Social Behavior is, like Interaction Process Analysis, used to code interpersonal behavior; Structural Analysis of Social Behavior, however, has 108 categories compared to Interaction Process Analysis's 12. Structural Analysis of Social Behavior gives more detailed information than Interaction Process Analysis, but requires the coders to make more decisions when classifying a behavior.

Whether a researcher uses a broadly or narrowly focused coding system depends on two factors. The first is the amount of information known about the behavior or situation being studied. The less one knows, the more useful a broader system is to ensure that all relevant behaviors are coded. With well-understood behavior or situations, one has enough information to decide on which behaviors to focus and to develop a finely grained coding system that can cover all aspects of the behavior. The second factor is the degree of detail the research requires. Do you, as the researcher, need a broad or narrow focus in order to test your hypothesis?

NUMBER OF CODING CATEGORIES   Generally speaking, fewer rather than more categories make for a better coding system. Although using more categories allows finer distinctions to be made between behaviors, when categories are very similar two coders might put the same behavior into different categories, thereby reducing reliability of measurement. Confusion of categories is especially likely when coding must be done quickly, as when observers code behavior while it happens. If the behavior is recorded verbatim (as on videotape), confusion can be less problematic, because coders can review the record to check their work. Some complex systems, such as Structural Analysis of Social Behavior, reduce the confusion by allowing coding at more than one level; higher level, broader categories can be used when circumstances make detailed coding difficult.

DEGREE OF INFERENCE REQUIRED   A coding system requires a high degree of inference if coders must make decisions about the meaning or intensity of a behavior rather than simply putting the behavior itself into a category. For example, if coders are required to categorize behavior as "aggressive" or "nonaggressive," they are making inferences about what a behavior means in terms of a hypothetical construct. Consider the behavior "Hits other person between shoulder blades with flat of hand." This action could be aggressive, or it could be a friendly greeting. Inferences of intensity refer to decisions about how much of a construct a behavior represents. For example, on a 7-point scale, how aggressive is a slap on the back? Because coders can differ in the inferences that they make about a behavior, they should code only the behavior itself: what happens, not what it means (Hoyt & Kerns, 1999). One way to prevent coders from having to make inferences is to draw up a list of behaviors that represent the construct that has been checked for content-related validity. Coders indicate which behaviors occur during the period of observation or how often each behavior occurs; because every coder uses the same list of behaviors, there can be no disagreement about which should be counted. One such checklist, from a study of children's aggression, is shown in Box 10-4.

UNIT OF BEHAVIOR   The term *unit of behavior* refers to the issue of what constitutes a single, codable behavior: When does a behavior begin, and when does it end? Because life is a continuous flow of events in which one behavior merges into another rather than a set of discrete behaviors, it can be hard to say when one behavior ends and another begins. Consider this hypothetical reason for stopping smoking: "I was always getting short of breath, so I decided to stop for a while; then my doctor advised me to quit permanently." Using Straits's (1967) coding system (Box 10-3), is this one reason or two? If one, should it be coded as "Current health reason" or as "Advised by doctor"? Ideally, a coding system will have an objective basis for determining the unit of behavior. In the case of the smoking data, for example, you could establish the rule "Code only the first thought expressed in an answer." But it is often not possible to construct such

BOX 10-4   Checklist of Aggressive Behaviors

Physical

1. Hits, slaps, or strikes with body part above waist

2. Hits, slaps, punches, or strikes with a held object

3. Kicks, steps on, sits on, lies on, or trips with body part below waist

4. Bites or spits

5. Pushes, holds, pulls, grabs, drags, or chokes

6. Snatches property of another (without damage to that property)

7. Damages the property of another

8. Tries to create a reaction, that is, teases, annoys, or interferes in the activity of another (except where chasing is involved and 11 or 12 is scored)

9. Threatens with some part of the body

10. Threatens with a held object

11. Chases another

12. Chases with a held object

13. Growls, grimaces, or makes sounds of dislike or anger toward another

Source: Joy, Kimball, & Zabrack, 1986, p. 340.

14. Throws or kicks an object at another, except as required (for example, ball in game)

Verbal

1. Disparages; makes remarks of dislike; finds fault with or censures; condemns; humiliates; laughs at the misfortunes of; mocks; attributes bad qualities to; or curses another; or expresses the desire that he or she be the victim of imperious events

2. Verbally tries to claim a possession of another

3. Rejects or denies some activity, privilege, or object to another

4. Threatens to hurt

5. Commands or demands another to do or not to do something in a loud, vigorous, or angry tone of voice

6. Argues with or is at cross-purposes with another, when this involves more than one statement separated by a rejoinder

7. Tells an authority figure about another's behavior (which the subject of observation apparently considered negative)

8. Shifts the blame for some activity (apparently considered negative) to another

9. Tries to cause injury to another via an agent

rules for behavioral observation studies, which deal with a continuous flow of behavior. In such cases, the unit of behavior must be left to the judgment of the coders, which may be somewhat variable and so introduce some unreliability into the coding.

CONCURRENT VERSUS AFTER-THE-FACT CODING   Coding can be conducted as the behavior occurs (concurrent coding), or the behavior can be recorded verbatim and the coding conducted from the record. After-the-fact coding is preferable because coders can review the record to ensure that they missed nothing and to check their codings. Records can also be stopped after a behavior occurs to allow coders more time to decide on the proper category for the behavior. These procedures generally result in more reliable coding. In some cases, however, verbatim records, especially those that identify the research participants, are not desirable, such as for privacy reasons. Concurrent coding is inescapable in such cases.

Developing Coding Systems

It is advisable to use an existing coding system whenever possible; not only does the use of an existing system enhance the ability to compare the results of own's own research with that of previous research, but the process of developing a new coding system can be long and laborious. However, because researchers must sometimes develop their coding systems, this section briefly discusses some rules for developing coding systems and the issue of reliability in coding.

RULES FOR DEVELOPING CODING SYSTEMS   Herbert and Attridge (1975) provide a list of 33 rules for developing coding systems. It is not possible to discuss all of them here, but three of the most fundamental are as follows:

1. *All terms, especially those related to the coding categories, must be clearly and unambiguously defined.* Coders cannot use a system reliably unless they fully understand what kinds of behaviors fall into each category. These definitions can be elaborate; Bales (1950), for example, uses 19 pages to define the 12 Interaction Process Analysis categories.

2. *There must be a category for every behavior.* When a coding system is first being developed, too many categories are better than too few; categories that turn out to be used only rarely can be combined with related categories or their behaviors can be relegated to an "Other" category. However, categories that make theoretically meaningful distinctions should always be retained. "Other" should be the least frequently used category; if it is not, some of the behaviors in it might constitute one or more meaningful categories. This situation could arise if a theory-based system overlooked important categories of behaviors.

3. *A behavior must fit into one and only one category.* If categories are too similar, the same behavior will be classified inconsistently, reducing the reliability of the coding system.

Adherence to these three basic rules will solve most of the problems involved in developing coding systems.

Reliability in Coding   The reliability of coding can be assessed in four ways (Weick, 1985). The most common way, discussed in Chapter 5, is interrater reliability, the degree to which two coders agree on the coding of the same data. Second, one can assess the degree to which one coder is consistent over time: Do codings at Time 1 agree with codings at Time 2? Third, one can look at interrater agreement across time. For example, do the codes assigned by Coder A at Time 1 agree with those assigned by Coder B at Time 2? Finally, one can look at within-coder consistency at the beginning and end of a coding period. For example, if coders work for 1 hour at a time, do the codes assigned during the first 15 minutes agree with those assigned during the last 15 minutes? The last three methods have one crucial limitation: They assume that the same behaviors occur at the same rate at both times (Methods 2 and 3) or at both the beginning and end of a rating period (Method 4). For this reason, interrater reliability is used most often. However, researchers can use the other methods to test the reliability of coders during training and practice sessions. Videotapes can be made and coders can code the same tape at, say, 2-week intervals, and Methods 2 and 3 can be applied to the codings. If the tapes are constructed so that the same behaviors occur at the same rate at the beginning and at the end, Method 4 can be used. These methods can serve as checks on the coders' understanding of the coding system before they work on real data and can be used to find flaws, such as ambiguous categories, in the coding system itself.

Given the characteristics of coding systems discussed earlier, Crano and Brewer (1986) suggest that the reliability of a coding system will be highest when

1. The system has a broad rather than narrow focus.
2. The unit of behavior is objectively defined rather than left to the coder's discretion.
3. The coding system has a small number of categories.
4. Coding is conducted after the fact rather than concurrently with the behavior.
5. Little or no inference is required.

Of course, it is not always possible to have all of these characteristics in a single coding system; research needs, such as a requirement for concurrent coding, might limit those that can be implemented. However, a coding system should have as many of these characteristics as possible.

Content Analysis

Content analysis is a "technique for making inferences by systematically and objectively identifying specific characteristics of messages" (Holsti, 1968, p. 601), such as those contained in speeches, letters, diaries, news reports, and entertainment media. Once these characteristics are determined, they can be related to each other or to characteristics of the sender or recipient of the message, or of the medium by which the message was sent. Lau and Russell (1980) and Peterson (1980), for example, examined the relationship between the outcomes of professional sporting events (win or lose) and the reasons the athletes and coaches gave for their performances (something about themselves or something about the situation).

The process of content analysis can be described in terms of four steps, which are briefly reviewed here; Holsti (1968, 1969), Krippendorff (1980), and R. P. Weber (1990) provide detailed descriptions of the process. An example of the use of content analysis is found in a study conducted by Gonzales and Meyers (1993), who sought to determine the characteristics that men and women want in dating partners and the characteristics that men and women think the other sex wants. They did so by examining how people presented themselves in personal ads and what their ads said that they wanted in others. Gonzales and Meyers investigated how these appeals for and offers of characteristics varied by the sex and sexual orientation of the advertisers.

The first step in content analysis is deciding on sources of data. Gonzales and Meyers used ads placed in free or low-cost newsprint publications; some targeted both a heterosexual and homosexual readership, such as New York City's *The Village Voice*, and others were targeted specifically at gay audiences, such as *Gay Chicago*. To maximize the representativeness of their sample of ads, they used publications from three

TABLE 10-1   Gonzales and Meyers's (1993) Coding Scheme

Category	Definition[a]	Examples[a]
Attractiveness		*Physical:* athletic, cute
		Social: classy, debonair
Financial security		generous, established
Expressive traits	"Characteristics generally considered to be more common among women than men"	affectionate, caring
Instrumental traits	"Any characteristic that is primarily goal or success oriented"	ambitious, competitive
Sincerity	"Committed, monogamous behaviors and characteristics that would prevent exploitation in an intimate relationship"	one-woman man, respectful
Sexual references	"Any reference to physical contact, explicit sexual behavior, fantasies, or sex-related physical characteristics"	

[a]Gonzales and Meyers did not provide narrative definitions for the attractiveness and financial security categories or specific examples for the sexual references category.

Note: Adapted from Gonzales & Meyers, 1993, pp. 133–134.

geographic regions: the West Coast (San Francisco), the Midwest (Chicago and Minneapolis), and the East Coast (New York City). The second step is to sample from the sources. Gonzales and Meyers collected more than 2,000 ads over an 8-month period. They divided the ads into 12 categories based on the advertiser's sex, the advertiser's sexual orientation, and the three geographic regions. They then randomly selected 25 ads from each category for analysis, resulting in a sample of 300 ads.

The third step is the development of a coding scheme for the content of material being analyzed. Gonzales and Meyers's coding scheme is shown in Table 10-1. They coded the terms used in the ads into six categories of characteristics—attractiveness, financial security, expressive traits, instrumental traits, sincerity, and sexual references—and according to whether the advertiser claimed to possess the characteristic (coded as an "offer") or asked for the characteristic in a dating partner (coded as an "appeal"). The fourth step is deciding how to measure the content of the material, that is, how to assign numerical values. Gonzales and Meyers used two measures: a dichotomous measure that indicated whether or not a category was mentioned in an ad and a continuous measure of the number of times each category was mentioned in each ad.

The results of Gonzales and Meyers's categorical analyses are shown in Table 10-2. They found that women were more likely to offer instrumental traits and ask for expressive traits and sincerity, and that gay advertisers of both sexes were more likely to include sexual references in their ads. They also found that heterosexual men were more likely to offer security than gay men, but that there was no sexual orientation difference for women, and that heterosexual women were more likely than members of any of the other groups to ask for financial security.

Gonzales and Meyers could have tried to collect data such as these through a self-report questionnaire. However, content analysis provided them with several advantages

TABLE 10-2   Number and Percentage of Advertisers Who Offered and Solicited Characteristics in Each of Six Content Categories

Ad Contents	HETEROSEXUAL		HOMOSEXUAL	
	Men (n = 75)	Women (n = 75)	Men (n = 75)	Women (n = 75)
Attractiveness offer	47	53	47	42
	(63%)	(71%)	(63%)	(56%)
Attractiveness appeal	34	34	33	21
	(45%)	(45%)	(44%)	(28%)
Security offer[ac]	40	32	23	32
	(53%)	(43%)	(31%)	(43%)
Security appeal[bc]	4	24	5	8
	(5%)	(32%)	(7%)	(11%)
Expressiveness offer	26	23	21	32
	(35%)	(31%)	(28%)	(43%)
Expressiveness appeal[b]	16	33	12	22
	(21%)	(44%)	(16%)	(29%)
Instrumentality offer[b]	10	22	14	23
	(13%)	(29%)	(19%)	(31%)
Instrumentality appeal	11	20	11	13
	(15%)	(27%)	(15%)	(17%)
Sincerity offer	12	6	9	11
	(16%)	(8%)	(12%)	(15%)
Sincerity appeal[b]	9	14	5	13
	(12%)	(19%)	(7%)	(17%)
Sexual offer[a]	2	1	21	7
	(3%)	(1%)	(28%)	(9%)
Sexual appeal[a]	2	2	21	8
	(3%)	(3%)	(28%)	(11%)

Note: Gonzales & Meyers, 1993, p. 135.

[a]Significant ($p < .05$) main effect for sexual orientation.

[b]Significant main effect for gender.

[c]Significant gender $\times$ sexual orientation interaction.

over the questionnaire methodology. First, they were able to collect data from a group of people from whom it might have been difficult to recruit participants, lesbians and gay men. Second, it was relatively easy for them to get data samples from geographically diverse regions. Third, they were able to collect data on variables, such as sexual appeals and offers, that people might have been reluctant to provide on a questionnaire due to social desirability concerns. Finally, they were able to collect data on variables, such as desire for security, that they might not have thought to ask about on a questionnaire.

SUMMARY

Research in natural settings, or field research, is conducted to obtain data that are more representative of people's true responses to natural situations than data collected in the laboratory. However, field settings provide lower control over independent, dependent, and extraneous variables and over assignment of research participants to conditions of the independent variable. Natural setting research can take a number of forms, including field experiments, quasi-experiments, natural experiments, observational and interview studies, and archival research.

Field experiments attempt to achieve a balance between naturalism and control by manipulating an independent variable in a natural setting and observing natural behavior in response to the independent variable. In conducting a field experiment, the researcher must choose a setting that contains research participants who have the desired characteristics and that will allow implementation of the independent variable in a controlled and plausible manner. The researcher must also obtain permission to use the setting. The independent variable can be manipulated using either the street theater strategy, in which everyone in the setting is exposed to the independent variable, or the accosting strategy, in which one person is singled out as a participant. In designing a field experiment, the researcher must be concerned with potential problems of construct validity, control over extraneous variables, and vulnerability to outside interference.

Natural experiments attempt to achieve naturalism in treatments and setting by taking advantage of events outside the researcher's control that, in effect, manipulate an independent variable. In a quasi-experiment, the researcher manipulates an independent variable using naturally occurring groups as the experimental and control groups. Both techniques use the same research designs. In the nonequivalent control group design, natural groups comprise the experimental and control groups in a group comparison approach. The researcher must ensure that the members of the experimental and control groups are equivalent on the dependent variable prior to the introduction of the independent variable and on extraneous variables. Whenever possible, this equivalence is determined by a pretest. Trying to match people from groups that are not equivalent on a pretest of the dependent variable is a mistaken strategy because it introduces the possibility of regression toward the mean on the posttest. The time series approach, which uses either an interrupted time series design or a control series design, is akin to a single-case experiment: Scores for the dependent variable are plotted before and after the introduction of an independent variable, and the effect of the independent variable is gauged by the amount of change in postintervention scores.

Naturalistic observation seeks to attain naturalism in behavior, settings, and treatments by studying people's natural behavior in natural settings with minimum interference by the researcher. Naturalistic observation research can vary along the dimensions of participation and deception, resulting in four categories of naturalistic observation. In complete participant observation, the researcher becomes a full member of the research setting without telling the other members of her or his role as researcher. The participant as observer becomes a full member of the setting but is open about the researcher role. The observer as participant enters into the research setting but interacts with members of the setting no more than is necessary to collect data, usually being open about the researcher role. In nonparticipant observation, the researcher takes no part in the research setting, passively observing, either overtly or covertly, what happens. Naturalistic observation research can suffer from cognitive biases of the observer, such as selective attention, selective interpretation of events, and selective recall; poor recordkeeping, especially in complete participant observation; reactivity; influencing events; and adverse effects on the researcher.

Interviews can be used to develop descriptions of experiences, describe processes, learn how people interpret events, and integrate multiple perspectives on events. Interviews can be classified by degree of structure: unstructured interviews proceed like conversations, semistructured interviews are based on question guides, and structured interviews contain specific questions asked in a specific order. Standardization of interviews enhances the validity of data collection. While conducting an interview, the interviewer must accomplish five interpersonal tasks: establish rapport with the interviewee, listen analytically, probe inadequate responses, motivate the respondent, and maintain control of the interview. Because group members exchange ideas in group interviews, group interviews can provide information and insights that might not be found with individual interviews.

Archives are records or documents that describe the characteristics or behaviors of individuals, groups, or organizations, and consist of statistical archives, survey archives, and written and electronic records. Archival data allow researchers to study populations not usually available to them with relative ease and few ethical problems. However, archival research can be limited by difficulty of access to the data sources, validity of the data, and the inability to rule out alternative explanations for findings. In addition, one must be wary of the ecological fallacy in aggregate data: inferring individual level processes from group level data.

Coding systems are used to classify open-ended data. The ideal coding system has a broad rather than narrow focus, deals with units of behavior that are objectively defined, has a small number of categories, is used for after-the-fact coding, and requires little inference. However, all of these characteristics are not always achievable in a particular coding system; each system must be designed to fit the needs of the research being conducted. Once coded, data can be analyzed either qualitatively or by using a quantitative content analysis.

QUESTIONS AND EXERCISES FOR REVIEW

1. How do field research settings differ from laboratory settings? What advantages and disadvantages do these characteristics confer on field research?
2. How does a field experiment differ from a laboratory experiment?
3. What issues must one consider in choosing a research setting for a field experiment and implementing an independent variable in a field setting?
4. Describe the problems and limitations of conducting field experiments.
5. What are the similarities and differences between natural experiments and quasi-experiments?
6. Describe the nonequivalent control group design. What problems is a researcher likely to face in conducting a study using this design? Why is matching a mistaken strategy when

groups are initially different on the dependent variable? How can a degree of randomization of participant characteristics be achieved in this design?

7. Describe the interrupted time series and control series designs. Given your knowledge of single-case experiments, how could these designs be improved?

8. What are the dimensions of naturalistic observation and the categories of observer roles derived from them?

9. Describe the problems and limitations of conducting naturalistic observation research.

10. Describe the types of information that interviews can provide.

11. Describe the types of interviews, their relative advantages and disadvantages, and their most appropriate uses.

12. What aspects of interview procedures should be standardized? How does the standardization of each procedure contribute to the validity of the research?

13. What interpersonal tasks must interviewers accomplish? How does each task contribute to the validity of the research?

14. What types of archives are available to researchers, and what types of data do they contain?

15. What are the characteristics of coding systems? How are these characteristics related to the reliability of coding systems?

16. What are the relative advantages and disadvantages of theory-based and ad hoc coding systems?

17. State the three basic rules for constructing coding categories.

18. Describe the process of content analysis.

19. Reconsider the hypothesis you chose for Question 15 in the previous chapter. Describe the relative advantages and disadvantages of testing it using field research methods. How would you test the hypothesis using naturalistic observation, a field experiment, a natural experiment, and a quasi-experiment? What are the advantages and disadvantages of each of those approaches? Are archives a viable data source? Why or why not?

11 SURVEY RESEARCH

ASKING QUESTIONS
Open- and Closed-Ended
  Questions
Question Wording
  Use the Language of
    Research Participants
  Avoid Unnecessary Negatives
  Ask Only One Question at a
    Time
  Avoid Leading and Loaded
    Questions
  Be Specific
  Do Not Make Assumptions
  Address Sensitive Topics
    Sensitively

OBTAINING ANSWERS
Levels of Measurement
  Measurement Levels
  Information Content
  Statistical Tests
  Ecological Validity
Response Formats
  Comparative Rating Scales
  Itemized Rating Scales
  Graphic Rating Scales

  Numerical Rating Scales
Choosing a Response Format

MULTI-ITEM SCALES
Advantages of Multi-Item Scales
Types of Multi-Item Scales
  Likert Scales
  Thurstone Scales
  Guttman Scales
  The Semantic Differential

RESPONSE BIASES
Question-Related Biases
  Scale Ambiguity
  Category Anchoring
  Estimation Biases
  Respondent Interpretations
    of Numerical Scales
Person-Related Biases
  Social Desirability
  Acquiescence
  Extremity
  Halo and Leniency
  Interpreting Responses

QUESTIONNAIRE DESIGN
Question Order
  Question Sequencing
  Context Effects
Layout of Questionnaires
Instructions
Using Existing Measures
  Response Formats
  Context Effects

QUESTIONNAIRE
ADMINISTRATION
Methods of Data Collection
  Group Administration
  Mail Questionnaires
  Personal Interviews
  Telephone Interviews
  Focus Groups
  Computer Administration
Comparing the Methods

SURVEY DATA ARCHIVES

SUMMARY

QUESTIONS AND EXERCISES
FOR REVIEW

In the most general sense, survey research is the process of collecting data by asking questions and recording people's answers. Surveys can be conducted for a variety of purposes, two of which predominate. One purpose is the estimation of **population parameters**, or the characteristics of a population. For example, the goal of a survey might be to determine the percentage of people who hold supporting and opposing positions on social issues, such as nuclear power; the percentage who perform certain behaviors, such as smoking cigarettes; or the demographic characteristics of the population, such as sex, age, income, and ethnicity. The U.S. census, public opinion polls, and the biennial General Social Survey (GSS) conducted by the University of Chicago's National Opinion Research Center are all surveys directed at estimating population parameters. The second purpose for which a survey might be conducted is hypothesis testing. Researchers might be interested in the correlations between the answers to questions or between characteristics of respondents and their answers. Surveys can be conducted specifically for the pupose of hypothesis testing, or researchers might use data from survey archives, such as those described in the previous chapter, to test their hypotheses. Experiments can also be conducted by survey methods when the independent variable is manipulated by manipulating the information that research participants receive: People in different conditions of the independent variable receive different versions of the survey that contain the appropriate information for their condition of the independent variable.

Surveys can also be classified into two broad categories based on the way respondents are recruited. Respondents in **sample surveys** are selected in ways that are designed to produce a respondent sample whose characteristics closely mirror those of the population from which the sample was drawn. National public opinion polls and the GSS are examples of sample surveys: They use techniques described in the next chapter to obtain respondent samples from each region of the United States who reflect the gender, ethnic group, and age distributions of the population. Respondents in **convenience surveys** consist of members of whatever group or groups of people that the research found it convenient to sample from. Most self-report research in the behavioral sciences uses convenience surveys, primarily of college students. The data from sample surveys can be used either to estimate population parameters or to explore relationships between variables. Because the samples used in convenience surveys are not representative of a population, they cannot be used to estimate population parameters but are commonly used in hypothesis-testing research.

This chapter provides an overview of several key issues in survey research. It first describes the process of writing questions and creating question response formats, and the advantage of using multi-item scales, especially when measuring hypothetical constructs. It next discusses the problem of response biases and then reviews the principles of questionnaire design and administration. The chapter concludes with a brief look at survey data archives as a research resource. One chapter cannot cover all the information you would need to know before conducting survey research, so before getting started you should consult one of the specialized books on the topic. The books by Babbie (1990) and Mangione (1995) are good starting points.

ASKING QUESTIONS

Survey researchers collect data by asking questions. The questions, or items, are compiled into questionnaires that can be administered to respondents in a variety of ways, as discussed later in this chapter. These items are composed of two parts. The *stem* is the question or statement to which the research participant responds, and the *response options* are the choices offered to the respondent as permissible responses. Consider the following item:

> The university should not raise tuition under any circumstances.
>
> *Agree*   *Disagree*

In this example, "The university should not raise tuition under any circumstances" is the stem and "*Agree*" and "*Disagree*" are the response options. This section discusses stem (or question) writing, and the next section discusses formats for response options. The phrasing of the question is extremely important because differences in phrasing can bias the responses made by research participants. In fact, the issue of question phrasing is so important that entire books have been written on the topic (for example, see Converse & Presser, 1986; Schuman & Presser, 1996; Sudman & Bradburn, 1982). In this section there is space to touch on only a few of the major issues; if you plan to write your own questions, you should consult one of the books on the subject.

Open- and Closed-Ended Questions

Questions can be grouped into two broad categories. Open-ended questions, such as essay questions on an exam, allow respondents to say anything they want to say and to say it in their own words. Closed-ended questions, such as multiple-choice exam questions, require respondents to select one response from a list of choices provided by the researcher. Researchers generally prefer closed-ended questions because the response options can be chosen to represent categories of interest to the researcher and because the options can be designed to be easily quantified. However, in three circumstances open-ended questions are more useful than closed-ended questions. One such circumstance is when asking about the frequency of sensitive or socially disapproved behaviors. Sudman and Bradburn (1982), for example, found that people reported higher frequencies of a variety of drinking and sexual behaviors in response to open-ended questions than in response to closed-ended questions. A second circumstance is when you are unsure of the most appropriate response options to include in closed-ended questions on a topic or with a particular participant population. Schuman and Presser (1996) therefore recommend using open-ended questions in preliminary research and using the responses to those questions to design response options for closed-ended questions. This strategy can reveal response options the researchers did not think of. Conversely, the response options included in closed-ended questions might remind respondents of responses they might not think of spontaneously. Finally, as discussed in more detail later, open-ended questions can assess some types of judgments more accurately than can closed-ended questions.

Table 11-1   Effect of Question Wording on Responses to Survey Questions

Question	Percent in Favor of Sending Troops
If a situation like Vietnam were to develop in another part of the world, do you think the United States should or should not send troops?	17.4
If a situation like Vietnam were to develop in another part of the world, do you think the United States should or should not send troops to stop a communist takeover?	35.9

Note: From Schuman & Presser (1996).

Question Wording

A major lesson survey researchers have learned over the past 75 years is that the way in which a question is phrased can strongly affect people's answers. Consider the two questions shown in Table 11-1. Half the respondents to surveys conducted in the late 1970s were asked the first question; the other half were asked the second question. Notice that adding the phrase "to stop a communist takeover" increased the approval rate for intervention from 17% to 36%. Let's examine a few basic rules of question writing.

USE THE LANGUAGE OF RESEARCH PARTICIPANTS   The questions used in survey research are usually written by people who have at least a college education and frequently by people who have a graduate education. As a result, the question writers' vocabularies may differ significantly from those of their respondents in at least two ways. First, researchers use many technical terms in their professional work that are unknown or that have different meanings to people outside the profession. Using such terms in questions will usually result in confusion on the part of respondents. Second, researchers' normal English vocabulary is likely to be larger than that of their participants, and using what might be called an intellectual vocabulary can also lead to misunderstanding. As Converse and Presser (1986, p. 10) note, the "polysyllabic and Latinate constructions that come easily to the tongue of the college educated" almost always have simpler synonyms. For example, "main" can be used for "principal" and "clear" for "intelligible." It is also wise to avoid grammatically correct but convoluted constructions such as "Physical fitness is an idea the time of which has come" (Fink & Kosecoff, 1985, p. 38). "An idea whose time has come" might irritate grammarians, but will be clearer to most people. When people fail to understand a question, they will interpret it as best they can and answer in terms of their interpretation (Ross & Allgeier, 1996). Consequently, respondents might not answer the question that the researcher intended to ask.

Because of the possibility that some respondents will not understand or will misinterpret questions, it is important to pretest questionnaires to assess respondents' understanding of the questions. Samples of respondents from the population in which the questionnaire will be used should be used for pretests. Sudman, Bradburn, and Schwarz (1996) describe a number of methods for assessing the comprehensibility of questionnaire items; Box 11-1 lists a few of them.

BOX 11-1   Some Techniques for Assessing the Comprehensibility of Questionnaire Items

- Have respondents read each question, give their responses, and then explain how they decided on their responses. For example, ask "Tell me exactly how you arrived at your answer . . . how did you work it out . . . how exactly did you get to it?" (Sudman et al., 1996, p. 19). This technique is sometimes called the *think aloud method*.

- Directly ask respondents what the item meant to them. For example, Ross and Allgeier (1996) asked their respondents, "What I would like you to do is tell me what you thought the item was actually asking you. I'm only interested in your interpretation. What did you think the item was asking when you were responding to it?" (p. 1593).

- Ask respondents to define specific terms used in items. Be sure to let them know that you are trying to identify unfamiliar words and terms, so "I don't know" is an appropriate response.

- When you administer the questionnaire to the research sample, for each item record the number of respondents who ask for clarification, give incomplete responses, or give responses that suggest they misinterpreted the item.

AVOID UNNECESSARY NEGATIVES   Using negative constructions in questions can lead to confusion. Consider this hypothetical example: "Do you agree or disagree that people who cannot read well should not be allowed to teach in public schools?" Whether respondents agree or disagree, it's impossible to tell what they're agreeing or disagreeing with. Although this is an extreme example, researchers are sometimes tempted to use negative constructions as a way of balancing questions to control for some people's tendencies to agree with whatever position they are presented with. Very often, however, a little searching will turn up alternatives. If our example were changed to "Do you agree or disagree that only people who read well should be allowed to teach in public schools?" the meaning of the responses would be clearer.

ASK ONLY ONE QUESTION AT A TIME   A **double-barreled question** asks for two or more pieces of information at once. Consider the following question used in a national opinion poll in 1973: "Do you think that President Nixon should be impeached and compelled to leave office, or not?" (Wheeler, 1976, p. 182). Impeachment is the investigation and indictment of an official by the House of Representatives for an alleged offense; removal from office is a possible punishment if the official is found guilty after trial by the Senate. It would certainly be possible to agree that an official's actions should be investigated but to disagree that removal from office is the appropriate penalty if the official is found guilty. This question also illustrates the vocabulary problem: A concurrent poll found that less than 50% of its respondents knew the meaning of impeachment (Wheeler, 1976).

Questions can become double-barreled through implication as well as the use of the word *and*. Consider the following example given by Lewin (1979, p. 137):

Your class functions as a stable, cohesive group, with a balance of leadership, which facilitates learning.

Always   Often   Sometimes   Rarely   Never

This question asks for four pieces of information: perceived group stability, perceived group cohesiveness, type of leadership used in the group, and the effects of these factors, if any, on learning. Always ensure that each question used on a scale asks for only one piece of information; otherwise, you never know which question respondents are answering.

AVOID LEADING AND LOADED QUESTIONS A **leading question** implies that a certain response is desired. For example, "Do you agree that . . ." implies that agreement is the desired response. Notice that the questions used as examples so far in this section have been balanced; that is, they suggest that either agreement or disagreement is an acceptable response (for example, "Do you think that . . . or not?" "Do you agree or disagree that . . . ?").

A **loaded question** leads the respondent by implication. For example, people tend to agree with positions attributed to well-respected people, such as "Do you agree or disagree with the President's position that . . . ?" Loading can also appeal to social values, such as freedom, and terms with strong positive or negative connotations can bias responses, as in this example provided by Sudman and Bradburn (1982, p. 7):

> Are you in favor of allowing construction union czars the power to shut down an entire construction site because of a dispute with a single contractor, thus forcing even more workers to knuckle under to union agencies?

Although this example is extreme, question loading can also be subtle. Rasinski (1989), for example, found that 64% of respondents to a series of surveys agreed that too little money was being spent on assistance to the poor, whereas only 23% agreed that too little was being spent on welfare. Clearly, *welfare* has a more negative connotation than *assistance to the poor*, even though both terms denote providing money to people in need. Table 11-2 lists some other pairs of phrases that Rasinski found to elicit different agreement rates.

TABLE 11-2 Examples of Phrasing Receiving Different Agreement Rates in Surveys

Too little money is being spent on . . .	*Percent Agreeing*
Solving problems of big cities	48.6
Assistance to big cities	19.9
Protecting Social Security	68.2
Social Security	53.2
Improving conditions of Blacks	35.6
Assistance to Blacks	27.6
Halting rising crime rates	67.8
Law enforcement	56.0
Dealing with drug addiction	63.9
Drug rehabilitation	54.6

Note: From Rasinski (1989).

TABLE 11-3   Effect of Different Degrees of Question Specificity on Survey Responses From a Poll Conducted in 1945

Question	Percent Answering Yes or Favor
Do you think the government should give money to workers who are unemployed for a limited length of time until they can find another job?	63
It has been proposed that unemployed workers with dependents be given $25 per week by the government for as many as 26 weeks during one year while they are out of work and looking for a job. Do you favor or oppose this plan?	46
Would you be willing to pay higher taxes to give unemployed people up to $25 a week for 26 weeks if they fail to find satisfactory jobs?	34

Note: $25 in 1945 is the equivalent of $230 in 2000. From Sudman & Bradburn, 1982, p. 4.

BE SPECIFIC   People's belief systems are very complex. One result of this complexity is that people's beliefs about general categories of objects can be very different from their beliefs about specific members of those categories. For example, you might like dogs in general but detest your neighbor's mutt that barks all night. The effect of question specificity on response can be seen in the examples shown in Table 11-3, taken from a poll conducted in 1945. You must therefore ensure that your questions use the degree of specificity necessary for the purposes of your research.

DO NOT MAKE ASSUMPTIONS   It is easy to write questions that include unwarranted assumptions. For example, the question "Do you agree or disagree with U.S. trade policy toward Canada?" assumes the respondent knows what that policy is. Similarly, asking, "What is your occupation?" assumes that the respondent is employed. People are quite willing to express opinions on topics with which they are unfamiliar; for example, Sudman and Bradburn (1982) reported that 15% of the respondents to one survey expressed opinions about a fictitious civil rights leader. Therefore, it is generally a good idea to verify that a respondent is familiar with a topic before asking questions about it. However, such verification questions should be tactful and not imply that the respondent should be familiar with the topic. Such an implication could lead the respondent to make up an opinion in order not to appear uninformed.

ADDRESS SENSITIVE TOPICS SENSITIVELY   Sensitive topics are those likely to make people look good or bad, leading respondents to underreport undesirable behaviors and to overreport desirable behaviors. Sudman and Bradburn (1982) suggest some ways to avoid biased responses, a few of which are shown in Box 11-2.

As you can see, good questions can be difficult to write. This difficulty is one reason why it is usually better to try to find well-validated scales and questions than to create your own. If you must write your own questions, take care to avoid biases such as those described here.

BOX 11-2   **Some Techniques for Reducing Biased Responses to Sensitive Questions**

To avoid the underreporting of undesirable behaviors:

- Imply that the behavior is common, that "everybody does it." For example, "Even the calmest parents get angry with their children some of the time. Did your children do anything in the past week to make you angry?"

- Assume the behavior and ask about frequency or other details. For example, "How many cans or bottles of beer did you drink during the past week?"

- Use authority to justify the behavior. For example, "Many doctors now think that drinking wine reduces heart attacks. How many glasses of wine did you drink during the past week?"

To avoid the overreporting of desirable behaviors:

- Be casual, such as by using the phrase "Did you happen to . . . ?" For example, "Did you happen to watch any public television programs during the past week?" Such phrasing implies that failure to do so is of little importance.

- Justify not doing something; imply that if the respondent did not do something, there was a good reason for the omission. For example, "Many drivers report that wearing seat belts is uncomfortable and makes it difficult to reach switches on the dashboard. Thinking about the last time you got into a car—did you use a seat belt?"

Source: Sudman & Bradburn (1982).

OBTAINING ANSWERS

Survey researchers ask questions to obtain answers. As noted earlier, these answers can be either open-ended or closed-ended. Most survey questions are designed to elicit closed-ended responses. This section discusses two issues related to closed-ended responses: levels of measurement and the relative merits of various closed-ended response formats.

Levels of Measurement

Researchers use questionnaires to measure the characteristic of respondents: their attitudes, opinions, evaluations of people and things, their personality traits, and so forth. **Measurement** consists of applying sets of rules to assign numbers to these characteristics. Several different rules could be applied in any situation. To measure student achievement, for example, the researcher might use any of three rules: (1) Classify students as having either passed or failed, (2) rank order students from best to worst, or (3) assign each student a score (such as 0 through 100) indicating degree of achievement. Each rule provides more information about any particular student than did the preceding rule, moving from which broad category the student is in, to whom the student did better and worse than, to how much better or worse the student did. Because of these increasing amounts of information content, these rules are called **levels of measurement** (also sometimes referred to as *scales of measurement*).

MEASUREMENT LEVELS A construct can be measured at any of four levels of information content. From lowest to highest, these levels are called *nominal, ordinal, interval,* and *ratio*. **Nominal level measurement** sorts people or things into categories based on common characteristics. These characteristics represent different aspects of a variable, such as gender or psychiatric diagnosis. As a result, nominal level data are usually reported in terms of frequency counts—the number of cases in each category—or percentage of cases in each category. To facilitate computerized data analysis, the categories are often given numbers (or scores); for example, "female = 1 and male = 2." These numbers are completely arbitrary. In this example, someone receiving a score of 2 does not have more gender than someone receiving a score of 1; he is only different on this characteristic.

Ordinal level measurement places people or things in a series based on increases or decreases in the magnitude of some variable. In the earlier example, students were arranged in order of proficiency from best to worst, as in class standings. As a result, ordinal level data are usually reported in terms of rankings: who (or what) is first, second, and so forth. Notice that while ordinal level measurement provides comparative information about people, such as "Mary did better than Phil," it does not quantify the comparison. That is, it does not let you know *how much* better Mary did. Because of this lack of quantification, one cannot mathematically transform ordinal level data, that is, perform addition, subtraction, multiplication, or division. As a result, most inferential statistics, such as the *t* test, which are based on these transformations, are normally considered inappropriate for ordinal level data.

Interval level measurement assigns numbers (scores) to people and things such that the difference between any two adjacent scores (such as 1 and 2) is assumed to represent the same difference in the amount of a variable as does the difference between any other two adjacent scores (such as 3 and 4). In other words, the people using an interval level measure perceive the intervals between scores to be equal. Thus, if Chris scores 5 on a variable measured at the interval level, Mary scores 3, and Phil scores 1, we can say Mary was better than Phil to the same degree that Chris was better than Mary. For this reason, interval level measures are used to assess magnitudes and amounts of hypothetical constructs, such as IQ or how much one person likes another.

In addition, interval level scores can be added to and subtracted from each other, multiplied and divided by constants, and have constants added to or subtracted from them; they cannot, however, be multiplied or divided by each other. For example, we could *not* say that Mary's score was three times better than Phil's or that someone with a score of 20 on the Beck (1972) Depression Inventory is twice as depressed as someone with a score of 10. These transformations are impossible because interval level data lack a true zero point; that is, one can never truly know when the variable being measured is totally absent. For example, if a student gets a score of zero on a test, that does not mean that he (or she) totally lacks knowledge of the subject matter. Rather, it means that he could not answer any of the questions on the test (an operational definition of the hypothetical construct of knowledge); there were probably other possible questions he could have answered. Therefore, the test score of zero does not necessarily represent total lack of knowledge; that is, it does not necessarily represent a true zero point.

Ratio level measurement, like interval level measurement, assigns equal interval scores to people or things. In addition, ratio measures have true zero points, and so can be multiplied and divided by each other. Therefore, it is appropriate to say that a ratio level score of 10 represents twice as much of a variable as does a score of 5. Some ratio level measures used in psychological research include the speed and frequency of behavior, the number of items recalled from a memorized list, and hormone levels. However, most measures of psychological states and traits and of constructs such as attitudes and people's interpretations of events are interval level at best, although ratio level measurement can sometimes be achieved, albeit with great difficulty. Gescheider, Catlin, and Fontana (1982), for example, were able to construct ratio level measures of the perceived severity of crimes and of punishments for crimes.

Measures of the same construct at different levels can differ from one another on three characteristics—information content, appropriate statistical tests, and ecological validity. It is important to bear these considerations in mind when choosing a level of measurement.

INFORMATION CONTENT   Higher level measures contain more information than do lower level measures; they also contain all the information lower levels provide. For example, you could measure people's heights and make ratio level comparisons, such as Mary is 1.2 times taller than Peter (ratio level), measure height but not make ratio comparisons (interval level), rank people by height (ordinal level), or classify them as short or tall (nominal level). You cannot go the other direction (for example, from ordinal to interval) without collecting additional information, in this case the actual differences in heights among people.

This difference in information content has two implications. First, the conclusions you can validly draw on the basis of measures constructed at one level of measurement, such as ratio, would be invalid if drawn on the basis of a lower level of measurement, such as interval. For example, you can say things such as "Group A improved twice as much as Group B" only if a ratio level measure is used. Second, higher level measures tend to be more sensitive to the effects of independent variables than are lower level measures. Consider the following hypothetical example, which uses the data shown in Table 11-4. Researchers conduct a study comparing the opinions of two groups of people (perhaps liberals and conservatives) on a political issue. Members of the groups are asked whether they favor or oppose a particular position on the issue, with the results shown in the top part of Table 11-4. Given this outcome, the researchers would conclude that there is no difference in opinion between the groups: 50% of the people in each group favor the position and 50% oppose it. If, however, the researchers asked people to put their opinions into one of the six categories shown in the bottom part of Table 11-4, with the frequency of response as shown for each category, they can analyze their results as ordinal level data. They would then conclude that the members of Group B have more favorable opinions than the members of Group A, $p = .002$. A difference was detected in the second case but not the first because the ordinal measure contained more information than the nominal measure, in this case information about the respondents' relative degree of favorability toward the issue.

STATISTICAL TESTS   Assumptions underlie statistical tests. The t test, for example, assumes that the scores in the two groups being compared are normally distributed. However, nominal level measures are not normally distributed, and ordinal level data

TABLE 11-4   Hypothetical Opinion Data

Analyzing these data at the nominal level and at the ordinal level lead to different conclusions.

	GROUP A	GROUP B
Nominal Level Data		
Favor	50%	50%
Oppose	50%	50%
Ordinal Level Data		
Strongly favor	2	16
Moderately favor	2	2
Slightly favor	16	2
Slightly oppose	2	16
Moderately oppose	2	2
Strongly oppose	16	2

frequently are not, and so violate this assumption (as well as others). Therefore, some authorities hold that one can only use statistics that are designed for a particular level of measurement when using data at that level. Other authorities, however, hold that there is no absolute relationship between level of measurement and statistics. See Michell (1986) for a review of this debate.

On a more practical level, statisticians have investigated the extent to which the assumptions underlying a particular statistic can be violated without leading to erroneous conclusions (referred to as the **robustness of a statistic**). The results of this research indicate that *under certain conditions*, ordinal and dichotomous (two-value nominal) data can be safely analyzed using parametric statistics such as the *t* test and analysis of variance (Davison & Sharma, 1988; Lunney, 1970; J. L. Myers, DiCecco, White, & Borden, 1982). Before applying parametric statistics to nonparametric data, however, you should carefully check to ensure that your data meet the necessary conditions.

ECOLOGICAL VALIDITY   The issue of ecological validity deals with the extent to which a research situation is similar to the natural situation to which the results of the research are to be applied (see Chapter 14). Ecological validity is related to levels of measurement because the natural level of measurement of a variable may not contain enough information to answer the research question or may not be appropriate to the statistics the researcher wants to use to analyze the data. The researcher then faces a choice between an ecologically valid, but (say) insensitive, measure and an ecologically less valid, but sufficiently sensitive, measure. Consider, for example, research on juror decision making. The natural level of measurement in this instance is nominal: A juror classifies a defendant as guilty or not guilty. A researcher conducting a laboratory experiment on juror decision processes, however, might want a more sensitive measure of perceived guilt and so might ask subjects to rate their belief about how likely it is that the defendant is guilty on an 11-point scale (interval level measurement). The researcher has traded off ecological validity (natural measurement level) to gain sensitivity of measurement. As discussed in Chapter 2, such tradeoffs are a normal part of the research process and so are neither good nor bad per se. However, researchers should make their tradeoffs only after complete consideration of the relative gains and losses resulting from each possible course of action. Sometimes the result of this consideration is the discovery of a middle ground, such as using both nominal and interval level measures of juror decisions (for example, see Bordens, 1984).

Response Formats

There are four categories of closed-ended response formats, commonly referred to as *rating scales*: the comparative, itemized, graphic, and numerical formats. Let's look at the characteristics of these formats.

COMPARATIVE RATING SCALES   In **comparative scaling,** respondents are presented with a set of stimuli, such as five brands of automobiles, and are asked to compare them on some characteristic, such as quality. Comparative scaling can be carried out in two ways. With the **method of paired comparisons,** raters are presented with all possible pairings of the stimuli being rated and are instructed to select the stimulus in each pair that is higher on the characteristic. Figure 11-1 shows a hypothetical paired comparisons scale for five brands of automobiles. The score for each stimulus is the number of times it is selected. A major limitation of the method of paired comparisons is that it becomes unwieldy with a large number of stimuli to rate. Notice that with five stimuli, the scale in Figure 11-1 had to have 10 pairs; the number of required pairs is $n(n - 1)/2$, where n is the number of stimuli. Consequently, 20 stimuli would require 190 pairs. With a large number of similar judgments to make, people can become bored and careless in their choices. Although there is no absolute rule about the maximum number of stimuli to use in the method, Crano and Brewer (1986) suggest no more than 10 (resulting in 45 pairs).

One solution to the problem of numerous pairs of stimuli lies in the **method of rank order.** With this method, respondents are given a list of stimuli and asked to rank them from highest to lowest on some characteristic. However, selecting the proper ranking for each stimulus can be a daunting task for respondents who are faced with a large number of stimuli. One way to simplify the task is to have respondents alternately choose the best and worst stimulus relative to the characteristic being rated. For example, if respondents had to rank 20 colors from the most to least pleasing, you would have them first choose their most and least preferred of the 20 colors, assigning those colors ranks 1 and 20, respectively. You would then have them consider the remaining 18 colors and choose their most and least preferred of those, giving those colors ranks 2 and 19, respectively. The process continues until all colors have been chosen.

Three conditions must be met for comparative scaling to provide reliable and valid results. First, the respondents must be familiar with all the stimuli they compare. If a respondent is not familiar with a stimulus, the ranking of that stimulus will be random

Instructions: Listed below are pairs of brand names of automobiles. For each pair, indicate the brand you think is of higher quality by putting an "X" on the line next to its name. Please make one choice in each pair and only one choice per pair; if you think the choices in a pair are about equal, mark the one you think is of higher quality even if the difference is small.

Set 1
_____ Chevrolet
_____ Buick

Set 2
_____ Ford
_____ Oldsmobile

Set 3
_____ Chevrolet
_____ Pontiac

Set 4
_____ Chevrolet
_____ Ford

Set 5
_____ Buick
_____ Pontiac

Set 6
_____ Chevrolet
_____ Oldsmobile

Set 7
_____ Ford
_____ Buick

Set 8
_____ Oldsmobile
_____ Buick

Set 9
_____ Ford
_____ Pontiac

Set 10
_____ Oldsmobile
_____ Pontiac

FIGURE 11-1   Hypothetical Paired Comparisons Rating Scale

and therefore not reflect where it stands on the characteristic. For example, people who have never driven Fords cannot judge their quality relative to other brands of automobiles. Second, the characteristic on which the stimuli are being rated must be unidimensional; that is, it must have one and only one component. Note that the example in Figure 11-1 violates this rule: automobile quality is made up of many components, such as physical appearance, mechanical reliability, seating comfort, the manufacturer's reputation, and so forth. If a rating characteristic has several components, you have no way of knowing which component any respondent is using as a basis for making ratings. To the extent that different respondents base their ratings on different components, the ratings will be unreliable. This situation is similar to the specificity problem in question phrasing. Finally, the respondents must completely understand the meaning of the characteristic being rated. For example, when rating automobiles on mechanical reliability, each respondent must define reliability in the same way. It is therefore best if the researcher defines the characteristic being rated for the respondents.

Notice that comparative scaling results in data at the ordinal level of measurement. Consequently, the ratings represent relative rather than absolute judgments. That is, a stimulus that raters perceive to be mediocre might be ranked highest because it is better than all the others despite its low absolute quality: It might be seen as "the best of a bad lot."

ITEMIZED RATING SCALES   **Itemized rating scales** are multiple-choice questions: The item stem asks a question, and the respondent chooses an answer from the options the researcher presents. A primary use of itemized scales is for classification—you can ask research participants to classify themselves as to sex, marital status, or any other variable of interest. Itemized scales can also be used to assess hypothetical constructs. Harvey and Brown (1992) present a theory of social influence that postulates five influence styles that every person uses to some degree. The degree to which any person uses each style is assessed with a multi-item scale composed of a set of social influence situations; each situation is followed by a set of possible responses to the situation. Each response represents one of the social influence styles. For example,

> If I have made a suggestion or proposal and a person reacts negatively to it, I am likely to
>
> a. Accept the person's position and try to reexamine my proposal, realizing that our differences are largely due to our individual ways of looking at things, rather than take the reaction as a personal affront.
> b. Suggest the best course of action and make clear the results of not following that course of action.
> c. Feel upset about the disagreement but will go along with the other person's ideas and allow him or her to express ideas fully.
> d. Point out the requirements of the situation but avoid becoming involved in fruitless argument.
> e. Search for a compromise position that satisfies both points of view.
> (Adapted from Harvey and Brown, 1992, p. 147)

Respondents choose the response most similar to the one they would make in the situation. Respondents' scores for each style can be calculated as the total number of times that a response indicative of a style was chosen.

Itemized rating scales generally provide data at the nominal level of measurement. The data can become ordinal if choices representing a single characteristic are cumulated across items, as in the Harvey and Brown example. People can then be ranked on how often they chose the dimension as characteristic of themselves. Itemized rating scales can also provide ordinal level data if the response options are ordered along some dimension; for example,

> Put an "X" on the line next to the phrase that best describes your political orientation:
>
> _____ Very conservative
>
> _____ Moderately conservative
>
> _____ Slightly conservative
>
> _____ Slightly liberal
>
> _____ Moderately liberal
>
> _____ Very liberal

Itemized rating scales must be developed carefully to ensure that all the relevant response options are presented to research participants. Failure to include all options will reduce the validity of the measure—respondents who don't skip the item because it doesn't include an appropriate response option will use an inaccurate option. For example, when asked to choose from a list of five options the most important thing for children to learn to prepare for life — to obey, to be well liked, to think for themselves, to work hard, and to help others who need help — 62% of the respondents to a survey chose "to think for themselves." However, when another sample of respondents was asked the same question in an open-ended format, "to think for themselves" was mentioned by only 5% of the respondents. It ranked seventh in frequency of being mentioned; none of the first six characteristics mentioned were on the itemized list (Schuman & Presser, 1996). An incomplete list of options can also lead to biased research results that confirm old stereotypes rather than provide new knowledge. As Bart (1971) pointed out, allowing women to describe their sexual roles only as "passive," "responsive," "aggressive," "deviant," or "other" does not allow for responses such as "playful," "active," and so forth.

GRAPHIC RATING SCALES   With **graphic rating scales,** (also called *visual analog scales*), people indicate their responses pictorially rather than by choosing a statement as with itemized rating scales or, as we will see, by choosing a number with numerical rating scales. Figure 11-2 shows some examples of graphic rating scales. With the feeling thermometer — Figure 11-2(a) — respondents rate their evaluations of a stimulus, such as a political candidate, from warm (favorable) to cold (unfavorable); respondents indicate their feelings by drawing a line across the thermometer at the appropriate point. The simple graphic rating scale — Figure 11-2(b) — is used in the same way as the feeling thermometer: The respondent marks the line at the appropriate point. The scale is scored by measuring the distance of the respondent's mark from one end of the line. The segmented graphic rating scale — Figure 11-2(c) — divides the line into segments; the respondent marks the appropriate segment. This format simplifies scoring because a numerical value can be assigned to each segment. The Smiley Faces scale, Figure 11-2(d), (Butzin & Anderson, 1973) can be used with children who are too young to understand verbal category labels or how to assign numerical values to concepts. As with the segmented graphic rating scale, the researcher can give each face a numerical value for data analysis.

Graphic rating scales provide ordinal level data. Even though some formats, such as the feeling thermometer and segmented graphic rating scale, divide the scale into *physically* equal intervals, one cannot assume that the intervals are *psychologically* equal to the respondents, as is required of interval level data. Interval level data can, however, be obtained with some forms of numerical rating scales.

NUMERICAL RATING SCALES   With **numerical rating scales,** respondents assign numerical values to their responses. The meanings of the values are defined by verbal labels called **anchors.** Figure 11-3 shows some hypothetical numerical rating scales. There are three elements to the design of a numerical rating scale: the number of scale points, the placement of the anchors, and the verbal labels used as anchors.

In principle, a numerical rating scale can have from 2 to an infinite number of points. In practice, the upper limit seems to be 101 points (a scale from 0 to 100). Two factors determine the number of points to use on a scale. The first is the required **sensitivity of measurement.** A sensitive measure can detect small differences in the level of a variable; an insensitive measure can detect only large differences. In general, scales

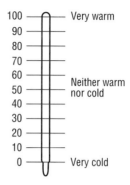

100 ── Very warm
90
80
70
60
50 ── Neither warm
40   nor cold
30
20
10
0 ── Very cold

(a) Feeling Thermometer

Happy ────────────────────── Sad

(b) Graphic Rating Scale

Happy ____ : ____ : ____ : ____ : ____ Sad

(c) Segmented Graphic Rating Scale

(d) Smiley Faces Scale

Note: (a) From Judd et al., 1991, p. 150; (d) from Lewin, 1979, p. 171.

FIGURE 11-2   Examples of Graphic Rating Scales

with more rating points are more sensitive than scales with only a few points. More points allow the raters finer gradations of judgment. For example, a 2-point attitude scale that allows only "Agree" and "Disagree" as responses is not very sensitive to differences in attitudes between people — those who agree only slightly are lumped in with those who agree strongly and those who disagree only slightly with those who disagree strongly. If you are studying the relationship between attitudes and behavior, and if people with strongly held attitudes behave differently from people with weakly held attitudes, you will have no way of detecting that difference because people with strongly and weakly held attitudes are assumed to be identical by your scale. In addition, respondents might be reluctant to use a scale they think does not let them respond accurately because there are too few options. People sometimes expand scales that they

Indicate your current mood by circling the appropriate number on the following scale:

Sad	1	2	3	4	5	6	7	Happy

How would you rate your performance on the last test?

9	8	7	6	5	4	3	2	1
Excellent		Good		Passable		Inferior		Terrible

The university should not raise tuition under any circumstances.

+3	+2	+1	−1	−2	−3
Agree	Agree	Agree	Disagree	Disagree	Disagree
very much	moderately	slightly	slightly	moderately	very much

FIGURE 11-3   Examples of Numerical Rating Scales

perceive as being too compressed by marking their responses in the space between two researcher-supplied options.

The second factor related to the number of scale points is the usability of the scale. A very large number of scale points can be counterproductive. Respondents can become overwhelmed with too many scale points and mentally compress the scale to be able to use it effectively. I have found, for example, that when people are given a scale ranging from 0 to 100, many will compress it to a 13-point scale using only the 0, 10, 20, 25, 30, 40, 50, 60, 70, 75, 80, 90, and 100 values. Research has found that people generally prefer to have from 5 to 9 points on a scale (Cox, 1980). With fewer than 5 points, people feel they cannot give accurate ratings; with more than 9 points, they feel they are being asked to make impossibly fine distinctions. In addition, although the reliability of a scale increases as points are added from 2 to 7, there is little increase after 7 points (Cicchetti, Showalter, & Tyrer, 1985). A scale of 5 to 9 points is therefore probably optimal.

As Figure 11-3 shows, the anchors for a numerical rating scale can be placed only at the end points or at the end and intermediate points. The use of intermediate anchors has two advantages. First, they more clearly define the meaning of the scale for respondents. When anchors are used only at the end points, respondents might be unsure of the meaning of the difference between two points on the scale. From the respondent's point of view, it can be a question of "What am I saying if I choose a 3 instead of a 4?" Perhaps because of this greater clarity of meaning, numerical rating scales that have anchors at each scale point show higher reliability and validity than scales with other anchoring patterns (Krosnick, 1999b).

The second advantage of intermediate anchors is that, in combination with the proper selection of labels for the anchors, they can increase the level of measurement of the scale. When numerical scales have only end point anchors or have intermediate anchors arbitrarily chosen by the researcher, ordinal level measurement results. There is no basis for assuming that simply because the mathematical differences between the scale points are equal that respondents perceive them as psychologically

TABLE 11-5   Anchors for 5-Point Equal-Appearing Interval Scales of Agreement-Disagreement, Evaluation, Frequency, and Amount

Scale Point	Agreement-Disagreement[a]	Evaluation[a]	Frequency[a]	Amount[b]
5	Very much	Excellent	Always	All
4	On the whole	Good	Frequently	An extreme amount
3	Moderately	Passable	Sometimes	Quite a bit
2	Mildly	Inferior	Seldom	Some
1	Slightly	Terrible	Never	None

[a] From Spector, 1992, p. 192.

[b] From Bass, Cascio, & O'Connor, 1974, p. 319.

equal. However, the verbal labels used as anchors can be chosen so that the difference in meaning between any two adjacent anchors is about equal to the difference in meaning between any other two adjacent anchors (Bass, Cascio, & O'Connor, 1974; Spector, 1976, 1992). Table 11-5 shows some approximately equal interval anchors for 5-point scales of agreement–disagreement, evaluation, frequency, and amount. These 5-point scales can be expanded to 9-point scales by providing an unlabeled response option between each pair of labeled options, as shown in the second scale in Figure 11-3. Bass et al. (1974) and Spector (1976) give additional anchor labels and their relative scale values.

Choosing a Response Format

Which response format is best? The answer to that question depends primarily on the purpose of the rating scale. If the purpose is to determine the relative position of the members of a set of stimuli along a dimension, then a comparative format is best. The method of paired comparisons is better with a small number of stimuli, and ranking is better with a large number of stimuli. If the purpose is to locate an individual or a single stimulus along a dimension, a numerical rating scale with equal interval anchors is probably best because it can provide interval level data. Itemized scales place people and stimuli into specific categories. Despite these differences, the results of stimulus ratings using different formats are highly correlated (Newstead & Arnold, 1989), suggesting that format might not have a large effect on the conclusions drawn about relationships between variables.

MULTI-ITEM SCALES

A **multi-item scale** is composed of two or more items in rating scale format, each of which is designed to assess the same variable. A respondent's scores on the items are combined—usually by summing or averaging—to form an overall scale score. A multi-item scale can be composed of two or more multi-item **subscales**, each of which measures a component of a multidimensional variable. A self-esteem scale, for example, could have subscales for global self-esteem, social self-esteem, academic self-esteem, and so forth. Each subscale would provide a subscale score for the component that it measures. This section discusses the advantages of using multi-item scales and describes the four types of these scales.

Advantages of Multi-Item Scales

Multi-item scales have several advantages over single items as measures of hypothetical constructs. First, as just noted, multi-item scales can be designed to assess multiple aspects of a construct. Depending on the research objective and the theory underlying the construct, the subscale scores can be either analyzed separately or combined into an overall scale score for analysis. A second advantage of multi-item scales is that the scale score has greater reliability and validity than does any one of the items of which it is composed. This increased reliability and validity derive from the use of multiple items. Each item assesses both true score on the construct being assessed and error. When multiple items are used, aspects of the true score that are missed by one item can be assessed by another. This situation is analogous to the use of multiple measurement modalities discussed in Chapter 5. Generally speaking, as the number of items on a scale increases, so does the scale's reliability and validity, if all items have a reasonable degree of reliability and validity. Adding an invalid or unreliable item decreases those characteristics of the scale.

Finally, multi-item scales provide more sensitivity of measurement than do single-item scales. Just as increasing the number of points on an item can increase its sensitivity, so can increasing the number of items on a scale. In a sense, multi-item scales provide more categories for classifying people on the variable being measured. A single 9-point item can put people into 9 categories, one for each scale point; a scale composed of five 9-point items has 41 possible categories—possible scores range from 5 to 45—so that finer distinctions can be made among people. This principle of increased sensitivity applies to behavioral measures as well as self-reports. Let's say that you are conducting a study to determine if a Roman typeface is easier to read than a Gothic typeface. If you asked participants in the research to read just one word printed in each typeface, their responses would probably be so fast that you could not detect a difference if one existed. However, if you had each participant read 25 words printed in each typeface, you might find a difference in the total reading time, which would represent the relative difficulty of reading words printed in the two typefaces.

Types of Multi-Item Scales

Multi-item scales can take many forms. This section describes the four major types: Likert scales, Thurstone scales, Guttman scales, and the semantic differential.

LIKERT SCALES Likert scales are named for their developer, Rensis Likert. Also known as **summated rating scales**, they are, perhaps, the most commonly used form of multi-item scale. A Likert scale presents respondents with a set of statements about a person, thing, or concept and has them rate their agreement or disagreement with the

TABLE 11-6   Example of a Likert-Type Scale

(Circle One)

Item		Strongly Agree (4)	Agree (3)	Disagree (2)	Strongly Disagree (1)
2.	The best way to handle people is to tell them what they want to hear. (+)	SA	A	D	SD
10.	When you ask someone to do something for you, it is best to give the real reasons for wanting it rather than giving reasons that might carry more weight. (−)	SA	A	D	SD
15.	It is wise to flatter important people. (+)	SA	A	D	SD
17.	Barnum was very wrong when he said there's a sucker born every minute. (−)	SA	A	D	SD
18.	It is hard to get ahead without cutting corners here and there. (+)	SA	A	D	SD

Note: Respondents do not see the information in parentheses. From Christie & Geis, 1970, pp. 17–18.

statements on a numerical scale that is the same for all the statements. To help control for response biases, half the statements are worded positively and half are worded negatively. Respondents' scores on a Likert scale are the sums of their item responses. Table 11-6 shows some items from Christie and Geis's (1970) Machiavellianism scale, which assesses people's tendencies to use manipulative tactics to influence others. The numbers in parentheses by the anchors indicate the numerical values assigned to the response options; the plus and minus signs in parentheses after the items indicate the direction of scoring. Items with minus signs are **reverse scored**; that is, their numerical values are changed so that a high number indicates a higher score on the characteristic being assessed. In the example in Table 11-6, 1 would become 4, 2 would become 3, 3 would become 2, and 4 would become 1. Reverse scoring can be accomplished by using the formula $R = (H + L) − I$, where R is the reversed score, H is the highest numerical value on the scale, L is the lowest value, and I is the item score.

As Dawis (1987) notes, the term *Likert scale* is frequently misused to refer to any numerical rating scale with intermediate anchors. However, Likert scaling is defined by the process by which items are selected for the scale, not by the response format. Only a scale with items that have been selected using the following four steps is a true Likert scale:

1. Write a large number of items representing the variable to be measured. The items represent the extremes of the variable, such as high or low self-esteem; moderate levels of the variable will be assessed as low levels of agreement with these extremes. The items have a numerical rating scale response format with intermediate anchors.

2. Administer the items to a large number of respondents. Dawis (1987) suggests at least 100, but some statistical procedures that can be used for item selection, such as factor analysis, require more respondents (recall Chapter 8). Record respondents' item scores and total scale scores.

3. Conduct an **item analysis**. This analysis selects the items that best discriminate between high and low scorers on the scale; items that discriminate poorly are thrown out. This procedure ensures the internal consistency of the scale. The criterion for item selection is the item-total correlation: the correlation of the item score with a modified total score; the total score is modified by subtracting the score of the item being analyzed. No item with an item-total correlation below .30 should be used in the final version of the scale (J. P. Robinson, Shaver, & Wrightsman, 1991a).

4. The items with the highest item-total correlations comprise the final scale. There should be a sufficient number of items to provide an internal consistency coefficient of at least .70 (J. P. Robinson et al., 1991a).

An important assumption underlying Likert scale construction is that the scale is unidimensional; if the scale assesses a multidimensional construct, the assumption is that each subscale is unidimensional. That is, every item on the scale or subscale measures just one construct or just one aspect of a multidimensional construct. When the items on a scale measure more than one aspect of a construct, the meaning of the overall scale score can be ambiguous. Assume, for example, that a self-esteem scale measures both social and academic self-esteem. There are two ways for a respondent to get a middle-range score on the scale: by scoring in the middle on both aspects of self-esteem or by scoring high on one and low on the other. These two types of scores define self-esteem differently; they are not equally valid unless the theory of self-esteem on which the scale is based holds that the distinction between these aspects of self-esteem is unimportant. The number of dimensions represented in a scale can be investigated using factor analysis. Factor analysis of a Likert scale should result in one factor if the items were intended to measure only one construct, or one factor for each aspect of the construct if the items were intended to form subscales measuring different aspects of the construct. Spector (1992) presents a detailed description of the development of a Likert scale.

The popularity of the Likert approach to scaling is probably due to its possessing several desirable features, one or more of which are absent in the other approaches to scaling. First, Likert scales are easy to construct relative to other types of scales. Even though the Likert process has several steps, other processes can be much more laborious. Second, Likert scales tend to have high reliability, not surprising given that internal consistency is the principal selection criterion for the items. Third, Likert scaling is highly flexible. It can be used to scale people on their attitudes, personality characteristics, perceptions of people and things, or almost any other construct of interest. The other scaling techniques are more restricted in the types of variables with which they can be used. Finally, Likert scaling can assess multidimensional constructs through the use of subscales; the other methods can assess only unidimensional constructs.

THURSTONE SCALES   L. L. Thurstone was the first person to apply the principles of scaling to attitudes. **Thurstone scaling**, like Likert scaling, starts with the generation of a large number of items representing attitudes toward an object. However, these items represent the entire range of attitudes from highly positive through neutral to highly negative, in contrast to Likert items, which represent only the extremes. Working independently of one another, 20 to 30 judges sort the items into 11 categories representing their perceptions of the degree of favorability items express. The judges are also

TABLE 11-7   Example of a Thurstone Scale

Scale Value	Item
1.2	I believe the church is a powerful agency for promoting both individual and social righteousness.
2.2	I like to go to church for I get something worthwhile to think about and it keeps my mind filled with right thoughts.
3.3	I enjoy my church because there is a spirit of friendliness there.
4.5	I believe in what the church teaches but with mental reservations.
6.7	I believe in sincerity and goodness without any church ceremonies.
7.5	I think too much money is being spent on the church for the benefit that is being derived.
9.2	I think the church seeks to impose a lot of worn-out dogmas and medieval superstitions.
10.4	The church represents shallowness, hypocrisy, and prejudice.
11.0	I think the church is a parasite on society.

Note: On the actual questionnaire, the items would appear in random order and the scale values would not be shown.

instructed to sort the items so that the difference in favorability between any two adjacent categories is equal to that of any other two adjacent categories; that is, they use an interval-level sorting procedure. The items used in the final scale must meet two criteria: (1) They must represent the entire range of attitudes, and (2) they must have very low variance in their judged favorability. Respondents are presented with a list of the items in random order and asked to check off those they agree with; they do not see the favorability ratings. Respondents' scores are the means of the favorability ratings of the items they chose. Sample items from one of Thurstone's (1929) original attitude scales are shown in Table 11-7 along with their scale values (favorability ratings).

Thurstone scales are rarely seen these days, primarily because of their disadvantages relative to Likert scales. Thurstone scales are more laborious to construct than Likert scales, and they tend to be less reliable than Likert scales of the same length (Tittle & Hill, 1967). In addition, Thurstone scaling assumes that the attitude being assessed is unidimensional; the technique provides no way to set up subscales for different aspects of an attitude. A third limitation inherent in Thurstone scaling is that the judges' attitudes influence their assignment of scale values to items (Hovland & Sherif, 1952): People rate statements that are close to their own opinions more favorably than divergent opinions, despite instructions to "be objective." It is therefore essential that judges represent a cross section of opinions on the attitude being scaled. Finally, the scale values that judges assign to items can change over time; Dawes (1972), for example, found some significant changes in the rated severity of crimes from 1927 to 1966. Such changes limit the "reusability" of Thurstone scales.

GUTTMAN SCALES   With a **Guttman scale** (named for Louis Guttman, who developed the theory underlying the technique), respondents are presented with a set of ordered attitude items designed so that a respondent will agree with all items up to a point and disagree with all items after that point. The last item with which a respondent agrees represents the attitude score. The classic example of a Guttman scale is the Bogardus (1925) Social Distance Scale, a measure of prejudice, part of which is shown

TABLE 11-8   Bogardus (1925) Social Distance Scale

Directions: For each race or nationality listed, circle the numbers representing each classification to which you would be willing to admit the *average* member of that race or nationality (not the *best* members you have known or the *worst*). Answer in terms of your first feeling reactions.

	To Close Kinship by Marriage	To My Club as Personal Chums	To My Street as Neighbors	To Employment in My Occupation	To Citizenship in My Country	As Visitors Only to My Country	Would Exclude from My Country
English	1	2	3	4	5	6	7
Black	1	2	3	4	5	6	7
French	1	2	3	4	5	6	7
Chinese	1	2	3	4	5	6	7
Russian	1	2	3	4	5	6	7
etc.							

Note: Adapted from Bogardus, 1925, p. 301.

in Table 11-8. On the Social Distance Scale, acceptance of a group at any one distance (such as "To my street as neighbors") implies acceptance of the group at greater distances; the greater the minimum acceptable social distance, the greater the prejudice. Behaviors can also be Guttman scaled if they represent a stepwise sequence, with one behavior always coming before the next; DeLamater and MacCorquodale (1979), for example, have developed a Guttman scale of sexual experience. Guttman scaling is rarely used because few variables can be represented as a stepwise progression through a series of behaviors or beliefs.

THE SEMANTIC DIFFERENTIAL   The **semantic differential** (Osgood, Suci, & Tannenbaum, 1957) is a scale rather than a scaling technique, but is widely used because of its flexibility and so deserves discussion. In their research on the psychological meanings of words (as opposed to their dictionary definitions), Osgood et al. found that any concept could be described in terms of three dimensions: evaluation, representing the perceived goodness or badness of the concept; activity, represented whether the concept is perceived as active or passive; and potency, representing the perceived strength or weakness of the concept. A concept's standing on each dimension is assessed by having respondents rate the concept on sets of bipolar adjective pairs such as *good-bad*, *active-passive*, and *strong-weak*. Because it represents one aspect of attitudes, evaluation tends to be the most commonly used rating dimension, and the scale takes the form of a set of segmented graphic rating scales; for example:

My voting in the forthcoming election is

Good	____ : ____ : ____ : ____ : ____ : ____ : ____	Bad
Foolish	____ : ____ : ____ : ____ : ____ : ____ : ____	Wise
Pleasant	____ : ____ : ____ : ____ : ____ : ____ : ____	Unpleasant

(Ajzen & Fishbein, 1980, p. 55).

Each item is scored on a 7-point scale, usually ranging from $+3$ to -3, and respondents' scale scores are the sums of their item scores. Notice that the items are balanced so that the positive adjective of each pair is on the right half the time; these items must therefore be reverse scored.

The semantic differential represents a ready-made scale that researchers can use to measure attitudes toward almost anything and therefore bypasses the item selection stage of scale development. Its validity has been supported by almost 50 years of research. However, great care must be taken to ensure that the adjective pairs one chooses for scale items are relevant to the concept being assessed. For example, although *foolish-wise* is relevant to the evaluation of a person, behavior, or concept, it would be much less relevant to the evaluation of a thing, such as an automobile. Osgood et al. (1957, pp. 53–55) list a large variety of evaluative adjective pairs that one can choose from. Finally, Ajzen and Fishbein (1980) warn that many scales used in research are incorrectly called *semantic differential scales*. Although these scales use the semantic differential format, they include arbitrarily chosen adjective pairs rather than pairs that have been demonstrated to represent the rating dimension. Such scales are of unknown validity.

RESPONSE BIASES

A **response bias** exists when a person responds to an item for reasons other than the response's being a reflection of the construct or behavior being assessed by the content of the item. Response biases obscure a person's true score on a measure and therefore represent a form of measurement error; better measures are less affected by response biases. Response biases can be categorized in two ways. Question-related biases are caused by the ways in which questions or response options are worded; person-related biases result from respondent characteristics.

Question-Related Biases

The earlier section of this chapter that discussed question wording described some of the ways in which question stems can bias responses. This section describes four types of response bias that can result from item response options: scale ambiguity effects, category anchoring, estimation biases, and respondent interpretations of numerical scales.

SCALE AMBIGUITY   Problems with scale ambiguity can occur when using numerical or graphic rating scales to assess frequency or amount. Anchor labels such as "frequently" or "an extreme amount of" can have different meanings to different people. Consider the following hypothetical question:

How much beer did you drink last weekend?

5	4	3	2	1
A great amount	Quite a bit	A moderate amount	A little	None

People evaluate frequency and amount relative to a personal standard (Newstead & Collis, 1987): To some people, one can of beer in a weekend might be a moderate amount and six cans of beer in a weekend a great amount; to another person, six cans might be moderate and one can a little. One possible solution to this problem is to use an ordered, itemized scale, such as

How much beer did you drink last weekend?

_____ None

_____ 1 or 2 cans

_____ 3 to 6 cans

_____ 7 to 12 cans

_____ 12 to 24 cans

_____ More than 24 cans

Although using this response format can resolve some of the problems associated with the measurement of frequency and amount, it can lead to another form of response bias, category anchoring.

CATEGORY ANCHORING   **Category anchoring** occurs when respondents use the amounts provided in the response options as cues for what constitutes an appropriate response, based on the range of values on the scale. Schwarz (1999) distinguishes between two types of itemized scales. *Low-range scales* start at zero or a very low value and increase until reaching a "greater than" value, such as in a question that asks how many hours of television a person watches per day and provides response options that start at "Up to ½ hour" and increase in half-hour increments to "More than 2½ hours." *High-range scales* start at a higher value and increase until reaching a "greater than" value, such as in a television-watching question that provides response options that start at "Up to 2½ hours" and increase in half-hour increments to "More than 4½ hours." Scales such as these are problematic because people tend to give lower responses with low-range scales and higher responses with high-range scales. For example, Schwarz, Hippler, Deutsch, and Strack (1985) found that 30% of respondents using the high-range scale just described reported watching more than 2½ hours of television per day, whereas none of the respondents using the low-range scale did. In comparison, 19% of the people responding to an open-ended version of the question reported watching more than 2½ hours of television per day.

Another problem that can arise is that people see an option phrased in terms of "more than" a certain amount as representing an excessive amount and that endorsing it will make them look bad (Sudman & Bradburn, 1982). Finally, respondents may use the scale range to interpret the question stem, assuming that questions using low-range scales refer to events that happen rarely and that questions using low-range scales refer to events that happen frequently (Schwarz, 1999). For example, Schwarz, Strack, Müller, and Chassein (1988) found that people who were asked to report the frequency of irritating events assumed the question referred to major irritants when responding on low-range scales, whereas people responding on high-range scales assumed the question referred to minor irritants. Schwarz (1999) recommends using open-ended questions to assess frequency and amount as a solution for both of these problems.

ESTIMATION BIASES   Open-ended questions asking for frequency and amount have their own problem. Unless the behavior being assessed is well represented in people's memory, they will estimate how often something occurs rather than counting specific instances of the behavior. A problem can occur because memory decays over time, making long-term estimates less accurate than short-term estimates. It is therefore advisable to keep estimation periods as short as possible (Sudman et al., 1996).

RESPONDENT INTERPRETATIONS OF NUMERICAL SCALES   As Figure 11-3 showed, scale values can be either all positive numbers or a combination of positive and negative numbers. Just as respondents can use the range of itemized response categories to interpret the question, they can use the range of values on a numerical rating scale in the same way. For example, when people were asked to rate how successful they were in life, 34% responding on a -5 to $+5$ scale chose a value in the lower part of the scale range (-5 to 0), whereas only 13% of those responding on a 0 to 10 scale chose a value in the lower part of the scale range (0 to 5; Schwarz, 1999). Schwarz explains that

> this difference reflects differential interpretations of the term "not at all successful." When this label was combined with the numeric value "0," respondents interpreted it to reflect the absence of outstanding achievements. However, when the same label was combined with the numeric value "-5," and the scale offered "0" as the midpoint, they interpreted it to reflect the presence of explicit failures. . . . In general, a format that ranges from negative to positive numbers conveys that the researcher has a bipolar dimension in mind, where the two poles refer to the presence of opposite attributes. In contrast, a format that uses only positive numbers conveys that the researcher has a unipolar dimension in mind, referring to different degrees of the same attribute. (p. 96)

Therefore, be certain of which meaning you want to convey when choosing a value range for a numerical rating scale.

Person-Related Biases

Person-related response biases reflect individuals' tendency to respond in a biased manner. There are five classes of person-related response biases: social desirability, acquiescence, extremity, halo, and leniency (W. H. Cooper, 1981; Paulhus, 1991).

SOCIAL DESIRABILITY   **Social desirability response bias,** the most thoroughly studied form of response bias, is a tendency to respond in a way that makes the respondent look good (socially desirable) to others. Paulhus (1991) has identified two forms of social desirability response bias. Self-deceptive positivity is "an honest but overly positive self-presentation" (p. 21). That is, some people respond in ways that put them in a more positive light than is warranted by their true scores on the construct, but they do so unknowingly, believing the overly positive responses to be true. However, impression management is "self-presentation tailored to an audience"; that is, some people "purposely tailor their answers to create the most positive social image" (p. 21). Self-deceptive positivity is an aspect of personality and so is consistent across time and situations, whereas the type and amount of impression management that people engage in vary with the demands of the situation and the content of the measure. For example, people are more likely to try to "look good" during an interview for a job they really want than during an interview for a less desirable job. This distinction between the two forms of social desirability response bias has an important implication for measurement.

Paulhus (1991) notes that self-deceptive positivity is a part of some personality traits such as self-esteem and achievement motivation. Consequently, measures of such constructs should *not* be totally free of self-deceptive positivity: such a measure would not be fully representative of the construct. However, most measures should be free of impression management bias; the exceptions, of course, are measures of impression management or of the few constructs, such as self-monitoring (Snyder, 1986), that have an impression management component.

Because social desirability response bias is caused by motivation to make a good impression on others, the bias is reduced when such motivation is low. Consequently, collecting data in ways that make respondents feel anonymous, such as by using anonymous questionnaires (Krosnick, 1999a) and computer-administered questionnaires (Joinson, 1999), is an effective way of controlling social desirability response bias.

ACQUIESCENCE   **Acquiescence response bias** is a general tendency either to agree or to disagree with statements, such as items on a self-report measure. People who show a tendency to agree are called "yea-sayers," and those who show a tendency to disagree are called "nay-sayers." Although acquiescence response bias includes the tendency to disagree, it is named after "acquiescence," or agreement, because that aspect has received the most attention. For example, respondents to a survey answered one of two versions of a question about their perceptions of the cause of crime: whether it is caused by individuals' characteristics (such as personality) or by social conditions. As Table 11-9 shows, respondents tended to agree with the statements regardless of which cause was mentioned first.

Acquiescence is a problem because it can make the meaning of scores on a measure ambiguous. For example, assume that a measure assesses anxiety by asking people whether they have experienced certain symptoms; respondents answer yes or no to each question. If someone gets a high score (that is, gives a large proportion of yes responses), does the score indicate a high level of anxiety or a yea-saying bias?

TABLE 11-9   An Example of Acquiescence Response Bias

Question Form	Percent Agreeing
Individuals are more to blame than social conditions for crime and lawlessness in this country.	59.5
Social conditions are more to blame than individuals for crime and lawlessness in this country.	56.8

Note: From Schuman & Presser (1996).

Acquiescence response bias is more likely to manifest itself when people lack the skill or motivation to think about answers, when a great deal of thought is required to answer a question, and when respondents are unsure about how to respond and so consistently agree or disagree as a way of resolving the uncertainty (Krosnick, 1999a). Writing questions that are clear and easy to answer will therefore help to reduce acquiescence response bias. Because acquiescence response bias has its strongest impact on dichotomous (yes/no or agree/disagree) questions, the use of other types of response formats will also help to alleviate its effects (Krosnick, 1999a).

The most common way of controlling for acquiescence response bias is through the use of a balanced measure. In a balanced measure, on half the items agreement leads to a higher score (called "positive items") and on half the items disagreement leads to a higher score ("negative items"). For example, a dominance scale could include items such as "I frequently try to get my way with other people" and "I frequently give in to other people." Because agreement with one type of item leads to a higher score and agreement with the other type of item leads to a lower score, the effect of acquiescence on positive items will be balanced by its effect on the negative items. However, writing balanced questions can be difficult because questions intended to have opposite meanings may not be interpreted that way by respondents. Consider, for example, the questions shown in Table 11-10. Both questions ask respondents about their attitudes toward public speeches in favor of communism. They are also balanced in that the first question asks whether such speeches should be forbidden and the second asks whether they should be allowed. However, more people endorsed not forbidding the speeches than endorsed allowing the speeches.

EXTREMITY Extremity response bias is the tendency to give extreme responses on a measure; for example, to use only the end points (1s and 7s) on a 7-point scale. Extremity response bias is primarily a function of the respondent rather than of an interaction of respondent and scale characteristics, as are social desirability and acquiescence, so it is difficult to establish controls for it. However, an understanding of extremity response bias is important for interpreting the results of research. There is some evidence that the members of some groups of people are more likely to use the end points of rating scales than are members of other groups. For example, on the average, women make more extreme ratings than do men, children and adolescents make more extreme ratings than do adults, people who have not attended college make more extreme ratings than college graduates, and African Americans make more extreme ratings than European Americans (Bachman & O'Malley, 1984; D. L. Hamilton, 1968; Shulman, 1973). Other group differences may also exist. Therefore, differences between groups on rating scale measures may be a result of extremity response differences (that is, differences in the use of the scale) rather than differences on the constructs, especially when there is no a priori reason to expect differences.

HALO AND LENIENCY A halo bias occurs when a respondent sees a stimulus as being positive or negative on some important characteristic and that evaluation influences ratings of other characteristics (W. H. Cooper, 1981). For example, a physically attractive person might be judged as more intelligent than is actually the case. The halo bias will have the greatest effect when the characteristic being rated is not easily observable, not clearly defined for the respondent, involves relations with other people, or is of some

TABLE 11-10 Illustration of the Difficulty of Writing Balanced Questions

Question Form	Percent in Favor of Speeches
Do you think the United States should forbid public speeches in favor of communism?	60.1
Do you think the United States should allow public speeches in favor of communism?	43.8

Note: From Schuman & Presser (1996).

moral importance (R. Rosenthal & Rosnow, 1991). **Leniency bias,** related to halo bias, occurs when respondents overestimate the positive characteristics and underestimate the negative characteristics of people (or other stimuli) whom they like.

Interpreting Responses

Because of these biases and other factors, when interpreting the ratings made by respondents it is important to avoid what Dawes and Smith (1985) call the *literal interpretation fallacy*. This fallacy consists of taking the meanings of scale anchors at face value. Scale anchors, even interval-scaled anchors, are simply markers that help respondents find an appropriate point at which to mark the scale; they have no inherent meaning. For example, consider a situation in which respondents are asked to rate an automobile using one of five terms—*excellent, very good, good, poor, very poor*—but the true opinion of some respondents is that "fair" best describes a particular model. Because "fair" is not an option, respondents with leniency biases might choose *good* as their response because they are unwilling to go any lower. Other respondents might choose *good* because that option is the closest to their true opinion. In neither case is the chosen response a literal representation of the respondents' beliefs.

QUESTIONNAIRE DESIGN

Once the questions for a survey have been written, they are compiled into questionnaires, lists of questions that the respondents to the survey will be asked to answer. Questionnaire construction is a very complex process of which only a brief overview can be given here. Before designing your own questionnaire, you should carefully read some books on survey research, such as those by Babbie (1990), Dillman (1978), and Sudman and Bradburn (1982), which extensively discuss questionnaire design. This section looks at some issues concerning question order, the layout of questionnaires, questionnaire instructions, and the use of existing measures in questionnaires.

Question Order

The order in which questions appear in a questionnaire is very important for two reasons. First, a confusing questionnaire will be demoralizing to respondents, resulting in low completion rates. Second, the order in which questions are presented can affect people's responses to them.

QUESTION SEQUENCING   The clarity of a questionnaire can be enhanced by careful sequencing of questions. It should start out with questions that are easy to answer, but that are also interesting to the respondents, clearly important, and clearly related to the stated purpose of the research. Consequently, although demographic questions such as those concerning sex, age, education, and so forth are easy to answer, they may not be perceived to be interesting, important, or relevant, and so should be reserved to the end. The main questions should be grouped by topic. Providing respondents with homogeneous groups of questions keeps them focused on the topic at hand and enhances recall. There must also be clear transitions between topics so that respondents can refocus their attention properly, and the transition should emphasize the relevance of the new topic to reinforce respondents' motivation.

Within a topic, questions should move from the general to the specific. For example, a set of questions dealing with job satisfaction should start out by asking respondents about their overall level of satisfaction and then ask about specific areas of satisfaction, such as satisfaction with pay, supervisors, working conditions, and so forth. Respondents tend to perceive general questions as being more relevant to the purpose of the research (which is usually expressed in general terms); general questions are also easier to answer and provide a context for the more specific questions.

Question order becomes an especially difficult issue when order is contingent on the answer to a question. For example, a lead-in question might be "Did you drink any alcoholic beverages during the past week?" Respondents who answer yes then go on to one set of follow-up questions, whereas those who answer no go on to a different set of follow-up questions. In such cases, instructions must make very clear what the respondent or interviewer is to do next. For example, if the lead-in question was Number 21, the instructions might be "If you answered YES to Question 21, go on with Question 22. If you answered NO to Question 21, skip ahead to Question 31 on page 8." Using differently colored pages can also aid respondents and interviewers in finding the correct question to answer next; for example, the instructions just given could end, "on page 8 (the green page)." Structure contingent questions so that respondents or interviewers always move forward in the questionnaire; moving back and forth can be confusing. Babbie (1990) suggests structuring contingent questions graphically, as in the example shown in Figure 11-4, to make it easier to find the next question.

CONTEXT EFFECTS   A context effect occurs when responding to one question affects the response to a later question. For example, Schuman and Presser (1996) found that 61% of respondents answered yes to this question when it was used as a lead-in question for the topic of abortion: "Do you think it should be possible for a pregnant woman to obtain a *legal* abortion if she is married and does not want any more children?" However, when that question followed a more specific one about abortion in the case of a child who was likely to be born with a birth defect (to which 84% of the respondents said yes), only 48% said yes to the more general question.

Sudman et al. (1996) note that context effects are unavoidable because using context to interpret meanings is an integral part of everyday conversational processes, and a questionnaire is a type of conversation between the researcher and the respondent. A number of factors influence the strength of context effects, including the content and number of preceding questions, the specificity of the question being asked, and the con-

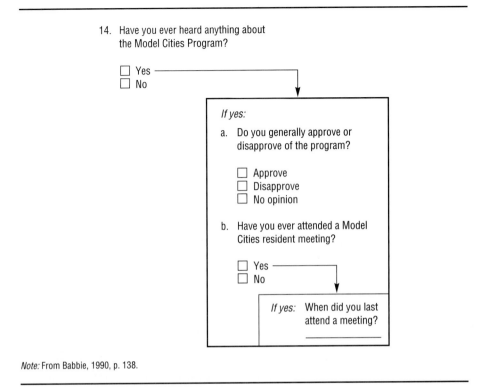

14. Have you ever heard anything about
the Model Cities Program?

☐ Yes
☐ No

If yes:

a. Do you generally approve or
disapprove of the program?

☐ Approve
☐ Disapprove
☐ No opinion

b. Have you ever attended a Model
Cities resident meeting?

☐ Yes
☐ No

If yes: When did you last
attend a meeting?

_____

Note: From Babbie, 1990, p. 138.

FIGURE 11-4   A Graphically Structured Contingent Question
This format can make it easier for respondents to determine which question to answer next.

tent of instructions and other information (such as that on a consent form) given to respondents. If there is reason to suspect that context might affect some questions, it is a
good practice to pretest several versions of the questionniare using different question orders. The order producing the least variation in response can then be used in the final
version of the questionnaire. See Sudman et al. (1996) for a complete discussion of context effects.

Layout of Questionnaires

The physical layout of a questionnaire and its questions can enhance the ease with
which respondents can use it. Here are a few guidelines drawn from several sources
(Babbie, 1990; Dillman, 1978; F. J. Fowler, 1988; Sudman & Bradburn, 1982):

1. *Use closed-ended questions to the greatest extent possible.* In F. J. Fowler's (1988)
opinion, the answers to open-ended questions "usually are incomplete, vague, and
difficult to code, and therefore are only of limited value as measurements" (p. 103).
However, as noted earlier, open-ended questions are better when asking about frequency or amount.

2. *Use a consistent item format*; a mixture of formats can confuse respondents. For example, have all ratings made on either 5-, 7-, or 9-point scales; don't use one number of points for some scales and a different number of points for other scales. To the greatest extent possible, have respondents answer questions in the same way, such as by circling a number, making a check mark, or writing a number on a line.

3. *Use a vertical item format whenever possible*. That is, arrange response options down the page rather than across the page. People sometimes overlook options when they read across. An exception to this rule is the *matrix question* format, in which one general question is applied to several specific situations. In this case, as shown in Figure 11-5, the specific situations are arranged vertically and the response options are arranged horizontally following each situation. This format conserves space and is easy for respondents to use, but it can tempt them to simply go down a column marking the same response for each situation.

4. *When placing questions on a page, don't crowd them together*; leave enough space to clearly indicate where one question ends and the next begins. Also, use a typeface that is large enough to be easily read by your respondents; questionnaires to be completed by members of older or visually impaired populations may require especially large print. Avoid fancy fonts that might be difficult to read.

5. *Don't split questions or response options between pages*. People might think that the question or their options end at the bottom of the page.

Instructions

The instructions that come with a questionnaire, whether it be self-administered or interviewer administered, affect the validity of the data. Instructions that are confusing or hard to follow will result in errors and lead people to abandon the task. Babbie (1990) divides the instructions used in questionnaires into three categories. General instructions tell respondents how to answer the questions. They explain the response formats and scales used in self-administered questionnaires, and tell people how to answer open-ended questions. For example, should a response be brief or lengthy? Introductions to topics explain the topic areas to respondents and tie the topics into the overall purpose of the research. These introductions can function as transitions between topics, focusing respondents' attention on the new topic. Specific instructions are used for questions that use a different response format than the one explained in the general instructions. For example, a question might ask respondents to make rankings rather than ratings or to use a matrix rather than a vertical response layout. As with all instructions, those for questionnaires should use repetition and examples to enhance respondents' understanding of the task. At a minimum, give an example of how to use each response format. As in other research, pilot studies are crucial in survey research for identifying and fixing problems with procedures and materials.

Using Existing Measures

Frequently, questionnaires are composed entirely or in part of existing measures, such as personality inventories or attitude scales or of questions from other surveys. Using ex-

Q-7   Much has been said about the quality of life offered by various sizes of cities. Which
      of the following do you think is best on each of the characteristics listed below?

Small *means* below 10,000 people is best
Medium *means* 10,000 to 49,999 people is best
Large *means* 50,000 to 149,999 people is best
Very Large *means* 150,000 or more people is best

		Size of city which is best (Circle your answer)			
1	Adequacy of medical care	Small	Medium	Large	Very Large
2	Adequacy of public education	Small	Medium	Large	Very Large
3	Adequacy of police protection	Small	Medium	Large	Very Large
4	Place in which to raise children	Small	Medium	Large	Very Large
5	Protection of individual freedon and privacy	Small	Medium	Large	Very Large
6	Lowest costs for public services (like water, sewer, and police)	Small	Medium	Large	Very Large
7	Friendliness of people to each other	Small	Medium	Large	Very Large
8	Community spirit and pride	Small	Medium	Large	Very Large
9	Equality of opportunities for all residents, regardless of race	Small	Medium	Large	Very Large
10	General mental health of residents	Small	Medium	Large	Very Large
11	Recreational and entertainment opportunities	Small	Medium	Large	Very Large
12	General satisfaction of residents	Small	Medium	Large	Very Large
13	Respect for law and order	Small	Medium	Large	Very Large

Note: From Dillman, 1978, p. 140.

FIGURE 11-5   Example of a Matrix Question

isting measures rather than creating your own is usually a good idea for several reasons: The degrees of reliability and validity of existing measures are already known, using measures that other researchers have used makes it easier for you to compare your results with those of previous research, and the process of developing a reliable and valid new measure is long and arduous (see, for example, DeVellis, 1991). However, when combining existing measures into a single questionnaire, two issues become important: the response format to use and the possibility of context effects.

RESPONSE FORMATS   Different measures are likely to use different response formats. For example, some will use 5-point scales and others will use 11-point scales; some will have anchors only at the end points, others will have anchors at each scale point (recall Figure 11-3). These differences create a dilemma: On the one hand, each measure was validated using its own response format, making the response format an integral part of the measure; on the other hand, using multiple response formats in one questionnaire is likely to confuse respondents and cause them to make erroneous responses.

This problem is especially severe when, for example, one attitude measure uses higher numbers to indicate agreement with item stems and another measure uses higher numbers to indicate disagreement. In such circumstances it is best to use a single response format for all items regardless of their source. This procedure will minimize confusion for respondents, thereby reducing errors in the data, and will have little impact on the validity of scores on the measures. As noted earlier, scores using different response formats for a measure are highly correlated (Newstead & Arnold, 1989).

CONTEXT EFFECTS   Just as one item can influence the responses to another item, completing one measure can influence scores on another measure. These mutual influences can lead to spurious correlations between the measures. For example, Council and his colleagues have found that a correlation between reported childhood traumas, such as sexual abuse, and adult symptoms of psychopathology emerges when the trauma survey is completed before the symptom survey but not when the symptom survey is completed first. Council (1993) concluded that "presenting the trauma survey first would prime memories of victimization and lead to increased symptom reporting" (p. 32). Council also cites research that shows that context effects can reduce correlations between measures.

These kinds of context effects occur when research participants fill out two (or more) questionnaires they believe are related to one another, such as when the questionnaires are presented as part of the same study. Therefore, one way to prevent context effects is to keep research participants unaware that the questionnaires are related until they have completed both. This separation of the questionnaires can be accomplished by having two data collection sessions, one for each questionnaire, that the respondents think are part of different studies. Another approach is to have participants complete both questionnaires in the same session, but to psychologically separate the questionnaires by presenting them as belonging to different studies but being administered at one time for the sake of convenience. Their independence is reinforced by having respondents complete separate consent forms for each questionnaire. Because both of these procedures involve deception, participants must be thoroughly debriefed after all the data have been collected.

A third possible control measure is to counterbalance the order of presentation of questionnaires administered in the same session: Half the participants complete one measure first, and the other half complete the other measure first. The researcher can then compare the correlation between the measures completed in one order with the correlation found when the measures are completed in the other order. If the correlations are equivalent, context effects are unlikely to be a problem; significantly different correlations would indicate a context effect. However, as with the counterbalancing of more than two conditions in a within-subjects experiment (recall Chapter 7), counterbalancing more than two measures in a questionnaire is exceedingly difficult. Therefore, a final control measure is to randomly intermix the items from each measure when compiling the questionnaire. However, this procedure complicates the scoring of the measures because items from a given measure will not be adjacent to one another. There is no one best method for dealing with intermeasure context effects, but you should always take steps to control them.

QUESTIONNAIRE ADMINISTRATION

Once a questionnaire has been constructed, it must be administered to respondents. This section describes the ways in which survey data can be collected and compares their relative advantages and disadvantages.

Methods of Data Collection

Six methods can be used to collect survey data: group-administered questionnaires, mail questionnaires, personal interviews, telephone interviews, focus groups, and computer-administered questionnaires. This section outlines the principal advantages and disadvantages of each method and the following section compares the methods. See Judd et al. (1991) for a more detailed summary of the advantages and disadvantages of these methods.

GROUP ADMINISTRATION   In the group administration method, as the name implies, respondents are brought together in one or more groups to complete questionnaires. This method is best suited for research situations in which the respondents are a "captive audience," such as in research using college student participants or in surveys of organizations whose members are colocated, such as the employees of a company.

Compared to the other methods, the use of group-administered questionnaires is inexpensive, the main cost being the reproduction of the questionnaires. This cost can be lowered by using standardized answer sheets (the so-called IBM forms) and reusing the questionnaire booklets for new groups of respondents. Because people participate in groups, data collection is fast relative to the methods that require individual data collection. Group-administered questionnaires also usually have a high response rate, with almost 100% of all respondents returning questionnaires. Responses to group-administered questionnaires can be completely anonymous, which can be of great importance in some situations.

With written questionnaires, there is no room for interviewer bias, the people administering the questionnaires need only minimal training, and it is easy to supervise them during data collection. The questionnaire itself can be fairly long, but be careful not to induce boredom in respondents: Writing out answers to printed questions does not arouse a high degree of motivation for the task. You can also control the context in which the questionnaire is administered, minimizing the possibility of distractions that could take respondents' attention away from the questions. And you can control the order in which respondents answer questions by dividing the questionnaire into sections and having respondents return one section before being given the next. Unlike with telephone interviews, you can use visual aids, but only those that can be easily explained and responded to in writing.

A major drawback of group-administered questionnaires is that it can be difficult to motivate respondents to answer the questions fully and correctly. For example, there is no way of preventing people from skipping questions. Motivation may be especially problematic with coerced respondent samples such as college students recruited from subject pools. The problem is compounded in the group setting because complete anonymity facilitates random responding and may contribute to a lackadaisical attitude toward the task. Even with well-motivated respondents, it is impossible to probe inadequate responses, and the group situation might inhibit people from asking for clarification of questions lest they appear foolish in front of the group. Because it is usually impossible to bring randomly selected respondents together for the group administration of a questionnaire, this method almost always uses a convenience sample with its attendant problem of low representativeness. However, you can use random or systematic sampling when surveying members of organizations. Finally, and very importantly for some forms of research, the validity of the data is totally dependent on the respondents' reading and writing ability.

MAIL QUESTIONNAIRES   Mail questionnaires can be used when the researcher has a list of valid addresses for the people to be surveyed. They are therefore frequently used for surveys of members of organizations whose members are geographically dispersed, such as professional associations. Mail questionnaires can also be used for surveys of the general public, using telephone directories or city directories as sources of names and addresses. However, the U.S. Postal Service will no longer attempt to deliver mail to apartment residents unless the apartment number is shown as part of the address. Because telephone directories generally do not show apartment numbers, using them as sources of addresses might result in a high rate of undelivered questionnaires.

As with group-administered questionnaires, there can be no interviewer bias effects on the responses to mail questionnaires and the respondents can have complete anonymity. Mail questionnaires can also include visual aids, but again only those that can be explained and responded to in writing. There is, of course, no need to train or supervise interviewers. Mail surveys can also be relatively inexpensive, adding only postage costs to those of reproducing the questionnaire.

There is of course no way to probe inadequate responses unless respondents give up their anonymity and provide a telephone number that the researcher can call for further information. Similarly, there is no way for respondents to ask for clarification of questions unless you provide a telephone number. You cannot control the order in which respondents answer the questions or the context in which they answer them. For example, there is no way to know whether a response to an opinion question represents only the respondent's own view on the issue or if the respondent consulted with someone, such as his or her spouse, before answering. Mail survey research also requires a fairly long time to complete because the questionnaire may sit on a respondent's table for days or weeks before being filled out. Finally, like group-administered questionnaires, mail questionnaires are totally dependent on the respondents' reading and writing abilities.

A potential shortcoming of the use of mail questionnaires is their low response rate: An average of only 47% of the people who receive mail questionnaires return them, compared to an average of 82% of people asked who consent to personal interviews and an average of 72% who consent to telephone interviews (Yu & Cooper, 1983). Low response rates can threaten the validity of the research because the people who do return questionnaires might not be representative of the initial sample. The low return rate probably derives from recipients' having little motivation to complete the questionnaire, although Dillman (1978) suggests that proper design of both the questionnaire

TABLE 11-11   Effective and Ineffective Techniques for Increasing Response Rates to Mail Surveys

Increases Response Rates	No Effect on Response Rates
Monetary incentives	Offer of survey results
Nonmonetary premium or gift	Return deadline
Prenotification	Special appeal in cover letter
Personalized cover letter	Promise of anonymity
Follow-up letter or card	Use of colored paper
Stamped rather than business reply return envelope	

Note: From Fox et al. (1988), Yammarino et al. (1991), and Yu & Cooper (1983).

and cover letter can enhance motivation by emphasizing the importance of both the survey and the respondent's contribution to it. Low respondent motivation also suggests that the questionnaire should be kept as short as possible.

Because low response rates are the great bane of mail surveys, a great deal of research has been directed at developing methods for increasing response rates (Fox, Crask, & Kim, 1988; Yammarino, Skinner, & Childers, 1991; Yu & Cooper, 1983). The first column of Table 11-11 shows some of the factors that increase response, and the second column shows some factors that one might expect to increase response, but that do not. Some of the more effective techniques—such as notifying respondents in advance that they will be asked to take part in a survey, including money or coupons as incentives, sending follow-up requests to people who do not respond initially, and using stamped rather than business reply envelopes—can greatly increase the cost of the survey. Personally addressing the envelope and cover letter is also helpful, indicating a special interest in the addressee's response. However, be *very* careful if you use a computerized database and mailing list program to address envelopes and personalize the cover letter. Many databases include both organizations and people, and while a survey recipient might find a letter that starts "Dear Dr. Department of Psychology" to be amusing, such a letter is not likely to motivate the person to complete the questionnaire. If you are planning to conduct a mail survey, consult Babbie (1990), Dillman (1978), and Mangione (1995), which contain a wealth of information on the mechanics of the process.

PERSONAL INTERVIEWS   Although the personal interview, with hordes of interviewers pounding the pavement and knocking on doors, is the archetype of survey research, it has been largely supplanted by telephone interviews. Nonetheless, it has many advantages and is still used for many research purposes.

The main advantage of personal interviews is the high level of respondent motivation that a skilled interviewer can generate, resulting in high response rates and a high-quality sample of respondents. A personal interview can be long, and there is ample opportunity for the interviewer to probe inadequate responses and for the respondent to ask for clarifications. The interviewer can also use visual aids that require more explanation than those that can be used in written questionnaires. The interviewer has complete control of the order in which questions are asked and often of the interview context. Finally, the success of the personal interview does not depend on the respondents' abilities to read and write.

Because respondents are contacted individually and in person, with the interviewers having to travel from respondent to respondent, personal interviews are very costly and data collection can take a long time. There is also a high degree of risk that interviewer bias will contaminate responses, resulting in the need for well-trained interviewers, which also adds to the cost of the method. Moreover, it is rarely possible to supervise interviewers while they collect data. Another drawback is the lack of respondent anonymity, which might result in reluctance to discuss certain issues. Finally, although the development of laptop computers has made it possible to use them to record data from personal interviews (Saris, 1991), use them sparingly: Some respondents might find the presence of a computer distracting, and it might detract from the person-to-person atmosphere that is a major plus of the personal interview.

TELEPHONE INTERVIEWS   Telephone interviews have almost all the advantages of personal interviews, but they can be conducted at a lower cost and completed more quickly. Because interviewer and respondent do not interact face-to-face, there is also less opportunity for interviewer bias to affect responses. In addition, telephone interviewing can be assisted by computers in two ways. First, random digit dialing can be used to draw a completely random sample of respondents and makes possible inclusion of people with unlisted numbers. Although only people who have telephones can be sampled, those people constitute over 90% of the U.S. population (Quinn, Gutek, & Walsh, 1980). Second, survey questions can be presented to telephone interviewers via computer terminals and the interviewers can enter responses directly into the database.

Telephone interviews also share some of the disadvantages of personal interviews. Telephone interviewers require a fair degree of training, especially in gaining potential respondents' cooperation after they answer the telephone. In contrast, supervision of interviews is easy to carry out. As with personal interviews, respondent anonymity is all but impossible; unlike personal interviews, however, telephone interviews cannot make use of visual aids. If you are considering conducting a telephone interview, consult Dillman (1978), which includes a very detailed discussion of the mechanics of the process.

FOCUS GROUPS   A **focus group** is a semistructured group interview that deals with a specific topic or experience that is familiar to the members of the group. The goal is to determine the group members' perceptions of and affective responses to that topic or experience. The interviewer (called a *moderator* in this context) encourages the participants to talk freely and to interact, with the expectation that the participants will build on each others' comments (Krueger, 1994; Stewart & Shamdasani, 1990). Focus groups are used extensively in market research as a means of evaluating products and services and of getting the reactions of members of a study population to a proposed survey instrument. They can also be used to generate hypotheses for research by exploring questions such as why people do (or do not) behave in certain ways.

Focus groups share most of the advantages of personal interviews, but the group context allows data to be gathered more quickly and at a lower cost. Like the personal interview, the focus group is vulnerable to interviewer bias, so moderators must be well trained; in addition, the moderator must be able to keep discussion flowing freely while maintaining a focus on the research question. However, if the room in which the group meets is equipped with a one-way mirror or television camera, the moderator's performance can be supervised. Also, as with the personal interview, anonymity is impossible. People who participate in focus groups are generally highly motivated, but recruitment can be a problem: Potential group members are contacted by telephone and are often reluctant to respond to a request from a stranger to take part in an unfamiliar experience. Focus groups can also suffer the disadvantages of the group context. The interviewer cannot explore any one person's comments in depth, and people may be reluctant to discuss certain topics in a group setting. In addition, there can be problems of group dynamics: people who try to dominate the discussion, people with axes to grind, and people who ramble on without saying anything of substance. Krueger (1994) and Stewart and Shamdasani (1990) discuss the mechanics of running focus groups.

COMPUTER ADMINISTRATION   It is often possible to administer questionnaires by computer. Researchers can accomplish this by using a single computer that every respondent uses in turn, a group of computers connected to a local area network, or the Internet. Computer-administered questionnaires share most of the advantages and disadvantages of group-administered questionnaires, but they provide the additional advantages of lower cost (no printing or data-entry expenses) and less vulnerability to social desirability response bias (Joinson, 1999). However, unless the researcher proctors the computer room, respondents cannot ask questions. The use of hypertext mark-up language (HTML) programming to create survey forms has the additional advantages of allowing the computer to prompt respondents to answer questions they skipped and of providing some clarifying information in the forms of links to "frequently asked questions" pages and definitions of terms. Internet surveys raise additional issues that are discussed in the next chapter's section on Internet research.

Comparing the Methods

Table 11-12 compares the six methods for collecting survey data on the dimensions that we discussed. For most general survey purposes, the telephone interview is probably the best all-around performer. As Quinn et al. (1980) note, its "generally favorable comparison with face-to-face interviews in terms of response rates, overall quality of data, and quality of data on sensitive issues should make telephone interviewing the most efficient, inexpensive, and methodologically sophisticated form of collecting survey data" (p. 152). Mail surveys can be used when mailing lists are available for homogeneous but geographically dispersed groups, such as professional organizations, or if cost is an especially important factor. Personal interviews are better when one is dealing with populations that are hard to reach by other means, such as members of deviant groups, or if the study population is geographically concentrated, reducing the cost of personal interviewing. Group-administered questionnaires are, as noted, generally used

TABLE 11-12   Comparison of Survey Data Collection Methods

Dimension of Comparison	Group Administration	Mail Questionnaire	Personal Interview	Telephone Interview	Focus Group	Computer Administration
Cost	Low	Low to moderate	High	Moderate	Moderate to high	Low to moderate
Data quality						
Response rate	High	Low	High	Moderate to high	Low to moderate	Low to moderate
Respondent motivation	Low to high	Low	High	High	High	Moderate to high
Interviewer bias	None	None	Moderate	Low	Moderate	None
Vulnerability to social desirability response bias	Some	Some	High	High	High	Low
Sample quality	Low to high	Low to moderate	High	Moderate to high	Moderate to high	Low to high
Possible length	Moderate	Short	Long	Long	Long	Moderate
Ability to clarify questions	Moderate	Low	High	High	High	Low
Ability to probe responses	None	Low	High	High	High	Low
Ability to use visual aids	Some	Some	High	None	High	High
Time needed for data collection	Low to moderate	High	High	Low	Low to moderate	Low
Interviewer training	Low	None	High	High	High	None
Interviewer supervision needed	High	Not required	Low	High	Moderate	None
Respondent anonymity	High	High	Low	Low	Low	Low to high
Ability to use computers	Moderate	None	Possible	High	Low	High
Dependence on respondents' reading and writing ability	High	High	None	None	None	High
Control of context	High	None	High	High	High	None to high
Control of question order	Some	None	High	High	High	Some

Note: Adapted from Judd et al., 1991, p. 223.

with "captive audiences." Focus groups can be especially useful for getting feedback on proposed research from members of the study population. The group can review the research proposal and comment on ethical or other issues the researcher overlooked, and can comment on the clarity of proposed questionnaires. Focus groups can also be used in evaluation research to obtain clients' perceptions of services provided by the program under evaluation (Krueger, 1988). As with all other aspects of research, the choice of a survey methodology requires the researcher to examine the goals of the research and to decide which method has the combination of advantages and disadvantages that will most facilitate the research while hindering it the least. Finally, the use of computers to administer surveys can reduce costs and limit the effects of social desirability response bias.

SURVEY DATA ARCHIVES

Survey data archives contain the records of surveys conducted by U.S. government agencies, such as the Census Bureau, and by survey research organizations, such as the University of Chicago's National Opinion Research Center (NORC) and the University of Michigan's Institute for Social Research (ISR). Survey archives contain people's responses to survey questions and demographic data about the respondents, such as age, sex, ethnicity, and income. For example, NORC maintains a computerized archive of the records of the General Social Survey (GSS), which has been conducted on at least a biennial basis since 1973 (NORC, 1998). These data (and the data of most survey archives) are kept on computer files that can be accessed through many college and university research centers. For instance, Himmelstein and McRae (1988) used GSS data to study the relationship between people's socioeconomic status and the liberal versus conservative nature of their views on social issues such as environmental protection, abortion, and nuclear power.

Survey archives are useful because unlike many of the types of archival data discussed in Chapter 10, most of the time they were collected for research purposes; consequently, great care was taken to ensure the validity of the questions included and of the data collection procedures. However, there are sometimes exceptions, such as when surveys are conducted to collect data to be used to influence legislation of litigation. In such cases the goals of the survey may intentionally or unintentionally influence the data collected, such as through the use of biased questions. Survey archives also provide an inexpensive source of data for answering research questions. The data have already been collected, usually from a representative sample of the national population, and are usually in a form, such as diskettes or CD-ROMs, that are readable by desktop computer statistical packages. Finally archives may contain longitudinal data and periodic surveys such as the GSS often include questions that remain consistent from year to year, allowing cross-sectional comparisons across time.

The use of archived survey data also has a major limitation: The data available in an archive might not provide high-quality operational definitions of hypothetical constructs. To cover as many topics as possible, surveys often assess constructs with single-item measures of unknown reliability and validity, although there are some exceptions (see, for example, Herek & Capitanio, 1996). Because of this limitation and others, you must carefully evaluate the data from a survey archive before using them for your research. Box 11-3 lists some criteria for evaluating archived survey data.

How can you find archived survey data to use in your research? As noted above, many college and university social science research centers can access GSS or ISR data sets. Stewart and Kamins (1993) and Zaitzow and Fields (1996) describe a number of other survey archives that researchers can use, and Clark and Maynard (1998) describe archives that are available on-line.

BOX 11-3   Criteria for Evaluating Archived Survey Data

- *What was the purpose of the original study?* Data collected for some purposes, such as influencing legislation or litigation, may be biased in ways that support the purpose.

- *How valid was the data collection process?* Unless there is documentation that includes information which allows you to evaluate the quality of the data collection process, such as how respondents were sampled (see Chapter 12) and the validity of measures, you should not use the data.

- *What information was collected?* Unless the data set includes all the variables you need to test your hypothesis, including demographic data to provide information about the generalizability of results, and unless the operational definitions used in the survey adequately represent the hypothetical constructs you are studying (see Chapter 5), the data may be of limited usefulness.

- *When were the data collected?* Because social attitudes and social processes can change over time, the relationships between variables found using old data sets might not represent the ways in which the variables are currently related (see Chapter 14).

Source: Stewart & Kamins (1993).

SUMMARY

Survey research is the process of collecting data by asking questions and recording people's answers. Important issues in survey research are question wording, question response formats, the use of multi-item scales, response biases, questionnaire design, and questionnaire administration.

Survey questions must be written carefully because the phrasing of the questions, and sometimes of the response options used in closed-ended questions, can bias the answers given by respondents. In writing questions, you must be careful to use language familiar to your respondents, avoid negatively worded questions, ask only one question at a time, avoid biased words and phrases, be specific, avoid making assumptions, and address sensitive topics sensitively. When writing response scales, it is important to decide on the appropriate level of measurement — nominal, ordinal, interval, or ratio — based on considerations of the information content provided by the level, its ecological validity, and the statistical tests to be used with the data.

There are four formats for closed-ended scale response options: comparative, itemized, graphic, and numerical. These formats typically provide data at the ordinal level of measurement, but judicious choice of anchors for numerical scales can result in interval level measurement. Choice of response format for a scale must be dictated by the purpose of the research. However, some evidence suggests that open-ended questions are better for assessing frequency and amount. When interpreting responses, one should not take the meanings of anchors literally: Several biases can affect how respondents use the anchors to select a response.

Hypothetical constructs are usually assessed using multi-item rating scales, which are generally more reliable and valid than single-item scales. The most commonly used technique for constructing multi-item scales is the Likert approach, which maximizes the internal consistency of the scale. The Thurstone approach uses interval-scaled items, and the Guttman approach uses items that represent a sequential ordering of beliefs or behaviors. Of these approaches, only the Linkert technique allows the development of a scale that can assess multidimensional or multifaceted constructs through the use of subscales. The semantic differential is a well-developed multi-item graphic rating scale widely used to assess the evaluative component of attitudes.

Response biases can threaten the validity of survey and other types of self-report data. Question-related response biases include scale ambiguity, in which respondents judge amount and frequency relative to their own behavior; category anchoring, in which respondents use the categories of itemized response scales as cues to how to respond; estimation biases, which occur when people cannot, or are not motivated to, count specific instances of a behavior; and respondent interpretations of numerical scales, which may lead them to make assumptions about the types of behavior the question asks about. Person-related response biases inlcude social desirability, in which respondents give answers they think will make them look good; acquiescence, the tendency to consistently agree or disagree with statements; extremity, the tendency to consistently use the end points of a scale; and halo and leniency, the tendencies to answer all questions the same way and to give positive ratings. Also, one should not interpret scale anchors literally.

When designing questionnaires, group questions according to topic and move from general to more specific issues. Be vigilant for context effects, in which answering one question can bias the response to later questions. When the order of questions is contingent on the answer to a prior question, special care must be taken to ensure that instructions clearly indicate how the respondent is to proceed. The questionnaire itself must be formatted so as to be easy to use. Instructions must be clearly written and include transitions between topics that will motivate respondents to answer the questions. It is a good idea to use existing questionnaires in your research, but when combining existing questionnaires, use a consistent response format and use controls to reduce context effects.

Survey data can be collected in six ways; although each method has its advantages and disadvantages, each also has situations to which it is best suited. The group administration of written questionnaires is best suited for situations in which respondents can be easily brought together in groups. Although fast and inexpensive, group administration does not contribute to respondent motivation and can normally be used only with convenience samples. Mail questionnaires are suitable for situations when an address list exists for a geographically dispersed group. Although inexpensive relative to interviews, research using mail questionnaires can take a long time to complete and can have a low response rate. Personal interviews tend to be best for hard-to-reach populations or if the study population is geographically concentrated. Personal interviewing can provide high-quality data but tends to be slow and expensive. Telephone interviewing is best for most general purposes, providing high-quality data at relatively low cost. Focus groups are used to assess people's perceptions and evaluations of products or services in a group context. They collect data more quickly than personal interviews but cannot explore any one person's views in depth. Computer-administered questionnaires minimize social desirability response bias and are very inexpensive.

There are a number of survey data archives that store survey data. Using these archives for research can allow one to have a nationally representative sample at low cost. However, the archived data may not include all the variables you need and hypothetical constructs may be measured poorly.

QUESTIONS AND EXERCISES FOR REVIEW

1. How do sample surveys and convenience surveys differ?
2. How do closed-ended and open-ended questions differ? What are their relative advantages and disadvantages? Under what circumstances is it better to use open-ended questions, and under what conditions are closed-ended questions preferable?
3. Wheeler (1976) has said that by carefully manipulating the wording of a question, one can get any response pattern that one desires. Choose an issue and a position, pro or con, on the issue. Write two opinion survey questions on the issue, one that you think will result mostly in agreement with your chosen position and one that you think will result mostly in disagreement. What question-wording principles did you exploit in constructing your questions?
4. Take the same issue that you dealt with in Question 3 and try to write two unbiased questions on it. Exchange your questions with a classmate and analyze each other's questions based on the principles of question wording.
5. Name and define the four levels of measurement. What characteristics of levels of measurement must the researcher bear in mind when choosing a level?
6. What are the relative advantages and disadvantages of the two methods of comparative scaling? What conditions must be met if comparative scaling is to provide reliable and valid results?
7. How can preliminary research using open-ended questions be used to improve the content-related validity of itemized rating scales?
8. How are graphic rating scales and numerical rating scales similar? How do they differ? Describe the ways in which itemized rating scales can be constructed to provide data similar to that from numerical scales.
9. How can the measurement sensitivity of rating scales be increased?
10. What level of measurement results from each scale response format? Under what conditions can interval and ratio level measurement be achieved?
11. What advantages do multi-item scales have over single-item scales?
12. Describe the development processes for Likert, Thurstone, and Guttman scales. How are these types of scales similar and how do they differ? Likert is currently the predominant approach used in developing multi-item scales. Describe the characteristics of Likert scaling that have led to its popularity.
13. Describe the structure and use of the semantic differential.
14. How do scale ambiguity, category anchoring, and estimation biases affect responses to survey questions? What steps can the researcher take to reduce these biases?
15. Find a survey that has been used at your college or university. Are any of the questions likely to induce response biases? If so, how can those questions be rewritten to reduce response bias?
16. What are the most common forms of respondent-related response biases? What can be done to reduce the influence of these biases on responses to survey questions?
17. What is the literal interpretation fallacy?
18. Describe the principles for ordering questions in questionnaires. What are context effects? How can they be controlled?

19. How should questionnaires be laid out?
20. What types of instructions are used in questionnaires?
21. Obtain a copy of a questionnaire that has been used in research at your college or university, and evaluate the effectiveness of its question ordering, instructions, and layout. What suggestions would you make for improving the questionnaire?
22. What are the advantages of using existing measures in research? What considerations are important when conbining existing measures in a questionnaire?
23. Describe the methods of survey data collection. Compare and contrast the advantages and disadvantages of each method. What type of situation is each best suited for?
24. What are survey data archives? What are the advantages and disadvantages of using archived survey data in research? What criteria can researchers use to evaluate archived survey data?

12 DATA COLLECTION

RESEARCH PARTICIPANTS
Populations and Samples
Sampling
  Probability Sampling
  Nonprobability Sampling
  Purposive Sampling
  Snowball Sampling
Sample Size
  Statistical Power
  Determining Sample Size

RESEARCH PROCEDURES
Effective Research Settings
  Coherence
  Simplicity
  Psychological Involvement
  Consistency
Effective Instructions
  Be Clear
  Get Participants' Attention
  Check Participants'
    Understanding
"Debugging" the Procedure
  The Research Proposal
  Rehearsal
  Pilot Studies

The Data Collection Session
The Postexperimental Interview
  The Ethical Function
  The Educational Function
  The Methodological Function
  The Discovery Function
  Conducting the Interview
Research Assistants

USING THE INTERNET TO
COLLECT DATA
Forms of Internet Data Collection
Advantages of Internet Research
  Economy and Ease of Data
    Collection
  Access to Research
    Participants
  Potential for Increased
    Internal Validity
  Public Research Methods
Disadvantages of Internet
  Research
  Participant Sampling
  Limits on Experimental
    Stimuli and Response
    Modes

Lack of Control Over the Data
  Collection Environment
Participant Attrition
Sabotage
Participant Recruitment
  E-mail Solicitation
  Announcements
  Listing on Research
    Directories
  Search Engines
  Control Over Recruitment
  Expiration Dates
  Web Site Design
The Validity of Web-Based Data
Ethical Issues
  Voluntary Participation
  Informed Consent
  Monitoring Participants for
    Harm
  Privacy
  Debriefing

SUMMARY

QUESTIONS AND EXERCISES
FOR REVIEW

Having selected a hypothesis to test and a research strategy to use in testing it, the researcher embarks on data collection. This is the most interesting and enjoyable phase of research, and often the most challenging, for it is here that researchers meet and interact with their research participants. In this chapter, we will briefly look at three aspects of this process: research participants, research procedures, and using the Internet to collect data.

RESEARCH PARTICIPANTS

Some of the most important questions that researchers face are those dealing with research participants. This section examines the issues to consider in answering three of those questions: What population should I use? How should I sample from that population? How many participants will I need?

Populations and Samples

When we conduct research, we want our results to apply to a certain group of people. This group might be very broad, such as the entire population of the world, or it might be very narrow, such as the students attending a particular college or university, or the group can fall somewhere between these extremes, such as all people in the United States who possess a particular characteristic, such as depression. Regardless of how broadly or narrowly we define this group, it constitutes the **target population** for our research. Frequently, target populations for behavioral science research are defined in terms of hypothetical constructs, such as depression. In such cases, we must operationally define the target population in terms of some manifest variable. For example, we could operationally define depression in terms of psychiatric diagnosis. The people who meet our operational definition of the target population constitute the **study population**. For most research, the study population is so large that it is impossible to collect data from all of its members. We therefore select a **research sample** from the study population from whom we collect our data. Figure 12-1 shows the relationships among the target population, study population, and research sample.

The distinctions among the target population, study population, and research sample are important because the definition of the study population and the sampling process can affect the validity of the research. To the extent that the measure used to define the study population suffers from measurement error, the members of the study population will not correctly represent the target population, reducing the extent to which the results of the research will apply to the target population as a whole. For example, not everyone who is depressed is seen by a mental health professional and receives a diagnosis of depression, some diagnoses of depression might be erroneous, and some people who are depressed might receive some other diagnosis. Therefore, researchers must be careful to use only the most valid measures available when defining the study population.

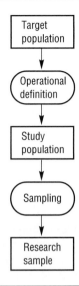

FIGURE 12-1   Moving From Target Population to Research Sample
The *target population* is the group of people to whom we want the results of our research to apply (such as depressed people), the *study population* consists of those members of the target population who fit a particular operational definition of the target population (such as having a psychiatric diagnosis of depression), and the *research sample* consists of the members of the study population who participate in the research.

In addition, to the extent that researchers' operational definitions of the target population differ, their findings might differ, leading to apparent contradictions among the results of studies. Widom (1988), for example, has pointed out that the operational definition of *abused child* can vary greatly from study to study. One consequence of this variation is that estimates of the incidence of child abuse range from 500,000 cases per year to 2,300,000 cases per year. As Widom notes, one cannot expect convergence in findings among studies unless the studies use similar study populations. A third potential problem lies in the sampling procedure: The research sample might not be representative of the study population and therefore not representative of the target population. Chapter 5 discussed the issues surrounding the validity of measurement; now let's turn to the question of sampling.

Sampling

There are a large number of techniques that you can use to draw a research sample from a study population (Henry, 1990). Most of these techniques can be described in terms of two dimensions: probability versus nonprobability sampling and simple versus stratified sampling. In **probability sampling** every member of the study population has a known probability of being selected for the research sample; in **nonprobability sampling,** the probability of a person's being chosen is unknown. **Simple sampling** assumes that the method used to draw the research sample will provide a reasonable cross section of the study population in terms of personal characteristics, such as sex, race, and so forth, that are important to the research; **stratified sampling** structures the research sample so that the sample contains the same proportion of each important characteristic as the study population. In addition to the sampling techniques defined by these dimensions, researchers can use purposive sampling, in which they select participants based on characteristics important to the research, and snowball sampling, in which current participants recommend people they know as future participants. Let's examine these techniques.

PROBABILITY SAMPLING   The basic forms of probability sampling begin with a list of all the people in the study population, such as a roster of all the students attending a particular college or university. This list is called a **sampling frame.** The researchers then decide how many people they want to participate in the research (N) and select N names from the list. With **simple random sampling,** the researchers use a table of random numbers to do the selecting. Each name on the list is given a unique identification number, ranging, for example, from 001 to 999. Starting randomly in the table of random numbers, the researchers look at the last three digits of the first random number and select for the sample the person whose identification number matches those digits. They then go on to the next random number, selecting for the sample the person whose identification number matches its last three digits. Random number digits that are outside the range of identification numbers are skipped, as are those that match identification numbers already selected. The process continues until the desired number of participants is sampled. Each person in the sampling frame therefore has an equal probability—$1/N$—of being selected for the sample.

For **stratified random sampling,** the sampling frame is arranged in terms of the variables to be used to structure the sample. Let's say that the researchers want to ensure that the makeup of the research sample exactly reflects the makeup of the student body in terms of class (freshman, sophomore, and so on), sex, and ethnic group. The researchers draw up a **quota matrix** reflecting all possible combinations of these variables, such as the matrix shown in Figure 12-2. Each person in the sampling frame is categorized by these variables and assigned to the appropriate cell in the quota matrix; for example, all first-year Asian-American women would be assigned to the upper left-hand cell in Figure 12-2. The researchers then sample randomly from each cell of the matrix, with each cell being sampled in proportion to its representation in the population. For example, if first-year Asian women constitute 1% of the study population and the desired sample size is 1,000, then 10 first-year Asian-American women would be randomly selected for the sample.

Simple and stratified random sampling can be very difficult and time consuming to carry out, especially if the assignment of identification numbers and the selection of participants are done by hand rather than with the assistance of a computer. Even computer-assisted random sampling can be laborious if the list comprising the sampling frame is not already available on a computer file and must be entered manually. A simple alternative to random sampling is **systematic sampling.** With systematic sampling, you start with a sampling frame and select every nth name, where n equals the

	Women				Men			
	Asian American	African American	Latino	European American	Asian American	African American	Latino	European American
Freshmen								
Sophomores								
Juniors								
Seniors								

FIGURE 12-2 Quota Matrix for Sampling by Sex, Ethnicity, and Class
Each person in the sampling frame is categorized by sex, ethnicity, and class and is assigned to the appropriate cell; researchers then sample randomly from each cell in proportion to its representation in the population.

proportion of the frame that you want to sample. For example, for a 10% sample, you would go down the list selecting every 10th name. Systematic sampling can also be stratified, such as by selecting every nth man and every nth woman to stratify the sample by sex. A danger in systematic sampling is a problem known as *periodicity*: The sampling frame is arranged so that some characteristic appears with the same pattern as the sampling interval, resulting in a biased sample. For example,

> in a housing development or apartment house every eighth dwelling unit may be a corner unit. If it is somewhat larger than the others its occupants can be expected to differ as well. If the sampling [interval] also happens to be [eight], one could obtain a sample with either all corner units or no corner units depending on the [starting point]. (Blalock, 1979, p. 559)

Fortunately, periodicity is rarely found in practice, but you should still carefully examine lists to be used for systematic sampling to guard against the problem.

A major problem inherent in random and systematic sampling is that you must have a list of the entire study population to use as a sampling frame. Therefore, these sampling approaches can normally be used only with relatively small study populations, such as the students enrolled in a particular college or university. But what if you define your study population as all the college and university students in the United States? There is no comprehensive listing of this population. The answer to this problem is **cluster sampling.** With cluster sampling, you first identify groups or clusters of people who meet the definition of the study population; in our example, the clusters would be colleges and universities. You then take a random sample of the clusters and use all members of the sampled clusters as research participants. When the clusters themselves are large, sampling can also be conducted within clusters. When membership lists are available, random or systematic sampling can be used. Otherwise, you would use **multi-stage cluster sampling,** in which clusters are sampled within clusters. For example, for a face-to-face survey in a geographic area, census tracts form the initial clusters; census blocks are sampled within tracts, houses or apartment buildings within blocks, apartments within apartment buildings, and people within apartments or houses. Cluster samples can also be stratified; in the college and university example, you could stratify by public versus private institution and by size. Census tracts or blocks could be stratified by their ethnic composition as reflected in census data.

Probability sampling is the ideal form of sampling because if done carefully it will provide a pool of potential research participants whose characteristics are near-perfect reflections of those of the study population. Probability sampling can therefore provide a sample that is highly representative of the population. This high degree of representativeness is only potential, however, because it may be impossible to contact some members of the potential participant pool and others may refuse to participate when contacted. To the extent that refusals and other causes of "lost" potential participants are related to participant characteristics, the people who actually participate in the research will not be representative of the population. For example, Doob and Macdonald (1979) identified high- and low-crime city and suburban areas in and around Toronto. A door-to-door survey was conducted of randomly selected adults from randomly selected households in each area. Despite these stringently random sample-construction procedures, 70% of the respondents to the survey were women. It is therefore important to compare the characteristics of the people who take part in the research to the characteristics of the population that was sampled using whatever data are available — usually demographic information — to assess the degree to which the people who took part in the research represent the population.

Even when you can be fairly confident of obtaining a representative group of participants, probability sampling can be very difficult to carry out unless the study population is relatively small, such as the membership of an organization. Data collection based on probability sampling can also be very expensive if a geographically diverse population, such as that of a nation, is being sampled. In addition, if members of the sample do not live near the researcher, the research must be carried to them, rather than having them come to the researcher. Consequently, the research must often be based on questionnaires, limiting the forms that experimental manipulations can take and limiting measurement to self-reports.

NONPROBABILITY SAMPLING Probability sampling is used infrequently in behavioral science research, partly because of the costs involved and partly because of the limitations it places on experimental manipulations and the types of measures that can be used. Consequently, researchers are more likely to use **nonprobability** or **convenience samples**. As the latter term implies, nonprobability samples consist of people from whom the researcher finds it convenient to collect data. For example, researchers might select depressed people as their target population for a study and define the study population as people who score above a certain point on a self-report depression inventory. However, rather than trying to draw a probability sample from that population, the researchers administer the depression inventory to students at the university where they teach and use those who score above the cutoff as the research sample. University students are selected as research participants not because they are necessarily representative of the target population, but because the researchers find it easy to collect data from them. When researchers use essentially anyone who happens to be convenient as research participants, they are said to have conducted **haphazard sampling.** Haphazard samples can also be stratified using a quota matrix such as that shown in Figure 12-2, in which case they are known as **quota samples.**

Convenience samples are not restricted to college students. Marketing researchers often use "mall intercept interviews," recruiting as participants people walking in shopping malls. Researchers also sometimes ask people in shopping malls, airport waiting areas, and other public places to answer questionnaires, or they recruit participants through newspaper advertisements.

Convenience samples are generally easy to acquire and inexpensive for data collection. As noted in Chapter 3, college and university students are frequently drafted as research participants to form convenience samples. Members of convenience samples can usually come to the researcher's laboratory, enabling the researcher to use complex experimental manipulations and behavioral and physiological measures. However, the researcher has no way of knowing the degree to which the members of a convenience sample are representative of the target population. The more the characteristics of the members of the sample differ from those of the members of the target population, the less likely the results of the research are to apply to the target population. Chapter 14 discusses this problem of generalizability in detail; for now, let's just note that the validity of convenience sampling is highly controversial.

PURPOSIVE SAMPLING   In **purposive sampling** the researcher uses her or his judgment to select the membership of the sample based on the goals of the research. Purposive sampling is frequently used in case study research, in which researchers often want to study typical or critical cases. A typical case, as the term implies, is one that the researcher believes is representative of the average case. For example, a researcher might choose a school for a case study because the demographic characteristics of its students and faculty appear to be representative of most of the schools in the district. A critical case is one that has one or more characteristics of special interest to the researcher. For example, a researcher might choose a school as the test case in a comparative case study because it represents a particular level of an independent variable, such as funding; other schools with different levels of funding could be chosen as control or comparison cases. Purposive sampling can be further used to select individuals within the school as sources of data by targeting for interview "key informants" who have special knowledge that is of interest to the researcher.

SNOWBALL SAMPLING   The final form of sampling is known as **snowball sampling.** In this procedure, people who are initially selected for a sample on the basis of convenience or purposive sampling nominate acquaintances whom they think might be willing to participate in the research. The nominees who agree to participate are then asked to nominate other potential participants. The size of the sample therefore grows like a rolling snowball, hence its name. This procedure is frequently used in developmental research: Once a group of parents whose children are at the age required for the research has been identified, those parents can recommend other people who have children of the same age as research participants and might even encourage friends and relatives to participate. Snowball sampling is also used to construct samples of hard-to-reach populations whose members might otherwise be unidentifiable, such as illegal drug users.

Sample Size

In addition to deciding on how to sample research participants, the researcher must also decide how many people to sample. The question of sample size is closely related to the question of statistical power, so we must begin there.

STATISTICAL POWER   You will recall that the outcome of a statistical test, such as the *t* test, represents the probability that the results found for the research sample reflect the results that would have been found if the entire study population had participated in the research. Statistical testing has traditionally focused on the probability of deciding that the independent variable had a real effect on the dependent variable when, in fact, the effect found in the sample was due to error. As shown in the top part of Table 12-1, the *Type I error* rate, or alpha level, usually set at .05, represents the probability of making this kind of error. If the statistical test indicates no effect of the independent variable — that is, alpha is greater than .05 — there is also a probability that the independent variable would have had an effect in the population, but, due to error, that effect was not found in the research sample. As shown in the bottom part of Table 12-1, the error caused by incorrectly concluding that the independent variable had no effect is called a *Type II error*; the probability of a Type II error is represented by beta, which, like alpha, can range from 0 to 1. **Statistical power,** represented by 1 − beta, is therefore the probability of correctly deciding that an independent variable had no effect. In other words, if a statistical test has insufficient power, it is possible to erroneously conclude that the independent variable had no effect on the dependent variable. You therefore must have high statistical power in order to avoid false negative results.

The power of a statistical test depends on several factors, including the alpha level chosen for the test, the size of the effect that the independent variable has on the dependent variable, and the size of the research sample. This discussion will assume that alpha equals .05 and that an independent variable can have a small, or medium, or large effect. The operational definition of effect size depends on the statistical test, but we will consider a small effect to be equivalent to a correlation of .10 between the independent and dependent variables, a medium effect to be equivalent to a correlation of .30, and a large effect to be equivalent to a correlation of .50 (J. Cohen, 1988). Unfortu-

TABLE 12-1   Type I and Type II Errors

A Type I error is erroneously concluding that an independent variable had an effect; a Type II error is erroneously concluding that an independent variable *did not* have an effect.

	REAL EFFECT OF THE INDEPENDENT VARIABLE	
	Relationship	*No Relationship*
Conclusion Drawn From Data		
Relationship	Correct decision	Type I error (probability = alpha)
No relationship	Type II error (probability = beta)	Correct decision

nately, much behavioral science research has inadequate statistical power. For example, J. S. Rossi (1990) found that research published in four major psychology journals in 1982 had an average statistical power of only .17 for small effects, .57 for medium effects, and .83 for large effects. This means that if an independent variable has only a small effect on a dependent variable, researchers are not detecting that effect 83% of the time, and when an independent variable has a medium effect, researchers are not detecting it 43% of the time.

DETERMINING SAMPLE SIZE   One way for researchers to improve the likelihood of detecting the effect of an independent variable is by conducting high-power research; one way of increasing power is to ensure an adequate sample size. In order to determine sample size, ask four questions. First, what effect size are you trying to detect with your research? This target effect size is the **critical effect size** (Kraemer & Thiemann, 1987). There are several approaches to answering this question. One approach is to decide on the smallest effect you consider important to the theory or application your research is testing. For example, if you set your critical effect size at $r = .25$ using this approach, you are saying that any correlation smaller than .25 is equivalent to a correlation of zero for the purpose of answering your research question. Minimum critical effect sizes can be important in applied research because an intervention (that is, an independent variable) that doesn't have a certain minimum impact might not be cost effective to implement. A second approach to deciding on the critical effect size is to use the average effect size found in previous research using your independent and dependent variables. A form of literature reviewing discussed in Chapter 16, called a *meta-analysis*, calculates mean effect sizes for bodies of research. If no meta-analysis has been published, you could conduct one yourself. Finally, lacking any theoretical, applied, or empirical basis for setting a critical effect size, you could simply use a medium effect size and probably be all right. Lipsey (1990) found that the average effect size found across 186 meta-analyses of research on mental health and educational interventions fell right in the middle of the medium range.

The second question to ask is, What alpha level will I use? The smaller the alpha (for example, .01 versus .05), the lower the statistical power will be and the larger the sample you will need to achieve a given level of power. By convention, most research sets alpha at .05. The third question is, Will I use a one-tailed or two-tailed statistical test? A one-tailed looks for either a positive relationship between the independent and dependent variables or a negative relationship, but not for both simultaneously. A two-tailed test looks for both. Use of a one- or two-tailed test depends on whether you have a directional or nondirectional hypothesis (see Chapter 4). A two-tailed test has less power than a one-tailed test, and so requires a larger sample size to achieve a given level of power. The final question is, What level of power do I want? Generally speaking, the higher the power, the better. One would certainly want power to exceed .50, giving a better than 50% chance of detecting an effect; J. Cohen (1992) suggests a level of .80.

To give you an idea about the relationship between sample size and statistical power, Table 12-2 gives the minimum total sample sizes needed to detect small, medium, and large effects at three levels of power. The table assumes that alpha equals .05, that two-tailed tests are used for t and r (ANOVA uses only a one-tailed test), and that there are equal group sizes for the t test and ANOVA. Notice that a reasonable level of

TABLE 12-2   Sample Sizes for Three Levels of Statistical Power for Detecting Small, Medium, and Large Effects of an Independent Variable for Alpha = .05

t Test (2-tailed)[a]

	POWER		
	.7	.8	.9
Small effect	620	786	1052
Medium effect	100	128	170
Large effect	40	52	68

Correlation Coefficient (2-tailed)

	POWER		
	.7	.8	.9
Small effect	616	783	1046
Medium effect	66	84	112
Large effect	23	28	37

2 × 2 ANOVA[a]

	POWER		
	.7	.8	.9
Small effect	884	1096	1446
Medium effect	144	180	232
Large effect	60	72	92

Note: Small effect is equivalent to a correlation of .10, medium effect to a correlation of .30, and large effect to a correlation of .50. Adapted from J. Cohen, 1988.

[a] Numbers indicate total sample size (not number per group) and assume equal-size groups.

statistical power for a small effect requires an extremely large sample. Therefore, it might not be very useful to test independent variables that are likely to have small effects when there are not a large number of potential participants. The sample sizes in Table 12-2 are taken from a book by J. Cohen (1988) that contains sample size tables for a variety of statistical tests, a wide range of critical effect sizes, and a wide range of power levels (see also J. Cohen, 1992).

A sample of a particular size represents a tradeoff between ease of data collection (smaller samples are easier to deal with in terms of time and money than are larger samples) and protection against making a Type II error (larger samples provide more protection than do smaller samples). Kraemer and Thiemann (1987) summarized these tradeoffs in terms of what they called six "facts of life":

- The more stringent the significance level, the greater the necessary sample size. More subjects are needed for a 1 percent level test than for a 5 percent level test.

- Two-tailed tests require larger sample sizes than one-tailed tests. Assessing two directions at the same time requires a greater investment.

- The smaller the critical effect size, the larger the necessary sample size. Subtle effects require greater efforts.

- The larger the power required, the larger the necessary sample size. Greater protection from failure requires greater effort.

- The smaller the sample size, the smaller the power, i.e., the greater the chance of failure. . . .

- If one proposes to [use] a sample size of 20 or fewer subjects, one must be willing to take a high risk of failure, or be operating in an area in which the critical effect size is large indeed. (p. 27)

RESEARCH PROCEDURES

Previous chapters have discussed several aspects of the mechanics of research: measuring variables (Chapter 5), controlling threats to internal validity (Chapter 6), manipulating variables (Chapter 7), and issues in conducting research in natural settings (Chapter 10). This section looks at some additional aspects of carrying out a study, which did not fit neatly into other chapters: the characteristics of effective research settings, effective instructions for participants, "debugging" the research procedures, running a data collection session, the postexperimental interview, and supervising research assistants.

Effective Research Settings

An effective research setting is one that contributes to the validity of the data collected in it. Chapter 10 discussed some characteristics of an effective setting for field research; let us look now at four factors that contribute to the effectiveness of any research setting, be it a laboratory or field setting: coherence, simplicity, psychological involvement, and consistency (Aronson, Ellsworth, Carlsmith, & Gonzales, 1990).

COHERENCE   A coherent research setting is one that participants experience as a smooth, logical flow of events, all of which are focused on the purpose of the research. Participants must understand how each event they experience, such as performing a task or filling out a questionnaire, is related to the purpose of the research as it has been explained to them. I say, "as it has been explained to them," because if the research procedures involve deception, the events must appear to be related to the cover story that explained the research to the participants. A lack of understanding or feelings of ambiguity about their experience will raise participants' levels of anxiety and start them wondering about what is happening to them. These feelings and thoughts will distract participants from what the researcher wants them to think, feel, or do, and so threaten the validity of their responses. For the same reason, the researcher should keep participants' attention focused on the task at hand and not bring up side issues, such as by giving a well-focused explanation of the research task and then saying something along the lines of "Oh, by the way, we're also interested in how this relates to X." If X is important, it should be fully integrated into the explanation; if unimportant, it should not be mentioned to the participants.

The exception to maintaining a smooth flow of events throughout a data collection session is when a planned disruption is part of the research. Latané and Darley (1970), for example, investigated the variables related to people's responses to emergencies by arranging for a simulated emergency to interrupt what participants thought was an experiment on some other topic. In this case, the disruption was intended to ensure the participants' complete psychological involvement in the research, a characteristic of effective research settings that will be discussed shortly.

SIMPLICITY   The apocryphal philosopher Murphy is credited with formulating one of life's most basic laws: "Anything that can possibly go wrong, will go wrong." A corollary to that law is that the more complex something is, the more there is that can, and so will, go wrong. Consequently, it is wise to keep research settings and the events that take place in them as simple as possible. For example, don't use complicated electronic or mechanical apparatus for data collection when more simple means are available—it might make research participants nervous, and equipment failure means loss of data. Don't use complex social manipulations involving several confederates when simple alternatives are possible—if one confederate blows his or her lines or fails to show up for a research session, those data are lost. In addition, a complex set of events or a complex explanation of the study is likely to be confusing, and therefore distracting, to research participants. Aronson et al. (1990) propose a rule for testing the simplicity of a research setting: "Pretest the experimental rationale and procedure on one's friends; if they react with blank stares, it is unlikely that a subject will be able to follow it, and some revision is in order" (p. 186).

PSYCHOLOGICAL INVOLVEMENT   An effective research setting arouses and engages participants' interest in what is happening to them and what they are doing; it gets them fully involved psychologically. Lack of involvement leads participants into distraction and boredom, resulting in low motivation and lack of validity in response to the independent variable. One way to make research involving is to make it realistic; this is one reason for using field settings even for experimental research. However, Aronson and Carlsmith (1968) distinguished between two forms of realism in research. A research setting has **experimental realism** if it leads participants to become psychologically involved in what is happening, if it forces them to take things seriously, and if it has an impact on them. A research setting has **mundane realism** if the events occurring in the setting are likely to occur in some natural setting. As Chapter 14 shows, many researchers consider mundane realism important to the generalizability of research results. However, Aronson and Carlsmith do not consider mundane realism sufficient for the creation of an effective research setting. As they see it, "The mere fact that an event is similar to events that occur in the real world does not endow it with importance. Many events that occur in the real world are boring and unimportant. Thus it is possible to put a subject to sleep if an event is high on mundane realism but remains low on experimental realism" (p. 22).

Mundane and experimental realism are independent concepts: A research situation might be high on both, low on both, or high on one but low on the other. For example, Milgram's (1974) obedience experiments, described in Chapter 3, were low on mundane realism (people are almost never asked to give severe electrical shocks to other people) but high on experimental realism (participants' psychological involve-ment in the research setting was shown by their stressful reactions to giving the shocks). Conversely, Wegner, Wenzloff, Kerker, and Beattie (1981) manipulated their indepen-dent variable by having participants read fictitious newspaper headlines, undoubtedly a realistic and mundane task, but one not likely to capture people's interest to a great de-gree. Much research on memory has been conducted by having research participants memorize nonsense syllables, a task that is neither part of daily life nor likely to be very psychologically involving. In contrast, consider Murray's (1963) research in which col-lege students took part in a discussion with a confederate posing as another student who challenged the participants to defend their cherished values and personal philosophies of life. Such an experience is both highly involving and likely to happen either in class or in discussions with other students, and it is therefore high on both experimental and mundane realism.

You have probably noticed that achieving a high degree of experimental realism can be at odds with the principle of simplicity. Milgram's (1974) research, for example, used both a complex scenario involving a researcher, one or more confederates and a real participant, and a fair amount of complex apparatus—a phony shock generator, a signaling system, tape recorders, hidden data recorders, and, in some experiments, an intercom system. Here, as in other aspects of research design, you must decide on the appropriate tradeoff between two at least somewhat incompatible but desirable charac-teristics: Is the degree of experimental realism gained by an increase in complexity worth the increased likelihood of things going awry and the attendant loss of data? One way to assess the tradeoff is by conducting detailed rehearsals and pilot studies, discussed later in this chapter.

Although experimental realism and participant involvement are important, Aron-son et al. (1990) point out that participants should not be so involved in the situation that they overlook the independent variable: "For example, if the experimenter wants to arouse aggression in a subject by having an obnoxious confederate deliver an inordi-nate amount of distracting stimulation while the subject is working on a task, the task [should not be] so exciting and absorbing that the subject will . . . disregard the noxious stimuli" (p. 187).

CONSISTENCY Finally, a good research setting provides a consistent experience for each research participant. Everyone has the same experience up to the point at which the in-dependent variable is introduced so that everyone is in the same psychological state be-fore being introduced to their condition of the independent variable. This consistency of pre-manipulation experience minimizes situational variables as possible sources of extraneous variance in the dependent variable, making the effect of the independent variable easier to detect. Each participant must also have the same experience within their condition of the independent variable, thereby ensuring the reliability of the ma-nipulation, which contributes to its construct validity. Unreliable manipulations, like unreliable measures, contain a high degree of random error and so are less likely to be valid representations of the hypothetical construct that the experimenter is trying to manipulate. Consistency can be achieved by developing detailed scripts for the proce-dures in each condition of the independent variable, carefully rehearsing experimenters and confederates, and by monitoring their performance during data collection. As noted in Chapter 10, field research trades off some of this consistency for an increase in naturalism.

Effective Instructions

Instructions to research participants are an essential component of research. Instructions orient participants to what will happen during the data collection session, tell them how to perform research tasks and how to complete self-report measures, and can be used to manipulate the independent variable. To meet these goals effectively, instructions must be clear, must get and hold participants' attention, and must be accompanied by procedures that check participants' understanding of the instructions.

BE CLEAR   When writing instructions, whether they are to be delivered orally or in writing, strive to be as clear, complete, and simple as possible. One way to increase participants' understanding of instructions is through repetition. Butler (1986; Butler & Jones, 1986) found that repetition of instructions dramatically improved research participants' ability to correctly perform a variety of research tasks. A single presentation of instructions resulted in an average error rate of 55%, two presentations reduced the error rate to 26%, and three reduced it to 10%; further repetition resulted in no increase in performance accuracy. Examples also help. Butler and Jones (1986), using a difficult task, found that one presentation of instructions without an example resulted in an 80% error rate, whereas the error rate was 40% when an example was included. The clarity of instructions can be validated with Aronson et al.'s (1990) "blank stare" test: Read them to friends; if you get blank stares in return, you need to revise the instructions.

GET PARTICIPANTS' ATTENTION   Getting and holding participants' attention involves the same behaviors as getting and holding attention in any conversation: maintaining eye contact, speaking clearly, emphatically, and fluently, and speaking with an appropriate degree of animation. In other words, *talk* to the participants, don't merely read to them from a script in a monotone, and don't mumble or stumble over unfamiliar words and phrases. The more familiar you are with the instructions, the easier it is to deliver them in a natural, conversational manner. Therefore, always rehearse instructions until you are thoroughly familiar with them and can deliver them clearly.

CHECK PARTICIPANTS' UNDERSTANDING   Don't assume that participants understand even the best-designed and best-presented instructions; always check to ensure their understanding. At a minimum, solicit questions. However, don't say, "Do you have any questions?" or worse, "You don't have any questions, do you?" Such inquiries invite a "No" response. It's better to ask, "What questions do you have?" which implies that it is reasonable to have questions and that you expect them. When the instructions are complex, it is useful for the experimenter to ask questions of the participants to check their understanding or to ask them to perform the research task to demonstrate their understanding. Probes of this nature should focus on aspects of the instructions that are likely to be particularly troublesome to participants. These problem areas can be identified during pilot testing, to be discussed shortly.

"Debugging" the Procedure

"Debugging" is a term coined by computer programmers for the process of finding errors or "bugs" in programs. The term has been borrowed by researchers to refer to the process of finding problems in research procedures. Debugging is accomplished in three steps: the research proposal, rehearsal, and pilot studies.

THE RESEARCH PROPOSAL   The research proposal is a detailed discussion of the background and hypotheses for a piece of research and a detailed description of the procedures to be used in testing the hypotheses (see Chapter 4). The debugging process starts by having colleagues read the proposal with an eye to finding any problems that the researcher overlooked. Colleagues might note problems in the derivation of hypotheses, they might be able to suggest important extraneous variables the researcher overlooked, they might know of better operational definitions, or they might be aware of problems with the materials or apparatus that the researcher intends to use. Colleagues' suggestions on these and other potential problem areas can be used to fix the problems before time and effort are expended in setting up the research.

REHEARSAL   Once the research procedure looks good on paper, it's time to try it out in practice, using rehearsals or "dry runs" that do not include research participants. It can be useful to think of data collection as a stage play with the research procedure as the script. As with a theatrical rehearsal, the research rehearsal should proceed as if it were the real thing, with the researcher giving instructions out loud, walking around the room distributing questionnaires, operating equipment, and so forth, and with confederates playing their roles, all as specified in the research procedures. Rehearsals provide the researcher with practice so that data collection sessions proceed smoothly and with the opportunity to find procedural problems not apparent in the research proposal. For example, as a graduate student I once worked as an experimenter on a project that required me to operate two pieces of equipment simultaneously. This was not a problem in itself, because it was easy to operate each device with one hand. However, when I started rehearsing the procedure, I found that the laboratory was arranged (from a previous research project) so that the two pieces of equipment were 10 feet apart! Needless to say, the experiment was put on hold until I could rearrange the lab. Rehearsals should continue until the entire procedure runs smoothly without any "blown lines," forgotten "stage business," overlooked "props," or other disruptions.

PILOT STUDIES   A **pilot study** is a preliminary piece of research conducted with a sample of research participants drawn from the study population. Pilot studies can be used for several purposes. First, they can consist of observational or correlational research conducted to determine if it would be worth the time and effort to conduct an experiment. For example, recall Middlemist, Knowles, and Matter's (1976) study of the effect of invasions of personal space in men's rooms on anxiety, described in Chapter 3. Before they designed their rather complex experiment involving both a confederate and a hidden observer, they conducted an observational study to determine if naturally occurring invasions of personal space were correlated with latency of urination. Because the correlational data were consistent with their hypothesis, they went ahead with an experimental test of the causal role of personal space invasion. The pilot study also gave the researchers the opportunity to interview participants to determine the participants' feelings about being observed under such circumstances.

Second, pilot studies can be conducted to test the validity of experimental manipulations. The dependent variable in such pilot studies is a measure of the hypothetical construct that the researchers want their manipulation to affect. Recall, for example, C. Seligman, Finegan, Hazlewood, and Wilkinson's (1985) pizza delivery study described in Chapter 10. They intended their explanations of why the delivery driver was early or late to manipulate customers' perceptions of whether the early or late delivery was due to the actions of the driver or due to situational factors. They tested the effectiveness of the manipulation by approaching people in their university's library and asking them to rate the explanations as to whether they appeared to reflect characteristics of the delivery driver or of the situation. Because this pilot manipulation check supported the validity of their procedure, they used it in their study.

Finally, pilot studies are conducted as a final test of research procedures prior to beginning data collection. Such pilot studies are useful because the researcher can solicit the participants' cooperation in the process by telling them at the outset that they are assisting in a test of the research procedures and asking them to note any aspects of the procedures they find difficult to understand and any tasks they find difficult to perform. The researcher can also interrupt the course of events at various points to collect information from participants. For example, the researcher can give pilot participants the instructions for the study and then ask if they have any difficulty in understanding what they are to do or in carrying out the instructions. Pilot studies can also help to detect any demand characteristics present in the research setting or procedures—aspects of the setting or procedures that "push" participants to respond, or to avoid responding, in certain ways. For example, Aronson et al. (1990) describe a pilot study for an experiment in which college students were asked to look at photographs of three men and pick out the one who was Jewish:

> Subjects became upset, arguing that it was impossible to recognize Jews on the basis of appearance. . . . On the basis of the information gained from these pilot subjects, the experimenters changed the test so that the subjects were asked to pick out schizophrenics rather than Jews, and from then on the experiment ran smoothly. (p. 234)

When such problems arise in a pilot study, ask the participants for suggestions on how to improve the clarity of the instructions or the nature of a problematic task. You can also develop probes to test participants' understanding of instructions for problem areas that cannot be changed.

Pilot studies also give the researcher an opportunity to determine whether the participants are interpreting things as intended. For example, does a questionnaire item have the same meaning to them as to the researcher? Ross and Allgeier (1996), for example, found that male college students interpreted some items on a frequently used sexual experiences questionnaire to have as many as six possible meanings each, some of which were contradictory. For instance, 37% of the participants interpreted the question "Have you ever had a women misinterpret the level of sexual intimacy you desired?" to mean the woman overestimated the man's desired level of sexual contact and 25% interpreted it to mean underestimation of the desired level of contact.

Participants might also interpret the procedures used to manipulate the independent variable in a different way from that intended by the researcher, resulting in an invalid manipulation. For example, Dane (1990) tells of a study he was conducting in which he wanted to see if physiological arousal affected men's perceptions of women's attractiveness. He manipulated arousal by sitting either 3 inches from the participants in the high-arousal condition or across the room from participants in the low-arousal condition. He got what seemed to be very strange results that made it appear that participants in the high-arousal condition were not paying attention to the photographs they were supposed to be rating. Therefore, as Dane (1990) tells the story,

> I called some of [the participants], interviewed them, and discovered that indeed many of them were not concentrating on the women in the photograph. It seems that my results were caused by the participants' beliefs about what was being studied. Most of the participants in the high arousal condition thought that because I was sitting very close to them, I was studying some aspect of homosexuality. They admitted to completing the ratings as quickly as they could so that they could get out of the room. (p. 210)

Pilot studies also let researchers know how much time is required for the research tasks and the data collection session as a whole. Researchers might find, for example, that a task takes participants more time to complete than was anticipated, so the research session must be lengthened. To fit a research session into their schedules, participants must be informed well in advance of the total time they will be asked to donate. Total time is also important when participants come from subject pools. In such circumstances, students are often given credit for research participation in terms of the amount of time they contribute; researchers have an obligation to these students to provide the correct amount of credit.

The last few sessions of the final pilot study conducted should function as "dress rehearsals" for the data collection sessions. As in a theatrical dress rehearsal, these sessions should be conducted without interruption except to answer participants' questions. These complete run-throughs allow a final smoothing of the rough edges of the procedures.

A common question that arises concerning pilot studies is that of the number of research participants to include. There is no absolute answer to this question; it depends on the goal of a particular study. If you are doing preliminary observational work, as Middlemist et al. (1976) did, or checking the validity of a manipulation, as C. Seligman et al. (1985) did, you want to have enough data to provide enough statistical power to be able to have confidence in your results. The number of participants therefore depends on the minimum effect size that you consider important for your goal. When collecting information from participants to improve procedures, you should probably keep collecting data and modifying procedures until participant comments indicate that no additional substantial improvements can be made. Finally, dress rehearsals should continue until the experimenter and any confederates can play their roles with minimal error.

In planning a research project, be sure to budget sufficient time for pilot studies. Let me emphasize the plural—*studies*, not just one study. Piloting is an iterative process: A problem is identified, a fix is implemented, and then the new procedure must be tested. A number of iterations of the process might be required before the entire procedure runs smoothly.

The Data Collection Session

In this section, I just want to remind you about some aspects of conducting a data collection session. First, be sure to dress neatly. A "power suit" is not required, but at the other extreme, a dirty sweatshirt and tattered blue jeans hardly present a professional appearance. People do judge you by the clothes you wear, and if your attire does not convey to participants the impression that you consider the research to be serious business, they will not take it seriously either. Next, be sure to arrive at the research site, be it a laboratory, a classroom, or some other setting, completely prepared to conduct the research. If you are using questionnaires, check the number on hand sufficiently far in advance (several days, if necessary) to ensure that you have enough available for your participants. Don't forget to bring enough pencils and, if they are used, answer sheets. If you are using any apparatus, such as a polygraph, get to the research site early enough to thoroughly test the equipment and to calibrate it, add paper or ink, and take care of any other routine maintenance before the participants arrive.

Finally, be sure to treat your research participants politely, unless the experimental manipulation calls for something else. Remember, these people are donating their time to help you with your research. Greet all your participants, answer their questions completely and courteously (even questions about things you've already covered several times), and thank them when their participation ends. Never let a data collection session run over the allotted time; your participants probably have other obligations. If you can't make a scheduled session, notify your participants as far in advance as possible if you have their telephone numbers or electronic mail addresses. Otherwise, arrange to have someone meet them at the research site and explain the problem. At a minimum, have someone leave a polite note. If participants were to receive some form of credit, be sure to inform them how to obtain it. In short, treat your research participants as you would like to be treated in the same circumstances.

The Postexperimental Interview

At the close of a data collection session, the researcher should conduct a **postexperimental interview** with the participants. This interview has four functions: ethical, educational, methodological, and discovery. This section will examine each of these functions and then outline a procedure for the interview.

THE ETHICAL FUNCTION   As discussed in Chapter 3, the researcher has a number of ethical obligations to research participants after data collection. Two of these obligations are fulfilled as part of the postexperimental interview. First, the researcher must alleviate any adverse effects of the research, such as by reassuring participants whose self-esteem may have been threatened by the research procedures. Second, if deception was used, the researcher must debrief the participants, explaining the nature of the deception and the reasons for it. You might want to go back and review the section in Chapter 3 on debriefing to refresh your memory on these topics.

THE EDUCATIONAL FUNCTION   As noted in Chapter 3, the researchers' postresearch ethical obligations include educating research participants about the nature of research in general and of the research in which they participated in particular. Because this educational benefit is frequently the only direct benefit received by participants drafted from subject pools, researchers have a special obligation to those participants. Sieber (1992) suggests that the educational function of the postexperimental interview include

> a brief, nontechnical presentation on (a) the purpose of the study, (b) the relation of the purpose to the condition(s) in which subjects participated, (c) what is known about the problem and what hypotheses are being tested, (d) the dependent and independent variables, and (e) why the study is of theoretical or practical importance. At this time, subjects also might be given a one- or two-page description of the topic and the research, expanding on what they had already been told. (pp. 40–41)

The researchers should also solicit questions about the explanation, make themselves available to participants who want to discuss the research further, and provide the name and telephone number of someone to call if they have questions later. Not all research participants, especially those who take part in studies using group-administered questionnaires, will be motivated to stay and listen to an oral presentation about the research. In this and other cases of minimal-risk research, a handout might be sufficient to meet the educational obligation.

Although researchers generally believe that they present good debriefings, participants frequently complain that debriefings are inadequate. They say that the debriefings they have experienced were too brief, difficult to understand, used terms that were unfamiliar to them, and did not put the research into a context understandable to them, such as the potential applications of the research results (Brody, Gluck, & Aragon, 2000). Brody et al. also found that participants reported that the researchers treated the debriefing process as a burdensome obligation rather than as an opportunity to educate participants and that the researchers appeared to be uninterested in answering questions. Therefore, regardless of whether the debriefing is oral or written, pretest it with colleagues and pilot study participants to ensure that it is clear and complete, present it in a professional manner, and be sure to encourage participants to ask questions.

THE METHODOLOGICAL FUNCTION   The postexperimental interview can be used to administer manipulation checks, and to assess the degree to which participants were affected by demand characteristics or misperceptions of the research situation or were suspicious about any deceptions that were used. Although pilot studies can provide researchers with information about the effectiveness of their manipulations in general, manipulation checks conducted after a research session can assess their effectiveness for individual participants. What is effective for most people will not necessarily be effective for all people. Chapter 6 discussed demand characteristics and noted that they can reduce the validity of participants' responses. Misperceptions of the purpose of the research can also reduce response validity, as illustrated by Dane's (1990) experience, cited earlier. To the extent that participants are suspicious of deception, feeling that something is "not right" about the research situation, the manipulation of the independent variable is invalid.

The postexperimental interview can therefore help the researcher sort out effective research sessions—in which everything went as intended—from ineffective sessions in which something went wrong. What should you do about data from "spoiled" sessions?

If the postexperimental interview suggests that the manipulation of the independent variable did not work as intended, then you should probably discard the data from that session. However, if data from a substantial number of participants must be discarded on this basis — say, more than 20% — there may be something wrong with the design of the research, and you should try to find alternative designs that are less susceptible to demand characteristics, misperceptions, or suspiciousness. Aronson et al. (1990) recommend that researchers set specific criteria for excluding participants' data before data collection begins to ensure objectivity in the process. For example, decide in advance the factors that indicate if research participants are unduly suspicious of a deception.

THE DISCOVERY FUNCTION   Postexperimental discussions with research participants can sometimes suggest new hypotheses to researchers or lead them to look at old hypotheses in new ways. Dane (1990), for example, tells of how his participants' mistaken belief that his research dealt with homosexuality led him to begin a research project investigating people's responses to others whom they believe are homosexual. While conducting research on learning, C. J. Martin (cited in Christensen, 2001) found that some of his participants could memorize a list of nonsense syllables in one try — a highly unusual feat. When he asked them during postexperimental interviews how they were able to do it, they described a specific learning strategy that C. J. Martin, Boersma, and Cox (1965) investigated in a follow-up study. It is always useful to find out what your participants think about your research and the hypotheses you are testing; unencumbered by the blinders of accepted theory and methodology, they can provide new and useful insights.

CONDUCTING THE INTERVIEW   These four functions are integrated into three steps that make up the postexperimental interview (Aronson et al., 1990). These steps are outlined here; Aronson et al. (1990) and J. Mills (1976) provide detailed guidance. The first step is probing for effects of demand characteristics, suspiciousness, and misperception. Aronson et al. (1990) suggest that this step proceed by using three increasingly specific questions. First, ask participants what questions they have about the study or the procedures used. Participants' questions can give hints about problems that the researcher can pursue with his or her own questions. The answers to the participants' questions should be complete and truthful, thereby contributing to the educational function. Next, the researcher should specifically ask if the participant "found any aspect of the procedure odd, confusing, or disturbing" (Aronson et al., 1990, p. 316). If this probe does not bring out any problems, then the researcher can ask, "Do you think that there may have been more to this experiment than meets the eye?" (p. 316). Aronson et al. point out that almost everyone will answer yes to this kind of question (it is obviously high on demand characteristics). Therefore, you must be careful to sort out problems that are plausible, given the nature of the research, from responses that a participant might make to give a socially desirable answer to the question.

Participants' responses to these probes can be used as a lead-in to the second step, explaining the research. If deception is used, the explanation will combine the ethical function of debriefing with the educational function of providing participants with information about the research (J. Mills, 1976). As already noted, in nondeceptive research, the oral explanation can be brief and supplemented with a handout.

The third step is soliciting participants' help in improving the research. Ask them for their comments on and criticisms of the research; as already mentioned, these comments can suggest topics for future research and may reveal methodological problems that have not yet come out in the interview. Aronson et al. (1990) note that this procedure can allow participants to voice qualms about the procedure or any deception that was used; you can then take further steps to alleviate these negative feelings. Finally, ask the participants not to discuss the research with anyone who might take part in it. As discussed in Chapter 6, knowledge of hypotheses or procedures can lead to reactivity and invalidate participants' responses. Explain the reasons for confidentiality clearly and completely; such candor both educates participants about the problems of research and motivates them to comply with the request. The effectiveness of such requests is a matter of some debate (Aronson et al., 1990), but Aronson et al. suggest that some of the noncompliance problem can be alleviated by telling participants what they *can* say if friends ask them about their research experience. For example, the experimenter could tell participants that they can describe the research task or some other superficial aspect of the procedure. Giving participants something explicit to say, such as "I watched a videotape and filled out a questionnaire about what I saw," spares them the embarrassment of having to give friends an evasive response, such as "I'd prefer not to discuss it." It also relieves them of the problem of having to invent an uninformative description of the experiment.

If two or more participants take part in the same research session, Aronson et al. (1990) recommend that they be interviewed separately. They note that it is difficult to assess two people's reactions simultaneously, thus leaving the door open to the researcher's missing a crucial word, gesture, or tone of voice. Also, someone might feel inhibited about asking a question or voicing a concern that the other people being interviewed don't mention. In addition, in deception experiments participants might be embarrassed by being dehoaxed, and perhaps in their minds being made to look foolish, in front of a peer. Finally, although we have been discussing the postexperimental interview in terms of a face-to-face interaction, written questionnaires can also play a role, especially as a starting point for further discussion. Questionnaires, especially anonymous questionnaires, can also allow participants to make comments that they might be reluctant to bring up in a face-to-face conversation. For example, politeness might inhibit someone from saying something along the lines of "That was the stupidest cover story imaginable" in an interview, but the person might feel freer to express critical comments in writing. Candor can be enhanced by having someone not associated with the experiment, such as a departmental secretary or office assistant, administer and collect the questionnaire.

Research Assistants

So far, our discussion of research procedures has assumed that you, the person who designed the study, will be the person who collects the data. Sometimes, however, you might have research assistants who collect data for you. If so, you will be responsible for your assistants' training in preparation for data collection and for how they treat research participants. In training your assistants, you must ensure that they are completely

BOX 12-1   Guidelines for Supervising Research Assistants

- Set clear goals and objectives, such as the number of data collection sessions each assistant will conduct during a semester.

- Set clear expectations for behavior, such as dress, punctuality, and interactions with research participants.

- Clearly define each person's role in the research process, such as who collects data, who enters data, who analyzes data, who supervises whom, and so forth.

- Compile a laboratory manual that explains policies and procedures, give one to each assistant, and hold a meeting to check their understanding of its contents and to answer questions. Malfese et al. (1996) provide a sample outline for a lab manual.

- Have a system for communicating with and among assistants. A periodic meeting can be very useful.

- Being a researcher will be a new (and perhaps stressful) role for most assistants, so monitor them carefully for signs of uncertainty or stress and provide appropriate guidance.

- Be alert for signs of conflicts between assistants, and take immediate action to resolve them.

- Provide assistants with periodic performance feedback so that they know what they are doing correctly and incorrectly. Provide corrective feedback tactfully.

Source: Adapted from Malfese et al. (1996).

familiar with the research equipment and procedures and are able to answer participants' questions. It can be useful for you to take the role of research participant and have your assistants collect data from you. This procedure lets you both assess your assistants' levels of training and, by looking at the study from a participant's point of view, catch any unforeseen problems with the procedures and materials. Also, ask your assistants any questions that participants might bring up so that you can see how well your assistants can answer them. You might also want to create problems for your assistants, such as by hiding a stopwatch left on a table, to see how well they can deal with unanticipated "glitches."

When your assistants interact with research participants in pilot studies and during data collection, you should monitor their performance, both to ensure that they are following the correct research procedures and to ensure that they are treating participants courteously. It is best to do this directly, such as by sitting in the corner of the room when a group-administered questionnaire is being administered or by observing through a one-way mirror. If direct observation is not possible, you could interview research participants about your assistants' behavior after explaining your supervisory role or by using a questionnaire. Make these assessments fairly frequently at the outset of data collection and periodically thereafter.

When discussing your observations with your assistants, be sure that your feedback is constructive. Be polite, point out what they did well in addition to any problems you noted, and give them specific guidelines for improving their performance. Always bear in mind that in this situation you are a teacher as well as a researcher, so you have an obligation to provide your assistants with an effective learning experience. Box 12-1 provides some guidelines for supervising research assistants.

USING THE INTERNET TO COLLECT DATA

Researchers are constantly looking for ways to collect data from a wide range of participants at minimal cost. The Internet (or World Wide Web) is quickly becoming a medium for doing so. When the first edition of this book was published in 1996, almost no research was being conducted over the Internet, although a few researchers had used electronic mail (e-mail) to distribute surveys (Krantz & Dalal, 2000). In contrast, on June 1, 2000, the American Psychological Society's Web page that lists studies being conducted on the Internet (http://psych.hanover.edu/APS/exponnet.html) contained links to 86 sites, some of which had multiple studies in progress. These studies covered a wide range of topics in psychology, including neuropsychology, cognition, personality, sensation and perception, and social psychology. Internet research can take a variety of forms, for example, experiments (Senior, Phillips, Barnes, & David, 1999), using known groups to test the validity of personality measures (Buchanan & Smith, 1999a), attitude and behavior surveys (Bailey, Foote, & Throckmorton, 2000), participant and nonparticipant observation (Sharf, 1997), and focus groups (Gaiser, 1997).

Following a brief introduction to the ways in which researchers can collect data over the Internet, this section presents some of the issues involved in using the Internet for data collection: the advantages of Web-based research, participant recruitment over the Web, the validity of data collected over the Internet, and ethical issues in Internet research. This section will not deal with programming and other technical issues; those are well covered in two books by Birnbaum (2000b, 2000c).

Forms of Internet Data Collection

Internet research has taken three basic forms. In the first form, a researcher uses e-mail to send surveys to potential research participants; the participants then return their responses via e-mail. For example, Parks and Floyd (1996) surveyed members of on-line discussion groups to investigate the characteristics of people who formed on-line friendships. This approach gives the researcher no control over how the respondent completes the questionnaire (such as the order in which the questions are answered). It can also arouse negative reactions in recipients who view unsolicited messages as electronic junk mail ("spam" in Internet jargon) and provides little anonymity for respondents unless special precautions are taken because their e-mail addresses are attached to their replies (Cho & LaRose, 1999).

The second form of Internet research has potential participants come to a Web site where they first see a page that describes the research, after which they move on to a page on which they give informed consent to participate. Participants then go to pages where the data are collected in the form of either a survey or an experiment, followed by a debriefing page. For example, Bailey et al. (2000) used this method to collect data on sexual attitudes and behavior and on variables hypothesized to be related to those attitudes and behaviors. This Web site–based form of research is generally preferred over e-mail surveys because it is less intrusive for participants, is more amenable to anonymous data collection (but not perfect in this regard), and gives the researcher more control over the presentation of experimental stimuli and the types of data that can be collected (Cho & LaRose, 1999; Schmidt, 1997).

The third form of Internet research is analogous to observational research: The researcher logs into a chat room or subscribes to a mailing list or bulletin board and observes users' behavior in the form of their comments and postings and their responses to others' comments and postings. For example, Sharf (1997) observed discussions of an on-line breast cancer support group to identify the types of topics discussed. As Miskevich (1996) notes, "These discussions are like a golden egg laid in the lap of the social scientist — open and candid discussions of alternative religious beliefs and behavior, discussions of different sexual proclivities, explorations of political beliefs and their expression in certain contexts" (p. 241). However, such observational research can raise ethical questions concerning invasion of privacy and voluntary participation in the research.

Advantages of Internet Research

Researchers who use the Internet to collect data have noted a number of advantages that the medium provides. These include economy and ease of data collection, accesses to nonstudent and special populations, the potential for increasing some aspects of the internal validity of research, and the public nature of the research process.

ECONOMY AND EASE OF DATA COLLECTION   Just as the introduction of the desktop computer was supposed to create the paperless office, data collection using the Internet (and data collection via computers generally) allows for paperless surveys and other forms of research. When researchers use computers to collect data there is no need for physical copies of surveys or data record forms: Participants enter their responses directly into a computer file, eliminating printing costs. Similarly, Internet surveys eliminate the postage costs of mail surveys. Furthermore, the data files can be transferred directly to the computer program used to analyze the data, thereby eliminating the errors that can creep in when data are transcribed from paper records to computer files.

Data collection over the Internet can also make data collection easier for both the researchers and the participants (Reips, 2000). Because Web pages are usually available 24 hours a day, 7 days a week, researchers do not need to schedule blocks of time for data collection. Similarly, participants can take part in the research when it is convenient for them to do so.

Internet research may be especially beneficial to researchers at small colleges and universities, where the potential number of research participants is small, and to researchers at institutions that do not have subject pool systems. Even when college student participants are readily available, many studies require collection data from one participant at a time. In such circumstances, data collection may have to be carried out over a long period of time, reducing the timeliness of the research results. In contrast, the Internet can provide a large number of participants very quickly (Smith & Leigh, 1997). As Birnbaum (2000a) reported, "Compared to my usual research, which typically takes 6 months to collect data for 100 college students, it was quite pleasant to collect 1224 sets of data in 4 months and 737 in the next 6 weeks" (p. 25).

ACCESS TO RESEARCH PARTICIPANTS   Perhaps the most common population of research participants for behavioral science research is college students (Sears, 1986). The In-

ternet allows researchers to extend their potential populations beyond the college student base. Internet research participants tend, on the average, to be older than college
students, to have more diverse educational backgrounds, and to exhibit more geographic diversity (e.g., Krantz & Dalal, 2000). In addition, purposive sampling of listservers and newsgroups can provide access to populations that are often hard to reach,
such as lesbians and gay men, people with disabilities or chronic diseases, and so forth
(Reips, 2000; Smith & Leigh, 1997). However, the costs of computers and Internet access mean that participation by members of low-income populations will be limited.

POTENTIAL FOR INCREASED INTERNAL VALIDITY   As Chapter 6 noted, demand characteristics and experimenter effects can be a problem for the internal validity of research.
However, when data are collected over the Internet, research participants do not interact with an experimenter, removing the problems that arise when experimenters
treat participants differently or inadvertently emit cues that could affect participants'
responses (Reips, 2000). Similarly, data collected in the absence of an experimenter and
other participants may be less vulnerable to social desirability response bias, especially
when the participants are confident of the anonymity and confidentiality of their responses (Binik, Mah, & Kiesler, 1999). For example, Joinson (1999) found a substantial reduction in scores on a standard measure of social desirability response bias when
college students completed the scale over the Internet compared to paper-and-pencil
administration, and Bailey et al. (2000) found that college student respondents to an
Internet survey were more likely to report sensitive behaviors, such as same-sex sexual
contact, than were college student respondents to a paper-and-pencil survey.

When data are collected by means of forms at a Web site, careful construction of
the data collection program can reduce data problems caused by participant response
errors (Schmidt, 1997). For example, the program could prompt users to answer survey
questions they had skipped. It could also screen responses and ask for correction of
seemingly out-of-range values in free-response data, such as a college student who reports being 8 years old.

Finally, Internet research participants may be more highly motivated than participants recruited through subject pools because Web participants are true volunteers, can
take part in the research in comfortable, familiar environments (such as their homes),
and can ensure their own privacy (Reips, 2000). However, Reips also notes that many
people who visit a research Web site will do so more from curiosity than from interest
in participating in research, and so may start a study but not complete it. Reips therefore offers some suggestions for discouraging people who are unlikely to complete the
study from beginning it, such as by forewarning potential participants if a study will take
more than a few minutes to complete.

PUBLIC RESEARCH METHODS   Chapter 1 noted that one of the key values of science is that
research methods are made public so that everyone can examine them and draw their
own conclusions about the validity of those methods. Reips (2000) points out that Web
research is the ultimate in public research: Anyone can visit the research site and experience for themselves exactly how those data were collected and see the exact nature
of experimental stimuli and the exact wording of survey questions. This situation stands
in sharp contrast to other forms of research, in which the reader of a research report is
(of necessity) given only a brief description of the methodology employed. Even after

data collection has been completed, the site can be maintained for a certain length of time after the results of the research have been published so that interested persons can visit it.

Disadvantages of Internet Research

Although using the Internet for research provides a number of advantages for researchers, it also has its disadvantages. These include biased participant sampling, limits on the types of experimental stimuli and response modes that can be used, lack of control over the data collection environment, participant attrition, and the potential for sabotage of the research project.

PARTICIPANT SAMPLING   Clearly, people who participate in Internet research do not constitute a random sample of the population but, like college students, are a sample who are easy to access and convenient to use in the research. However, as Smith and Leigh (1997) note, researchers are willing to accept the possible biases inherent in college student samples in exchange for easy access to research participants. Smith and Leigh go on to note that in Internet research, the bias inherent in convenience sampling is offset somewhat by access to a research population that is broader in terms of age than are college student samples. Also, research comparing the results of Internet research with the results of more traditional research (usually using college student samples) has almost always found similar results (Krantz & Dalal, 2000). These findings suggest, then, that the sampling biases in Internet research are no different than those deriving from traditional research methods. However, the costs of computers and Internet access mean that participation by members of low-income populations will be limited.

LIMITS ON EXPERIMENTAL STIMULI AND RESPONSE MODES   In the laboratory, researchers can manipulate the stimuli that participants respond to in a variety of ways, including the use of visual materials, sounds, the presence and actions of others, odors, touch, and pain. Of these, only visual and auditory stimuli can currently be presented by computers. Similarly, in the laboratory researchers can observe and measure a variety of participant responses to stimuli, including vocal and written responses, facial expressions, eye and other body movements, and behavior toward confederates. Currently, technology allows most Internet users to respond only via key presses and mouse movements. These technological limitations place severe constraints on the kinds of experimental research that can be conducted over the Internet.

LACK OF CONTROL OVER THE DATA COLLECTION ENVIRONMENT   In laboratory research, the researchers have complete control over the situations in which they collect their data. Field researchers can choose their research settings and sometimes can control the specific circumstances under which they collect their data. Internet researchers, however, have very little control over the data collection environment (Reips, 2000). Internet participants may be at home, at work, at school, or in a public library; they may be alone or with others; they may be in a tranquil setting or one replete with distractions. From a technological perspective, variations in the computer hardware and software used by research participants can cause variations in the fidelity of graphics, color, and sound reproduction (Plous, 2000; Welch & Krantz, 1996). All of these factors can affect the accuracy of the data collected.

Another control issue in Internet research derives from the lack of interaction between the researcher and the participant. Although this lack of interaction can reduce demand characteristics and experimenter effects, it also prevents participants from asking questions concerning their roles in the research. Similarly, researchers cannot query participants to determine if they understand the instructions for the study, nor can they observe participants' behavior to see if they are following the instructions (Birnbaum, 2000a; Reips, 2000). Consequently, instructions for Internet studies must be extremely clear and carefully pretested to identify and remove any sources of ambiguity and misunderstanding.

A final potential problem is that participants can, either intentionally or inadvertently, participate in a study more than once. For example, Pasveer and Ellard (1998) had one participant who submitted a questionnaire 10 times. There are several technological solutions to this problem, each of which has its advantages and disadvantages (Reips, 2000; Schmidt, 1997; Smith & Leigh, 1997). In addition, careful design of the data collection site might prevent some such problems. Pasveer and Ellard noted that participants might expect some form of feedback after submitting their data and, if no feedback occurs, resubmit the data thinking that a network error prevented the researchers' computer from receiving the data. Pasveer and Ellard therefore recommend that researchers send some type of feedback, even if only a "thank you" note, when participants submit data.

PARTICIPANT ATTRITION   The traditional research situation, in which the researcher and participant interact face-to-face, contains a number of what might be called binding factors that commit the participant to completing the study. Most of these factors — such as personally agreeing to participate in the research, being in a setting (the laboratory) that reduces distractions, the psychological if not physical presence of the researcher, and the need for course credit — are absent in much Internet research (Reips, 2000). Consequently, Internet participants may be more likely to fail to complete a study than traditional research participants: In a survey of on-line researchers, Musch and Reips (2000) found attrition rates that ranged from 1% to 87%, with an average of 34%. It is therefore very important for Internet researchers to design studies that screen out uncommitted participants and capture participants' interest (Reips, 2000).

SABOTAGE   Hackers — people who break into and modify Web sites — are an unfortunate fact of Internet life. Although many hackers are motivated by curiosity and break into computer systems just to see what is there, others are motivated by malice or a deviant sense of humor and sabotage the systems they enter. Hackers can cause two types of damage in a research Web site. They can alter experimental stimuli or survey questionnaires, undermining the validity of the independent variable, or they can modify data either as it is collected or after it is stored, undermining the validity of the dependent variables. It therefore behooves Internet researchers to ensure that all possible safeguards are in place to prevent unauthorized access to the research site and to check the site periodically to ensure that no vandalism has occurred (Hewson, Laurent, & Vogel, 1996).

Participant Recruitment

Although it might be tempting to take what could be called a *Field of Dreams* approach to recruiting participants for Internet research—"Build it [the Web site] and they will come"—a proactive approach is likely to be more productive. This section describes four methods for participant recruitment: e-mail, posting announcements to electronic mailing lists and bulletin boards, listing the research on directories, and designing the research site so that it can be easily located by search engines. It also discusses three related issues: problems of control over participant recruitment, project expiration dates, and effective Web site design.

E-MAIL SOLICITATION   The oldest form of participant recruitment is using e-mail to solicit people's participation. When e-mail first became widely available, survey researchers would send out surveys by e-mail and wait for the responses to arrive. However, response rates to e-mail surveys are generally lower than the rates for other survey media because recipients often see surveys as a form of electronic junk mail (Cho & LaRose, 1999). Also, some Internet service providers charge users for incoming as well as outgoing e-mail, so an unsolicited survey would, as Martin (1996) points out, be equivalent to sending a mail survey postage due or calling collect for a telephone survey. A more effective technique for recruiting participants is to send an e-mail message explaining the research and requesting participation; if the person agrees, a survey can then be sent. If the survey (or an experiment) is on a Web site, then the request for participation can include the site's Web address (Cho & LaRose, 1999).

How can one locate e-mail addresses for recruiting participants? Cho and LaRose (1999) discuss several methods. A technique that should be avoided is called trolling: using a computer program to gather addresses from electronic mailing lists, chat rooms, newsgroups, and personal home pages. Although this method is effective in gathering addresses, most Internet users consider it to be an unethical practice that invades their privacy. In fact, trolling is considered to be such a severe violation of Internet etiquette that some Internet service providers prohibit it under penalty of the offender's losing Internet access through that provider. Another source of addresses is public e-mail directories that operate like telephone directories of Internet users. However, people solicited through these directories may also react negatively to research solicitations because the directories advertise themselves in ways that imply that the information they contain will be used only for personal, not commercial or research, purposes. A final source of addresses is organizational e-mail lists. In contrast to surveys based on other sources of e-mail addresses, surveys of organization members can result in very respectable return rates when the topic of the survey is relevant to the mission or functioning of the organization.

ANNOUNCEMENTS   Another way to recruit participants is by posting an announcement about the research on electronic mailing lists (listservers) and bulletin boards (newsgroups). This technique is especially useful if one is trying to recruit members of specific populations because mailing lists and newsgroups are organized around specific topics (Cho & LaRose, 1999). However, because mailing list and newsgroup subscribers tend to be suspicious of what appears to be advertising, it is a good idea to get the approval of the mailing list or newsgroup moderator before posting an announcement and to mention that approval in the announcement (Michalak & Szabo, 1998; Smith & Leigh, 1997). Smith and Leigh also recommend posting notices of one's intent to recruit participants and to ask for subscribers' feedback on the appropriateness of using their mailing lists or newsgroups as sources of research participants. For announcements to be effective, they should be clearly relevant to the purpose of the group and the results should provide some potential benefit to the group (Michalak & Szabo, 1998). Because the membership of mailing lists and newsgroups is somewhat fluid, the announcement should be reposted periodically, but not so frequently as to appear intrusive. The list or group moderator can provide advice on the most appropriate posting interval (Michalak & Szabo, 1998).

LISTINGS ON RESEARCH DIRECTORIES   Participants can also be recruited by listing the research on directories of research projects such as those maintained by the American Psychological Society (http://psych.hanover.edu/APS/exponnet.html) and Yahoo! (http://dir.yahoo.com/Social_Science/Psychology/Research/Tests_and_Experiments/). The directories contain the titles and sometimes one-line descriptions of the studies listed and links to the research Web sites.

SEARCH ENGINES   A search engine is a computer program that scans the Internet for Web pages that contain key words supplied by the person conducting the search and returns links to those pages. Alta Vista, Excite, and Lycos are some of the most commonly used search engines. The likelihood of a search engine locating a research page can be enhanced by having a clearly descriptive title for the page and including key words in a META tag, which lists terms that can be read by search engines but are not visible on the page itself.

CONTROL OVER RECRUITMENT   In a traditional research project, the researcher can exert some control of the characteristics of people who participate in the research by controlling recruitment procedures. Web researchers have somewhat less control, especially when data are collected via a Web site, because anyone can find the site through a search engine even if the researchers try to limit recruitment to specific categories of people through announcements on carefully selected mailing lists and newsgroups. In addition, people other than the researchers can post the site's URL (Uniform Resource Locator, or Web page address) on other Web sites, mailing lists, and newsgroups, with the result that people other than members of targeted groups participate in the research (Birnbaum, 2000a). If a specific population is needed for the research, it is therefore advisable to screen responses, such as by asking for relevant demographic data to ensure that participants are members of the targeted groups and then use only the responses of those participants.

EXPIRATION DATES   Michalak and Szabo (1998) advise Web researchers to include an expiration date—the last date on which data will be collected—in announcements of studies. The expiration date will prevent the frustration potential participants might experience when they try to access a research site and find that it is no longer in operation. Similarly, if a site is listed on a research directory, the researchers should notify the directory administrator so that the listing can be removed. Alternatively, the data collection pages could be replaced by one that explains that data collection has ended and provides a summary of the research results when they are available.

WEB SITE DESIGN   Participant recruitment and motivation can be greatly affected by a Web site's attractiveness and ease of use (Plous, 2000; Reips, 2000). Box 12-2 provides some tips for designing an effective data collection Web site.

The Validity of Web-Based Data

A question that concerns Internet researchers is that of the validity of their data. Not only are those data being collected by a novel means that could affect results, but the demographic characteristics of participants differ from those of the most commonly used research population (college students; Krantz & Dalal, 2000) and people tend to behave differently on the Internet than in in-person interactions, primarily by being less inhibited and more self-disclosing (Joinson, 1999). Several studies have addressed the question of data validity by examining the extent to which the results of Web-based studies match those of laboratory studies. Based on their review of that research, Krantz and Dalal (2000) concluded that the results of all forms of research conducted over the Internet—surveys, correlational studies, and experiments—converge very well with the results of their laboratory counterparts. In addition, a smaller number of studies have examined the psychometric properties (such as reliability and factor structure) of personality scales administered over the Internet and have found them to be similar to the psychometric properties of the same scales administered in a paper-and-pencil format (Buchanan & Smith, 1999b; Davis, 1999; Pasveer & Ellard, 1998). It would therefore seem that data collected in well-designed Internet research is as valid as data collected by traditional means.

Ethical Issues

Internet researchers are bound by the same principles, rules, and guidelines as other researchers (see Chapter 3), including Institutional Review Board (IRB) approval. However, some ethical principles, such as informed consent and monitoring participants for harm, are more difficult to implement in Internet research. Others, such as voluntary participation and privacy, may be more salient to participants in Internet research than to participants in traditional research.

VOLUNTARY PARTICIPATION   For most Internet studies, voluntary participation is not an issue. Recipients of e-mail surveys are free to choose whether to return them, and visitors to research Web sites are free to choose whether to take part in the study and can terminate their participation at any time simply by closing the browser window. However, studies that observe and record discussions in chat rooms and on mailing lists and newsgroups raise the same question of voluntary participation as do other forms of observational research (see Chapter 10).

BOX 12-2   Tips for Designing an Effective Data Collection Web Site

Keep download time to a minimum. Remember that a page that loads instantaneously from your hard drive might take much longer over a modem link. Many people will not wait for a slow page to download. Therefore,

- keep pages as short as possible;
- keep graphics files as small as possible; and
- avoid using animation.

Do not put advertising banners on the page. Advertising not only distracts users from the content of the page, it also gives the page a commercial rather than a scientific appearance.

Emphasize the professional nature of your site. For example,

- prominently display the name of your college or university;
- provide an e-mail address for users to contact you;
- explain the procedures used to keep data anonymous or confidential;
- offer feedback to research participants;
- solicit feedback from visitors to the site; and
- post the date on which the site was last modified.

Make the site easy to use. For example,

- avoid using frames to divide the main browser window into two or more sections (many people find frames to be confusing);
- avoid the use of browser plug-ins that are not distributed with most browsers (if they are necessary, provide a link to a download site);
- if Java or Java Script are required, remind users to enable them (some people disable Java because of security concerns);
- use HTML tags that can be read even by older versions of browsers;

- do not put important information in banners (people associate banners with advertising and so ignore them); and
- do not use pop-up windows that open automatically (people also associate these with advertising and close them without reading the contents).

Make the pages easy to read. For example,

- use short text lines (long lines can be difficult to read);
- use font styles, font sizes, and text and background colors that promote readability, and remember that most people's computers support only a limited range of fonts;
- use both upper- and lowercase letters (text that is all uppercase is difficult to read);
- keep images and tables small enough to accommodate small monitors; and
- use only the basic 216-shade color palette (some browsers or computers may not render other colors accurately).

Check to ensure that the site works regardless of the hardware or software used to view it. For example, does it work

- on both IBM-compatible and Macintosh computers;
- with different browsers, such as America Online, Internet Explorer, and Netscape Communicator; and
- on monitors with different resolutions?

Have some members of the target participant population review the Web site for usability (such as words that need defining) and acceptability (such as disliked images), and use their feedback to improve the site.

Source: Adapted from *Jakob Nielson's Alert Box* (http://www.useit.com/alertbox/), Plous (2000), and Reips (2000).

Technically, on-line discussions constitute public behavior because, in most cases, anyone can log into a chat room or subscribe to a mailing list or newsgroup. However, the participants in these discussions often assume that their postings are equivalent to private conversations among the participants, especially when they are using their home computers to participate (Binik et al., 1999; Sharf, 1999). Consequently, participants in on-line discussions are likely to view researchers who lurk (observe without participating) in chat rooms or on mailing lists or newsgroups as voyeurs who are invading the participants' privacy (Cho & LaRose, 1999; Sharf, 1999). Because of these concerns, recommendations for researchers conducting observations of on-line behavior include obtaining the consent of group or list moderators, identifying themselves as researchers, explaining the purpose of their research and how the results will be used, and terminating the research if a substantial number of discussion participants object to it. Researchers should also periodically repeat the notification of research in progress because the membership of on-line groups changes frequently (Cho & LaRose, 1999; Michalak & Szabo, 1998; Sharf, 1999).

INFORMED CONSENT   The principle of informed consent requires that potential research participants have all information relevant to deciding whether to take part in research. One piece of that information that gets taken for granted in traditional research is that the people collecting the data are bona fide researchers. This information is typically conveyed by the context of the research: Data are collected at a college or university, or in field research an official of the organization in which the research is conducted vouches for the researchers. However, the use of false identities is common on the Internet, so potential research participants must be able to verify the researchers' credentials (Binik et al., 1999; Cho & LaRose, 1999). Cho and LaRose suggest that a simple way to provide such verification is to use a Web page to collect data and to base that Web page on a college or university Web site. They point out that most people trust the integrity of educational institutions, so an ".edu" on the end of the domain name of the site where research is being conducted will enhance the researchers' credibility to potential participants. Michalak and Szabo (1998) also recommend that researchers describe any support they receive from sources outside their institutions, such as grant agencies and corporations. Some people might not want to participate in research sponsored by organizations whose policies or practices they object to.

Another informed consent issue is how to obtain consent without using a physical consent form. It is, of course, very easy to provide potential participants with the necessary information, but they cannot sign a form. Michalak and Szabo (1998) suggest putting the informed consent form on a Web page and having participants indicate their consent by clicking on an "agree" button that would then take them to the data collection page. Michalak and Szabo point out that this procedure is similar to that used by software companies: End-user licensing agreements inform people who purchase their software that breaking the seal on the package indicates their commitment to abide by the terms and conditions of use for the software.

Perhaps the thorniest issue in informed consent for Internet research is verifying that participants are legally able to give consent to participate (Binik et al., 1999; Smith & Leigh, 1997). In the United States, persons under the age of 18 cannot legally give their consent to participate in research; however, large numbers of Internet users are minors. There is no absolute solution to this problem. Smith and Leigh (1997) recruited participants by posting notices on newsgroups, but only after contacting the newsgroup moderators and verifying that the vast majority of subscribers were adults. Alternative procedures would be to include an age restriction in the description of the study and to ask participants to report their ages, recording only the data from those who report being at least 18 years of age.

MONITORING PARTICIPANTS FOR HARM   One of a researcher's obligations is to monitor participants during a study for signs of unanticipated negative effects. Such monitoring is impossible in Internet research, so alternative procedures must be used. One course of action would be to refrain from using potentially upsetting research materials, such as pictures of victims of violence, and not ask questions on potentially upsetting topics, such as being the victim of abuse. This approach limits the research topics that can be studied but maximizes participant protection. If such materials or questions are essential to the research, then potential participants should be clearly warned about the potentially upsetting material. Binik et al. (1999) also suggest including contact information for an appropriate crisis line, which could be included as part of both the informed consent and debriefing procedures.

PRIVACY   Chapter 3 discussed the researcher's obligation to protect the confidentiality of the data provided by research participants. Internet users are likely to see confidentiality as part of the broader issue of privacy. Privacy is of special interest to Internet users because Web servers can be programmed to collect data about visitors to a Web site, such as the Internet identification number (IP address) of the visitor's computer and the visitor's e-mail address (Cho & LaRose, 1999). It is therefore extremely important to inform potential research participants about the procedures used to protect the anonymity or confidentiality of the information they provide. Michalak and Szabo (1998) also recommend informing potential participants how the data will be reported: Knowing that no individual responses will be published, only average group scores and summaries of free-response data will help people unfamiliar with the research process better understand how their privacy will be protected.

An important privacy concern arises in observational research when researchers record quotations from on-line discussions (a practice called harvesting) and use them in their research reports without the permission of the person being quoted. Members of on-line discussion groups consider harvesting to be an extremely severe invasion of privacy; quotations should never be used without permission (Michalak & Szabo, 1998; Sharf, 1999).

DEBRIEFING   Debriefing is quite easy in Web site–based research: After participants submit their data, they can be sent to a page that thanks them for their participation and explains the purpose of the research. Michalak and Szabo (1998) suggest the debriefing page also solicit comments on the research and provide the researchers' e-mail address and perhaps an e-mail link. Smith and Leigh (1997) further suggest that the page include information on the IRB's role in protecting research participants and information on how to contact the researchers' IRB so that participants can direct any complaints or reservations they have about the research to the IRB.

SUMMARY

Two major aspects of data collection are the selection of research participants and research procedures. Researchers want to be able to apply the results of research to a target population—a particular group of people. When this group is operationally defined, it constitutes the study population from which researchers draw the research sample. The sample can be drawn using either a probability sampling technique, in which the likelihood of any member of the study population's being selected for the sample is known, or a nonprobability sample, in which the likelihood of selection is unknown. Probability samples are highly representative of the population, but nonprobability samples are less expensive and easier to acquire, and so are used much more frequently in psychological research.

Researchers must also determine the appropriate sample size. Sample size is important because of its relationship to statistical power: The larger the sample, the more likely the research will show a significant effect of the independent variable if that variable has an effect in the study population. If sample size is too small, the research might fail to detect the effect of the independent variable. Determination of sample size is based on the magnitude of the expected effect of the independent variable, the alpha level used, use of a one- or two-tailed significance test, and the desired level of statistical power.

Proper research procedures include an effective research setting, effective instructions, debugging the procedures, running the data collection session, and the post-experimenter interview. Effective research settings are coherent—providing a smooth, logical flow of events—simple, psychologically involving for participants, and consistent across participants. Effective instructions are clear, get and hold participants' attention, and include checks on participants' understanding. The process of debugging the research procedures begins with the research proposal, which colleagues can review for problems. Rehearsals allow the researcher and any confederates to familiarize themselves with the mechanics of the procedures and to identify and work out any kinks. As a final step, pilot studies are used to collect preliminary data, to test the validity of experimental manipulations, and to conduct a final test of the research procedures. Pilot studies also give the researcher an opportunity to determine whether participants perceive the research situation as intended and to determine the time needed for a data collection session.

During data collection, researchers should present a professional appearance and act in a professional manner, treating participants politely. The postexperimental interview has four functions: an ethical function of debriefing and removing adverse effects, an educational function of informing participants about the research, a methodological function that assesses the validity of the session, and a discovery function that uses participants' comments to shed new light on the research. These four functions can be integrated into a three-step process: probing for problems, explaining the research, and asking participants' help in improving the research. Finally, researchers must carefully train and supervise their research assistants.

Internet research offers a potentially rich new source of data. Internet research can take the form of experiments, observational studies, interviews, and surveys. it offers the advantages of economy and ease of data collection, access to research participants who might not otherwise be sampled, the potential for increased internal validity, and the use of public research methods. However, it has the disadvantages of biased participant sampling, limits on the kinds of experimental stimuli and response modes that can be used, lack of control over the data collection environment, participant attrition, and the risk of sabotage. Despite these limitations, research indicates that Web-based data are as valid as data collected in laboratory research. Participants for Internet research can be recruited in a number of ways, including e-mail solicitation, announcements, and listings on research directories. Internet researchers must be sensitive to a number of ethical issues including voluntary participation, informed consent, participant welfare, participant privacy, and debriefing.

QUESTIONS AND EXERCISES FOR REVIEW

1. Describe the relationships among the target population for research, the study population, and the research sample.
2. Muehlenhard, Powch, Phelps, and Giusti (1992) and Widom (1988) have pointed out the importance of good operational definitions of the target population for rape and child abuse research. What other areas of research that you are familiar with have defined the target population differently in different studies? What effects do these differences seem to have had on the results and interpretation of the research?
3. Describe the advantages and disadvantages of probability and nonprobability sampling. How do stratified and unstratified sampling procedures differ? Under what conditions are purposive and snowball sampling used?
4. What implications do you see of the predominance of convenience samples in psychological research? Consider such issues as using the results of the research for testing theories and solving applied problems.
5. Why is sample size important in research design? What factors must a researcher consider when determining sample size for hypothesis-testing research?
6. Describe the characteristics of an effective research setting. What kinds of tradeoffs might have to be made among these factors?
7. Choose a recent article describing a study on a topic that interests you. How would you rate the study on its levels of experimental and mundane realism? What suggestions do you have for improving these characteristics?
8. Describe the characteristics of effective instructions for research participants.
9. Go back to the study you chose for Question 7, and write a set of instructions for participants. Test these instructions on a friend who is not familiar with behavioral science research. Based on your friend's reactions and comments, how effective were your instructions? How could you improve them?
10. What steps are involved in debugging research procedures? What are the purposes and uses of pilot studies?
11. Describe the functions of the postexperimental interview. What should happen in each step of the interview?
12. Describe the postexperimental interview you would design for use with the study you chose for Question 7. Why did you structure it as you did?
13. What responsibilities do researchers have toward their research assistants?

14. What are the ways in which researchers can collect data over the Internet? What are the advantages and disadvantages of Internet research?
15. What means can researchers use to recruit participants for Internet research? Compare and contrast the advantages and disadvantages of the recruitment options.
16. Explain the ethical issues that are most salient in Internet research.
17. Locate and participate in two Internet studies on the same or similar topics. Critique their research procedures in terms of the issues discussed in this chapter.

13 INTERPRETING RESEARCH RESULTS

DESCRIBING THE RESULTS OF RESEARCH

The Nature of the Relationship
  Types of Relationships
  Predicted and Observed Relationships
Real Versus Chance Relationships
  Inferential Statistics
  Testing the Proper Statistical Hypothesis
Effect Size and Importance
  Effect Size
  Practical Significance

INFERENCE IN BEHAVIORAL SCIENCE RESEARCH

Knowledge as a Social Construction
  The Constructionist Viewpoint
  Constructing Theories
  Bias in Interpreting Data

Making Valid Inferences
  Measurement and Statistics
  Empiricism
  Causality
  Generalization

NULL RESULTS

Uses of the Null Hypothesis
  Testing Theories
  Research Validity
  Testing Generalizability
Prejudice Against the Null Hypothesis
Possible Sources of Type II Errors
Accepting the Null Hypothesis
  Common Criteria
  Predicted Null Results
  Unexpected Null Results

INTEGRATING THE RESULTS OF RESEARCH

Identifying Implications for Theory
  Comparison With Prior Research
  Comparison With Theoretical Predictions
Identifying Implications for Research
  Research Procedures
  New Research Questions
Identifying Implications for Application

SUMMARY

QUESTIONS AND EXERCISES FOR REVIEW

Research does not end with the collection of data. By themselves, data are merely numbers or sets of observation notes; to be useful, these numbers and notes must be imbued with meaning, they must be transformed from data to knowledge. The process of infusing data with meaning is referred to as *inference*; Figure 13-1 illustrates the steps in this process. If the figure looks familiar, that is because it was also part of Figure 4-3, which illustrated the process of developing a hypothesis. In hypothesis development, we go down the ladder of inference, using deduction to derive specific and concrete predictions about the effects of independent variables from a general and abstract theory. When interpreting the results of the research, we use induction to go up the ladder from the specific and concrete results to their meaning for the general and abstract theory.

Interpretation of research results can be divided into three broad steps. First, you must describe the results of the research, analyze the data, and compare the results of statistical analyses to the statistical hypotheses. Next, you must draw conclusions about the results, extending the results of the data analysis to the research hypothesis and research problem and considering the implications of null results. Finally, you must integrate those results into the "big picture" of theory, application, and research.

DESCRIBING THE RESULTS OF RESEARCH

In describing the results of a piece of research, we want to answer three questions: What is the nature of the relationship between the independent and dependent variables? Is the relationship real, or is it due to chance? How big an effect did the independent variable have? Although these questions will be discussed separately, they are, of course, related to one another. For example, the questions of the nature of the relationship and of effect size are moot if the effect is not real, and without conducting the appropriate statistical analyses you cannot determine if some forms of relationships, such as one variable mediating the relationship between two other variables, exist.

The Nature of the Relationship

The first thing to consider in describing the results of research is the nature of the relationship found between the independent and dependent variable. You must answer two questions: (1) What type of relationship did you find? (2) How well did the relationship you observed match the one you predicted?

TYPES OF RELATIONSHIPS   Of the three questions, the nature of the relationship is, perhaps, the easiest to describe. As you will recall from Chapter 7, relationships between variables can be broadly categorized as linear or curvilinear. The nature of the relation-

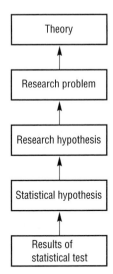

Theory

Research problem

Research hypothesis

Statistical hypothesis

Results of
statistical test

Note: Adapted from Wampold et al., 1990, p. 362.

FIGURE 13-1   Inference in Research
Use the statistical hypothesis to determine the implications of the results of the statistical test for the research hypothesis, and then determine the implications of the outcome of the research—whether or not the hypothesis was supported—for answering the research problem and for the theory.

ship between the independent and dependent variables can be determined by drawing a graph plotting the mean scores of groups that experienced the different conditions of the independent variable. Chapter 1 showed that theories can postulate that a third variable either mediates or moderates the relationship between an independent and a dependent variable. Mediated and moderated relationships must be tested by conducting the appropriate statistical analysis: partial correlation or multiple regression analysis for mediation (Chapter 8) or a factorial design to detect the interaction postulated by a moderated relationship (Chapter 7).

PREDICTED AND OBSERVED RELATIONSHIPS   Once you have determined the nature of the relationship found (or observed) in the data, you must compare it to the relationship the hypothesis predicted. To make this comparison, you must have a firm idea of the way in which your research hypothesis relates to the statistical hypothesis—that is, what the results should look like if the hypothesis is correct. You might want to review the discussion of research and statistical hypotheses in Chapter 4. One way to make this link is through a diagram of the expected outcome of the study. For example, recall the Bransford and Johnson (1972) experiment, discussed in Chapter 7, that examined the effects of the context in which information is presented on memory for the information. The researchers predicted (research hypotheses) that knowing the context before receiving the information would result in better recall than would receiving the context

TABLE 13-1   Expected Outcome Diagram and Results for Bransford and Johnson's (1972) Experiment II

	CONDITION OF THE INDEPENDENT VARIABLE		
	Context Before	*Context After*	*No Context (Control)*
Expected outcome	+	0	0
Results	5.8	2.6	2.8

Note: A + in the Expected Outcome row indicates a mean that is expected to be greater than that for the control condition; a 0 indicates a mean expected to be equal to the control condition. The Results row shows the mean memory score for each condition.

after the information or receiving no context (essentially, a no-treatment control group). Further, they predicted that there would be no difference between the context-after and no-context conditions.

Table 13-1 shows the expected outcome diagram and the results for one of Bransford and Johnson's (1972) studies. On the "expected outcome" line of the diagram, a "0" indicates that the mean score for a condition is expected to be the same as for the control condition. A "+" indicates a condition expected to have a significantly larger mean than the control condition, and a "–" could be used to indicate a condition expected to have a significantly smaller mean than the control condition. Double pluses ("++") or double minuses ("––") could be used in more complex designs to indicate even more extreme means. As you can see, Bransford and Johnson's observed means fit their predicted results.

Similar diagrams can be constructed for research designed to compare theories. Whitley, McHugh, and Frieze (1986), for example, compared three explanations for the finding that women often attribute their successes and failures to other causes than do men. Table 13-2 shows a diagram of the outcomes predicted by the three models; an "x" indicates a causal explanation—ability, effort, luck, or characteristics of the task—for which each model predicts sex differences. It turned out that Whitley et al.'s results failed to support any of the models. Constructing outcome diagrams for complex studies, especially those using factorial designs with more than two independent variables, can be very difficult. However, they are worth the effort in the long run because they make it easier to see how well the results of the research conform to the predictions the hypotheses made.

Real Versus Chance Relationships

An examination of the pattern of the observed relationship between the independent and dependent variables that exists in the research sample is not sufficient for deciding that the relationship reflects the effect of the independent variable rather than chance factors, such as sampling error. **Inferential statistics,** such as the *t* test and analysis of variance (ANOVA), are designed to help the researcher decide if the rela-

TABLE 13-2   Sex Differences in Causal Attributions Predicted by Three Different Theoretical Perspectives. An x indicates the factor on which a theory predicts that women will score higher than men.

	THEORETICAL PERSPECTIVE		
	General Externality	*Self-Derogation*	*Low Expectancy*
Success			
Ability			x
Effort			x
Luck	x	x	
Task ease	x	x	
Failure			
Low ability		x	x
Lack of effort		x	
Bad luck	x		
Task difficulty	x		x

Note: From Whitley et al., 1986, p. 106.

tionship found in the sample is a real relationship, resulting from the effect of the independent variable.

INFERENTIAL STATISTICS   Inferential statistics tell us, roughly speaking, how likely it is that the results found in our sample are due to chance rather than to the effect of the independent variable. If we set a criterion level of likelihood for deciding that a relationship is real, then we can use inferential statistics as decision-making tools. If the likelihood of the sample relationship's having occurred by chance exceeds the criterion, we decide that there is no effect of the independent variable; if the likelihood of error falls short of the criterion, then we decide that the relationship is real, caused by the independent variable. By convention, the criterion for behavioral science research is the .05, or 5%, level: If there is a likelihood greater than 1 in 20 of the sample results having occurred by chance, then we decide that the independent variable had no effect; if the likelihood is less than 1 in 20, then we decide that the independent variable had an effect. A common question is "Why is the criterion set at .05? Why not .10 or .025?" Cowles and Davis (1982) note that this criterion developed slowly in conjunction with the field of statistics, on the basis of what seemed reasonable to pioneering statisticians. They also point out that 95% certainty represents how sure most people want to be before they accept something as true.

Because the .05 criterion represents a probability of error, a decision that the independent variable did have an effect and a decision that the independent variable did not have an effect could both be wrong. As noted in the previous chapter, deciding that a relationship exists, when in fact it does not, constitutes a Type I error; conversely, deciding that a relationship does not exist, when in fact it does, constitutes a Type II error. As also noted, given the low statistical power of much research, behavioral science researchers do not appear to be very concerned about the likelihood of making a Type II error. This lack of concern for statistical power can lead to an interesting, if frustrating, outcome for research. Let's say that a study's Type I error rate exceeds the .05 criterion so that the researchers cannot conclude that the independent variable had an effect on the dependent variable. However, if the study has the average statistical power of .57 (J. S. Rossi, 1990), neither can the researchers conclude that the independent variable did *not* have an effect; such a conclusion would have a 43% chance of being wrong! The researchers can therefore draw no firm conclusions from the research. Taking statistical power into consideration before collecting data is therefore essential.

TESTING THE PROPER STATISTICAL HYPOTHESIS   No matter how well designed a study is, its statistical analysis is meaningless if the proper statistical hypothesis is not tested. Chapter 4 looked at one aspect of this issue, in the discussion of deriving statistical hypotheses that are congruent with the research hypotheses. Because the ladder of inference shown in Figure 13-1 begins with deciding, on the basis of the statistical test, whether or not the research hypothesis was supported, the validity of the entire chain of inference rests on conducting a proper statistical test and properly interpreting the results of the test.

A common problem of statistical inference arises when a study includes more than two conditions of the independent variable. As noted in Chapter 7, the statistical test for multiple-group studies—ANOVA—tests the hypothesis that at least one of the possible comparisons between groups is significant, but it cannot tell us which comparison that is. ANOVA is therefore an **omnibus test:** It tests everything at once. However, as R. Rosenthal and Rosnow (1991) point out, researchers are almost never interested in everything at once; rather, they are interested in comparisons between specific groups. Consider, for example, the results of the Bransford and Johnson (1972) experiment shown in Table 13-1. An ANOVA of the scores in the three groups presents a statistically significant result, $F(2, 48) = 11.56, p < .001$; there is definitely a difference somewhere among those groups. However, knowing that there is a difference somewhere did not help Bransford and Johnson; they had hypothesized very specific differences. The way to test for those specified differences is through **planned comparisons** of means that test the specific between-means differences of interest to the researcher. Bransford and Johnson's hypotheses called for two planned comparisons, one testing whether the context-before (B) group had better recall scores than the context-after (A) and no-context (N) groups, and the other testing whether the context-after and no-context group means were equal. The first contrast takes the form $2B - (A + N)$ and is statistically significant, $t(48) = 5.880, p < .001$. The second contrast takes the form $A - N$ and is not significant, $t(48) < 1$; note, however, that a firm conclusion of no difference would depend on the power of the analysis.

When researchers have hypotheses that predict specific patterns of differences between groups, it is usually more useful to ignore the results of the omnibus test and to focus their attention on the planned comparisons (R. Rosenthal & Rosnow, 1991). In Bransford and Johnson's (1972) study, just described, the conditions of the independent variable differed qualitatively; when the conditions differ quantitatively, there are planned comparisons to determine the significance of linear and curvilinear effects. Planned comparisons can also be developed and tested for factorial designs. See R. Rosenthal and Rosnow (1991, chap. 21) for more information on planned comparisons.

Effect Size and Importance

Traditionally, the analysis of data from behavioral science research has focused on the statistical significance of the results. However, as Hays (1973) notes, one needs more information than statistical significance to fully understand the results of research:

> All that a significant result implies is that one has observed something relatively unlikely given the hypothetical situation. Everything else is a matter of what one does with this information. Statistical significance is a statement about the likelihood of the observed result, nothing else. It does not guarantee that something important, or even meaningful, has been found. (p. 384)

This limitation on the meaning of statistical significance for the interpretation of the results of research has led researchers to take two other criteria into consideration: effect size and practical significance.

EFFECT SIZE   As noted in the previous chapter, the term **effect size** refers to the magnitude of the impact an independent variable has on a dependent variable in experimental research and to the size of the relationship between two variables in nonexperimental research. In research using continuous-scale independent variables, effect size is usually operationally defined as the Pearson product–moment correlation r, the absolute value of which varies on a continuous scale from zero to one. In research using categorical independent variables, effect size is usually operationally defined as the difference between two conditions of the independent variable, such as the experimental and control conditions, divided by the standard deviation of all the scores. This effect size indicator, referred to as d, is a continuous-scale variable that can range from zero, indicating absolutely no effect of the independent variable, to infinity. There are also specific effect size indicators for different statistical tests, all of which, including d, can be mathematically transformed into r (R. Rosenthal & Rosnow, 1991). In essence, effect size measures indicate how much of the variance in the dependent variable is caused by or is accounted for by the independent variable. The more variance an independent variable accounts for, the stronger a cause (or, in the case of correlational research, potential cause) it is of the dependent variable.

Looking at the results of research in terms of effect size has a number of advantages (Prentice & Miller, 1992). First, as already noted, effect size measures indicate how much impact an independent variable has on a dependent variable. Second, as the previous chapter pointed out, there are conventions for what constitutes a small, medium, and large effect so that the terms *small*, *medium*, and *large* become objective rather than subjective descriptions of effect size. As a result, when a researcher says that an independent variable had a "large effect" the term *large* means the same thing to everyone who reads the research report. Third, effect sizes can provide an indicator of the practical significance or importance of an effect if one assumes that a large effect is also an important effect. As discussed shortly, researchers do not universally accept this assumption. Fourth, effect size measures are standardized; that is, they are expressed in standard deviation units so that an independent variable that has an impact of .30 on a dependent variable measured on a 9-point scale will also have an impact of .30 on a dependent variable measured on a 5-point scale (assuming, of course, that both measures assess the same amount of true score). Consequently, researchers can use effect size measures to assess the impact of an independent variable across two or more studies, using a process called meta-analysis, discussed in Chapter 16. Finally, again as noted in the previous chapter, effect sizes can be used in the analysis of statistical power to determine the appropriate sample size for a study.

These benefits of effect size analysis have led to an increasing focus on effect size as an indicator of the impact of an independent variable, with the implicit assumption that a large effect size always indicates a large impact. However, Prentice and Miller (1992) point out that there are two situations in which a small effect size could reflect a strong impact of the independent variable. One such situation is when a weak manipulation results in a small effect: The fact that the weak manipulation had *any* effect could indicate a strong impact of the conceptual independent variable. Prentice and Miller cite what is known as the "minimal group effect" (Tajfel, Billig, Bundy, & Flamant, 1971) as an example of this situation. Research before Tajfel et al.'s work had shown that people favor members of their own groups over members of other groups, with most of the research being conducted with *group* operationally defined as one that was important to the person's self-concept. Tajfel et al. demonstrated the pervasiveness of the group membership effect by randomly dividing research participants into groups. One would expect that arbitrarily formed groups would have little importance to people relative to natural groups and so should provide little motivation for people to express in-group favoritism. Nonetheless, members of these arbitrary groups showed the same type of in-group favoritism as members of natural groups. Therefore, even the minimal level of group identification brought about by being randomly assigned to a group of strangers can elicit in-group favoritism, suggesting that such favoritism is a basic human characteristic.

A second situation in which a small effect size could indicate an impressive effect of the independent variable is when one would expect the dependent variable to be resistant to influence by the independent variable. For example, although people who are physically attractive are generally rated more positively than people who are less attractive (Hatfield & Sprecher, 1986), one would expect attractiveness to have little effect on hiring decisions when attractiveness is irrelevant to job performance. Nonetheless, given two people with equal qualifications, the more attractive person is more likely to be hired (Cash, Gillen, & Burns, 1977). The ability of attractiveness to overcome the barrier of relevance to have an impact on personnel decision making demonstrates its importance to that process.

As these examples show, although effect sizes can indicate the magnitude of the impact of independent variables, they need to be interpreted in the context of the operational definitions used in the research. As Prentice and Miller (1992) conclude, "Showing that an effect holds even under the most unlikely circumstances possible can be as impressive as (or, in some cases, perhaps even more impressive than) showing that it accounts for a great deal of variance" in the dependent variable (p. 163).

PRACTICAL SIGNIFICANCE   Even though an independent variable may have a statistically significant effect on a dependent variable and even though that effect might be large, it still may not be important. The **practical significance** of an effect (also called *clinical significance* in psychotherapy research) is a value judgment about its importance for theory or application. The criterion for practical significance is the minimum impact considered to be important by people who have an interest in the research. For example, "The clinical significance of a treatment refers to its ability to meet standards of efficacy set by consumers, clinicians, and researchers" (Jacobson & Truax, 1991, p. 12). Clearly, this criterion will vary as a function of the independent and dependent variables in the research, their operational definitions, and the purpose of the research, but the criterion can and should be set in advance of the research.

Frequently, the criterion for practical significance will be a large effect size, but in some situations even a small effect can have practical significance. For example, small effects can sometimes add up over time to result in large effects. Abelson (1985) uses professional baseball players as an example of this situation: Although the correlation between players' batting skill and getting a hit at any one time at bat is only .06—indicating almost no relation between skill and getting a hit—skill definitely affects players' batting performance over a season or a career. This kind of cumulative effect can also be seen in variables of more professional interest to behavioral scientists: Although correlations between measures of attitudes and behavior and between measures of personality and behavior are low for any one situation, when behaviors are cumulated across time and situations the correlations increase greatly. Fishbein and Ajzen (1975) found, for example, that correlations between the trait of religiosity and individual religious behaviors were small, averaging around .10, but that when behaviors were cumulated across time, the correlation became .63.

A second situation in which small effect sizes can have practical significance is when a small effect is applied to a very large population. For example, the correlation between taking aspirin and avoiding heart attack is only .03, representing a decrease in the population heart attack rate of 3.4% (R. Rosenthal & Rosnow, 1991). Although these effects are small, if the at-risk population for heart attacks consisted of about 750,000 people in any one year (U.S. Bureau of the Census, 1992), then a 3.4% reduction in heart attacks would result in 25,500 fewer heart attacks per year, certainly an important effect!

Finally, Chow (1988) points out that even a small effect of an independent variable can be important when testing theories. Especially in the early stages of testing a theory, it might be useful to know that an independent variable has any effect, even a small one, if that knowledge will help to advance the development of the theory. Conversely, when even a small effect cannot be found under the most auspicious conditions, the theory can be rejected (Mook, 1983).

Let's summarize this section by noting that in coming to understand the results of a study, you must ask yourself several questions: What is the nature of the relationship between the independent and dependent variables? Does the observed relationship match the predicted relationship? Is the relationship statistically significant; that is, is it a real relationship? How large an effect did the independent variable have? Does this effect meet the criterion for practical significance?

INFERENCE IN BEHAVIORAL SCIENCE RESEARCH

In the context of psychological research, **inference** is the process of drawing conclusions about hypothetical constructs and the relationships between them on the basis of manifest variables and their relationships. It is the process of moving from the concrete and specific to the abstract and general. This section discusses two issues related to inference: knowledge as a social construction and some guidelines for making valid inferences.

Knowledge as a Social Construction

Chapters 1 and 4 noted the influence of personal epistemologies and biases on theory construction and hypothesis formulation. Researchers' beliefs about the nature of knowledge and their personal biases can also affect the ways in which they interpret data.

THE CONSTRUCTIONIST VIEWPOINT   Scientific knowledge can be viewed in two ways. In the **logical positivist** view, knowledge consists of a set of absolute facts that, once discovered, remain unchanging and unchangeable for all time. Knowledge, in a sense, exists in the world. In the other, or **constructionist,** view, knowledge consists of a set of interpretations of observations. These interpretations can, and do, vary from person to person; two people can draw opposite conclusions from the same set of observations. In this view, knowledge resides in the mind of the observer. As Scarr (1985) puts it,

> We [as scientists] do not discover facts; we invent them. Their usefulness to us depends both on shared perceptions of the "facts" (consensual validation) and on whether they work for various purposes, some practical and some theoretical. (p. 499)

Or, as Diesing (1991) puts it, somewhat more extremely, "Social science data are usually somewhat ambiguous, like the ink blots in a Rorschach test, so [different] people . . . will make different things of them" (p. 274). The constructionist view of knowledge currently dominates the social and behavioral sciences (Diesing, 1991).

This constructionist viewpoint has two implications for interpreting behavioral science data. First, it implies that people interpret observations and construct theories to fit in with the zeitgeist — the prevailing social values and needs of the time. Second, the ambiguous nature of data leaves the door open to bias in interpreting research results and constructing theories.

CONSTRUCTING THEORIES   In the constructionist view of knowledge, scientific theories reflect the societies in which the scientists live. People construct theories in ways that support the worldview commonly held in society. These theories do not represent distortions of facts, because in the constructionist view, facts themselves are ambiguous and open to multiple interpretations. Rather, the socialization process that everyone goes through from childhood through adulthood teaches people to interpret data in ways that reflect the values of the society.

For example, Duckitt (1992a) notes that during the 20th century, psychologists have developed a variety of theories to explain racial prejudice, each theory focusing on a different psychological process. These theories would arise, direct research for a time, and then lapse into relative obscurity. Duckitt (1992a) notes that

> these shifts in emphasis . . . do not seem to be fully explained in terms of the evolution of knowledge and the emergence of newer and better theories. Typically, older perspectives and theories are not refuted or even shown to be seriously inadequate. Although displaced from the mainstream of psychological interest, they are not discarded. In fact, it is widely acknowledged that they remain relevant and even important in accounting for prejudice. (pp. 1182–1183)

> An important determinant of these shifts was that historical events and circumstances made certain issues and questions about prejudice particularly salient for social scientists and that the different approaches at particular periods therefore represented attempts to answer fundamentally different questions about the nature and causation of prejudice. (p. 1191)

Table 13-3 shows Duckitt's (1992b) analysis of the interaction between social and historical events and changing emphases on the factors causing prejudice. In the first quarter of the 20th century, psychological theories justified prejudice as a natural response to "inferior peoples." The Nazi racial ideology and its resultant genocide led, in the 1950s, to theories that explained prejudice as a behavioral consequence of an inadequate personality. In the 1980s, the continued presence of prejudice, despite two decades of social and educational programs aimed at its demise, led to theories that explained prejudice in terms of inevitable outcomes of normal psychological processes. New social forces in the future will, perhaps, result in new explanations for prejudice. As researchers we therefore need to be aware of the influence that the zeitgeist can have on the interpretations we make of our data and to consider alternative explanations that go against the tenor of the times.

BIAS IN INTERPRETING DATA   The ambiguous nature of psychological data makes it easy for bias to creep unnoticed into the interpretation of those data. Bias can take two forms. One form is theoretical bias:

> Each scientist approaches scientific problems with a theoretical viewpoint, whether explicit or implicit. Theory guides inquiry through the questions raised, the framework of inquiry, and the interpretation of results. Each scientist seeks to find "facts" to assimilate into his or her world view. Thus, each of us is biased by human tendency to seek "facts" that are congruent with our prior beliefs. (Scarr, 1985, p. 499)

Pyke and Agnew (1991) use two interpretations of some data reported by Money and Ehrhardt (1972) to illustrate theoretical bias. Money and Ehrhardt studied 25 children who, although genetically female (XX chromosomal pattern), were prenatally exposed to androgens (masculinizing hormones), which resulted in their being genitally ambiguous at birth; that is, they showed a combination of male and female primary sexual characteristics. After surgery, the children were raised as girls. However, as they grew up, their behavior was more "boylike" than the behavior of a matched control

TABLE 13-3   Historical Evolution of the Psychological Understanding of Prejudice

Social and Historical Problem	Social Scientific Question	Image of Prejudice	Theoretical Orientation	Research Orientation
Up to the 1920s: White domination and colonial rule of "backward peoples"	Identifying the deficiencies of "backward peoples"	A natural response to "inferior peoples"	"Race theories"	Comparative studies of the abilities of different races
The 1920s and 1930s: The legitimacy of White domination challenged	Explaining the stigmatization of minorities	Prejudice as irrational and unjustified	Conceptualizing prejudice as a social problem	Measurement and descriptive studies
The 1930s and 1940s: The ubiquity of White racism in the United States	Identifying universal processes underlying prejudice	Prejudice as unconscious defense	Psychodynamic theory: Defensive processes	Experimental
The 1950s: Nazi racial ideology and the holocaust	Identifying the prejudice-prone personality	Prejudice as an expression of a pathological need	Individual differences	Correlational
The 1960s: The problem of prejudice in the American South	How social norms and influences determine prejudice	Prejudice as a social norm	Sociocultural: Social transmission of prejudice	Observational and correlational
The 1970s: The persistence of U.S. racism and discrimination	How prejudice is rooted in social structure and intergroup relations	Prejudice as an expression of group interests	Sociocultural: Intergroup dynamics of prejudice	Sociological and historical research
The 1980s: The inevitability and universality of prejudice and intergroup conflict	What universal psychological processes underlie intergroup conflict and prejudice	Prejudice as an inevitable outcome of social categorization	Cognitive perspective	Experimental

Note: Adapted from *The Social Psychology of Prejudice* by J. Duckitt, 1992, p. 48. New York: Praeger. Copyright 1992 by John Duckitt. Adapted by permission of the Greenwood Publishing Group, Inc., Westport, CT.

group. For example, the girls prenatally exposed to the hormone were more interested in athletics, were more likely to play with boys, and showed a greater preference for toys usually marketed to boys. Pyke and Agnew point out that theorists who hold different views about the origins of sex differences make very different interpretations of these findings. On the one hand, sociobiologists, who hold that sex differences in social behavior are largely determined by biological and genetic factors, use these results as support for their theories. For example, E. O. Wilson (1978) wrote that these results "suggest that the universal existence of sexual division of labor is not entirely an accident of cultural evolution" (p. 132). On the other hand, theorists who favor cultural explanations of sex differences in social behavior also interpret the same data to fit their own theories. For example, Mackie (1983) noted that although the average behavior of the girls prenatally exposed to androgens was more "masculine" than the average behavior of the members of the comparison group, their behavior nonetheless fell within the normal range for girls in U.S. society and their female gender identities were not seriously disrupted. That is, the girls still behaved and thought of themselves in ways culturally defined as female despite their exposure to masculinizing hormones. To Mackie, these findings indicated that culture was more important than biology in determining sex differences in behavior and self-concept.

The other form of bias is personal: We all grow up learning that certain things are true, and these beliefs can affect our interpretations of data. For example, Sherwood and Nataupsky (1968) studied 82 psychologists who had conducted research on racial differences in IQ scores. They categorized the researchers into three broad categories: environmentalists, who believed the differences were caused by environmental factors, such as differences in education; hereditarians, who believed that the differences in scores reflected genetic differences in intelligence; and middle-of-the-roaders, who believed the data were inconclusive. Sherwood and Nataupsky found a number of differences in the personal backgrounds of members of these groups, especially when hereditarians were compared to the others. Hereditarians tended to be older at the time their research was conducted, to have been born first rather than later in the family, to have had fewer foreign-born grandparents, to have had better-educated parents, to have grown up outside of cities, and to have gotten better grades as undergraduates. "Taken together these biographical data would seem to indicate that investigators whose research was categorized as concluding that Negroes are innately inferior intellectually came from higher socioeconomic backgrounds" (Sherwood & Nataupsky, 1968, p. 57). As Sherwood and Nataupsky note, their research cannot show that the differences in data interpretation were caused by the researchers' differences in background. However, it is not unreasonable to believe that everyone learns some prejudices and that these prejudices can affect the interpretation of ambiguous data.

Behavioral scientists concerned with bias in the interpretation of research results, especially intergroup bias, have noted several forms of bias in data interpretation (Denmark, Russo, Frieze, & Sechzer, 1988; Eichler, 1988; McHugh, Koeske, & Frieze, 1986). Although examples of these biases are drawn from research on sex differences, they are applicable to any research that focuses on differences between social groups. One form of bias is accepting any statistically significant group difference as an important group difference. As already noted, statistically significant differences are not necessarily large, and large differences are not necessarily important. A second bias is assuming that group differences are biological differences—that is, assuming that the observed differences have some biological or genetic cause without having data to support that assumption. Sex, race, and other such physical variables are confounded with a number of cultural variables, and the effects of the two sets of variables are usually impossible to sort out. Always bear in mind that research on group differences such as these is correlational; causality cannot be determined. Third, research or theory might apply the results of research conducted with members of one group to members of another group without evidence that the generalization is valid: What is true for women might not be true for men, and vice versa.

Research on social group differences very often involves comparing a relatively advantaged group to a relatively disadvantaged group in a search for the causes of the disadvantage. A fourth form of bias, *victim blame*, arises when the members of the disadvantaged group are blamed for their own disadvantage without sufficient evidence to support that interpretation. For example, as Table 13-3 shows, the race psychology of the early 20th century blamed prejudice on the "innate inferiority" of the targets of prejudice. Finally, one must be careful not to use biased language in describing the results of research. For example, is the same behavior labeled as "assertive" when exhibited by the members of one group, but as "aggressive" when exhibited by the members of another group?

Bias in our interpretation of data is usually unconscious, reflecting our personal worldviews (MacCoun, 1998), and so can be difficult for us to notice. Therefore, a good way to avoid bias is to have another person review your interpretations of your data. People who adhere to different theoretical perspectives than one's own or who are perceptive in picking out biased interpretations are especially valuable in this regard.

Making Valid Inferences

The likelihood of making biased inferences can be reduced, and the likelihood of making valid inferences increased, by carefully considering the nature of the research that was conducted. The most basic consideration, of course, is internal validity; none of the threats to internal validity discussed in Chapter 6 should be present in the research. The present discussion will assume that the research was well designed and will focus on some common pitfalls in interpreting the results of even the best designed research. It will consider the proper interpretation of measures and statistics, the importance of basing interpretations on empirical evidence, avoiding causal interpretations of correlational data, and the generalizability of results.

MEASUREMENT AND STATISTICS   When interpreting the results of research, it is important to bear the level of measurement of the dependent variable in mind. Be careful, for example, not to draw ratio level conclusions from interval or lower level data, such as by saying something like "The attitudes of the experimental group changed twice as much as the attitudes of the control group." Attitudes and other hypothetical constructs are almost always measured at the interval level or lower.

Also, be wary of exaggerating differences between groups. As already noted, people can tend to assume that statistical significance implies a large effect of the independent variable or that the effect has practical importance. Always make these decisions separately from one another, using criteria set in advance of the study whenever possible. Researchers can also tend to think of the members of the experimental and control groups as being homogeneous in their responses to the independent variable. That is, in what might be called the **fallacy of the mean,** we tend to think of the group mean scores as the "experimental group score" and the "control group score," attributing the same score to each member of the group. In fact, of course, there will always be variability within the groups, and some members of each group will almost always score within the range of scores of the other group. To take a concrete example, the average height of men is greater than the average height of women, but there is great variability of height in both sexes and some women are taller than some men. It is therefore just as incorrect to say that the experimental group scored higher than the control group, implying that *all* members of the experimental group scored higher than *all* members of the control group, as it is to say that men are taller than women, implying that *all* men are taller than *all* women.

Be careful when drawing conclusions from research that includes more than two groups. As noted earlier, the overall or omnibus *F* ratio provides no information about which groups are different from which other groups. Similarly, be careful when drawing conclusions about research when the statistical test is not significant. A nonsignificant test means that you cannot conclude that the independent variable had an effect. However, unless statistical power is reasonably high, neither can you conclude that it did *not* have an effect. If alpha is greater than .05 and power is less than .8, then you may not want to draw firm conclusions from the research. Null results (alpha greater than .05) will be discussed in more detail shortly.

EMPIRICISM   Chapter 1 pointed out that the principle of empiricism in research seeks to ensure that all conclusions are based on sound objective evidence. In interpreting the results of research, we must therefore be very careful about the quality of the evidence. For example, every conclusion must have supporting evidence. If you want to say that the average score of the experimental group is higher than that of the control group, do the mean scores and the result of the statistical test support that conclusion? If you want to say that the effect of the independent variable is large or important, what criterion are you using?

Also, be very careful about drawing firm conclusions about hypothetical constructs or their relationships from operational definitions and their relationships. Remember that any operational definition is an imperfect representation of the construct and that the relationships between operational definitions are only imperfect representations of the relationships between the hypothetical constructs. Above all, you should have evidence of the construct validity of operational definitions before drawing firm conclusions about hypothetical constructs. For example, Zuckerman (1990) suggests that almost all research on racial differences is of dubious value because there is no well-validated operational definition of race. Race, by the way, is a hypothetical construct: Although skin tone can be directly and objectively measured, the division of people into racial groups on that basis is, like all hypothetical constructs, a convenience of the scientific (and, in this case, popular) imagination (Zuckerman, 1990).

Finally, it is important to think descriptively rather than evaluatively about the results of research. There is a tendency for people to think that if there is a difference between groups, one group is necessarily better than the other. This tendency can be a particular problem when there is no objective criterion for what constitutes a "good" level of a behavior. For example, men, on the average, give themselves more credit for success at achievement tasks than women, on the average, give themselves. But does this mean that on the average women lack a proper appreciation of their abilities, or does it mean that on the average men think too well of themselves? Or does it mean that, on the average, men and women fall at different ends of a normal or reasonable range of self-evaluation? Descriptively, men's average score is higher than women's average score; evaluatively, any of the three interpretations could be correct depending on how you define reasonable self-evaluation. In fact, the difference, while generally consistent across studies and statistically significant, is quite small, averaging .13 standard deviation (Whitley et al., 1986). In the absence of objective or generally accepted criteria for making evaluative judgments of behavior, a descriptive approach to the interpretation of results is probably best.

CAUSALITY   When trying to draw causal conclusions from research, it is important to bear in mind the limitations of the research design. For example, never draw causal conclusions from correlational research. As noted in Chapter 7, some research designs resemble experiments on the surface but are actually correlational studies because their independent variables are measured rather than manipulated. All personality variables fall into this category, as do personal characteristics of research participants, such as sex, ethnicity, and so forth. Only true experiments can determine causality. It is also important to remember that most behaviors have multiple causes; therefore, any study is likely to find only one cause of a behavior, not the only cause. Even for studies with multiple independent variables, other causes may not have been included in the research design. Also, be alert to the possibility of alternative explanations for the results: Were other possible causes of the behavior confounded with the independent variable?

GENERALIZATION   We want the results of our research to apply beyond the particular conditions of the research. The term **generalizability** refers to the degree that the results of research can be applied to other populations, settings, operational definitions of the variables, and so forth. The next chapter will discuss the problems of generalization in some detail. For now, note that it is very important not to overgeneralize results; that is, in the absence of supporting evidence, you should not draw firm conclusions about the degree to which your results apply to other circumstances.

NULL RESULTS

Null results are said to have occurred in research when the independent variable does not have a statistically significant effect, that is, when there is no difference between the experimental and control conditions. Because most research is designed to find an effect for the independent variable, null results are a disappointment to most researchers. However, as will be shown, no-difference outcomes can be important to both theory and the research process; also, as discussed in the next section, researchers have a prejudice against testing and accepting the **null** (no difference) **hypothesis** in research.

Uses of the Null Hypothesis

A null hypothesis can be useful in three ways: It can test theory, support the validity of a study, and support the generalizability of a theoretical principle.

TESTING THEORIES   As noted in Chapter 1, theories postulate sets of relationships between variables; they also—sometimes explicitly, more often implicitly—postulate the lack of a relationship between two variables. For example, Chapter 8 showed that a mediational hypothesis predicts no relationship between the independent and dependent variables when the mediating variable is controlled (R. M. Baron & Kenny, 1986). In this case, confirmation of the null hypothesis supports the theory. In addition, theories may postulate or imply the lack of direct relationships between variables; in such cases, null results support the theory and the presence of relationships contradicts it. Finally, of course, the failure to find support for a predicted relationship calls the theory being tested into question, indicating that it needs revision or, when lack of support is pervasive and consistent, that it should be abandoned.

RESEARCH VALIDITY   Null hypotheses are also used to support the validity of research. The internal validity of a study can be demonstrated by showing that an alternative explanation for the results is incorrect — that is, that a potential confounding variable had no relationship with the dependent variable. Unless this null hypothesis of no relationship can be supported with data, the validity of the research is open to challenge. Also, Chapter 5 noted that discriminant validity is a component of the construct validity of a measure. That is, to demonstrate construct validity, you must be able to show that a measure is not related to variables, such as social desirability response bias, to which it should not be related. Support for the null hypothesis of no relationship to irrelevant variables supports the construct validity of the measure.

TESTING GENERALIZABILITY   Finally, if a theoretical principle is generalizable, it operates in the same way across settings, populations, operational definitions, and so forth. To be generalizable across sex, for example, an independent variable's effect should be the same for men and women; that is, there should be no difference between men and women in response to the variable. Support for the null hypothesis of no sex difference supports the generalizability of the effect.

Prejudice Against the Null Hypothesis

Despite the utility of the null hypothesis, there appears to be a prejudice against accepting the validity of null results. For example, Atkinson, Furlong, and Wampold (1982) found that only 39% of the researchers they surveyed would recommend publication of a well-designed study that failed to support the hypothesis, compared to the 82% who would recommend publication if the same study supported the hypothesis. In addition, the respondents rated the quality of the null results version of the study as being of lower quality than the positive results version. Even high statistical power does not add to the acceptability of no-difference research (Yeaton & Sechrest, 1987a). It is quite likely, then, that research that fails to support the proposed hypothesis does not get published and therefore does not become part of the scientific knowledge base.

This prejudice against the publication of null results could be having at least two undesirable effects on psychology as a science (Greenwald, 1975). First, if unpublished null results are correct — that is, there is, in fact, no relationship between the independent and dependent variables — then studies that find a relationship represent Type I errors. Consequently, erroneous theories are accepted as correct, retarding the progress of behavioral science. Greenwald (1975, p. 13) cites several examples of what he calls "epidemics of Type I error" in which incorrect hypotheses prevailed until large numbers of failures to replicate the original results were reported.

The second undesirable effect of prejudice against the null hypothesis is wastage of resources. Unless researchers are aware that a hypothesis cannot be supported, they are likely to conduct research on it only to obtain null results. There is then a 28% chance that those researchers will abandon the problem (Greenwald, 1975), leaving still other

BOX 13-1   Possible Sources of Type II Errors. (These potential sources of error must be ruled out before you can accept the null hypothesis.)

The Independent Variable

1. Is there evidence for the construct validity of the operational definition of the independent variable (Chapter 7)? If the operational definition is not an adequate representation of the hypothetical construct, then one should not expect an effect. In experimental research, this question can be answered by manipulation checks conducted during pilot studies or concurrently with data collection. In addition, pilot studies and the postexperimental interviews should be used to ensure that research participants interpreted the manipulation as intended (Chapter 12). In correlational research, construct validity should be assessed as described in Chapter 5. When participants are divided into groups based on personal characteristics, the classification criteria must be well defined. For example, Widom (1988) suggests that many contradictory results found in research on the psychological effects of child abuse stem from different studies' using different operational definitions of abuse.

2. Was the independent variable implemented properly (Chapter 7)? That is, did the participants in the experimental and control groups receive the experiences they were supposed to during data collection? For example, R. A. Feldman, Caplinger, and Wodarski (1983) describe a study that compared two interventions for antisocial youth to a control group and found no effect for the independent variable. However, investigation of the treatment programs found that the interventions were not conducted properly and that the control group actually received a form of treatment.

3. Was the manipulation strong enough to have an effect on the dependent variable (Chapter 7)? If the experimental and control conditions are very similar, one would not expect an effect. In correlational research, was there a restriction in the range of the scores on the independent variable (Chapter 8)?

4. Was the manipulation salient to the research participants (Chapter 7)? If the independent variable tends to blend in with the rest of the research situation, participants cannot notice it, and, therefore, they cannot respond to it. Similarly, if aspects of the situation distract participants' attention from the independent variable, it cannot have an effect.

The Dependent Variable

1. Is there evidence for the construct validity of the operational definition of the dependent variable (Chapter 5)? As with the independent variable, if the operational definition of the dependent variable does not adequately reflect the hypothetical construct, one should not expect an effect.

---

researchers to test and be frustrated by the same hypothesis. Resources that could be used on more fruitful research have been squandered. In contrast, Greenwald's case studies of Type I error epidemics suggest that if researchers carefully replicate null results that have theoretical importance, then they can overcome the prejudice and get their results into the scientific knowledge base.

Why does this prejudice exist? There are at least two reasons (Greenwald, 1975). First, most theories are expressed in terms of the presence rather than the absence of relationships. Consequently, researchers tend to think of theory testing in terms of finding rather than not finding relationships. Null results are therefore seen as sources of disappointment rather than as sources of information about the theory. Second, the meaning of null results can be ambiguous because they could represent Type II errors. Therefore, studies designed to test the null hypothesis must be carefully designed to

BOX 13-1 *(continued)*

2. Is the measure of the dependent variable sensitive enough to detect an effect of the independent variable? An insensitive measure will not detect an effect (Chapter 11).

3. In correlational research, is there a restriction in the range of scores on the dependent variable (Chapter 8)?

Research Design

1. Was the research designed in such a way as to detect a curvilinear relationship between the independent and dependent variables? If the research is designed so that only a linear effect can be found—using only two levels of the independent variable or a simple correlational design—a curvilinear effect will look like a null result (Chapters 7 and 8).

2. Were the extraneous variables controlled? Extraneous variables can increase the error variance of a statistical test and reduce its power to detect an effect of the independent variable (Chapter 7).

3. Was the research designed to detect the effect of a moderator variable if theory or prior research suggested that one might have an effect? The independent variable might have an effect in one condition of the moderator variable, but not in another. If the research design used only the latter condition of the

moderator variable, the independent variable will not have an effect (Chapter 7).

4. Was the research designed to detect the presence of mediating variables if a theory or prior research suggests they might be present (Chapter 8)? If two mediating variables have opposite relationships to the dependent variable—one positive, the other negative—they could cancel each other out. For example, Sheets and Braver (1999) found that two variables mediated the relationship between a man's status in an organization and the degree to which women interpreted his behavior as constituting sexual harassment: his power in the organization and the degree to which he was perceived to have positive personal characteristics. However, the man's having more organizational power led to *increased* perceptions of sexual harassment whereas having more positive characteristics led to *decreased* perceptions of harassment. As a result, a simple test of the effect of organizational status of perceptions of sexual harassment was not statistically significant.

5. Was the sample size large enough to provide a reasonable level of statistical power (Chapter 12)? Remember, without sufficient statistical power, one cannot say that the null hypothesis was supported even if the results of the statistical test are not significant.

minimize the possibility of Type II error. Research that unexpectedly obtains null results should be carefully examined for the possibility of Type II error, and it should be replicated both exactly and conceptually in order to confirm the initial results and determine if the null results were a function of the particular method used to test the hypothesis.

Possible Sources of Type II Errors

Before accepting the null hypothesis, you must carefully examine the research to ensure that it did not include factors that could lead to a Type II error. What factors can lead to Type II errors and so must be ruled out in order to accept the null hypothesis? A number of potential sources of Type II errors have been discussed so far in this book, although they were not originally presented in that context. Box 13-1 recapitulates these points in the form of questions you should ask about a study whenever it produces null results; the chapters in which the issues are discussed are shown in parentheses. Overlooking factors such as these may lead you to erroneously accept the null hypothesis.

Accepting the Null Hypothesis

Given the possible sources of Type II errors shown in Box 13-1, under what conditions can we accept the null hypothesis with reasonable confidence? There are two situations in which we might want to do so: when we predict no effect of the independent variable and when we unexpectedly find no effect. Let's first examine criteria for accepting the null hypothesis that are common to both situations, then look at additional criteria that apply to each situation.

COMMON CRITERIA   A number of criteria must be met if one is to accept either a predicted or unexpected null result (T. D. Cook, Gruder, Hennigan, & Flay, 1979; Greenwald, 1975; Harcum, 1990). The first criterion, as for all research, is proper design of the study; none of the possible alternative explanations for null results listed in Box 13-1 should be present in the research. Second, there should be sufficient statistical power to detect an effect of the independent variable if it has an effect. As noted in the previous chapter, J. Cohen (1992) suggests a power of at least .8. This level is probably sufficient for an unexpected null result, the context in which Cohen was writing. However, if you predict the null hypothesis, you should probably set a power level as strict as the alpha level for a predicted research hypothesis; that is, power should probably be at least .95.

Because a very sensitive, high-power study could provide statistically significant but trivial results, you should establish a criterion for the minimum effect size required for practical significance (Greenwald, 1975). You can then conduct a statistical test to determine if the effect size found in the research is significantly different from this criterion effect size (Fowler, 1985). If high statistical power cannot be achieved, such as when a rarely occurring phenomenon is being studied or when measures are by their natures insensitive, Yeaton and Sechrest (1987b) suggest that a contrast effect can support the null hypothesis. A contrast effect occurs when one treatment, such as relaxation therapy, has no effect on a dependent variable, such as respiratory functioning in asthmatic children, while an alternative treatment, such as medication, has an effect under the same adverse research conditions.

PREDICTED NULL RESULTS   When predicting a null result, in addition to the criteria just listed, you should ensure that there is a good theoretical or empirical basis for the prediction (Harcum, 1990). Predictions of null results, just like predictions of positive effects of independent variables, should derive logically from the theory being tested and should function to advance the development of the theory (recall Chapter 4).

UNEXPECTED NULL RESULTS   Unexpected null results occur despite theoretical and empirical evidence suggesting that the research hypothesis should be supported. You should therefore want very strong evidence that the independent variable did not, in fact, have an effect (Yeaton & Sechrest, 1987b). If the common criteria just listed are met, three other factors support a true null result. One is a very small effect size; the closer it is to zero, the less likely it is that the independent variable had an effect. The second factor is consistency with other empirical findings. However, given the prejudice against publication of null results, such convergent research might be hard to find. Finally, you should conduct replications to confirm the null result. Such replications should not only give the independent variable a fair chance of having an effect and so overturn the initial null result, but should also bend over backward to give the independent variable an opportunity to have an effect; in essence, the deck should be stacked as much in favor of the research hypothesis as good research procedures allow. If the independent variable still has no observable effect under even the most favorable conditions, it probably has no effect at all (Mook, 1983).

INTEGRATING THE RESULTS OF RESEARCH

Research studies are not conducted in a vacuum. As noted in Chapter 4, they derive from prior theoretical, empirical, and applied work, and the results of each study must be integrated into this broader body of knowledge. There are no set rules for this process; however, it should be guided by the purposes of the research and the research problem developed during the hypothesis generation process discussed in Chapter 4 and laid out in the research proposal. You must link each theoretical, methodological, and applied issue identified in the proposal as a topic of investigation to the results of the research, and must think through the implications of the research results for each of these issues. Similarly, you must think through the implications for each of these areas of any unexpected results or discoveries. This process is both one of the most creative and one of the most difficult parts of research and will serve as the nucleus of the Discussion section of your report of the research.

Identifying Implications for Theory

Research hypotheses are based on both predictions derived from a theory and previous research that has tested the theory. Consequently, as illustrated in Figure 13-2, the results of your research, the results of previous research, and the similarities to and differences between the results of your research and those of previous research all have implications for the theory being tested. Therefore, although linking your results to those of previous research and linking your results to theory are discussed separately, in practice the two processes take place simultaneously.

COMPARISON WITH PRIOR RESEARCH   The first question to ask is "How well do my results agree with those of previous research?" If your results fit in well, then you can move on to consider the implications of the combination of your results and those of prior research for theory, as discussed later. If your results do not agree well with those of prior research, then you must ask why. Answering this question requires a careful consideration of the similarities and differences of your research and the prior research. For example, was your hypothesis somewhat different? Did you use different

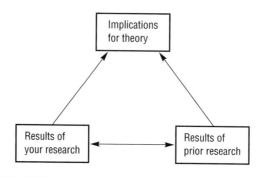

FIGURE 13-2   Linkages Between Results of Your Research, Results of Prior Research, and Implications for Theory
The results of your research, the results of previous research, and the similarities to and differences between the results of your research and those of previous research all have implications for the theory being tested.

operational definitions or a different study population or research setting? Recall the Whitley (1982) study described in Chapters 4 and 7 that resolved an apparent contradiction in the results of two studies testing the same hypothesis using similar procedures by showing that the operational definitions used were different enough to cause the contradiction.

COMPARISON WITH THEORETICAL PREDICTIONS   Again, the first question is "How well do my results agree with the predictions made by the theory?" Were all the predictions supported, only some, or none? If the research compared two or more theories, how well supported were the predictions made by each? Here is where the predicted outcome diagram illustrated in Tables 13-1 and 13-2 comes into play. Given the results of your research, those of prior research, and the relations between them, you now must ask three more questions. First, should the theory be modified and, if so, how? J. Cooper and Fazio (1984) present an excellent description of how cognitive dissonance theory developed and changed based on the results of research that delimited the conditions under which its predictions would hold. Second, are there limits to the generalizability of the theory? Does it operate similarly for all populations and in all settings? If not, under what conditions is it most effective? Finally, what does the research say about the application of the theory? Does it meet its applied goals, and are there new, previously unidentified, applications for it?

Identifying Implications for Research

The results of a study can have implications for future research on the topic that was investigated. These implications can deal with research procedures or new research questions.

RESEARCH PROCEDURES   The results of a study, either alone or in combination with those of other studies, sometimes suggest that the measures, manipulations, or procedures used to study a problem are inadequate and need to be changed. Such findings indicate that researchers should direct their efforts toward improving operational definitions or research procedures before doing further research on the topic. For example, T. D. Cook et al. (1979) noted that research on an attitude phenomenon known as the "sleeper effect," in which a persuasive communication has no immediate effect but attitude change does occur later, was hampered because the operational definitions used in the research did not adequately represent the hypothetical constructs. The poor operational definitions initially used led to conflicting results among studies; development of better operational definitions led to a more consistent set of results.

NEW RESEARCH QUESTIONS   No study ever answers, or can even address, all the research questions on a topic. You must therefore ask the question "What else do I need to do?" For example, what related theoretical issues do you now need to address? Perhaps your research addressed one step in a causal sequence proposed by theory; what step or steps should you address next? Does your research suggest that the theory being tested ties into other theories (see Chapter 1)? If so, what linkages does your research suggest and how should they be tested? Does the theory need to be tested in new settings or with new study populations? If your research had unexpected results, what kind of further research is needed to confirm them and to understand their meaning for theory or application?

Identifying Implications for Application

When the goal of the research was to test the effectiveness of an intervention, questions parallel to those for identifying implications for theory arise: Does the intervention have the predicted effect? How well do the results of your research agree with those of previous research? Do you need to modify the intervention, and, if so, how? Are there limits on the use of the intervention in terms of settings, populations, and so forth? If the goal of the research was to gather information on a problem, how should that information be used to address the problem? When the goal of the research was theory testing, you should still think about the potential applications of the theory and about how those applications could be tested empirically.

SUMMARY

Four aspects of the interpretation of research results are describing the results, drawing inferences from the results, null results, and integrating the results into the body of existing theory and research. When describing the results of research, include the nature of the relationship between the independent and dependent variables, the likelihood that the observed relationship occurred by chance, the size of the relationship, and the importance of the relationship. Relationships can be linear or curvilinear and can be moderated or mediated. When interpreting the results of research, compare the relationship found in the data to that predicted by the research hypothesis and use inferential statistics to determine if the observed relationship is real or occurred by chance. Be careful, however, to test the proper statistical hypothesis, the one that reflects the comparisons required by the research hypothesis, using focused contrasts rather than omnibus statistical tests.

Given a sufficiently sensitive research design—a high-impact independent variable, a sensitive dependent measure, a large number of research participants—even a very small effect of the independent variable can be statistically significant. It is therefore often useful to consider the size of the effect when interpreting the results of research. Effect sizes indicate the magnitude of the impact of the independent variable, and there are conventions for what constitute small, medium, and large effects. Effect sizes can be compared and cumulated across studies, and they can be used to determine appropriate sample sizes for future research. It is important to bear in mind, however, that effect size is a function not only of the impact of the independent variable as a hypothetical construct, but also of the operational definitions of the independent and dependent variables. Consequently, you should interpret effect sizes within the context of the research procedures. Also, be careful not to confuse effect size with importance. Small effect sizes can be important when they cumulate across time to have large effects, when a small effect applied to a large population results in a large effect in the population, and when they test theoretical propositions.

Inference in behavioral science research is the process of drawing conclusions about hypothetical constructs and the relationships between them on the basis of manifest variables and their relationships. Because these inferences involve interpretations of data, different people can draw different conclusions from the same data. Consequently, theories reflect the social values of the times during which they are constructed, and the interpretation of data can be contaminated by theoretical and personal biases. Bias can be minimized and valid interpretations maximized by interpreting data carefully. Pay careful attention to the levels of measurement used in the research, avoid the fallacy of the mean, and properly interpret the results of the statistical test. Carefully consider the degree of validity of the measures and manipulations used in the research, and think about results descriptively rather than evaluatively. Finally, draw causal conclusions only from experimental research, and be careful not to overgeneralize results.

Null results occur when no statistically significant relationship is found between the independent and dependent variables. Although null results are often disappointing, null hypotheses play important roles in psychological research: They can test theory, ensure validity, and test the generalizability of results. Despite these uses, the null hypothesis is generally not valued by researchers, and studies with null results are rarely published. Consequently, nonsupportive information is rarely disseminated about theories. An important source of the reluctance to accept null results is their ambiguity—there are many alternative explanations for the lack of an effect of the independent variable. For the null hypothesis to be accepted as valid, the research must have been properly conducted and there must have been sufficient statistical power. If the researcher predicts null results, there should be theoretical or empirical justification for the prediction. Unexpected null results should be carefully replicated.

The conclusions drawn from research results must be fitted into the existing body of knowledge. Carefully compare the results of your research to those of prior research and to the predictions derived from theory. Then determine the implications of those results for modifying theory, for designing research, for new research, and for application.

QUESTIONS AND EXERCISES FOR REVIEW

1. What is an expected outcome diagram? How is it used in interpreting the results of research?
2. Describe the functions of inferential statistics in research. What types of decision errors can occur when inferential statistics are used?
3. Describe the inferential problem posed by the use of omnibus statistical tests. How can researchers avoid this problem?
4. Explain the distinction between statistical significance and effect size. What are the advantages of computing effect sizes? How can a small effect size actually indicate a large impact of the independent variable?
5. Explain the distinction between effect size and the practical significance of an effect. How does one determine practical significance? How can small effects have practical significance?
6. Explain the constructionist viewpoint on scientific knowledge. What does this viewpoint imply for the interpretation of behavioral science data?
7. Describe instances of bias in the interpretation of behavioral science data with which you are familiar. Do these instances represent theoretical or personal bias? What factors might be indicative of bias in the interpretation of research results?
8. What factors should you consider in making valid inferences from research results?
9. Describe the uses of the null hypothesis. What consequences result from the prejudice against the null hypothesis? Why does this prejudice exist?
10. What are the possible sources of Type II errors in research?
11. Describe the criteria for accepting null results as valid.
12. What issues should you consider in identifying the implications of research results for theory, research, and application?
13. Interpretation of results is, perhaps, the most difficult part of research, and it requires some practice. Try this exercise, adapted from Drew (1976):
    a. Copy a journal article reporting the results of an empirical study. Pick one that covers a topic that interests you, is familiar to you, uses a simple design, and that you find relatively easy to read. You can repeat this exercise with more complex studies as you gain experience.
    b. Tape paper over the pages of the Discussion section of the article, which contains the authors' interpretations of their results.
    c. Carefully read the introduction, which presents the background and hypotheses for the study, the Method section, which describes how the research was conducted, and the Results section.
    d. Write your own interpretation of the results, considering the authors' hypotheses, their methodology, their rationale for their hypotheses, and *your* knowledge of the research topic and of research methods.
    e. Uncover the authors' discussion, and compare your interpretation to theirs. If your interpretation differs, what might have caused the differences?

14 THE EXTERNAL VALIDITY OF RESEARCH

THE CONCEPT OF EXTERNAL
VALIDITY
Aspects of External Validity
Components of External Validity
   The Structural Component
   The Functional Component
   The Conceptual Component

THE STRUCTURAL COMPONENT
OF EXTERNAL VALIDITY
Setting Factors
   The Physical Setting
   Reactivity
   Researcher Attributes
   Coparticipant Attributes
   Ecological Validity
Participant Sample Factors
   Convenience Sampling
   Restricted Sampling
   Volunteer Participants
   Person-by-Situation
      Interactions
   Ecological Validity

Research Procedure Factors
   Artificiality
   Operational Definitions
   Levels of the Independent
      Variable
   Ecological Validity
Cultural Factors
Time Factors
   Time Sampling
   Changes Over Time

THE FUNCTIONAL AND
CONCEPTUAL COMPONENTS
OF EXTERNAL VALIDITY
The Functional Component
The Conceptual Component
Relationships Among the
   Components of External
   Validity

ASSESSING EXTERNAL
VALIDITY
Assessing Generalizability
Assessing Ecological Validity
   The Components of
      Ecological Validity
   Success Criteria

LABORATORY RESEARCH,
NATURAL SETTING RESEARCH,
AND EXTERNAL VALIDITY
Laboratory Research and
   Ecological Validity
   Purposes of Research
   Ecological Validity as an
      Empirical Question
   Natural Settings and
      Generalizability
   Structural Versus Functional
      and Conceptual
      Verisimilitude
   Analog Research
   Philosophies of Science and
      Naturalism in Research
External Validity and Internal
   Validity

SUMMARY

QUESTIONS AND EXERCISES
FOR REVIEW

Every research study is unique: It is carried out in a particular setting, using particular procedures, with a particular sample of participants, at a particular time. At the same time, studies are often conducted to determine general principles of behavior that are expected to operate in a variety of circumstances. An important question, therefore, is the extent to which the findings from any one study apply in other settings, at other times, with different participants, when different procedures are used.

This question represents the issue of **external validity.** This chapter first considers the concept of external validity and defines its components. It then considers each of the components of external validity in more detail. After that are discussed ways of assessing the external validity of research. The chapter concludes by examining the continuing controversy over the applicability of the results of laboratory research to natural settings and by considering the relationship between internal validity and external validity.

THE CONCEPT OF EXTERNAL VALIDITY

The concept of external validity can be expressed as a question: Are the findings of a study specific to the conditions under which the study was conducted, or do they represent general principles of behavior that apply under a wide-ranging set of conditions? Because of this focus on how broadly findings apply, the term *generalizability* is often used synonymously with *external validity;* however, I will use the term *generalizability* to refer to a specific aspect of external validity. This section examines the two most common ways in which the term *external validity* is used and identifies and defines the components of external validity.

Aspects of External Validity

T. D. Cook and Campbell (1979) identify two aspects of external validity. One aspect they call "generalizing across," which refers to the question of whether the results of a study pertain equally to more than one setting, population, or subpopulation, such as to both men and women. The other aspect they call "generalizing to," which refers to the question of whether the results of a study pertain to a particular setting or population, such as hospitalized psychiatric patients.

To a large extent, basic researchers are more interested in the "generalizing across" aspect of generalizability than in the "generalizing to" aspect. This focus derives from their interest in discovering general principles of behavior and theories that will apply regardless of population, setting, or operational definition. If a principle does not operate as expected under a particular set of circumstances, those circumstances are incorporated into the theory as **boundary,** or limiting, **conditions.**

Somewhat in contrast to the basic researchers' focus on "generalizing across," applied researchers are more interested in the "generalizing to" aspect of generalizability.

This focus derives from their interest in using theory and research to solve problems in particular settings (such as psychology clinics, the criminal justice system, and schools) that are inhabited by particular populations (such as therapists and patients; police officers, defendants, attorneys, judges, and jurors; and teachers, students, parents, and administrators). Consequently, applied researchers place a high value on what Brunswik (1956) called the ecological validity of research. The term **ecological validity** refers to the degree to which the conditions under which research is carried out mimic the conditions found in a natural setting to which they are to be applied. The strictest interpretation of the concept of ecological validity holds that only the results of research conducted in the setting itself are valid for application to that setting.

This discussion will distinguish between the generalizing-across and the generalizing-to aspects of external validity by referring to the generalizing-across aspect as **generalizability** and the generalizing-to aspect as *ecological validity*. However, as T. D. Cook and Campbell (1979) note, these aspects are closely related, so be careful not to overemphasize the difference between them. After all, if a principle generalizes across variations in a set of conditions, such as participant populations, then it generalizes to each of those conditions. For example, if a principle generalizes across sex of research participant, it is applicable to both women and men.

Components of External Validity

The differing views of external validity on the part of basic and applied researchers have led to a somewhat acrimonious debate over the applicability of laboratory-based theories and research findings to natural settings. Some of the issues in this debate are considered in the last section of this chapter. The aspect of the debate discussed in this section is the nature of the concept of external validity, especially in its sense of ecological validity. Vidmar (1979) has suggested that external validity has three components: a structural component that is relevant to both generalizability and ecological validity, and functional and conceptual components that are more relevant to ecological validity. These relationships are illustrated in Figure 14-1.

THE STRUCTURAL COMPONENT   The **structural component** of external validity is concerned with the method by which a study is carried out, including factors such as the setting in which the study is conducted, the research procedures used, and the nature of the participant sample. The findings of a particular study are high on the generalizability aspect of external validity to the extent that they remain consistent when tested in new studies that use different methods. That is, studies that test the same hypothesis should get reasonably similar results regardless of differences in settings (such as laboratory or field), research procedures (such as operational definitions), and research participants (such as college students or factory workers). Conceptual replication of research (discussed in Chapter 4) is therefore one way of testing the generalizability of research. Research findings are high on the ecological validity aspect of external validity to the extent that they can be replicated in a particular natural setting, using the procedures normally used in that setting and with the people usually found in the setting.

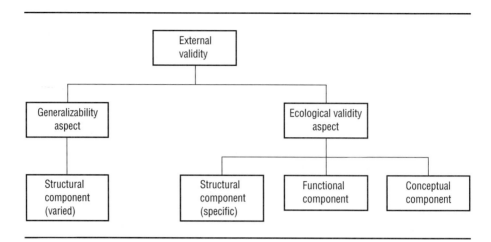

FIGURE 14-1   The Meanings of External Validity
External validity has two components: generalizability, which deals with questions of whether the results of
a particular study can be replicated under different conditions, and ecological validity, which deals with the
question of whether a finding can be applied in a particular setting. Generalizability therefore focuses on
whether different aspects of the structure of research (such as settings, procedures, and participant populations) lead to differences in findings, whereas ecological validity focuses on the similarity between a study and
a natural setting to which its results will be applied. This similarity includes similarity in the structure of the research and natural settings, similarity in the psychological processes operating in the settings, and similarity
in the issues studied in the research setting and those of importance in the natural setting.

Consider, for example, a laboratory study on the effects of college student participants' having a say in setting task goals on the satisfaction they derive from performing
the task, with satisfaction assessed by a paper-and-pencil measure. The generalizability
of the results of the study could be tested by having students at another college participate or not participate in setting goals for a different task and assessing their satisfaction
using a different paper-and-pencil measure. The ecological validity of the results could
be tested by seeing if they apply in a particular factory with the people who work there,
using a naturalistic indicator of satisfaction such as the number of grievances filed by
the workers. Notice that a test of the ecological validity of a research finding is essentially a conceptual replication of that finding and is therefore also a test of the finding's
generalizability. The second section of this chapter examines some factors that can affect the structural component of external validity.

THE FUNCTIONAL COMPONENT   The **functional component** of external validity is the degree to which the psychological processes that operate in a study are similar to the psychological processes at work in a particular natural setting. Because of its focus on the
degree to which a component of research mimics a component of a natural setting,
the functional component of external validity pertains primarily to questions about the
ecological validity of research results. For example, the question of whether people who
participate in mock jury research, whose decisions have no effect on anyone's life, process evidence and make decisions in the same way as real jurors, whose decisions have

TABLE 14-1   The Structural, Functional, and Conceptual Components of External Validity

Component	Focus	Issue Addressed
Structural	Methodology	Are the results of research consistent across variations in settings, procedures, populations, etc.?
Functional	Psychological processes	Are the psychological processes that operate in research settings similar to those operating in applicable natural settings?
Conceptual	Research question	Is the research question under investigation one of importance in the applicable natural setting?

important effects on people's lives, is a question of the functional validity of mock jury research. The third section of this chapter discusses the functional component of external validity.

THE CONCEPTUAL COMPONENT   The **conceptual component** of external validity is the degree to which the problems studied in research corresponds to problems considered important in a natural setting. Like questions concerning the functional component of external validity, those concerning the conceptual component of external validity arise primarily in the context of ecological validity. For example, researchers who study crowding are often interested in its psychological effects, such as stress. However, people in natural settings who must deal with crowded conditions, such as prison administrators, are more interested in its behavioral effects, such as aggression (Ruback & Innes, 1988). Therefore, from the viewpoint of prison administrators, research on the psychological effects of crowding is low on conceptual validity. The third section of this chapter discusses the conceptual component of external validity along with the functional component.

Let's recapitulate the discussion so far. As Figure 14-1 showed, external validity has two aspects: generalizability, or the extent to which research results hold up across variations in the structure of studies, and ecological validity, or the extent to which research results can be applied to a particular natural setting. Table 14-1 summarizes the three components of external validity. Issues of structural validity apply to questions of both generalizability and ecological validity, whereas issues of functional and conceptual validity apply primarily to questions of ecological validity. Vidmar (1979) used the term *verisimilitude* to refer to the similarity between research settings and natural settings and thus to the ecological validity of research. I will also use the terms *structural, functional,* and *conceptual verisimilitude* when discussing ecological validity.

THE STRUCTURAL COMPONENT OF EXTERNAL VALIDITY

Epstein (1980) suggests that researchers want to generalize their findings across four structural dimensions: settings, participant samples, research procedures, and time; cultures can also be included in this list. The setting concerns the physical and social environment in which the research takes place. Participants are the people from whom data are collected and who can represent different subgroups or classes of people, such as sex or race. Research procedures include operational definitions, instructions, and tasks. Time represents the possibility that relationships between variables may not be stable, but may change as a function of historical events or social change. Culture concerns the shared history, traditions, and worldview of a social group. To the extent that research findings represent general principles of behavior, they should be relatively stable across each of these dimensions. The following sections discuss some of these factors that can affect the external validity of research.

Parenthetically, note that although these factors are sometimes called "threats to external validity," it is more accurate to consider them sources of study-to-study extraneous variation in tests of the same hypothesis. The better a hypothesis holds up across these variations, the more likely it is to be generally applicable; failures to hold up suggest limits on its applicability.

Setting Factors

Research settings vary considerably from study to study. Not only can the physical setting (and its potential for reactivity) vary, but even within settings such factors as characteristics of the researcher and of the other people taking part in the research with the participant can vary from study to study. This section discusses the effects of these setting factors on generalizability and ecological validity.

THE PHYSICAL SETTING   Aspects of the physical setting can affect research participants' responses to the independent variable and thereby affect the generalizability of the results of research conducted in the setting. R. Rosenthal (1976), for example, found that research participants' evaluations of an experimenter varied as a function of the room in which they made their evaluations. Behavior can be altered by as seemingly minor a factor as the presence or absence of a mirror in the laboratory room (Wicklund, 1975); people become more concerned with making a good impression under such circumstances. Cherulnik (1983) notes that this finding can have important implications for researchers who use "one-way" mirrors to observe people's behavior: The participants' behavior may change even if the participants don't deduce that they are under observation. Physiological measures, such as blood pressure, can also be affected by the physical setting (Biner, 1991). The environment can influence behavior in many ways (Darley & Gilbert, 1985); to the extent that aspects of research environments interact with the independent variable, people's responses can vary from setting to setting. It is therefore important to examine the research environment for any factors that might interact with the independent variable to affect the dependent variable.

REACTIVITY   As noted in Chapter 6, the term *reactivity* refers to people's tendency to change their behavior when they know they are observed. To the extent that research settings are differentially reactive, responses to the same independent variable may differ between those settings. Researchers have developed a number of techniques for reducing the reactivity of the research setting, such as naturalistic observation, field experiments, and various forms of deception. Even when participants are fully aware of being in an experiment, reactivity can often be reduced by creating a high degree of experimental realism: manipulating the independent variable in such an engaging manner that subjects become so psychologically involved in the situation that they give realistic responses (see Chapter 12).

RESEARCHER ATTRIBUTES   It should come as no surprise that people's behavior is affected by the characteristics of the persons with whom they interact. In a research study, the participant interacts with the experimenter, and the experimenter's characteristics can affect the participant's responses. For example, variation in sex of experimenter has been associated with variation in the accuracy of task performance, the reporting of intimate information, and response to projective tests, among other variables (Rumenik, Capasso, & Hendrick, 1977). The race of the experimenter can affect expression of prejudicial attitudes (Summer & Hammonds, cited in R. Rosenthal, 1976) and physiological response (A. S. Bernstein, 1965). In addition to gender and race, other experimenter characteristics, such as personality, values, and experience, can affect participants' behavior (R. Rosenthal, 1976). However, Barber (1976) points out that the effects of these nonphysical experimenter attributes may be relatively small. As noted in Chapter 6, researchers can assess the impact of experimenter attributes by using multiple experimenters and including the experimenter as a factor in the data analysis.

COPARTICIPANT ATTRIBUTES   When people participate in an experiment in groups, the potential exists for them to be influenced by each other's behavior and personal characteristics. Even when they don't speak to each other, coparticipants' physical characteristics, such as race and gender, might have an influence on behavior. McGuire (1984) has shown, for example, that when someone is the sole member of his or her gender or race in a group, that characteristic becomes more salient to the person. This salience phenomenon has been found to affect responses to personality inventories (Cota & Dion, 1986) and could have other effects as well. Solutions to this problem include making participant groups as homogeneous as possible and having people participate individually rather than in groups.

ECOLOGICAL VALIDITY   In terms of ecological validity, the physical, social, and psychological structure of a research setting, especially a laboratory setting, can be very different from that of a natural setting, such as the workplace or the clinic. Consequently, behavior in the usually less complex laboratory setting may be very different from that in the natural setting (Bouchard, 1976). This difference may be especially important in settings that may be designed to influence the processes that take place there, such as the psychology clinic (Kazdin, 1997). In the social structure of the laboratory, the research participant is usually cut off from his or her natural social network, and is often placed in the position of being a passive recipient of the researcher's manipulations rather than being proactive and interactive with other people (Argyris, 1980). The most ecologically valid research setting from the structural point of view, therefore, is the natural setting of the behavior or process of interest. Lacking access to the natural setting, the research setting should be as similar to it as possible, that is, be characterized by what Aronson and Carlsmith (1968) call mundane realism (see

Chapter 12). For example, jury research might take place in the mock courtroom of a law school.

Participant Sample Factors

Although research settings show a high degree of variability in their characteristics, research participants are often quite homogeneous in their demographic, social, and psychological characteristics, which can be very different from those of the population in general. This section considers some of the effects of that homogeneity on the generalizability and ecological validity of research results.

CONVENIENCE SAMPLING   As Chapter 12 noted, much behavioral science research uses convenience sampling; that is, participants are chosen on the basis of availability rather than on the basis of representativeness of the population as a whole or of a particular subpopulation. The most convenient participants for most researchers are college students, which has led to the assumption that the results of such research are ungeneralizable to other populations (see Sears, 1986, for example). Because this question is closely related to that of ecological validity, it will be addressed as part of that discussion and the conclusion of this section.

RESTRICTED SAMPLING   Sometimes participant samples are restricted to one category of persons, such as men, people of European descent, or young adults. For example, men have appeared as research participants much more often than have women (Gannon, Luchetta, Rhodes, Pardie, & Segrist, 1992), and 90% of all research on aggression has used male participants, whereas only half has used female participants (McKenna & Kessler, 1977); in contrast, studies of social influence have primarily used women as participants (Eagly & Carli, 1981). However, Gannon et al. (1992) report that behavioral science research has increasingly included women in recent years. Racial minorities have been so rarely included in behavioral science research that Guthrie (1998) titled his history of African Americans in psychology *Even the Rat was White*. In sharp contrast to the increasing inclusion of women in behavioral science research, Graham (1992) reports that studies published in prestigious journals are currently less likely to include African Americans than studies published 25 years ago. The age of participants is also frequently restricted. Sears (1986) found that only 17% of adult subjects in social psychological research were older than the average college student. Thus, it may be difficult to generalize much of behavioral science research across subpopulations because of the predominance of European-American male college students as research participants.

VOLUNTEER PARTICIPANTS   As noted in Chapter 6, people who volunteer to participate in research differ from nonvolunteers in many ways, such as need for approval, psychological adjustment, need for achievement, IQ, and birth order (R. Rosenthal & Rosnow, 1975). To the extent that these factors interact with the independent variable, there will be a lack of generalizability to nonvolunteers. Even when people are required to participate in research, as are many introductory psychology students, elements of volunteerism remain. People are generally allowed to choose which of several experiments to participate in, and certain types of people are attracted to certain types of studies. For example, men are more likely to volunteer for studies on "masculine" topics such as power and competition, and women for "feminine" topics such as revealing feelings and moods (Signorella & Vegega, 1984). People who volunteer for sex research are more sexually experienced and have more liberal sexual attitudes than nonvolunteers (Farkas, Sine, & Evans, 1978). Because participants can withdraw from research after they learn about the procedures to be used, they can "devolunteer"; Wolchik, Braver, and Jensen (1985), for example, found that volunteer rates for sex research dropped from 67% to 30% for men and from 38% to 13% for women when the procedures required some undressing. These problems point out the importance of reporting participant refusal and dropout rates and of taking the characteristics of "survivors" into account when interpreting results: The results of the research may apply only to people with these characteristics.

PERSON-BY-SITUATION INTERACTIONS   The possibility that the characteristics of volunteer participants might interact with the independent variable to affect the results of a study is an example of the broader case of the person-by-situation interaction: Different types of people, such as those with different personality characteristics, might respond differently to the same independent variable (Cronbach, 1975). Thus, the results of a study might apply only to one type of person if only that type is represented in the study. For example, Aronson, Willerman, and Floyd (1966) found that a person's making a mistake led to lower evaluation of the person when the person was of low status. However, later research revealed that this effect was found only for research participants of average self-esteem; High and low self-esteem participants did not give lower evaluations to a low-status person (Helmreich, Aronson, & LeFan, 1970). It can be useful, therefore, for researchers to carefully examine any project they propose to carry out to determine if the personal characteristics of participants might interact with the independent variables to affect the outcome.

ECOLOGICAL VALIDITY   Much criticism of the ecological validity of behavioral science research has centered around the use of research participants who are unrepresentative of the populations to which the results of the research might be applied. Sears (1986), for example, points out that most research in social psychology has used college students in the 18–22 age range as participants; other studies suggest that the same pattern holds true for other areas of behavioral science (Dipboye & Flanagan, 1979; Endler & Parker, 1991). As Sears notes, late adolescents differ from the population in general and from specific populations of interest to many applied researchers, such as factory workers, managers, and psychiatric patients. College students are not even representative of late adolescents in general. To the extent that the participants in research differ from the population to which the results of the research might apply, the research is low on structural verisimilitude. Because only a relatively small amount of research is intended to apply solely to college students, their use as research participants is often taken as an a priori indicator of low ecological validity.

Although the most ecologically representative participant sample consists of people from the natural setting of interest, these people are not always available for research.

However, for some research an alternative strategy may be to carefully select college students for similarity to the people in the natural setting of interest. Gordon, Slade, and Schmitt (1986), for example, suggest employing research participants with demographic, personality, and interest profiles as similar as possible to those of members of the natural setting population. Thus, psychopathology research could select college student participants on the basis of appropriate clinical criteria (Sanislow, Perkins, & Balogh, 1989). Gordon et al. also suggest using "nontraditional" students who have the appropriate work experience or background for industrial and organizational research. Because one factor that leads to differences in response by college student and natural setting research participants is experience with naturalistic tasks, Gordon, Schmitt, and Schneider (1984) recommend training naive participants on the task; such training can greatly reduce differences in response. Finally, because college student and natural setting participants might interpret the experimental task differently, thus leading to different responses, Adair (1984) suggests debriefing participants on the perceptions, meanings, and understandings they impute to the research situation, and comparing these factors with those of people from the natural setting.

Research Procedure Factors

The procedures used in research can affect its external validity in several ways: The use of artificial procedures can limit the ecological validity of its results and incomplete sampling from the possible operational definitions, and range of values of a construct can limit the generalizability of the research results.

ARTIFICIALITY The contention that the setting, tasks, and procedures of laboratory experiments are artificial, and therefore do not generalize to "real-world" phenomena (for example, see Argyris, 1980), is an important aspect of ecological validity and so will be discussed in that context at the end of this section. In brief, however, note that laboratory research tends to isolate people from their accustomed environments, to present them with relatively simple and time-limited tasks, and to allow them only limited response modes, such as 7-point scales. Most forms of research, including nonlaboratory methods, are in some degree artificial and can vary in artificiality within a method. These variations can affect generalizability across studies.

OPERATIONAL DEFINITIONS Because any construct can have more than one operational definition, any one operational definition can be considered a sample drawn from a population of possible operational definitions (Wells & Windschitl, 1999). Just as response to a stimulus can vary from person to person, so too can one person's response vary from operational definition to operational definition. Although these effects are probably subtle, they can sometimes be large. For example, the correlation between the personality constructs of sex role orientation and self-esteem can vary greatly depending on the operational definitions used (Whitley, 1988). The solution to this problem is relatively simple when dealing with dependent variables in an experiment: Use multiple operational definitions of the construct and test commonality of effect through a multivariate analysis (Tabachnick & Fidell, 1996). As noted in Chapter 7, multiple operational definitions of the independent variable are also possible through the use of multiple exemplars of a category, such as by using two men and two women to represent the categories male and female, in a nested design. This procedure is methodologically and statistically complex, but it improves the generalizability of the results. Multiple operational definitions can also be used in correlational research, using latent variable analysis (see Chapter 8).

LEVELS OF THE INDEPENDENT VARIABLE   Just as it is important to sample from the population of operational definitions, it is important to cover the entire range of the independent variables. As noted in Chapter 7, an experiment using only two levels of a quantitative independent variable assumes a linear relationship between the independent and dependent variables; however, this linear relationship may or may not reflect the true state of nature. Recall the conflicting results of the two studies of the effect of high or low responsibility for a crime on assigned punishment, discussed in Chapter 7. DeJong, Morris, and Hastorf (1976) found a linear relationship between the variables, whereas R. S. Feldman and Rosen (1978) found no relationship. Feldman and Rosen's failure to replicate DeJong et al.'s results could be interpreted as challenging the external validity of those results: They did not appear to hold outside of DeJong et al.'s research context. However, DeJong et al. had operationally defined low and high responsibility as almost no responsibility and almost total responsibility, whereas Feldman and Rosen had used 50% responsibility and almost total responsibility as their operational definitions. When all three levels of responsibility are used, a curvilinear relationship is found: low punishment when there is almost no responsibility, but higher and equal punishment at the two higher levels of responsibility (Whitley, 1982). Both DeJong et al.'s and Feldman and Rosen's studies therefore lacked external validity because neither accurately modeled the true responsibility-punishment relationship. Other phenomena require even more levels of the independent variable to provide an accurate picture of their relationships with dependent variables. For example, the relationship between time spent in the dark and visual adaptation to darkness requires at least five "levels" of time to be properly described (Matlin, 1988). Although using the extremes of an independent variable is often desirable in order to achieve a strong manipulation, it is also wise to include intermediate levels to test for nonlinear effects.

ECOLOGICAL VALIDITY   Sears (1986) suggests that dependence on college students as research participants has led researchers to use artificial, academic tasks that differ considerably from those that most people perform in natural settings. One example of these tasks is the use of experimental simulations, such as the Prisoner's Dilemma game used in research on conflict and conflict resolution (Schlenker & Bonoma, 1978). In addition, laboratory research has participants take a short-term time perspective on tasks, and, unlike natural situations, participants generally suffer no consequences for poor performance or for harm done to others (Fromkin & Streufert, 1976). When participants interact with people other than the experimenter, these people are usually strangers—confederates of the experimenter or ad hoc groups of other research participants—rather than members of natural acquaintance networks. The demands of experimental control may require artificial means of communication between subjects, such as intercoms (Darley & Latané, 1968), or the observation of a videotaped stimulus person rather than face-to-face interaction (Whitley & Greenberg, 1986). Such artificial conditions could elicit artificial responses from research participants, thereby limiting the application of the results of the research to natural settings.

Another aspect of procedural artificiality is that dependent measures are often assessed in ways that are highly artificial and restrictive to the participants' behavior. For example, rarely in a natural setting do people express aggression by pushing a button on a machine that (supposedly) generates an electric shock, or express their attitudes on 7-point scales—common occurrences in laboratory research on these topics. In addition to being behaviorally restrictive, these methods force participants to respond in terms of the researcher's theoretical or empirical model rather than in their own terms. For example, much early research on how people perceived the causes of their successes and failures asked research participants to rate the extent to which ability, effort, luck, and task difficulty—theoretical dimensions of causes—affected their performance on a task, ignoring the many other possible influences people may perceive as relevant (Elig & Frieze, 1979). Finally, the construct being assessed may not resemble the appropriate natural construct. For example, in simulated jury research, to obtain a continuous dependent measure compatible with an analysis-of-variance design, simulated jurors may be asked to make punishment decisions, such as years in prison, rather than the dichotomous guilty–not guilty decisions made by real jurors (Bray & Kerr, 1982).

Also related to the procedural verisimilitude of research is the manner in which research participants are classified on the basis of personal characteristics, such as personality. For example, most research on depression uses responses to relatively brief questionnaires to classify participants, whereas most psychiatric patients are classified on the basis of clinical judgment (Coyne & Gotlib, 1983). To the extent that natural setting and research procedures lead to different classifications, structural verisimilitude is lost.

Cultural Factors

Human behavior is a function not only of the psychological factors and immediate situations normally studied by psychologists, but also of the person's cultural environment. As Matsumoto (2000) shows, responses to similar stimuli can vary greatly from culture to culture. Milgram (1961), for example, found higher levels of conformity to group norms among Norwegians than among French, who showed higher levels of conformity than did Americans. Similarly, Forgas and Bond (1985) found different relationships between demographic, attitudinal, and personality variables and interpretations of others' behavior in Chinese and Australian research participants that reflected differences in broader cultural patterns. There are also differences among American subcultures; for example, male-female relations tend to be more egalitarian among African Americans than European Americans (Adams, 1983). Consequently, researchers and consumers of research must be sensitive to the possibility of cross-cultural differences when interpreting and applying the results of research.

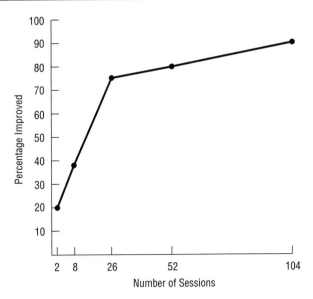

Note: Adapted from Howard et al., 1986, p. 160.

FIGURE 14-2   Relation of Number of Sessions of Psychotherapy and Percentage of Patients Improved
The results of studies based on therapy lasting from 2 to 26 sessions do not generalize to therapy lasting
more than 26 sessions.

Time Factors

Time can affect the external validity of research results in two ways: through problems
in time sampling in research design and through changes in relationships between variables over time.

TIME SAMPLING   Willson (1981) notes that time can be an important factor in the design of research. Some behaviors are cyclic, their frequency rising and falling at regular
intervals. For example, Willson points out that automobile accidents occur more frequently during the winter months in northern states because of adverse weather conditions. Any research aimed at preventing accidents must therefore take seasonal
variations in driving conditions into account: The effectiveness of preventive measures
instituted during summer might not generalize to winter. Research design must also take
into account the amount of time required for an independent variable to have an effect.
For example, Figure 14-2 shows the relationship between the number of psychotherapy
sessions and the cumulative percentage of patients who improve (Howard, Kopta,
Krause, & Orlinski, 1986). This relationship suggests that the results of psychotherapy
research would not generalize across studies that used between 2 and 26 sessions:
Because the outcome of therapy differs substantially among studies based on 2, 8, and

26 psychotherapy sessions, conclusions drawn on the basis of a 2-session study might not apply to psychotherapy that lasted 8 sessions; similarly, the results of an 8-session study might not apply to psychotherapy that lasted 26 sessions. However, the percentage of patients who improve changes little from 26 to 104 sessions, suggesting that you could make generalizations about the effectiveness of therapy that lasted at least 26 sessions.

CHANGES OVER TIME   Beliefs and behaviors change over time; three commonly cited examples are criteria for physical attractiveness (Hatfield & Sprecher, 1986), sexual mores (D'Emilio & Freedman, 1988), and gender roles (Basow, 1992). Such changes led Gergen (1973) to classify the study of the sociocultural aspects of behavior as the study of history, holding that cultural change makes it impossible to identify immutable laws of social behavior. Although this view has not been generally accepted (see Blank, 1988, for a history of the debate), researchers should be sensitive to the possibility of the obsolescence of research findings and should conduct replication studies for findings that may be vulnerable to change (for example, see Simpson, Campbell, & Berscheid, 1986).

THE FUNCTIONAL AND CONCEPTUAL COMPONENTS OF EXTERNAL VALIDITY

Although Vidmar first distinguished between the structural, functional, and conceptual components of external validity in 1979, most discussions of external validity have focused on its structural component, especially in relation to ecological validity. Nonetheless, the other components have important implications for external and ecological validity; let's briefly examine some of them.

The Functional Component

As noted earlier, the functional component of external validity, or functional verisimilitude, deals with the question of the extent to which the psychological processes that affect behavior in the research situation are similar to those that affect behavior in the natural situation. Jung (1981) cites experimental research on the effects of television violence on aggressive behavior as an example of research that is relatively low on functional verisimilitude. Although the experiments are high on structural verisimilitude because they use real television programs, the experimental requirement of random assignment of participants to conditions lessens their functional verisimilitude. Random assignment is designed to balance individual differences across groups; however, if individual differences determine who does and does not watch violent television programming in natural situations, the experiment no longer accurately models the natural process, and functional verisimilitude is lost. One such factor related to watching violent television programs is trait aggressiveness: Children who have a history of aggressiveness prefer violent television programs to nonviolent programs (Milavsky, Stipp,

Kessler, & Rubens, 1982). As important as functional verisimilitude is, it can some-times be difficult to assess. For example, legal restrictions limit access to real juries so that functional comparisons cannot be made between the processes that affect real jury decisions and the processes observed in simulated juries (Bermant, McGuire, McKinley, & Salo, 1974).

The Conceptual Component

As noted, the conceptual component of external validity, or conceptual verisimilitude, deals with the question of the degree to which the problems studied in research on a topic correspond to problems found in the natural situation. Kazdin (1997), for example, questions the conceptual verisimilitude of laboratory studies of systematic de-sensitization of phobias because such studies usually deal only with mild fears of small animals, whereas clinical phobias are much more severe and center around a greater va-riety of stimuli. Similarly, the "subclinical" depression usually studied in college stu-dents may be conceptually quite different from the forms of depression found in clinical populations (Depue & Monroe, 1978).

Conceptual verisimilitude can be especially important for researchers who want their work to be applied to "real-world" problems—if the researcher's conceptual sys-tem does not match that of the policy makers who are expected to implement the re-search in the applied setting, the results of the research will not be used. As you will recall from Chapter 4, Ruback and Innes (1988) suggest two ways in which researchers' and policy makers' conceptions of research differ. The first difference is found in policy makers' need for research involving independent variables that they can change. As Ruback and Innes note, these variables, which they call *policy variables*, may or may not be the most important determinants of behavior in a situation; however, they point out, if a variable cannot be changed, knowledge about its effects cannot lead to policy changes. Researchers, however, more often focus on variables that can be manipulated in the laboratory, which Ruback and Innes call *estimator variables*; however, these vari-ables are not useful to policy makers because there is no way policy makers can control them. For example, in terms of factors affecting the accuracy of eyewitness testimony, the degree of anxiety experienced by a witness during a crime is an estimator variable because the criminal justice system cannot control it; however, the time between the witnessing of the crime and the giving of testimony can be controlled, and so is a pol-icy variable.

The second difference is in what Ruback and Innes (1988) refer to as the *utility* of the dependent variables used—the degree to which the behavior studied is of direct in-terest to the policy maker. For example, prison authorities are more interested in pris-oner violence, illness, and mortality than they are in prisoners' perceptions of control over their environment, which may be of greater interest to the researcher because of its empirical or theoretical importance. Ruback and Innes's analysis suggests that for re-search to be high on conceptual verisimilitude, it must be high on both the number of policy variables investigated and on the utility of the dependent variables.

Relationships Among the Components of External Validity

It is important to bear in mind that structural, functional, and conceptual components of external validity are not entirely independent of one another; all three are necessary to accurately model a natural situation. One aspect of this interdependence is illustrated by Hendrick and Jones's (1972) distinction between chronic and acute manipulations of independent variables. **Chronic manipulations** are those which are found in natural situations and which often result from an accumulation of small effects over time, have been experienced for some time, and are expected to continue into the future; examples are anxiety, self-esteem, and stress. In contrast, experiments normally involve **acute manipulations,** which result from a single event, occur relatively suddenly, and end with the research situation; in fact, ethical considerations require that they end then. For example, using a threat of electric shock to manipulate anxiety constitutes an acute manipulation of anxiety. Acute manipulations thus lack structural verisimilitude because of their time-limited nature. This time limitation may, in turn, call other aspects of ecological validity into question. Conceptual verisimilitude questions the equivalence of long- and short-term anxiety at the construct level, and finds they are probably not equivalent (for example, see Spielberger, Vagg, Barker, Donham, & Westberry, 1980). Functional verisimilitude questions whether the processes involving long- and short-term anxiety are equivalent, and finds they are probably not (for example, see Millman, 1968). One threat to ecological validity may therefore imply others. Conversely, conceptual verisimilitude may require structural verisimilitude. The study of policy-relevant variables, such as the impact of crowding on illness rates, may often be practical only in natural settings (for example, see Ruback & Carr, 1984).

ASSESSING EXTERNAL VALIDITY

The more often that tests of a hypothesis result in similar findings when conducted in a variety of settings using a variety of procedures with a variety of participants over time and across cultures, the more confidence we can have in the generality of the hypothesis. Note that external validity is therefore a characteristic of a set of findings or of a theory, not of an individual study; individual studies function as tests of the generalizability and ecological validity of theories (Cronbach, 1975). This section looks at some of the issues involved in assessing the generalizability and ecological validity of research results.

Assessing Generalizability

By conducting multiple tests of a hypothesis, a researcher can determine the circumstances under which the hypothesis is supported and those under which it is not. This process allows the researcher not only to determine the boundary conditions of the hypothesis, but also to generate and test new hypotheses concerning the rules governing those conditions. Thus, one could interpret the finding that Americans' stereotypes of nationality groups change over time (Karlins, Coffman, & Walters, 1969) as evidence of "psychology as history," or one could use it to test hypotheses about the nature of stereotypes and why they change over time (Secord & Backman, 1974). In addition, replicating the effect of an independent variable using different operational definitions, settings, populations, and procedures enhances the construct validity of the principle being tested. The more varied the conditions under which the effect is replicated, the more likely it is that the effect observed is due to the abstract hypothetical construct than to the concrete conditions under which the research is carried out.

One indicator of a possible lack of generalizability of a hypothesis is an interaction effect in a factorial design: One independent variable has an effect only under certain conditions of the other independent variable. Conversely, the generalizability of an effect across an external validity variable such as setting, procedures, or participant characteristics can be tested by including that variable as a factor in the design. If, for example, sex of participant interacts with topic in an opinion conformity experiment (Eagly & Carli, 1981), then you know that sex differences don't generalize across topics and that topic differences don't generalize across women and men. The large number of factors that affect the external validity of research may lead you to despair of being able to generalize the results of any piece of research: After all, it would be impossible to control all these factors in one study. However, at least three steps can be taken: (1) include generalization factors, such as sex or race of participant, in the study's design; (2) design research projects to systematically replicate findings as a test of their generalizability when the appropriate factors cannot be included in a single design; and (3) interpret the results of research in light of the limits its design places on generalization.

Assessing Ecological Validity

In trying to determine the ecological validity of a theory or of a set of research findings, you must ask two questions: To what degree is each of the components of ecological validity represented in the research on the issue, and what standard should be used to determine if a principle has been successfully replicated in a natural setting?

THE COMPONENTS OF ECOLOGICAL VALIDITY   If the issue of ecological validity is relevant to the evaluation of a theory or piece of research, then you must assess the degree to which the research exhibits conceptual, functional, and structural verisimilitude. On the conceptual level, you must determine the policy relevance of the independent variables and the utility of the dependent variables (see Chapter 4). On the functional level, you must decide how similar the psychological processes involved in the research setting are to those involved in the natural setting. On the structural level, you must evaluate the naturalism of the manipulations or measures of the independent variables, of the measures of the dependent variables, of the research population, and of the characteristics of the research setting. Remember that ecological validity is not an all-or-nothing decision: Each of the components (and subcomponents of structural verisimilitude) can vary along a continuum of similarity to the natural setting (Tunnell, 1977). For example, some populations used in research on a topic are quite similar to the natural populations to which the research might be applied; others are less similar. The amount of confidence that you can have in generalizing to populations not used in the research depends on the similarity of the research and natural populations. Such issues of degree of similarity apply to making generalizations to outcome, treatment, and setting variables that were not used in the research.

Success Criteria   You must also decide what kind of outcome from a natural setting study indicates that a theory or principle has been successfully applied in the setting. J. P. Campbell (1986) notes that successful application or generalization of a theoretical principle or the results of a laboratory study can be defined in at least five ways:

1. Empirical results obtained in the field are *identical* to those obtained in the laboratory.
2. The *direction* of empirical relationships found in the field are the same as those found in the laboratory.
3. The *conclusions* drawn about a specific question are the same for field studies as they are for laboratory studies.
4. The *existence* of a particular phenomenon can be demonstrated in the laboratory as well as the field.
5. Data from the laboratory can be used to justify or support the *application* of a particular practice or program in an operational setting. (p. 270)

Campbell believes that many people tend to think of ecological validity in terms of the first meaning, but suggests that the third and fifth meanings may be the most useful because even exact replications rarely obtain results absolutely identical to those of the original study.

LABORATORY RESEARCH, NATURAL SETTING RESEARCH, AND EXTERNAL VALIDITY

For at least the last half century, behavioral scientists have been engaged in a debate over the roles of laboratory and natural setting research in developing an externally valid body of knowledge. This section discusses two aspects of this debate: laboratory researchers' views on the ecological validity of research and the relationship between external validity and internal validity.

Laboratory Research and Ecological Validity

The discussion of the structural component of external validity noted a number of factors that can limit the ecological validity of the results of laboratory research, such as the artificiality of the research setting and procedures and the widespread use of convenience samples from potentially unrepresentative populations. Some commentators have taken these characteristics of laboratory research as a priori evidence of its external invalidity (Argyris, 1980; Sears, 1986). These critics take the position that if the conditions of research do not faithfully mimic the conditions of a natural setting in which the behavior or process being studied is found, then the results of the research lack external validity. In essence, these critics equate external validity with ecological validity.

As you might expect, researchers who engage in laboratory research do not share that view. This section will present four arguments that have been given in defense of traditional laboratory procedures: that ecological validity, especially when defined solely in terms of structure, is irrelevant to, and in some cases may hinder, the purposes of research, that ecological validity is an empirical question, that conducting research in natural settings does not guarantee its external validity in the sense of generalizability, and that the structural component of external validity is inappropriately given priority over the functional and conceptual components. This section also examines analog research, which attempts to enhance the functional verisimilitude of laboratory research, and considers the roles of scientists' personal philosophies of science in the ecological validity debate.

PURPOSES OF RESEARCH   The defenders of the traditional laboratory experiment point out that research has many goals and that the laboratory environment is more conducive to achieving some goals, whereas the field environment is more conducive to achieving other goals. Specifically, these commentators point to four goals that are better pursued in the laboratory: testing causal hypotheses, falsifying theoretical propositions, dissecting complex phenomena, and discovering new phenomena.

Berkowitz and Donnerstein (1982) state that "laboratory experiments are mainly oriented toward testing some causal hypothesis . . . and are not carried out to determine the probability that a certain event will occur in a particular population" (p. 247). That is, laboratory research is carried out to test the validity of what one hopes are universal theoretical principles; whether members of a particular population undergoing a particular application of a theory in a particular setting show a particular response is an important question, but it is not the type of question asked by laboratory research. As Oakes (1972) wrote in regard to participant samples,

> A behavioral phenomenon reliably exhibited is a genuine phenomenon, no matter what population is sampled in the research in which it is demonstrated. For any behavioral phenomenon, it may well be that members of another population that one could sample might have certain behavioral characteristics that would preclude the phenomenon being demonstrated with that population. Such a finding would suggest a restriction of the generality of the phenomenon, but it would not make it any less genuine. (p. 962)

In fact, very few researchers, either those who are laboratory oriented or those who are field oriented, would claim that their results would apply to all people in all situations; rather, they would say that it is the purpose of programmatic applied research carried out by people knowledgeable of the applied situation to determine the conditions governing the applicability of a theory (Cronbach, 1975).

A second purpose of experimentation is to allow falsification of invalid hypotheses (Calder, Phillips, & Tybout, 1981). If a laboratory experiment provides the most favorable conditions for the manifestation of a phenomenon and the phenomenon still does not occur, it is unlikely to occur under the usually less favorable natural conditions (Mook, 1983). For example, Higgens and Marlatt (1973) conducted a laboratory experiment to test the hypothesis that alcoholics drink to reduce tension and anxiety.

They tried to establish conditions favorable to confirmation of the hypothesis by using threat of electric shock to induce an extremely high level of anxiety in the participants in their research, making alcoholic beverages readily available to participants, and eliminating the use of other forms of tension reduction such as escape from the situation. When their experiment failed to support the hypothesis, Higgens and Marlatt (1973) concluded that "threat of shock did not cause our subjects to drink under these circumstances. Therefore, the tension reduction hypothesis, which predicts that it should have done so, either is false or is in need of qualification" (p. 432). Conversely, one could demonstrate the strength of a phenomenon by showing that it occurs despite artificially strong barriers to it (Prentice & Miller, 1992).

Experiments can also be used to dissect complex naturally occurring variables into their component parts to determine which of the components are crucial to a variable's relationship with another variable. This finer-grained knowledge increases understanding of the relationship and may help to tie it into a theoretical network (Mook, 1983). For example, by randomly assigning research participants to the roles of prisoner and guard in a simulated prison, Haney, Banks, and Zimbardo (1973) were able to remove the effects of self-selection from the role acquisition process and thereby study the influence of situational demands on behavior. Similarly, the artificial controls of laboratory research allowed Lowen and Craig (1968) to specify the reciprocal effects of leader and subordinate behavior.

A final purpose of experimentation is what Henshel (1980) calls its *discovery* function: seeking out previously unknown relationships between variables under conditions that do not exist in natural settings. Because experimental control permits the arrangement of variables in novel configurations, the researcher can create unique physical or social environments to answer "what if" questions. As Henshel puts it, the researcher "seeks to discover [relationships] that are capable of existing, if only the outside world provided the appropriate conditions" (p. 472). Henshel cites brain wave biofeedback as an area of research and application that developed through the discovery process — that is, of testing the effects of highly artificial conditions. He notes that research high in ecological validity would never have detected brain wave biofeedback: "Neither humans nor other organisms are capable of monitoring their own brain waves in the slightest extent without special, artificial arrangements. [The discovery] required experimenters who wondered what *would* happen *if* humans could see their own brain wave output" (p. 473; emphasis in original).

ECOLOGICAL VALIDITY AS AN EMPIRICAL QUESTION   Several analysts of the ecological validity debate have pointed out that the ecological validity of research is fundamentally an empirical question (for example, see Anderson, Lindsay, & Bushman, 1999). That is, the question of whether a particular finding can be applied to a specific setting or population is testable. Such tests have frequently supported the ecological validity of laboratory research. For example, Anderson et al. (1999) examined the results of 21 meta-analyses (see Chapter 16) that compared the average effect sizes found in laboratory and field research in psychology. Anderson et al. found that the average effect sizes for the lab and field studies were generally quite similar and were highly correlated, $r = .73$. They concluded that "the psychological laboratory is doing quite well in terms of external validity; it has been discovering truth, not triviality. Otherwise, correspondence between field and lab effects would be close to zero" (p. 8). Generalizability of results to a particular setting should therefore always be tested, never accepted or rejected out of hand.

NATURAL SETTINGS AND GENERALIZABILITY An often overlooked aspect of the ecological validity debate is that conducting research in a natural setting is no guarantee of its generalizability (Banaji & Crowder, 1989; Locke, 1986). That is, any research carried out in a natural environment is done so in a particular setting, with a particular set of participants, using a particular set of procedures, just as in laboratory research. Therefore, the results are no more or less likely than those of a laboratory experiment to apply to other settings (either natural or laboratory), participants, or procedures. For example, just as laboratory research has been described in McNemar's (1946) classic phrase as "the science of the behavior of sophomores" (p. 333), Dipboye and Flanagan (1979) characterized natural setting research in industrial and organizational psychology as "a psychology of self-report by male, professional, technical, and management personnel in productive-economic organizations" (p. 146), reflecting the modal procedures, participants, and settings used in that field of applied research. As Oakes (1972) noted regarding participant populations, "*any* population one may sample is 'atypical' with respect to some behavioral phenomenon. But the point is that we cannot really say a priori what population is 'more typical'" (p. 962; emphasis in original). Banaji and Crowder (1989) suggest that generalizability and ecological validity are independent dimensions of research and give examples of natural setting studies with low generalizability and of artificial setting studies with high generalizability.

STRUCTURAL VERSUS FUNCTIONAL AND CONCEPTUAL VERISIMILITUDE Locke (1986) states that "ecological representativeness of the type implied in the [ecological] validity thesis is an invalid standard" (p. 7) that focuses on structural issues while ignoring functional issues. In his view, to determine the applicability of research to natural settings one must identify the essential features of the settings that need to be replicated in the lab, such as essential participant, task, and setting characteristics. This process would not involve trying to reproduce the natural settings exactly but, rather, abstracting out of the settings those elements that are required for the phenomenon to occur. In Locke's view, then, it is the functional component of external validity—the similarity of the psychological processes in the natural and research situations—that is the key to ecological validity because it allows for generalization across a variety of natural settings.

ANALOG RESEARCH Research that attempts to extract essential aspects of a natural setting and reproduce them in the laboratory is often referred to as **analog research** because it attempts to establish conditions that are analogous to those in the natural setting:

> An analogue is designed to preserve an explicit relationship between the laboratory setting and some real-world situation of interest; for every feature of the external situation that is considered theoretically relevant, there is a corresponding feature contained in the laboratory situation. In this sense, an analogue is like a roadmap of a particular geographic region, where there is a one-to-one correspondence between features on the map and specific features of the actual terrain (e.g., highways, rivers, mountains, etc.) but where other features

that exist in the natural setting (e.g., trees, houses) are not represented on the map. If the features represented in the analogue situation have been appropriately selected, subjects' responses to that situation should provide an accurate "mapping" of their responses to the corresponding situation in real life. (Crano & Brewer, 1986, p. 106)

The key feature of analog research is therefore the theoretical relevance of the variables under investigation. These variables may or may not be operationalized in ways that reflect their natural manifestations, but analog research generally attempts to maximize mundane realism (or structural verisimilitude) while engaging participants' interest and attention by maximizing experimental realism in ways that enhance functional verisimilitude. Emphasis on the theoretical relevance of the variables studied also enhances the conceptual verisimilitude of the research relative to the theory being tested. Interestingly, maintaining conceptual verisimilitude can lead to research procedures that appear to be of low structural verisimilitude. For example, Vredenburg, Flett, and Krames (1993) suggest that college students constitute an ideal research population for testing theories concerning the role of stress in causing depression:

> Being young and having a high chronic level of negative affective distress are two factors that increase the likelihood of experiencing a major depression. Because 1st-year college students tend to be quite young and the transition to college involves a great deal of stress, it seems that college student populations may be particularly appropriate for investigators interested in the initial development of depression. It cannot be denied that college students encounter many, if not all, of the major stressors believed to precipitate bouts of depression. (p. 335)

However, just as the structural component is not the defining criterion for external validity, neither are the functional and conceptual components. As noted earlier, there is no guarantee that *any* piece of research will apply to a specific set of circumstances. Only research conducted under those circumstances can validate a theoretical or empirical principle for a specific situation (for example, see Yuille & Wells, 1991); other research can only suggest that the principle *might* apply.

PHILOSOPHIES OF SCIENCE AND NATURALISM IN RESEARCH   The debate over the external validity of laboratory research has been going on for over 50 years and is unlikely to be resolved easily or quickly. This situation exists because the debate may, to some extent, be a function of personal beliefs about the nature of scientific knowledge. Some people's philosophies may bring them to prefer the laboratory approach, whereas other people's philosophies may bring them to prefer research in natural settings (Kimble, 1984; Krasner & Houts, 1984). To the extent that the debate involves such basic philosophical differences, it may be unreconcilable. For example, Sears's (1986) statement that Berkowitz and Donnerstein's (1982) argument that "experimental, rather than mundane realism is sufficient to test causal hypotheses . . . seems less obvious to me than it does to them" (p. 520) appears to reflect a basic epistemological position. However, perhaps the debate should not be resolved: Some epistemologists contend that the truth is best found through vigorous debate among partisan adherents of opposing viewpoints (MacCoun, 1998), and debates about the advantages and disadvantages of various research methods keeps attention focused on conducting high-quality research (Ilgen, 1986).

Nonetheless, it is important to note that there is no necessary contradiction between the positions of the adherents of laboratory research and those of the adherents of naturalistic research; the difference is one of viewpoints. As noted at the beginning of this chapter, basic researchers are primarily interested in the extent to which results can be replicated under a variety of conditions; natural settings represent a subset of all the possible conditions under which an effect could be replicated. To the basic researcher, therefore, a natural setting study is just one more source of evidence about the validity and limitations of the theory being tested. Applied researchers, however, are more interested in a specific setting or category of settings, such as factories, and the people and events naturally found in that setting. To the applied researcher, then, natural setting research is the most useful research because it provides information about the specific setting of interest and the behavior of the people in that setting. The more general principles of behavior studied by the basic researcher are, to some extent, outside the applied researcher's scope of interest, except as general guides and starting points for what might work in that setting.

External Validity and Internal Validity

The debate over how essential ecological validity is to behavioral science research tends to pass over a point that we made in Chapter 2: Both external validity, especially naturalism, and internal validity, especially control over extraneous variables, are desirable characteristics of research, but it is impossible to maximize both simultaneously. For example, enhancing the internal validity of a study by carefully controlling all possible sources of extraneous variance increases its artificiality, which can limit the generalizability and ecological validity of its results. Conversely, maximizing the ecological validity of a study by conducting it in a natural setting opens the door to threats to its internal validity, such as those discussed in Chapters 6 and 10. As McGrath (1981) wrote, "One cannot plan, or execute, flawless research. All strategies, all designs, all methods, are . . . flawed" (p. 209).

However, T. D. Cook and Campbell (1979) point out that although there will be a tradeoff between them, internal validity should take precedence over external validity when you design research. Whether the research is being conducted to test a theoretical proposition in a laboratory setting or to test the effectiveness of a treatment in a natural setting, the researcher's most basic goal is to be able to draw valid conclusions about the effect of the independent variable on the dependent variable. Only by being able to rule out plausible alternative explanations for effects—that is, by maintaining appropriate standards of internal validity—can the researcher achieve this goal. No matter how ecologically valid a piece of research is, its results are useless if you cannot be confident of the accuracy of the conclusions drawn from them.

Although the requirements of internal and external validity are sometimes at odds with one another, it is possible to determine the generalizability of a theory or principle while maintaining confidence in the accuracy of the conclusions that one draws about it. The researcher can reconcile these requirements by conducting programmatic research that systematically tests a hypothesis using procedures that maintain internal validity while determining the boundary conditions under which a theory or principle operates. These boundaries can consist of operational definitions, populations, settings, or the interaction of any of these. For any one study within the program, the researchers must decide what level of tradeoff between control and naturalism gives them the kind of information they need at that point in the research program. For example, after noting the ways in which their procedures for selecting participants, their use of a laboratory setting, and the rather contrived nature of the research task limited the structural verisimilitude of their study of parent-child interactions in families with alcoholic fathers, Jacob, Krahn, and Leonard (1991) explained that "we chose to implement these procedures in order to maximize the clarity and specificity of interpretations that could be made" from the data (p. 177). That is, they chose to give up some degree of naturalism to conduct a well-controlled, clear test of their hypotheses, free of the effects of the extraneous variables that a more naturalistic approach would entail. In addition, Jacob et al. explained how this one study filled a particular niche in a broad-based and systematic investigation of alcoholism and family interactions that also included more naturalistic investigations (Jacob, Seilhamer, & Rushe, 1989).

Let's conclude this discussion of generalizability by considering Cronbach's (1975) view of its role in the process of research and knowledge generation:

> Instead of making generalization the ruling consideration in our research, I suggest that we reverse our priorities. An observer collecting data in one particular situation is in a position to appraise a practice or proposition in that setting, observing effects in context. . . . As he goes from situation to situation, his first task is to describe and interpret the effect anew in each locale, perhaps taking into account factors unique to that locale. . . . As results accumulate, a person who seeks understanding will do his best to trace how the uncontrolled factors could have caused local departures from the modal effects. That is, generalization comes late, and the exception is taken as seriously as the rule. (pp. 124–125)

SUMMARY

The external validity of research is the extent to which research results can be applied outside the specific context in which the data were collected. The generalizability of research is the extent to which the results of a study can be replicated under new conditions. The ecological validity or naturalism of research includes the issue of the extent to which theories or sets of findings can be applied to specific natural situations. The concept of external validity has three components: the structural, the functional, and the conceptual.

Five sets of structural factors can affect the generalizability and ecological validity of the results of a study. Setting factors include characteristics of the physical setting, reactivity, researcher attributes, and coparticipant attributes. Participant sample factors include convenience sampling, restricted sampling, use of volunteer participants, and person-by-situation interactions. Research procedure factors include artificiality, operational definitions, and levels of the independent variable. Culture can have a strong impact on the results of behavioral science research, as can the time sampling of behavior and changes in cultural values over time. The functional and conceptual components of external validity apply primarily to questions of ecological validity. The functional component concerns the similarity of the psychological processes that affect behavior in the natural and research settings, and it is related to the concept of experimental realism. The conceptual component concerns the degree to which the problem studied in the research situation corresponds to a problem found in a natural situation.

The external validity of research can be assessed by including generalization factors as part of a factorial design; an interaction would indicate a limitation on generalizability. Programmatic research can systematically test a hypothesis under different conditions. It is important to bear in mind, however, that simply because an independent variable has the same outcome under different conditions, it does not necessarily follow that the same psychological process was operating under both sets of conditions.

Some laboratory researchers contend that the importance of ecological validity, especially the structural aspect, has been overemphasized by its proponents. They note that some important purposes of research—testing of causal hypotheses, falsification of theoretical propositions, discovery of new phenomena, and dissection of complex phenomena—would be impossible in natural settings. They also point out that the ecological validity of research is an empirical question and that naturalism does not guarantee external validity. Finally, they suggest that functional and conceptual verisimilitude, which can be achieved in the laboratory, are more important than structural verisimilitude, the basis for most criticisms of laboratory research.

The ecological validity debate probably cannot be resolved, because the people on either side have differing philosophies of science. Nonetheless, the debate underscores the need for programmatic research that tests hypotheses under a variety of conditions that test the causal roles of the variables involved, delimit the boundary conditions of the theory, and test the theory's applicability to specific situations.

QUESTIONS AND EXERCISES FOR REVIEW

1. What characteristics of the research setting can affect the external validity of a study? Characteristics of the experimenter can affect the behavior of research participants—is the reverse possible? That is, can the characteristics of participants affect the experimenter's behavior? If so, what characteristics might be important and what effects could they have on the research?

2. What characteristics of the research setting, research procedure, and participant sample can affect the external validity of a study? In what ways can these factors enhance and detract from the generalizability and ecological validity of the results of the study?

3. Discuss the advantages and disadvantages of using college students as research participants. Overall, does this procedure have a positive, negative, or no effect on the external and ecological validity of research? Is there a place for college student data in the programmatic investigation of a hypothesis? If so, what would it be? If not, why not?

4. How can cultural differences influence the results of behavioral science research? What effects can changes in cultural values over time have?

5. How can variations in the time sampling of behavior lead to inconsistencies in the results of studies? What criteria should researchers use in determining whether external validity has been achieved?

6. Describe the ways in which the external validity of research can be assessed.

7. How might you go about testing the functional verisimilitude of research? If tests of a hypothesis in a laboratory and in a field setting had the same results, would that indicate functional verisimilitude? Why or why not?

8. Which factors contribute to the conceptual verisimilitude of research?

9. Discuss the relative importance of structural, functional, and conceptual verisimilitude to the overall concept of ecological validity. Are any of them more important than the others? What are your reasons for taking this position? Are functional and conceptual verisimilitude sufficient for ecological validity, as some people contend? Why or why not?

10. Describe the positions taken by laboratory researchers in the ecological validity debate. To a large degree, the debate centers around the relative importance of control and naturalism in research. What is your position on this issue? What are your reasons for taking that position? How are your reasons related to your philosophy of science, as discussed in Chapter 1?

11. Describe a strategy for conducting research that would optimize its internal, external, and ecological validity. Choose a hypothesis that interests you, and describe how you would test it using your strategy.

15 EVALUATION RESEARCH

GOAL DEFINITION
Needs Assessment
  Identifying Problems
  Developing Solutions
Evaluability Assessment
  Goal Specification
  Proximal Versus Distal
    Outcomes
  The Role of Stakeholders
  The Role of Theory

PROGRAM MONITORING
The Target Population
Program Implementation
  Sources of Implementation
    Failure
  Assessing Implementation
  Client Resistance
Unintended Effects
Program Monitoring and
  Program Development

IMPACT ASSESSMENT
Criteria for Evaluating Impact
  Degree of Change
  Importance of the Change
  Costs of the Program
  Acceptability of the Program
Answering Research Questions
  Is the Program Effective?
  What Aspects of the Program
    Are Important?
  How Can the Program Be
    Improved?
  How Valid Is the Theory of the
    Program?
Research Strategies
  True Experiments
  Quasi-Experiments
  Threats to Internal Validity
  Preexperimental Designs
  The Single-Case Strategy
Interpreting Null Results
  Sources of Null Results
  When "Null" Results Are
    Not Null

EFFICIENCY ANALYSIS
Cost-Benefit Analysis
Cost-Effectiveness Analysis

INFORMATION UTILIZATION
Criteria for Research Utilization
  Relevance
  Truth
  Utility
The Political Context
  Ritual Evaluations
  Stakeholder Interests

MEASURING CHANGE
Difference Scores
Reliability of Difference Scores
The Reliable Change Index

SUMMARY

QUESTIONS AND EXERCISES
FOR REVIEW

The knowledge generated by theory and research in the behavioral sciences is often applied in attempts to solve practical problems. Psychotherapies are developed from theory and research on abnormal psychology, organization development interventions derive from theory and research in industrial and organizational psychology, and educational reforms are based on theory and research on the teaching-learning process. Some interventions are directed at bringing about change in individuals or in small groups of people. Other programs are intended to have a broader impact on the general social framework of a city, state, or country. Such broad-based programs include Project Head Start, designed to improve preschoolers' readiness for our educational system, educational television programs, such as Sesame Street, designed to enhance young children's basic cognitive and social skills, and school desegregation programs, designed to improve the educational opportunities of minority group students.

Evaluation research, or **program evaluation,** is the application of social and behavioral research methods to determine the effectiveness of a program or an intervention. Effectiveness can be defined in terms of four questions (Lambert, Masters, & Ogles, 1991):

• To what extent did the program achieve its goals? Goal achievement can be defined relative to a no-treatment or placebo control group or to the effectiveness of some other intervention designed to achieve the same goals.

• What aspects of the program contributed to its success? Most intervention programs are complex, composed of many parts. An evaluation can be conducted to determine which of those parts are critical to the success of the program and which could be eliminated without harming the program's effectiveness.

• How can the effects of a program be improved? For example, if a successful 10-week program is increased in length to 20 weeks, is there a commensurate increase in benefit?

• How valid is the theory underlying the program? Many interventions are explicitly based on theory, and all include at least an implicit model of the processes by which the program should have an effect. The validity of the theory underlying the program has implications for the generalizability of the program and for interpreting situations in which the program has no effect.

Evaluation research has emerged as a major branch of the behavioral sciences; consequently, only a brief overview of the field can be conducted in a single chapter. This chapter, then, examines the five stages of evaluation research — defining the goals of the program, monitoring the implementation of the program, assessing the program's impact, analysis of the cost efficiency of the program, and utilization of the results of the evaluation — and, because an effective intervention implies bringing about change, some issues in the measurement of change. More detailed information is available in the texts by Posavac and Carey (1997), P. H. Rossi, Freeman, and Lipsey (1999), and Weiss (1998).

GOAL DEFINITION

Every intervention program has goals—it was put into operation to accomplish something. To evaluate the degree to which a program has attained its goals, those goals must be defined both conceptually and operationally. Goal definition begins with **needs assessment,** the process of determining that a problem exists and of designing a solution for the problem—the intervention program. An **evaluability assessment** examines a program to determine the information necessary to conduct an evaluation. An important part of goal definition is the inclusion of goals as defined by all the **stakeholders** in the program, the people who are affected by the program and its success or failure. Finally, it is important to explicate the theory underlying the program.

Needs Assessment

Before program administrators set goals for their programs, they have to know what needs the program must meet. The needs assessment aspect of goal definition involves identifying the problems that a program must solve and developing possible solutions for it to implement.

IDENTIFYING PROBLEMS   Every intervention program begins with a needs assessment, the determination that a problem exists and that something should be done about it. The determination that a problem exists can derive from many sources. *Social indicators* are continuing measures of various social phenomena such as crime rates, unemployment rates, admissions to psychiatric care facilities, and so forth. An increase in a negative social indicator, such as crime rates, could lead to the determination that crime is a problem. Problems can also be identified through surveys conducted to assess people's perceptions of needed community services. Finally, the determination that a problem exists could stem from a policy maker's intuition that something is wrong. Regardless of the source of the perception of need, careful research should be conducted to verify that a need in fact exists. If a program is implemented to solve a nonexistent problem, it cannot be effective: If the problem rate is zero or near-zero, it cannot go any lower. For example,

> After a social intervention designed to prevent criminal behavior by adolescents was put in place in a midwestern suburb, it was discovered that there was a very low rate of juvenile crime . . . in the community. The planners had assumed that because juvenile delinquency was a social problem nationally, it was a problem in their community as well. (P. H. Rossi et al., 1999, p. 121)

DEVELOPING SOLUTIONS   Once a problem has been identified, a solution—an intervention program—must be developed. Two important considerations in solution development are identifying the **client population** (the people to be served by the intervention) and the content of the program (the services to be provided to the client population).

It is important to identify the client population because if the service is delivered to the wrong people, the problem cannot be solved. For example,

> A birth control project was expanded to reduce the reportedly high rate of abortion in a large urban center, but the program failed to attract many additional participants. Subsequently it was found that most of the intended urban clients were already being adequately served and a high proportion practiced contraception. The high abortion rate was caused mainly by young women who came to the city from rural areas to have abortions. (P. H. Rossi et al., 1999, p. 122)

To design an effective change program, you must know the causes of the phenomenon to be changed so that the program can manipulate the causes in ways that can bring about the desired change. Ideally, program design will be based on theory and research that address policy-relevant independent variables and high-utility dependent variables (Ruback & Innes, 1988; recall Chapter 4). Although such theory-based program designs may be common for "micro" level interventions such as psychotherapy, organization development interventions, and educational interventions developed by scientist-practitioners, they are not as common for interventions aimed at broader social problems, which are often developed by policy makers not trained in the social and behavioral sciences. As P. H. Rossi et al. (1999) note,

> Defining a social problem and specifying the goals of intervention are . . . ultimately political processes that do not follow simply from the inherent characteristics of the situation. . . . For instance, in an analysis of legislation designed to reduce adolescent pregnancy . . . the U.S. General Accounting Office . . . found that none of the pending legislative proposals defined the problem as involving the fathers of the children in question; every one addressed adolescent pregnancy as an issue of young mothers. (p. 125)

Evaluability Assessment

Once a problem has been identified and a program has been developed to address the problem, the next step in the evaluation process is evaluability assessment. In this step, the evaluation team identifies the types of information needed to determine how much impact the program had and why it had that level of impact (M. F. Smith, 1989; Wholey, 1987). To conduct an evaluation, the evaluators must know

- The goals of the program, the expected consequences of achieving those goals, and the expected magnitude of the impact of the program on the consequences
- The theory of the program that links the elements of the program to the expected consequences, explaining how the program will have its effects
- The implementation guidelines for the program, explaining how the program is to be carried out so that it has the expected consequences; that is, how the theory will be put into practice
- The resources the program needs to achieve its goals effectively

During the evaluation process, the evaluation team will collect data on all these issues in order to understand why an effective program worked and why an ineffective program did not. Evaluations that look only at outcomes cannot answer the question of why a program succeeds or fails. This question is important because a negative evaluation outcome, in which a program appears to have no effect, can have causes other than a poorly designed program; if these other causes of failure can be removed, the program could be effective. Now, let's look at the process of specifying the goals of the program; the issues of theory, implementation, and resources will be considered shortly.

GOAL SPECIFICATION   To evaluate the success of a program, you must be able to measure goal attainment; to be measurable, goals must be clear, specific, and concrete. Most programs have some kind of statement of goals in the form of a mission statement, public relations materials, or part of the funding application. However, as Weiss (1998), notes:

> Some programs lack official statements. If the evaluator asks program staff about goals, they may discuss them in terms of the number of people they intend to serve, the kinds of service they will offer, and similar process information. For program implementers, these are program goals in a real and valid sense, but they are not the primary currency in which the evaluator deals. She is interested in the intended *consequences* of the program.
>
> Other programs have goal statements that are hazy, ambiguous, or hard to pin down. Occasionally, the official goals are merely a long list of pious and partly incompatible platitudes. Goals, either in official documents or program managers' discussion, can be framed in such terms as *improve education, enhance the quality of life, improve the life chances of children and families, strengthen democratic processes.* Such global goals give little direction for an evaluator who wants to understand the program in detail. (p. 52; emphasis in original)

In such cases, it becomes part of the evaluation researcher's job to elicit specific measurable goals from the program's staff.

To illustrate the process of goal specification, let's take the example of the goal *improve education.* As shown in Box 15-1, first of all there can be many viewpoints on what constitutes educational improvement. Every program involves a variety of stakeholders,

BOX 15-1   Goal Specification. A broadly stated goal can have many different meanings based on the point of view taken and how it is operationally defined.

Goal	Possible Meanings for Students
"Improve education"	Students enjoy classes.
	Students know more.
Possible Points of View	Students can apply knowledge.
School board	Students show more interest.
School administrators	
Teachers	**Possible Behavioral Indicators of Interest**
Parents	Students participate in class discussions.
Students	Students ask more questions.
	Students do outside reading.
	Students talk to parents about subject.

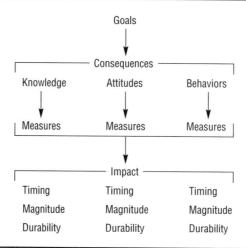

FIGURE 15-1 Program Goals, Consequences, and Impact
A program can have many different consequences, the impact of which can be assessed in terms of timing, magnitude, and durability.

and, as discussed shortly, every stakeholder group can have a different set of goals for the program. Potential stakeholders in educational programs include the school board, school administrators, teachers, parents, and students. Looking at Box 15-1, you can see that from the students' viewpoint, educational improvement can have many possible meanings, each of which, such as interest in the material, can have several behavioral consequences. Each consequence can, of course, be measured in several ways. If this process of goal specification sounds familiar, look back at Figure 4-2, which dealt with the process of refining a topic into a research question. In each case, the researcher is trying to move from generalities to specifics. One difference, as will be discussed, is that while the typical research project focuses on one or a few research questions, the evaluation research project seeks to assess as many of the program's goals as possible.

Figure 15-1 shows the issues to consider in goal specification (Shortell & Richardson, 1978; Weiss, 1998). Each abstract goal must be specified in terms of specific consequences that can be operationally defined. Consequences can fall into three categories: knowledge, or what clients should know as a result of the program; attitudes, or what clients should believe as a result of the program; and behaviors, or what clients should do as a result of the program. Measures must then be selected or developed for each specified consequence (recall Chapter 5). The specification process must also lay out the expected impact the program will have on each measure. Impact specification consists of stating the expected timing of effects, magnitude of effects, and durability of effects.

Timing concerns when during the course of a program an effect should occur. Consider, for example, Figure 15-2, which shows the cumulative percentage of psychiatric patients rated as improved as a function of the number of therapy sessions. If one defined program success as improvement in at least 50% of the patients, then a psy-

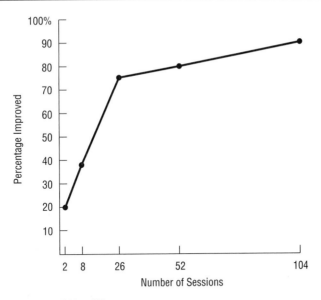

Note: Adapted from Howard et al., 1986, p. 160.

FIGURE 15-2   Relation of Number of Sessions of Psychotherapy and Percentage of Patients Improved
How successful a program appears to be may be a function of when outcomes are measured.

chotherapy program would require at least 10 sessions to be successful; if the success criterion was improvement in 75% of the patients, then at least 26 sessions would be required. Magnitude concerns the question of how much of an impact a program should have, or the effect size of the program (see Chapter 13). As with other research, the smallest effect size that would have practical significance should be specified for each measure. Durability concerns the question of how long the effects should last after clients leave the program: Should the effect be permanent or temporary? Should the magnitude of the effect stay the same after the client leaves the program, or should it be expected to diminish? If it should diminish, at what minimum level should it be maintained? What is a reasonable follow-up period over which to assess the maintenance of effects?

A final aspect of goal specification is determining the relative importance of the goals and their consequences. In any program, some goals are going to be more important than others, and within goals some consequences are going to be more important than others. Specifying the relative importance of goals is necessary for two reasons. First, the resources for conducting the evaluation might not support the assessment of all goals or of all consequences of a goal. Agreement on the relative importance of goals and consequences allows the evaluation team to focus on the most important ones. Second, if the evaluation finds that some goals have been achieved and others not, determining the degree of program success can be based on the relative importance of the attained versus nonattained goals. Getting people to specify the relative importance of goals and consequences can be a difficult process, but there are standard techniques to facilitate the process (see, for example, Edwards & Newman, 1982).

PROXIMAL VERSUS DISTAL OUTCOMES   In considering the consequences or outcomes of a program, it can be useful to distinguish between proximal and distal outcomes. **Proximal outcomes** are direct effects of the program and can be expected to occur while the clients are taking part in the program. **Distal outcomes** are indirect effects of the program and occur only after the client has completed the program, occur in environments not controlled by the program, or occur at a higher level of analysis than that addressed by the program. Consider, for example, the sex education program diagrammed in Figure 15-3. The program is designed to increase teenagers sexual knowledge and to induce more positive attitudes toward using contraception. These knowledge and attitude changes represent proximal outcomes. Changes in knowledge and attitudes are expected to result in changes in sexual and contraceptive behavior, which can also be considered reasonably proximal effects of the program, but are also somewhat distal because the program cannot affect them directly. More distal expected outcomes are fewer pregnancies among the program's clients and a lower overall teenage pregnancy rate.

Distal outcomes are also called **social impact outcomes** (Kazdin, 1997) because they take place in the client's broader social environment outside the program and are often reflected in social indicators. Because distal effects take place outside the scope of the program, they can be considered indicators of the program's ecological validity, answering the question of whether the program affects clients' behavior outside the limited environment of the program itself. For example, no matter how much the example sex education program changed its clients' sexual knowledge, if that knowledge does not result in behavioral changes, the program has been ineffective in terms of society's concerns about teenage pregnancy. This example also indicates a limitation on a program's ability to bring about distal effects: Not all causes of the distal effect are under the program's control. For example, not only a young woman's sexual and contraceptive knowledge and attitudes affect her sexual and contraceptive behavior—so do those of her sexual partner, who is not included in the program. Despite this problem, however, intervention programs can have significant distal effects (for example, see Kazdin, 1997).

THE ROLE OF STAKEHOLDERS   As noted earlier, every intervention program has stakeholders who have interests in the outcome of the program. Common stakeholder groups in a program include (P. H. Rossi et al., 1999):

- *Policy makers* who decide whether the program should be started, continued, expanded, curtailed, or stopped ~Legislature
- *Program sponsors,* such as government agencies and philanthropic organizations, that fund the program Department of Corrections
- *Program designers* who decide on the content of the program ?
- *Program administrators* who oversee and coordinate the day-to-day operations of the program That Steve guy
- *Program staff* who actually deliver the program's services to its clients
- *Program clients* who use the services of the program parolees

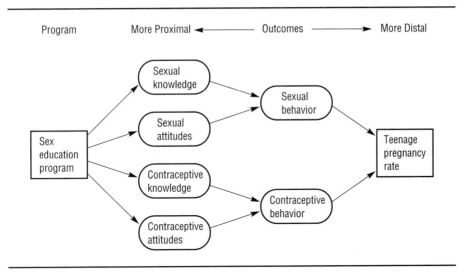

Program   More Proximal ◄——————— Outcomes ———————► More Distal

FIGURE 15-3   Theory of Program Effects for Hypothetical Sex Education Program
The program is designed to change sexual and contraceptive knowledge and attitudes, which are expected to affect behavior and thereby reduce the pregnancy rate.

- *Opinion leaders* in the community who can influence public attitudes toward the program and public perceptions of its success or failure

Each of these groups can have different, and sometimes conflicting, goals and expected consequences for the program. To take a simple example, Edwards and Newman (1982) describe the decision to select a site for a drug abuse treatment program. In terms of relative importance, the program staff rated good conditions for the staff, such as large offices, commuting convenience, and availability of parking, as being about twice as important as easy access for clients, which they rated as being about twice as important as adequate space for secretaries. It would not be surprising if two other stakeholder groups — the clients and secretaries — rated the relative importance of these aspects of the site differently! A successful evaluation requires that the evaluation team identify all the stakeholder groups, determine their goals and expected consequences for the program, and resolve conflicts in goals and in the relative importance of goals. Failure to do so can result in a situation that will allow a stakeholder group that doesn't like the outcome of the evaluation to reject it as flawed. As Weiss (1998) notes, this aspect of the evaluation requires that evaluators have excellent negotiation and mediation skills.

THE ROLE OF THEORY   As shown in Figure 15-4, the theory of a program specifies what kinds of treatments should be provided to clients. The theory also specifies the expected outcome of the treatment in terms of variables relevant to the theory and those relevant to the program's goals. Finally, the theory specifies the moderating variables that can limit the effectiveness of the treatment and the mediating variables that come between the treatment and the outcomes. For example, Hackman and Oldham's (1980) model of job design describes interventions that should lead to improved work motivation and

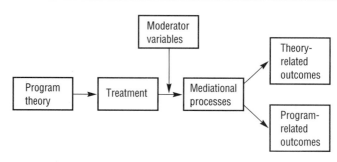

Note: Adapted from Wholey, 1987, p. 18.

FIGURE 15-4   Role of Program Theory in Evaluation
The theory specifies the treatment and the variables that moderate and mediate the effect of the treatment on the program's expected outcomes.

job satisfaction. However, the model also specifies that these effects will be found only for people who have the skills required to do the job well and who expect to get high levels of satisfaction from doing their jobs. These worker characteristics moderate the effect of the treatment. In Figure 15-3, sexual and contraceptive knowledge, attitudes, and behavior are mediator variables that come between the treatment and its expected effects: The treatment changes knowledge and attitudes, which change behavior, which in turn affects the pregnancy rate.

An intervention program may be designed around an existing theory, or the theory might be implicit in the components and goals of the program. In the latter case, the evaluation team must help the designers, administrators, and staff of the program expli-cate the theory. Conducting a theory-based evaluation requires the measurement of es-timator variables, such as those shown in ovals in Figure 15-3, as well as measurement of the consequences of the program and, in some cases, measurement or manipulation of policy variable components of the program as independent variables. As you will re-call from Chapter 4, policy variables are aspects of the situation that program adminis-trators can manipulate, whereas estimator variables are outside administrators' control but still affect program outcomes. Estimator variables are often psychological states, as illustrated by the more proximal outcomes in Figure 15-3, and, as shown in the figure, mediate the impact of the treatment.

Including the program theory in the evaluation has several advantages (Chen, 1990; Weiss, 1998). First, if the program is based on an existing theory, the program functions as a test of the validity of the theory, as in the action research model described in Chapter 2. Second, testing the effects of the various components of the program al-lows one to determine which components are necessary to accomplish the goals of the program and which are not. Eliminating unneeded components can reduce the cost of the program. Third, the theory should specify the conditions necessary for the program to bring about its intended effects, as does Hackman and Oldham's (1980) model of work redesign. If the conditions necessary for the success of the program are not met, it cannot succeed. Finally, if a program is not effective, the theory might suggest reasons why. For example, a program might not have had its intended effects on the estimator variables that were supposed to affect the dependent variables. If the hypothetical program illustrated in Figure 15-3 did not result in a lower pregnancy rate, maybe the program did not have the intended effect on the participants' sexual and contraceptive knowledge or behavior.

PROGRAM MONITORING

A program must be carried out as designed; otherwise, it will not have its intended effect. Program monitoring involves continuing assessment of how well the program is being implemented while it is being carried out. This process is also called **process evaluation** or **formative evaluation** because monitoring evaluates the process or form of the program, in contrast to **summative evaluation,** which addresses the overall effectiveness of the program relative to its goals. The following sections briefly examine three major aspects of program monitoring—delivery of services to the intended client (or target) population, program implementation, and unintended effects—and consider the implications of program monitoring for carrying out the program and for the evaluation process.

The Target Population

Every program is designed to have an effect on a certain group of people, such as adolescents or substance abusers. If a program is not reaching the members of this **target population,** it cannot affect them. The fact that a program has been established does not mean it is reaching its target population; a program should therefore include an advertising component to ensure that members of the target population know about the program and an outreach component to persuade them to make use of the program (P. H. Rossi et al., 1999).

Once potential clients are aware of the program and begin to use it, there can be problems of bias in accepting people into the program. It is not uncommon for programs to enroll clients selectively, leaving some subgroups of the target population unserved. Selective enrollment usually operates to ensure that only those potential clients who appear most likely to benefit from the program or with whom the program staff feel most comfortable enter the program. This process has three consequences. First, not all the people in need of the program's services receive them, and those who do receive the services often need them less than those not selected. Second, selective enrollment threatens the internal validity of the evaluation. Evaluations frequently use members of the target population who are not enrolled in the program as the control group in an experimental or quasi-experimental research design. If the characteristics of the program enrollees differ from those not enrolled, these characteristics are confounded with the treatment and control conditions of the research design, presenting alternative explanations for the outcome of the evaluation. Finally, selective enrollment threatens the generalizability of the program: If the evaluation finds the program to be effective but the program enrolls only a subgroup of the target population, there is no way of knowing if it will be effective for the other members of the target population. For example, would a pregnancy prevention program that is effective for European-American teenagers also be effective for members of minority groups? There is no way to know unless minority group members are included in the program when it is evaluated.

These potential problems mean that the evaluation team must check to ensure that the program is reaching all members of the target population. This checking starts with the program goals: Whom is the program supposed to serve? The team can then review program records and interview clients to determine the characteristics of clientele being served. These characteristics can be checked against the program goals and against results of surveys of potential clients not enrolled in the program. If the enrolled clients differ from the target population described in the goals or from unenrolled potential clients, the team must modify the program to reach these groups.

Program Implementation

The assessment of program implementation deals with the question of whether the program is being carried out as designed: that is, to compare what is *actually* happening in the program to what is *supposed to* happen. A program consists of a specific set of experiences that each client undergoes; if clients are not receiving these experiences, the program is not being implemented properly. For example, R. A. Feldman, Caplinger, and Wodarski (1983) evaluated the effectiveness of two treatment programs for antisocial youths. The programs organized youths into groups supervised by an adult leader. One program used traditional group social work, focusing on group processes, organization, and norms, whereas the other program used behavior modification techniques, using reinforcement contingencies to change behavior. A third, minimal-treatment "program" was actually a placebo control condition, in which no structured intervention was supposed to take place. However, process evaluations indicated that only 25% of the leaders in the group social work program and 65% of the leaders in the behavior modification program implemented their treatments correctly. In addition, 44% of the leaders in the placebo program carried out some form of systematic intervention. It was not very surprising, therefore, that the summative evaluation found few differences in the effects of the three treatment programs. This section briefly examines three aspects of implementation: sources of implementation failure, assessing implementation, and client resistance to the program.

Sources of Implementation Failure   Kazdin (1997) notes three potential sources of implementation failure. The first is a lack of specific criteria and procedures for program implementation. Every program should have a manual that describes the program's procedures, techniques, and activities in detail. The manual can also provide the evaluation team with a basis for determining the degree to which the program is being implemented. The second potential source of implementation failure is an insufficiently trained staff. The staff must be thoroughly trained and tested on their ability to carry out the program as described in the manual. Finally, inadequate supervision of staff provides opportunity for treatments to drift away from their intended course. Any program must, to some degree, be tailored to each client's needs; however, it cannot be tailored to the extent that it departs from its intended form.

A fourth source of failure can arise in situations in which a novel treatment program is implemented with a staff who do not believe in its effectiveness, who are used to doing things differently, or who feel threatened by the new procedure. Such a situation can lead to resistance to or even sabotage of the program by the staff. For example,

> A program was established by a state legislature to teach welfare recipients the basic rudiments of parenting and household management. The state welfare department was charged with conducting workshops, distributing brochures, showing films, and training caseworkers on how low-income people could better manage their meager resources and become better parents. . . .
>
> As a result of . . . political battles [among stakeholder groups], the program was delayed and further delayed. Procrastination being the better part of valor, no parenting brochures were ever printed; no household management films were ever shown; no workshops were held; and no caseworkers were ever trained.
>
> In short, *the program was never implemented. . . . But it was evaluated!* It was found to be ineffective, and was killed. (Patton, 1986, pp. 124, 125; emphasis in original)

ASSESSING IMPLEMENTATION   The assessment of implementation is not an easy matter. Programs are complex, and absolute criteria for correct implementation are rarely available. Nonetheless, criteria for deciding whether a program has been properly implemented must be established, even if they are somewhat arbitrary (Kazdin, 1997). For example, R. A. Feldman et al. (1983) randomly sampled and observed meetings held by group leaders during three phases of their treatment programs for antisocial youth.

> The observers [who were blind to the treatments] were asked to mark which of three leadership styles best exemplified each leader's behavior. Respectively, the selection categories described leader behaviors that typically were associated with the minimal, behavioral, and traditional methods of group treatment. . . .
>
> . . . A treatment method was considered to be *unimplemented* when the observer recorded the proper leadership style for none or only one of the three treatment periods. In contrast, an *implemented* method was one in which the group leader properly applied the assigned method for at least two of the three treatment periods that were observed. (R. A. Feldman et al., 1983, p. 220; emphasis in original)

As in the case of the goals and desired consequences of the program, implementation criteria should be established in consultation with stakeholder groups to ensure that all points of view on proper implementation have been considered (Patton, 1986).

CLIENT RESISTANCE   Resistance to a program can come not only from staff, but also from clients and potential clients (see, for example, Harvey & Brown, 1996; Patton, 1986). For example, many members of disadvantaged groups highly distrust programs sponsored by government agencies and other "establishment" groups, and so may be suspicious of the goals of the program and reluctant to take part. Resistance also arises when people are uncertain about the effects of the program, resulting from anxiety over having to deal with the unfamiliar new program and, in some cases, disruption of daily routines. The structure and implementation of the program can also arouse client resistance or reluctance to use the services. Some of these factors include

- Inaccessibility, such as a lack of transportation, restricted operating hours, or locating the service delivery site in an area that clients perceive as dangerous
- Threats to client dignity, such as demeaning procedures, unnecessarily intrusive questioning, and rude treatment
- Failure to consider the clients' culture, such as lifestyles, special treatment needs, and language difficulties
- Provision of unusable services, such as printed materials with a reading level too high for the clients or with a typeface too small to be read by visually impaired clients

Client resistance can be reduced by taking two steps (Harvey & Brown, 1996; Patton, 1986). The first is including all stakeholder groups in the design of the program to ensure that all viewpoints are considered. Focus groups, described in Chapter 11, can be used for this purpose by providing members of stakeholder groups with information about the goals and structure of the program and soliciting their comments and suggestions. The program can then be modified to address concerns the group members raise. Second, information programs can be used to alleviate potential clients' uncertainties over the program by explaining any unchangeable aspects of the program that caused concern for members of the focus groups. Focus groups can also suggest ways to present the information that will facilitate acceptance of the program by members of the target population. Even when these steps have been taken, however, process evaluations should include assessment of clients' perceptions of the program and the sources of any reservations they express about it.

Unintended Effects

Every program is intended to bring out certain effects, as defined by its goals and their consequences. Programs also bring about unintended effects, and one function of process evaluation is the identification of these side effects (Weiss, 1998). D. T. Campbell (1969b) presents a classic case of unintended effects. In 1956 the governor of Connecticut ordered the state police to crack down on speeders and encouraged judges to suspend the driving licenses of offenders as a way of reducing highway deaths. As the broken line in Figure 15-5 indicates, the program was successfully implemented: The number of speeding violations declined after the program was started. However, the two solid lines in Figure 15-5 suggest the program had at least two unintended negative consequences: Fewer drivers charged with speeding were found guilty, and the frequency of people driving with a suspended license increased.

In the worst case, unintended effects can exacerbate the problem a program was intended to alleviate. For example, there have been a number of programs designed to reduce problem behaviors, such as delinquency and alcohol and tobacco use, among adolescents. Dishion, McCord, and Poulin (1999) conducted a series of evaluations of

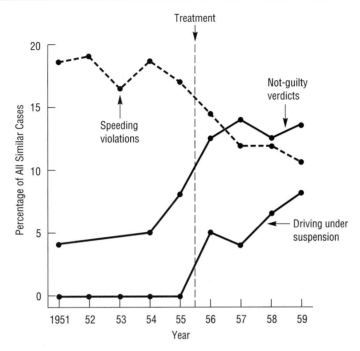

Note: Data from D. T. Campbell, 1969b.

FIGURE 15-5   Intended and Unintended Effects of an Intervention
The Connecticut speeding crackdown had its intended effect of increasing the number of speeding tickets written (broken line) but had the unintended effects of more "not guilty" verdicts when those tickets went to court and more arrests for driving with a suspended license.

one such program that used a group-based format to promote prosocial goals and self-regulation of behavior among teenagers. Although "many of the short-term effects were quite positive" (Dishion et al., 1999, p. 757), Dishion et al. found that over a 3-year follow-up period, the teens in the intervention group were *more* likely than those in a placebo control group to increase their tobacco and alcohol use and to engage in delinquent and violent behavior. In addition, the teenagers "with the highest initial levels of problem behavior were more susceptible to the [unintended negative] effect" (Dishion et al., 1999, p. 758).

Unintended positive effects are also possible but are, perhaps, less likely to be reported because they are not defined as problems. Process evaluation must be able to identify unintended effects, both positive and negative. Because these effects often cannot be identified in advance, the evaluation team must conduct observations, personal interviews, and surveys with all stakeholder groups throughout the course of the program in order to detect them.

Program Monitoring and Program Development

Program monitoring is conducted to ensure that the program is being carried out as designed and to identify departures from the design. If problems are noted, program administrators will take steps to correct them. While these corrections are good for the program and, indeed, are the desired outcome of process evaluation, they can create a dilemma for the summative evaluation. On the one hand, corrections ensure proper implementation of the program and its theory, so the summative evaluation can determine the effectiveness of the program as designed. On the other hand, summative data collected while the program was off track may have to be discarded as "bad," not reflecting the true effects of the program. Discarding data not only offends the aesthetic sense that most researchers have concerning the proper conduct of research, it also means additional work: The discarded data must be replaced by collecting data from clients of the revised program. However, such "bad" data need not always be discarded. These cases can be considered to represent the effects of an alternate form of the program that can be compared to the effects of the program as designed. For example, if improper implementation led to the omission of a component from the program, the data from that version of the program, when compared to the full program, can indicate the importance of the component: If both versions of the program are successful, then the omitted component is not a necessary part of the program.

IMPACT ASSESSMENT

The impact assessment stage of evaluation research addresses the question of how much effect the program had on its clients in terms of achieving its goals. Data are collected and analyzed in order to make a summative evaluation of the program's effect. Four aspects of impact assessment are criteria for evaluating the impact of a program, designs for answering the questions posed in evaluation research, choice of research methods, and interpretation of null results.

Criteria for Evaluating Impact

What standards can one use to decide whether a program is effective or ineffective? Kazdin (1997) suggests four sets of criteria, outlined in Box 15-2: the degree of change brought about by the program, the importance of the change, the costs of the program, and the acceptability of the program to stakeholders.

DEGREE OF CHANGE   The simplest way of looking at program impact is in degree of change brought about relative to each of the goals and desired consequences of the program. The change experienced by each client of the program relative to a goal can be averaged across clients to provide an index of the program's effect on that goal. The mean change can be tested for statistical significance to determine if it represents real change, and can be compared to the mean change found in a control group to deter-

BOX 15-2   Categories of Evaluation Criteria

Degree of Change
Importance of Change
   Proportion of clients who meet goals
   Number of goals achieved per client
   Durability of outcome
Cost of the Program
   Costs of administration
     Duration of treatment
     Method of providing treatment
     Required qualifications of staff

Cost to clients
   Monetary
   Negative side effects of program
Cost to staff: Negative side effects
Acceptability of Program to Stakeholders

Source: Adapted from Kazdin, 1997.

mine if the program had an effect over and above those of history, maturation, and so forth (see Chapter 6). In addition, you can calculate an effect size index as an indicator of the degree of a program's effect.

However, be cautious in using mean change as an indicator of a program's effect. As noted in Chapter 13, an average score can obscure individual differences in response to a treatment. A program could have positive effects for some clients and negative effects for other clients, leading to no mean change. Conversely, a program that had large effects for a few clients and no effect for the rest could result in a statistically significant mean change. It is therefore useful to supplement analyses of mean change with other indicators of effectiveness, such as the percentage of clients who show an important degree of change.

IMPORTANCE OF THE CHANGE   As noted in Chapter 13, neither statistical significance nor effect size necessarily says anything about the practical importance of an effect. Program administrators are most likely to define effect importance in terms of the percentage of clients who meet the program's goals: The more clients who meet the goals, the more effective the program (Jacobson & Truax, 1991; Kazdin, 1997). Goal attainment can be operationally defined either in terms of meeting some preset criterion of improvement or relative to the level at which an outcome is found in a criterion population. For example, Klosko, Barlow, Tassinari, and Cerny (1990) compared the effects of psychotherapy and medication for panic attacks with two control groups. The two treatments brought about the same amount of change in terms of mean scores on a set of outcome measures. However, using an absolute measure of improvement—zero panic attacks over a 2-week period—87% of the psychotherapy group had improved compared to 50% in the medication group and 36% and 33% in the two control groups.

Jacobson and Truax (1991) suggest three possible ways of operationally defining improvement relative to a criterion population. Under the first definition, a client would be considered improved if his or her outcome score fell outside the range of scores of an untreated control population, with "outside the range" defined as two or more standard deviations above the mean of the untreated group. That is, improvement is defined as no longer needing the program; for example, a psychotherapy patient improves to the point of no longer being considered dysfunctional. Under the second definition, the score of a client determined to be improved would fall within the range of scores of a population not in need of treatment, with "within the range" defined as no more than two standard deviations below the mean of the criterion group. That is, improvement is defined in terms of joining the criterion population; for example, a psychotherapy patient improves to the point of being considered "normal." Under the third definition, the score of a client determined to be improved would fall closer to the mean of the population not in need of treatment than to the mean of the population in need of treatment. That is, a client improves but may still need treatment. Nezu and Perri (1989) used the second definition to evaluate the effectiveness of a treatment for depression and found that 86% of the treated clients scored within the normal range on a commonly used measure of depression compared to 9% of the members of an untreated control group.

A second indicator of the importance of the change brought about by a program is the number of goals achieved. Most programs have multiple goals, and a more effective program will achieve more of its goals or at least more of its goals defined as important. For example, the evaluation of the first year of *Sesame Street* found the program did not meet one of its stated goals: The "achievement gap"—disadvantaged children's doing less well in primary school than better-off children—it was designed to reduce increased rather than decreased. Yet the skill levels of the disadvantaged children did improve, which itself could be considered a significant accomplishment of the program, especially given its relatively low cost (T. D. Cook et al., 1975).

A third indicator of importance is the durability of the outcomes. It is not unusual for program effects to decay over time, with the greatest effect being found immediately after completion of the program. For this reason, every program evaluation must include appropriate follow-up data to determine the longer-term effects of the program. Evaluation of goals that are distal in time, such as the academic effects of preschool enrichment programs, may require very long term follow-ups. Follow-up research can be arduous because it may be difficult to locate clients once they complete the program and to keep track of members of control groups. Nonetheless, follow-ups are essential for evaluating the effectiveness of a program (Dishion et al., 1999).

COSTS OF THE PROGRAM   A second set of factors to consider in evaluating a program is its costs. Cost-efficiency analyses will be discussed later; for the present let's consider some types of costs that can be assessed. Perhaps the most obvious source of costs is the monetary cost of administering the program: the number of dollars the funder must lay out to provide the treatment. Although these costs are best assessed by accountants, program evaluation research can investigate a number of factors that can affect them, such as the optimum length of treatment. If a 26-week program has essentially the same effect as a 52-week program, then twice as many clients can be served in a year at the same cost. Another factor affecting the cost of a program is the method of providing treatment. For example, group treatment that is just as effective as individual treatment can be provided at less cost. A third testable cost factor is the required level of professional qualification of the staff. Does effective treatment require staff with doctoral degrees, or will master's level training or even nonprofessional staff suffice? The higher the technical qualifications of the staff, the more they must be paid and the more the program costs. As Kazdin (1997) points out, a number of highly successful programs, such as Alcoholics Anonymous, are run by nonprofessionals.

Programs also entail costs to clients. Some are monetary costs directly related to program participation, such as any fees or deposits the program requires and the cost of transportation to the program site. Other monetary costs are indirect, such as child care costs while a client attends the program. Other costs might be psychological or social in nature, such as lowered self-esteem from perceiving oneself as being in need of help, impolite treatment by program staff, frustrations caused by red tape and understaffing, and disruptions of one's day-to-day life caused by attending the program. Finally, don't overlook costs to staff, especially in terms of negative side effects of providing services. An understaffed program can quickly result in high levels of stress for the staff, and constantly having to deal with troubled and sometimes frustrating clients can lead to burnout.

ACCEPTABILITY OF THE PROGRAM　　A program can be highly effective in terms of bringing about the intended changes, but if potential clients don't like the program, they won't use it. Similarly, if a program is perceived to be unpleasant to work in, it will be difficult to recruit well-qualified staff. The acceptability of the program to other stakeholders can also affect its viability. Patton (1986), for example, tells of a parenting skills training program for low-income families that was effectively killed by leaders of welfare rights organizations who perceived it as an unwarranted interference in people's lives. It is therefore very important for evaluation research to assess the acceptability of a program to all stakeholder groups. Information on sources of dissatisfaction can be used to improve the program, and comparison of two programs that are equally effective on other criteria could find that one is more acceptable, and therefore more likely to be used, than the other. Without utilization, even the best designed program will be a failure.

Answering Research Questions

As noted at the beginning of this chapter, evaluation research can ask four questions about a program. Table 15-1 shows that each of these questions can be addressed by an appropriate research design. Kazdin (1997) described these designs in the context of psychotherapy outcome research, but they apply to the evaluation of any type of program.

IS THE PROGRAM EFFECTIVE?　　This is, of course, the most basic question in program evaluation. It is usually addressed using the **program package design** in which the program is compared to a no-treatment or waiting-list control group. The concept of "program package" acknowledges that programs are often complex, consisting of several aspects or components that could be investigated separately. However, this strategy ignores those complexities, looking at the effects of the program as a whole. The **comparative outcome design** is used to compare the effectiveness of two different programs that have the same goals, addressing the question of which program is more effective, and includes

TABLE 15-1   Program Evaluation Designs

Evaluation Question	Evaluation Designs	Basic Requirements
Is the program effective (or more effective than another program)?	Program package	Treatment versus no-treatment or waiting-list control group
	Comparative outcome	Two or more different programs designed to have the same outcome
What aspects of the program are important?	Dismantling	Two or more treatment groups that vary in the components of the program they receive
	Client and program variation	Program as applied to different client groups in different settings, and so on
How can the program be improved?	Constructive	Two or more treatment groups that vary in the components of the program they receive
	Parametric	Two or more treatment groups that differ in the degree of one or more components of the program
How valid is the program theory?	Any of these	Inclusion of estimator as well as policy variables

Note: Adapted from Kazdin, 1997, p. 142.

a control condition against which to evaluate the effects of both programs. For example, the Klosko et al. (1990) study described earlier compared the effectiveness of psychotherapy and medication as treatments for panic disorder to two control conditions.

WHAT ASPECTS OF THE PROGRAM ARE IMPORTANT?   A complex program might have some components that are required for it to be effective and other components that contribute little or nothing to its effectiveness. The **dismantling design** tests the necessity of including a component in a program by comparing a client group that experiences a version of the program which includes that component to a client group that experiences a version of the program which does not include that component. For example, Nezu and Perri (1989) compared two versions of a social problem-solving treatment for depression, one that consisted of the entire treatment program and one that omitted a component that the theory underlying the treatment held to be important for success of the treatment. They found that at the end of treatment, 86% of the people who had experienced the full treatment could be classified as nondepressed, compared to 43% of the people who experienced the partial treatment, and 9% of the members of a waiting-list control group. These results supported the importance of the omitted component of the treatment program.

   The **client and program variation design** addresses issues such as whether a program is equally effective for all client groups or whether it is equally effective if implemented in different ways, such as with professional versus nonprofessional staff. For example, Kadden, Cooney, Getter, and Litt (1989) hypothesized that alcoholics with different levels of psychological impairment would respond better to different types of treatment programs. They postulated that patients with lower degrees of impairment would benefit more from group therapies in which they interacted with each other, whereas patients with greater degrees of impairment would benefit more from coping-skills training that emphasized relapse prevention. Kadden et al. compared high- and low-impairment patients and the two types of treatment in factorial design and found an interaction that supported their hypothesis: The patients who underwent the treatment that the researchers' theory held should lead to more improvement given their level of impairment drank less over a 6-month period than the patients who underwent the treatment that the theory suggested would be less effective.

HOW CAN THE PROGRAM BE IMPROVED?   Even effective programs can sometimes be improved, and two designs can be used to evaluate the effects of program changes. With the **constructive design,** a component is added to a successful program to determine if the addition will improve goal attainment. In parallel to the dismantling design, a client group exposed to the expanded program is compared to a client group undergoing the standard program; a no-treatment or waiting-list control group can also be included in the design. Rather than varying the content of a program, the **parametric design** varies the degree to which clients experience a component of the program. For example, a short version of the program might be compared to a long version, or a version in which clients participate three times a week might be compared to one in which clients participate once a week.

HOW VALID IS THE THEORY OF THE PROGRAM?   The validity of the theory underlying a program can be evaluated by any of these designs if the effects of theoretically relevant variables are assessed. For example, theoretically relevant estimator variables can be assessed as part of a treatment package or comparative design to see if they have the mediating effects hypothesized by the theory. Theoretically relevant policy variables can be manipulated in the other four designs, and theoretically relevant client variables can be included in a client variation design. Therefore, the effectiveness of a program and the validity of the theory underlying it can be tested simultaneously in an action research paradigm.

Research Strategies

The minimum requirement for an evaluation research study is a 2 × 3 factorial design with a treatment group and a control group assessed on the dependent measures at three points: pretreatment, at the end of treatment, and a follow-up some time after the end of treatment. The pretest ensures that the treatment and control groups are equivalent at the outset of the research and provides a starting point against which to assess the impact of the program. The follow-up is conducted to determine the extent to which the effects of the program endure over time. Depending on the goals of the research, there can, of course, be more than two groups and additional assessments can be made during treatment and at multiple follow-ups.

Any of the research strategies discussed in Chapters 7 through 10 can be used to evaluate a program, but quasi-experimental designs (Chapter 10) predominate. In a review of reports of 175 published program evaluations, Lipsey, Crosse, Dunkle, Pollard, and Stobart (1985) found that 39% used quasi-experiments, almost all of which were nonequivalent control group designs, 19% used true experiments with program participants randomly assigned to treatment and control groups, and 11% used preexperimental designs that consisted of a pretest and a posttest of a treatment group but had no control group. The remaining studies were equally divided among qualitative evaluations, studies that had no pretest, and subjective evaluations. This section briefly overviews some of the issues involved in choosing among the research strategies.

TRUE EXPERIMENTS   In principle, the true experiment is the ideal strategy for program evaluation research because it can most definitely determine if the program caused any changes that are observed among the program's clients. However, as Lipsey et al. (1985) found, it is infrequently used for evaluation purposes, perhaps because many practitioners perceive experimental controls such as random assignment of participants to conditions and control of situational variables to be impractical to implement under the natural setting conditions in which programs operate (Boruch, 1975). However, as Chapter 10 pointed out, field experiments are quite often used in research in general and can also be used for program evaluation; Boruch (1975), for example, lists over 200 program evaluations that used experimental designs. In addition, many programs—such as psychotherapy, substance abuse treatment, and educational programs—are carried out in relatively controlled environments such as clinics and schools that are quite amenable to random assignment of people to conditions and to experimental control over situational variables.

There are, however, also situations that, while offering less control over situational variables, allow random assignment of people to conditions (T. D. Cook & Campbell, 1979; Posavac & Carey, 1997). For example,

- When program resources are scarce and not all potential clients can be served, randomly choosing who gets to use the program may be the fairest way of allocating the resources; determining who is most in need might be virtually impossible. Consider, for example, the lotteries that some colleges and universities hold to allocate rooms in dormitories for which there are more applicants than spaces.

- Scarce program resources can result in a first-come-first-served approach to allocating resources, and people are put on a waiting list until there is space for them in the program. In such a situation, assignment to treatment or the waiting list might be quasi-random, leading to the use of people on the waiting list as a control group, as in much psychotherapy research.

- Other forms of natural quasi-randomization can also occur, such as when patients admitted to a hospital or other in-patient treatment facility are assigned to wards or other units. Different versions of a program can be instituted in different units and other units used as control groups.

- Sometimes people have no preference among alternative versions of a program and so essentially give permission to be randomly assigned.

• In some situations, there is a legitimate power basis for randomly assigning people to conditions, such as when an organization development intervention is conducted. Employers have the authority to make reasonable changes in employee working conditions or procedures and so to randomly assign people to experimental and control conditions of an intervention.

When planning an evaluation, always be alert to aspects of the program that might allow random assignment of clients to conditions and permit the researcher to control extraneous variables. The knowledge about causality gained from a true experiment is usually well worth any inconvenience its use engenders.

QUASI-EXPERIMENTS   The quasi-experiment, especially the nonequivalent control group design, is the most commonly used evaluation research strategy (Lipsey et al., 1985), perhaps because of the ease with which educational, industrial, and similar interventions can use one natural unit, such as a classroom, as a treatment group and another natural unit as a control group. This convenience comes, however, at the cost of not being completely able to rule out preexisting differences between the groups as alternative explanations for the results of the evaluation (see Chapter 10).

Another reason for the extensive use of quasi-experiments in evaluation research is that many evaluations are designed and conducted after a program has been instituted rather than being built into the program. Consequently, control groups must be formed after the fact and constructed so that they can be used to rule out alternative explanations for the program's effect. Cordray (1986) calls these designs *patched-up quasi-experiments* because the control groups are selected in ways that patch over holes in the internal validity of the research. Posavac and Carey (1997) provide the example of an after-the-fact evaluation of a college's junior year abroad program on the maturity level of seniors; the hypothesis was that foreign study would enhance international understanding. There were several problems to be faced in conducting this evaluation. Because the request for the evaluation was made after the students had returned from their year abroad, no pretest could be conducted; the evaluation could not use the next group leaving because of a short deadline for completing the evaluation. Consequently, the evaluators had to compare the returning seniors to seniors who had not studied abroad. However, self-selection then became a threat to internal validity: Students who choose to study abroad are different from those who choose not to. But self-selection could be controlled by comparing sophomores who apply for foreign study to the returned seniors. However, using sophomores as a control group raises maturation as a threat to internal validity; therefore, a maturation control group of sophomores who did not apply for foreign study was added to the design. The result was the 2×2 design shown in Table 15-2. As the bottom row of the table shows, seniors' international understanding scores would be expected to increase by 5 points if they did not study abroad; however, the scores of those who took part in the program increased by 15 points relative to sophomores who intended to study abroad, indicating an effect for the program.

THREATS TO INTERNAL VALIDITY   Experiments and quasi-experiments are designed to avoid as much as possible the threats to internal validity discussed in Chapter 6. However,

TABLE 15-2   Example of a Patched-Up Quasi-Experimental Design

To assess the effects of a junior-year-abroad program, seniors who participated in the program were compared to seniors who had not; self-selection was controlled by comparing sophomores who intended to enter the program with those who did not.

| | MATURATION LEVEL | |
Self-Selection	Sophomores	Seniors
Students who will study or have studied abroad	50	65 (treatment group)
Students who have not studied or do not plan to study abroad	40	45

Note: From Posavac & Carey, 1997, p. 178.

additional threats to internal validity can develop in the course of an intervention program (T. D. Cook & Campbell, 1979). Four of these threats affect only the control group, so their effects are sometimes referred to as **control group contamination.** One such problem is **treatment diffusion:** Members of the control group learn about the treatment from members of the treatment group and try to apply the treatment to themselves. For example, while conducting an evaluation of the effectiveness of a Students Against Drunk Driving (SADD) program, Klitzner, Gruenewald, Bamberger, and Rossiter (1994) found that students at one of the control schools had formed their own SADD group. This problem can be avoided in quasi-experiments by using treatment and control groups that are geographically separated and unlikely to communicate, as was done by J. Greenberg (1990) in his study of the effects of explaining management decisions to employees on employee morale (described in Chapter 10). If treatment diffusion does occur, the "contaminated" control participants can be treated as an additional condition in the study and their outcomes compared to those of the members of the treatment and "pure" control groups.

A second problem is attempts by staff to compensate the control group for being deprived of the benefits the treatment group received. Recall, for example, that R. A. Feldman et al. (1983) found that 44% of the members of their control group received some sort of systematic intervention from the program staff. As with treatment diffusion, it may be possible to treat the "contaminated" control participants as an additional condition in the research.

Third, control group members who are aware that they are part of a control group might feel rivalry with the treatment group and work to outdo them on the posttest. For example, in an evaluation of the effects of an employee incentive program on job performance, Petty, Singleton, and Connell (1992) found that managers and employees who were supposed to constitute the control group learned about the experiment and tried to outperform the employees in the treatment group.

A fourth potential problem is the converse of rivalry, resentful demoralization: Members of the control group learn that they are being deprived of a program that could benefit them and so reduce any efforts they may have been making to solve their problem themselves. Posavac and Carey (1997) give the example of a job skills program designed to increase employment: Members of the control group might feel that people in the program have an unfair advantage in job hunting and so reduce their own efforts in that direction. Because most programs are designed to have a greater impact than normal self-help efforts, when members of a control group stop such activities because of their knowledge of their control status, they no longer provide the baseline required for a valid evaluation of the program.

A final threat is **local history,** which can affect either the control group or the experimental group. Chapter 6 pointed out that history as a threat to internal validity is an event outside the research that affects the dependent variable. Local history is an event that affects only the treatment or only the control group and so is local to it. This threat is obviously strongest in quasi-experiments in which the treatment and control groups are geographically separated. For example, one of J. Greenberg's (1990) indicators of employee morale was turnover—the number of employees who quit. If a number of desirable jobs had become available in one of the cities in which the factories participating in his study were located, the factory in that city might have experienced increased turnover regardless of whether it constituted the experimental group or a control group. The effects of this threat can be reduced if the treatment and control groups each consist of several naturally occurring groups, each in a different location: It is unlikely that the same local history event would affect all the sites within a condition.

The members of an evaluation team cannot detect and deal with these threats unless they are familiar with how the treatment is being implemented, how participants, especially control participants, are responding to being part of a study, and what events are occurring in the study environment. Such familiarity can come only through a well-planned process evaluation designed before the program is started and conducted while the program is under way.

PREEXPERIMENTAL DESIGNS   Lipsey et al. (1985) found that 11% of their sample of evaluation studies used what T. D. Cook and Campbell (1979) refer to as a preexperimental design, a pretest-posttest design without a control group. Such a design is preexperimental because without a control group there is no way to assess the impact of the internal validity threats discussed in Chapter 6. Why, then, would anyone use such a design? There are two reasons. First, it is sometimes impossible to come up with a no-treatment control group. For example, the treatment might be made available to all members of the population, comprising what T. D. Cook et al. (1975) called a "universally available social good" (p. 22), such as television programming. If everyone is exposed to the treatment, there can be no control group; in such a case, only pretest-posttest comparisons can be made of the treatment group. One can, however, also conduct correlational analyses of the relationship of program variables to outcome variables. For example, T. D. Cook et al. found that children who more frequently watched *Sesame Street* scored higher on the outcome measures. Second, Posavac and Carey (1997) suggest that preexperiments can be used as inexpensive pilot studies to determine if a more expensive full evaluation is necessary. They also suggest that program administrators and staff might be more accepting of an evaluation that does not include a no-treatment group and that positive results from such a study might make administrators and staff more amenable to a more rigorous evaluation.

Although preexperimental evaluations can be done and are done, they should be avoided if at all possible: The conclusions that can be drawn from their results will be too weak to be worth the effort. If a preexperimental evaluation must be done, then the results must be very carefully interpreted in light of the internal validity threats discussed in Chapter 6 and the limitations of correlational research discussed in Chapter 8.

THE SINGLE-CASE STRATEGY   Although Lipsey et al. (1985) did not mention any evaluations using the single-case approach, such evaluations are frequently used in psychotherapy outcome evaluations (Kazdin, 1997). Single-case experiments may be especially amenable to use in evaluation because they can be designed to answer any of the four evaluation questions (Hayes & Leonhard, 1991). For example, alternating treatment designs can be used to assess the effectiveness of a treatment, using an A-B-A approach, and treatments can be compared using an A-B-A-C-A design. The single-case approach can be used with very large units of analysis as well as with individuals.

McSweeney (1978), for example, examined the effect of the institution of a 20¢ charge for local directory assistance calls in Cincinnati. The study was essentially a single-case natural experiment using an A-B design with the city of Cincinnati as the case being studied. The number of directory assistance calls for the 12 years prior to the institution of the charge constituted the baseline (A) condition, and the three following years constituted the experimental (B) condition. As shown by the line of open circles in Figure 15-6, the number of directory assistance calls for local numbers decreased sharply after the 20¢ charge went into effect. McSweeney also included the number of long-distance directory assistance calls, for which no charge was added, as a control condition. As shown by the line of filled-in circles in Figure 15-6, no change occurred for those calls.

This study also illustrates the use of archival data in evaluation research: The call data came from telephone company records. Yin (1993, 1994) discusses how well-designed case studies can be used for evaluation by carefully selecting test and control cases. The results of single-case evaluation research must, of course, be interpreted in the light of the limitations on single-case research discussed in Chapter 9.

Interpreting Null Results

It is not uncommon for an evaluation to find that a program had no effect. Lipsey et al. (1985), for example, found that 37% of the 175 published evaluation studies that they reviewed found no program effect. They also noted that this figure is probably an underestimate because of the bias against publishing null results. This section considers two issues concerning null results in evaluation studies: sources of null results and situations in which null results might not be so null.

SOURCES OF NULL RESULTS   Weiss (1998) suggested that null results in evaluation research come from three sources. The first is program failure, a true null result: The program does not bring about the desired effect. However, before reaching this conclusion, the evaluation team must consider two other sources of null results stemming from Type II errors. One source of Type II error is implementation failure, discussed earlier:

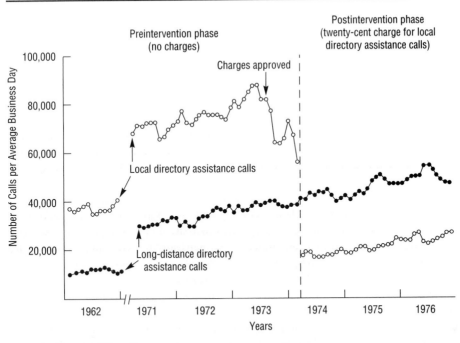

Note: From McSweeney, 1978, p. 49.

FIGURE 15-6 A Single-Case Evaluation Design
The number of local directory assistance calls in Cincinnati declined after a 20¢ charge went into effect, but there was no change in the number of long-distance directory assistance calls, which remained free of charge.

Was the program implemented as designed? Did the program have all the resources necessary for its success?

The second source of Type II errors is evaluation failure: poor research. Evaluation research is prone to the same Type II error problems that can affect all research (see Chapter 13). Lipsey et al. (1985) suggest that low statistical power is a rampant problem; the average power for the studies they reviewed was .28 for a small effect, .63 for a medium effect, and .81 for a large effect. Given that most interventions have a medium effect (Lipsey, 1990), it is thus not surprising that 37% of evaluations found null results. Other common problems include the use of measures of unknown reliability, validity, and sensitivity (Lipsey et al., 1985). Evaluators must also be sensitive to the content validity of their research: They must be certain to include measures of all the outcomes considered to be important by all stakeholder groups. A program might have effects on some outcomes but not others, and if an outcome is not measured the evaluation cannot show that the program had an effect on it. Finally, the evaluation must use appropriate operational definitions. For example, one goal of school desegregation is the improvement of interracial relationships. Relationship quality has been assessed in two ways in school desegregation research (Schofield & Whitley, 1983): as the number of other-race children whom students name as best friends (peer nomination method) and as interval level ratings of how much each child likes all the members of his or her class with ratings averaged by race of the rated children (roster-and-rating method). Peer nomination studies tend to show more racial bias than roster-and-rating studies, but

> while cross-racial best friendships may be desirable, they go beyond the degree of interpersonal intimacy which desegregation as a social policy is designed to bring about. . . . As such, best friendships may not be an appropriate criterion for success in achieving the social goals of school desegregation. (Schofield & Whitley, 1983, p. 249)

WHEN "NULL" RESULTS ARE NOT NULL   The term *null results* is typically used to mean that there is no difference in outcome between a treatment group and a control group or between two treatment groups, both of which perform better than a control group. However, in the latter case—the relative effectiveness of two treatments—outcome is not the only evaluation criterion. For example, two treatments could have the same level of outcome, but one could be delivered at a lower cost, could achieve its results more quickly, or could be more acceptable to clients or staff. For example, Bertera and Bertera (1981) compared the effectiveness of two versions of a counseling program for people being treated for high blood pressure. The program's counselors encouraged participants to take their medication, control their weight, and reduce sodium intake; noncompliance with these aspects of treatment is a major problem in treating hypertension. One version of the program had counselors call their clients every 3 weeks to give the reminders, to answer clients' questions, and to give other advice as requested; the other version of the program had clients come to a clinic every 3 weeks for face-to-face counseling sessions. A greater proportion of participants in both versions of the program achieved clinically significant reductions in blood pressure than did members of a no-counseling control group, and the magnitude of the program's effect was the same in both versions of the program. However, the telephone version cost $39 per improved client compared to $82 per improved client for the face-to-face version. Therefore, do not be too quick to draw conclusions of no difference between treatments without considering variables not related to outcome that could have an impact on a decision to continue or terminate a program.

EFFICIENCY ANALYSIS

The efficiency analysis stage of program evaluation compares the outcomes produced by a program to the costs required to run the program. Note that efficiency analysis is descriptive: It provides information about costs and outcomes. Efficiency analysis does *not* address the question of whether the outcomes are *worth* the cost; that question of the value of the program is a policy or administrative question, not a scientific question. The purpose of program evaluation is to provide policy makers and administrators with the information they need to make such value judgments, not to make the judgments for them. Likewise, the question of the monetary cost of a program is an accounting question, not a psychological question. The determination of the dollar costs is an extremely complex process (Posavac & Carey, 1997; P. H. Rossi et al., 1999) and so is best left to accounting professionals. In this section we will briefly examine the two major forms of efficiency analysis, cost-benefit analysis and cost-effectiveness analysis.

Cost-Benefit Analysis

Cost-benefit analysis compares the dollar cost of operating a program to the benefits in dollars provided by the program. The use of cost-benefit analysis is predicated on the assumptions that all outcomes can be expressed in monetary terms or that the only important outcomes are those that can be expressed monetarily. The monetary benefits derived from a program can be estimated with different degrees of directness, as three examples will show. Schnelle et al. (1978) directly estimated the benefit derived from police use of helicopter patrols in a high-crime neighborhood. They subtracted the average burglary loss per day for the days that the patrols were in place ($161) from the average loss per day for comparable periods when the patrols were not being conducted ($494). The net benefit of $333 per day came at a cost of $126 per day for the helicopter patrols, giving a benefit-cost ratio of 2.6 to 1: Householders saved $2.60 in burglary costs for every dollar spent in conducting the patrols.

A bank interested in computing the benefit derived from providing free day care to the children of employees had to use a more indirect method (Solomon, 1988). They compared the turnover rate of employees who used the bank's day care program to employees who used other day care options. Based on a turnover rate of 2.2% for the users of the bank's day care compared to 9.5% for users of other day care, the evaluator estimated that providing day care saved the bank $157,000 per year in turnover costs. Users of the bank's day care also used an average of 1.7 fewer sick days per year and took an average of 1.2 weeks less maternity leave, for an additional savings of $35,000. This benefit of $192,000 per year came at an operating cost to the bank of $105,000 per year, for a benefit-cost ratio of 1.8 to 1.

Much more indirect benefit estimates were used in a cost-benefit analysis of a preschool intervention program for disadvantaged children who were followed through age 19. W. S. Barnett (1985) used data on differences between treatment and control participants to estimate that dollar value of the following social outcomes:

- Savings in child care time of the parents of the program participants
- Savings in special education costs required by the control participants but not by the program participants
- Savings in criminal or delinquent behavior prevented by the program
- Earnings differences resulting from higher employment rates of program participants
- Savings in the costs of welfare and economic dependency services not used by program participants

Barnett estimated a net benefit of $10,077 per program participant compared to a cost of $4,963, for a benefit-cost ratio of 2 to 1.

Cost-Effectiveness Analysis

The goals and outcomes of intervention programs are not always, and perhaps are only rarely, expressible in terms of money. More often, goals are psychological or social in nature, such as a reduction in psychological distress, a reduction in substance abuse in a community, or an increase in educational achievement. **Cost-effectiveness analysis** compares the cost of a program to the size of its outcomes rather than to the dollar benefit derived from those outcomes. For example, T. D. Cook et al.'s (1975) evaluation of the educational effects of *Sesame Street* found that the program's effect, while real, was also fairly small. However, they noted that the cost of the program was also small, about $1 per year per regular viewer in 1971 dollars. P. H. Rossi et al. (1999) suggest that cost-effectiveness analysis is most useful for comparing and choosing among programs that have similar goals: The program that produces the greatest effect at the least cost would be preferable to its competitors. Recall, for example, Bertera and Bertera's (1981) study, described earlier, which found that a telephone counseling program was as effective as a face-to-face program but cost about half as much.

INFORMATION UTILIZATION

The purpose of evaluation research is to provide policy makers with information about a program. The policy makers can then use this information to make decisions about the continuation, termination, or modification of the program. But is the information derived from program evaluations actually used in this way? Dooley (1995) notes that there is a general perception among evaluation researchers that not much use is made of their work, but also notes that there is little research on the actual utilization rate of evaluation research.

Part of the perception that results are not used by policy makers might lie in the fact that "utilization" actually has at least three meanings (Leviton & Hughes, 1981). **Instrumental utilization** is what most people mean by the use of research results: The results of the research are directly used for making decisions or solving problems. However, the results of program evaluation research may actually be used more frequently in two other ways (Leviton & Hughes, 1981; P. H. Rossi et al., 1999). **Conceptual utilization** is involved when the information influences a policy maker's thinking about an issue even if it doesn't have a direct influence on decisions about the issue. For example, although a particular program might be continued or discontinued for reasons other than the results of the evaluation, those results might influence future policy making on issues related to the program and its effects. Finally, the **persuasive utilization of evaluation results** is their use as evidence in attempts to convince others to support a political position or to defend a political position from attack. Chapter 1 looked at examples of such political use of research.

Because most researchers think of utilization in terms of decision making, this section briefly examines two sets of factors that influence the instrumental and conceptual use of research results: characteristics of the research and the political context of the evaluation.

Criteria for Research Utilization

The results of evaluation research are more likely to be used for decision making to the degree that they meet three criteria (Leviton & Hughes, 1981; Weiss, 1984): relevance, truth, and utility.

RELEVANCE   Relevant evaluation research addresses the needs of all stakeholder groups. For example, it assesses the degree to which the program meets its clients' need for services, it provides the information that program administrators need on the implementation of the program and the effectiveness of the various elements of the program, and it provides the information that policy makers need on the implementation of the program, the overall effectiveness of the program, and the resources required by the program (Leviton & Hughes, 1981). Evaluation relevance is rooted in the inclusion of all stakeholder groups in all stages of the evaluation from definition of goals, desired outcomes, and measures, through the choice of research methods, to the interpretation of the results of the evaluation into policy recommendations (Patton, 1986). Relevance requires that the stakeholders "own" the evaluation, in the sense that the evaluation team is their agent in gathering information that they will use to make decisions.

TRUTH   True research produces valid results; it adheres to the principles of construct validity, internal validity, external validity, ecological validity, and statistical conclusion validity. Equally important, the stakeholders must *perceive* the research to be valid and to accept its results as valid information. To some extent, research results are perceived as valid to the extent that they agree with other information available to the user of the research and to the extent that they meet the user's expectations for the outcome of the research (Weiss, 1984). Perceived validity is also a function of the extent to which the user has faith in the research process as a means of providing valid information and has faith in the researchers as being motivated by fairness and impartiality rather than having a prejudice in favor of or against the program (Leviton & Hughes, 1981). Patton (1986) suggests that stakeholders' faith in the research process and in the researchers increases as a function of the degree to which they help determine the goals of the evaluation and the procedures used to evaluate goal attainment.

UTILITY   As discussed in Chapter 4, research is perceived to be useful to the extent that it focuses on policy variables as independent variables and on high-utility dependent variables. In addition, a useful program evaluation provides information that can aid in program development (Posavac & Carey, 1997). For example, being able to answer the question "Why did the program work?" assists in generalizing the program to other client groups, other staff, and other locations. Being able to answer the question "Why did the program not achieve its goals or not all of its goals?" assists in identifying ways of improving the program. As you have seen, answering "why" questions about programs requires the incorporation of tests of the program theory and relevant estimator variables, such as client characteristics, into the evaluation. Finally, useful evaluation research is designed to provide informative no-difference results if they should occur. For example, by comparing two versions of a program, an evaluation can determine if one version provides its outcomes at less cost, even if the outcomes themselves are the same in both versions of the program.

The Political Context

Unlike most basic research, and even much academic-based applied research, evaluation research is conducted in a social environment pervaded by political motivations.

The term *evaluation* implies that there will be winners and losers from the process, and, indeed, people's incomes, power, and prestige can be negatively affected by the cancelation of a program or enhanced by its continuation or expansion. Not surprisingly, therefore, the quality of evaluation research is not the only, or even the most important, factor affecting its use; politics also play a role. The political ramifications of evaluation research are manifold (P. H. Rossi et al., 1999; Weiss, 1984); here I will mention two: ritual evaluation and stakeholder interests.

RITUAL EVALUATIONS   One political factor affecting the use of evaluation research is the conduct of what Weiss (1984) calls *ritual evaluations*, which are carried out although no one has any intention of applying their results to the program. These evaluations might be required by law or regulations, they might be done because an evaluation seems like the right thing to do at the time, or the results of an evaluation might be seen as useful for persuasive purposes. As a consequence of the ritual nature of such evaluations,

> should the evaluation show weaknesses when the expectation was for program success, a first line of defense is usually to file away the report in the expectation that nobody else will want to know. When there were no expectations at all, but just ritualistic adherence to "correct procedure," few . . . people [in charge of the program] can be expected to read even the executive summary [of the report]. (Weiss, 1984, pp. 160–161)

When an evaluation has been ordered by an outside authority, reaction to an unfavorable evaluation might be akin to guerrilla warfare. For example, Archer, Pettigrew, and Aronson (1992) relate the troubles they had after completing an evaluation of utility-company-sponsored energy conservation programs for the California Public Utilities Commission (PUC). Their findings were highly critical of some of the programs. One result:

> The mere fact that our review was critical came to dominate meetings [with utility company officials]. The goal of the utilities was simple: to undermine the potential impact of the report, using any arguments necessary. The utilities seemed bent on preventing any criticism from entering the PUC record in order to minimize any possible fiscal damage at later rate hearings. (Archer et al., 1992, p. 1234)

STAKEHOLDER INTERESTS   As shown by Archer et al.'s (1992) experience, the vested interests of stakeholders in a program can strongly affect the acceptance of the results of an evaluation. Stakeholders will loudly trumpet information favorable to their interests and attempt to suppress or downplay unfavorable information, extensively using selective citation of findings (Crossen, 1994). For example, Zimring (1975) conducted an evaluation of the effects of the federal Gun Control Act of 1968 but noted that

> the study will be of little use to the most fervent friends and foes of gun control legislation. It provides data they do not need. Each group uses the Act's presumed failure to confirm views already strongly held. Enthusiasts for strict federal controls see the failure of the law as proof that stricter laws are needed, while opponents see it as evidence that no controls will work. (p. 133)

MEASURING CHANGE

Change is a basic issue in program evaluation: Change is what the program being evaluated is supposed to bring about in its clients. However, the question of the proper way to measure change has long been controversial; Cronbach and Furby (1970) went so far as to suggest that psychologists should not attempt to measure change. This section looks at two issues in the measurement of change: the reliability of change (or difference) scores and the types of change that can be found when change is assessed using self-report measures.

Difference Scores

Change is most commonly measured in terms of a **difference score:** a person's score on a measure at a posttest minus that person's score on the measure at a pretest. However, as simple as a difference score is to compute, statisticians have long been reluctant to endorse it as a measure of change. This reluctance stems from the conclusion first drawn by Lord (1956) that "differences between scores tend to be much more unreliable than the scores themselves" (p. 420) and echoed by methodologists ever since (see Allison, 1990). The problem is, of course, that low reliability implies low validity (recall Chapter 5), so that if difference scores are unreliable they are unlikely to be valid indicators of change. Although the conclusion drawn by Lord (1956) and his successors is grounded in a large body of research (Rogosa, Brandt, & Zimowski, 1982), more recent analyses of the issue have led to more optimism about using difference scores to assess change. This discussion will examine two of these approaches: the assessment of the reliability of difference scores and the use of a reliable change index.

Reliability of Difference Scores

Some statisticians have concluded that the extreme unreliability of difference scores that has been found in research on the subject resulted from the researchers' having examined unusual measurement situations. In order for difference scores to be reliable, they must reflect individual differences in change. However, most research on difference scores that led to the pessimistic conclusion about their reliability has been conducted under conditions of little individual difference in change; that is, all the participants in the research exhibited the same amount of change (Rogosa et al., 1982; Rogosa & Willett, 1983). When there is more person-to-person variation in the degree of change that occurs from pretest to posttest, the difference scores can be reliable if certain statistical conditions are met.

Rogosa and Willett (1983) have shown that the reliability of a difference score increases

- As the reliability of the measure increases
- As the correlation between the pretest scores and the difference scores increases
- As the correlation between the pretest scores and the posttest scores approaches zero

Rogosa and Willett (1983) provide a formula for computing the reliability of a difference score given this information. For example, given a measure with a reliability of .8, a pretest-difference correlation of .4, and a pretest-posttest correlation of zero, the reliability of the difference score is .74, or 93% of the reliability of the measure itself.

Assessing the reliability of difference scores for a measure requires two steps. First, select the most reliable measure available. Second, if possible, compute the reliability of difference scores for the measure using data from other studies. If it is low, stop: Low reliability indicates low validity, and there is no point in trying to draw valid conclusions from an invalid measure of change. If no prior data are available, conduct a pilot study to collect the necessary data for a reliability check.

The Reliable Change Index

Jacobson and Truax (1991) report another approach to difference scores, which they call the **reliable change index (RCI).** The RCI is a person's difference score on a measure divided by the standard error of the difference for the measure; the standard error of the difference is computed from the standard error of measurement of the measure. Because the RCI requires a reasonable estimate of the population standard error of measurement, it can be used only with standardized measures (see Chapter 5). However, because all published psychological tests are standardized, this requirement does not impose a significant limitation on the use of the RCI. If the value of the RCI is greater than 1.96, then the probability that the difference score reflects only random change is less than .05; that is, the change found is likely to be real change.

Researchers can use the RCI in two ways for program evaluation. First, they can compare the mean RCI scores of a treatment group with that of a control group to determine the average amount of reliable change brought about by the treatment. Note, however, that a mean RCI score, like the mean of any other variable, can obscure individual differences in response to the treatment. To alleviate this problem, researchers can use the RCI in a second way, comparing the proportions of people in the treatment and control groups who show reliable change. This procedure answers the question "Does the treatment cause more people to show reliable change than no treatment or an alternative treatment?" A more refined analysis could divide research participants into three groups: those who show no reliable change, those who show change that is reliable but not practically significant, and those whose change is both reliable and practically significant. Jacobson and Truax (1991) give the example of couples who took part in a marital therapy program: Forty-six percent of the couples showed change that was both reliable and clinically significant and so were considered recovered, 27% showed reliable change but did not meet the criterion for recovery and so were considered improved, and 27% did not show reliable change and so were considered unimproved. The RCI therefore represents a very useful tool for program evaluation when outcomes are assessed using standardized measures.

SUMMARY

Five steps of evaluation research are goal definition, program monitoring, impact assessment, efficiency analysis, and information utilization. Two issues in the measurement of change are the reliability of difference scores and the types of change found with subjective measures. Evaluation research applies social and behavioral science research methods to answer four questions concerning an intervention program: the extent to which a program is meeting its goals, the aspects of the program that contribute to its success, ways in which the program can be improved, and the validity of the theory underlying the program.

The first step in program evaluation is defining the goals of the program. Goal definition has two aspects. The first is needs assessment, identifying problems that need to be addressed and developing solutions to the problems. Solution identification includes defining the target population for the intervention and determining the content of the program. The second aspect of goal definition is evaluability assessment, collection of the information needed in order to conduct the evaluation. This information includes specifying the goals of the program, the theory of the program, implementation guidelines for the program, and the resources the program requires. Goal specification transforms abstract program goals into concrete indicators of program effects. This process must consider the viewpoints of all stakeholder groups and develop goals and effect indicators from those points of view. It must also determine the relative importance of the goals and take into account both the proximal and distal goals of the program. Inclusion of the program theory allows a test of the theory and of the importance of the program components, specifies the conditions under which the program should be most effective, and can provide insight into why a program did not have its intended effects.

The second stage of evaluation research is program monitoring, ensuring that the program is carried out as designed. Program monitoring has three aspects. The first is ensuring that the program reaches its intended client population. The second aspect is ensuring that the program is implemented completely and properly. Four sources of implementation failure are lack of specific implementation criteria, insufficiently trained staff, inadequate supervision of staff, and staff resistance. Implementation can also fail because clients resist the program. The third aspect of program monitoring is the identification of unintended effects. When program monitoring detects implementation problems, the program is changed to bring it back on track. These changes can be troublesome for the evaluation because the data collected while the program was off track cannot be used to evaluate the properly implemented program.

The third stage of evaluation research is assessing program impact. The first issue relevant to impact assessment is the choice of impact criteria. Four sets of criteria are the degree of change brought about by the program, the importance of the change, the costs of the program, and the acceptability of the program to stakeholders. The second issue is choice of research design; six designs—program package, comparative outcome, dismantling, client and program variation, constructive, and parametric—are available to answer the four evaluation questions. The third issue is choice of research strategy. Any research strategy can be used for program evaluation, but additional controls must be instituted to avoid control group contamination as a threat to internal validity.

Finally, possible reasons for null results in evaluation research are theory failure, implementation failure, and evaluation failure. Also, if two programs do not differ in impact, they may differ on other evaluation criteria, such as cost or acceptability.

The fourth stage of evaluation research is efficiency analysis, a comparison of a program's outcomes to its costs. Efficiency analysis can take two forms. Cost-benefit analysis compares the monetary benefits of a program to its monetary costs. Cost-effectiveness analysis compares the magnitude of the nonmonetary effects of a program to its monetary costs and is especially well suited to comparing two programs that have the same goals.

The last stage of evaluation research is utilization of its results. Policy makers are most likely to use information they perceive as relevant to their needs, valid, and directly applicable to program development. However, even information that meets these criteria may not be used if the evaluation is conducted only to meet mandated requirements or conflicts with stakeholder interests.

An important issue in the measurement of change is the reliability of difference scores. Before using difference scores to assess change, compute their reliability, and use them only if the reliability is adequate. Or compute the reliable change index for standardized measures to assess the likelihood that a difference score represents only random variation in the score across time.

QUESTIONS AND EXERCISES FOR REVIEW

1. What four questions concerning program effectiveness does evaluation research investigate? Briefly describe the five stages of evaluation research.
2. Describe the process of needs assessment.
3. Describe the process of goal specification. What roles do stakeholders and program theory play in this process? Explain the importance of the distinction between proximal and distal goals.
4. What problems are involved in ensuring that a program reaches its target population? How can a program's success in reaching its target population be evaluated?
5. How can the success of program implementation be assessed? Describe the sources of implementation failure. What procedures can program administrators use to overcome these sources of failure?
6. Explain the problem of unintended effects in evaluation research. What procedures can evaluators use to detect such effects?
7. Explain the dilemma that process or formative evaluation can create for summative evaluation. How can this dilemma be resolved?
8. Which categories of criteria can be used to evaluate the impact of a program? Why is using multiple evaluation criteria desirable?
9. Describe the six evaluation research designs. What program effectiveness question does each design answer?
10. Describe the minimum requirement for an evaluation research design. How can this requirement be met by using the research strategies described in Chapters 7 through 10? What are the advantages and disadvantages of each strategy for evaluation research?
11. What additional threats to internal validity can arise in evaluation research?
12. Describe the circumstances under which a preexperimental design might be used for evaluation research. What are the limitations of this approach?

13. Describe the possible sources of null results in evaluation research. How can program theory and the use of multiple evaluation criteria shed light on the meaning of null results?

14. How do cost-benefit analysis and cost-effectiveness analysis differ? What are the advantages and disadvantages of each of these approaches to efficiency analysis?

15. Describe the ways in which the results of program evaluation can be used. Describe the factors affecting the use of evaluation results. Given the limitations on utilization, is program evaluation a worthwhile endeavor? Why or why not?

16. The discussion of unintended effects noted that the evaluation of the first year of *Sesame Street* had an ambiguous outcome: The skills of disadvantaged children who watched the program increased, but the gap between their skill level and that of advantaged children who watched the program widened. In your opinion, did this outcome make the program a success or failure? Would your answer be different if the program goals had been defined differently? How could the political context of evaluation affect the decision about the success of the program?

17. Describe two ways of dealing with the problem of the potential unreliability of difference scores.

16 INTEGRATIVE LITERATURE REVIEWING

DEFINING THE RESEARCH
QUESTION
Types of Questions
  What Is the Average Effect of
    an Independent Variable?
  What Factors Moderate That
    Effect?
  Is the Effect Found Under
    Specific Conditions?
The Scope of the Question
Approaches to Answering
  Questions

DATA COLLECTION

DATA EVALUATION
Include All Studies
Include Only Published Studies
Include Only Valid Studies
  Internal Validity
  Theoretical Validity
  Ecological Validity
  Evaluating Validity
Stratified Sampling
Expert Judgment

DATA ANALYSIS
Operationally Defining Study
  Outcome
  Effect Size
  Multiple Outcome Categories
  Two Outcome Categories
Classifying Studies
Analyzing Patterns of Flaws
Level of Analysis
Choosing a Technique
  Types of Studies That Can Be
    Reviewed
  Objectivity Versus
    Subjectivity
  Precision of Results
  "Best Evidence" Literature
    Reviewing

DATA INTERPRETATION
The Effect of Judgment Calls
The Correlational Nature of
  Moderator Variable Analyses
Publication Biases

EVALUATING LITERATURE
REVIEWS

UNDERSTANDING META-
ANALYSIS
Defining the Research Question
Data Collection
Data Evaluation
Data Analysis
Interpretation

SUMMARY

QUESTIONS AND EXERCISES
FOR REVIEW

As of 1980, almost 900 studies had been conducted on the relationship between perceptual speed and the job performance of clerical workers (Schmidt, 1992). A reasonable question to ask is "What have all these studies told us about that relationship?" Given that not all the results of the studies were consistent—some supported the existence of a relationship, others did not—another reasonable question is "What caused these inconsistencies?" An **integrative literature review** attempts to answer such questions by collecting all the available information on a topic and organizing it to show the current state of knowledge on the topic and to identify gaps in knowledge that need to be filled.

Literature reviews can be conducted to fulfill a number of purposes and a review can fulfill more than one purpose. One purpose is summarizing new theories, findings, research methods, and data analysis techniques on a topic. For example, the *Annual Review of Psychology* tries to update the state of knowledge in every major field of psychology every 4 to 5 years. A second purpose of literature reviews is identifying linkages between theories and developing new theories from the knowledge provided by existing theories and research. Sternberg (1986), for example, conducted a comprehensive review of theories and research on the topic of love and distilled the resulting large mass of sometimes conflicting information into a parsimonious three-factor theory of love. A third purpose of literature reviewing is evaluating the validity of a theory by summarizing the research evidence for and against its propositions. Similarly, the validity of competing theories on a topic can be compared by analyzing the results of research conducted on the topic to see which theory the research best supports. Marks and Miller (1987), for example, compared the evidence underlying four theoretical explanations for a phenomenon known as the *false consensus effect*: the tendency for people to overestimate the degree to which others share their opinions and beliefs.

A final purpose of literature reviewing, and the one that will be the focus of this chapter, is summarizing the research evidence on a hypothesis or set of related hypotheses. Such summaries have several goals. One goal is determining how well the hypothesis is supported. As noted before, every study has its flaws; no study can be perfect and so by itself cannot provide a complete answer to a research question—the outcome of a single study could be the result of its flaws rather than of the effect of the independent variable. However, if several studies of a hypothesis, each with its own flaws but each also having strengths that compensate for the weaknesses of the others, all come to the same conclusion, then it is unlikely that the overall result is an artifact resulting from design flaws. The consensus of a number of studies as shown by a literature review therefore provides the best estimate of the effect of an independent variable. Nonetheless, some studies in a set will support the hypothesis and others will not; therefore, a related goal of literature reviewing is determining the causes of inconsistencies in research results. Sometimes the cause is methodological, such as the use of different operational definitions in different studies, and sometimes the cause is a variable that moderates the effect of the independent variable, such as when men respond differently from women. In such a case, the use of all-male samples in some studies and all-female samples in other studies will lead to apparently conflicting results. Once the summary is completed, the literature reviewer can draw implications for theory, research, and application. For example, the discovery of moderating variables might require modification to theories, the literature review might show that a commonly used operational definition has validity problems, or the review might indicate that an intervention works better for some types of people or in some situations than it does for other people or in other situations.

The results of literature reviews can be used in several ways. Chapter 4 discussed one use: Literature reviews provide the background for new research studies. Literature reviews are also used to inform other scientists about the current state of knowledge about a theory or topic and to identify gaps in knowledge that need to be filled by research. For example, a review might find that important aspects of a theory have not been tested or have not been properly tested. Such reviews can also address the generalizability of research results by determining how consistent they are across such factors as research strategies, operational definitions, research settings, and participant populations. Reviews of this kind are published in journals such as *Psychological Bulletin*. Finally, reviews of evaluation studies can provide information that can be used in making policy decisions by identifying what programs work and the conditions affecting the quality of program outcomes. For example, the Office of Technology Assessment, created by

Congress to provide its members with scientific information relevant to proposed legislation, makes extensive use of literature reviews to organize and summarize the results of research on issues that it investigates.

This chapter examines the process of conducting integrative literature reviews, a form of research whose goal is to draw overall conclusions concerning the validity of a hypothesis based on the results of studies that have tested the hypothesis. As Jackson (1980) noted, "Reviewers and primary researchers share a common goal . . . to make accurate generalizations about phenomena from limited information" (pp. 441–442). In **primary research,** that information is the data collected from research participants; in literature reviewing, the information is the results of a set of studies testing a hypothesis. Because they share a common goal, primary researchers and literature reviews take similar steps to reach the goal. As in empirical research, there are five steps to literature reviewing: defining the research question, data collection, data evaluation, data analysis, and interpretation of results. This chapter first discusses these steps as they apply to literature reviews and then considers in more detail the statistical approach to literature reviewing known as meta-analysis. More detailed discussions of the process of literature reviewing can be found in Light and Pillemer's (1984) pioneering book and in the books by H. M. Cooper (1998), Lipsey and Wilson (2001), and H. M. Cooper and Hedges (1994).

DEFINING THE RESEARCH QUESTION

Literature reviews, like all research, start with a question. There are three issues to consider in formulating a literature review question (Light & Pillemer, 1984): the type of question you want to answer, the scope of the question, and the approach to take to answering the question.

Types of Questions

Literature reviews can address three questions: What is the average effect of an independent variable on a dependent variable, what factors moderate that effect, and is the effect found under specific sets of conditions?

WHAT IS THE AVERAGE EFFECT OF AN INDEPENDENT VARIABLE?   This question concerns what, in analysis-of-variance designs, would be called a main effect (recall Chapter 7). That is, ignoring such factors as differences among studies in research strategies, participant populations, operational definitions, and settings, what effect does an independent variable have on a dependent variable, and how large is that effect? Although this is a rather simplistic way of looking at the effect of a variable, this "main effects" approach to literature reviewing can serve two purposes. One purpose is to guide social policy making, which is often more interested in the overall effect of a variable than in the factors that moderate its effects (Light & Pillemer, 1984). For example, consider a hypothetical policy question such as "Should public funds be used to pay for psychotherapy services?" Because the question is one of whether the services should be funded at all, policy makers will want to know if psychotherapy in general is effective and therefore deserving of funding. Questions concerning moderator variables, such as whether some types of therapy are more effective for some types of people or problems, are too narrow to form the basis for a broad social policy. Paraphrasing Masters (1984), Guzzo, Jackson, and Katzell (1987) frame the issue in this way:

> Policy makers voice a need for "one-armed" social scientists who give straight, unqualified answers when asked for advice. Instead, they too often encounter a response such as, "Well, on the one hand thus and so is the case, but on the other hand this and that may hold." Unlike scientists, who often prefer to dwell on the contingencies that make global generalizations impossible, policy makers must seek to find the most justifiable generalizations. (p. 412)

Policymakers may consider interactions especially irrelevant when the moderator is an estimator variable, over which they have no control (recall Chapter 4). However, the consideration of relevant policy variables as potential moderators is essential to any applied meta-analysis (Light & Pillemer, 1984).

A second purpose of main effects literature reviewing is to identify general principles that can guide research. For example, a general finding that there are sex differences in nonverbal communication skills implies that sex of research participant should be controlled in such studies in order to minimize extraneous variance.

WHAT FACTORS MODERATE THAT EFFECT?   This is the question of the generalizability of an effect: Does the independent variable have the same effect under all conditions? In analysis-of-variance terms, this is the question of whether an interaction exists between the independent variable whose effect is being reviewed and some other variable. Ideas for the potential moderator variables to consider in a literature review can come from a number of sources (Mullen, Salas, & Miller, 1991). One source of ideas is the theories that deal with the independent variable; these theories might postulate the existence of moderator variables and so predict that research should find certain interactions. For example, Hackman and Oldham's (1980) Job Characteristics Model of work motivation holds that interventions based on the model will be more effective for certain types of people — those high in what Hackman and Oldham call growth need strength — than for others. Reviews of the literature on the effectiveness of the model should therefore compare the outcomes of studies conducted with people high in growth need strength with studies conducted with people low in growth need strength. This procedure both tests the theory and examines its impact under the conditions that it specifies as crucial to its effectiveness.

Potential moderator variables can also be identified from the reviewer's knowledge of research on the topic and from prior literature reviews. For example, the reviewer might know that the results of research on a topic vary as a function of research setting. Similarly, potential mediator variables may emerge from the studies being reviewed: As the reviewer reads through them, she may see patterns of relationships between factors such as study characteristics and the magnitude of the impact of the independent variable. Finally, one can apply "one's intuition, insight, and ingenuity" (Jackson, 1980, p. 443) to the problem: The reviewer might have hypotheses of his own to test in the review.

A shortcoming of many literature reviews is a tendency to look primarily for simple interactions, those involving only one moderator variable (Shadish & Sweeney, 1991). As Shadish and Sweeney point out, however, interactions among moderator variables can be important. They use the example of reviews of psychotherapy outcome research, which have generally found that behavioral and nonbehavioral therapies have equal effects in terms of recovery rates. That is, these reviews concluded that type of treatment does not interact with condition of the independent variable (treatment versus control) to affect outcome: An equal proportion of people improve with each type of therapy when compared to control groups. However, Shadish and Sweeney's review found that type of therapy interacts with therapy setting to affect outcome: Behavioral therapies have twice the effect of nonbehavioral therapies when the research is conducted in university settings, but there is no difference in effect size when the research is conducted in nonuniversity settings. To be able to identify possible moderator variables, literature reviewers need to be thoroughly familiar with both the theoretical and empirical issues related to the topic of the review. Reviewers new to a topic should seek the advice of people who are experts on it.

IS THE EFFECT FOUND UNDER SPECIFIC CONDITIONS?   This is the question of the ecological validity of an effect (recall Chapter 14); that is, how well can a broad principle be applied to a specific type of situation? The answer to this question can be used to assist in deciding if an intervention should be implemented under a given set of circumstances: Has previous research shown it to be effective or ineffective under those, or similar, circumstances?

The Scope of the Question

The issue of scope deals with how narrowly or broadly the question is defined. For example, is the review to be limited to just one operational definition of the independent variable, or will multiple operational definitions be considered? Will the review be limited to one dependent variable, or will the independent variable's effects on several dependent variables be assessed? Will the review include just one or more than one operational definition of each dependent variable? Will it include only one research strategy or will all strategies be included? The answers to questions such as these will depend to some extent on the purpose of the literature review. For example, only experiments can test causality, so a review that asks a causal question might be limited to or give more emphasis to experiments. A review that is too narrow in scope—for example, a review limited to one operational definition each of the independent and dependent variables—may lead to conclusions with little generalizability. Yet a review that is too broadly defined might become impossible to complete, with the reviewer overwhelmed by a huge number of studies. As with many other aspects of literature reviewing, and research in general, defining the scope of the review is a judgment call that must be guided by the reviewer's knowledge of the topic under review.

Approaches to Answering Questions

Light and Pillemer (1984) suggest that there are two broad approaches to conducting literature reviews, although any review can involve a combination of the two. With the hypothesis-testing approach, the reviewer starts with a specific hypothesis about the relationship between an independent variable and a dependent variable, and tests the hypothesis against the results of research. For example, Loher, Noe, Moeller, and Fitzgerald (1985) tested the hypotheses that application of Hackman and Oldham's (1980) Job Characteristics Model would lead to increases in job satisfaction and that it would be more effective for people high in growth need strength. They found that the model had a moderate positive impact overall and that its impact was, as the theory predicted, greater for people high in growth need strength.

The second approach is exploratory, in which the reviewer focuses on an outcome and searches the relevant literature to determine which independent variables consistently produce the outcome. For example, Whitley and Schofield (1986) asked "What variables predict the use of contraception by adolescents?" Their review found 25 reasonably consistent predictors for young women and 12 for young men. One drawback of the exploratory approach is that the predictors found can be intercorrelated so that controlling for one or more might remove the effects of others (recall the discussion of multiple regression analysis in Chapter 8). Therefore, any relationships found using an exploratory literature review should be confirmed by collecting new data. When

Whitley (1990a) did this, he found that only three of the variables independently predicted contraceptive use by young women and only one predicted contraceptive use by young men.

The choice between the hypothesis-testing and exploratory approaches to literature reviewing depends to a large extent on the purpose of the review and the nature of the research being reviewed. For example, the hypothesis-testing approach can be used only when the reviewer has a specific hypothesis in mind, derived from theory, from prior empirical work, or from her own insight or experience. The exploratory approach can be used to identify important independent variables in order to develop new theories from existing research or, as Whitley and Schofield (1986) did, to catalog independent variables in an area of research that has been generally unguided by theory and to determine which appear to have effects and which do not.

DATA COLLECTION

Data collection for a literature review consists of locating studies that deal with the hypothesis or topic of interest. Chapter 4 discussed this process, going over the various indexes available for locating research reports; you might want to review that discussion before going on.

Although the methods discussed in Chapter 4 provide useful starting points for collecting data for an integrative literature review, they do not provide a complete listing of relevant research. M. C. Rosenthal (1994), for example, discusses what she calls "the fugitive literature"—research reports in the form of technical reports, unpublished manuscripts, papers presented at conventions, and dissertations and theses—that are often not covered by the more commonly used indexes. Rosenthal's chapter provides several strategies for locating these kinds of studies.

In addition, indexes do not always provide a complete listing of all the published studies on a topic. Durlak and Lipsey (1991), for example, noted that computer searches of indexes overlooked 67% of the studies relevant to a literature review that they conducted. People doing literature reviews therefore often find it useful to conduct what Green and Hall (1984) call a source-by-source search: Identify all the journals that are likely to carry research reports on your topic, and examine every issue of every journal for relevant articles. Such a procedure is laborious and time consuming, but Green and Hall believe it is the best way of being certain to have located all relevant published studies.

DATA EVALUATION

Once you have collected the studies relevant to your hypothesis, you must decide which ones to include in your literature review. Although your initial impulse might be to include all the studies, there are other options (Light & Pillemer, 1984): including only published studies, including only highly valid studies, stratified sampling of studies, and using experts' judgments to choose studies. Let's look at the advantages and disadvantages of these options.

Include All Studies

Including all the relevant studies in the literature review has the distinct advantage of completeness: All the available data will be used in drawing conclusions. There are, however, several potential disadvantages to this approach (Light & Pillemer, 1984). First, it might be difficult or impossible to locate all relevant studies. As noted, few unpublished studies are indexed, making it very difficult to locate them, and the benefit derived once they are found might not be worth the effort. Second, including all studies in the review will give equal weight to both highly valid and poor research. Conclusions drawn from the latter studies should be qualified by consideration of the alternative explanations for their results posed by the threats to their internal validity. However, if all studies are lumped together, valid results are confounded with potentially invalid results. Finally, if there is a very large number of studies on a topic, it might be impossible to include all of them, especially if the time available for conducting the review is limited.

Include Only Published Studies

Most literature reviews include only published studies or make only limited attempts to locate unpublished studies, such as through the use of the ERIC database discussed in Chapter 4. Published studies are easy to locate because they are indexed. In addition, the peer review process provides some screening for methodological validity, although the process, in which other scientists evaluate the quality of a research report as a condition of publication, is not perfect. Considering only published studies also limits the number of studies you must deal with.

The disadvantage of including only published studies in the review is that it brings into play the publication biases discussed in Chapter 13. As noted then, there is a bias against publishing null results (Greenwald, 1975). Because studies finding no statistically significant difference between the conditions of the independent variable — that is, those with small effect sizes — are unlikely to be published, those that are published may overestimate the true effect of the independent variable, resulting in a literature review that gives a distorted picture of the relationship between the independent and dependent variables (Schmidt, 1992). White (1982), for example, conducted a literature review of studies of the relationship between socioeconomic status (SES) and IQ scores, and discovered that unpublished studies found an average correlation of .29, studies published in journals found an average correlation of .34, and studies published in books found an average correlation of .51.

Another form of publication bias is in favor of studies whose results are consistent with accepted theory (Greenwald, Pratkanis, Leippe, & Baumgardner, 1986). Studies that challenge the explanations of phenomena provided by popular theories tend to be evaluated more strictly than studies that support the theory and so are less likely to get published. Garcia (1981), for example, recounts the difficulties he encountered in getting the results of research on the biological constraints on classical conditioning published. Many of his problems stemmed from his challenges to principles that had long been accepted without question. Consequently, a literature review aimed at evaluating a theory is less likely to turn up data that challenge the theory if it includes only published studies.

Include Only Valid Studies

As noted earlier, including all studies in a literature review, or even only all published studies, may result in using studies that have threats to their validity. Consequently, literature reviewers frequently attempt to assess the validity of the studies conducted on a topic. Reviewers are generally most concerned with internal validity, theoretical validity, and ecological validity; they assess generalizability with analyses of the effects of moderator variables.

INTERNAL VALIDITY   Because the results of studies that suffer from internal validity problems might not accurately reflect the true relationship between the independent and dependent variables, including them in a literature review could threaten the validity of the conclusions drawn from the review. For example, White (1982) noted the studies he thought were of low internal validity found an average correlation of .49 between SES and IQ scores, whereas the highly valid studies found an average correlation of .30. Consequently, literature reviews usually evaluate the internal validity of the research they review and give more weight to those considered more valid. Some reviewers completely exclude from consideration studies they consider invalid.

THEORETICAL VALIDITY   You can also evaluate studies on their theoretical validity (T. D. Cook & Leviton, 1980). That is, some theories specify conditions that must be met in order for predictions made by the theories to be fulfilled. As already noted, Hackman and Oldham (1980) say that their theory of work performance will apply only to a certain type of person but not to other types of people. A true test of the validity of a theory can take place only if the conditions that it sets for itself are met. T. D. Cook and Leviton (1980) cite the example of research on the "sleeper effect" in persuasion, the finding that attitude change is sometimes delayed until well after the persuasive message is received:

> If all past studies of the sleeper effect were included in a review without regard to how well the necessary conditions for a strong test of the effect were met, one would probably conclude from the many failures to obtain the effect that "it is time to lay the sleeper effect to rest.". . . And the number of failures to obtain the effect would be psychologically impressive. Yet the very few studies that demonstrably met the theory-derived conditions for a strong test of the effect all obtained it . . . , and one can surmise that these studies should be assigned greatest inferential weight because of their higher theoretical relevance. (pp. 460–461)

ECOLOGICAL VALIDITY   Finally, when the literature review is aimed at determining the applicability of a principle to a specific situation, the reviewer will want to assess the ecological validity of the studies relative to that situation. The studies that were not conducted under conditions reasonably similar to those in the situation to which the principle is going to be applied could be eliminated from or given less weight in the review.

EVALUATING VALIDITY   Excluding studies from consideration in a review on the basis of their validity raises the question of what constitutes a study that is sufficiently valid to be included in the literature review. As noted in Chapter 2, no study can be perfect (McGrath, 1981); as a result, even experts can disagree about the degree of validity of a study. Therefore, selecting studies for inclusion in a literature review on the basis of their validity might be overly restrictive: A methodological flaw in a study does not necessarily mean its results are biased, only that the conclusions you can draw from it are less certain than the conclusions that can be drawn from a better study (Jackson, 1980). In addition, as R. Rosenthal (1990a) points out, "Too often, deciding what is a 'bad' study is a procedure richly susceptible to bias or to claims of bias. . . . 'Bad' studies are too often those whose results we don't like or . . . the studies [conducted by] our 'enemies' " (p. 126).

What, then, should you do when you face a set of studies that vary on their validity? Mullen et al. (1991) suggest a three-step approach. First, exclude those studies that are so flawed in terms of internal or construct validity that no valid conclusions can be drawn from them. For example, a study might use a measure that later research has shown to be invalid; because the wrong construct was measured, the study does not really test the hypothesis under review. Second, establish an explicit set of criteria for judging the degree of validity of the studies under review. For example, a study that randomly assigned participants to conditions of the independent variable would be considered of higher internal validity than a study that allowed participants to select themselves into conditions. Criteria could also be established for ecological or theoretical validity. Third, classify the studies as to their degree of validity, being sure to check the reliability of the classification system, and analyze the results of the studies within validity categories. Using this approach, you can determine if degree of validity affected the results of the studies, as did White (1982). If there are large discrepancies in results on the basis of degree of validity, you might want to give more weight to the high-validity studies when drawing conclusions.

Stratified Sampling

If the number of studies on a topic is so large that including all of them in a review would be unduly burdensome or would make it impossible to complete the review in the time available, you can classify (or stratify) the studies on the basis of important characteristics, such as the operational definitions or participant samples used, and randomly sample studies from each category for inclusion in the review (Light & Pillemer, 1984). This approach will result in a review based on a sample of studies whose characteristics are reasonably representative of the characteristics of all the studies. As a result, the conclusions drawn from such a review should be similar to those drawn from a review of all the studies. The drawback of this approach is that it might not be possible to classify all the studies on all the relevant characteristics; the information needed might not be available for some studies. If all the studies cannot be classified, a sample based only on the classifiable studies might be biased.

Expert Judgment

Another solution that Light and Pillemer (1984) suggest to the overabundance of studies problem is to have acknowledged experts on the topic under review choose the best and most relevant studies for review. This approach capitalizes on the experts' knowledge and experience and ensures that the review will focus on studies that are valued by experts in the field. However, studies chosen by experts might reflect biases that the experts hold, such as favoring studies that use large numbers of participants or that are well known over other studies that are equally or more relevant or valid.

DATA ANALYSIS

Once the studies are selected for inclusion in the literature, the reviewer must synthesize or combine their results. This synthesis has two aspects. First, the reviewer must determine the overall effect of the independent variable as shown by the results of the studies: On the average, does the independent variable have an effect or not? Second, the reviewer must determine the factors that moderate, or lead to differences in, the results of the studies. For example, does the independent variable have an effect in one situation, such as a laboratory environment, but not in another, such as field settings? To accomplish these tasks, the reviewer must make several sets of decisions: how to operationally define the outcomes of studies, how to classify studies on possible moderating variables, how to assess flaws in research designs, how broadly to define the independent and dependent variables, and how to conduct the data analysis.

Operationally Defining Study Outcome

A literature review combines the outcomes of studies to draw conclusions about the effect of an independent variable. The first step in this process is operationally defining study outcome in a way that allows the reviewer to directly compare the results of different studies even though those studies might have used different operational definitions of the independent and dependent variables. For example, studies of the relationship between television violence and aggression in children have used a wide variety of operational definitions of both constructs (Hearold, 1986). How can you compare the results of studies and draw overall conclusions in such circumstances? You must develop an operational definition of study outcome that can be applied to the studies under review. Three operational definitions are commonly used (Jackson, 1980): effect size, multiple outcome categories, and a dichotomous categorization based on whether the results of the study supported or did not support the hypothesis.

EFFECT SIZE   Jackson (1980) recommends effect size as the ideal operational definition of study outcome because, as Chapter 13 noted, it provides a precise index of the impact of the independent variable on the dependent variable. Two effect size measures are commonly used in literature reviews. When the independent variable is categorical, such as the experimental versus control conditions in an experiment, the standardized difference in the means of the two conditions, indicated by the symbol d, is used as the operational definition of outcome. The difference d is computed as the mean of the experimental condition minus the mean of the control condition divided by the pooled, or combined, standard deviation of the conditions. Therefore, d indicates the number of standard deviations that separate the means of the two conditions. Typically, d is given a plus sign if the results are in the direction predicted by the hypothesis being tested in the review, and a minus sign if the results are opposite to the prediction. Take a hypothetical example: The hypothesis is that boys are more aggressive than girls, and a study finds a mean aggression score of 16.5 for boys and 10.9 for girls with a pooled standard deviation of 12.8. The effect size d would be computed as $(16.5 - 10.9)/12.8 = +.437$. When the independent variable is continuous, such as scores on a personality questionnaire, then the Pearson product moment correlation, r, is used as the effect size indicator. Given an effect size for each study, you can answer the question of the overall effect of the independent variable by computing the mean effect size across studies (Lipsey & Wilson, 2001).

Both d and r require that the dependent variable in the study be continuous; however, there are also effect size indicators for categorical dependent variables that can be mathematically transformed to d and r (for example, see R. Rosenthal, 1991). And d and r can also be converted to one another: $r = d/\sqrt{d^2 + 4}$. For example, the d of $+.437$, computed earlier, is equivalent to an r of $+.213$.

MULTIPLE OUTCOME CATEGORIES   One problem with the use of effect size as an operational definition of study outcome is that studies do not always report an effect size or the statistical information required to compute one. This kind of nonreporting is especially likely when the independent variable did not have a statistically significant effect. When exact effect sizes are not available, Jackson (1980) suggests the use of multiple outcome categories as a secondary tactic. A study would be put into one of five categories depending on the statistical significance of its outcome: (1) the results were statistically significant and supported the hypothesis, (2) the results were not statistically significant but did support the hypothesis, (3) the independent variable had no effect, (4) the results were not statistically significant and contradicted the hypothesis, or (5) the results were statistically significant and contradicted the hypothesis. Once all studies have been categorized, you can examine the distribution of outcomes to draw conclusions about the effect of the independent variable.

TWO OUTCOME CATEGORIES   Unfortunately, not all studies provide sufficient information to allow the reviewer to use five outcome categories. Sometimes the best the reviewer can do is categorize studies as either supporting or not supporting the hypothesis based on the statistical significance of the results and draw conclusions about the effect of the independent variable by counting the "votes" for and against the hypothesis. This vote-counting approach to literature reviewing has a serious drawback: It is highly susceptible to Type II errors—incorrectly accepting the null hypothesis (Hedges & Olkin, 1985). Statistical significance is strongly affected by sample size. Consequently, two studies could find identical effect sizes for an independent variable, but the study using a large sample could have a statistically significant result while the study with a small sample could have a statistically nonsignificant result. For example, an r of .25 would be statistically significant with a sample size of 100 but not with a sample size of 50. Although the outcomes are identical in terms of effect size, the first study would be classified as supporting the hypothesis and the second as not supporting it. J. S. Rossi (1990) describes an example of this problem. He reported the results of two literature reviews of the same set of studies, one using the vote-counting method to operationally define study outcome and one using effect sizes. The vote-counting review concluded that the research was inconsistent, sometimes finding an effect for the independent variable and sometimes not finding an effect; however, the effect size analysis concluded that the independent variable did have an effect, albeit a small one equivalent to a correlation of about .18. Furthermore, Rossi noted that

> the average power of [the studies reviewed] was .375, suggesting that 37.5 percent of [the] studies should have found statistically significant results, in good agreement with the observed rate of significance of 41.7 percent. . . . This analysis suggested that the sample sizes of [the] studies were inadequate to ensure detection of the effect in most studies but were sufficient to guarantee some statistically significant results. (p. 652)

The five-category approach described earlier is also susceptible to Type II errors, but it is less susceptible than the vote-counting method because it uses more categories.

In summary, note that the use of effect sizes is perhaps the ideal approach to literature reviewing. It precisely estimates the degree of effect of the independent variable and avoids the problem of Type II errors. However, not all quantitative studies provide the statistical information required to compute effect sizes, and qualitative research is not intended to provide precise estimates of effect size. In these cases, the researcher must take a categorical approach to operationally defining study outcome.

Classifying Studies

As noted, literature reviewing has two goals: identifying the overall effect of an independent variable and identifying the factors that moderate its effect. To achieve the second goal, you must first identify possible moderator variables, such as participant population and research setting, and then classify each study on each variable. For example, one study might use a college student sample in a laboratory setting and another might use a non–college-student sample in a field setting. Because a study might not clearly fall into only one category, classifying studies can sometimes involve relatively subjective judgments (Wanous, Sullivan, & Malinak, 1989). Consequently, you must be careful to check the reliability of the classifications, just as you would check the reliability of behavioral observations or the reliability of the classifications made in a content analysis. Once the studies have been classified, you can compare the typical outcome in one category with the typical outcome in another. For example, an independent variable might have an effect in laboratory settings but not in natural settings.

However, you must also be alert for confounds among moderator variables, such as the confound between participant population and research setting in the example just given. These comparisons of outcomes between categories of studies can identify limits on the generalizability of an effect.

Analyzing Patterns of Flaws

In addition to establishing the degree of validity of each study in a literature review as discussed earlier, it is important to look for patterns of design flaws within the set of studies being reviewed. A set of studies might all point to the same conclusion, but if the studies have one or more validity threats in common, the consistency in their results could come from the shared flaw rather than from the effect of the independent variable (Salipante, Notz, & Bigelow, 1982). Salipante et al. recommend conducting a **design flaw analysis** by creating a matrix, such as shown in Table 16-1, in which the rows represent the studies being reviewed and the columns represent potential validity threats. The columns in Table 16-1, for example, represent some of the internal validity threats identified by T. D. Cook and Campbell (1979) that Chapter 6 discussed; the matrix could, of course, be expanded to include other threats to internal validity, threats to ecological, construct, and theoretical validity, and possible confounds. In Table 16-1 an "x" indicates that the threat did not arise because the research design precluded it; for example, pretest sensitization is not a threat if the study did not use a pretest. A "√" indicates that the study included a specific control for or an assessment of the effects of

TABLE 16-1 Sample Matrix for Assessing Validity Threats

			THREATS TO INTERNAL VALIDITY			
Study	History	Maturation	Testing	Statistical Regression	Selection	Mortality
A			x		√	
B	√	√	x	x		
C	√	√	√			
D	√		√	√	√	
E			x		√	
F					√	
G					√	
H			x	√	√	
I	√		x	x		
J	√		x	x		
K	√		x	x		

x = design precludes threat
√ = study included control for or assessment of threat

Note: Adapted from Salipante et al., 1982, p. 344.

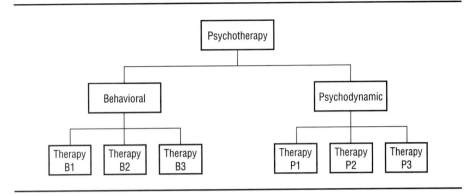

FIGURE 16-1 Defining a Concept at Different Levels of Abstraction
In this example, the concept of "psychotherapy" can be defined very generally, encompassing all types of therapy, at an intermediate level, as broad categories of therapies such as behavioral and psychodynamic, or very narrowly as specific therapies within categories.

the threat. A large number of blanks in a column therefore indicates that the entire set of studies suffered from a common flaw; consequently, conclusions drawn about the effects of the independent variable must be tempered by consideration of the flaw as a possible alternative explanation for the effects found. For example, Table 16-1 shows that the research reviewed (a set of quasi-experiments) generally did not control for the effects of maturation and mortality. As noted at the beginning of this chapter, literature reviews are important because they let us draw conclusions from a set of studies each of which has strengths that compensate for the weaknesses of the others. The design flaw matrix lets you be sure that all weaknesses are compensated, that none affect all or most of the studies.

Level of Analysis

An important decision that literature reviewers must make is determining the appropriate conceptual level of analysis at which to define the independent and dependent variables. Let's say you want to conduct a literature review on the effectiveness of psychotherapy. As shown in Figure 16-1, the hypothetical construct of psychotherapy could be operationally defined at different levels of abstraction. For example, you could simply define psychotherapy as a general concept and not investigate whether different types of therapy, such as behavioral and psychodynamic therapy, have different effects. Or you could decide to compare the relative effectiveness of behavioral and psychodynamic therapy, but not investigate the relative effectiveness of specific therapeutic techniques within these general categories. Or, of course, you could conduct a very fine-grained analysis in which you compared the effectiveness of specific techniques within each of the categories. Similarly, dependent variables can be defined at various levels of abstraction.

The inappropriate combining of effect sizes or other definitions of outcome across different independent variables, dependent variables, and operational definitions of the variables is sometimes referred to as the problem of "mixing apples and oranges" (T. D. Cook & Leviton, 1980). This criticism was directed initially at a review of psychotherapy outcome studies (M. L. Smith & Glass, 1977) that combined effect sizes across different types of therapy (for example, mixing the apples of behavior therapy with the oranges of psychodynamic therapy) after initial analyses indicated no difference in outcome by type of therapy. Glass (1978) defended this approach by noting that both behavior therapy and psychodynamic therapy are subcategories of the general concept of psychotherapy and that this higher order concept was the independent variable of interest in the review; in short, it is permissible to mix apples and oranges if you're interested in the effects of fruit. Such higher order combination of effect sizes is generally considered appropriate as long as two cautions are borne in mind: that such "mixed" independent variables can at times be somewhat artificial or remote from real applications (Bangert-Downs, 1986) and that effect sizes should be examined within types of independent variable to determine if effect sizes differ as a function of the type of independent variable or if moderators affect different independent variables differently (Shadish & Sweeney, 1991). Recall Shadish and Sweeney's finding that research setting interacted with type of psychotherapy to affect recovery rates.

It is more difficult to justify mixing across dependent variables, as M. L. Smith and Glass (1977) also did, on the principle that in psychotherapy outcome was outcome regardless of whether the outcome was defined in terms of clinicians' judgments, clients' self-reports, or independent assessments of behavior. This tactic is risky because any one independent variable can have greatly divergent impacts on different types of dependent variables. As Bangert-Downs (1986) notes,

> Treatments may influence many phenomena but averaging measures of all these phenomena only confuses our picture of the treatment. A drug may cure cancer but make colds worse. Averaging these effects would obscure important information about the drug and produce a single effect size that is difficult to interpret. (p. 397)

Averaging outcomes across different operational definitions of a single independent or dependent variable is less controversial: If the operational definitions are valid indicators of the construct, the studies being reviewed should get the same pattern of results regardless of the operational definition used. It is extremely useful, however, to check this assumption of equivalence of operational definitions by treating operational definition as a moderator variable in the literature review. If no difference in outcome is found as a function of operational definition, the outcomes of the different operational definitions can be combined for further analysis; if differences are found, you must assess the implications of those differences for the validity of the research being reviewed. If, for example, there is evidence that one operational definition is more valid than another, then research using the more valid definition should be given more weight when drawing conclusions.

Choosing a Technique

There are two techniques for synthesizing the results of studies once outcome has been operationally defined and the studies have been classified on the moderator variables.

The traditional approach has been the **narrative literature review,** in which the reviewer considers the outcomes of the studies and the relationships of the moderator variables to the outcomes, and provides a narrative description of the overall effect of the independent variable and of the variables that appear to moderate that effect. Commonly, these conclusions are supported by "vote counts" of studies supporting and not supporting the hypothesis, both overall and within conditions of moderator variables. The last 25 years have seen the emergence of a literature review technique called **meta-analysis.** Meta-analysis reviews the literature on a hypothesis by computing mean effect sizes for an independent variable, both overall and within conditions of moderator variables. You can also compute the statistical significance of a mean effect size and of the difference between the mean effect sizes in different conditions of a moderator variable. Meta-analysis therefore takes a more statistical or quantitative approach to literature reviewing, whereas the narrative literature review takes a more qualitative approach.

The development of meta-analysis has led to a fair degree of controversy and conflict between advocates of the narrative literature review, who see meta-analysis as being an overly mechanistic and uncreative approach to literature reviewing, and the advocates of meta-analysis, who see the narrative literature review as too subjective and imprecise (J. Greenberg & Folger, 1988). However, a comparison of the techniques shows that they tend to be complementary — the strengths of one compensating for the shortcomings of the other — rather than competing. Let's consider some of the points of comparison between narrative literature reviews and meta-analyses.

TYPES OF STUDIES THAT CAN BE REVIEWED   The narrative literature review can consider the results of both qualitative and quantitative studies in coming to its conclusions. Meta-analysis, as a quantitative technique, can only consider the results of studies that provide quantitative results. Consequently, meta-analysis must ignore entire bodies of research in fields such as clinical, counseling, and industrial-organizational psychology that make extensive use of case studies and single-case experiments. The exclusion of such studies from a literature review can severely limit the conclusions that you can draw, especially if qualitative and quantitative studies come to different conclusions about the effect of an independent variable. Such conflicts are not unlikely given the differences in philosophy, data collection, and data analysis evidenced in the two approaches to research (Guzzo et al., 1987). Note, however, that some researchers are looking for ways to include the results of single-case research in meta-analyses (Bullock & Tubbs, 1987; Swanson & Sachse-Lee, 2000).

Meta-analysis faces a similar problem of data exclusion when quantitative studies do not provide the information necessary to compute an effect size. This situation is especially likely to occur when the effect of the independent variable is not statistically significant; researchers often simply note that the difference between conditions was not significant and move on to report the (presumably more important) statistically significant effects. The number of studies that must be excluded from a meta-analysis can sometimes be substantial; to give but two examples, Burger (1981) could compute effect sizes for only 7 of 22 studies (32%) and Guzzo, Jette, and Katzell (1985) for only 98 of 207 studies (47%). The exclusion of such no-difference studies can have substantial effects on the conclusions drawn from a meta-analysis. For example, Marks and Miller (1987) described a meta-analysis that concluded that there was no support for one theoretical explanation for the false consensus effect, but they noted that several studies supporting that explanation were excluded from the meta-analysis because effect sizes could not be computed for them. It is therefore important to use extreme caution when interpreting conclusions from meta-analyses that had to exclude a substantial number of studies due to lack of data.

Meta-analysis's dependence on effect sizes can also limit its ability to evaluate interactions. As Mullen et al. (1991) point out, it can be difficult to find the data required to test theory-based interactions. If the interaction was tested as part of the original research, then the research report must provide the data necessary to compute the a priori contrast for the interaction predicted by theory. Such data are less likely to be available than are main effects data, especially since only a subset of studies testing the theory is likely to include any one moderator variable. If the interaction was not tested as part of the original research, you would have to find studies that were characterized by different conditions of the moderator variable and compare the mean effect sizes in the two groups of studies, just as you would test for the effects of a methodological moderator. However, it is often impossible to determine if a study was conducted in a way that represents one or another condition of the moderator variable. Lacking that data needed to evaluate interactions, all you can do is look at main effects; this problem would also apply to narrative literature reviews.

Meta-analysis has also given little attention to the role of mediating variables — those that come between an independent and dependent variable in a causal chain — from either a theoretical or methodological perspective (Shadish, 1996). As with moderating variables, the problem is often that there is not a sufficient number of studies that include all the important potential mediators to allow a good test of their effects. However, techniques do exist for testing mediational hypotheses using meta-analysis and should be applied to appropriate research questions (Shadish, 1996).

OBJECTIVITY VERSUS SUBJECTIVITY   Advocates of meta-analysis generally view it as a more objective means of drawing conclusions about the effects of an independent variable compared to the narrative literature review (for example, see Green & Hall, 1984). This view is based on meta-analysis's using statistical tests to determine the overall effect of an independent variable and the effects of any potential moderator variables. The conclusions of narrative reviews, however, are not based on a predefined criterion of whether or not effect occurs, such as the probability values used in statistical analyses but, rather, on the subjective judgment of the literature reviewer. This judgment can be affected by the theoretical and other biases of the reviewer; decisions based on statistics are free of such biases.

However, while it is true that the mathematical aspects of meta-analysis are relatively free of bias, the meta-analyst, like the narrative literature reviewer, must make a number of subjective decisions before getting to the data analysis stage of the review. Wanous, Sullivan, and Malinak (1989) list 11 decisions that must be made in a meta-analysis, 8 of which are subjective judgments that also must be made by narrative literature reviewers. Some of these decisions are listed in Box 16-1. Different decisions made at such choice points can easily lead to contradictions between the conclusions drawn from a meta-analysis and narrative literature review of a hypothesis (T. D. Cook & Leviton, 1980), to contradictions between the conclusions drawn by two meta-analyses

BOX 16-1   Some Judgment Calls in Literature Reviewing

Defining the scope of the review, such as in terms of which independent and dependent variables to include.

Establishing criteria for including studies in the review, such as using only published studies.

Defining the scope of the search for studies, such as using only computerized databases.

Deciding which moderator variables to consider.

Categorizing the studies on each moderator variable, such as quality of the research.

Source: Adapted from Wanous et al., 1989, Table 1.

(Wanous et al., 1989), and, of course, to contradictions between the conclusions of two narrative literature reviews (T. D. Cook & Leviton, 1980). Also bear in mind that, as noted in Chapter 13, the interpretation of the results of research—what it means in theoretical and practical terms—is always a subjective judgment open to the influence of the personal and theoretical biases of whoever is making the interpretation. It would appear, then, that meta-analysis has only a narrow advantage in objectivity over the narrative literature review, limited to conclusions about the statistical significance of the effects of the independent and moderator variables.

PRECISION OF RESULTS   The advocates of meta-analysis also believe that it provides more precise information about the magnitude of the effect of an independent variable—expressed as a mean effect size—than does the narrative literature review, which generally provides only a broad yes-or-no conclusion. In addition, the use of effect sizes in meta-analysis reduces the likelihood of making a Type II error: deciding that the independent variable had no effect when there was insufficient statistical power to detect an effect. The vote-counting approach taken by most narrative literature reviews, in contrast, must depend entirely on the statistical power of the studies being reviewed to avoid Type II errors.

However, a number of factors limit the precision with which meta-analysis can estimate the size of the effect of an independent variable. First, as already noted, publication biases might inflate the Type I error rate present in the studies reviewed. Although this is also a problem for a vote-counting approach, it may be a greater problem for meta-analysis because it will lead to an inflated estimate of the mean effect size. To the extent that the effect size is used as an indicator of the importance of the effect, its importance will be overestimated, perhaps leading to faulty policy decisions (Bangert-Downs, 1986). Second, the mean effect size can be very sensitive to outliers—values that are unusually large or unusually small—especially when only a few studies are included in a meta-analysis. Light and Pillemer (1984) give the example of a meta-analysis (Burger, 1981) that found a mean d of .63 based on the results of seven studies. However, one study had an unusually large d of 4.01; with this value dropped, the mean d became .33, which might be a better estimate of the true effect size. Finally, as also noted, it might not be possible to compute effect sizes for all studies. Consequently, these studies cannot be included in the meta-analysis, and their exclusion reduces the precision with which the mean effect size found in the meta-analysis estimates the true effect of the independent variable.

The degree of precision gained by meta-analysis over the narrative literature review comes at the cost of requiring effect sizes from a relatively large number of studies (Durlak & Lipsey, 1991). As with any variable, the precision with which a mean effect size estimates the population effect size depends on the number of observations. Although meta-analysis cumulates results over a large number of research participants and thereby gains statistical power, the studies are also likely to vary widely in their operational definitions, participant populations, settings, and other methodological characteristics, which will lead to variance in effect sizes, thereby reducing the precision of the estimate of the true effect size (T. D. Cook & Leviton, 1980). To determine how much of this variance is attributable to these methodological factors, they must be treated as moderator variables in the analysis. The power of a meta-analysis to detect the effect of a moderator variable depends on both the number of studies and the average sample size of the studies (Hunter & Schmidt, 1990). For example, a power of .80 requires 33 studies in each condition of the moderator variable when the average sample size is 20, 13 studies in each condition when the average sample size is 50, and 7 studies in each condition when the average sample size is 100. A narrative literature review can be conducted on fewer studies because it does not aspire to the higher degree of precision desired by meta-analysts, although this lesser precision should be reflected in more tentative conclusions.

Meta-analysis attains precision by focusing on numbers—effect sizes—which has led some observers (for example, T. D. Cook & Leviton, 1980; Wanous et al., 1989) to caution against mindless number-crunching in meta-analysis: paying so much attention to effect sizes, their mean, and their statistical significance that one loses sight of the meaning of the numbers. It is easy, for example, to become so entranced by the seemingly precise "bottom line" provided by a mean effect size that one overlooks the limitations that moderator variables might put on the accuracy of that statistic or the degree to which the mean might be influenced by publication and other biases (T. D. Cook & Leviton, 1980). Therefore, always pay careful attention not only to the numbers produced by meta-analyses but also to the substantive meaning of those numbers, the limitations of the studies that produced them, and limitations of meta-analysis as a method. For this reason, Wanous et al. (1989) recommend that one do a narrative literature review before conducting a meta-analysis. The narrative review provides an overview of the important issues on the topic and sensitizes the reviewer to the limitations of the studies under review and to factors that require attention as potential moderator variables.

"BEST EVIDENCE" LITERATURE REVIEWING   Both narrative literature reviews and meta-analyses have strengths and weaknesses; the most important of these are summarized in Table 16-2. Both meta-analysis and the narrative literature review can synthesize the results of quantitative studies; they differ in their approaches, however. The meta-analysis computes mean effect sizes whereas the narrative review categorizes study outcomes as supporting or not supporting the hypothesis. However, meta-analysis cannot synthesize the results of qualitative research because there is no way to estimate an effect size, whereas the narrative review can use those results because its conclusions are

TABLE 16-2　Comparison of Narrative Literature Review and Meta-Analysis

	Narrative	Meta-Analysis
Can analyze quantitative studies	Yes	Yes
Can analyze qualitative studies	Yes	No
Precision of conclusions	Low	High[a]
Vulnerability to Type I errors through publication bias	High	High
Vulnerability to Type II errors in studies reviewed	High	Low
Needs statistical information about outcome of studies	No	Yes
Number of studies required	Few	Many
Efficiency for large number of studies	Low	High

[a]Within the limits described in the text.

not based on effect sizes. The conclusions drawn from a meta-analysis are more precise in the sense that meta-analysis can describe the magnitude as well as the existence of the effect of an independent variable. Meta-analyses are also less likely to be affected by Type II errors in the studies reviewed because meta-analyses do not take the statistical significance of individual studies' results into account in drawing conclusions. These advantages also contain an element of weakness because meta-analyses can include only studies that provide the necessary statistical information, whereas the narrative review can consider the results of studies that do not provide that information. In addition, meta-analyses, like all other statistical techniques, can suffer from insufficient statistical power if the number of studies is too small. Again, because of its nonstatistical nature, the narrative review can draw at least tentative conclusions from a smaller number of studies. In practical terms, more studies might be available for a narrative review because it can include qualitative studies and quantitative studies that don't provide the statistical information required for meta-analysis.

In summary, then, meta-analysis gains statistical precision at the cost of inclusiveness and the narrative review gains inclusiveness at the cost of statistical precision. The ideal literature review would therefore use the strengths of each technique to balance the weaknesses of the other by using both qualitative and quantitative elements in a review of the best evidence bearing on a hypothesis, providing what Slavin (1986) calls "best evidence" research synthesis. As Light and Pillemer (1984) observe in the context of program evaluation,

> Both numerical and qualitative information play key roles in a good [literature review]. Quantitative procedures appeal to scientists and policy makers who experience feelings of futility when trying to develop a clear statement of "what is known." But using them does not reduce the value of careful program descriptions, case studies, narrative reports, or expert judgment, even though this information may be difficult to quantify. We cannot afford to ignore any information that may provide solid answers. For most purposes, a review using both numerical and narrative information will outperform its one-sided counterparts. For example, formal statistical analysis is often needed to identify small effects across studies that are not apparent through casual inspection. . . . But qualitative analyses of program

characteristics are necessary to explain the effect and to decide whether it matters for policy. (pp. 9–10)

Best evidence synthesis would first use the narrative approach to provide an overview of the theoretical, applied, and empirical issues that have guided research in the field. This overview would identify potential theoretical and methodological moderator variables that you would have to take into consideration in drawing conclusions about the effect of the independent variable, and it would identify appropriate criteria for deciding which studies to include in the review. For example, you would exclude studies that used operational definitions that were subsequently shown to be invalid. Once you have located studies, you can put them into three categories: those for which an effect size can be computed for a meta-analysis, those that used quantitative procedures but for which an effect size cannot be computed, and those using qualitative procedures. You can then use design flaw analysis to identify patterns of flaws (if any) across studies. You can use this information to categorize studies to see if outcomes vary as a function of design flaws and to determine the limits of the conclusions that can be drawn from the studies. The reviewer would then synthesize the results for each category of studies, using quantitative or qualitative methods as appropriate. You can subject quantitative studies that report no effect for the independent variable, and for which no effect size can be computed, to an analysis of their statistical power, to see if that might be a problem. Next, compare the results of the syntheses across categories of studies to see if they are consistent. If they are not, you need to see if there was any apparent reason for the inconsistencies. Finally, you interpret the results of the literature review in terms of the theoretical, applied, and empirical implications of its results.

DATA INTERPRETATION

Because the literature review is a form of research, the final stage of the literature review is the same as that of all research—drawing conclusions from the data and laying out the implications of those conclusions for theory, research, and application. Chapter 13 discussed that process, so the next section simply considers a few limitations on interpreting the results of literature reviews.

The Effects of Judgment Calls

First, literature reviewing is a process that involves a fairly large number of judgment calls, decisions that one person may make in one way and another person may make in another (Wanous et al., 1989). For example, if two people were to review the research on the same hypothesis, they might make different decisions about which studies to include in their reviews. One person might choose to include only published studies, whereas the other might also include any unpublished research that could be found. One consequence of this judgmental factor in literature reviewing is that the different decisions made by different reviewers may lead to different results in the literature reviews and different conclusions being drawn about the hypothesis being tested. Wanous et al. (1989), for example, describe four pairs of literature reviews that came to opposite conclusions and show how different decisions at various judgment points could have led to those conflicting conclusions.

Because differences in judgment calls can produce such large differences in conclusions, it is extremely important for literature reviewers to clearly specify the decisions they make at each point in the review process (Halvorsen, 1994). Literature reviewers should report the operational definitions of variables included in the review. For example, in reviewing the effects of psychotherapy, specify exactly what kinds of treatments were considered to be therapies for the purpose of the review and the kinds of therapies put into each subcategory used, such as behavior or psychodynamic therapies. Similarly, specify the operational definitions of the dependent variables, such as anxiety or depression. Another factor that reviewers should report is the criteria for including studies in the review or excluding them from consideration. These criteria could include study characteristics such as validity level and participant population. Reviewers should also tell readers the methods they used to locate studies, such as computer searches of indexes (in which case the key words used should be reported), bibliographic searching, and source-by-source searching (specifying the sources searched). Finally, the reviewer should report the methods used to analyze the data, including the specific statistical techniques used for a meta-analysis. This information should be detailed enough that another person could exactly replicate the literature review. Such information allows readers to judge the adequacy of the review procedures and the validity of the conclusions that the reviewer draws.

The Correlational Nature of Moderator Variable Analyses

A second point to bear in mind when interpreting the results of a literature review is that any relationships that are found between moderator variables and study outcomes are correlational, not causal (Mullen et al., 1991). That is, a literature review can at best demonstrate only that there is a relationship between a moderator variable and study outcomes, not that the moderator variable caused the difference in outcomes. For example, if a literature review found that a hypothesis tended to be supported in laboratory settings but not in natural settings, the only way to determine if type of setting caused the difference in outcomes would be to conduct an experiment with type of setting as an independent variable. In addition, as already noted, conditions of a moderator variable might be confounded with other characteristics of the studies. For example, the research participants in the laboratory settings might have been college students and those in natural settings, older adults. The only way to determine which variable actually moderated the effect sizes would be through an appropriately designed experiment.

Publication Biases

Finally, it is important to temper the conclusions drawn from literature reviews with consideration of the possible effects of publication biases. As noted earlier, publication

BOX 16-2   Evaluating Literature Reviews

Question Formulation

1. What is the purpose of the literature review?

   a. To summarize theories or methods

   b. To integrate theories and develop new knowledge

   c. To evaluate the validity of a theory

   d. To summarize evidence on a hypothesis

2. Is the hypothesis clearly stated so that the results of studies can be unambiguously classified as supporting or not supporting it?

3. Are all relevant theories thoroughly analyzed to identify variables that moderate study outcome and to identify the conditions required for an adequate test of the hypothesis?

4. Is all relevant research thoroughly analyzed to identify methodological variables (such as operational definitions, research settings, research strategies, participant populations) that might moderate study outcome?

Data Collection

1. Is the scope of the search for studies clearly stated? That is, are there clear rules regarding the characteristics of studies that are considered for inclusion in the review?

2. Are all relevant sources of studies checked? These include

   a. Indexes

   b. Previous literature reviews of the hypothesis

   c. Reference lists and bibliographies from the studies already located

   d. A manual search of relevant journals

3. Is the proper search term used with indexes? Are all variants on the terms (such as both singular and plural) and synonyms checked?

Data Evaluation

1. Are the criteria used to include and exclude studies clearly stated? Are these criteria appropriate? What biases might these criteria bring to the conclusions drawn from the review?

2. How many studies are excluded from the review relative to the total number located? Is the remaining sample large enough to allow valid conclusions to be drawn?

---

bias in favor of statistically significant outcomes may lead the literature reviewer to overestimate the impact of an independent variable. Conversely, insufficient statistical power in the studies reviewed might lead to an underestimation of the independent variable impact. Finally, you must be aware of any design flaws that are common to the studies reviewed and to interpret the results of the literature review with these flaws in mind. A set of studies might point to a common conclusion, but a common flaw would cast doubt on that conclusion.

EVALUATING LITERATURE REVIEWS

The preceding description of the process of conducting a literature review implies a set of criteria that you can use to evaluate the quality of a literature review. Box 16-2 summarizes these criteria in the form of a set of questions you can ask as you read a literature review.

BOX 16-2   *(continued)*

Data Analysis

1. What literature review technique is used, narrative, meta-analysis, or best evidence? Is it appropriate to the purpose of the review and the nature of the research being reviewed, such as the number of quantitative and qualitative studies that have been conducted?

2. What is the mean (meta-analysis) or modal (narrative review) outcome of the studies?

3. How much variance is there in the study outcomes? Are there any outliers that increased the variance or skewed the mean?

4. Are moderator variables used to try to explain the variance in study outcomes?

5. Are clear rules established for classifying studies according to the moderator variables? Are these rules applied reliably?

6. Are there enough studies within each category of the moderator variables to permit reliable conclusions to be drawn?

7. Have the studies been analyzed to determine if there are any common design flaws that might call into question the validity of their overall results?

8. Is a list of studies used in the review included in the report? Does the list include how each study was classified on each moderator variable? In a meta-analysis, is the effect size for each study included?

Interpretation

1. Are the interpretations appropriate given the scope of the review, the types of studies included in the review (such as restriction to one participant population), and the limitations of the review technique? For example, do the conclusions drawn from a narrative review reflect an awareness of the possibility of Type II errors? Does a meta-analysis acknowledge the possibility of inflated mean effect sizes due to publication biases?

2. Are clear implications drawn for theory, research, and application?

3. Are all possible interpretations of the findings considered? For example, does a review of correlational research consider both directions of causality and the possibility of third-variable influences? Are all theoretical perspectives considered?

4. Is the impact of any common design flaws given full consideration?

5. Have possible confounds among moderator variables, such as having only college students participate in laboratory studies and participants who were not in college in field studies, been considered in interpreting the impact of moderator variables?

UNDERSTANDING META-ANALYSIS

As discussed earlier, meta-analysis statistically combines the results of a set of studies of the same hypothesis to come to an overall conclusion about the effects of the independent variable and to identify variables that might moderate its effects. Meta-analysis has been increasingly used as a literature-reviewing tool over the past 25 years, especially in applied areas of behavioral science, which account for about 78% of meta-analyses (H. M. Cooper & Lemke, 1991). Although this rise in the use of meta-analysis makes it look like a new technique, the basic principles have been around since the 1930s (Olkin, 1990); however, only relatively recently have statisticians given much attention to its formal development. Because of the increasing importance of meta-analysis as a means of reviewing research literature, it is important to clearly understand the technique's strengths and weaknesses so that you can correctly interpret the results of published meta-analyses. Therefore, this section examines a sample meta-analysis. In addition, Durlak and Lipsey (1991) provide a "practitioner's guide" to meta-analysis that discusses the important issues in the field in more detail than space allows here.

The statistical procedures for conducting a meta-analysis are fairly complex, so I won't discuss them. Hedges and Becker (1986) provide a nice, readable overview of the statistical procedures, H. M. Cooper (1998) and Lipsey and Wilson (2001) present more detailed "how to" descriptions, H. M. Cooper and Hedges (1994) and Hunter and Schmidt (1990) give somewhat more technical presentations, and, for those interested, Hedges and Olkin (1985) present the statistical theory underlying meta-analysis. In addition, B. T. Johnson (1993) and Mullen (1993) have written computer programs to analyze data for meta-analyses.

Let's examine the process of conducting a meta-analysis by looking at one conducted by B. T. Johnson and Eagly (1989). Their meta-analysis is not especially better or worse than others that could have been chosen, but it does illustrate the process of meta-analysis well. It also illustrates the use of multiple moderator variables in analyzing effect sizes and the use of theory-based moderator variables in understanding the results of a body of research. This exploration of Johnson and Eagly's work will be organized in terms of the five stages of literature reviewing.

Defining the Research Question

Johnson and Eagly (1989) drew their research question from the field of attitude change and persuasion. The question was one that has been the subject of over 50 years of theory and research: When people face a persuasive message designed to change their attitudes on an issue, does the degree to which they are personally involved in the issue affect the degree to which their attitudes change? In other words, is it easier or harder to persuade people who have a strong personal involvement in the issue under discussion to change their minds?

Johnson and Eagly (1989) began their review of the research on this question by noting that there are three theoretical approaches to answering this question, each of which has used a different operational definition of "issue involvement" in its research. One theoretical perspective focuses on what Johnson and Eagly called "value-relevant involvement," which defines involvement as the degree to which the message recipient personally identifies with the issue under discussion; the issue is closely related to the recipient's personal values and self-definition. In "outcome-relevant involvement," the issue has an important, direct impact on the recipient's life but is not necessarily linked to his or her personal value system. For example, if the message recipients are college students, involvement might be manipulated by a message dealing with raising tuition at their college (high involvement) versus raising tuition at a distant college (low involvement). With "impression-relevant involvement," the message recipient wants to make a favorable impression on the person sending the persuasive message; that is, the recipient wants to "look good" to the persuader.

Johnson and Eagly (1989) also noted that the quality of the message—whether it used strong, relevant, and logical arguments to support its position versus weak, irrelevant, and illogical arguments—could moderate the relationship between issue involvement and persuasion, and that the three theories made different predictions about the form the interaction would take. Value-relevance theory holds that there should be no interaction between message strength and involvement: More highly involved people should be less easy to persuade regardless of the form the message takes. Impression-relevance theory also makes a simple prediction: Neither involvement nor argument strength should affect persuasion. Because the message recipients simply want to look good to the persuader, they will tell the persuader what they think he or she wants to hear, but their true attitudes are not affected. Outcome-relevance theory makes a complex prediction: When arguments are strong, highly involved people will be more persuaded than less involved people because they will give more thought to the arguments; when arguments are weak, highly involved people will be less persuaded than less involved people because they will be offended by the poor arguments the persuader made. (This is an oversimplification of outcome-relevance theory, but a full explanation would take up too much space; see Johnson and Eagly, 1989, pp. 292–293, for more detail.)

Based on their analysis of these theories, Johnson and Eagly (1989) decided to conduct a meta-analysis of the research on the relationship between issue involvement and persuasion to see which theory was best supported. Because of the theoretical importance of the operational definition of issue involvement and argument strength, they used these variables as moderators in their analysis. Note that Johnson and Eagly used a narrative literature review to identify the important theoretical issues relevant to their topic. As shown below, the results of the narrative review defined the structure of their meta-analysis.

Data Collection

Johnson and Eagly (1989) began their search for studies relevant to their research question by defining the type of study they wanted: "To examine the effects of the three types of involvement, we endeavored to locate all studies that had manipulated or assessed message recipients' involvement and related this independent variable to the persuasion induced by a communication" (p. 294). They used four strategies to locate studies. First, they conducted computer searches of six indexes using the search term *involvement*. They also checked the reference lists and bibliographies of relevant literature review articles, books, and book chapters. In addition, they looked through the tables of contents of journals that published the largest number of involvement studies. Finally, they checked the reference lists and bibliographies of the studies they had located by other means. Although it would be interesting and useful to know the total number of studies they located, Johnson and Eagly do not report that information.

Data Evaluation

Johnson and Eagly (1989) established four criteria for including studies in their review:

> (a) subjects were adults or adolescents not sampled from abnormal populations; (b) subjects received a persuasive message; (c) subjects indicated their [degree of] acceptance of the position advocated in the message; and (d) involvement . . . was used in the analysis of persuasive effects. (p. 295)

Johnson and Eagly also established 13 criteria for excluding studies from the review, starting with "studies with obviously confounded manipulations" (p. 294) and including studies with any of 10 other methodological inadequacies. Johnson and Eagly clearly defined both "obviously confounded" and the other methodological faults. They also excluded studies that used extremely simple persuasive messages on theoretical grounds: "The theories underlying . . . involvement research . . . have been tailored to account for the persuasion that occurs when people are exposed to relatively complex messages" (p. 294). Finally, they excluded studies for which they could not compute an effect size. After these exclusion criteria were applied, Johnson and Eagly had a sample of 38 studies with which to conduct their analysis.

Data Analysis

Because meta-analysis is a set of techniques rather than a single method of combining results across studies (see Bangert-Downs, 1986, for a comparison of methods), Johnson and Eagly (1989) had to select a technique. They chose to define effect size in terms of d (they could, of course, have chosen r) and computed the mean effect size for the entire set of studies and within the conditions of the moderating variables. (In the following discussion, I include the equivalent r value for each d since many people find r easier to understand.) In addition, they weighted the d from each study by the study's sample size, thereby giving more importance to larger samples in computing the mean value for d. This is a standard procedure in meta-analysis because a study using a large sample provides a more accurate estimation of the true effect size than does one using a small sample.

Johnson and Eagly (1989) found a mean d for all 38 studies of $-.21$ ($r = -.10$), indicating that higher involvement in the issue led to less persuasion. These results are consistent with value-relevance theory. When the studies were categorized on the basis of operational definition of involvement, Johnson and Eagly found that the mean d was $-.48$ ($r = -.23$) for value-relevance studies, $.02$ ($r = .01$) for outcome-relevance studies, and $-.17$ ($r = -.08$) for impression-relevance studies. These results indicate that higher involvement led to less persuasion for value- and impression-relevant involvement (but less so for impression relevance) and that involvement had no relationship to persuasion when involvement was defined in terms of outcome. These results are consistent with the prediction made by value-relevance theory, but not with predictions made by outcome- and impression-relevance theories. Note an important point illustrated by this set of results: *A main effect for a moderator variable in meta-analysis is equivalent to an interaction between the moderator variable and the independent variable being examined in the meta-analysis.* That is, the relationship between the independent variable (issue involvement, in the example given) and the dependent variable (persuasion) changes depending on the condition of the moderator variable (involvement type). The meta-analysis with involvement type as a moderator variable was therefore equivalent to a 2 (high versus low involvement) $\times$ 3 (involvement type) factorial design in an experiment.

Because both impression-relevance and outcome-relevance theories make specific predictions about argument strength, the best test of the theories comes only when both

TABLE 16-3   Mean *d* Values and Equivalent *r* Values for Effect of Involvement on Persuasion Moderated by Involvement Type and Argument Strength

	TYPE OF INVOLVEMENT		
	Value-Relevant	*Outcome-Relevant*	*Impression-Relevant*
Strong arguments	$-.28\ (-.14)^*$	$.31\quad(.15)^*$	$-.17\ (-.08)$
Weak arguments	$-.58\ (-.28)^*$	$-.26\ (-.13)^*$	$-.17\ (-.08)$

Note: *r* is in parentheses.
$^*p < .05$.

moderators are included in the analysis. These results are shown in Table 16-3. For value-relevant involvement, higher involvement resulted in less persuasion regardless of argument strength, although this effect was stronger for weak arguments. For outcome-relevant involvement, higher involvement resulted in more persuasion in response to strong arguments and less persuasion in response to weak arguments. For impression-relevant involvement, involvement was not related to persuasion regardless of argument strength. These results are all consistent with the predictions made by the respective theories.

Interpretation

Johnson and Eagly (1989) made a number of theoretical and methodological interpretations of these results and of other results not discussed here. One major conclusion to be drawn from the portion of their meta-analysis examined here is that there are three different types of issue involvement, each of which has different effects on persuasion when considered in conjunction with argument strength. For our purposes, however, let's consider two lessons that their findings have for the interpretation of meta-analyses and literature reviews in general. First, these results illustrate the importance of conducting a thorough theoretical analysis of the hypothesis to be reviewed in order to identify moderator variables. Notice that the conclusions you would draw from the meta-analysis change as you move from an analysis without any moderators, to one that includes one moderator, to the final analysis with both moderators. A less thorough theoretical analysis might have overlooked a moderator variable and so led to incorrect conclusions.

The second lesson illustrated by Johnson and Eagly's (1989) findings is the importance of methodological moderators, in this case different operational definitions of the independent variable (which also happen to have theoretical relevance in this instance). When different operational definitions are ignored and if argument strength is included as a moderator variable (a situation not included in Johnson and Eagly's analysis but one that can be examined with the information Johnson and Eagly provide), none of the theories would have been supported very well and there would appear to be a mass of contradictions among the results of the studies. Including the operational definition of involvement as a moderator variable resolves many of those contradictions. Note that this is an example of the apples-and-oranges problem discussed earlier: Value relevance, impression relevance, and outcome relevance are all forms of issue involvement and therefore could be considered, in Glass's (1978) terms, "fruit." However, in this case the type of fruit makes a big difference in terms of the conclusions one draws from the analysis.

SUMMARY

Literature reviews can be conducted to fulfill a number of purposes: summarizing new theories, findings, research methods, and data analysis techniques for a topic; identifying linkages between theories and developing new theories from existing knowledge; evaluating the validity of theories; and summarizing the research evidence on a hypothesis or set of hypotheses. The last purpose has several goals: determining how well the hypothesis (or hypotheses) is supported, determining the factors that lead to differences in outcomes across studies, and identifying the implications of the review for theory, research, and application. The results of the review can be used to decide how theories should be modified, to identify new topics for research, and to inform policy decisions.

Viewed as a form of research, the literature review has five steps. The first step is defining the research question. Literature reviews can address three questions: What is the average effect of an independent variable? Under what conditions does the independent variable have its effects (external validity)? Does an independent variable have an effect under a specified set of conditions (ecological validity)? The scope of the question must also be carefully defined. A question that is too narrow might not produce a generalizable answer, but one that is too broad might be impossible to complete — there will be too much information to deal with. Finally, literature reviews can either test specific hypotheses or be exploratory, attempting to identify the independent variables that affect a given dependent variable.

The second step in a literature review is data collection. Chapter 4 described this process; also note that to find all the research that has been conducted on a topic, literature reviewers must go beyond the use of the standard indexes to other techniques such as source-by-source searching.

The third step is data evaluation, deciding which studies to use in the literature review. Five options exist. The first is to include all studies in the literature review; however, it might be impossible to locate all relevant studies, and this procedure could give equal weight to both good and poor research in reaching conclusions. The second option is to include only published studies. This approach makes it easy to locate studies, but the studies used in the review will reflect any publication biases that might exist. A third option is to include only valid studies, but this approach raises the question of how to grade studies on validity. Often literature reviewers categorize studies in terms of level of validity and check to see if study outcomes vary as a function of validity. The fourth option, which can be used when there is an overwhelming number of studies to review, is to stratify the studies on important characteristics and randomly sample studies within strata. Finally, you can ask experts to choose the best or most important studies for inclusion in the review, but the studies reviewed will then reflect any biases the experts hold.

The fourth step in literature reviewing is data analysis, which involves several tasks. The first task is choosing an operational definition of study outcome. Effect size is probably the best definition because it is precise and not affected by the statistical power of the studies reviewed; however, not all studies report effect sizes or the information needed to compute them. When effect sizes are not available, studies can be classified according to the degree to which they support the hypothesis; however, these classification systems are vulnerable to Type II errors when studies have low statistical power. The second task is classifying studies on potential moderator variables to determine if they are related to study outcomes. The third task is analyzing the validity of the studies to determine if there is a common flaw that could challenge the accuracy of the conclusions drawn from the review. The fourth task is determining the proper level of abstraction at which to define the independent and dependent variables. Choosing too high a level can result in combining the results of studies whose independent or dependent variables are too conceptually different to provide meaningful overall results.

The final task is choosing a technique for summarizing the results of the studies and relating variation in outcomes to moderator variables. Narrative literature reviews take a qualitative approach, with the reviewer verbally summarizing the results of the studies and the effects of the moderator variables. Meta-analyses are quantitative reviews based on average effect sizes across all studies and differences in average effect sizes between conditions of moderator variables. Meta-analysis and narrative literature reviews complement one another in that the strengths of one often compensate for the shortcomings of the other. The most useful approach to literature reviewing is to use the techniques in tandem.

The final step in literature reviewing is interpreting the results of the data analysis. Four points should be borne in mind. First, literature reviewing involves a large number of judgments, each of which can influence the conclusions drawn from the review. Second, any relationships found between moderator variables and study outcomes are correlational, not causal. Third, the results of literature reviews can be influenced by publication biases and the statistical power of the studies. Finally, design flaws that are common to a large number of the studies can limit the validity of the conclusions drawn from the review.

In conclusion, Box 16-2 lists some questions you can use to evaluate the quality of literature reviews, both meta-analyses and narrative reviews.

QUESTIONS AND EXERCISES FOR REVIEW

1. Describe the purposes of literature reviews. What are the goals of a literature review designed to summarize the evidence bearing on a hypothesis? In what ways can the results of a literature review be used?
2. Explain the three questions a literature review can answer. How does the question addressed in a literature review affect its scope and the approach taken to answering the question?
3. Guzzo et al. (1987) have stated that policy makers prefer simple, main effects conclusions from literature reviews. What do you see as the advantages and disadvantages of this

approach to research synthesis? Is it proper for scientists to provide apparently simple answers, or should they insist on more complex analyses? Explain your answers.

4. Describe the strategies for deciding what studies to include in a literature review. What are the advantages and disadvantages of these strategies?

5. What is "theoretical validity"? How can the degree of theoretical validity of the studies included in a literature review affect the conclusions drawn?

6. Describe the ways of operationally defining study outcome. What are the advantages and disadvantages of each? What role does statistical power play in this process?

7. Describe the process of design flaw analysis. Why is this process important to the validity of a literature review?

8. What problems are involved in determining the most appropriate level of analysis at which to define the independent and dependent variables in a literature review?

9. Compare and contrast the narrative and meta-analytic approaches to literature reviewing. How are these approaches affected by such issues as the types of studies each can handle and the objectivity and precision of the results each approach produces?

10. What factors affect the interpretation of the results of a literature review? Explain their effects.

11. What is "best evidence" literature reviewing? How can the strengths of meta-analysis and the narrative literature review compensate for the other technique's weakness?

12. In *Psychological Bulletin*, look up a literature review on a topic that interests you. Critique it using the guidelines in Box 16-2. What are its strengths and weaknesses?

17 WRITING RESEARCH REPORTS

THE RESEARCH REPORT
Structure
Content
   Before Writing
   The Introduction
   The Method Section
   The Results Section
   The Discussion Section
   The Title and Abstract
Writing for Nonresearchers
   Establishing Credibility
   Relevance
   Statistics
   Making Recommendations

JOURNAL ARTICLES AND
CONVENTION PRESENTATIONS
The Journal Article
   Choosing a Journal
   Preparing the Manuscript
   Submitting the Manuscript
   Peer Review
   Editorial Response
   Revising the Manuscript
   After Acceptance
   Dealing With Rejection

Convention Presentations
   The Abstract
   Oral Presentation
   Poster Session
Reviewing Manuscripts
   The Reviewer's Task
   Writing the Review

ETHICAL ISSUES IN
PUBLICATION
Authorship Credit
Plagiarism
Multiple Publication

SUMMARY

QUESTIONS AND EXERCISES
FOR REVIEW

The knowledge generated by the research process has value only if it is communicated to people who can put it to use in the form of theory development and practical application. Consequently, scientists throughout history have endeavored to disseminate the results of their research to their colleagues. Today there are three primary media of scientific communication: books, journals, and presentations at professional meetings or conventions. In most of the behavioral sciences, the primary media for communicating the results of research studies are journal articles and convention presentations; except for long case studies, books tend to be reserved for theoretical presentations, literature reviews, and handbooks for application. This chapter discusses the process of preparing research reports for journal publication and for presentation at professional meetings. It begins by discussing the structure and content of the research report, follows by describing the publication and presentation processes, and concludes by discussing ethical issues in publication.

THE RESEARCH REPORT

Research reports exist to tell other people what scientists learn in the course of their research. The report begins by stating the research question and justifying the investigation: What makes it important enough to justify the resources expended on the investigation, to justify the cost of publication, and to justify others' spending their time reading it? The report continues with a description of how the question was investigated so that readers can evaluate the validity of the research and of the knowledge that it produced. Next come the results of the investigation: the data that provide a basis for answering the question. The report concludes with a discussion of the meaning of the data, the answers they provide to the research questions.

This section discusses five aspects of writing a research report: the structure of the report or outline it follows, the content of the report, evaluation criteria for research reports, and considerations in writing reports for nonresearchers. In this chapter, I cannot teach you how to write a research report; writing skill comes only through writing, being critiqued by more experienced writers, rewriting, and then continuing that process until you have a satisfactory manuscript. I can, however, provide some general guidelines to follow. D. J. Bem (1987) and Sternberg (1993) give more detailed guidance, and I strongly recommend that you read them carefully.

Another invaluable resource is the American Psychological Association's *Publication Manual* (APA, 1994). The *Publication Manual* (popularly called the APA style manual) provides both detailed guidance on the format a research report should use and many examples. It also contains excellent advice on writing style, including examples of poor style and suggested improvements. All manuscripts submitted to journals published by the APA must follow the guidelines of the *Publication Manual*, and many other journals also require that manuscripts be submitted in APA format. Also, universities frequently require dissertations and theses in psychology and related fields to use APA format, and many professors require its use for papers submitted for their courses. There-fore, keep a copy of the *Publication Manual* close at hand whenever you write a paper, whether for a class, your degree, or publication.

Although the APA *Publication Manual* is commonly used in the behavioral sci-ences, other professional associations, such as the American Sociological Association, and some journals have stylistic requirements that differ from those of the APA. Stylis-tic requirements are usually listed in a section called "Notice to Contributors" or a sim-ilarly titled section of each issue of a journal. Before writing for a particular journal, be sure to check its requirements.

Structure

Frequently, the hardest part of writing a paper is deciding on its structure: what infor-mation to provide and the order in which to provide it. Fortunately, there is a standard structure or outline for research reports in the behavioral sciences: introduction, method, results, and discussion, with the Method section being subdivided into partic-ipants, materials, and procedures, and all preceded by a title and abstract and followed by a reference list (see Box 17-1). D. J. Bem (1987, p. 175) notes that as a consequence of this outline, "An article is written in the shape of an hourglass. It begins with broad general statements, progressively narrows down to the specifics of your study, and then broadens out again to more general considerations." (See Figure 17-1 and Box 17-2.) If you follow this general-to-specific-to-general progression in your writing, readers will see that your research report flows smoothly from one point to the next and that every-thing comes together into a coherent whole.

Content

The structure of a research report provides its skeleton; its content puts the meat on those bones. This section examines the parts of a research report, the type of informa-tion that goes in each part, and some guidelines for the effective presentation of that information.

BOX 17-1 Outline of a Research Report

Title	Method
Authors	Participants
Abstract	Materials
Introduction	Procedure
	Results
	Discussion
	References

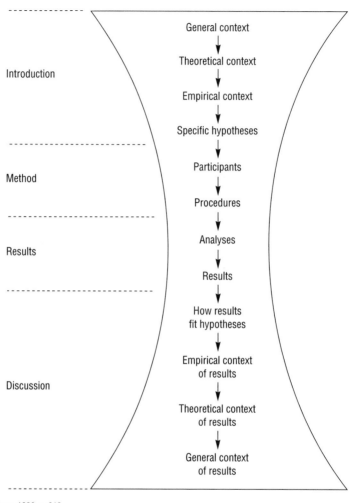

Introduction

General context
↓
Theoretical context
↓
Empirical context
↓
Specific hypotheses
↓

Method

Participants
↓
Procedures
↓

Results

Analyses
↓
Results
↓

Discussion

How results
fit hypotheses
↓
Empirical context
of results
↓
Theoretical context
of results
↓
General context
of results

Note: From Dane, 1990, p. 213.

FIGURE 17-1   The Hourglass Analogy of the Research Report

BEFORE WRITING   Before writing a research report, you have several questions to answer. The first is "Which report should you write?" As D. J. Bem (1987) notes in regard to writing a journal article, "There are two possible articles you can write: (1) the article you planned to write when you designed your study or (2) the article that makes the most sense now that you have seen the results. They are rarely the same, and the correct answer is (2)" (pp. 171–172). In conducting research, two processes frequently occur that make the final research project different from the planned research project. First, researchers may have to modify their original design or procedures because of problems found during pilot studies. A research report could describe all these false starts and cor-

BOX 17-2   Example of the "Hourglass" Analogy of the Research Report

The introduction begins broadly:	"Individuals differ radically from one another in the degree to which they are willing and able to express their emotions."
It becomes more specific:	"Indeed, the popular view is that such emotional expressiveness is a central difference between men and women. . . . But the research evidence is mixed . . ."
And more so:	"There is even some evidence that men may actually . . ."
Until you are ready to introduce your own study in conceptual terms:	"In this study, we recorded the emotional reactions of both men and women to filmed . . ."
The Method and Results sections are the most specific, the "neck" of the hourglass:	"(Method) One hundred male and 100 female undergraduates were shown one of two movies . . ." "(Results) Table 1 shows that men in the father-watching condition cried significantly more . . ."
The Discussion section begins with the implications of your study:	"These results imply that sex differences in emotional expressiveness are moderated by two kinds of variables . . ."
It becomes broader:	"Not since Charles Darwin's first observations has psychology contributed as much new . . ."
And more so:	"If emotions can incarcerate us by hiding our complexity, at least their expression can liberate us by displaying our authenticity."

Source: D. J. Bem, 1987, pp. 175–176.

rections, but doing so would distract readers from the final outcome of the research and perhaps leave them confused about the final form taken by the research. Researchers therefore report only the final form of the research that led to the data being presented in the report.

The second process that can occur is that you discover something unexpected in your data that deserves to be reported. For readers to understand the implications of the discovery, it must be placed in context. Because the finding was unexpected, that context is lacking in your original research plan and must be added to the research report. If the finding is of special importance and the data supporting it are strong, the research report may be written to highlight the discovery rather than the original hypotheses. As Bem (1987) puts it, "Your overriding purpose is to tell the world what you have learned from your study. If your results suggest a compelling framework for their presentation, adopt it and make the most instructive findings your centerpiece" (p. 173).

The second question is "For whom should you write?" Who is your audience? Researchers typically write for other researchers, particularly for those who are experts on the specific topic of the research. Consequently, much scientific writing is opaque to nonexperts because the writer assumes the reader has a detailed understanding of the theoretical and empirical issues involved. However, many nonexperts may also want to read the research report. At some time you have probably been frustrated by trying to read an article that assumes a background you do not yet have. Even scientists in fields closely related to the topic of a report may not be familiar with the theories and methods involved. Bem (1987) therefore encourages writers to explain everything so that the information in a research report is accessible to anyone who wants it:

> Good writing is good teaching. . . . No matter how technical or abstruse your article is in its particulars, intelligent nonpsychologists with no expertise in statistics or experimental design should be able to comprehend the broad outlines of what you did and why. They should understand in general terms what was learned. And above all, they should appreciate why someone — anyone — should give a damn. (p. 174)

The Results section of an article, which deals with statistics, will by its nature be difficult for nonexperts to follow. However, the introduction and the Method and Discussion sections, which lay out the background, procedures, and meaning of the research, should be accessible to a wider audience.

The final preliminary question is "How should you write?" Scientific writing should project an image of an author who "is of good sense, good moral character, and good will" (S. Friedman & Steinberg, 1989, p. 27). There are four components to this image. The first is reason: the logical development of arguments supporting the points you want to make, the use of evidence to support those points, and the avoidance of direct or indirect emotional appeals, such as through value-laden language. The second component is objectivity, acknowledging the shortcomings of your research along with its strong points. The third component is fairness, considering all aspects of an issue and all possible interpretations of your results, not only those that you favor. The final point is caution in asserting claims, not making statements that cannot be supported by your results or other evidence, such as by making wide-ranging but inappropriate generalizations. Most people who read what you write will not know you, so they draw conclusions about your ability as a scientist not only by the quality of your work but also by how you present it. Readers will interpret writing that appears unreasoned, subjective, unfair, or reckless as indicating an unscientific attitude on the part of the writer.

THE INTRODUCTION   The introduction tells the reader what the study is about and why it was conducted. D. J. Bem (1987) divides the introduction into three parts: the opening statement, the literature review, and the conclusion. The opening statement must be a strong, clear statement of the theme of your report that grabs readers' attention and makes them want to continue reading. Bem (1987) suggests four rules for opening statements:

1. Write in English prose, not psychological jargon.
2. Don't plunge unprepared readers into the middle of your problem or theory. Take the time and space necessary to lead them up to the formal or theoretical statement of the problem step by step.
3. Use examples to illustrate theoretical points or to introduce unfamiliar conceptual or technical terms. The more abstract the material, the more important such examples become.
4. Whenever possible, try to open with a statement about people (or animals), not psychologists or their research. (p. 176)

BOX 17-3   Examples of Poor and Good Opening Statements for a Research Report

Poor

Research in the forced-compliance paradigm has focused on the effects of predecisional alternatives and incentive magnitude.

Poor

Festinger's theory of cognitive dissonance has received a great deal of attention during the past 20 years.

Source: Adapted from D. J. Bem, 1987, pp. 176–177.

Good

The individual who holds two beliefs that are inconsistent with one another may feel uncomfortable. For example, the person who knows that he or she enjoys smoking but believes it to be unhealthy may experience discomfort arising from the inconsistency or disharmony between these two thoughts or cognitions. This feeling of discomfort has been called *cognitive dissonance* by social psychologist Leon Festinger (1957), who suggests that individuals will be motivated to remove this dissonance in whatever way they can.

Box 17-3 provides two examples of bad opening statements and one good opening statement on the same topic. Notice that the first poor example uses technical terms, such as "forced-compliance paradigm," "predecisional alternatives," and "incentive magnitude" that might be meaningless to someone who lacks a background in the particular area of theory and research being discussed. In contrast, note how the good opening statement implicitly defines a novel term, "cognitive dissonance," by leading up to it with familiar terms such as "beliefs," "inconsistency," and "discomfort" and by providing an example of the process. The second poor opening is a cliché that focuses on research and researchers, whereas the good opening statement catches the readers' attention by discussing human behavior in the context of everyday life.

The literature review is the heart of the introduction, laying out the theoretical and empirical background for the research, addressing four questions. It is not necessary to answer these questions in the order in which they are listed, but the literature review should address each of them. The first question is "What is the research question being investigated?" Following the hourglass analogy presented in Figure 17-1, you must lead the reader from the general context of the research through its theoretical and empirical background to a specific hypothesis.

The second question is "What is already known about the research question?" The literature review describes the theoretical and empirical background of the research, laying out the bases of the hypotheses. The literature review must show where the hypotheses came from, citing theory and research to support your statements. For example, R. A. Baron (1983) conducted a study to determine the effect of pleasant artificial scents such as perfumes and colognes on the evaluation of job applicants; Figure 17-2 shows a portion of the introduction of his research report. Notice that Baron starts his report with a strong statement about human behavior (1 in Figure 17-2) and follows that statement with a summary of the research on it (2). He then links that research to the topic of his study, citing perfumes and colognes as means of enhancing attractiveness (3). Next comes the specific research question: Are artificial scents actually

"Sweet Smell of Success"? The Impact of Pleasant Artificial Scents on Evaluations of Job Applicants

Robert A. Baron
Purdue University

Each year, manufacturers of clothing, cosmetics, and other grooming aids spend huge sums in an effort to convince consumers that use of their products will yield important benefits. Interestingly, a large body of research concerned with the impact of personal attractiveness suggests that to some degree, these claims may be justified (Berscheid & Walster, 1978). For example, it has been found that individuals who are attractive in personal appearance have an advantage over those who are not in hiring decisions (Dipboye, Arvey, & Terpstra, 1977). Similarly, attractive persons are often perceived as possessing more positive traits (e.g., greater potential for success) than unattractive ones (e.g., Cash, Gillen, & Burns, 1977). Additional evidence suggests that these advantages do not exist in all situations or under all circumstances. In particular, females may experience negative rather than positive effects as a result of physical attractiveness (e.g., Heilman & Saruwatari, 1979). Yet the benefits of attractiveness appear to be general enough in scope to suggest that efforts to enhance one's personal appearance are often worthwhile.

Typically, people try to enhance their appeal to others through appropriate dress, cosmetics, and various forms of personal grooming. In addition, they often adopt another tactic—the use of perfume or cologne. Advertisements for these artificial scents indicate that they can enhance one's attractiveness and so contribute to both personal happiness and career success. And the millions of dollars spent on such products each year suggest that many consumers accept the accuracy of these claims.

But are these claims actually valid? Do perfumes and colognes yield the uniformly beneficial outcomes so often predicted? Surprisingly, no empirical evidence on these questions exists. While the behavioral impact of naturally occurring scents has been extensively studied (e.g., pheromones; Leshner, 1978), little research has focused on the effects of artificial aromas (Levine & McBurney, Note 1). More to the point, no investigation has sought to determine the impact of such scents in work-related settings. The present research was designed to attain preliminary evidence on such effects. Specifically, it sought to determine whether wearing pleasant artificial scents can affect the ratings assigned to job candidates during employment interviews. Past research on related topics suggests that such effects might arise in two distinct ways.

First, because perfume and cologne are pleasant, they may induce positive moods among interviewers. These reactions, in turn, may enhance liking for interviewees (Clore & Byrne, 1974). Second, the use of artificial scents may lead interviewers to make negative attributions about the traits of people who use them (see Harvey & Weary, 1981). For example, individuals who wear perfume or cologne to a job interview may be perceived as overly concerned with their appearance or as manipulative. To the extent such perceptions occur, evaluations of job candidates may be reduced.

Note: From R. A. Baron, 1983, pp. 709–710.

FIGURE 17-2 Excerpt from Example Introduction

helpful in enhancing attractiveness (4)? Baron concludes his literature review by noting that there has been no research on this specific question (5), but he describes two conflicting predictions that could be derived from theories of interpersonal attraction and impression formation (6).

For a literature review to be effective, it must meet a number of criteria. First, the literature reviewed must be current; nothing makes a poorer impression on a reader than citing research and theory that is out of date. If your most recent citation is more than 2 years old, you might have a problem with being current unless you are absolutely sure there have been no empirical or theoretical developments since that source was published.

Second, make sure you stay focused on your topic. It is very easy to get off on tangential issues in an attempt to be comprehensive in reviewing the literature; address only the issues that are directly relevant to your research.

Third, your literature review must be complete, covering all the relevant issues. For example, make sure your literature reviews includes all the independent, mediating, moderating, and dependent variables you used in your research. Fourth, being complete means covering all the relevant issues, not describing in detail every study ever done on the topic. The APA *Publication Manual* (1994) recommends citing the one or two best examples of research that support a particular point you are making. Note in Figure 17-2 how Baron (1983) makes extensive use of "e.g.," which means "for example"— he doesn't cite all possible studies that support his points, only the most relevant examples. The *Publication Manual* also suggests supporting general principles, such as "Men are typically found to be more aggressive than women," by citing literature reviews rather than specific studies. Sometimes it is necessary to describe the procedures and results of particular studies, such as when your research is replicating all or part of the study. In such cases, make your summary of the study as concise as possible. Writing concise but accurate summaries of research is not easy; see D. J. Bem (1987) and S. Friedman and Steinberg (1989, chap. 10) for hints and examples.

A fifth criterion the literature review must meet is accuracy. When you cite a study as supporting your point, be sure the study really does support it. The only way to ensure accuracy is by reading the study itself. Summaries in literature reviews and textbooks can be very inaccurate, glossing over details of procedures and findings that might be crucial to your literature review but of little importance to the point being made by the author of the secondary source (recall Chapter 4). Finally, your literature review must be balanced; it should not ignore any research that does *not* support the points you are trying to make. Such research should be cited, and you should demonstrate why the criticisms it makes do not apply in your case.

The third and fourth questions addressed in the literature review go together: What will your study add to what is already known? Why is your study important? How you go about answering these questions depends on the type of study you're doing. When testing hypotheses derived from a theory, you must show that the hypotheses represent a test of the validity of the theory, that failure to confirm the hypotheses would require a revision of theory. If your hypotheses test two competing theories, you must show how the results of the study would support one theory but not the other. When your research deals with a relatively open-ended question rather than specific hypotheses, you must similarly convince your readers that the question has theoretical, applied, or empirical importance. When conducting replication research, you must demonstrate why the replication is necessary. For example, was an important population or setting not studied? Does your research have improved statistical power or better measures? Is there some reason for suspecting that different operational definitions will lead to different results? Has a relevant independent or dependent variable been overlooked in previous research? In short, you must convince the reader that your hypotheses matter, that they will make a substantial contribution to knowledge.

The final part of the introduction is the conclusion. Here you provide a brief overview of your study and state your hypotheses or research questions. For example, Hodgins and Koestner (1993) concluded the introduction to their study of the relation

BOX 17-4   Checklist for the Introduction

1. Did you cite relevant, recent research?

2. Did you read and cite primary (original) sources rather than secondhand accounts (summaries of studies in texts)?

3. Have you critically commented on the limitations of that research? What were the weaknesses of that work? Are critiques of past research accurate?

4. Is it clear how the work you have cited relates to your hypothesis or study? Is it clear how this study will build on previous work? How does this study fit in the context of past research?

5. Have you cited enough sources?

6. Is your hypothesis clear? If you are including a variable, but have no hypothesis relating to this variable, this may indicate a problem. Your hypothesis should concern a relationship between two or more variables. Note that (a) those variables should be carefully defined and (b) those variables should be measurable.

7. Is the reason for making the hypothesis clear? Why are you making this prediction? Is that logic clear? Why might previous research or theory make that prediction? Note that to make such arguments you may have to clearly define relevant concepts and theories.

8. Is it clear why your research hypothesis should be tested? Is it clear why the problem is important?

9. Is it clear that your study intends to test the hypothesis? Is it clear why your study is the best way to test this hypothesis?

10. Do ideas follow logically? Or do they appear to jump around? If ideas seem to jump around, try

    a. Outlining your introduction.

    b. Grouping together studies that seem to "go together." Then write a sentence describing the main conclusion or similarity shared by these studies. This will be your topic sentence. Write your topic sentence and then use the studies to provide evidence or support for that sentence.

    c. Using subheadings.

    d. Summarizing the point you are trying to make before moving on to your next point (e.g., "Thus, the evidence suggests that _____. However, existing research can be criticized for _____.")

11. Can the reader anticipate the rest of your paper from your introduction?

Questions for Either Introduction or Method Section

1. Is it clear why you used the measures you used? Do you have evidence they are valid, well accepted, or follow from how the concept is defined?

2. Is it clear why you used the procedures you used?

3. Is it clear why you used the design you used? Is it clear that this study is the best way to test the hypothesis?

Source: Adapted from M. Mitchell & Jolley, 1992, p. 499.

of early childhood experience to one's ability to decode or "read" other people's nonverbal behavior in this way:

> In summary, early temperament, parental warmth and strictness, and family harmony at age 5 were used to predict adult nonverbal sensitivity at age 31. It was expected that adult decoding ability would be related to family harmony, an authoritative parenting style (high warmth and moderate strictness), and easy temperament. (p. 467)

In summary, your introduction is your opportunity to grab your readers' attention and to make them want to read about your research. It provides the background for your research, culminating in hypotheses that flow logically from the theoretical and empirical bases you describe. Box 17-4 contains a checklist you can use to evaluate the introductions you write.

THE METHOD SECTION The Method section is, in one way, the easiest part of a research report to write—you simply describe how you went about collecting your data. In doing so, you must answer five questions: *Who* were the research participants? *What* materials did you use? *When* did you collect the data? *Where* did you collect the data (that is, the setting)? *How* did you collect the data? (The introduction answered the question of *why* you did the study.) The difficult part of writing the Method section is answering these questions clearly yet concisely. To help you describe your method clearly, the Method section can be divided into four subsections, two of which are always present and two of which are optional. These subsections follow this outline:

Method

    Overview (or Design) (optional)

    Participants (or Subjects) (required)

    Materials (or Apparatus) (optional)

    Procedure (required)

The Method section of a research report sometimes starts with an optional subsection called "overview" or "design." This subsection outlines the general plan of the research design and provides readers with a framework for understanding the rest of the methodological information. An overview is especially helpful when complex designs are used. For example, Al-Zahrani and Kaplowitz (1993) examined the relationship between culture and people's tendencies to see behavior as being caused by psychological characteristics of the person performing the behavior (whom they call "the actor") or as being caused by something in the person's environment. These perceptions are referred to as "attributions." Al-Zahrani and Kaplowitz (1993) describe their design this way:

Design of the Experiment

    Each subject completed a form describing eight situations and was asked to make attributions about each.

    Within-subject variables. The eight scenarios varied on three dimensions: 1. whether the actor in the vignette was known personally to the subject . . . or was described only by nationality . . . ; 2. whether the situation involved achievement . . . or morality . . . ; and 3. whether the [behavior] was positive . . . or negative. . . .

    Between-subjects variables. We employed three between-subjects variables: 1. respondent's culture (American or Saudi) . . . ; 2. whether the personally known actor was oneself or a family member; and 3. whether the actor who was known only by nationality was a member of [the subject's culture or the other culture]. (pp. 225–226)

For somewhat less complex studies, the overview can often be stated more succinctly. For example, Monteith (1993) examined the effects of performing behaviors that are discrepant from their beliefs on high- and low-prejudiced individuals. She described her design in this way: "The design was a 2 (gender: men or women) × 2 (prejudice: low or high) × 2 (discrepancy activation: activated or not activated) between-subjects factorial. Eight men and women at each prejudice level were randomly assigned to each of the discrepancy conditions" (p. 472).

The "participants" subsection (the term *participants* is now preferred over *subjects* for research with human participants) is part of every Method section. It describes the participants in the research, providing information on number, sex, age, and other characteristics. If participants are selected based on some criterion, such as clinical diagnosis or attitude, the basis for selection must be described. For example,

> As part of a larger mass survey, several hundred introductory psychology students completed the [Heterosexual Attitudes Toward Homosexuals] questionnaire. . . . Participants also recorded their sexual orientation. Heterosexual individuals scoring relatively low or high in prejudice were identified as eligible participants. Forty low . . . and 39 high . . . prejudiced subjects were then randomly selected and successfully recruited for participation. (Monteith, 1993, p. 479)

The participants subsection should also list any incentives that were offered in exchange for participation, such as monetary payments or credit for completion of a course requirement. Finally, if the data from any participants were not analyzed, you should tell the reader how many participants and the reason. For example, people may have been told about the study by a friend, may not have been taken in by a deception, or may not have followed instructions. At the end of the participants subsection, the reader should have a clear picture of the number and characteristics of the people who participated in your study.

The participants subsection can be followed by an optional subsection called "materials" or "apparatus." The term "materials" is used to refer to printed materials such as questionnaires and "apparatus" to refer to mechanical or electronic devices. If you use questionnaires, personality assessment instruments, and so forth, the materials subsection describes them and presents evidence for their reliability and validity. The description typically includes the number of items, response format (such as a 7-point scale), and scoring procedures. If you use equipment, such as a tachistoscope or polygraph, describe them in the apparatus subsection by giving the manufacturer and model number. If you built the equipment yourself, you must completely describe it. For example, Butler and Steuerwald (1991) conducted an experiment on people's preferences for windows of different sizes and constructed a scale model of a view from inside an office (because current practice uses metric units of measurement, I've added them in brackets):

> The apparatus was a 1/12 scale model 55 in. [140 cm] × 22.5 in. [57 cm] × 10 in. [25 cm] which sat on a table. . . . The side "walls" of the model were adjustable allowing the width of the space to be manipulated. Four panels on the back "wall" (from the subject's point of view) were movable, allowing the size of a rectangular "window" to be adjusted. . . . Light was provided . . . by one desk lamp (100 watt incandescent bulb) positioned above the model. . . . Contents of the space included scaled office furniture (i.e., desks and chairs). . . . The model and the furniture were constructed of wood, posterboard, and foamboard. Everything was white, including the furniture. . . . A rear projection screen [for manipulating the "view" from the office] was positioned approximately 8 inches [20 cm] behind the

[model]. A slide projector was positioned approximately 15 feet [4.6 m] behind the screen. (pp. 337–338)

Very complex apparatus can be illustrated using a line drawing or photograph (Butler and Steuerwald, for example, included a photograph with their description); common types of equipment, such as stopwatches and office furniture, do not need to be described in detail. Information about materials and apparatus, if it is brief, can be integrated into the next subsection, procedure.

Every research report must include a procedure subsection that describes when, where, and how the research was conducted. The research setting should be described in sufficient detail that the reader can understand any influences it may have had on participants' behavior. If participants completed a questionnaire in a classroom, the description "classroom setting" is usually sufficient; aspects of laboratory settings that can influence behavior, such as furniture arrangements in studies of interpersonal distance, require more detailed description; a field setting should be described in sufficient detail that the reader can clearly picture it. As with descriptions of apparatus, a photograph or drawing can clarify descriptions of research settings. For example, C. E. Brown (1981) supplemented this setting description for his study of factors influencing invasions of personal space in a shopping mall with the diagram in Figure 17-3:

The experiment was conducted during a time of moderate traffic density (Thursday evening, May 25, 1979). A major thoroughfare funneled a majority of incoming shoppers through a 13-foot (3.96 m) wide area, limited by a wall on one side and an enclosure for rentable baby carriages on the other. . . . Two confederates stood facing one another perpendicular to oncoming shoppers 6 feet (1.83 m) apart and approximately 3.5 feet (1.07 m) from the wall or the railing of the enclosure. Two white male observers 42 feet (12.80 m) and 48 feet (14.63 m) away, respectively, stood unobtrusively beside a large fountain. (p. 104)

The major portion of the procedure subsection describes how you went about collecting your data. The clearest way to do this is to take your readers through the study as if they were participants. Provide a chronological description of what happens to the participants from the moment they arrive for the study to the moment they leave. For example, Figure 17-4 reproduces the procedure subsection from R. A. Baron's (1983) "Sweet Smell of Success" study. Notice the detailed, step-by-step explanation of the participants' experience during the study. The procedure subsection also contains the operational definitions of the independent and dependent variables (1 and 2 in Figure 17-4), as well as any manipulation checks or pretests that were conducted on the operational definition of the independent variables (3). If an independent variable is manipulated by providing information to participants, either orally or in writing, those instructions should be provided verbatim. In addition, you should maintain copies of written materials, such as questionnaires and transcripts of oral instructions, so you can provide them to others who might want to use them in their research. The APA (1994) recommends that researchers maintain these materials for at least 5 years after publishing the report of the research.

The procedure subsection also describes any special control measures that were instituted for demand characteristics or to prevent other confounds (see Chapter 6). Also report any deviations from normal research procedures. For example, Baron (1983) informed his readers that "subjects were randomly assigned to [conditions] as

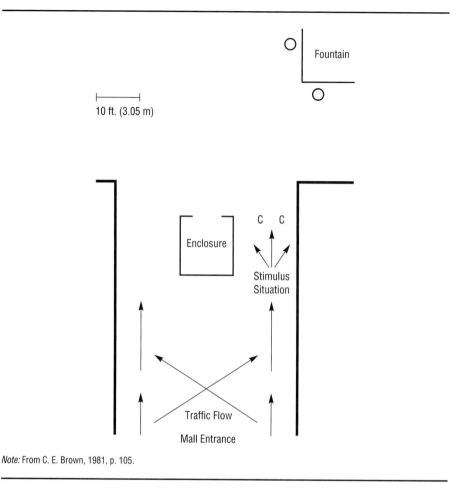

Fountain

10 ft. (3.05 m)

Enclosure

C   C

Stimulus
Situation

Traffic Flow

Mall Entrance

Note: From C. E. Brown, 1981, p. 105.

FIGURE 17-3   Suburban Shopping Mall Setting
Observers (O) recorded whether incoming shoppers walked through or around conversing African American, European American, or mixed-race male confederates (C).

they appeared for their appointments with one exception: Because of the lingering qualities of the two scents employed, it was necessary to conduct scent and no-scent sessions on alternate days" (p. 710).

Finally, you should discuss any ethical issues raised by your procedure. For example, if deception was involved, how was the debriefing conducted? What steps were taken to alleviate adverse effects? How was informed consent obtained? If it was not obtained, why not? How was confidentiality maintained? If these or any of the other issues discussed in Chapter 3 arise in your research, you must justify any potential harm that your research procedures posed to participants. The ethical controversies described in Chapter 3 over the Jacob, Krahn, and Leonard (1991) and Middlemist, Knowles, and Matter

"Sweet Smell of Success"? The Impact of Pleasant Artificial
Scents on Evaluations of Job Applicants

Robert A. Baron
Purdue University

The employment interview. The study was described as being concerned with the manner in which individuals form first impressions of others. Within this general context, the subject played the role of a personnel manager and interviewed the confederate, who played the role of job applicant. The job in question was described as an entry-level management position involving a wide range of activities (e.g., visits to various plants and customer sites, preparation of written reports). During the interview the subject (i.e., the interviewer) read a series of questions to the applicant (i.e., the confederate). The questions were typed on index cards and were quite straightforward. For example, one asked, "What are the major goals you are seeking in your career?" Another was, "How do you get along with other people?" The confederate's responses to each question were prepared in advance and thoroughly memorized. Thus, they were identical for all subjects. These replies were designed to be simple and noncontroversial and were found, during pretesting, to be both reasonable and believable by participants.

1 | *Dependent measures.* Following the final interview question, the subject was taken to a separate room where he or she rated the applicant on a number of different dimensions. Four of these were directly job related (personal suitability for the job, qualifications for this position, potential for future success, and an overall recommendation about hiring). Four other items related to personal characteristics of the applicant (intelligence, warmth, friendliness, and modesty). Three additional dimensions were concerned with the applicant's physical appearance (grooming, neatness, attractiveness). Subjects also rated their liking for the applicant, the extent to which their evaluations of his or her qualifications were affected by this person's appearance, and their own effectiveness as an interviewer. All ratings were made on 7-point scales.

Presence or absence of pleasant scent. In the scent-present condition, the confederates applied two small drops of the appropriate perfume or cologne behind their ears prior to the start of each day's sessions. In the scent-absent condition, they did not make use of these substances. In both conditions, the confederates refrained from employing any scented cosmetics of their own. The two scents used were *Jontue* for the female accomplices and *Brut* for the males. These products were chosen through pretesting in which 12 undergraduate judges (8 females, 4 males) rated 11 popular perfumes and colognes presented in identical plastic bottles. Judges rated the pleasantness of each scent and its attractiveness when used by a member of the opposite sex. Jontue and Brut received the highest mean ratings in this preliminary study. Further, they were rated above the neutral point on both dimensions by all participants. | 2

Additional pretesting indicated that two small drops of these products placed behind the ear produced a noticeable but far-from-overpowering aroma. Because data were collected in sessions lasting from 2 to 3 hours, little fading of these scents occurred in most cases. On those few occasions when data collection occupied a longer interval, an additional single drop of scent was applied. The confederates dressed neatly in all cases, in a manner suitable for an informal job interview (they wore slacks and a blouse). They did not wear more formal clothing because it was felt that such behavior, unusual for a college campus, might arouse suspicion among subjects. | 3

Note: From R. A. Baron, 1983, p. 710.

FIGURE 17-4   Example Procedure Subsection of a Method Section

(1976) studies might have been prevented if their articles had more fully explained their ethical safeguards.

In summary, the Method section of your research report should provide enough information to allow another researcher to replicate your study. Box 17-5 contains a checklist to help you write a good Method section.

BOX 17-5 Checklist for the Method Section

Participants

1. Is it clear how many participants you studied? How many were men and how many were women?

2. Is it clear how participants came to be in your study and how they were compensated?

3. Is it clear how they were assigned to each condition?

4. How many were eliminated? Why?

Procedure

1. Is it written in chronological order (what happened to the subjects first, second, third, etc.)? In other words, is the procedure a step-by-step description of the experience participants underwent? Usually, you should write the procedure from the participants' viewpoint. This makes it easier for readers to put themselves in the participants' shoes and to understand what really happened.

2. Is it clear what the stimuli were that participants were exposed to?

3. Is it clear how control or comparison groups ruled out alternative explanations?

4. Is there any evidence of the quality of your measure?

   a. Reliability?

   b. Validity?

   c. How it avoids problems with biases, such as self-report biases?

5. If your measure is commonly used, have you cited evidence to that effect?

6. Is it clear what subjects were doing? What was the task? If using a paper-and-pencil measure, did you list example items? That is, is it clear what your measure is? You may want to have a separate measures subsection.

7. Do you describe any procedures used to avoid demand characteristics?

8. If you are using a commonly used procedure, do you cite this fact?

9. Is it clear what design you are using? If you have a complicated design, you may want a separate design section. *Note:* You may want to combine information about your design and your participants into one participants and design subsection.

10. Does the reader have a general idea of instructions given to participants? Key instructions, such as those that differentiate between conditions, should be included verbatim.

11. Could someone repeat your study based on reading the Method section?

Source: Adapted from M. Mitchell & Jolley, 1992, pp. 519–520.

THE RESULTS SECTION   Like the Method section, in one way the Results section is easy to write: You simply describe what you found as a result of your method. However, as with the Method section, the problem comes in presenting the results clearly and concisely. This section discusses three aspects of presenting the results of research: types of results to present, organization of the Results section, and the use of tables and figures.

Five types of results can be reported. Three of these are "preliminary" in that they provide information needed to evaluate the validity of the research, but do not bear on the hypotheses. Sometimes you will want to report descriptive statistics, such as the

THE RESEARCH REPORT   563

BOX 17-6   Outline of the Results Section

I. Manipulation check
   A. What were the data?
   B. How were the data analyzed?
   C. If the manipulation worked, what effects should this analysis find?
   D. What were the results: means, standard deviations, statistical test, degrees of freedom, test value, p value?
      1. State the main effects, followed by interactions.
      2. State the overall measures, followed by components.
   E. What does this outcome mean?
      1. Describe the outcome operationally.
      2. If a scale is used, how do the means relate to scale anchors?
      3. What do these results say about the effectiveness of the manipulation?
   F. Summarize the manipulation checks.
   G. Provide a transition to the next section.
II. First hypothesis
   A. What were the data?
   B. How were the data analyzed?
   C. If the hypothesis is correct, what effects should this analysis find?
   D. What were the results: means, standard deviations, statistical test, degrees of freedom, test value, p value?
      1. State the main effects, followed by interactions.
      2. State the overall measures, followed by components.
   E. What does this outcome mean?
      1. Describe the outcome operationally.
      2. If a scale is used, how do the means relate to scale anchors?
      3. What do these results say about the validity of the hypothesis?
   F. Summarize the results for the first hypothesis.
   G. Provide a transition to the next section.
III. Second hypothesis
IV. Other findings

mean and standard deviation on a variable, for all participants in the research. For example, you might want to show that your research sample was similar to the norming sample for a standardized measure. If you develop your own measure, you will want to report any reliability or validity data collected from your research sample; reliability or validity evidence collected in previous research or a pilot study should be reported in the Method section when you describe the measure. The third type of preliminary results are those for manipulation checks: evidence for the construct validity of the operational definition of your independent variables. The fourth type of results you report are the outcomes of the tests of your hypotheses: Were they supported or not? Finally, you will want to report any important results you did not predict. For example, were there any unexpected sex of participant effects?

Your Results section should be organized to present first the preliminary results, then the results bearing on your hypotheses, and finally any other important results you found. As shown in Box 17-6, when presenting your results, you should provide certain types of information to the reader. First, what were the data used to check the manipulation or test a particular hypothesis? What measure did you use? Next explain the design used to analyze those data; for example, R. A. Baron (1983) used a 2 (sex of research participant) $\times$ 2 (sex of person interviewed) $\times$ 2 (presence or absence of scent) factorial design. When the same statistical design is used to analyze all the data, you can present it in an introductory sentence or paragraph at the beginning of the Results section. If the statistical technique is likely to be unfamiliar to your readers, provide a brief explanation of it, with a reference to a more complete description in a book or journal article.

The third piece of information the reader needs is a reminder of what the outcome of the statistical test should be if the manipulation worked or the hypothesis is correct. Remember, your hypotheses were presented back in the introduction, and the intervening Method section might have caused your readers to forget the exact nature of the hypothesis. You could say, for example, "If the manipulation were successful, we would expect to find participants in the negative mood condition scoring higher than participants in the positive mood condition on the subscales of the Multiple Affect Adjective Check List." After reminding your readers of the hypothesis and how it will be reflected in your measure, then present the results of the statistical test: means and standard deviations for each condition of the independent variable, the type of statistical test used (for example, t, F, and so on), the degrees of freedom for the test, its magnitude, and the p value associated with an outcome of that magnitude. When you use preplanned or post hoc contrasts of means (recall Chapter 7), report the results of those tests after the results of the overall test. The information about the statistical test is often present in this shorthand form: "$t(28) = 2.04, p < .05$." Because computerized data analyses can provide exact p values rather than the broad categories found in statistical tables, it is becoming the norm to present exact values, such as "$F(3, 223) = 5.24, p = .002$." It is also becoming common to include an indicator of effect size, such as d or r.

You should conclude your presentation with a narrative description of these results. For example, "As predicted by our first hypothesis, men made a larger number of aggressive statements (mean = 6.8, s.d. = 2.1) than did women (mean = 3.6, s.d. = 1.9), $d = 1.6$." Note two characteristics of this sentence: First, it is stated operationally ("a larger number of aggressive statements"), not in terms of a hypothetical construct (such as "more aggressive"); interpretations of the results go in the Discussion section. Second, it tells the reader how the results relate to the hypothesis: These results confirmed it. When the dependent measure is a scale, it is helpful to interpret mean scores for the reader in terms of the scale anchors. For example, "Men had a mean score of 4.5 on the happiness scale, which falls halfway between 'Somewhat happy' and 'Moderately happy.' "

When presenting results, move from the general to specific, presenting main effects before interactions and, when appropriate, overall scores on a measure of a complex construct before the component scores. You can organize the presentation of your main results in a number of ways: by hypothesis, by independent variable, or by dependent variable. Use the organization that most clearly presents the outcome of your study; you may have to experiment a little and get feedback from other people before deciding on a final organization. It is extremely helpful to use headings to subdivide your Results section. For example, you might have subsections titled "Manipulation Checks," "Hypothesis 1," "Hypothesis 2," and "Other Findings." At the end of each subsection, briefly summarize your findings and provide a transition to the next subsection. For example, "Having found support for the first hypothesis on all dependent measures, let us now examine the results for the second hypothesis."

When your results are complex, such as when you have an interaction effect, or you report the effect of the same independent variables on several dependent variables, it helps readers to follow your results if you present them using a table or figure. Consider, for example, this excerpt from R. A. Baron's (1983) results ("M" is shorthand for "mean"):

> The interaction [between sex of participant and scent] was significant for ratings of intelligence and friendliness, $F(1, 37) = 4.50, 4.54, p < .05$. . . . Men rated the applicants as lower on intelligence ($M = 5.10$) and friendliness ($M = 6.10$) when wearing perfume or cologne ($M = 5.44$) than when not wearing these substances ($M = 6.68$). In contrast, females rated the applicants higher in intelligence ($M = 5.64$) and friendliness ($M = 5.85$) when wearing perfume or cologne ($M = 4.08$) than when not wearing such substances. . . .
>
> An additional item on the questionnaire asked subjects to rate their liking for the applicants. An ANOVA on these data yielded a significant interaction between sex of subject and scent, $F(1, 37) = 4.28, p < .05$. Consistent with findings reported earlier, this interaction reflected the fact that males reported liking the applicant less in the presence of a pleasant scent ($M = 3.56$) than in its absence ($M = 5.10$). In contrast, females reported liking the applicants more in the presence of such scent ($M = 5.21$) than in its absence ($M = 4.62$). (p. 711)

The mixture of numbers and text in this passage makes it somewhat difficult to follow, and in the first paragraph, it is difficult to determine which means go with which conditions. Now consider Table 17-1, which presents the same results; it is now clear which means go with which conditions. Interaction effects are often most clearly shown when portrayed in the form of a graph or figure, such as Figure 17-5, which shows the results of R. A. Baron's (1983) study for his liking measure. In fact, the figure offers a somewhat different interpretation of the results from that made by Baron: only men are influenced by the presence of scent (note that the "female" line is almost flat) and that the sex difference occurs only in the presence of the scent.

TABLE 17-1   Selected Results from R. A. Baron (1983)

Compare this tabular presentation with the narrative presentation in the text.

	SCENT		
	Present	Absent	Interaction F(1, 37)
Intelligence			4.50*
Male participants	5.10	5.44	
Female participants	4.08	5.64	
Friendliness			4.54*
Male participants	6.10	6.88	
Female participants	5.85	5.30	
Liking			4.28*
Male participants	3.56	5.10	
Female participants	5.10	4.62	

*$p < .05$.

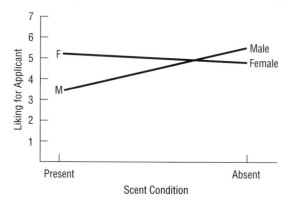

Note: Based on data from R. A. Baron, 1983.

FIGURE 17-5   Graph of Scent Condition by Sex of Participant Interaction for Liking Ratings

In summary, the Results section tells your readers what you found in your study. Box 17-7 contains a checklist to help you write a Results section.

THE DISCUSSION SECTION   The Discussion section is, perhaps, the most difficult part of the research report to write. It is here that you must interpret the results of the research in terms of what they mean for theory, research, and application. In doing so, you must ensure that you address each issue that you raised in the introduction plus any new issues raised by your results, such as unexpected findings. In structure, the Discussion section is the bottom of the hourglass shown in Figure 17-1: You move from specific results to the general implications of those results.

Open your discussion with a summary of your results. This summary should be completely nonstatistical so that readers who could not follow the technicalities of the Results section can understand the essence of your findings. For example, Whitley and Gridley (1993) opened their discussion of a complex statistical analysis of the relationships among self-esteem, psychological masculinity, and depression in this way: "The first-order confirmatory factor analysis indicated that masculinity was a construct separate from self-esteem. However, the hierarchical analysis indicated that masculinity, self-esteem and mild depression could be conceptualized as different manifestations of a single underlying construct" (p. 366).

Then tell your readers what these results mean in terms of theory, research, and application. If your results are consistent with theoretical predictions and prior research, what does this say about the validity of the theory? If your results are not consistent with previous work, you need to address the question of why. For example, is the theory incorrect? If so, in what ways is it incorrect and how should it be changed to make it more valid? Are conflicts between your results and those of previous research caused by methodological differences? If so, what are those differences, how did they lead to the conflict, and what does the conflict mean for theory and future research? For example, consider this excerpt from R. A. Baron's (1983) discussion:

> Past research has called attention to the fact that job applicants' appearance and grooming can strongly affect the interview process. . . . The present results extend this previous work by indicating that the direction of such effects is *not* uniformly positive. On the contrary, it appears that interviewers may sometimes react negatively to efforts at self-enhancement by job applicants. Further, such reactions appear to stem from complex cognitive mechanisms as well as from current affective states. (p. 712)

As you lay out your interpretations, especially interpretations of results that are inconsistent with the theory and research on which you based your study, you may find yourself returning to the library to find the proper theoretical and empirical niche for your results. For example, Whitley and Gridley (1993) interpreted their results in terms of the "Big Five" theory of personality traits (John, 1990), an interpretation that did not occur to them until they had seen the pattern of relationships among the variables uncovered by their data analysis.

As you explain the meaning of your results, be sure not to overlook any reasonable alternative explanations for your findings, such as those provided by theories other than the one you favor or by aspects of your procedures. As an example of the latter, recall that different path models can fit the same data (see Chapter 8) and that nonequivalent control group quasi-experimental designs allow for selection biases (see Chapter 10). While considering these alternative explanations, don't forget to point out any evidence you have to refute them. Anticipate any reasonable criticisms of your work, and show why those criticisms don't, in fact, apply.

Similarly, acknowledge any limitations on the generalizability of your results but, again, also point out facts that reduce the severity of those limitations. For example, R. A. Baron (1983), while acknowledging the artificiality of his laboratory research setting, points out that

> Several steps were taken to enhance the generalizability of the present research. The description of the job in question was quite realistic, and the questions asked during the interview were similar to ones that might well be posed to actual job candidates. The perfume or cologne worn by confederates were popular national brands, and the amount used was carefully adjusted to reflect levels typically applied under ordinary life conditions. These precautions, and the fact that earlier studies employing simulated interviews have often yielded valuable results . . . , suggest that the present findings may possess considerable generality. (pp. 712–713)

Be careful when discussing the limitations of your research not to shoot yourself in the foot. On a number of occasions, after reading that part of a research report's discussion, I have asked myself, "If the study was that bad, why are the researchers bothering to report it?" In most of these cases, the limitations were actually not as severe as the authors had made them seem. In fact, the positive aspects of the research far outweighed the limitations; the authors simply did not point that out.

Your discussion must also consider any unexpected findings from your research: Why did they occur and what do they mean? Once again, you will find yourself returning to the library to consult relevant theory and research.

Be sure to point out any practical implications of your results, whether those results were predicted or unexpected. For example, R. A. Baron (1983) noted that "the practical implications of the present findings for applicants seem clear: Use artificial scents

BOX 17-7   Checklist for the Results Section

1. Is it clear what data were used? In other words, is it clear how participants' behaviors or responses were converted into scores?

2. Is it clear what analysis was used on these scores?

3. Is the analysis justifiable?

   a. Do data meet the assumptions of the test (observations independent, appropriate scale of measurement)?

   b. Have others used or recommended that test in similar circumstances? If so, you might cite their work.

4. Is it clear why the analysis was done? That is, what hypothesis is being tested by the analysis? You will often want to remind the reader of your hypothesis. After reading the Method section, the reader may have forgotten the hypothesis described in the introduction. Furthermore, sometimes an analysis is not done to test a hypothesis. For example, an analysis might be done to show the measure or manipulation is valid or the data meet the assumption of the test. In such cases, you

should clearly explain why you are doing that analysis.

5. Does your presentation of results follow this general format?

   a. Statement of hypothesis or relationship to be discovered.

   b. Statement of whether hypothesis was supported or relationship uncovered.

   c. Report of statistical significance, indicating whether proof of relationship was found. After reporting whether result was significant, should report statistic (F, t, χ^2, etc.), degrees of freedom, value of statistic, and probability value ($p < .05$).

   d. Means, percent, or other summary, descriptive statistics to give better understanding of relationship. The means help reader understand direction of the relationship and give some indication of its size. You may choose to use tables or graphs to convey this information, especially if there are many means or the relationship is complex.

Source: Adapted from M. Mitchell & Jolley, 1992, p. 534.

and other grooming aids with caution, for their impact may sometimes be negative" (p. 712).

Finally, make recommendations for future research. It has become a cliché to end a research report with a call for more research, but recommendations for investigating specific research questions are useful. Box 17-8 lists some types of research that can be derived from a study.

Just as you opened your research paper with a strong statement about human behavior, you should also close it with such a statement (D. J. Bem, 1987; Sternberg, 1993). You want your reader to leave with something to remember you by. Consider, for example, the following:

> The timeworn contention that errors in the laboratory have no consequences in the real world may, in fact, prove to be more than harmless optimism. Our human history of conflict and carnage attests to both the ubiquity and the virulence of social misunderstanding; if we fail to acknowledge that the roots of these events lie in ourselves, and not in our stars, then we may be doomed to witness their endless repetition. (Gilbert & Osborne, 1989, p. 947)

BOX 17-7 *(continued)*

6. Are the degrees of freedom correct?

7. Is it clear how the results relate to the hypothesis? The results should provide a clear "scorecard" for the hypothesis. That is, do the results tell a story about how much support the hypothesis got? Or is the reader simply bombarded with statistics?

8. Do you do more than just state that a result is significant? That is, do you include summary statistics (means, percentages, etc.) to help the reader see the pattern of your results? That is, saying the results were significant does not tell us who did better.

9. Are tables or graphs needed to make the pattern of results easier to understand? Tables and graphs are probably necessary to help the reader understand any interactions you have.

10. Are there relationships that you hypothesized but did not report? There should not be!

11. Did you do and report appropriate follow-up tests?

12. Did you confuse the value of your test statistic (F, t, r) with the p value? Remember, the p value refers to how likely it is that your results could be obtained by chance. If the results were extremely unlikely to be due to chance, you would conclude the variables are really related. Thus, if you got a p value of .001, you would be relatively confident your results are not due to chance. Note that if you have a large F, t, or r, you will probably have a small p value (because that would indicate a big relationship in your sample, and having a big relationship in your sample is unlikely if there is really no relationship). Conversely, a small r, F, or t value will probably be accompanied by a large p value (because a small relationship in the sample could quite easily be due to chance).

In summary, the Discussion section of your research report is where you show how your research fits into and contributes to the body of psychological knowledge. Box 17-9 contains a checklist to help you evaluate the discussion sections you write.

THE TITLE AND ABSTRACT   Although the title and abstract come first in a research report, they are written last; you write them last because they describe and summarize the research report. A good title is short (no more than 15 words) and tells the reader what the report is about; it should tell the reader the independent and dependent variables studied in the research. Consider, for example, the title of C. E. Brown's (1981) report: "Shared Space Invasion and Race." It is short (only five words), but it describes the independent and dependent variables studied (race and the invasion of personal space). Butler and Steuerwald's (1991) study was more complex, so the title of their report was longer: "Effects of View and Room Size on Window Size Preferences in Models." The title is only 12 words long but nonetheless describes two independent variables (view and window size) and the dependent variable (window size preferences). Sometimes the title of a report is broken down into two parts, the main title and a subtitle, usually

BOX 17-8   Possible Recommendations for Future Research

1. Improvements in design:

    Increasing power by using more participants, more homogeneous participants, within-subjects design, more standardized procedures, and/or more sensitive measures

    Using a design that will establish causality (experimental rather than correlational)

    Different, more involving tasks

    More complex, realistic, or more carefully designed stimulus materials

    More objective measures to rule out subject or researcher biases

    More valid measures

    More specific measures of the construct to pinpoint the exact effect of the treatment (a global measure of memory being replaced with a measure of encoding and a measure of retrieval)

    More valid manipulations

    Placebo conditions and double-blind conditions to rule out demand characteristics

    More specific measures

2. Longer-term consequences

3. Whether related factors have the same effect

4. The extent to which the results generalize to different levels of the treatment variable to different age groups, genders, situations, tasks, settings, and/or a broader sample

5. Research applying the finding to an applied problem

6. Manipulations that might moderate the observed relationship between the variables

7. Possible mediating factors, usually cognitive or physiological variables that intervene between stimulus and response

8. Ruling out alternative explanations for the findings or for competing explanations of an unexpected finding

9. Research investigating the psychological processes underlying observed phenomena

Source: Adapted from M. Mitchell & Jolley, 1992, pp. 536–537.

---

separated by a colon, such as "Unemployment, Distress, and Coping: A Panel Study of Autoworkers" (V. L. Hamilton, Hoffman, Broman, & Rauma, 1993). The main title before the colon provides the general topic of the research, in this case the relationships among unemployment, stress, and coping, and the subtitle gives more specific information about the research, in this case the method used (a panel study, a form of longitudinal research) and the participant population (autoworkers). Again, note the brevity of the title: nine words.

The abstract summarizes the research report. It has two purposes. The first is to provide a more complete description of the research than the title provides so that readers can decide if the report includes the information they need on the variables described in the title. The second purpose is to provide a framework for reading the article: Because the readers know in a general way what the report will say, they will find it easier to understand and to relate to what they already know about the topic. Your abstract should be short (150 words maximum) in order to conserve space in computerized databases such as *PsycINFO*. Despite this brevity, the abstract must convey five pieces of information: your hypothesis or research question, the nature of your research participants, your procedures, your results, and an outline of your interpretation of your

BOX 17-9   Checklist for the Discussion Section

1. Did you briefly summarize results? Is the first paragraph closely tied to the results? Do nonsignificant results stay nonsignificant?

2. Are all the comparisons you make (group 1 > group 5) backed up by analyses specifically testing these comparisons? Do you confuse the meaning of main effects and interactions? That is, do you say, "The elaborative rehearsal group did better than the rote rehearsal group, as shown by the rehearsal by type of information interaction?"

3. Did you relate results to your hypothesis and to the points you made in the *introduction?* That is, do they have relevance for previous theory or research? Have you connected your results and your study back to the problems stated in the introduction?

Source: Adapted from M. Mitchell & Jolley, 1992, p. 538.

4. Have you answered the question "What are the implications of this study?"
   a. Theoretical?
   b. Practical?
   c. Future research?

5. Are there alternative interpretations for your results? Remember, there are always many explanations for null results. Discuss these alternatives.

6. Do you try to explain unexpected findings?

7. Are there other studies that should be done?
   a. To address alternative interpretations?
   b. To improve the study (if it were to be redone, what would you do differently)?
   c. To extend the research by using different types of subjects, additional variables, or additional levels of variables?

8. Is it evident that you have given some thought to your results? That you have tried to make them meaningful?

results. The abstract must provide the essence of the introduction and the three sections of your research report: Method, Results, and Discussion. However, to conserve space the abstract usually does not summarize the literature review part of the introduction or include citations to other works. Notice how R. A. Baron's (1983) title and abstract, shown in Figure 17-6, provide a complete yet concise summary of his research.

Writing for Nonresearchers

The discussion of the design of applicable research in Chapter 4 noted that such research should focus on policy variables as independent variables and on high-utility dependent variables (Ruback & Innes, 1988). Research reports intended for audiences of practitioners require a similar focus if the practitioners are to read the reports and make use of the information in them. In addition, practitioners want clear and detailed descriptions of how the independent variables can be manipulated in natural settings so that they can translate the research into practice. Unfortunately, much behavioral science research does not seem to meet the needs of practitioners. Price (1985), for example, classified only 17% of the articles he surveyed from a set of prestigious organizational science journals as relevant to the needs of practitioners. Posavac (1992)

**"Sweet Smell of Success"? The Impact of Pleasant Artificial
Scents on Evaluations of Job Applicants**

Robert A. Baron
Purdue University

Male and female subjects interviewed male or female applicants for an entry-level management position. Applicants were actually confederates of the researcher who wore or did not wear a measured amount of a popular perfume or cologne. Following the interview, subjects rated each applicant on a number of job-related dimensions (e.g., to what extent is this individual qualified for the job?) and personal characteristics (e.g., how friendly is this person?). Results indicated that sex of subject and the presence or absence of scent interacted in affecting ratings of the applicants. Males assigned lower ratings to these persons when they wore perfume or cologne than when they did not; females showed the opposite pattern. Moreover, this was true both for job-related and personal characteristics. These and other results are interpreted as reflecting greater difficulty on the part of males than females in ignoring extraneous aspects of job applicants' appearance or grooming.

Note: From R. A. Baron, 1983, p. 709.

FIGURE 17-6   Example Title and Abstract

identified four common problems in reporting research to nonresearchers: establishing the researcher's credibility, focusing on relevant variables, overuse of statistics, and making recommendations.

ESTABLISHING CREDIBILITY   A key to persuading nonresearchers to use the results of research is establishing the researcher's credibility relative to the research topic as a practical matter. Many practitioners view researchers as people who deal only in abstract concepts and have no understanding of what happens in applied settings on a day-to-day basis. Morrow-Bradley and Elliott (1986), for example, found that over one third of the practicing psychotherapists whom they surveyed said that published research on psychotherapy was not relevant to them because "in general, psychotherapy researchers do not do psychotherapy" (p. 193). The respondents to the survey said that as a consequence of this lack of practical experience, psychotherapy research lacked ecological validity in terms of research questions, independent variables, and dependent variables. To be credible to nonresearchers, then, research reports must exhibit a sensitivity to the problems practitioners face in their work. This sensitivity can be conveyed by emphasizing the researcher's practical experience with the topic that was investigated and, as discussed next, by focusing on issues and variables that the practitioners view as most relevant.

RELEVANCE   Perceived relevance derives not only from the use of ecologically valid research questions, variables, and methods, but also from the way in which the research is presented to the reader. As Posavac (1992) notes, researchers focus on the internal validity in presenting the results of research, whereas practitioners want to know how to apply those results:

> Normally, [researchers] emphasize the theory, the quality of the research design, and measurement issues related to the dependent variable. . . . Applied readers want to be assured that the research design and [data] analyses were sound, but their primary interest centers on the independent variable. They want to know what was done to get a positive consumer

reaction, the high level of patient compliance with medical care, or the enthusiastic employee reaction to a reorganized work environment. . . . The independent variable represents a prototype of an intervention, a teaching technique, or a policy that people might try to apply. (p. 274)

To achieve this kind of relevance, the research report must clearly explain how the independent variable was manipulated and link that manipulation to actions that can be taken in applied settings (Morrow-Bradley & Elliott, 1986).

This emphasis on practical implementation does not mean that practitioners find theoretical analyses useless; on the contrary, almost half of Morrow-Bradley and Elliott's (1986) respondents classified "research that emphasizes how research findings fit into a specific theoretical orientation" as extremely or very useful (p. 194). However, as Price (1985) notes, practitioners expect researchers to establish the link between theory and practice. Writing about research in organizational science, he notes that "while many links between theoretical concepts and organizational problems are easy to make, it certainly helps if the [researcher] makes an attempt to relate [research] findings to problems or dilemmas in organizations" (p. 127).

STATISTICS   Many practitioners, especially those not trained in the behavioral sciences, do not have the statistical sophistication of most researchers. Consequently, it is incumbent on the researcher to present descriptive and inferential statistics in ways that are relevant to the audience and that minimize misunderstandings. For example, researchers' focus on hypothesis testing leads them to place a great deal of emphasis on aggregate statistics (such as means), statistical tests, and the statistical significance of results. Practitioners have other interests. For example, two of the complaints about published research voiced by Morrow-Bradley and Elliott's (1986) respondents were that "the frequent use of only aggregate statistics (means, F values, etc.) does not include important results, for example, how many [clients] changed" and that "a significant statistical result may be clinically insignificant, yet this information usually is not reported" (p. 193).

Posavac (1992) points out that many nonresearchers have difficulty interpreting statistics as they are normally used in research reports. Table 17-2 lists some of the more common statistical misinterpretations he has encountered in his experience as an applied researcher. Posavac has two suggestions for dealing with this kind of problem. The first is to be aware of the types of misinterpretations that can arise and to clearly explain the meaning of the statistics in terms of the variables of interest to the reader. For example, you might explain that an effect size of .45 standard deviation means that 67% of the members of the experimental group scored higher than the average person in the control group, but also that 33% of the members of the experimental group scored lower than the average member of the control group. The second suggestion is, especially when dealing with an audience of nonscientists, simply to highlight the most important results in the body of the report and relegate details of the statistical analysis to an appendix.

MAKING RECOMMENDATIONS   Price (1985) notes that most researchers are reluctant to make strong recommendations about actions to take on the basis of the results of their research. As Masters (1984) noted, because of their awareness of the inherent

TABLE 17-2   Misinterpretations of Standard Reporting Terminology of Statistical Analyses

Standard Reporting Practice	*Communication Problem Observed*
Using a numerical mean from a scale	A client question was "Is 5.5 out of 7 good or bad?"
Using a numerical mean	Information users forget that the actual values are not all essentially equal to the mean; variance is a hard concept.
Reporting two group means	Clients vastly underestimate the overlap in the scores from two groups.
Reporting the amount of overlap between experimental and control groups, or any two groups	Since most clients don't understand variance, they overestimate the degree that their services will lead people to change.
Reporting statistical significance	Information users confuse significant with meaningful or important findings.
Noting that a comparison is not statistically significant	Many clients think that a nonsignificant finding means that there are no differences between groups.

Note: From Posavac, 1992, p. 276.

limitations of the research process and of the complexity of the factors influencing any one variable, researchers are reluctant to make simple, straightforward recommendations for action. Nonetheless, for practitioners to practice, they must take action and so applied researchers need to make recommendations for action. This is especially true in evaluation research: One of the evaluation researcher's functions is to make recommendations for improvement. Researchers' recommendations must meet two criteria (Posavac, 1992). First, they must be acceptable to the people who must implement them; one way to increase acceptance is to include stakeholders in the process of formulating recommendations. Second, implementing the recommendations must be within the power and resources of the practitioner; a practitioner might not have the authority to make certain changes or might not have the required budget. Again, stakeholder input can keep recommendations within the limits of implementation.

JOURNAL ARTICLES AND CONVENTION PRESENTATIONS

Once a research project has been completed and the research report written, it is time to communicate the results of the research to people who have an interest in the topic. The two most common media of communication used by researchers, especially for communication with other researchers, are the journal article and the presentation at a convention or meeting of a professional association. This section examines these two communication media.

The Journal Article

The journal article is the most prestigious form of publication in most of the social sciences. One reason for this prestige may be the relatively small number of articles accepted for publication in professional journals. For example, the average acceptance rate for APA-sponsored journals in 1998 was 23% ("Summary Report," 1999). In addition, articles published in professional journals undergo rigorous review by experts on the paper's topic before it is accepted for publication. Acceptance therefore reflects experts' endorsement of the quality of the research. Let's take a look at the process by which research reports get into print.

CHOOSING A JOURNAL   The first step the researcher faces in the publication process is choosing a journal to which to submit the manuscript of the research report for publication. Choosing a journal is not always an easy process: Literally hundreds of journals publish behavioral science research (for example, see APA, 1993), and publication in some journals brings more prestige than publication in other journals. Because journals are often specialized, publishing articles only on certain topics or only research that uses certain methods, prospective authors must ensure that their articles fall within the publication scope of the journals to which they submit their work. Every journal includes in each issue information concerning the types of articles it will consider for publication. This information is sometimes found inside the front cover of the issue, or included in a section called "Editorial Policy," "Information for Contributors," or something similar; it is also contained in guides to journals, such as that compiled by the APA (1993). Submissions that do not fall within the scope of the journal will be returned without being considered for publication, so be sure to carefully match your research report to a journal. S. L. Garfield (1979), for example, reported that 20% of the articles submitted during his tenure as editor of the *Journal of Consulting and Clinical Psychology* were returned without review because they were not appropriate to the journal.

PREPARING THE MANUSCRIPT   Your manuscript represents you to the journal editor and to the reviewers. It is therefore extremely important that the manuscript make a favorable impression on them; a sloppy manuscript will make them wonder if your research procedures were equally sloppy. Be sure your manuscript is completely free of errors in spelling, word usage, grammar, and punctuation. These days, it is common to write manuscripts on a computer using a word processing program that includes a spelling checker. To the extent that the manuscripts I review are representative, many people seem to substitute the spelling checker for proofreading; as a result, the manuscripts frequently contain spelling errors. Why? Because a computerized spelling checker will pass as correct any word in its dictionary, even if that word represents a typographical error. For example, a spelling checker will accept "their" in place of "there" and "four" in place of "for." Computerized grammar checkers can also be highly inaccurate (Pogue, 1993). Computers are no substitute for human proofreading.

You must also ensure that your manuscript is typed in the proper format. Most psychology journals require authors to use the APA (1994) format, but some journals vary slightly from that format, while journals in other fields may use quite different formats. Most journals in sociology, for example, use the format prescribed by the American Sociological Association, which is similar to, but in many ways differs from, the APA format. Check a journal's formatting requirements before you submit your manuscript; these requirements are usually found in the journal's "Information for Contributors" section.

SUBMITTING THE MANUSCRIPT   When the manuscript is properly prepared, send it to the journal's editor; the editor's address is included in the journal's "Information for Contributors" section. This section will also tell you how many copies of the manuscript to send (varying from three to five depending on the journal), whether there is a submission fee and how much it is, and whether you have to send anything else, such as a self-addressed postcard that the editor will use to acknowledge receipt of the manuscript. You should also enclose a letter to the editor with your submission, giving the title of the article and a one- or two-sentence description of its topic. And you must include the name, mailing address, telephone number, and, if available, the electronic mail (e-mail) address of the **corresponding author**—the person whom the editor will contact concerning the manuscript.

When the editor receives your manuscript, he or she may handle it personally or send it to an associate editor or to an **action editor** for processing; associate editors and action editors are the editor's deputies and have full authority to make decisions concerning the acceptance or rejection of manuscripts. The editor will acknowledge receipt of the manuscript and assign a number to it; use this number in all correspondence with the editor concerning your manuscript. The editor then sends the manuscript out for **peer review:** Two to four experts will critically read the manuscript and make recommendations to the editor about whether or not it should be accepted for publication. The editor will send copies of their comments to the corresponding author along with the decision concerning the manuscript.

Some journals use a process called **blind** (or **masked**) **review,** or offer it to authors as an option. In a blind review, the authors format the manuscript so that it does not contain information identifying them; consequently, the reviewers cannot be influenced by the authors' reputations in making their recommendations. When a journal offers blind review as an option to authors, they must specifically request it when submitting the manuscript. Whenever blind review is used—whether as a general policy of the journal or as an option to the authors—it is the authors' responsibility to format the manuscript so that it does not reveal their identities. If the nature of the article makes disguising the authors' identities impossible—as when the article reports one in a series of experiments and refers to earlier work by the authors—the corresponding author should note this in the letter to the editor included with the manuscript. Not all journals use blind review; check each journal's "Information for Contributors" section.

PEER REVIEW   To make a decision about the acceptability for publication of a manuscript, an editor needs information about both the theoretical and methodological soundness of the research. Therefore, some of the people who review a manuscript are experts on the theory underlying it, and others are experts on the methodology and statistical analyses used (J. P. Campbell, 1982). Because of this difference in focus, different reviewers will make differing criticisms about a manuscript (D. W. Fiske & Fogg, 1990). Although some people find this lack of agreement about "what's wrong with my manuscript" disconcerting, these differing viewpoints meet the editor's information needs (Campbell, 1982; Fiske & Fogg, 1990). Also, as Fiske and Fogg noted after analyzing reviewers' comments on 153 manuscripts, "Saying that two reviewers typically do not agree [about what is wrong with a manuscript] does not mean that they disagree. An attempt to locate explicit disagreements turned up only a few instances in which one reviewer said a given aspect of the paper was satisfactory but another found a problem" (p. 597). For a description of how a reviewer goes about evaluating a manuscript, see Schwab (1985).

In considering the theoretical and methodological soundness of the research reported in a manuscript, what kinds of problems do reviewers typically find? Studies of the review process (Fiske & Fogg, 1990; Gottfredson, 1978; Lindsey, 1978) and reviewers' and editors' experiences (Campbell, 1982; Daft, 1985) indicate five major categories of common problems. The first set of problems is typically found in the introduction and centers around development of the research question. These problems include lack of a theoretical or empirical rationale for the research, inadequate explanation of how the research question was derived from prior theory and research, an incomplete or outdated literature review, and incorrect descriptions of theories or prior research. The second set of problems comes from the Method section and includes problems such as poor control of extraneous variables, lack of evidence for the validity of measures and experimental manipulations, and problems with the sample of research participants, such as its being too small or not appropriate to the research question. The third set of problems deals with statistics: using the wrong analysis for the type of data, using an analysis that doesn't answer the research questions, and making incorrect interpretations of the results of statistical tests. The fourth set of problems comes from the Discussion section and includes making interpretations that are not supported by the data, overlooking implications of the data, and not clearly linking the results of the research to the questions posed in the hypotheses.

The final set of problems relates not to the content of the article but, rather, to how the contents are presented: failure to clearly describe the logic underlying hypotheses and interpretations, failure to make logical connections and transitions between points made in the introduction and discussion, incorrect use of technical terms, poor organization, and so forth. Such presentation problems made up two thirds of the criticisms that Fiske and Fogg (1990) found in their analysis of manuscript reviews.

What can authors do to prevent these problems? Problems in developing the research question and designing the research can often be headed off by writing a prospectus of the research and having colleagues read it and comment on it (see Chapter 4). Similarly, you can consult with knowledgeable colleagues about statistical analyses and ask them to read a draft of the research report to identify any problems in the discussion. Finally, you can simply be careful about writing; as Fiske and Fogg (1990) note, "Criticisms of presentation are corrigible. Many of them [can be] prevented by more careful review by the authors themselves and also by frank critiquing from a number of colleagues" (p. 593). Von Békésy (1960) has a further suggestion:

> An even better way [to prevent research errors] is to have an enemy. An enemy is willing to devote a vast amount of time and brain power to ferreting out errors both large and small, and this without any compensation. The trouble is that really capable enemies are scarce; most of them are only ordinary. Another trouble with enemies is that they sometimes develop into friends and lose a great deal of their zeal. It was in this way that the writer lost his three best enemies. (pp. 8–9)

EDITORIAL RESPONSE   Once the editor has the comments and recommendations of all the reviewers of a manuscript, she or he must make a decision about its acceptability for publication. The editor has four options. The first is to accept the manuscript without revision; this happens with less than 2% of manuscripts (Eichorn & VandenBos, 1985). The second option is to accept the manuscript contingent on the authors' making revisions specified by the editor based on the reviewers' comments. These revisions are generally minor, often requiring the authors to describe procedures in more detail, to explain certain points more fully, or to shorten the manuscript. The third option is called "revise and resubmit": The editor rejects the article as it is, but allows the authors the option of making substantial revisions and resubmitting it; the resubmission will undergo the entire review process as if it were a new manuscript. A "revise and resubmit" decision occurs when the reviewers think that the research question is important, but that the article has major but correctable problems. These problems typically involve data analyses, interpretations of results, or severe presentation problems. If the editor decides the manuscript is not of sufficient quality to warrant publication in the journal, it will be rejected. By the time you receive the editor's decision on your manuscript, 6 to 9 months will have passed.

REVISING THE MANUSCRIPT   The most optimistic responses you are likely to get from an editor are acceptance contingent on revision and revise and resubmit. In either case, carefully read the comments made by the reviewers, especially those highlighted in the editor's letter to you, and any additional comments made by the editor. Occasionally— but rarely (D. W. Fiske & Fogg, 1990)—reviewers will make contradictory recommendations; in such a case, the editor will normally provide some advice. To the extent possible, you should incorporate the reviewers' and the editor's comments into your revision of the manuscript: They are experts, so their advice will almost always improve the manuscript. However, you should also bear two points in mind. First, it is *your* manuscript; if you strongly believe your way of doing something is better than the way the reviewers recommended, then you can stick with it. However, you must weigh the possible cost of noncompliance—rejection of the manuscript—against the advantage to be gained by doing things your way. Second, sometimes reviewers are just plain wrong. If you are sure you are right and have evidence to support your way of doing things, stick with it, but explain your decision and the reasons for it to the editor when you return the revised manuscript.

When you return the revised manuscript to the editor, whether in response to an acceptance contingent on revision or a revise-and-resubmit decision, include a letter specifying the changes you have made. Note each change, the page in the revised manuscript on which it occurs, and the reviewer (usually designated by a letter) who suggested the change. When reviewers number their comments, you should also refer to the comment number. If you decide not to make a recommended change, fully explain the reason for your decision, citing any evidence you have to back it up. For example, if a reviewer said that a statistical analysis was performed incorrectly, you could cite a statistics book that supports the way you did it.

If the original decision on your manuscript was to accept contingent on revisions, either the editor may accept the revised manuscript based on the revisions you made and your explanation of them, or the editor may send it back to the original reviewers for further comment. Additional revisions may be recommended. As noted earlier, a revised and resubmitted manuscript is treated as if it were a new submission. The editor may send it back to the original reviewers, may use new reviewers, or may use a combination of old and new reviewers. This cycle of submission, review, resubmission, and new review can go on for some time, although many journals allow only one resubmission of a manuscript.

AFTER ACCEPTANCE   Once the editor receives the manuscript in its final form, it is sent to the publisher of the journal. The publisher may be either a professional association or a commercial publishing house. At the publisher the **production editor** for the journal schedules the manuscript for publication in a particular issue of the journal and sends a copy of the manuscript to a **copy editor.** The copy editor checks the manuscript for proper spelling, grammar, and punctuation, makes note of any ambiguities, and puts the manuscript into the journal's publication format. The production editor will then ask the authors to clear up any ambiguities noted by the copy editor, such as a work's having one date when cited in the text of the manuscript and a different date in the reference list. Respond promptly to these queries because you and the production editor are now working against a deadline to get the issue of the journal published on time.

The copyedited manuscript is sent to the printer, who sets it in type and sends you **page proofs.** The page proofs are a facsimile of how the article will look in print. *Check the proofs carefully:* Typesetters make errors, even to the point of omitting entire paragraphs (that has happened to me twice); don't forget to check the tables and the reference list. Many journals now require authors to send a computer disk containing a word-processor file of the article along with the final version of the manuscript. The copy editor's changes are entered into the electronic version of the manuscript, which is then sent to the printer for computerized typesetting. Even when computerized typesetting is used, be sure to check your page proofs carefully — the word-processing file you send is changed at both the copyediting and typesetting stages, so errors can still sometimes creep in. Correct any errors by following the instructions that come with the page proofs and return the corrected proofs by the stated deadline (usually 2 days). The next time you see your article it will be as part of the journal. This will occur anywhere from 12 to 24 months after your original submission of the manuscript. There are, however, exceptions. For example, if your article is on a topic that is the theme of a special issue of the journal, then the editor might advance the publication of the article so that it can be part of the special issue.

To get a feel for the publication process, you might want to read Cummings and Frost's (1985) chapter 28, which contains the case histories of two manuscripts (one that was accepted for publication and one that was rejected) and includes the texts of the manuscripts, the correspondence between author and editor, reviewers' comments, the authors' responses to those comments, and the copy editor's comments and queries on the accepted manuscript. It also includes reflections by the authors and the editor on the manuscript review and publication processes.

DEALING WITH REJECTION   I have never known a researcher who has not had a manuscript rejected by a journal, and the more experience researchers have, the more rejections they have received. For example, Robert Douglas (1992), a much-published and much-cited psychologist, estimates that he has had three rejections for every published manuscript. Therefore, here is a little advice on dealing with rejection. First, don't take it personally. Unfortunately, not all reviewers are tactful in their comments and a few are downright nasty. Even tactful, constructive criticism can be a disappointment when you have put a lot of work into what you and your colleagues thought was a good manuscript. However, remember that it's your manuscript, not you, that the reviewers didn't like, and you may be able to improve the manuscript. That thought brings us to our second point: Don't be overly pessimistic about a rejection; just because one journal didn't want your article doesn't mean that another won't. After receiving a rejection letter, wait a few days to get over your disappointment and then look at your manuscript in the light of the reviewers' comments. You will often find you can revise the manuscript and submit it, much improved, to another journal; this will be especially true if you find the problem is with the presentation of the information rather than with the content. Almost all the research I have written up has been published, albeit after several rejections and revisions in some cases. In fact, after I have written up a piece of research, I make up a list of potential journals to send it to, rank ordered by preference. If one journal rejects the article and I think it's salvageable, I revise it and send it to the next. However, as Sternberg (1993) says, "If your article is being rejected across the board, you need at least to consider the possibility that you don't need to go to the supermarket for your next turkey" (p. 180). I've had a few of those, too.

Convention Presentations

Journal publication is a slow process; researchers often want a faster means for communicating the results of their research. Professional meetings or conventions provide such a means. Conventions have many purposes, one of which is the dissemination of the results of recently completed research. Let's look at the process of submitting a proposal to a convention.

THE ABSTRACT   Once a year, professional associations send out "calls for papers," requesting that their members submit proposals for presentations at the next meeting. Nonmembers can usually also submit proposals under the sponsorship of a member. For research reports, the proposal takes the form of a long abstract that summarizes the research and is divided into the same four sections as a journal article. Each convention has its own format for the abstract and imposes a limit on its length, usually between 400 and 1,000 words. This length limitation places a premium on the authors' being able to describe their research succinctly yet clearly. Like journal submissions, convention abstracts are usually peer reviewed. However, the proposal is either accepted or rejected outright—there is no opportunity to revise—and the author is not told the reasons for the rejection. Conventions use these procedures because they must handle a large number of submissions in a short period of time with limited resources. If accepted, a convention paper can be presented either orally or as part of a poster session.

ORAL PRESENTATION   Oral presentations are organized into panels of researchers who present the results of research on related topics. Panel members have between 10 and 20 minutes each (depending on the policy of the convention) to present their research. Adhere strictly to these limits; if you use too much time, someone else loses time. In addition, reserve one or two minutes at the end of your talk to answer questions from the audience. When making an oral presentation, be sure to speak to your audience rather than read from a prepared script. People who read their presentations tend to slip into a monotone, thereby losing their audiences. Also, don't include references in your talk; they break up the flow of your presentation and reduce the amount of time you have for the content of your presentation. Put as much information as you can onto overhead slides and show your audience your results; don't read out long lists of numbers. Estes (1993) gives some excellent suggestions for the organization of slides. Finally, be sure to have copies of your paper, complete with all the references and numbers you left out of your talk, to give to people who want more detailed information.

POSTER SESSION   A **poster session** is a visual, rather than oral, presentation of your work. Like oral presentations, poster sessions are organized by topic. However, presenters are each given a 4- by 6-foot board on which to display the results of their research. There will be several dozen such "posters" in a room; presenters stand next to their displays and discuss their work with the members of the "audience," who walk from poster to poster. This format allows much more give-and-take between audience and presenter than does an oral presentation. The key to a successful poster is simplicity: Post an outline of each section of your report, giving only essential information, and use tables and figures to present your results. You can explain details to people when they stop by. Make sure your poster is large enough to read from a distance; you want to grab the attention of passersby who will not want to crowd together to read small print close up. Estes's (1993) advice concerning slides for oral presentations is equally pertinent to poster displays: Keep them simple and pictorial. As with an oral presentation, have copies of your complete paper to give to people who want them.

Reviewing Manuscripts

At some time in your professional career, you may be asked to be a peer reviewer for an article submitted to a journal or for abstracts submitted for a professional meeting. Such a request is especially likely if you follow an academic career and publish your own research: Editors frequently choose as reviewers people whose research is cited in the manuscript under review. This section briefly outlines the reviewer's task and discusses some considerations about writing reviews.

THE REVIEWER'S TASK   In broad terms, the reviewer's task is to provide the editor with information that will help him or her decide if the manuscript is of enough scientific value to be published. However, when one gets down to specifics, the reviewer's task can be quite detailed; Campion (1993), for example, lists 223 criteria for evaluating research articles. For present purposes, though, let's briefly consider six broad categories of criteria, organized in terms of the outline of the research article, how well the article is written, and the article's overall contribution to knowledge.

The first questions the reviewer asks concern the introduction: Does the article deal with a topic that has theoretical or applied importance? Are the research questions or hypotheses clearly stated? Does the literature review provide an adequate rationale for the questions or hypotheses; that is, is it clear how the authors arrived at them? Have the authors considered all the relevant theoretical and empirical work in developing their questions and hypotheses? Have they overlooked any important moderating or mediating variables?

When evaluating the Method section, reviewers should ask whether the design of the research and the procedures used provided an adequate test of the hypotheses or adequate answers to the research questions. Was an appropriate research setting (such as laboratory or field) and research population used? Were all the variables reliably and validly measured or manipulated? Were the necessary controls in place to avoid threats to internal validity and other confounds, and to rule out plausible alternatives to the independent variable as the cause of the outcomes that were observed?

In considering the Results section, ask if all the relevant information, such as means, standard deviations, and correlations, has been reported. Were the appropriate statistical tests used to analyze the data? Were the results of the tests correctly interpreted?

The focus in evaluating the Discussion section is on the proper interpretation of the results. Did the authors draw valid conclusions from their data, or did they make interpretations that their data do not support? Have they overlooked any important aspects of their results? Are their interpretations tempered by a reasonable consideration of the inherent limitations of the procedures they used to collect the data?

In more global terms, the reviewer must ask if the article is well written: Is it both clear and concise? Finally, does the article make an important contribution to knowledge; does what it tell us have important implications for theory and application?

WRITING THE REVIEW   Once you have answered these kinds of questions, you must write your review. The review will generally consist of two parts: a global evaluation and specific comments. In the global evaluation, the editor will ask you to rate the overall quality of the article, usually using one or more numeric rating scales. The editor will also ask you to make a recommendation about the fate of the manuscript in terms of the categories discussed earlier: accept as is, accept pending revision, revise and resubmit, or reject.

In addition, the editor will want you to provide a narrative evaluation consisting of your perceptions of the manuscript's strengths and weaknesses. In writing this section, bear four considerations in mind. First, be tactful; if you think that the authors have made a mistake, point it out as gently as possible. Treat them the way you would like to be treated under the same circumstances. Second, be even-handed, pointing out the things the authors did well as well as mentioning the manuscript's shortcomings. Too often in evaluating others' work, reviewers focus on the weaknesses and overlook the strengths. Remember that, of necessity, every piece of research will have limitations; the critical question is whether the strengths of the research outweigh those limitations. Third, be constructive. If you find a problem with the research, can it be remedied? If so, how? An important function of the review process is to help researchers improve their research. Finally, be fair in your review; try to evaluate the research on its merits even if it challenges your own work or a theory you favor. Fairness in reviewing also includes competence: If you think you do not have the proper background to do a good job of evaluating the manuscript, you shouldn't. If for any reason you feel you are not an appropriate choice as a reviewer, promptly contact the editor so that she or he can find another reviewer.

ETHICAL ISSUES IN PUBLICATION

Within the scientific community, publication, especially in the form of journal articles, increases people's reputations and, frequently, their employability. In general, the greater the number of publications and the better the reputation of the journals in which you publish, the more positive is the effect on your reputation. Because publication is a route to rewards in science, ethical issues arise concerning the fair allocation of those rewards in terms of assigning credit for the work and improper inflation of publication records.

Authorship Credit

Listing someone as an author on a publication or convention paper is a statement that the person made a significant scientific contribution to the research. The order in which the authors are listed implies the degree of their contribution: The greater the contribution, the higher the person comes in the list; being the first or sole author of a publication carries the greatest prestige. Consequently, the question of whether or not a person receives authorship credit and the order of authorship raise the issue of the fair allocation of credit for the work. Authorship disputes are the most common of the ethical controversies in publication (Keith-Spiegel & Koocher, 1985). The assignment of authorship credit may be a special problem when students and faculty members work jointly on a research project because of the greater power of the faculty member (Fine & Kurdek, 1993).

Because of the potential problems in authorship credit, the APA (1992, 1994) has issued specific guidelines concerning the assignment of credit. Authorship is reserved for those who have made "substantial scientific contributions" to the research; knowledge in a footnote people who make contributions to the research project that are not substantial enough to warrant authorship credit. Box 17-10 lists some of the research activities that the APA (1994) recognizes as deserving of authorship credit and those that are more properly recognized by acknowledgment. However, the activities listed in Box 17-10 are only guidelines; on occasion, one of the activities listed in the acknowledgment section of Box 17-10 is sufficiently important to the research to deserve authorship credit.

BOX 17-10   Examples of Research Activities Deserving of Authorship Credit and Footnote Acknowledgment

Activities deserving of authorship	Activities deserving footnote acknowledgment
Formulating the problem or hypothesis	Designing or building apparatus
Organizing and conducting the statistical analysis	Advising on the statistical analysis
Interpreting the results	Running the statistical analysis under the direction of another
Writing a major portion of the paper	Collecting the data
Source: Adapted from APA, 1994, pp. 294–295.	Modifying or structuring a computer program
	Arranging for research participants

Because a number of disputes have arisen over the proper order of authorship of publications based on doctoral dissertations, the APA has issued specific authorship guidelines for this situation:

1. Only second authorship is acceptable for the dissertation supervisor.
2. Second authorship may be considered *obligatory* if the supervisor designates the primary variables or makes major interpretative contributions or provides the data base.
3. Second authorship is a courtesy if the supervisor designates the general area of concern or is substantially involved in the development of the design and measurement procedures or substantially contributes to the write-up of the published report.
4. Second authorship is *not* acceptable if the supervisor provides only encouragement, physical facilities, financial support, or editorial contributions.
5. In all instances, agreements should be reviewed before the writing for publication is undertaken and at the time of submission. If disagreements arise, they should be resolved by a third party. (quoted in Keith-Spiegel & Koocher, 1985, p. 354)

The current APA ethical code (1992) implicitly extends these guidelines to master's theses. However, because the thesis adviser often has a much greater level of input into a thesis project than a dissertation adviser has into a dissertation project, first authorship may sometimes be appropriate for the faculty member. In such cases, the faculty member's first authorship should have the full and free agreement of the student.

Whenever two or more researchers work together on a project, it is always best to discuss authorship credit early on in the project and work out an agreement. When researchers deserve equal credit, it is common to list them randomly or alphabetically and to explain that procedure in a footnote. When a long-term project results in a series of publications, order of authorship can be rotated among those making equal contributions.

Plagiarism

Plagiarism is the act of taking someone else's work or ideas and passing them off as one's own. Plagiarism in the form of the misappropriation of someone's written work is a violation of copyright law and the aggrieved party can, under some circumstances, sue for damages. Ideas are not protected by law, but "intellectual theft" is unethical and ruinous to the reputation of anyone caught at it. Although a few cases of plagiarism involve outright copying, most result from an author's careless failure to cite the source of a quotation or idea (Koocher & Keith-Spiegel, 1998). Consequently, the best way to avoid plagiarism is to keep careful track of the sources of any information or ideas you use and credit the source when you publish work based on that information or those ideas. Such careful tracking of sources is important because people often do not recall the sources of information they use and so inadvertently attribute others' ideas to themselves (A. S. Brown & Murphy, 1989). People who act as peer reviewers must be especially careful not to accidentally appropriate ideas from the manuscripts they review (Sigma Xi, 1986). Because people review manuscripts that deal with their areas of expertise, it can be easy for them to confuse ideas read in manuscripts they reviewed with ideas of their own.

The plagiarism issue is complicated somewhat by what is known as the "fair use" doctrine: People can use copyrighted material in a reasonable manner without the permission of the copyright holder. "Reasonable manner" is usually considered to be the *limited* use of *short* quotations from a work if that work is properly cited. Long quotations, or a large number of short quotations from a single source, require permission from the copyright holder, as does the reproduction of tables and figures. Extensive paraphrasing of another's work with the addition of original material (such as comments on the work) is a violation of the fair use doctrine even if the source is cited. See Koocher & Keith-Speigel (1998) for a fuller discussion of these issues with examples.

Multiple Publication

The correlation between one's reputation as a scientist and the number of publications one has can lead to the temptation to publish the same work in different journals. Such multiple publication is unethical because it distorts the scientific knowledge base by making it appear there is more information available on the topic of the research than really exists (APA, 1994). However, there are three exceptions to the prohibition against multiple publication. First, it is quite proper to present a study at a convention and publish it in a journal later. Convention papers receive limited distribution, so subsequent journal publication, which will reach a wider interested audience, is in the best interest of science. The second exception is taking a technical article and rewriting it for publication in a nontechnical outlet. For example, a group of educational psychologists might want to communicate the results of their research to both psychologists and teachers. However, the information needs of the two audiences differ, as do their technical backgrounds, so two forms of publication are appropriate. Finally, sometimes editors will ask an author to write up a report of previously published material for their journals because they think the information will be useful to their readers, who may not have had access to the original publication. Whenever a study is published twice, however, the prior publication should be made clear to the editor and acknowledged in the article.

Another form of multiple publication is taking the data from a single study and breaking it into pieces in order to increase the number of resulting publications. This procedure is also improper because it makes it difficult for readers to get a clear and complete picture of the research and to evaluate its validity as a whole (APA, 1994). There are also a few exceptions to this rule. One is when the data for two separate studies are collected simultaneously, for example, as part of a large survey. Because the two sets of data concern separate hypotheses, it is proper to report them separately. A second exception is when an old data set is reanalyzed to test new hypotheses; however, the author should explicitly state that the study is based on previously published data and cite the original publication. Third, the results of long-term studies might be published incrementally so that other researchers know what progress is being made, and the results of a very complex study or set of studies might be easier to assimilate if published incrementally. Finally, sometimes an editor will want to publish only one part of a complex study. The remaining data can then be the basis of another article and submitted to a different journal. Under any of these circumstances, one should always cite previously published related work and indicate how the new study fits into the overall program of research.

SUMMARY

Three aspects of communicating the results of research are the research report, reporting research in journal articles and convention presentations, and ethical issues. The research report is divided into an introduction and three primary sections: Method, Results, and Discussion. When preparing a research report, write so that it clearly presents the most important results of your research in a way that any educated person can understand and that projects a scientific image of yourself and your work.

The introduction tells the reader what the study is about and why it was conducted. Start with a strong opening statement, logically develop the background of the hypothesis, and conclude with a clear statement of the hypothesis. The literature review portion of the introduction develops the hypothesis and must meet five criteria: It must be current, focused on the topic, complete, concise, and accurate. The literature review should also clearly indicate what your study will add to what is already known about the research question and why your study is important. The Method section tells the reader how you carried out your study. It often begins with an overview of the design and then describes the important characteristics of the research participants. Next, it describes the apparatus or materials used in the research and the procedures used to collect the data. It concludes with a discussion of any ethical issues important to the research and the safeguards used to protect participants.

The Results section reports the outcome of the research. For each set of results, report the data used to test the hypothesis, the design used to analyze the data, the expected outcome, the results of the statistical test, and a narrative description of those results. When your results are complex, present them in tables or figures. In the Discussion section, you interpret your results in terms of how they relate to theory and prior research, describe applications of the results, and describe further research that needs to be done on the research question. Also discuss possible alternative explanations for your results and any limitations of your research. The title and abstract describe and summarize your report for potential readers.

When writing for nonresearchers, you must first establish your credibility as a person who is familiar with the day-to-day problems in the practitioner's field. You must also report the research in a manner that focuses on variables of importance to practitioners and facilitates application of the principles tested in the research. Report statistics in terms familiar to the practitioner and carefully interpret them, to avoid misunderstandings. Finally, make clear recommendations for action.

When submitting a research report for publication in a professional journal, choose a journal appropriate to the topic of your research and prepare the manuscript according to the journal's requirements. The journal's editor will send the manuscript to reviewers who will evaluate its theory, methods, and clarity. If the journal accepts your manuscript pending revision or encourages you to revise and resubmit it, carefully consider the editor's and reviewers' comments and make any necessary changes. Once the article is accepted, answer all the copy editor's queries and carefully check and correct the page proofs. If your article is not accepted, consider whether it can be revised and submitted to another journal. Proposed convention presentations are evaluated on the basis of a long abstract. Presentations can be in the form of a talk or part of a poster session. When acting as a peer reviewer, do a complete review, covering all aspects of the manuscript. Also, strive to be tactful, evenhanded, constructive, and fair in writing the review.

Three ethical issues are important in professional writing. The first is fair allocation of authorship credit based on each person's scientific contribution to the work. The second issue is plagiarism; avoid it by carefully citing the sources of all information and ideas based on others' work. The third issue is multiple publications based on the same data; the practice is unacceptable under most circumstances.

QUESTIONS AND EXERCISES FOR REVIEW

1. Describe the structure of the research report.
2. Describe the factors to consider in answering these three questions that are preliminary to writing a research report: Which report should I write? For whom should I write? How should I write?
3. For the introduction and each of the three main sections of the research report,
   a. Describe the information that goes into it.
   b. Describe the common errors that peer reviewers find in it.
4. What criteria are used to evaluate the literature review portion of the introduction to the research report?
5. Into which subsections can the Method section of the research report be divided? Which subsections are required and which are optional?
6. What types of results can be included in a research report? In what order are they normally reported? What information should be reported for each hypothesis tested?

7. What are the characteristics of a good title? of a good abstract?
8. What factors should you take into account when writing for nonresearchers?
9. Describe the process by which a research report becomes published as a journal article.
10. How is a research report evaluated for presentation at a convention? Describe the convention presentation formats.
11. Describe the job of the peer reviewer: What does the reviewer look for in a manuscript, and how should the review be written?
12. Explain each of these three ethical issues in publication: authorship credit, plagiarism, and multiple publication.

18 THE PROFESSIONAL AND SOCIAL RESPONSIBILITIES OF SCIENTISTS

MALPRACTICE IN RESEARCH
Forms of Scientific Malpractice
   Data Forging
   Data Cooking
   Data Trimming
   Data Torturing
The Extent of the Problem
Motivations for Scientific
   Malpractice
   Personal Factors
   Institutional Factors
Problems of Detection and
   Enforcement
   Detection
   Enforcement
"Quis Custodiet Ipsos
   Custodes?"

MISTAKES AND ERRORS IN
RESEARCH
Consequences of Error
   Harm to Research
     Participants
   Harm to Science
   Harm to the Public

Sources of Culpable Error
   Incompetence
   Negligence
Correcting Mistakes and Errors

USING THE RESULTS OF
RESEARCH
The Application of Research
   Results
   Exploitation
   Wasting Resources
   Overgeneralization
   Failure to Apply Research
Influencing Decision Makers
   The Societal Mentor
   The Social Activist
   The Limits of Behavioral
     Science Knowledge
   The Expert Witness

Researchers' Responsibilities
   Conducting Research
   Reporting Research
   Societal Mentoring and Social
     Activism
   Monitoring the Use of Science
   Encouraging the Application
     of Research

RESEARCH AND THE COMMON
GOOD
Is Applied Research More Ethical
   Than Basic Research?
Should Research on Some Topics
   Be Banned or Restricted?
Is There an Ethical Obligation to
   Conduct Research?

SUMMARY

QUESTIONS AND EXERCISES
FOR REVIEW

The ethical responsibilities of scientists who conduct behavioral science research can be divided into two broad categories. The first category, discussed in Chapter 3, is our responsibilities for the welfare of research participants. The second category, which is the topic of this chapter, is our responsibilities to science as an institution and to society as a whole. This discussion of the professional and social responsibilities of scientists focuses on four issues: malpractice in conducting research, conducting valid research, the proper use of research results, and research and the common good.

MALPRACTICE IN RESEARCH

The term *scientist* calls up an image of someone who works to develop knowledge for the sake of knowledge or to develop knowledge to cure the ills of the world without giving thought to fame or fortune. Because these scientists are seekers after truth, they hold themselves to high standards of honesty: True knowledge is found only through rigorous and disinterested research. To some extent, of course, this stereotype portrays the scientist as better than human and motivated (unlike other people) only by pure goals and thus uncorrupted and incorruptible by worldly vices. But the average scientist is not necessarily morally different from the average person and so can be corrupted by visions of fame and fortune. Also like people in general, scientists can fall victim to wishful thinking and come to see their theories as more representative of the truth than their data would actually suggest. Both of these processes can tempt the scientist into improper research practices. Although these practices are often labeled "fraud" or "dishonesty," I prefer the term **scientific malpractice** because, like other forms of malpractice, it can stem not only from intentionally dishonest behavior, but also from wishful thinking and lack of competence. This section looks at some of the forms scientific malpractice can take, examines some of the factors that can motivate such behavior, considers the problems in detecting scientific malpractice and enforcing standards of research practice, and concludes with a question: Who will stand guardian of proper scientific behavior?

Forms of Scientific Malpractice

Malpractice in science is not a modern phenomenon. Broad and Wade (1982) list cases of suspected and documented malpractice among scientists—including such icons as Galileo, Newton, and Mendel—dating back to the second century B.C. As long ago as 1830, the English mathematician, scientist, and philosopher Charles Babbage (1830/1989) cataloged the three basic forms of scientific malpractice: data forging, data cooking, and data trimming. To these, J. L. Mills (1993) has added a fourth, data torturing. Let's consider each of these.

DATA FORGING   Data forgery consists of inventing data, of reporting the results of experiments that were never conducted. Because the forger collects no data, forging is clearly a form of fraud and intentional dishonesty. Consider the case of psychologist Stephen Breuning (R. Bell, 1992). Over a period of years, Breuning published research that purportedly tested the effectiveness of drug treatments for self-destructive mentally retarded children. These children have little voluntary control over their behavior, which often takes self-injurious forms such as continuously beating their heads against walls. The cause of these disorders is unknown, and treatment consists of either physical restraint or the prescription of strong tranquilizers to prevent self-injury. Breuning's research purportedly showed that the use of tranquilizers was not only ineffective, but also harmful: According to Breuning's reports, side effects were more severe than believed and children who were taken off the tranquilizers showed impressive IQ gains. In addition, Breuning published data that purportedly showed that stimulants were more effective than tranquilizers in controlling the children's behavior. However, investigations begun in 1983 revealed that almost none of the studies Breuning claimed to have conducted were actually carried out and that most of the data from other studies were fabricated. Breuning's record revealed "a chronic career of doctored research results and reports of research that was not carried out" (Holden, 1987, p. 1566). Although other researchers could not replicate Breuning's results (E. Garfield & Welljams-Dorof, 1990), his spurious "findings" received widespread publicity and resulted in at least one state's changing its policies regarding the use of drugs to treat mentally retarded children (R. Bell, 1992; Holden, 1987).

DATA COOKING   Data cooking consists of discarding data that don't support a study's hypothesis so that the study produces "better" results. Although it is reasonable to eliminate data from analysis when there is evidence that the data are invalid—such as when a piece of apparatus malfunctions, when a research participant doesn't follow instructions, or when a participant is suspicious of a deception—data should not be discarded simply because they do not fit the predictions the hypothesis made. An example of inappropriate data discarding in psychology can be found in the early days of research on cognitive dissonance theory. In a critique of that research, Chapanis and Chapanis (1964) pointed out that cognitive dissonance researchers had discarded data from as many as 82% of the participants in their studies, apparently because their responses to the independent variable did not fit the predictions the theory made. Chapanis and Chapanis concluded that some cognitive dissonance researchers considered inspection of the results to be sufficient to determine whether participants were or were not to be included in the data analysis. As they go on to point out,

> Unfortunately, this line of reasoning contains one fundamental flaw: *It does not allow the possibility that the null hypothesis may be correct.* The experimenter, in effect, is asserting that his dissonance prediction is correct and that the subjects who do not conform to the prediction should be excluded from the analysis. This is a foolproof method of guaranteeing positive results. (Chapanis & Chapanis, 1964, pp. 16–17; emphasis in original)

Subsequently, more rigorous research has validated most of the postulates of cognitive dissonance theory; however, it has also shown that much of what the early researchers considered "bad" data was the result of moderating variables (J. Cooper & Fazio, 1984). However, discarding these data made it impossible for them to discover those moderators.

DATA TRIMMING   **Data trimming** consists of changing data values so that they better fit the predictions made by the research hypothesis. Sir Cyril Burt, a pioneering educational psychologist, was accused posthumously of both forging and trimming IQ data to fit his theories concerning the heritability of intelligence (Hearnshaw, 1979). These accusations came about because the results he reported literally seemed too good to be true — the small random fluctuations in results normally found from study to study in behavioral science research were almost nonexistent.

DATA TORTURING   **Data torturing** is the improper exploitation of statistical tests: repeatedly analyzing the same data in different ways until something — anything — statistically significant emerges. This kind of repeated statistical testing of the same data is problematic because the more statistical tests that are conducted on a data set, the more likely that a chance relationship will be statistically significant (J. L. Mills, 1993). The researcher then reports only the statistically significant result, writing the research report so that the hypothesis predicts the (possibly random) significant result. Data torturing is hard to detect because the data are not altered in any way and because the torturing process is not reported in the research report. It may appear that calling data torturing a form of scientific malpractice is inconsistent with the advice given by D. J. Bem (1987) to report the most interesting findings of a study even if they weren't the results originally predicted. The search for unexpected findings is a legitimate part of scientific research. However, the results of such searches should be reported as after-the-fact findings, not as stemming from a priori hypotheses, and such findings should be replicated before being reported to reduce the likelihood that they represent chance, rather than real, relationships.

The Extent of the Problem

How big a problem is scientific malpractice? There is no way to answer this question accurately. As Bechtel and Pearson (1985) note, "Determining the amount of scientific fraud is like measuring the frequency of crime in society; only those crimes reported and recorded are counted" (p. 238). In this regard, reports of scientific misconduct have been increasing since the mid-1970s (R. Bell, 1992; Committee on Government Operations, 1990). However, there is no way to know whether the increased number of reports reflects an increased rate of misconduct or an increased rate of detection given the closer scrutiny that Congress has been giving to the ways in which the government funds research and the ways in which that money is spent. In contrast, a survey of faculty and graduate students in chemistry, civil engineering, microbiology, and sociology found that 7% of the respondents knew of at least one incident of research malpractice by a faculty member and that 15% knew of at least one incident by a graduate student during the 5 years preceding the survey (Swazey, Anderson, & Lewis, 1993). When one looks at behavioral science, the only data on the prevalence of scientific malpractice are subjective: The respondents to a survey of research psychologists conducted by Riordan and Marlin (1987) thought such incidents were rare.

Motivations for Scientific Malpractice

Bechtel and Pearson (1985) note that almost all the scientists who have been found to have committed malpractice

> share a common profile. All were male and white [with one exception]. . . . The average age was the middle to late thirties with the youngest and oldest being . . . ages 24 and 55. . . . The act most commonly perpetrated was some form of data manipulation, either the fabrication of non-existent results or fudging procedures to produce a desired outcome. Also, the institutions in which they were conducting their research are among the most prestigious universities and medical centers in the world. (p. 242)

Why do these successful scientists engage in malpractice? People who have studied the problem suggest that it stems from a combination of personal motivations of the scientists involved and flaws in science as a social institution.

PERSONAL FACTORS   The explanation most commonly given for scientific malpractice is mental aberration (Bechtel & Pearson, 1985; Broad & Wade, 1982). That is, the deviant scientist is seen by peers as mentally unstable, usually because of work pressures or stress; this is also the excuse most commonly offered by those caught committing research fraud. Rousseau (1992) also notes that some cases of malpractice could stem from a loss of objectivity: Researchers become so convinced their theories are correct that they assume any contradictory data must be wrong. They therefore "correct" the data to fit the theory.

INSTITUTIONAL FACTORS   Although it is convenient to blame the personality of the deviant for his or her deviance, such a "bad person" approach to the problem deflects attention from the social institutions in which the behavior takes place, in this case the institution of science (Bechtel & Pearson, 1985). Writing in the context of biomedical research, Bechtel and Pearson point out that professional schools, especially in medicine, foster a spirit of competition among students, rewarding only successful research projects and labeling as failures students whose hypotheses are not supported. This intellectual environment socializes students into believing that success, even fraudulent success, is more important than the proper practice of science. For professional researchers, success is the road to advancement, with success again being defined in terms of confirmed hypotheses. Much research, especially in the biomedical field, is expensive to conduct, and the grants that support research are contingent on continued success in finding the results that one predicts. Finally, a successful research career can be the road to fame and fortune: pay raises, speaking fees, consulting fees, book contracts, and perhaps even the Nobel Prize. It may be noteworthy that the most notorious cases of research malpractice have come from fields in which Nobel Prizes are awarded: medicine, chemistry, and physics.

Researchers in nonacademic settings may face especially strong pressures to produce the "right" results. As Adams (1985) notes in the context of evaluation research,

> Organizations might expect an evaluator to put organizational loyalty and performance as a team player above providing a candid portrayal of the evaluation findings. The evaluation unit might be expected to perform a "public relations" function—to promote and defend the organization—rather than to view it impartially. (p. 54)

Similarly, researchers working for pharmaceutical companies might feel pressured to produce "good" results—high effectiveness and minimal side effects—when evaluating a new drug awaiting approval by the Food and Drug Administration (R. Bell, 1992).

Broad and Wade (1982) also point out that much of the day-to-day labor on research projects is carried out by people they call "hired hands": research assistants and graduate students who are paid to conduct experiments, but who have little or no say in the design of the research. Consequently, they have no psychological investment in the research process and may be willing to fraudulently manipulate data to provide their employers with the results they want, thereby protecting their own jobs. Even when research assistants want to conduct research properly, their supervisors might encourage or require them to commit malpractice (Goodyear, Crego, & Johnston, 1992). As Goodyear et al. point out, these actions expose the research assistants to poor role models and the risk of having their reputations tainted: If the malpractice is exposed, the assistant may be held to be equally as or more culpable than the supervisor.

Problems of Detection and Enforcement

One reason why hard data on the prevalence of scientific malpractice are unavailable is that instances of malpractice are hard to detect and document. In addition, people may be reluctant to take action when they suspect malpractice has taken place.

DETECTION The scientific establishment holds that replication is a key safeguard against misconduct and an important tool for detecting it (Broad & Wade, 1982), but as Chapter 4 noted, behavioral scientists rarely conduct exact replications. Even when an attempted replication fails to confirm a finding, that failure to replicate provides ambiguous information at best: There is no way to know whether the results of the original research or those of the replication are erroneous. Scientists are likely to become suspicious of the validity of a finding only after repeated failures to replicate it. However, even a series of failed replications is not necessarily evidence of malpractice: The original results could have been a Type I error. In addition, as P. J. Friedman (1992) points out, malpractice does not necessarily lead to erroneous conclusions about the relationship between two variables: Forged, cooked, trimmed, or tortured data could reflect reality. In such a case, one would expect attempted replications to be successful and therefore not lead to suspicions about the original data. Despite the shortcomings of replication as a means of detecting malpractice, St James-Roberts (1976) noted that 26% of the cases of malpractice known to the respondents in a survey that he conducted were detected through failures to replicate.

However, St James-Roberts (1976) found that people most commonly came to suspect malpractice because of suspicious data: The data claimed by the researchers were simply too good to be true. In 33% of the cases, the data reported by the researcher fit the predictions made by the hypothesis much better than real data possibly could have done. It was, in fact, such "too good to be true" data that led to Breuning's downfall (Roman, 1988). A final way in which research malpractice comes to light is through guilt, often on the part of research assistants rather than the person in charge of the research, brought on by the possibility that falsified research results would lead to ineffective or dangerous treatments being applied to medical patients (Broad & Wade, 1982).

The problems of detection are complicated by the fact that even when malpractice is suspected, it may be very difficult to prove or disprove because the evidence can be ambiguous. Consider, for example, the case of Sir Cyril Burt, who, as noted earlier, was accused of both forging and trimming data on the heritability of intelligence. The original accusations were made by a British newspaper reporter and elaborated on by Hearnshaw (1979), who concluded that Burt was guilty of fraud. Hearnshaw's conclusions were accepted by most scientists because he was an admirer of Burt and, as he notes in his book, he initially expected to find evidence that would support Burt. However, ten years after the publication of Hearnshaw's book, Joynson (1989) uncovered evidence that refuted many of Hearnshaw's conclusions. Consequently, many observers now believe that although much of Burt's data is invalid, that invalidity stems more from the poor state of behavioral science research technology at the time he collected his data (the 1920s and 1930s) than from malpractice. See Green (1992) for a summary of Hearnshaw's and Joynson's views on Burt.

ENFORCEMENT   Even when research malpractice is detected, people may be reluctant to take action. One reason for this reluctance may be embarrassment over having to accuse a colleague of fraud. For example, a Nobel laureate in biology, Peter Medawar, was shown a rabbit that had supposedly received grafts of the corneas of its eyes. Broad and Wade (1982) quote his description of his reaction to the rabbit:

> I could not believe that this rabbit had received a graft of any kind, not so much because of the perfect transparency of the cornea as because the pattern of blood vessels in the ring around the cornea was in no way disturbed. Nevertheless, I simply lacked the moral courage to say at the time that I thought we were the victims of a hoax or confidence trick. (p. 155)

If even an eminent scientist is reluctant to make an accusation of fraud when presented with clear-cut evidence, it is unlikely that less professionally secure people will do so.

When credible accusations are made, administrators at the institutions at which the research took place have rarely been willing to conduct proper investigations of the charges (Committee on Government Operations, 1990). The usual administrative response has been to deny everything and to stonewall any outside attempts at investigation. Administrators have often appeared to be more interested in protecting the reputations of their institutions and protecting their eligibility for future grant money than in determining and revealing the truth. Even government agencies, such as the National Institutes of Health (NIH), may have stifled investigations of research fraud in the grants they administer in order to protect their institutional images (Committee on Government Operations, 1990).

Adding to these problems is the fact that even if someone is detected at research fraud and admits it, he is unlikely to be punished severely. At most, he will be asked to resign; more commonly, he will simply be told to behave himself in the future (Broad & Wade, 1982). As one Congressional committee concluded concerning the Stephen Breuning case, "The University of Pittsburgh Medical School [where Breuning was working at the time his fraud was discovered] conducted an inadequate investigation of Dr. Breuning and then allowed him to resign and continue his career, thus endangering the medical treatment of retarded children" (Committee on Government Operations, 1990, p. 13). As P. J. Friedman (1992) notes, such lack of punishment reinforces deviant behavior and sends a message to others that they can get away with malpractice. In the long run, however, Breuning's punishment was more severe: He pleaded guilty to fraud in federal court, was fined $11,352, was sentenced to 60 days in a halfway house and ordered to perform 250 hours of community service, and was banned from psychological research for 5 years (Committee on Government Operations, 1990). In addition, the University of Pittsburgh was required to pay back $163,000 in grant money awarded to Breuning for the research he fabricated.

A final problem in detecting fraud and enforcing ethical standards is that people who report fraud are more often punished than rewarded (Broad & Wade, 1982; Committee on Government Operations, 1990). For example, Dr. Robert Sprague, who detected and reported Breuning's fraud, had his research funds cut by NIH and was threatened with a lawsuit by the University of Pittsburgh (Committee on Government Operations, 1990). Whistle-blowers who worked at the institution where the frauds they reported took place have been fired (Broad & Wade, 1982). Such consequences are hardly likely to encourage the reporting of malpractice.

"Quis Custodiet Ipsos Custodes?"

"Who will watch the watchmen?" asked the Roman orator Cicero when the Praetorian Guard was accused of corruption. Revelations of research fraud raise a similar question: Who will watch us, the scientists, to ensure that we act honestly? Science is by nature often a solitary pursuit, so we must each watch ourselves, we must develop a sense of honor, a personal moral code that eschews dishonesty in research (Sigma Xi, 1986). As the authors of the Sigma Xi report on integrity in science point out, science is based on trust: We trust other scientists to conduct their research properly so that we can use their results in our own research and applications. We also hold the public good in trust: Technological progress takes place because the general public, who do not have the expertise to make independent judgments of the quality of scientific research, trust us, as scientists, not to mislead them. As Broad and Wade (1982) note, "No matter how small the percentage of scientists who might be fakers of data, it takes only one case to surface . . . for the public credibility of science to be severely damaged" (p. 12).

MISTAKES AND ERRORS IN RESEARCH

The discussion so far has focused on malpractice in research and the harm it can cause. Research that is poorly conducted can also cause harm; consequently, researchers have an ethical obligation to conduct valid research (Sieber, 1992). Mistakes are a normal part of science: "For the research scientist, every hypothesis is a new problem, a new opportunity to make mistakes" (P. J. Friedman, 1992, p. 18). In the behavioral sciences we freely acknowledge the possibility of making mistakes in the conclusions we draw in the form of statistical tests, which tell us the probability of our having made Type I and Type II errors. Such mistakes are unavoidable, deriving inevitably from our use of samples rather than entire populations to test hypotheses. Although we will sometimes draw mistaken conclusions because of sampling and measurement error, we have an obligation to take all the precautions we can to minimize the influences of other sources of error. Scientists guard against mistakes by using systematic research methods that are designed to prevent errors and by checking their results. These checks take the form of replication and of exposing the results of research to the critical review of peers through oral presentations, electronic mail discussion groups, and formal publication.

Mistakes, which are blameless, must be distinguished from culpable error, which is ethically unacceptable. P. J. Friedman (1992) sees the line between mistake and culpable error being crossed when accepted standards for replication and confirmation are ignored. Systematic carelessness and violations of good research practices are ethical failures in scientists. This section examines three aspects of the problem of error in research: some consequences of error, sources of culpable error, and correcting mistakes and errors.

Consequences of Error

Error in research certainly demonstrates a lack of skill on the part of the researcher, but why is it unethical? As noted in Chapter 3, a basic principle of research ethics is beneficence—prevention of harm and promotion of well-being. Research that is poorly designed and executed is unethical because it can harm research participants, science, and the public (R. Rosenthal, 1994).

HARM TO RESEARCH PARTICIPANTS   Poor research has the potential of causing two types of harm to participants (Koocher & Keith-Spiegel, 1998). First, because poorly designed research cannot provide valid information, it wastes participants' time and, to the extent that it involves discomfort, causes the participants to suffer for no purpose. The justification for allowing research participants to experience discomfort is the knowledge to be gained from the research; if valid knowledge is unattainable because of poor research, the discomfort is unjustifiable and therefore unethical. Second, research that is properly designed but poorly executed could lead to direct harm to participants if carelessness on the part of experimenters leads them to overlook or not properly implement any necessary safety precautions. For example, a lazy experimenter might fail to check that electrical equipment is properly grounded, exposing participants to the threat of shock.

HARM TO SCIENCE   If the results of poor research find their way into the scientific literature, they can harm science's search for knowledge. Because researchers base their work at least partially on what others have done, the erroneous results of others' research can lead investigators down false trails, causing them to waste time and resources that they could devote to more fruitful work. Unfortunately, even when a study is discovered to be in error, it is difficult to purge the results from the scientific knowledge base and prevent others from using the study as a basis for their research. For example, Pfeifer and Snodgrass (1990) found that every year an average of five articles that were published in biomedical journals are retracted or corrected because the results they reported were partially or entirely in error. Nonetheless, researchers continue to cite these articles up to 7 years after the correction or retraction is published (Pfeifer & Snodgrass, 1990). Pfeifer and Snodgrass attribute this problem to the lack of a standard method for listing corrections and retractions in indexes such as *Psychological Abstracts*.

HARM TO THE PUBLIC   As Keith-Spiegel and Koocher (1985) point out, when the popular media report the results of poor research, the general public accepts the results as accurate. Citing the example of a poorly designed and executed study that purportedly found a relationship between antisocial behavior and school achievement, Keith-Spiegel and Koocher (1985) note that

> the general public is unlikely to judge [research] quality and may focus only on the conclusions. Stress and fear may well be induced among readers with children who are having problems with school achievement and, almost as problematical, some teachers may believe that they have found a bizarre excuse for their inability to teach. Thus publicizing poorly formulated studies under the guise of *research* may cause widespread harm. (p. 386; emphasis in original)

Sources of Culpable Error

Culpable error can derive from two general sources: a lack of competence on the part of the researcher to design research and to analyze and interpret research data, and carelessness in carrying out research.

INCOMPETENCE   Incompetence in research is usually discussed in terms of a lack of ability to design internally valid research (for example, see Sieber, 1992). However, incompetence can take two other forms as well. Goodyear et al. (1992) identify what they call *subject matter competence* as an ethical issue: Researchers must be competent not only in the design of research but also in the subject matter area in which they are conducting research. Such competence is required for the researchers to formulate research questions of theoretical or applied value. As B. Freedman (1987) notes, "A study may be well-designed relative to its hypothesis, and therefore scientifically valid, but nonetheless be of no value . . . because the hypothesis itself is trivial or of no value" (p. 7). Research on trivial hypotheses is ethically questionable if it wastes the time of research participants and uses up resources that could be applied to testing more valuable hypotheses. The relative value of hypotheses is, to some extent, a subjective matter, but, as shown in Chapter 4, some general criteria do apply.

A third area of competence that is becoming identified as an ethical issue is competence in data analysis (P. J. Friedman, 1992; Goodyear et al., 1992). All quantitative research in the behavioral sciences uses statistical analyses to help researchers draw conclusions about the validity of their hypotheses. If the researchers carry out their statistical analyses incorrectly, such as by using a statistical technique that is inappropriate to the level of measurement of their data, they can reach erroneous conclusions. Some observers believe that the proliferation of computers and computerized data analysis has exacerbated this problem, making it easy for researchers to use complex data analysis techniques they don't fully understand, thereby increasing the risk of conducting an analysis incorrectly or of incorrectly interpreting the results. As P. J. Friedman (1992) notes, "The standard computer statistical packages . . . make it too easy for the average scientist to run inappropriate tests and get attractive numbers or graphs as results" (p. 23). This problem has led Gordon Sherman to suggest that researchers should not use computers to conduct data analyses unless they have sufficient statistical knowledge to carry out the analyses by hand; lacking that knowledge, they should consult a statistical expert who does have that level of understanding of the statistics being used (quoted in Sigma Xi, 1986).

NEGLIGENCE   Even the most competent researchers can fall into error if they carry out the research carelessly. Failure to completely analyze a theory can lead to hypotheses that are uninformative; failure to conduct an adequate literature review may lead researchers to overlook variables that must be controlled to adequately test their hypotheses; failure to completely think through research procedures can result in confounds, demand characteristics, or other sources of invalidity; and failure to check the data for accuracy can result in misleading statistical analyses. Researchers have an obligation not only to carry out these tasks correctly themselves, but also to ensure that any assistants to whom they assign these tasks also carry them out correctly. Scientists must constantly monitor their own and their assistants' work to ensure that no one falls prey to "the hope that the first superficially logical approach [to a problem] will work" (P. J. Friedman, 1992, p. 23).

Correcting Mistakes and Errors

Researchers who find mistakes or errors in their own or others' work have an obligation to correct them. Such corrections can take several forms. First, as P. J. Friedman (1992) notes, "If a theory or observation is refuted by subsequent work, either by the same investigators or a competing group, publication of the new result effectively corrects the previous error" (p. 20). In this regard, scientists have an ethical obligation not to suppress or withhold data they have collected that contradict findings they have previously published. Nonetheless, Swazey et al. (1993) found that 15% of the respondents to their survey knew of at least one case during the preceding 5 years in which researchers failed to report data that contradicted the results of their own prior research. A second form of correction takes place when researchers find a mistake or error in a study after it has been published. In such a case, the researchers should ask the journal to print a correction if the problem is in just one aspect of the research or, if the problem renders the entire study invalid, to print a retraction, notifying readers of the problem that was found (for example, see Hartlage, 1988). When readers find what appears to be an error in someone else's published research, they can write a critique of the article and submit it for publication to the journal that published the article. The critique will be reviewed like any other submission and if the reviewers and editor find it accurate and informative, it will be published (for example, see Whitley, 1992). In such instances, the authors of the article being critiqued will be afforded the opportunity of answering the criticisms (for example, Shaffer & Kerwin, 1992) and the journal's readers can judge the validity of the criticisms.

USING THE RESULTS OF RESEARCH

An important ethical question concerns the ways in which people use the results of research. Although knowledge itself is morally neutral, people can use it for either good or bad purposes. If it is used for bad purposes, the question then arises, how responsible for its misuse is the researcher who developed the knowledge? This section examines ways in which the knowledge generated by research can be misused either intentionally or unintentionally in application and in influencing decision makers, considers some of the potential harmful effects of erroneous media reports of research, and concludes by discussing researchers' responsibilities concerning the knowledge they create.

The Application of Research Results

This section looks at three ways in which psychological knowledge can be misapplied — by exploiting people, by wasting resources through ineffective treatments, and by overgeneralization — and considers the issue of whether it can be unethical *not* to apply the results of research.

EXPLOITATION   Behavioral science knowledge is used for exploitive purposes when it is used to manipulate people in ways that bring them harm or that benefit the manipulator to a greater degree than the people being manipulated (Kelman, 1965). The exploitive potential of behavioral science knowledge and the ethical implications of that potential have been long discussed by behavioral scientists (for example, see Rogers & Skinner, 1956; Diener & Crandall, 1978; Steininger, Newell, & Garcia, 1984) and have been illustrated by novelists in such works as *A Clockwork Orange* (Burgess, 1962), *Brave New World* (Huxley, 1932), and *1984* (Orwell, 1949). Although real-life misapplications of behavioral science knowledge probably never reach the extremes of their fictional counterparts, they can nonetheless be real and raise real ethical issues. For example, industrial and organizational research has developed a number of interventions that can increase the productivity and job satisfaction of workers. Although these are, in principle, desirable outcomes, the interventions that lead to them can be considered exploitive if they are implemented without the understanding of those affected and with the intention of getting more work out of people without a concomitant increase in rewards (Judd, Smith, & Kidder, 1991). This exploitive potential is one reason why unions often oppose such interventions (Schultz & Schultz, 1994).

Kelman (1965) notes that the manipulative potential of behavioral science knowledge raises a true ethical dilemma because manipulation can be used for either good or bad purposes:

On the one hand, for those of us who hold the enhancement of man's freedom of choice as a fundamental value, any manipulation of the behavior of others constitutes a violation of their essential humanity. This would be true . . . regardless of the "goodness" of the cause that this manipulation is designed to serve. . . . On the other hand, effective behavior change inevitably involves some degree of manipulation. . . . There are many situations in which all of us . . . would consider behavior change desirable: for example, childhood socialization, education, psychotherapy, racial integration, and so on. The two horns of the dilemma, then, are represented by the view that any manipulation of human behavior inherently violates a fundamental value, but that there exists no formula for so structuring an effective change situation that such manipulation is totally absent. (p. 33)

Kelman goes on to suggest that the use of behavioral science knowledge to influence others' behavior is ethical to the extent that the person being influenced can also exert influence on the person attempting to exert influence, the degree to which the influence benefits the person being influenced, and the degree to which the influence will increase the future freedom of the person being influenced. Even these criteria are somewhat problematical; for example, the influencer and the person being influenced might not agree on which outcomes constitute benefits (for example, see Fischhoff, 1990). As with all ethical dilemmas, the ultimate resolution can only be found in each individual's conscience.

WASTING RESOURCES   The issue of exploitation concerns the use of valid scientific knowledge to inappropriately control people's behavior. Conversely, you could derive a well-intended application from an incompletely validated theory and end up wasting money and resources because the theory is incorrect: The causal relationships that it proposes and that are the basis of the application do not, in fact, exist, and so the intervention is ineffective. For example, Alexander and Baker (1992) consider bilingual education to be an example of "how the education system picks up a correlation between two variables, imposes an unsupported causal theory on the correlation, derives an unsupported application of theory, and makes this fragile framework a cornerstone of policy" (p. 1742). Bilingual education programs teach children whose native language is not English in their native languages while they are learning to become fluent in English. The theory behind these programs is that learning in one's native language increases children's self-esteem by validating the importance of that language and that this leads to increased academic achievement. However, Alexander and Baker point out that there is no evidence that bilingual education affects self-esteem and no evidence that level of self-esteem causes achievement—in fact, the evidence suggests that achievement causes increases in self-esteem. Consequently, no well-designed evaluation has found that bilingual education increases academic achievement. Alexander and Baker consider the continuation of such ineffective programs to be an ethical issue because the money spent on them could be used for other programs of demonstrated effectiveness or for testing programs based on better-validated theories.

OVERGENERALIZATION   Chapter 14 discussed the problem of the generalizability of research. Generalizability becomes an ethical issue when knowledge derived from research conducted in a restricted setting is used without the replication required to test its external and ecological validity. Kimmel (1988) cites the example of a study that compared the verdicts arrived at by eight 12-person mock juries with those arrived at by eight 6-person mock juries. A U.S. Supreme Court decision that 6-person juries are acceptable under some circumstances was based in part on the findings of this research that 6-person and 12-person juries did not differ in their verdicts, in the time they took to reach their verdicts, and the number of issues discussed during deliberation. However, Kimmel (1988) notes, in presenting this research to the court, "The lack of power of statistical tests when samples are so small was not discussed, and the naive reader was not warned that such results should not be interpreted to mean that differences do not actually exist" (p. 120).

Overgeneralization is not limited to the use of research to influence policy decisions. Eyer (1992), for example, notes that the concept of mother-infant bonding was developed on the basis of findings of poor physical and psychological development in institutionalized children who were deprived of regular contact with adult caregivers. However, some scientists generalized the results to mean that too little maternal attention during a child's first year, even within a normal family context, would harm the child. Even though no research supported this generalization, it made its way into child care books, the popular press, the advice given by pediatric physicians and nurses, and even into hospital checklists for what constituted proper infant care. In addition, the widespread publicity given to the "need" for bonding induced guilt and anxiety among mothers who had to leave their infants in others' care when they went to work.

FAILURE TO APPLY RESEARCH   Although this discussion so far has focused on inappropriate application of research, many observers also point out that it can be unethical *not* to apply research when such application is warranted (for example, Diener & Crandall, 1978; Kimmel, 1988). For example, while mother-infant bonding was being heavily promoted, a great deal of well-validated information on child care was *not* being disseminated to parents (Clarke-Stewart, 1978). Failure to provide people with available benefits, while perhaps not as unethical as the doing of harm, is nonetheless an ethical failing.

Influencing Decision Makers

Reynolds (1979) notes that scientists play two roles in society. One role is that of scientist, a person who generates knowledge. The other role is that of citizen, a person who has an interest in promoting the common good as defined by his or her personal social values. In Reynolds's view, these two roles are expressed in the form of four professional philosophies regarding the role of the scientist in society. The autonomous investigator or basic researcher sees the scientist and citizen roles as independent: The scientist's role is to generate knowledge and not to worry about any implications this knowledge has for society. The applied scientist does research on topics related to social problems, but leaves to politicians and other decision makers the definition of those problems and policy decisions needed to solve them. The **societal mentor** views science as a means of providing information about societal problems: using scientific methods to identify potential problems and to generate knowledge that can be used to alleviate problems. Unlike the applied scientist, who stands somewhat apart from politics, the societal mentor engages in the political process, acting as social critic and advice giver. The **social activist** also sees a necessary connection between science and society, but advocates particular solutions to social problems based on his or her personal values. Unlike the societal mentor, who takes the role of neutral advice giver, the social activist uses the scientific process and scientific knowledge to justify solutions to social problems based on personal values. Reynolds points out that each of these philosophies has ethical implications; however, because the societal mentor and social activist directly involve themselves in the political process, let's examine some ethical implications of those roles.

THE SOCIETAL MENTOR   Taking the role of societal mentor implies that you intend to be a neutral advice giver, reviewing all the scientific evidence on both sides of an issue and pointing out the strengths and weaknesses of the evidence on each side. This role also includes pointing out which side, if any, is favored by the weight of the evidence, how strong that evidence is, and what kinds of further evidence might be needed to reach a reasonably firm decision about the course of action to take. The societal mentor will also advise decision makers that science cannot provide information on an issue when such advice is appropriate—for example, when the issue at hand is nonscientific, such as the issue of the relative value of the potential results of a decision, or when there is no available scientific information relevant to the issue.

In some cases, societal mentors act as individuals, by writing to members of Congress and to officials in the executive branch or by testifying at hearings. In other cases, the societal mentor role is institutionalized in the form of agencies established for that purpose, such as Congress's Office of Science and Technology (Saxe, 1986) or the National Research Council (see Swets & Bjork, 1990). Professional organizations can also take the role of societal mentor, such as when the American Psychological Association (APA) submits an *amicus curiae* (literally, "friend of the court") brief to an appellate court; Chapter 1 discussed some examples of these. Whenever a scientist presents him- or herself as a societal mentor, the people receiving the information will expect it to be complete, objective, and unbiased, with all the information pro and con clearly laid out and the strengths and weaknesses of the research supporting each side clearly explained; consequently, scientists taking that role have an ethical obligation to fulfill those expectations.

THE SOCIAL ACTIVIST   In contrast to the neutral societal mentor, the social activist advocates one side of an issue and uses science as a tool for gaining implementation of social policies in line with his or her personal values. In fulfilling this advocacy role, the social activist might select information to present to decision makers so that the evidence supporting the advocate's side appears more favorable than would otherwise be the case. For example, research contradicting the advocate's position might be ignored or the weaknesses of the research supporting the advocate's position might be downplayed while the weaknesses of opposing evidence might be overemphasized. To some extent, then, social activists may misrepresent the extent and quality of the research supporting their positions and thereby mislead decision makers.

The ethical status of such misrepresentations is somewhat ambiguous. On the one hand, social activists justify them on the grounds that there can be no such thing as neutral science, so that any advice anyone gives is necessarily biased. In addition, social activists deeply believe in the rightness of their positions and in the capability of research to generate knowledge demonstrating that correctness; consequently, they see themselves as doing the morally correct thing by pushing for the (in their view) morally correct policy (Diener & Crandall, 1978; Reynolds, 1979; Steininger et al., 1984). To the extent, then, that social activists present themselves as advocates for a particular position and not as neutral advisers, ethical problems may be reduced (Kendler, 1993). On the other hand, the APA (1992) code of ethics prohibits misrepresentation in any form for any purpose.

However, it *is* unethical to present oneself as a societal mentor while acting as an advocate. For example, the 1986 Attorney General's Commission on Pornography was established to review the scientific evidence on the effects of pornography and to recommend policy based on that evidence. However, some critics of the committee alleged that its membership appeared to be "stacked" with people favoring the suppression of pornography, and that the commission's official report was highly selective of the research evidence it used to support its conclusions and misrepresented the results of that research to make it appear that the research supported those conclusions more strongly than was actually the case (for example, see Linz, Donnerstein, & Penrod, 1987). Scientific organizations are not immune from the temptation to become advocates when mentoring is expected. The APA, for example, has been accused of selectively citing and misrepresenting the results of research in *amicus curiae* briefs it has submitted to the U.S. Supreme Court (Cameron & Cameron, 1988). Not only does this form of misrepresentation mislead decision makers, it may cause them to see all behavioral scientists as social activists and therefore to distrust any information they might provide (Kimble, 1989).

THE LIMITS OF BEHAVIORAL SCIENCE KNOWLEDGE   Many behavioral scientists are uncomfortable when they see colleagues taking on the social activist role because they believe activism implies that science can objectively identify the one correct social policy from a set of alternatives. That is, they see social activism as presuming that science can identify the morally correct course of action (Kendler, 1993). However, many scientists believe that although *scientists as individuals* can hold beliefs about what is morally correct and should act on those beliefs by advocating public policies congruent with them, *science as an institution* cannot say what policy is best (Kendler, 1993). They therefore see the social activist role itself as a misrepresentation, not necessarily of the content of scientific knowledge but of the capability of science to provide definitive answers to public policy questions. They believe that the most science can do is provide information about the potential outcomes of policy alternatives; it cannot say whether those outcomes are good or bad (Kendler, 1993).

However, Kendler (1993) suggests that even that potential contribution is circumscribed by two limitations. First, to determine the outcomes of a policy decision, one must decide how to measure them, and people can disagree over the appropriate criteria to use in evaluating a policy or in the operational definitions of those criteria. Consequently, people with different value positions on an issue can always dispute the validity of any scientific evidence. For example,

A psychologist cannot contend that a particular intelligence test is a valid measure of intelligence in the same sense that one can insist that DNA is the genetic material responsible for the laws of inheritance. Therefore, one can always argue that some other behavioral measure (e.g., creativity or aesthetic sensitivity) is a more valid index of intelligence. (Kendler, 1993, p. 1051)

The second limitation on behavioral science knowledge is that researchers' personal values can, as noted in Chapter 13, influence their interpretations of the outcome of research, with the result that two people can make conflicting interpretations of the same data. At a more basic level, the data themselves may be contaminated by the researcher's personal values. Perhaps somewhat cynically, Albee (1982) notes that

people, and especially social scientists, select theories that are consistent with their personal values, attitudes, and prejudices and then go out into the world, or into the laboratory, to seek facts that validate their beliefs about the world and about human nature, neglecting or denying observations that contradict their personal prejudices. (p. 5)

Because of these limitations and because of the risk that social activism might lead to distrust of behavioral science as an institution, some commentators recommend that behavioral science eschew any politically active role. As a psychologist, Kimble (1989) sees the problem this way:

Already in its short history, psychology has made important scientific contributions. The credibility acquired by reason of those accomplishments must not be mistaken for moral authority, however. It is a misuse of the credibility of psychology to use it as a basis to promote social prejudices or political goals, and the use of our status as psychologists for such purposes is an even worse misuse. The potential cost of these misuses is loss of the very credibility and status that allowed the misuse in the first place. (p. 499)

THE EXPERT WITNESS One forum in our society in which many participants are expected to be advocates is the courtroom. The norms of our legal system require the attorneys for the opposing sides in a trial to do their best to win and to present their side in the most favorable light possible and their opponent's side in the most unfavorable light possible within the bounds of the law and legal ethics. It is then up to the jury (or the judge in a nonjury trial) to decide who's right (for example, see Cohn & Udolf, 1979). This adversarial norm has led to some discussion of the ethical responsibilities of behavioral science researchers as expert witnesses, whose role is to provide specialized knowledge in order to help the jury or judge reach a decision (for example, see Loftus & Monahan, 1980).

The discussion centers around the conflict between the scientific norm of presenting all the information relevant to a question (as in the societal mentoring role) and the legal norm of presenting only the information favorable to your side and concealing to the extent legally permissible information favorable to the other side. Which norm should the scientist follow as expert witness? Some commentators (for example, Rivlin, 1973; Wolfgang, 1974) hold that one should adhere to the norms of the situation, and in the trial court context follow the legal norm of presenting only the evidence favorable to your side. Others hold that not only do scientific norms require one to provide all relevant information, but so does the witness's oath to tell the whole truth: "By selectively leaving out studies that are crucial to some particular question, the psychologist is failing to perform according to the oath. The 'whole truth' is not being told" (Loftus & Monahan, 1980, p. 279). However, Loftus and Monahan (1980) concede that the rules of evidence only require an expert witness to give an opinion on the issue at hand, not to lay out the scientific basis of that opinion. However, the judge in the case does have the authority to require the expert witness to provide additional information and "an opposing attorney is always free to ask this question: 'Do you know of any studies that show the opposite result?'" (p. 279).

Like many ethical issues, the question of what to say as an expert witness ends up being between individuals and their consciences. Loftus and Monahan (1980) do provide one guideline, however:

> Any resolution of this issue will . . . depend on the quality of the evidence on both sides of the case. If the expert is testifying that overcrowding produces psychological harm and 95 percent of all investigations support this conclusion, there may be no duty to confuse the jury and prolong the testimony with a discussion of the other 5 percent. However, if good, solid evidence exists to support the other position, the expert may have an ethical, even if not a legal, obligation to discuss it. (pp. 279–280)

Researchers' Responsibilities

What responsibilities do researchers have concerning the ways in which research—both their own and others'—is used? Ethical principles hold people responsible only for what they themselves do or say; we are, in general, not responsible for what others do with our research or the implications they draw from it (Reynolds, 1979; Steininger et al., 1984). However, we do have some general responsibility concerning the conduct and reporting of research, societal mentoring and social activism, monitoring the use of research, and encouraging the appropriate use of research.

CONDUCTING RESEARCH Diener and Crandall (1978) believe that although researchers are not responsible for all possible uses or misuses of their research, they should consider possible uses and misuses that can be made of it (see also Scarr, 1988). They recommend that if it is clear the results of research would be used for exploitive purposes, then the research should not be done. But what about more ambiguous situations? For example, if the results of research on racial and sex differences could be used to the detriment of members of racial minority groups and women, should that research be conducted (for example, see Baumeister, 1988; Zuckerman, 1990)? Answering this question requires a consideration of both social and scientific values and of the relative harm and good that could come from the research. Those considerations are discussed later in this chapter.

REPORTING RESEARCH When the results of research could be misused, researchers have two responsibilities concerning reports of that research. One responsibility is to consider whether the research should be reported at all. This question is a sensitive one, addressed later in this chapter. For now, simply note that some observers, such as Zuckerman (1990), recommend that potentially harmful research be held to higher standards of validity than those against which other research is judged—that is, that the validity criteria become more stringent as the potential for harm increases. The second responsibility is to clearly spell out the meaning of the research in a way that will minimize the possibility of misinterpretation. For example, Shedler and Block (1990) found a positive correlation between adolescents' experimenting with marijuana and psychological adjustment. They concluded their research report in this way:

> In presenting research on a topic as emotionally charged as drug use, there is always the danger that findings may be misinterpreted or misrepresented. Specifically, we are concerned that some segments of the popular media may misrepresent our findings as indicating that drug use might somehow improve an adolescent's psychological health. Although the incorrectness of such an interpretation should be obvious to anyone who has actually read this article, our concern about media misrepresentation requires us to state categorically that our findings do not support such a view, nor should anything we have said remotely encourage such an interpretation. (p. 628)

We should not, however, be too hopeful about the effectiveness of such warnings. Sieber (1993), for example, quotes one newspaper headline about the research: "Furor Over Report on Teenage Drug Use: Researchers said those who experimented were healthier than abstainers or abusers" (p. 23).

Even when it is unlikely that results could be misused, scientists who conduct research that has public policy or other applied implications should carefully explain the limits that methodology or research technology put on the application of their results. Catania, Gibson, Chitwood, and Coates (1990), for example, point out some limits on the use of sex research for developing policies for controlling the spread of AIDS, caused by problems in measuring sexual behavior. Researchers on applied topics have an obligation to explain what their research *cannot* say about a problem as well as what it *can* say, to point out the potential negative effects of implementing policies based on that research as well as the potential positive effects (Reynolds, 1979).

SOCIETAL MENTORING AND SOCIAL ACTIVISM When advising or commenting on social policy or when advocating a particular policy, scientists have an obligation to base their statements only on validated information that is clearly generalizable to the particular context to which it is to be applied (Kimmel, 1988; Loftus & Monahan, 1980). They also have an obligation to provide complete information, laying out both the positive and negative implications of research for the policy at issue and spelling out any limitations on its application based on such factors as settings, populations, and so forth. However, reasonable people may disagree, based on their individual value orientations, on what constitutes valid research, generalizable research, and harm and benefit. Therefore, scientists have an obligation to analyze their value positions on policy issues and to make clear their values and the potential effects of their values on positions that they take on policy issues or topics of public controversy (APA, 1992; Fischhoff, 1990; Kendler, 1993). For example, in the preface to their book on the role of genetic influences on psychological variables, Lewontin, Rose, and Kamin (1984) explain that they "share a commitment to the prospect of a creation of a more socially just—a socialist—society" (p. ix) and later state that "the ultimate tests [of science] are always twofold: tests of truth and social function" (p. 33). As Kendler (1993) comments, "Their [social philosophy] makes their conclusion that genetic predispositions play no role in IQ scores or in the etiology of schizophrenia understandable but nevertheless inconsistent with available evidence?" (p. 1051).

MONITORING THE USE OF SCIENCE   Thus far, the discussion has focused on preventing the misuse of research. Scientists also have an obligation to monitor the uses to which research—both their own and others'—is put and to speak out when it appears that research is being misapplied or misrepresented (Diener & Crandall, 1978; Steininger et al., 1984). As Wilcox (1987) notes,

> Even the clearest and least ambiguous research findings can be misunderstood or intentionally distorted, leading to a misrepresentation of those findings. It remains incumbent on psychologists to carefully scrutinize the uses to which psychological data are put, especially when the subject matter deals with issues around which our society has deep moral and ideological divisions. Direct, frank participation in such policy debates is one of the best means of preventing such misuses, especially when we portray the research in a complete and honest fashion, spelling out limitations as well as strengths. (p. 943)

Be alert not only for the misuse of scientific research but also for the nonuse of research data when they are needed. That is, sometimes people claim a scientific basis for some intervention or policy decision when no such basis exists. The scientist then has an obligation to point out the lack of research support for the intervention or decision. For example, the idea of repressed memories of child abuse has received a great deal of publicity. This hypothesis holds that some children are so traumatized by abuse that they repress their memories of it; these memories then surface many years later in psychotherapy. However, the research evidence suggests that such memories should be evaluated cautiously. For example, some of the incidents were said to have happened when the people reporting them were as young as 6 months of age, although people can rarely recall events that occur before age 2. Furthermore, people can "remember" events that never happened (Loftus, 1993). However, people sometimes do repress memories; the problem, as Loftus notes, is that there is no valid way of discriminating between true and false memories, so there is no way of checking for accuracy in any particular case. Nonetheless, several people have been convicted of child abuse on the basis of repressed memories, and some states have extended their statutes of limitations to allow prosecutions based on events recalled decades after they were said to have happened (Loftus, 1993).

ENCOURAGING THE APPLICATION OF RESEARCH   As noted earlier, the failure to apply knowledge when appropriate could deprive people of the benefits of that knowledge. It is therefore important that scientists not hold themselves aloof from the application of the knowledge that they and their colleagues generate, but to actively work for its application in situations where it can provide benefit (for example, Diener & Crandall, 1978; Judd et al., 1991; Kimmel, 1988; Reynolds, 1979; Steininger et al., 1984). This social engagement can take any number of forms depending on the personal values of the scientist and the roles in which she or he feels comfortable, such as active political involvement, writing to legislators and newspapers, paid and unpaid consulting, and teaching. The form of the involvement is less important than the involvement itself.

RESEARCH AND THE COMMON GOOD

To conclude this chapter and this book, I want to present you with three questions about the ethics of research in relation to the common good, or the needs and welfare of society. As with many ethical questions, there are no prescribed answers to these. Nonetheless, they are questions that researchers face from time to time, sometimes on a philosophical level and sometimes on a practical level, and so must answer for themselves. Let us therefore give them some consideration now.

Is Applied Research More Ethical Than Basic Research?

As discussed in Chapter 2, basic research seeks to develop general knowledge without regard for its practical utility, whereas applied research focuses on solving practical problems. Some scientists and philosophers of science (for example, Baumrin, 1970; Lewontin et al., 1984) believe that as long as society faces important problems, basic research is unethical. In their view, basic research harms society as a whole and some of society's individual members by diverting resources from applied research that could solve society's problems: Delaying solutions to problems prolongs the harm caused by the problems. This view further holds that one cannot justify basic research on the grounds that the knowledge it provides might help solve problems in the future because there is no way to know when or if that payoff will occur. Applied research, in contrast, is more likely to produce benefits and to do so more quickly.

Others (for example, Diener & Crandall, 1978) consider this view of basic research shortsighted, for three reasons. First, although the future potential of any one line of basic research is unknowable, the history of science has shown that important practical advances come only as a result of an understanding of basic processes. Diener and Crandall (1978) cite the case of chemistry: "As long as alchemists sought an applied end, to create gold, chemistry did not advance. But once chemists became concerned with understanding chemistry at a theoretical level, there were great leaps in knowledge" (p. 192). A second, related, argument against the applied-is-morally-better position is that trying to develop an intervention to solve a problem without understanding the basic processes involved is like groping in the dark: You don't know what direction to go, you might inadvertently cause harm, and when you are successful, you don't know the reasons for the success and so have no basis for judging the generalizability of the intervention. Finally, as noted in Chapter 2, the distinction between basic and applied research is somewhat artificial: You can combine the two in the form of action research and generate basic knowledge while trying to solve important practical problems. In addition, basic research can have directly applicable implications; recall Lassiter's findings based on basic research in attribution theory (described in Chapter 2) that camera angle can influence people's perceptions of the voluntariness of videotaped confessions (Lassiter & Dudley, 1991; Lassiter & Irvine, 1986).

Despite the compatibility and even interdependence of the basic and applied approaches to science, the argument over which is better continues. The argument may be unsolvable because to a large extent it is rooted in the basic philosophical division discussed in Chapter 1: the epistemological separation of applied, activist, humanistic science from that of basic, knowledge-for-its-own-sake, positivist science.

Should Research on Some Topics Be Banned or Restricted?

Earlier in this chapter I noted that the results of research can sometimes be misused, misrepresented, or misinterpreted and thereby cause harm. Two areas of research that some observers see as especially vulnerable to harmful misinterpretation or misrepresentation are gender and ethnic minority issues (for example, see Baumeister, 1988; Zuckerman, 1990). Harm in these instances takes the form of the development of information that could be interpreted as showing that one social group is in some way deficient relevant to other social groups, thereby reinforcing stereotypes and perhaps being used to justify discrimination. In addition, certain types of causal explanations for group differences could be used as justifications for failure to take action to correct problems (Lewontin et al., 1984; Nelkin, 1982). For example, a genetic explanation of racial differences in IQ scores and other indices of achievement could be used to justify inadequate educational services for low-scoring groups: If the "deficiency" is inborn, the reasoning would go, then attempts to alleviate it by environmental changes are doomed to failure and are wastes of resources. Finally, such misuses, misrepresentations, and misinterpretations of behavioral science data are harmful because they lead to social disharmony and conflict between segments of society, thereby weakening the social order (Saranson, 1984).

Sieber and Stanley (1988) refer to research on such topics as **socially sensitive research.** Sensitive research consists of "studies in which there are potential social consequences or implications, either directly for the participants in the research or for the class of individuals represented by the research" (p. 49). Although Sieber and Stanley define sensitive research in terms of both individuals and social groups, most discussions of these issues focus on consequences for social groups such as women, racial or ethnic minority groups, and so forth. The potential for harm from socially sensitive research has raised the question of whether the conduct of such research should be banned or restricted (Saranson, 1984) or whether restrictions should be placed on the publication and dissemination of the results of such research (Estes, 1992; Oden & MacDonald, 1978).

Chapter 3 addressed a version of this question, discussing the problems caused by the possibility of harming the people who participate in research. It was noted that the decision to conduct or not conduct a study must be based on a cost-benefit analysis, weighing the costs of the research in terms of harm to participants against the benefits to be derived from doing the research. As R. Rosenthal and Rosnow (1984) point out, one also must factor into the cost-benefit analysis the costs of *not* doing the research. For example, Scarr (1988) points out that restrictions on research on women and racial or ethnic minority groups prevent the development of information on their strengths as well as on their supposed deficiencies, thereby suppressing information that could be used to counter stereotypes or to inform policy decisions in a positive manner. Graham

(1992) and Loo, Fong, and Iwamasa (1988) further point out that failure to conduct research on racial or ethnic minority groups hinders the development of interventions that take into account the particular needs of members of the groups, such as those based in cultural differences. Graham (1992) also notes that a lack of research means there would be no valid information on which to base policy decisions:

> How will we be able to meet these challenges in the absence of a strong empirical base of research on ethnic minorities from which we can confidently draw? How will we be able to avoid oversimplifying complex topics, citing outdated findings, or perpetuating incorrect beliefs if a relevant database remains . . . inaccessible? As an African-American psychologist I find it disconcerting, for example, to hear and read so often in the popular press that Black children have a unique learning style or that they prefer cooperation to competition, when the empirical evidence supporting these conclusions is so thin. What we need . . . is a substantive African-American psychological literature that is both accurate and current. What we have instead are sets of isolated and outdated findings, often of questionable methodological soundness. (p. 638)

How can we strike a balance between preventing potential harm from the misuse of the results of socially sensitive research and potential harm from not developing necessary information by not conducting such research? Two procedures have been suggested. Sieber (1992) suggests conducting a cost-benefit analysis of the potential social effects of the research just as one conducts a cost-benefit analysis of the potential effects of the research on its participants; the research should be conducted only if the anticipated benefits outweigh the anticipated costs. Because members of different social groups can perceive the relative costs and benefits of research differently, Sieber recommends having the research reviewed at the question formulation, design, and interpretation stages by members of groups who are likely to be affected by its outcome. Although researchers can make their own social cost-benefit analyses, such decision-making procedures deny members of social groups the right to make decisions about research that will affect their lives, thereby denying them their autonomy and treating them as incapable of making such decisions (Scarr, 1988).

A second procedure is to limit the publication of research that may have socially harmful effects, through either self-censorship (Saranson, 1984) or editorial censorship (Oden & MacDonald, 1978). As Estes (1992) notes, such restrictions are contrary to the scientific ideal of building a knowledge base through the unhindered publication of research results and theoretical developments. But, he says, "A balance must be found between the need for free exchange of research results among scientists . . . and the need to be sure that no segment of our society has reason to feel threatened by the research or its publication" (p. 278). Zuckerman (1990) suggests that one way in which to strike such a balance is to require potentially harmful research to meet higher standards of methodological soundness and validity as a criterion for publication than does more innocuous research. Although some researchers see elevated standards for publication as unfair (for example, Scarr, 1981), are they actually less fair than a requirement for a cost-benefit analysis? Should we not require a certainty in the validity of research results that is in proportion to the risk of harm they present (Zuckerman, 1990)?

As with other ethical questions, the answer to this one can be found only within the researcher's personal value system. To the extent that you value knowledge for the sake of knowledge, social consequences will appear to be of lesser importance than the knowledge to be gained through research. To the extent that you see protection of less powerful social groups as part of the scientific role, knowledge will appear less important than the prevention of possible social harm.

Is There an Ethical Obligation to Conduct Research?

The previous section and Chapter 3 discussed ethical constraints on research and so focused on the question of when research should not be conducted. But within the boundaries of avoidance of harm, is there, in Darley's (1980) words, "an ethical imperative to do research" (p. 15)? That is, does accepting the role of scientist place on you an ethical obligation to conduct research? Behavioral science is both a science and a field of practice; that is, behavioral science knowledge is used as the basis for interventions and policy decisions. Do behavioral scientists therefore have an obligation to ensure that interventions and decisions based on behavioral science knowledge are both safe and effective? In essence, should behavioral science interventions meet the same requirements of safety and effectiveness as do medical interventions? Both, after all, affect people's lives. Consider, for instance, the principle of informed consent, which applies to psychotherapy and other interventions as well as to research (for example, see Koocher & Keith-Spiegel, 1998). The people affected by an intervention should give their informed consent to participate in it. But if there is no research on the safety or effectiveness of an intervention, how can one inform potential participants of anticipated risks and benefits with any degree of confidence? Without basic research on the principles underlying an experimental intervention, there is no basis for estimating its potential risks and benefits and so no way to obtain the informed consent of those affected by it. The ethical principles underlying the practice of behavioral science therefore imply an ethical obligation to conduct research.

If we do not do research to develop basic knowledge on which to base interventions and policy decisions and if we do not do action and evaluation research to test the safety and effectiveness of those interventions and decisions, do we not "leave those who are attempting social change the prey of hucksters who are willing to put forth undocumentable claims based on inadequate evidence" (Darley, 1980, p. 15)? Even at best, practice without research to guide its design and test its effectiveness proceeds on the basis of speculation rather than fact and the potential for both benefit and harm remains unknown (Snyder & Mentzer, 1978).

SUMMARY

The professional and social responsibilities of scientists include the problem of scientific malpractice, which can take four forms. Data forging consists of fabricating data, data cooking consists of discarding data that don't conform to the hypothesis, data trimming consists of changing data values so that they better fit the predictions made by the hypothesis, and data torturing consists of conducting statistical tests until a significant effect is uncovered. The actual extent of such practices is unknown, but about 7–15% of scientists in one survey reported knowing of at least one such incident. Malpractice is often attributed to work pressures, but the social structure of science, especially the practices of defining success in terms of confirmed hypotheses and of "hired hand" research, may also contribute. Research malpractice can be difficult to detect and often goes unpunished. Because science is often a solitary profession, the best protection against research malpractice is each scientist's personal sense of honor.

Mistakes are a normal part of research, but avoidable errors are ethical shortcomings. Culpable error can harm research participants by wasting their time and exposing them to unnecessary discomfort. Culpable error also harms science by contaminating its knowledge base with invalid data, and it can harm the public by engendering invalid beliefs about human nature. Scientists therefore have a moral obligation to be competent in the subject matter they study, in research design, and in statistical analysis. They also have an obligation to carefully adhere to proper research procedures when collecting data. Finally, scientists have an obligation to publicly correct research mistakes and errors when they are detected.

The application of research results has the potential for a number of ethical problems. Applications of psychological knowledge can be used to exploit people. Applications based on inadequately tested theories or overgeneralized research results can waste resources and lead to erroneous policy decisions. Finally, the failure to appropriately apply the results of research can deny the public of its benefits. The political use of research is a controversial issue because there is a basic philosophical division over the role of scientists in politics. Societal mentors see their role as one of providing a neutral, balanced overview of research on a topic and of carefully laying out the limits of its application. Social activists push a particular course of action, using scientific research and theory to justify it. A danger in social activism is that activists might, even unintentionally, misrepresent the state of knowledge about their issue, overemphasizing the strengths of their position and underemphasizing the positive aspects of alternative positions. Epistemologically, social activism is problematic because science, by its nature, cannot answer questions about the moral correctness of policies; moral decisions are based in personal values and so are outside the realm of science. Science can say only what the observable outcomes of a policy are or might be; it cannot say if those outcomes are good or bad. Scientists can, however, make such value judgments on the basis of their personal beliefs. The difficulty lies in separating scientific knowledge from personal belief.

Expert witnesses face an ethical dilemma: The norms of the courtroom often require one to be an advocate for one side, but scientific norms prescribe a balanced presentation of fact. Because there are no formal guidelines for resolving this dilemma, each expert witness must be guided by his or her personal sense of justice.

Scientists must carefully consider the social costs and benefits of conducting and reporting research as well as the scientific costs and benefits. When politically active, they must be open about whether they are taking an activist or mentoring role and carefully adhere to the requirements of the latter when taking it. Scientists must monitor the uses society makes of the knowledge gained through research and speak out when that knowledge is misused, misrepresented, or misinterpreted, and when inaccurate claims are made for the scientific basis of an intervention or a policy decision. Finally, scientists must encourage the appropriate application of scientific knowledge.

Every scientist faces three questions about the relationship of science to the common good: Is applied research more ethical than basic research? Should research on some topics be restricted or banned? Is there an ethical obligation to conduct research? Each of us must find an answer to these questions on the basis of our own philosophies and values.

QUESTIONS AND EXERCISES FOR REVIEW

1. Do the various forms of scientific malpractice reflect different degrees of dishonesty? For example, are data trimming, cooking, and torturing less dishonest than data forging, given that they are based on real data? What are your reasons for your answer?
2. What are the differences between the forms of scientific malpractice and legitimate research procedures such as discarding invalid data and exploratory data analysis?
3. What factors appear to motivate scientific malpractice? Is malpractice in response to external pressure less blameworthy than malpractice in pursuit of personal gain or fame? Why or why not?
4. What factors influence the detection of scientific malpractice and the enforcement of honest research practices?
5. Some people believe the concept of personal honor is outdated. Is it? Why or why not? How would you design a graduate curriculum to instill a sense of honor in apprentice scientists? If you believe honor is an outdated concept, what controls would you establish to ensure honesty in research?
6. How do normal research mistakes differ from culpable error? Why is culpable error an ethical shortcoming, while making a mistake is not? Why is negligence in research an ethical issue?
7. Describe the areas in which researchers must be competent.
8. How can mistakes and errors in published research be corrected?
9. How can the results of research be misused? Describe examples of misuse with which you are familiar. What about these uses makes them *misuses*? That is, in what ways could they cause harm?
10. Describe the similarities and differences between the societal mentor and social activist roles. Which role appeals to you personally? Why? How does your preference relate to your epistemological viewpoint?
11. Describe the ethical issues involved in societal mentoring and social activism. What limits does the nature of behavioral science knowledge place on these roles?
12. Describe the ethical choices facing the expert witness.
13. Describe the scientist's responsibilities relative to the conduct and reporting of socially sensitive research, societal mentoring and social activism, monitoring the use of research, and encouraging the appropriate application of research results.
14. What are your answers to the three questions concerning research and the common good? Explain your reasons for your answers. How does your epistemological position affect your answers? How did your political and social values affect your answers?

REFERENCES

Abelson, R. P. (1985). A variance explanation paradox: When a little is a lot. *Psychological Bulletin, 97,* 129–133.

Abramson, L. Y., Metalsky, G. I., & Alloy, L. B. (1989). Hopelessness depression: A theory-based subtype of depression. *Psychological Review, 96,* 358–372.

Abramson, L. Y., Seligman, M. E. P., & Teasdale, J. D. (1978). Learned helplessness in humans: Critique and reformulation. *Journal of Abnormal Psychology, 87,* 49–74.

Adair, J. G. (1984). The Hawthorne effect: A reconsideration of the methodological artifact. *Journal of Applied Psychology, 69,* 334–345.

Adams, K. A. (1983). Aspects of social context as determinants of black women's resistance to challenges. *Journal of Social Issues, 39*(3), 69–78.

Adams, K. A. (1985). Gamesmanship for internal evaluators: Knowing when to "hold 'em" and when to "fold 'em." *Evaluation and Program Planning, 8,* 53–57.

Ajzen, I., & Fishbein, M. (1980). *Understanding attitudes and predicting social behavior.* Englewood Cliffs, NJ: Prentice Hall.

Albee, G. W. (1982). The politics of nature and nurture. *American Journal of Community Psychology, 10,* 4–30.

Alexander, S., & Baker, K. (1992). Some ethical issues in applied social psychology: The case of bilingual education and self-esteem. *Journal of Applied Social Psychology, 22,* 1741–1757.

Alfred, R. H. (1976). The Church of Satan. In C. Y. Glock & R. N. Bellah (Eds.), *The new religious consciousness* (pp. 180–202). Berkeley: University of California Press.

Allen, M. J., & Yen, W. M. (1979). *Introduction to measurement theory.* Monterey, CA: Brooks/Cole.

Allison, P. D. (1990). Change scores as dependent variables in regression analysis. *Sociological Methodology, 20,* 93–114.

Alloy, L. B., Abramson, L. Y., & Viscusi, D. (1981). Induced mood and the illusion of control. *Journal of Personality and Social Psychology, 41,* 1129–1140.

Allport, G. W. (1961). *Pattern and growth in personality.* New York: Holt, Rinehart, & Winston.

Al-Zahrani, S. S. A., & Kaplowitz, S. A. (1993). Attributional biases in individualistic and collective cultures: A comparison of Americans with Saudis. *Social Psychology Quarterly, 56,* 223–233.

American College of Sports Medicine. (1995). *Guidelines for exercise testing and prescription* (5th ed.). Philadelphia: Lea & Febiger.

American Psychological Association [APA]. (1982). *Ethical principles in the conduct of research with human participants*. Washington, DC: Author.

American Psychological Association [APA]. (1992). Ethical principles of psychologists and code of conduct. *American Psychologist, 47,* 1597–1611.

American Psychological Association [APA]. (1993). *Journals in psychology* (4th ed.). Washington, DC: Author.

American Psychological Association [APA]. (1994). *Publication manual* (4th ed.). Washington, DC: Author.

Amir, Y., & Sharon, I. (1990). Replication research: A "must" for the scientific advancement of psychology. *Journal of Social Behavior and Personality, 5,* 51–69.

Anastasi, A., & Urbani, S. (1997). *Psychological testing* (7th ed.). Upper Saddle River, NJ: Prentice Hall.

Andersen, M. (1981). Corporate wives: Longing for liberation or satisfied with the status quo? *Urban Life, 10,* 311–327.

Anderson, C. A. (1989). Temperature and aggression: Ubiquitous effects of heat on occurrence of human violence. *Psychological Bulletin, 106,* 74–96.

Anderson, C. A., Lindsay, J. J., & Bushman, B. B. (1999). Research in psychological laboratories: Truth or triviality? *Current Directions in Psychological Science, 8,* 3–9.

Annas, G. J., Glantz, L. H., & Katz, B. F. (1977). *Informed consent to human experimentation*. Cambridge, MA: Ballinger.

Appelbaum, M. I., & McCall, R. B. (1983). Design and analysis in developmental psychology. In P. H. Mussen (Ed.), *Handbook of child psychology* (Vol. 1, pp. 415–476). New York: Wiley.

Archer, D., Pettigrew, T. F., & Aronson, E. (1992). Making research apply: High stakes public policy in a regulatory environment. *American Psychologist, 47,* 1233–1236.

Argyris, C. (1980). *Inner contradictions of rigorous research*. New York: Academic Press.

Aronson, E., Brewer, M., & Carlsmith, J. M. (1985). Experimentation in social psychology. In G. Lindzey & E. Aronson (Eds.), *Handbook of social psychology* (3rd ed., Vol. 1, pp. 441–486). New York: Random House.

Aronson, E., & Carlsmith, J. M. (1968). Experimentation in social psychology. In G. Lindzey & E. Aronson (Eds.), *Handbook of social psychology* (2nd ed., Vol. 2, pp. 1–79). Reading, MA: Addison-Wesley.

Aronson, E., Ellsworth, P. C., Carlsmith, J. M., & Gonzales, M. H. (1990). *Methods of research in social psychology* (2nd ed.). New York: McGraw-Hill.

Aronson, E., Willerman, B., & Floyd, J. (1966). The effect of a pratfall on increasing interpersonal attractiveness. *Psychonomic Science, 4,* 227–228.

Atkinson, D. R., Furlong, M. J., & Wampold, B. E. (1982). Statistical significance, reviewer evaluations, and the scientific process: Is there a (statistically) significant relationship? *Journal of Counseling Psychology, 29,* 189–194.

AuBuchon, P. G., & Calhoun, K. S. (1985). Menstrual cycle symptomatology: The role of social expectancy and experimental demand characteristics. *Psychosomatic Medicine, 47,* 35–45.

Babbage, C. (1989). *Reflections on the decline of science in England and on some of its causes*. New York: New York University Press. (Original work published 1830)

Babbie, E. (1990). *Survey research methods*. Belmont, CA: Wadsworth.

Bachman, J. G., & O'Malley, P. M. (1984). Yea-saying, nay-saying and going to extremes: Black-white differences in response style. *Public Opinion Quarterly, 48,* 491–509.

Bailey, R. D., Foote, W. E., & Throckmorton, B. (2000). Human sexual behavior: A comparison of college and Internet surveys. In M. Birnbaum (Ed.), *Psychological experiments on the Internet* (pp. 141–168). San Diego, CA: Academic Press.

Bakeman, R., & Gottman, J. M. (1989). *Observing interaction*. Cambridge, England: Cambridge University Press.

Bales, R. F. (1950). *Interaction process analysis*. Cambridge, MA: Addison-Wesley.

Bales, R. F., & Cohen, S. P. (1979). *SYMLOG: A system for the multiple level observation of groups*. New York: Free Press.

Baltes, P. B., Reese, H. W., & Nesselroade, J. R. (1977). *Life-span developmental psychology: Introduction to research methods*. Monterey, CA: Brooks/Cole.

Banaji, M. R., & Crowder, R. G. (1989). The bankruptcy of everyday memory. *American Psychologist, 44*, 1185–1193.

Bandura, A. (1982). Self-efficacy mechanism in human agency. *American Psychologist, 37*, 122–147.

Bangert-Downs, R. L. (1986). Review of developments in meta-analytic method. *Psychological Bulletin, 99*, 388–399.

Banister, P., Burman, E., Parker, I., Taylor, M., & Tindall, C. (1994). *Qualitative methods in psychology: A research guide*. Philadelphia: Open University Press.

Barber, T. X. (1976). *Pitfalls in human research*. New York: Pergamon Press.

Barlow, D. H., & Hersen, M. (1984). *Single case experimental designs* (2nd ed.). New York: Pergamon.

Barnett, P. A., & Gotlib, I. H. (1988). Psychosocial functioning and depression: Distinguishing among antecedents, concomitants, and consequences. *Psychological Bulletin, 104*, 97–126.

Barnett, W. S. (1985). *The Perry Preschool Program and its long-term effects*. Ypsilanti, MI: High/Scope Educational Research Foundation.

Baron, R. A. (1983). "Sweet smell of success"? The impact of pleasant artificial scents on evaluations of job applicants. *Journal of Applied Psychology, 68*, 709–713.

Baron, R. M., & Kenny, D. A. (1986). The mediator-moderator variable distinction in social psychological research: Conceptual, strategic, and statistical considerations. *Journal of Personality and Social Psychology, 51*, 1173–1182.

Bart, P. B. (1971). Sexism and social science: From the gilded cage to the iron cage, or, the perils of Pauline. *Journal of Marriage and the Family, 33*, 734–735.

Basow, S. A. (1992). *Gender stereotypes and roles* (3rd ed.). Monterey, CA: Brooks/Cole.

Bass, B. M., Cascio, W. F., & O'Connor, E. J. (1974). Magnitude estimations of expressions of frequency and amount. *Journal of Applied Psychology, 59*, 313–320.

Baumeister, R. F. (1988). Should we stop studying sex differences altogether? *American Psychologist, 43*, 1092–1095.

Baumrin, B. H. (1970). The immorality of irrelevance: The social role of science. In F. A. Korten, S. W. Cook, & J. I. Lacey (Eds.), *Psychology and the problems of society* (pp. 73–83). Washington, DC: American Psychological Association.

Baumrind, D. (1985). Research using intentional deception: Ethical issues revisited. *American Psychologist, 40*, 165–174.

Baxter, J. C. (1970). Interpersonal spacing in natural settings. *Sociometry, 33*, 444–456.

Baxter, L. A. (1992). Root metaphors in accounts of developing romantic relationships. *Journal of Social and Personal Relationships, 9*, 253–275.

Bechtel, H. K., Jr., & Pearson, W., Jr. (1985). Deviant scientists and scientific deviance. *Deviant Behavior, 6*, 237–252.

Beck, A. T. (1972). *Depression: Causes and treatment*. Philadelphia: University of Pennsylvania Press.

Beck, A. T., Steer, R. A., & Garbin, M. G. (1988). Psychometric properties of the Beck Depression Inventory: Twenty-five years of evaluation. *Clinical Psychology Review, 8*, 77–100.

Belar, C. D., & Perry, N. W. (1992). National conference on scientist-practitioner education and training for professional practice of psychology. *American Psychologist, 47*, 71–75.

Bell, P. A. (1992). In defense of the negative affect escape model of heat and aggression. *Psychological Bulletin, 111*, 342–346.

Bell, R. (1992). *Impure science*. New York: Wiley.

Bem, D. J. (1972). Self-perception theory. In L. Berkowitz (Ed.), *Advances in experimental social psychology* (Vol. 6, pp. 1–62). New York: Academic Press.

Bem, D. J. (1987). Writing the empirical journal article. In M. P. Zanna & J. M. Darley (Eds.), *The compleat academic* (pp. 171–201). New York: Random House.

Bem, S. L. (1974). The measurement of psychological androgyny. *Journal of Consulting and Clinical Psychology, 42*, 155–162.

Benjamin, L. S. (1979). Structural analysis of differentiation failure. *Psychiatry, 42*, 1–23.

Berkowitz, L. (1970). The contagion of violence: An S-R mediational analysis of some effects of observed aggression. *Nebraska Symposium on Motivation, 18*, 95–136.

Berkowitz, L., & Donnerstein, E. (1982). External validity is more than skin deep. *American Psychologist, 37*, 245–257.

Berkowitz, L., & Macauley, J. (1971). The contagion of criminal violence. *Sociometry, 34*, 238–260.

Bermant, G., McGuire, M., McKinley, W., & Salo, C. (1974). The logic of simulation in jury research. *Criminal Justice and Behavior, 1*, 224–233.

Bernstein, A. S. (1965). Race and examiner as significant influences on basal skin impedance. *Journal of Personality and Social Psychology, 1*, 346–349.

Bernstein, D. A., Borkovec, T. D., & Coles, M. G. H. (1986). Assessment of anxiety. In A. B. Ciminero, K. S. Calhoun, & H. E. Adams (Eds.), *Handbook of behavioral assessment* (2nd ed., pp. 353–403). New York: Wiley.

Bersoff, D. N. (1987). Social science data and the Supreme Court: *Lockhart* as a case in point. *American Psychologist, 42*, 52–58.

Bersoff, D. N. (1988). Should subjective employment devices be scrutinized? It's elementary, my dear Ms. Watson. *American Psychologist, 43*, 1016–1018.

Bertera, E. M., & Bertera, R. L. (1981). The cost-effectiveness of telephone vs. clinic counseling for hypertensive patients: A pilot study. *American Journal of Public Health, 71*, 626–629.

Bickman, L. (1981). Some distinctions between basic and applied approaches. In L. Bickman (Ed.), *Applied social psychology annual* (Vol. 1, pp. 23–44). Beverly Hills, CA: Sage.

Biner, P. M. (1991). Effects of lighting-induced arousal on the magnitude of goal valence. *Personality and Social Psychology Bulletin, 17*, 219–226.

Binik, Y. M., Mah, K., & Kiesler, S. (1999). Ethical issues in conducting sex research on the Internet. *The Journal of Sex Research, 36*, 82–90.

Binning, J. F., & Barrett, G. V. (1989). Validity of personnel decisions: A conceptual analysis of the inferential and evidential bases. *Journal of Applied Psychology, 74*, 478–494.

Birnbaum, M. H. (2000a). Decision making in the lab and on the Web. In M. Birnbaum (Ed.), *Psychological experiments on the Internet* (pp. 3–34). San Diego, CA: Academic Press.

Birnbaum, M. H. (2000b). *Introduction to behavioral research on the Internet*. Upper Saddle River, NJ: Prentice Hall.

Birnbaum, M. H. (Ed.). (2000c). *Psychological experiments on the Internet*. San Diego, CA: Academic Press.

Black, D. J., & Reiss, A. J. (1967). Patterns of behavior in police and citizen transactions. In A. J. Reiss (Ed.), *Studies of crime and law enforcement in metropolitan areas* (Vol. 2, Sec. 1). Washington, DC: U.S. Government Printing Office.

Blalock, H. M., Jr. (1979). *Social statistics* (Rev. 2nd ed.). New York: McGraw-Hill.

Blanchard, F. A., & Cook, S. W. (1976). Effects of helping a less competent member of a cooperating interracial group on the development of interpersonal attraction. *Journal of Personality and Social Psychology, 34*, 1245–1255.

Blank, T. O. (1988). Reflections on Gergen's "Social psychology as history" in perspective. *Personality and Social Psychology Bulletin, 14*, 651–663.

Bochner, S. (1979). Designing unobtrusive field experiments in social psychology. In L. Sechrist (Ed.), *Unobtrusive measurement today* (pp. 33–45). San Francisco: Jossey-Bass.

Bogardus, E. E. (1925). Measuring social distances. *Journal of Applied Sociology, 9,* 299–301.

Bogdan, R. (1972). *Participant observation in organizational settings.* Syracuse, NY: Syracuse University Press.

Bollen, K. A., & Barb, K. H. (1981). Pearson's r and coarsely categorized measures. *American Sociological Review, 46,* 232–239.

Booth-Kewley, S., & Friedman, H. S. (1987). Psychological predictors of heart disease: A quantitative review. *Psychological Bulletin, 101,* 343–362.

Bordens, K. S. (1984). The effects of likelihood of conviction, threatened punishment, and assumed role on mock plea bargain decisions. *Basic and Applied Social Psychology, 5,* 59–74.

Bordens, K. S., & Abbott, B. B. (1999). *Research design and methods* (4th ed.). Mountain View, CA: Mayfield.

Bornstein, M., Bellack, A. S., & Hersen, M. (1977). Social-skills training for unassertive children: A multiple-baseline analysis. *Journal of Applied Behavior Analysis, 10,* 183–195.

Boruch, R. F. (1975). On common contentions about randomized field experiments. In R. F. Boruch & H. W. Reicken (Eds.), *Experimental testing of public policy* (pp. 107–145). Boulder, CO: Westview.

Bouchard, T. J. (1972). A comparison of two group brainstorming procedures. *Journal of Applied Psychology, 56,* 418–421.

Bouchard, T. J., Jr. (1976). Field research methods: Interviewing, questionnaires, participant observation, systematic observation, unobtrusive measures. In M. D. Dunnette (Ed.), *Handbook of industrial and organizational psychology* (pp. 363–413). Chicago: Rand-McNally.

Boyle, G. J. (1985). Self-report measures of depression: Some psychometric considerations. *British Journal of Clinical Psychology, 24,* 45–59.

Bransford, J. D. (1979). *Human cognition.* Belmont, CA: Wadsworth.

Bransford, J. D., & Johnson, M. K. (1972). Contextual prerequisites for understanding: Some investigations of comprehension and recall. *Journal of Verbal Learning and Verbal Behavior, 11,* 717–726.

Braver, M. C. W., & Braver, S. L. (1988). Statistical treatment of the Solomon four-group design: A meta-analytic approach. *Psychological Bulletin, 104,* 150–154.

Bray, R. M., & Kerr, N. L. (1982). Methodological considerations in the study of the psychology of the courtroom. In R. M. Bray & N. L. Kerr (Eds.), *The psychology of the courtroom* (pp. 287–323). New York: Academic Press.

Breckler, S. J. (1990). Application of covariance structure modeling in psychology: Cause for concern? *Psychological Bulletin, 107,* 260–273.

Brehm, S. S., & Brehm, J. W. (1981). *Psychological reactance: A theory of freedom and control.* New York: Academic Press.

Britton, B. K. (1979). Ethical and educational aspects of participating as a subject in psychology experiments. *Teaching of Psychology, 6,* 195–198.

Broad, W., & Wade, N. (1982). *Betrayers of the truth.* New York: Simon & Schuster.

Brody, J. L., Gluck, J. P., & Aragon, A. S. (2000). Participants' understanding of the process of psychological research: Debriefing. *Ethics & Behavior, 10,* 13–25.

Brown, A. S., & Murphy, D. R. (1989). Cryptomnesia: Delineating inadvertent plagiarism. *Journal of Experimental Psychology: Learning, Memory, and Cognition, 15,* 432–442.

Brown, C. E. (1981). Shared space invasion and race. *Personality and Social Psychology Bulletin, 7,* 103–108.

Brunswik, E. (1956). *Perception and the representative design of psychological experiments.* Berkeley: University of California Press.

Buchanan, T., & Smith, J. L. (1999a). Research on the Internet: Validation of a World Wide Web mediated personality scale. *British Journal of Psychology, 90,* 125–144.

Buchanan, T., & Smith, J. L. (1999b). Using the Internet for psychological research: Personality testing on the World Wide Web. *Behavior Research Methods, Instruments, & Computers, 31,* 565–571.

Bullock, R. J., & Tubbs, M. E. (1987). The case meta-analysis method for OD. *Research in Organizational Change and Development, 1,* 171–228.

Burbach, D. J., Farha, J. G., & Thorpe, J. S. (1986). Assessing depression in community samples of children using self-report inventories: Ethical considerations. *Journal of Abnormal Child Psychology, 14,* 579–589.

Burger, J. M. (1981). Motivation biases in the attribution of responsibility for an accident: A meta-analysis of the defensive attribution hypothesis. *Psychological Bulletin, 90,* 496–512.

Burgess, A. (1962). *A clockwork orange.* New York: Norton.

Buss, A. H. (1971). Aggression pays. In J. L. Singer (Ed.), *The control of aggression and violence* (pp. 7–18). New York: Academic Press.

Butler, D. L. (1986). Automation of instructions in human experiments. *Perceptual and Motor Skills, 63,* 435–440.

Butler, D. L., & Biner, P. M. (1987). Preferred lighting levels: Variability among settings, behaviors, and individuals. *Environment and Behavior, 19,* 695–721.

Butler, D. L., & Jones, S. K. (1986). Instructions to human subjects: Effects of repetition on task errors. *Perceptual and Motor Skills, 63,* 451–454.

Butler, D. L., & Steuerwald, B. L. (1991). Effects of view and room size on window size preferences in models. *Environment and Behavior, 23,* 334–358.

Butzin, C. A., & Anderson, N. H. (1973). Functional measurement of children's judgments. *Child Development, 44,* 529–537.

Cacioppo, J. T., & Tassinary, L. G. (1990). Inferring psychological significance from physiological signals. *American Psychologist, 45,* 16–28.

Calder, B. J., Phillips, L. W., & Tybout, A. M. (1981). Designing research for application. *Journal of Consumer Research, 8,* 197–207.

Cameron, P., & Cameron, K. (1988). Did the American Psychological Association misrepresent scientific material to the US Supreme Court? *Psychological Reports, 63,* 255–270.

Campbell, D. T. (1969a). Prospective: Artifact and control. In R. Rosenthal & R. L. Rosnow (Eds.), *Artifact in behavioral research* (pp. 351–382). New York: Academic Press.

Campbell, D. T. (1969b). Reforms as experiments. *American Psychologist, 24,* 409–429.

Campbell, D. T., & Erlebacher, A. (1970). How regression artifacts in quasi-experimental evaluations can mistakenly make compensatory education look harmful. In J. Hellmuth (Ed.), *The disadvantaged child: Vol. 3. Compensatory education: A national debate.* New York: Brunner/ Mazel.

Campbell, D. T., & Fiske, D. W. (1959). Convergent and discriminant validation by the multitrait-multimethod matrix. *Psychological Bulletin, 56,* 81–105.

Campbell, D. T., & Stanley, J. C. (1963). *Experimental and quasi-experimental designs for research.* Chicago: Rand-McNally.

Campbell, J. P. (1982). Editorial: Some remarks from the outgoing editor. *Journal of Applied Psychology, 67,* 691–700.

Campbell, J. P. (1986). Labs, fields, and straw issues. In E. A. Locke (Ed.), *Generalizing from laboratory to field settings* (pp. 269–279). Lexington, MA: Lexington Books.

Campion, M. A. (1993). Article review checklist: A criterion checklist for reviewing research articles in applied psychology. *Personnel Psychology, 46,* 705–718.

Cannell, C. F., & Kahn, R. L. (1968). Interviewing. In G. Lindzey & E. Aronson (Eds.), *Handbook of social psychology* (2nd ed., Vol. 2, pp. 526–595). Reading, MA: Addison-Wesley.

Carver, C. S. (1989). How should multifaceted personality constructs be tested? Issues illustrated by self-monitoring, attributional style, and hardiness. *Journal of Personality and Social Psychology, 56,* 577–585.

Cascio, W. F. (1998). *Applied psychology in personnel management* (5th ed.). Upper Saddle River, NJ: Prentice Hall.

Cash, T., Gillen, B., & Burns, D. (1977). Sexism and "beautyism" in personnel consultant decision making. *Journal of Applied Psychology, 62,* 301–310.

Catania, J. A., Gibson, D. R., Chitwood, D. D., & Coates, T. J. (1990). Methodological problems in AIDS behavioral research: Influences on measurement error and participation bias in studies of sexual behavior. *Psychological Bulletin, 108,* 339–362.

Chafetz, J. S. (1978). *A primer on the construction and testing of theories in sociology.* Itasca, IL: Peacock.

Chapanis, N. P., & Chapanis, A. (1964). Cognitive dissonance: Five years later. *Psychological Bulletin, 61,* 1–22.

Chen, H. T. (1990). *Theory-driven evaluations.* Newbury Park, CA: Sage.

Cherulnik, P. D. (1983). *Behavioral research.* New York: Harper & Row.

Cho, H., & LaRose, R. (1999). Privacy issues in Internet surveys. *Social Science Computer Review, 17,* 421–434.

Chow, S. L. (1988). Significance test or effect size? *Psychological Bulletin, 103,* 105–110.

Christensen, L. (1977). The negative subject: Myth, reality, or prior experience effect? *Journal of Personality and Social Psychology, 35,* 392–400.

Christensen, L. (1988). Deception in psychological research: When is its use justified? *Personality and Social Psychology Bulletin, 14,* 664–675.

Christensen, L. (2001). *Experimental methodology* (8th ed.). Boston: Allyn and Bacon.

Christie, R., & Geis, F. L. (1970). *Studies in Machiavellianism.* New York: Academic Press.

Cicchetti, D. V., Showalter, D., & Tyrer, P. J. (1985). The effect of number of rating scale categories on levels of interrater reliability: A Monte Carlo investigation. *Applied Psychological Measurement, 9,* 31–36.

Clark, R., & Maynard, M. (1998). Research methodology: Using online technology for secondary analysis of survey research data—"Act globally, think locally." *Social Science Computer Review, 16,* 58–71.

Clarke-Stewart, K. A. (1978). Popular primers for parents. *American Psychologist, 33,* 359–369.

Cliff, N. (1983). Some cautions concerning the application of causal modeling methods. *Multivariate Behavioral Research, 18,* 115–126.

Cohen, J. (1988). *Statistical power analysis for the behavioral sciences* (2nd ed.). Hillsdale, NJ: Erlbaum.

Cohen, J. (1992). A power primer. *Psychological Bulletin, 112,* 155–159.

Cohen, J., & Cohen, P. (1983). *Applied multiple regression/correlation analysis for the behavioral sciences* (2nd ed.). Hillsdale, NJ: Erlbaum.

Cohen, R. J., Swerdlik, M. E., & Phillips, S. M. (1996). *Psychological testing* (3rd ed.). Mountain View, CA: Mayfield.

Cohn, A., & Udolf, R. (1979). *The criminal justice system and its psychology.* New York: Van Nostrand Reinhold.

Cole, D. A. (1987). Utility of confirmatory factor analysis in test validation research. *Journal of Consulting and Clinical Psychology, 55,* 584–594.

Committee on Government Operations, U.S. House of Representatives. (1990). *Are scientific misconduct and conflicts of interest hazardous to our health?* (House Report 101–688). Washington, DC: U.S. Government Printing Office.

Condon, J. W., & Crano, W. D. (1988). Inferred evaluation and the relation between attitude similarity and interpersonal attraction. *Journal of Personality and Social Psychology, 54,* 789–797.

Converse, J. M., & Presser, S. (1986). *Survey questions*. Newbury Park, CA: Sage.

Cook, S. W. (1976). Ethical issues in the conduct of research in social relations. In C. Selltiz, L. S. Wrightsman, & S. W. Cook (Eds.), *Research methods in social relations* (3rd ed., pp. 199–249). New York: Holt, Rinehart, and Winston.

Cook, T. D., Appleton, H., Connor, R. F., Shaffer, A., Tomkin, G., & Weber, S. J. (1975). *"Sesame Street" revisited*. New York: Russell Sage Foundation.

Cook, T. D., & Campbell, D. T. (1979). *Quasi-experimentation*. Chicago: Rand-McNally.

Cook, T. D., Gruder, C. L., Hennigan, K. M., & Flay, B. R. (1979). History of the sleeper effect: Some logical pitfalls in accepting the null hypothesis. *Psychological Bulletin, 86*, 662–679.

Cook, T. D., & Leviton, L. C. (1980). Reviewing the literature: A comparison of traditional methods with meta-analysis. *Journal of Personality, 48*, 449–472.

Cooper, H. M. (1998). *Integrating research* (3rd ed.). Thousand Oaks, CA: Sage.

Cooper, H. M., & Hedges, L. V. (Eds.). (1994). *The handbook of research synthesis*. New York: Russell Sage Foundation.

Cooper, H. M., & Lemke, K. M. (1991). On the role of meta-analysis in personality and social psychology. *Personality and Social Psychology Bulletin, 17*, 245–251.

Cooper, J., & Fazio, R. H. (1984). A new look at dissonance theory. In L. Berkowitz (Ed.), *Advances in experimental social psychology* (Vol. 17, pp. 229–267). New York: Academic Press.

Cooper, J., & Mackie, D. (1986). Video games and aggression in children. *Journal of Applied Social Psychology, 16*, 726–744.

Cooper, W. H. (1981). Ubiquitous halo. *Psychological Bulletin, 90*, 218–244.

Coovert, M. D., Penner, L. A., & MacCallum, R. (1990). Covariance structure modeling in personality and social psychological research: An introduction. In C. Hendrick & M. S. Clark (Eds.), *Research methods in personality and social psychology* (pp. 185–216). Newbury Park, CA: Sage.

Cordray, D. S. (1986). Quasi-experimental analysis: A mixture of methods and judgment. In W. M. K. Trochim (Ed.), *Advances in quasi-experimental design and analysis* (pp. 9–27). San Francisco: Jossey-Bass.

Cota, A. A., & Dion, K. L. (1986). Salience of gender and sex composition of ad hoc groups: An experimental test of distinctiveness theory. *Journal of Personality and Social Psychology, 50*, 770–776.

Council, J. R. (1993). Context effects in personality research. *Current Directions in Psychological Science, 2*, 31–34.

Council of National Psychological Associations for the Advancement of Ethnic Minority Interests. (2000). *Guidelines for research in ethnic minority communities*. Washington, DC: American Psychological Association.

Cowles, M., & Davis, C. (1982). On the origins of the .05 level of statistical significance. *American Psychologist, 37*, 553–558.

Cox, E. P., III. (1980). The optimal number of response alternatives for a scale: A review. *Journal of Marketing Research, 17*, 407–422.

Coyne, J. C., & Gotlib, I. H. (1983). The role of cognition in depression: A critical appraisal. *Psychological Bulletin, 94*, 472–505.

Crandall, C. S. (1994). Prejudice against fat people: Ideology and self-interest. *Journal of Personality and Social Psychology, 66*, 882–894.

Crano, W. D., & Brewer, M. B. (1986). *Principles and methods of social research*. Boston: Allyn & Bacon.

Critchfield, R. (1978, January). The culture of poverty. *Human Behavior*, pp. 65–69.

Cronbach, L. J. (1975). Beyond the two disciplines of scientific psychology. *American Psychologist, 30*, 116–127.

Cronbach, L. J. (1990). *Essentials of psychological testing* (5th ed.). Needham Heights, MA: Allyn & Bacon.

Cronbach, L. J., & Furby, L. (1970). How should we measure "change"— or should we? *Psychological Bulletin, 74,* 68–80.

Cronbach, L. J., & Meehl, P. E. (1955). Construct validity in psychological tests. *Psychological Bulletin, 52,* 281–300.

Crossen, C. (1994). *Tainted truth: The manipulation of fact in America.* New York: Simon & Schuster.

Csikszentmihalyi, M., & Larson, R. (1987). Validity and reliability of experience-sampling method. *Journal of Nervous and Mental Disease, 175,* 526–536.

Cummings, L. L., & Frost, P. J. (Eds.). (1985). *Publishing in the organizational sciences.* Homewood, IL: Irwin.

Daft, R. L. (1985). Why I recommended that your manuscript be rejected and what you can do about it. In L. L. Cummings & P. J. Frost (Eds.), *Publishing in the organizational sciences* (pp. 193–209). Homewood, IL: Irwin.

Dane, F. C. (1990). *Research methods.* Pacific Grove, CA: Brooks/Cole.

Danziger, K. (1990). *Constructing the subject: Historical origins of psychological research.* New York: Cambridge University Press.

Darley, J. M. (1980). The importance of being earnest—and ethical. *Contemporary Psychology, 25,* 14–15.

Darley, J. M., & Gilbert, D. T. (1985). Social psychological aspects of environmental psychology. In G. Lindzey & E. Aronson (Eds.), *Handbook of social psychology* (3rd ed., Vol. 2, pp. 949–991). New York: Random House.

Darley, J. M., & Latané, B. (1968). Bystander intervention in emergencies: Diffusion of responsibility. *Journal of Personality and Social Psychology, 8,* 377–383.

Davis, R. N. (1999). Web-based administration of a personality questionnaire: Comparison with traditional methods. *Behavior Research Methods, Instruments, & Computers, 31,* 572–577.

Davison, M. L., & Sharma, A. R. (1988). Parametric statistics and levels of measurement. *Psychological Bulletin, 104,* 137–144.

Dawes, R. M. (1972). *Fundamentals of attitude measurement.* New York: Wiley.

Dawes, R. M., Faust, D., & Meehl, P. E. (1989). Clinical versus actuarial judgment. *Science, 243,* 1668–1674.

Dawes, R. M., & Smith, T. L. (1985). Attitude and opinion measurement. In G. Lindzey & E. Aronson (Eds.), *Handbook of social psychology* (3rd ed., Vol. 1, pp. 509–566). New York: Random House.

Dawis, R. V. (1987). Scale construction. *Journal of Counseling Psychology, 34,* 481–489.

DeJong, W., Morris, W. N., & Hastorf, A. H. (1976). Effect of an escaped accomplice on the punishment assigned to a criminal defendant. *Journal of Personality and Social Psychology, 33,* 192–198.

DeLamater, J., & MacCorquodale, P. (1979). *Premarital sexuality.* Madison: University of Wisconsin Press.

D'Emilio, J., & Freedman, E. B. (1988). *Intimate matters: A history of sexuality in America.* New York: Harper & Row.

Dempster, F. N. (1988). The spacing effect: A case study in the failure to apply the results of psychological research. *American Psychologist, 43,* 627–634.

Denmark, F. L., Russo, N. F., Frieze, I. H., & Sechzer, J. A. (1988). Guidelines for avoiding sexism in psychological research: A report of the Ad Hoc Committee on Nonsexist Research. *American Psychologist, 43,* 582–585.

Depue, R. A., & Monroe, S. M. (1978). Learned helplessness in the perspective of the depressive disorders: Conceptual and definitional issues. *Journal of Abnormal Psychology, 87,* 3–21.

Deutsch, M., & Krauss, R. M. (1960). The effect of threat upon interpersonal bargaining. *Journal of Abnormal and Social Psychology, 61,* 181–189.

DeVellis, R. F. (1991). *Scale development*. Newbury Park, CA: Sage.

Diener, E., & Crandall, R. (1978). *Ethics in social and behavioral research*. Chicago: University of Chicago Press.

Diesing, P. (1991). *How does social science work?* Pittsburgh: University of Pittsburgh Press.

Dill, C. A., Gilden, E. R., Hill, P. C., & Hanselka, L. L. (1982). Federal human subjects regulations: A methodological artifact? *Personality and Social Psychology Bulletin, 8*, 417–425.

Dillman, D. A. (1978). *Mail and telephone surveys*. New York: Wiley.

Dipboye, R. T., & Flanagan, M. (1979). Research settings in industrial and organizational psychology: Are findings in the field more generalizable than in the laboratory? *American Psychologist, 34*, 141–150.

Dishion, T. J., McCord, J., & Poulin, F. (1999). When interventions harm: Peer groups and problem behavior. *American Psychologist, 54*, 755–764.

Dobson, K. S. (1985). The relationship between anxiety and depression. *Clinical Psychology Review, 5*, 307–324.

Doob, A. N., & Macdonald, G. E. (1979). Television viewing and fear of victimization: Is the relationship causal? *Journal of Personality and Social Psychology, 37*, 170–179.

Dooley, D. (1995). *Social research methods* (3rd ed.). Upper Saddle River, NJ: Prentice Hall.

Douglas, R. J. (1992). How to write a highly cited article without even trying. *Psychological Bulletin, 112*, 405–408.

Downs, C. W., Smeyak, G. P., & Martin, E. (1980). *Professional interviewing*. New York: Harper Collins.

Drew, C. J. (1976). *Introduction to designing research and evaluation*. St. Louis: Mosby.

Duckitt, J. (1992a). Psychology and prejudice: A historical analysis and integrative framework. *American Psychologist, 47*, 1182–1193.

Duckitt, J. (1992b). *The social psychology of prejudice*. New York: Praeger.

Durlak, J. A., & Lipsey, M. W. (1991). A practitioner's guide to meta-analysis. *American Journal of Community Psychology, 19*, 291–332.

Dworkin, R. J. (1992). *Researching persons with mental illness*. Newbury Park, CA: Sage.

Dwyer, C. A. (1979). The role of tests and their construction in producing apparent sex-related differences. In M. A. Wittig & A. C. Petersen (Eds.), *Sex-related differences in cognitive functioning* (pp. 335–353). New York: Academic Press.

Dyer, K., Christian, W. P., & Luce, S. C. (1982). The role of response delay in improving the discrimination performance of autistic children. *Journal of Applied Behavior Analysis, 15*, 231–240.

Eagly, A. H., & Carli, L. L. (1981). Sex of researcher and sex-typed communications as determinants of sex differences in influenceability: A meta-analysis of social influence studies. *Psychological Bulletin, 90*, 1–20.

Ebbesen, E. B., Duncan, D., & Konecni, V. J. (1975). Effects of content of verbal aggression on future verbal aggression: A field experiment. *Journal of Experimental Social Psychology, 11*, 192–204.

Educational Testing Service. (1981). *Guide to the use of the Graduate Record Examination*. Princeton, NJ: Author.

Edwards, W., & Newman, J. R. (1982). *Multiattribute evaluation*. Beverly Hills, CA: Sage.

Eichler, M. (1988). *Nonsexist research methods*. Boston: Allen & Unwin.

Eichorn, D. H., & VandenBos, G. R. (1985). Dissemination of scientific and professional knowledge: Journal publication within the APA. *American Psychologist, 40*, 1309–1316.

Elig, T. W., & Frieze, I. H. (1979). Measuring causal attributions for success and failure. *Journal of Personality and Social Psychology, 37*, 621–634.

Elliot, A. J., & Harackiewicz, J. M. (1994). Goal setting, achievement orientation, and intrinsic motivation: A mediational analysis. *Journal of Personality and Social Psychology, 66*, 968–980.

Elliott, R. (1983). Fitting process research to the practicing psychotherapist. *Psychotherapy: Theory, Research, and Practice, 20,* 47–55.

Endler, N. S., & Parker, J. D. A. (1991). Personality research: Theories, issues, and methods. In M. Hersen, A. E. Kazdin, & A. S. Bellack (Eds.), *The clinical psychology handbook* (2nd ed., pp. 258–275). New York: Pergamon.

Epperson, D. L., Bushway, D. J., & Warman, R. E. (1983). Client self-termination after one counseling session: Effects of problem recognition, counselor gender, and counselor experience. *Journal of Counseling Psychology, 30,* 307–315.

Epstein, S. (1980). The stability of behavior II: Implications for psychological research. *American Psychologist, 35,* 790–806.

Estes, W. K. (1992). Ability testing: Postscript on ability tests, testing, and public policy. *Psychological Science, 3,* 278.

Estes, W. K. (1993, March). How to present visual information. *APS Observer,* pp. 6–9.

Evans, J. D. (1985). *Invitation to psychological research.* New York: Holt, Rinehart, & Winston.

Exline, R. V. (1971). Visual interaction: The glances of power and preference. *Nebraska Symposium on Motivation, 19,* 163–206.

Eyer, D. E. (1992). *Mother-infant bonding: A scientific fiction.* New Haven, CT: Yale University Press.

Eysenck, H. J. (1972). Primaries or second-order factors: A critical consideration of Cattell's 16PF battery. *British Journal of Social and Clinical Psychology, 11,* 265–269.

Fabrigar, L. R., Wegener, D. T., MacCallum, R. C., & Strahan, E. J. (1999). Evaluating the use of exploratory factor analysis in psychological research. *Psychological Methods, 4,* 272–299.

Farkas, G. M., Sine, L. F., & Evans, I. M. (1978). Personality, sexuality, and demographic differences between volunteers and nonvolunteers for a laboratory study of male sexual behavior. *Archives of Sexual Behavior, 7,* 513–520.

Fassinger, R. A. (1987). Use of structural equation modeling in counseling psychology research. *Journal of Counseling Psychology, 34,* 425–436.

Fazio, R. H., Cooper, M., Dayson, K., & Johnson, M. (1981). Control and the coronary-prone behavior pattern: Responses to multiple situational demands. *Personality and Social Psychology Bulletin, 7,* 97–102.

Feather, N. T. (1985). Masculinity, femininity, self-esteem, and subclinical depression. *Sex Roles, 12,* 491–499.

Feldman, R. A., Caplinger, T. E., & Wodarski, J. S. (1983). *The St. Louis conundrum: The effective treatment of antisocial youths.* Englewood Cliffs, NJ: Prentice Hall.

Feldman, R. S., & Rosen, F. P. (1978). Diffusion of responsibility in crime, punishment, and other adversity. *Law and Human Behavior, 2,* 313–322.

Festinger, L. (1957). *A theory of cognitive dissonance.* Stanford, CA: Stanford University Press.

Festinger, L., & Carlsmith, J. M. (1959). Cognitive consequences of forced compliance. *Journal of Abnormal and Social Psychology, 58,* 203–210.

Fiedler, F. E. (1967). *A theory of leadership effectiveness.* New York: McGraw-Hill.

Fiedler, F. E., Bell, C. H., Chemers, M. M., & Patrick, D. (1984). Increasing mine productivity and safety through management training and organization development: A comparative study. *Basic and Applied Social Psychology, 5,* 1–18.

Fillenbaum, S. (1966). Prior deception and subsequent experimental performance: The "faithful" subject. *Journal of Personality and Social Psychology, 4,* 532–537.

Fine, M. A., & Kurdek, L. A. (1993). Reflections on determining authorship credit and authorship order on faculty-student collaborations. *American Psychologist, 48,* 1141–1147.

Fink, A., & Kosecoff, J. (1985). *How to conduct surveys.* Beverly Hills, CA: Sage.

Firebaugh, G. (1978). A rule for inferring individual-level relationships from aggregate data. *American Sociological Review, 43,* 557–572.

Fischhoff, B. (1990). Psychology and public policy: Tool or toolmaker? *American Psychologist, 45,* 647–653.

Fishbein, M., & Ajzen, I. (1975). *Belief, attitude, intention, and behavior.* Reading, MA: Addison-Wesley.

Fiske, D. W., & Fogg, L. (1990). But the reviewers are making different criticisms of my paper! Diversity and uniqueness in reviewer comments. *American Psychologist, 45,* 591–598.

Fiske, S. T., Bersoff, D. N., Borgida, E., Deaux, K., & Heilman, M. E. (1991). Social science research on trial: Use of sex stereotyping research in *Price Waterhouse v. Hopkins. American Psychologist, 46,* 1049–1060.

Fiske, S. T., & Taylor, S. G. (1991). *Social cognition* (2nd ed.). New York: McGraw-Hill.

Forgas, J. P., & Bond, M. H. (1985). Cultural influences on the perception of interaction episodes. *Personality and Social Psychology Bulletin, 11,* 75–88.

Forsyth, D. R. (1998). *Group dynamics* (3rd ed.). Pacific Grove, CA: Brooks/Cole.

Fowler, F. J., Jr. (1988). *Survey research methods* (Rev. ed.). Newbury Park, CA: Sage.

Fowler, F. J., Jr., & Mangione, T. W. (1990). *Standardized survey interviewing.* Newbury Park, CA: Sage.

Fowler, R. L. (1985). Testing for substantive significance in applied research by specifying nonzero effect null hypotheses. *Journal of Applied Psychology, 70,* 215–218.

Fox, R. J., Crask, M. R., & Kim, J. (1988). Mail survey response rate: A meta-analysis of selected techniques for inducing response. *Public Opinion Quarterly, 52,* 467–491.

Foxx, R. M., & Rubinoff, A. (1979). Behavioral treatment of caffeinism: Reducing excessive coffee drinking. *Journal of Applied Behavior Analysis, 12,* 335–344.

Freedman, B. (1987). Scientific value and validity as ethical requirements for research: A proposed explication. *IRB: A Review of Human Subjects Research, 9*(6), 7–10.

Freedman, J. L. (1984). Effect of television violence on aggression. *Psychological Bulletin, 96,* 227–246.

Friedman, P. J. (1992). Mistakes and fraud in medical research. *Law, Medicine, and Health Care, 20,* 17–25.

Friedman, S., & Steinberg, S. (1989). *Writing and thinking in the social sciences.* Englewood Cliffs, NJ: Prentice Hall.

Friend, R., Rafferty, Y., & Bramel, D. (1990). A puzzling misinterpretation of the Asch "conformity" study. *European Journal of Social Psychology, 20,* 29–44.

Fromkin, L. H., & Streufert, S. (1976). Laboratory experimentation. In M. D. Dunnette (Ed.), *Handbook of industrial and organizational psychology* (pp. 415–465). Chicago: Rand-McNally.

Gaiser, T. J. (1997). Conducting on-line focus groups: A methodological discussion. *Social Science Computer Review, 15,* 135–144.

Gannon, L., Luchetta, T., Rhodes, K., Pardie, L., & Segrist, D. (1992). Sex bias in psychological research: Progress or complacency? *American Psychologist, 47,* 389–396.

Garcia, J. (1981). Tilting at the paper mills of academe. *American Psychologist, 36,* 149–158.

Garfield, E., & Welljams-Dorof, A. (1990). The impact of fraudulent research on the scientific literature: The Stephen E. Breuning case. *Journal of the American Medical Association, 263,* 1424–1426.

Garfield, S. L. (1979). Editorial. *Journal of Consulting and Clinical Psychology, 47,* 1–4.

Gergen, K. J. (1973). Social psychology as history. *Journal of Personality and Social Psychology, 26,* 309–320.

Gescheider, G. A., Catlin, E. C., & Fontana, A. M. (1982). Psychophysical measurement of the judged seriousness of crimes and severities of punishments. *Bulletin of the Psychonomic Society, 19,* 275–278.

Ghiselli, E. E., Campbell, J. P., & Zedeck, S. (1981). *Measurement theory for the behavioral sciences.* San Francisco: Freeman.

Gilbert, D. T., & Osborne, R. E. (1989). Thinking backward: Some curable and incurable consequences of cognitive busyness. *Journal of Personality and Social Psychology, 57,* 940–949.

Gilligan, C. (1982). *In a different voice.* Cambridge, MA: Harvard University Press.

Gilovich, T. (1991). *How we know what isn't so.* New York: Free Press.

Glass, G. V. (1978). In defense of generalization. *Brain and Behavioral Sciences, 3,* 394–395.

Glesne, C., & Peshkin, A. (1992). *Becoming qualitative researchers.* White Plains, NY: Longman.

Gold, R. L. (1969). Roles in sociological observation. In G. J. McCall & J. L. Simms (Eds.), *Issues in participant observation* (pp. 30–39). Reading, MA: Addison-Wesley.

Goldberg, L. R. (1977). Admissions to the Ph.D. program in the department of psychology. *American Psychologist, 32,* 663–668.

Goldman, A. E., & McDonald, S. S. (1987). *The group depth interview.* Englewood Cliffs, NJ: Prentice Hall.

Goldman, B. A., & Saunders, J. L. (1997). *Directory of unpublished experimental measures* (Vol. 7). Dubuque, IA: Brown.

Gonzales, M. H., & Meyers, S. A. (1993). "Your mother would like me": Self-presentation in the personal ads of heterosexual and homosexual men and women. *Personality and Social Psychology Bulletin, 19,* 131–142.

Gonzalez, R., Ellsworth, P. C., & Pembroke, M. (1993). Response bias in lineups and showups. *Journal of Personality and Social Psychology, 64,* 525–537.

Goodall, J. (1978). Chimp killings: Is it the man in them? *Science News, 113,* 276.

Goodyear, R. K., Crego, C. A., & Johnston, M. W. (1992). Ethical issues in the supervision of student research: A study of critical incidents. *Professional Psychology: Research and Practice, 23,* 203–210.

Gordon, M. E., Schmitt, N., & Schneider, W. (1984). An evaluation of laboratory research on bargaining and negotiations. *Industrial Relations, 23,* 218–233.

Gordon, M. E., Slade, L. A., & Schmitt, N. (1986). The "science of the sophomore" revisited: From conjecture to empiricism. *Academy of Management Review, 11,* 191–207.

Gottfredson, S. D. (1978). Evaluating psychological research reports: Dimensions, reliability, and correlates of quality judgments. *American Psychologist, 33,* 920–934.

Graham, S. (1992). "Most of the subjects were white and middle-class": Trends in published research on African-Americans in selected APA journals, 1970–1989. *American Psychologist, 47,* 629–639.

Green, B. F. (1992). Exposé or smear? The Burt affair. *Psychological Science, 3,* 328–331.

Green, B. F., & Hall, J. A. (1984). Quantitative methods for literature reviews. *Annual Review of Psychology, 35,* 37–53.

Greenberg, J. (1990). Employee theft as a reaction to underpayment inequity: The hidden cost of pay cuts. *Journal of Applied Psychology, 75,* 561–568.

Greenberg, J., & Folger, R. (1988). *Controversial issues in social research methods.* New York: Springer.

Greenberg, J. S. (1983). *Comprehensive stress management.* Dubuque, IA: Brown.

Greene, E., & Loftus, E. F. (1984). What's in the news? The influence of well-publicized news events on psychological research and courtroom trials. *Basic and Applied Social Psychology, 5,* 211–221.

Greenwald, A. G. (1975). Consequences of prejudice against the null hypothesis. *Psychological Bulletin, 82,* 1–20.

Greenwald, A. G. (1976). Within-subjects designs: To use or not to use? *Psychological Bulletin, 83,* 314–320.

Greenwald, A. G., Pratkanis, A. R., Leippe, M. R., & Baumgardner, M. H. (1986). Under what conditions does theory obstruct research progress? *Psychological Review, 93,* 216–229.

Griffin, K. W., Botvin, G. J., Doyle, M. M., Diaz, T., & Epstein, J. A. (1999). A six-year follow-up study of determinants of heavy cigarette smoking among high-school seniors. *Journal of Behavioral Medicine, 22,* 271–284.

Grisso, T., Baldwin, E., Blanck, P. D., Rotheram-Borus, M. J., Schooler, N. R., & Thompson, T. (1991). Standards in research: APA's mechanism for monitoring the challenges. *American Psychologist, 46,* 758–766.

Gronlund, N. E. (1988). *How to construct achievement tests* (4th ed.). Englewood Cliffs, NJ: Prentice Hall.

Gruenfeld, D. H., & Preston, J. (2000). Upending the status quo: Cognitive complexity in U.S. Supreme Court justices who overturn legal precedent. *Personality and Social Psychology Bulletin, 26,* 1013–1022.

Gunst, R. F., & Mason, R. L. (1980). *Regression analysis and its applications.* New York: Dekker.

Guthrie, R. V. (1998). *Even the rat was white* (2nd ed.). Needham Heights, MA: Allyn & Bacon.

Guzzo, R. A., Jackson, S. E., & Katzell, R. A. (1987). Meta-analysis analysis. *Research in Organizational Behavior, 9,* 407–442.

Guzzo, R. A., Jette, R. D., & Katzell, R. A. (1985). The effects of psychologically based intervention programs on worker productivity. *Personnel Psychology, 38,* 275–292.

Hackman, J. R., & Oldham, G. R. (1980). *Work redesign.* Reading, MA: Addison-Wesley.

Hagenaars, J. A., & Cobben, N. P. (1978). Age, cohort, and period: A general model for the analysis of social change. *Netherlands Journal of Sociology, 14,* 59–91.

Halvorsen, K. T. (1994). The reporting format. In H. Cooper & L. V. Hedges (Eds.), *The handbook of research synthesis* (pp. 425–437). New York: Russell Sage Foundation.

Hamilton, D. L. (1968). Personality attributes associated with extreme response style. *Psychological Bulletin, 69,* 192–203.

Hamilton, V. L., Hoffman, W. S., Broman, C. L., & Rauma, D. (1993). Unemployment, distress, and coping: A panel study of autoworkers. *Journal of Personality and Social Psychology, 65,* 234–247.

Haney, C., Banks, W. C., & Zimbardo, P. G. (1973). Interpersonal dynamics in a simulated prison. *International Journal of Criminology and Penology, 1,* 69–97.

Harcum, E. R. (1990). Guidance from the literature for accepting a null hypothesis when its truth is expected. *Journal of General Psychology, 117,* 325–344.

Harris, F. C., & Lahey, B. B. (1982). Subject reactivity in direct observation assessments: A review and critical analysis. *Clinical Psychology Review, 2,* 523–538.

Hartlage, L. C. (1988). Notice. *American Psychologist, 43,* 1092.

Harvey, D. F., & Brown, D. R. (1996). *An experiential approach to organizational development* (5th ed.). Englewood Cliffs, NJ: Prentice Hall.

Hatfield, E., & Sprecher, S. (1986). *Mirror, mirror . . . : The importance of looks in everyday life.* Albany: State University of New York Press.

Hay, L. R., Nelson, R. O., & Hay, W. W. (1980). Methodological problems in the use of participant observers. *Journal of Applied Behavioral Analysis, 13,* 501–504.

Hayes, S. C., & Leonhard, C. (1991). The role of the individual case in clinical science and practice. In M. Hersen, A. E. Kazdin, & A. S. Bellack (Eds.), *The handbook of clinical psychology* (pp. 223–238). New York: Pergamon.

Haynes, S. N., & Horn, W. F. (1982). Reactivity in behavioral observation: A review. *Behavioral Assessment, 4,* 369–385.

Hays, W. L. (1973). *Statistics for the social sciences* (2nd ed.). New York: Holt, Rinehart, & Winston.

Hearnshaw, L. S. (1979). *Cyril Burt: Psychologist.* Ithaca, NY: Cornell University Press.

Hearold, S. (1986). A synthesis of 1043 effects of television on social behavior. In G. Comstock (Ed.), *Public communication and behavior* (Vol. 1, pp. 65–133). Orlando, FL: Academic Press.

Hedges, L. V., & Becker, B. J. (1986). Statistical methods in the meta-analysis of research on gender differences. In J. S. Hyde & M. C. Linn (Eds.), *The psychology of gender: Advances through meta-analysis* (pp. 14–50). Baltimore: Johns Hopkins University Press.

Hedges, L. V., & Olkin, I. (1985). *Statistical methods for meta-analysis*. Orlando, FL: Academic Press.

Heinsman, D. T., & Shadish, W. R. (1996). Assignment methods in experimentation: When do nonrandomized experiments approximate answers from randomized experiments? *Psychological Methods, 1*, 154–169.

Heinssen, R. K., Jr., Glass, C. R., & Knight, L. A. (1987). Assessing computer anxiety: Development and validation of the Computer Anxiety Rating Scale. *Computers in Human Behavior, 3*, 49–59.

Helmreich, R., Aronson, E., & LeFan, J. (1970). To err is humanizing—sometimes: Effects of self-esteem, competence, and a pratfall on interpersonal attraction. *Journal of Personality and Social Psychology, 16*, 259–264.

Hendrick, C., & Jones, R. A. (1972). *The nature of theory and research in social psychology*. New York: Academic Press.

Henninger, M. (1997). *Don't just surf: Effective research strategies for the Net*. Sydney, Australia: University of New South Wales Press.

Henry, G. T. (1990). *Practical sampling*. Newbury Park, CA: Sage.

Henshel, R. L. (1980). The purposes of laboratory experimentation and the virtues of deliberate artificiality. *Journal of Experimental Social Psychology, 16*, 466–478.

Herbert, J., & Attridge, C. (1975). A guide for developers and users of observation systems and manuals. *American Educational Research Journal, 12*, 1–20.

Herek, G. M. (1988). Heterosexuals' attitudes toward lesbians and gay men: Correlates and gender differences. *Journal of Sex Research, 25*, 451–477.

Herek, G. M., & Capitanio, J. P. (1996). "Some of my best friends": Intergroup contact, concealable stigma, and heterosexuals' attitudes toward gay men and lesbians. *Personality and Social Psychology Bulletin, 12*, 412–424.

Hewson, C. M., Laurent, D., & Vogel, C. M. (1996). Proper methodologies for psychological and sociological studies conducted via the Internet. *Behavior Research Methods, Instruments, & Computers, 28*, 186–191.

Higgens, R. L., & Marlatt, G. A. (1973). Effects of anxiety arousal on the consumption of alcohol by alcoholics and social drinkers. *Journal of Consulting and Clinical Psychology, 41*, 426–433.

Himmelstein, J. L., & McRae, J. A. (1988). Social issues and socioeconomic status. *Public Opinion Quarterly, 52*, 492–512.

Hochschild, A. R. (1973). *The unexpected community*. Berkeley: University of California Press.

Hodgins, H. S., & Koestner, R. (1993). The origins of nonverbal sensitivity. *Personality and Social Psychology Bulletin, 19*, 466–473.

Holden, C. (1987). NIMH finds a case of "serious misconduct." *Science, 235*, 1566–1567.

Hollenbeck, J. R., & Klein, H. J. (1987). Goal commitment and the goal-setting process. *Journal of Applied Psychology, 72*, 212–220.

Holmes, D. S. (1976a). Debriefing after psychological experiments: I. Effectiveness of postdeception dehoaxing. *American Psychologist, 31*, 858–867.

Holmes, D. S. (1976b). Debriefing after psychological experiments: II. Effectiveness of postdeception desensitization. *American Psychologist, 31*, 868–875.

Holsti, O. R. (1968). Content analysis. In G. Lindzey & E. Aronson (Eds.), *Handbook of social psychology* (2nd ed., Vol. 2, pp. 596–692). Reading, MA: Addison-Wesley.

Holsti, O. R. (1969). *Content analysis for the social sciences and humanities*. Reading, MA: Addison-Wesley.

Hopkins, K. D. (1982). The unit of analysis: Group means versus individual observations. *American Educational Research Journal, 19,* 5–18.

Hovland, C. I., & Sherif, M. (1952). Judgmental phenomena and scales of attitude measurement: Item displacement in Thurstone scales. *Journal of Abnormal and Social Psychology, 47,* 822–832.

Howard, K. I., Kopta, S. M., Krause, M. S., & Orlinski, D. E. (1986). The dose-effect relationship in psychotherapy. *American Psychologist, 41,* 159–164.

Hoyt, W. T., & Kerns, M. D. (1999). Magnitude and moderators of bias in observer ratings: A meta-analysis. *Psychological Methods, 4,* 403–424.

Huck, S. W., Cormier, W. H., & Bounds, W. G., Jr. (1974). *Reading statistics and research.* New York: Harper & Row.

Huck, S. W., & Sandler, H. M. (1979). *Rival hypotheses.* New York: Harper & Row.

Humphreys, L. (1975). *Tearoom trade* (Enlarged ed.). New York: Aldine.

Hunter, J. E., & Schmidt, F. L. (1990). *Methods of meta-analysis.* Newbury Park, CA: Sage.

Hunter, J. E., Schmidt, F. L., & Hunter, R. (1979). Differential validity of employment tests by race: A comprehensive review and analysis. *Psychological Bulletin, 86,* 721–735.

Huxley, A. (1932). *Brave new world.* London: Chatto & Windus.

Hyde, J. S. (1984). How large are gender differences in aggression? A developmental meta-analysis. *Developmental Psychology, 20,* 722–736.

Ilgen, D. R. (1986). Laboratory research: A question of when, not if. In E. A. Locke (Ed.), *Generalizing from laboratory to field settings* (pp. 257–267). Lexington, MA: Lexington Books.

Imber, S. D., Glanz, L. M., Elkin, I., Sotsky, S. M., Boyer, J., & Leber, W. R. (1986). Ethical issues in psychotherapy research: Problems in a collaborative clinical trials study. *American Psychologist, 41,* 137–146.

Jackson, G. B. (1980). Methods for integrative reviews. *Review of Educational Research, 50,* 438–460.

Jacob, T., Krahn, G. L., & Leonard, K. (1991). Parent-child interactions in families with alcoholic fathers. *Journal of Consulting and Clinical Psychology, 59,* 176–181.

Jacob, T., & Leonard, K. (1991). Experimental drinking procedures in the study of alcoholics and their families: A consideration of ethical issues. *Journal of Consulting and Clinical Psychology, 59,* 249–255.

Jacob, T., Seilhamer, R. A., & Rushe, R. (1989). Alcoholism and family interactions: A research paradigm. *American Journal of Drug and Alcohol Abuse, 15,* 73–91.

Jacobson, N. S., & Truax, P. (1991). Clinical significance: A statistical approach to defining meaningful change in psychotherapy research. *Journal of Consulting and Clinical Psychology, 59,* 12–19.

Janis, I. L. (1972). *Victims of groupthink.* Boston: Houghton Mifflin.

John, O. P. (1990). The "Big Five" factor taxonomy: Dimensions of personality in the natural language and questionnaires. In L. A. Pervin (Ed.), *Handbook of personality theory and research* (pp. 66–100). New York: Guilford.

Johnson, B. T. (1993). *DSTAT: Software for the meta-analytic review of research literatures.* Hillsdale, NJ: Erlbaum.

Johnson, B. T., & Eagly, A. H. (1989). Effects of involvement on persuasion: A meta-analysis. *Psychological Bulletin, 106,* 290–314.

Johnson, C. G. (1982). Risks in the publication of fieldwork. In J. E. Sieber (Ed.), *The ethics of social research: Fieldwork, regulation, and publication* (pp. 71–91). New York: Springer.

Joinson, A. (1999). Social desirability, anonymity, and Internet-based questionnaires. *Behavior Research Methods, Instruments, & Computers, 31,* 433–438.

Jones, R. A. (1985). *Research methods in the social and behavioral sciences.* Sunderland, MA: Sinauer.

Joswick, K. E. (1994). Getting the most from PsycLIT: Recommendations for searching. *Teaching of Psychology, 21*, 49–53.

Joy, L. A., Kimball, M. M., & Zabrack, M. L. (1986). Television and children's aggressive behavior. In T. M. Williams (Ed.), *The impact of television* (pp. 303–360). Orlando, FL: Academic Press.

Joynson, R. B. (1989). *The Burt affair.* New York: Routledge.

Judd, C. M., Smith, E. R., & Kidder, L. H. (1991). *Research methods in social relations* (6th ed.). Fort Worth, TX: Holt, Rinehart & Winston.

Jung, J. (1981). Is it possible to measure generalizability from laboratory to life, and is it really that important? In I. Silverman (Ed.), *Generalizing from laboratory to life* (pp. 39–49). San Francisco: Jossey-Bass.

Kadden, R. M., Cooney, N. L., Getter, H., & Litt, M. D. (1989). Matching alcoholics to coping skills or interactional therapies: Posttreatment results. *Journal of Consulting and Clinical Psychology, 57*, 698–704.

Kallman, W. M., & Feuerstein, M. J. (1986). Psychophysiological procedures. In A. R. Ciminero, K. S. Calhoun, & H. E. Adams (Eds.), *Handbook of behavioral assessment* (2nd ed., pp. 325–350). New York: Wiley.

Kanter, R. M. (1977). *Men and women of the corporation.* New York: Basic Books.

Karlins, M., Coffman, T. L., & Walters, G. (1969). On the fading of social stereotypes: Studies in three generations of college students. *Journal of Personality and Social Psychology, 13*, 1–16.

Kazdin, A. E. (1982). *Single-case research designs.* New York: Oxford University Press.

Kazdin, A. E. (1997). *Research design in clinical psychology* (3rd ed.). Needham Heights, MA: Allyn & Bacon.

Keith-Spiegel, P. (1983). Children and consent to participate in research. In G. B. Melton, G. P. Koocher, & M. J. Saks (Eds.), *Children's competence to consent* (pp. 179–211). New York: Plenum.

Keith-Spiegel, P., & Koocher, G. P. (1985). *Ethics in psychology.* New York: Random House.

Kellehear, A. (1993). *The unobstrusive researcher.* St. Leonards, Australia: Allen & Unwin.

Kelly, J. A., Furman, W., & Young, V. (1978). Problems associated with the typological measurement of sex roles and androgyny. *Journal of Consulting and Clinical Psychology, 46*, 1574–1576.

Kelman, H. C. (1965). Manipulation of human behavior: An ethical dilemma for the social scientist. *Journal of Social Issues, 21*(2), 31–46.

Kendall, P. C., & Beutler, L. E. (1991). Editorial comment on Jacob et al., "Parent-child interactions in families with alcoholic fathers." *Journal of Consulting and Clinical Psychology, 59*, 183.

Kendler, H. H. (1993). Psychology and the ethics of social policy. *American Psychologist, 48*, 1046–1053.

Kenny, D. A., Kashy, D. A., & Bolger, N. (1998). Data analysis in social psychology. In D. T. Gilbert, S. T. Fiske, & G. Lindzey (Eds.), *Handbook of social psychology* (4th ed., Vol. 1, pp. 233–265). Boston: McGraw-Hill.

Kerckhoff, A. C., & Back, K. W. (1968). *The June bug: A study of hysterical contagion.* New York: Appleton-Century-Crofts.

Kidd, G. R., & Greenwald, A. G. (1988). Attention, rehearsal, and memory for serial order. *American Journal of Psychology, 101*, 259–279.

Kidder, T. (1981). *The soul of a new machine.* Boston: Little, Brown.

Kimble, G. A. (1984). Psychology's two cultures. *American Psychologist, 39*, 833–839.

Kimble, G. A. (1989). Psychology from the standpoint of a generalist. *American Psychologist, 44*, 491–499.

Kimmel, A. J. (1988). *Ethics and values in applied social research.* Newbury Park, CA: Sage.

Kimmel, A. J. (1996). *Ethical issues in behavioral research.* Cambridge, MA: Blackwell.

Kite, M. E. (1992). Age and the spontaneous self-concept. *Journal of Applied Social Psychology, 22,* 1828–1837.

Klitzner, M., Gruenewald, P. J., Bamberger, E., & Rossiter, C. (1994). A quasi-experimental evaluation of Students Against Drunk Driving. *American Journal of Drug and Alcohol Abuse, 20,* 57–74.

Klosko, J. S., Barlow, D. H., Tassinari, R., & Cerny, J. A. (1990). A comparison of Alprazolam and behavior therapy in the treatment of panic disorder. *Journal of Consulting and Clinical Psychology, 58,* 77–84.

Knerr, C. R., Jr. (1982). What to do before and after a subpoena of data arrives. In J. E. Sieber (Ed.), *The ethics of social research: Surveys and experiments* (pp. 191–206). New York: Springer.

Knoke, D., & Bohrnstedt, G. W. (1994). *Statistics for social data analysis* (3rd ed.). Itasca, IL: Peacock.

Koocher, G. P. (1977). Bathroom behavior and human dignity. *Journal of Personality and Social Psychology, 35,* 120–121.

Koocher, G. P. (1991). Questionable methods in alcoholism research. *Journal of Consulting and Clinical Psychology, 59,* 246–248.

Koocher, G. P., & Keith-Spiegel, P. C. (1990). *Children, ethics, and the law.* Lincoln: University of Nebraska Press.

Koocher, G. P., & Keith-Spiegel, P. (1998). *Ethics in psychology* (2nd ed.). New York: Oxford University Press.

Kraemer, H. C., & Thiemann, S. (1987). *How many subjects?* Newbury Park, CA: Sage.

Krantz, J. H., & Dalal, R. (2000). Validity of Web-based psychological research. In M. Birnbaum (Ed.), *Psychological experiments on the Internet* (pp. 35–60). San Diego, CA: Academic Press.

Krasner, L., & Houts, A. C. (1984). A study of the "value" systems of behavioral scientists. *American Psychologist, 39,* 840–850.

Kratochwill, T. R. (1992). Single-case research design and analysis: An overview. In T. R. Kratochwill & J. L. Levin (Eds.), *Single-case research design and analysis* (pp. 1–14). Hillsdale, NJ: Erlbaum.

Kratochwill, T. R., & Levin, J. R. (Eds.). (1992). *Single-case research design and analysis.* Hillsdale, NJ: Erlbaum.

Kratochwill, T. R., Mott, S. E., & Dodson, C. L. (1984). Case study and single-case research in clinical and applied psychology. In A. S. Bellack & M. Hersen (Eds.), *Research methods in clinical psychology* (pp. 55–99). New York: Pergamon.

Kremer, J. F., & Stephens, L. (1983). Attributions and arousal as mediators of mitigation's effect on retaliation. *Journal of Personality and Social Psychology, 45,* 335–343.

Krippendorff, K. (1980). *Content analysis.* Beverly Hills, CA: Sage.

Krishef, C. H. (1991). *Fundamental approaches to single subject design and analysis.* Malabar, FL: Krieger.

Krosnick, J. A. (1999a). Maximizing questionnaire quality. In J. P. Robinson, P. R. Shaver, & L. S. Wrightsman (Eds.), *Measures of political attitudes* (pp. 37–57). San Diego, CA: Academic Press.

Krosnick, J. A. (1999b). Survey research. *Annual Review of Psychology, 50,* 537–567.

Krueger, R. A. (1994). *Focus groups* (2nd ed.). Thousand Oaks, CA: Sage.

Kruglanski, A. W. (1975). The human subject in the psychology experiment: Fact and artifact. In L. Berkowitz (Ed.), *Advances in experimental social psychology* (Vol. 8, pp. 101–147). New York: Academic Press.

Kuhn, T. S. (1970). *The structure of scientific revolutions* (2nd ed.). Chicago: University of Chicago Press.

Lamal, P. A. (1990). On the importance of replication. *Journal of Social Behavior and Personality*, 5, 31–35.

Lambert, M. J., Masters, K. S., & Ogles, B. M. (1991). Outcome research in counseling. In C. E. Watkins, Jr., & L. J. Schneider (Eds.), *Research in counseling* (pp. 51–83). Hillsdale, NJ: Erlbaum.

Landy, D., & Aronson, E. (1968). Liking for an evaluator as a function of his discernment. *Journal of Personality and Social Psychology*, 9, 133–141.

Landy, F. J. (1986). Stamp collecting versus science: Validation as hypothesis testing. *American Psychologist*, 41, 1183–1192.

Landy, F. J. (1989). *Psychology of work behavior* (4th ed.). Pacific Grove, CA: Brooks/Cole.

Lassiter, G. D., & Dudley, K. A. (1991). The *a priori* value of basic research: The case of video-taped confessions. *Journal of Social Behavior and Personality*, 6, 7–16.

Lassiter, G. D., & Irvine, A. A. (1986). Videotaped confessions: The impact of camera point of view on judgments of coercion. *Journal of Applied Social Psychology*, 16, 268–276.

Latané, B., & Darley, J. M. (1968). Group inhibition of bystander intervention in emergencies. *Journal of Personality and Social Psychology*, 10, 215–221.

Latané, B., & Darley, J. M. (1970). *The unresponsive bystander*. New York: Appleton-Century-Crofts.

Lau, R. R., & Russell, D. (1980). Attributions in the sports pages. *Journal of Personality and Social Psychology*, 39, 29–38.

Lawshe, C. H. (1975). A quantitative approach to content validity. *Personnel Psychology*, 28, 563–575.

Leak, G. K. (1981). Student perception of coercion and value from participation in psychological research. *Teaching of Psychology*, 8, 147–149.

Leavitt, F. (1991). *Research methods for behavioral scientists*. Dubuque, IA: Brown.

Lee, F., Hallahan, M., & Herzog, T. (1996). Explaining real life events: How culture and domain shape attributions. *Personality and Social Psychology Bulletin*, 22, 731–747.

Lee, F., & Peterson, C. (1997). Content analysis of archival data. *Journal of Consulting and Clinical Psychology*, 65, 959–969.

Lenneberg, E. H. (1962). Understanding language without ability to speak: A case report. *Journal of Abnormal and Social Psychology*, 65, 419–425.

Leviton, L. C., & Hughes, E. F. X. (1981). Research on the utilization of evaluations: A review and synthesis. *Evaluation Review*, 5, 525–548.

Lewin, M. (1979). *Understanding psychological research*. New York: Wiley.

Lewontin, B. C., Rose, S., & Kamin, L. (1984). *Not in our genes*. New York: Pantheon.

Lidz, C. W., Meisel, A., Zerabauel, E., Carter, M., Sestak, R. M., & Roth, L. H. (1984). *Informed consent: A study of decision-making in psychiatry*. New York: Guilford.

Liebow, E. (1967). *Talley's corner*. Boston: Little, Brown.

Light, R. J., & Pillemer, D. B. (1984). *Summing up: The science of reviewing research*. Cambridge, MA: Harvard University Press.

Lindsey, D. (1978). *The scientific publication system in social science*. San Francisco: Jossey-Bass.

Linz, D., Donnerstein, E., & Penrod, S. (1987). The findings and recommendations of the Attorney General's Commission on Pornography: Do the psychological "facts" fit the political fury? *American Psychologist*, 42, 946–953.

Lipsey, M. W. (1990). *Design sensitivity*. Newbury Park, CA: Sage.

Lipsey, M. W., & Wilson, D. B. (2001). *Practical meta-analysis*. Thousand Oaks, CA: Sage.

Lipsey, M. W., Crosse, S., Dunkle, J., Pollard, J., & Stobart, G. (1985). Evaluation: The state of the art and the sorry state of the science. In D. S. Cordray (Ed.), *Utilizing prior research in evaluation planning* (pp. 7–27). San Francisco: Jossey-Bass.

Locke, E. A. (1986). Generalizing from laboratory to field: Ecological validity or abstraction of essential elements? In E. A. Locke (Ed.), *Generalizing from laboratory to field settings* (pp. 3–9). Lexington, MA: Lexington Books.

Locke, E. A., & Latham, G. P. (1990). *A theory of goal setting and task performance.* Englewood Cliffs, NJ: Prentice Hall.

Lofland, J., & Lofland, L. H. (1995). *Analyzing social settings* (3rd ed.). Belmont, CA: Wadsworth.

Loftus, E. F. (1993). The reality of repressed memories. *American Psychologist, 48,* 518–537.

Loftus, E. F., & Monahan, J. (1980). Trial by data: Psychological research as legal evidence. *American Psychologist, 35,* 270–283.

Loftus, E. F., & Palmer, J. P. (1974). Reconstruction of automobile destruction: An example of the interaction between language and memory. *Journal of Verbal Learning and Verbal Behavior, 13,* 585–589.

Loher, B. T., Noe, R. A., Moeller, N. L., & Fitzgerald, M. P. (1985). A meta-analysis of the relation of job characteristics to job satisfaction. *Journal of Applied Psychology, 70,* 280–289.

Loo, C., Fong, K. T., & Iwamasa, G. (1988). Ethnicity and cultural diversity: An analysis of work published in community psychology journals, 1965–1985. *Journal of Community Psychology, 16,* 332–349.

Lord, F. M. (1956). The measurement of growth. *Educational and Psychological Measurement, 16,* 421–437.

Lowen, A., & Craig, J. R. (1968). The influence of level of performance on managerial style: An experimental object lesson in the ambiguity of correlational data. *Organization Behavior and Human Performance, 3,* 440–458.

Lunney, G. H. (1970). Using analysis of variance with a dichotomous dependent variable: An empirical study. *Journal of Educational Measurement, 7,* 263–269.

Lydon, J., & Dunkel-Schetter, C. (1994). Seeing is committing: A longitudinal study of bolstering commitment in amniocentesis patients. *Personality and Social Psychology Bulletin, 20,* 218–227.

Lykken, D. T. (1981). *A tremor in the blood: Uses and abuses of the lie detector.* New York: McGraw-Hill.

Lyon, D., & Greenberg, J. (1991). Evidence of codependency in women with an alcoholic parent: Helping out Mr. Wrong. *Journal of Personality and Social Psychology, 61,* 435–439.

MacCoun, R. J. (1998). Bias in the interpretation of and use of research results. *Annual Review of Psychology, 49,* 259–287.

MacCoun, R. J., & Kerr, N. L. (1987). Suspicion in the psychological laboratory: Kelman's prophecy revisited. *American Psychologist, 42,* 199.

Mackie, M. (1983). *Exploring gender relations.* Toronto: Butterworths.

Malfese, D. L., Murray, K. L., Martin, T. B., Peters, C. J., Tan, A. A., Gill, L. A., & Simos, P. A. (1996). Coordinating a research team. In F. T. L. Leong & J. T. Austin (Eds.), *The psychology research handbook* (pp. 311–324). Thousand Oaks, CA: Sage.

Mangione, T. W. (1995). *Mail surveys.* Thousand Oaks, CA: Sage.

Marascuilo, L. A., & Busk, P. L. (1987). Loglinear models: A way to study main effects and interactions for multidimensional contingency tables with categorical data. *Journal of Counseling Psychology, 34,* 443–455.

Marecek, J., Fine, M., & Kidder, L. (1997). Working between worlds: Qualitative methods and social psychology. *Journal of Social Issues, 53,* 631–644.

Maris, R. W. (1969). *Social forces in urban suicide.* Homewood, IL: Dorsey Press.

Marks, G., & Miller, N. (1987). Ten years of research on the false consensus effect: An empirical and theoretical review. *Psychological Bulletin, 102,* 72–90.

Marshall, C., & Rossman, G. B. (1989). *Designing qualitative research.* Newbury Park, CA: Sage.

Martin, C. J., Boersma, F. J., & Cox, D. L. (1965). A classification of associative strategies in paired-associate learning. *Psychonomic Science, 3,* 455–456.

Martin, J. A. (1996, December). Spam isn't just lunch meat any more, *Macworld, 13,* 185–187.

Martin, J. E., & Sachs, D. A. (1973). The effects of a self-control weight loss program on an obese woman. *Journal of Behavior Therapy and Experimental Psychiatry, 4,* 155–159.

Masters, J. C. (1984). Psychology, research, and social policy. *American Psychologist, 39,* 851–862.

Matlin, M. W. (1988). *Sensation and perception* (2nd ed.). Boston: Allyn & Bacon.

Matsumoto, D. (2000). *Culture and psychology* (2nd ed.). Belmont, CA: Wadsworth.

Maxwell, S. E., & Delaney, H. D. (1993). Bivariate median splits and spurious statistical significance. *Psychological Bulletin, 113,* 181–190.

McFatter, R. M. (1994). Interactions in predicting mood from extroversion and neuroticism. *Journal of Personality and Social Psychology, 66,* 570–578.

McGrath, J. E. (1981). Dilemmatics: The study of research choices and dilemmas. *American Behavioral Scientist, 25,* 179–210.

McGuire, W. J. (1964). Inducing resistance to persuasion. In L. Berkowitz (Ed.), *Advances in experimental social psychology* (Vol. 1, pp. 192–229). New York: Academic Press.

McGuire, W. J. (1973). The yin and yang of progress in social psychology: Seven koan. *Journal of Personality and Social Psychology, 26,* 446–456.

McGuire, W. J. (1984). Search for the self: Going beyond self-esteem and the reactive self. In R. A. Zucker, J. Arnoff, & A. I. Rabin (Eds.), *Personality and the prediction of behavior* (pp. 73–120). New York: Academic Press.

McGuire, W. J. (1985). Attitudes and attitude change. In G. Lindzey & E. Aronson (Eds.), *Handbook of social psychology* (3rd ed., Vol. 2, pp. 233–346). New York: Random House.

McGuire, W. J., & McGuire, C. V. (1982). Self-space: Sex differences and developmental trends in the social self. In J. Suls (Ed.), *Psychological perspectives on the self* (Vol. 1, pp. 71–96). Hillsdale, NJ: Erlbaum.

McHugh, M. C., Koeske, R., & Frieze, I. H. (1986). Issues to consider in conducting nonsexist psychological research. *American Psychologist, 41,* 879–890.

McKenna, W., & Kessler, S. (1977). Experimental design as a source of sex bias in social psychology. *Sex Roles, 3,* 117–128.

McNemar, Q. (1946). Opinion attitude methodology. *Psychological Bulletin, 43,* 289–374.

McSweeney, A. J. (1978). Effects of response cost on the behavior of a million persons: Charging for directory assistance in Cincinnati. *Journal of Applied Behavior Analysis, 11,* 47–51.

Meier, S. T. (1988). Predicting individual differences in performance on computer-administered tests and tasks: Development of the Computer Aversion Scale. *Computers in Human Behavior, 4,* 175–187.

Metalsky, G. I., Halberstadt, L. J., & Abramson, L. Y. (1987). Vulnerability to depressive mood reactions: Toward a more powerful test of the diathesis-stress and causal mediation components of the reformulated theory of depression. *Journal of Personality and Social Psychology, 52,* 386–393.

Meyer, J. P., & Mulherin, A. (1980). From attribution to helping: An analysis of the mediating effects of affect on expectancy. *Journal of Personality and Social Psychology, 39,* 201–210.

Michalak, E. E., & Szabo, A. (1998). Guidelines for Internet research: An update. *European Psychologist, 3,* 70–75.

Michell, J. (1986). Measurement scales and statistics: A clash of paradigms. *Psychological Bulletin, 100,* 398–407.

Middlemist, R. D., Knowles, E. S., & Matter, C. F. (1976). Personal space invasion in the lavatory: Suggestive evidence for arousal. *Journal of Personality and Social Psychology, 33,* 541–546.

Middlemist, R. D., Knowles, E. S., & Matter, C. F. (1977). What to do and what to report: A reply to Koocher. *Journal of Personality and Social Psychology, 35,* 122–124.

Milavsky, J. R., Stipp, H. H., Kessler, R. C., & Rubens, W. S. (1982). *Television and aggression.* New York: Academic Press.

Miles, M. B., & Huberman, A. M. (1984). *Qualitative data analysis*. Beverly Hills, CA: Sage.

Milgram, S. (1961). Nationality and conformity. *Scientific American, 205*(6), 45–51.

Milgram, S. (1974). *Obedience to authority*. New York: Harper & Row.

Milgram, S. (1977, October). Subject reaction: The neglected factor in the ethics of experimentation. *Hastings Center Report*, pp. 19–23.

Miller, P. M., Hersen, M., Eisler, R. M., & Watts, J. G. (1974). Contingent reinforcement of lowered blood/alcohol levels in an outpatient chronic alcoholic. *Behaviour Research and Therapy, 12*, 261–263.

Millman, S. (1968). Anxiety, comprehension, and susceptibility to social influence. *Journal of Personality and Social Psychology, 9*, 251–256.

Mills, J. (1976). A procedure for explaining experiments involving deception. *Personality and Social Psychology Bulletin, 2*, 3–13.

Mills, J. L. (1993). Data torturing. *New England Journal of Medicine, 329*, 1196–1199.

Mirvis, P. H., & Seashore, S. E. (1979). Being ethical in organizational research. *American Psychologist, 34*, 766–780.

Miskevich, S. L. (1996). Killing the goose that laid the golden eggs: Ethical issues in social science research on the Internet. *Science and Engineering Ethics, 2*, 241–242.

Mitchell, J. V., Jr. (Ed). (1983). *Tests in print III*. Lincoln: University of Nebraska Press.

Mitchell, M., & Jolley, J. (1992). *Research design explained* (2nd ed.) Fort Worth, TX: Harcourt Brace Jovanovich.

Mitroff, I. I., & Kilmann, R. H. (1978). *Methodological approaches to social science*. San Francisco: Jossey-Bass.

Money, J., & Ehrhardt, A. A. (1972). *Man and woman, boy and girl*. Baltimore: Johns Hopkins University Press.

Monteith, M. J. (1993). Self-regulation of prejudiced responses: Implications for progress in prejudice-reduction. *Journal of Personality and Social Psychology, 65*, 469–485.

Mook, D. G. (1983). In defense of external invalidity. *American Psychologist, 38*, 379–387.

Mooney, K. M., Cohn, E. S., & Swift, M. B. (1992). Physical distance and AIDS: Too close for comfort? *Journal of Applied Social Psychology, 22*, 1442–1452.

Morrow, L., Urtunski, P. B., Kim, Y., & Boller, F. (1981). Arousal responses to emotional stimuli and laterality of lesion. *Neuropsychologia, 19*, 65–72.

Morrow-Bradley, C., & Elliott, R. (1986). Utilization of psychotherapy research by practicing psychotherapists. *American Psychologist, 41*, 188–197.

Muehlenhard, C. L., Powch, I. G., Phelps, J. L., & Giusti, L. M. (1992). Definitions of rape: Scientific and political implications. *Journal of Social Issues, 48*(1), 23–44.

Mulkay, M., & Gilbert, G. N. (1986). Replication and mere replication. *Philosophy of the Social Sciences, 16*, 21–37.

Mullen, B. (1993). *Advanced BASIC meta-analysis*. Hillsdale, NJ: Erlbaum.

Mullen, B., Salas, E., & Miller, N. (1991). Using meta-analysis to test theoretical hypotheses in social psychology. *Personality and Social Psychology Bulletin, 17*, 258–264.

Murphy, L. L., Impara, J. C., & Plake, B. S. (Eds.). (1999). *Tests in print V*. Lincoln: University of Nebraska Press.

Murray, H. A. (1963). Studies of stressful interpersonal disputation. *American Psychologist, 18*, 28–36.

Musch, J., & Reips, U.-D. (2000). A brief history of Web experimenting. In M. Birnbaum (Ed.), *Psychological experiments on the Internet* (pp. 61–87). San Diego, CA: Academic Press.

Myers, J. L., DiCecco, J. V., White, J. B., & Borden, V. M. (1982). Repeated measures on dichotomous variables: Q and F tests. *Psychological Bulletin, 92*, 517–525.

Myers, R. H. (1986). *Classical and modern regression with applications*. Boston: Duxbury Press.

Nance, J. (1975). *The gentle Tasaday*. New York: Harcourt Brace Jovanovich.

National Commission for Protection of Human Subjects of Biomedical and Behavioral Research. (1978). *The Belmont report: Ethical principles and guidelines for the protection of human subjects of research* (DHEW Publication No. (OS) 78-0012). Washington, DC: U.S. Government Printing Office.

National Opinion Research Center [NORC]. (1998). *The General Social Survey* [On-line]. Retrieved July 24, 2000. Available World Wide Web: http://www.norc.uchicago.edu/gss/homepage.htm

Neisser, U. (1967). *Cognitive psychology*. New York: Appleton-Century-Crofts.

Neisser, U. (1981). John Dean's memory: A case study. *Cognition, 9*, 1–22.

Nelkin, D. (1982). Forbidden research: Limits to inquiry in the social sciences. In T. L. Beauchamp, R. R. Faden, R. J. Wallace, Jr., & L. Walters (Eds.), *Ethical issues in social science research* (pp. 163–174). Baltimore: Johns Hopkins University Press.

Neuliep, J. W., & Crandall, R. (1990). Editorial bias against replication research. *Journal of Social Behavior and Personality, 5*(4), 85–90.

Neuliep, J. W., & Crandall, R. (1993a). Everyone was wrong: There are lots of replications out there. *Journal of Social Behavior and Personality, 8*(6), 1–8.

Neuliep, J. W., & Crandall, R. (1993b). Reviewer bias against replication research. *Journal of Social Behavior and Personality, 8*(6), 21–29.

Newstead, S. E., & Arnold, J. (1989). The effect of response format on ratings of teaching. *Educational and Psychological Measurement, 49*, 33–43.

Newstead, S. E., & Collis, J. M. (1987). Context and the interpretation of quantifiers of frequency. *Ergonomics, 30*, 1447–1462.

Nezu, A. M., & Perri, M. G. (1989). Social problem-solving therapy for unipolar depression: An initial dismantling investigation. *Journal of Consulting and Clinical Psychology, 57*, 408–413.

Nickell, G. S., & Pinto, J. N. (1986). The Computer Attitude Scale. *Computers in Human Behavior, 2*, 301–306.

Nicks, S. D., Korn, J. H., & Mainieri, T. (1997). The rise and fall of deception in social psychology and personality research, 1921 to 1994. *Ethics & Behavior, 7*, 69–77.

Nisbett, R. E., & Wilson, T. (1977). Telling more than we can know: Verbal reports as data. *Psychological Review, 84*, 231–259.

Nolen-Hoeksema, S. (1987). Sex differences in unipolar depression: Evidence and theory. *Psychological Bulletin, 101*, 259–282.

Norman, D. A. (1988). *The psychology of everyday things*. New York: Basic Books.

Nye, R. D. (1999). *Three psychologies* (6th ed.). Pacific Grove, CA: Brooks/Cole.

Oakes, W. (1972). External validity and the use of real people as subjects. *American Psychologist, 27*, 959–962.

Oden, C. W., Jr., & MacDonald, W. S. (1978). The RIP in social scientific reporting. *American Psychologist, 33*, 952–954.

Ogloff, J. R., & Otto, R. K. (1991). Are research participants truly informed? Readability of informed consent forms used in research. *Ethics and Behavior, 1*, 239–252.

Olkin, I. (1990). History and goals. In K. W. Wachter & M. L. Straf (Eds.), *The future of meta-analysis* (pp. 3–10). New York: Russell Sage Foundation.

Ollendick, T. H. (1981). Self-monitoring and self-administered overcorrection. *Behavior Modification, 5*, 75–84.

Ollendick, T. H., Shapiro, E. S., & Barrett, R. P. (1981). Reducing stereotypic behavior: An analysis of treatment procedures utilizing an alternating treatments design. *Behavior Therapy, 12*, 570–577.

Orne, M. T. (1962). On the social psychology of the psychological experiment: With particular reference to demand characteristics and their implications. *American Psychologist, 17*, 776–783.

Orwell, G. (1949). *1984*. New York: Harcourt, Brace.

Osgood, S. E., Suci, G. J., & Tannenbaum, P. H. (1957). *The measurement of meaning*. Urbana: University of Illinois Press.

Parks, M. R., & Floyd, K. (1996). Making friends in cyberspace. *Journal of Communication, 46*, 80–97.

Parsonson, B. S., & Baer, D. M. (1992). The visual analysis of data, and current research into the stimuli controlling it. In T. R. Kratochwill & J. R. Levin (Eds.), *Single-case research design and analysis* (pp. 15–40). Hillsdale, NJ: Erlbaum.

Pasveer, K. A., & Ellard, J. H. (1998). The making of a personality inventory: Help from the WWW. *Behavior Research Methods, Instruments, & Computers, 30*, 309–313.

Patton, M. Q. (1986). *Utilization-focused evaluation* (2nd ed.). Beverly Hills, CA: Sage.

Patton, M. Q. (1990). *Qualitative evaluation and research methods* (2nd ed.). Newbury Park, CA: Sage.

Paulhus, D. L. (1991). Measurement and control of response bias. In J. P. Robinson, P. R. Shaver, & L. S. Wrightsman (Eds.), *Measures of personality and social psychological attitudes* (pp. 17–59). San Diego, CA: Academic Press.

Pedhazur, E. J. (1997). *Multiple regression in behavioral research* (3rd ed.). Fort Worth, TX: Harcourt College Publishers.

Penrod, S., Loftus, E. F., & Winkler, J. (1982). The reliability of eyewitness testimony: A psychological perspective. In N. L. Kerr & R. M. Bray (Eds.), *The psychology of the courtroom* (pp. 119–168). New York: Academic Press.

Peterson, C. (1980). Attribution in the sports pages: An archival investigation of the covariation hypothesis. *Social Psychology Quarterly, 43*, 136–141.

Peterson, C., & Seligman, M. E. P. (1984). Causal explanations as a risk factor for depression: Theory and evidence. *Psychological Review, 91*, 347–374.

Peterson, C., Seligman, M. E. P., & Valliant, G. E. (1988). Pessimistic explanatory style is a risk factor for physical illness: A thirty-five-year longitudinal study. *Journal of Personality and Social Psychology, 55*, 23–27.

Petty, M. M., Singleton, B., & Connell, D. W. (1992). An experimental evaluation of an organizational incentive plan in the electric utility industry. *Journal of Applied Psychology, 77*, 427–436.

Pfeifer, M. P., & Snodgrass, G. L. (1990). The continued use of retracted, invalid scientific literature. *Journal of the American Medical Association, 263*, 1420–1423.

Pfungst, O. (1965). *Clever Hans (the horse of Mr. von Osten)*. New York: Holt, Rinehart & Winston. (Original work published 1904)

Phares, V. (1992). Where's poppa? The relative lack of attention to the role of fathers in child and adolescent psychopathology. *American Psychologist, 47*, 656–664.

Piliavin, I. M., Rodin, J., & Piliavin, J. A. (1969). Good Samaritanism: An underground phenomenon? *Journal of Personality and Social Psychology, 13*, 289–299.

Piliavin, J. A., Dovidio, J. F., Gaertner, S. L., & Clark, R. P., III. (1981). *Emergency intervention*. New York: Academic Press.

Plake, B. S., & Impara, J. C. (Eds.) (1999). *Supplement to the thirteenth mental measurements yearbook*. Lincoln: University of Nebraska Press.

Platz, S. J., & Hosch, H. M. (1988). Cross-racial/ethnic eyewitness identification: A field study. *Journal of Applied Social Psychology, 18*, 972–984.

Plous, S. (2000). Tips on creating and maintaining an educational World Wide Web. *Teaching of Psychology, 27*, 63–70.

Podsakoff, P. M., & Farh, J. (1989). Effects of feedback sign and credibility on goal setting and task performance. *Organizational Behavior and Human Decision Processes, 44*, 45–67.

Pogue, D. (1993, November). Grammar crackers. *Macworld*, pp. 183–186.

Polivy, J., & Doyle, C. (1980). Laboratory induction of mood states through the reading of self-referent mood statements: Affective changes or demand characteristics? *Journal of Abnormal Psychology, 89*, 286–290.

Pomeroy, W. B. (1972). *Dr. Kinsey and the Institute for Sex Research.* New York: Harper & Row.

Pope, K. S., Keith-Spiegel, P., & Tabachnick, B. (1986). Sexual attraction to clients: The human therapist and the (sometimes) inhuman training system. *American Psychologist, 41*, 147–158.

Popovich, P. M., Hyde, K. R., Zakrajsek, T., & Blumer, C. (1987). Development of the Attitudes Toward Computer Usage Scale. *Educational and Psychological Measurement, 47*, 261–269.

Popper, K. R. (1959). *The logic of scientific discovery.* New York: Basic Books.

Porter, A. C., & Raudenbush, S. W. (1987). Analysis of covariance: Its model and use in psychological research. *Journal of Counseling Psychology, 34*, 383–392.

Posavac, E. J. (1992). Communicating applied social psychology to users: A challenge and an art. In F. B. Bryant, J. Edwards, R. S. Tinsdale, E. J. Posavac, L. Heath, E. Henderson, & Y. Suarez-Bakazar (Eds.), *Methodological issues in applied social psychology* (pp. 269–294). New York: Plenum.

Posavac, E. J., & Carey, R. G. (1997). *Program evaluation* (5th ed.). Upper Saddle River, NJ: Prentice Hall.

Prentice, D. A., & Miller, D. T. (1992). When small effects are impressive. *Psychological Bulletin, 112*, 160–164.

Price, R. L. (1985). A customer's view of organizational literature. In L. L. Cummings & P. J. Frost (Eds.), *Publishing in the organizational sciences* (pp. 125–132). Homewood, IL: Irwin.

Pyke, S. W., & Agnew, N. McK. (1991). *The science game* (5th ed.). Englewood Cliffs, NJ: Prentice Hall.

Quinn, R. P., Gutek, B. A., & Walsh, J. T. (1980). Telephone interviewing: A reappraisal and field experiment. *Basic and Applied Social Psychology, 1*, 127–153.

Rabinowitz, V. C., & Weseen, S. (1997). Elu(ci)d(at)ing epistemological impasses: Re-viewing the qualitative/quantitative debates in psychology. *Journal of Social Issues, 53*, 605–630.

Rasinski, K. A. (1989). The effect of question wording on public support for government spending. *Public Opinion Quarterly, 53*, 388–394.

Reed, J. G., & Baxter, P. M. (1992). *Library use: A handbook for psychology* (2nd ed.). Washington, DC: American Psychological Association.

Reips, U.-D. (2000). The Web experiment method: Advantages, disadvantages, and solutions. In M. Birnbaum (Ed.), *Psychological experiments on the Internet* (pp. 89–117). San Diego, CA: Academic Press.

Reisenzein, R. (1986). A structural equation analysis of Weiner's attribution-affect model of helping behavior. *Journal of Personality and Social Psychology, 50*, 1123–1133.

Reiss, A. J. (1968). Stuff and nonsense about social surveys and observation. In H. S. Becker, B. Geer, D. Riesman, & R. S. Weiss (Eds.), *Institutions and the person* (pp. 351–367). Chicago: Aldine.

Resnick, J. H., & Schwartz, T. (1973). Ethical standards as an independent variable in psychological research. *American Psychologist, 28*, 134–139.

Reynolds, P. D. (1979). *Ethical dilemmas and social science research.* San Francisco: Jossey-Bass.

Richter, M. L., & Seay, M. B. (1987). ANOVA designs with subjects and stimuli as random effects: Applications to prototype effects on recognition memory. *Journal of Personality and Social Psychology, 53*, 470–480.

Riger, S. (1992). Epistemological debates, feminist voices: Science, social values, and the study of women. *American Psychologist, 47*, 730–740.

Riordan, C. A., & Marlin, N. A. (1987). Some good news about some bad practices. *American Psychologist, 42*, 104–106.

Rivlin, A. (1973). Forensic social science. *Harvard Educational Review, 43*, 61–75.

Robbins, S. P. (1991). *Organizational behavior* (5th ed.). Englewood Cliffs, NJ: Prentice Hall.

Robinson, J. P., Shaver, P. R., & Wrightsman, L. S. (1991a). Criteria for scale selection and evaluation. In J. P. Robinson, P. R. Shaver, & L. S. Wrightsman (Eds.), *Measures of personality and social psychological attitudes* (pp. 1–16). San Diego, CA: Academic Press.

Robinson, J. P., Shaver, P. R., & Wrightsman, L. S. (Eds.). (1991b). *Measures of personality and social psychological attitudes*. San Diego, CA: Academic Press.

Robinson, W. S. (1950). Ecological correlations and the behavior of individuals. *American Sociological Review, 15*, 351–357.

Roese, N. J., & Jamieson, D. W. (1993). Twenty years of bogus pipeline research: A critical review and meta-analysis. *Psychological Bulletin, 114*, 363–375.

Rogers, C. R., & Skinner, B. F. (1956). Some issues concerning the control of human behavior: A symposium. *Science, 124*, 1057–1066.

Rogosa, D. R., Brandt, D., & Zimowski, M. (1982). A growth curve approach to the measurement of change. *Psychological Bulletin, 90*, 726–748.

Rogosa, D. R., & Willett, J. B. (1983). Demonstrating the reliability of the difference score in the measurement of change. *Journal of Educational Measurement, 20*, 335–343.

Rokeach, M. (1973). *The nature of human values*. New York: Free Press.

Roman, M. B. (1988, April). When good scientists turn bad. *Discover*, pp. 50–58.

Rosenblatt, A., & Greenberg, J. (1988). Depression and interpersonal attraction: The role of perceived similarity. *Journal of Personality and Social Psychology, 55*, 112–119.

Rosenthal, M. C. (1994). The fugitive literature. In H. Cooper & L. V. Hedges (Eds.), *The handbook of research synthesis* (pp. 85–94). New York: Russell Sage Foundation.

Rosenthal, R. (1976). *Experimenter effects in behavioral research* (2nd ed.). New York: Irvington.

Rosenthal, R. (1990a). An evaluation of procedures and results. In K. W. Wachter & M. L. Straf (Eds.), *The future of meta-analysis* (pp. 123–133). New York: Russell Sage Foundation.

Rosenthal, R. (1990b). Replication in behavioral research. *Journal of Social Behavior and Personality, 5*, 1–30.

Rosenthal, R. (1991). *Meta-analytic procedures for social research* (Rev. ed.). Newbury Park, CA: Sage.

Rosenthal, R. (1994). Science and ethics in conducting, analyzing, and reporting psychological research. *Psychological Science, 5*, 127–134.

Rosenthal, R., & Rosnow, R. L. (1975). *The volunteer subject*. New York: Wiley.

Rosenthal, R., & Rosnow, R. L. (1984). Applying Hamlet's question to the ethical conduct of research: A conceptual addendum. *American Psychologist, 39*, 561–563.

Rosenthal, R., & Rosnow, R. L. (1991). *Essentials of behavioral research* (2nd ed.). New York: McGraw-Hill.

Ross, L., Lepper, M. R., & Hubbard, M. (1975). Perspectives in self-perception and social perception: Biased attributional processes in the debriefing paradigm. *Journal of Personality and Social Psychology, 32*, 880–892.

Ross, R. R., & Allgeier, E. R. (1996). Behind the paper/pencil measurement of sexual coercion: Interview-based clarification of men's interpretations of Sexual Experiences Survey items. *Journal of Applied Social Psychology, 26*, 1587–1616.

Rossi, J. S. (1990). Statistical power of psychological research: What have we gained in 20 years? *Journal of Consulting and Clinical Psychology, 58*, 646–656.

Rossi, P. H., Freeman, H. E., & Lipsey, M. W. (1999). *Evaluation* (6th ed.). Thousand Oaks, CA: Sage.

Rousseau, D. L. (1992). Case studies in pathological science. *American Scientist, 80*, 54–63.

Ruback, R. B., & Carr, T. S. (1984). Crowding in a women's prison: Attitudinal and behavioral effects. *Journal of Applied Social Psychology, 14*, 57–68.

Ruback, R. B., & Innes, C. A. (1988). The relevance and irrelevance of psychological research: The example of prison crowding. *American Psychologist, 43*, 683–693.

Rubin, H. J., & Rubin, I. S. (1995). *Qualitative interviewing.* Thousand Oaks, CA: Sage.

Rubin, Z., & Mitchell, C. (1976). Couples research as couples counseling: Some unintended effects of studying close relationships. *American Psychologist, 31*, 17–25.

Rumenik, D. K., Capasso, D. R., & Hendrick, C. (1977). Experimenter sex effects in behavioral research. *Psychological Bulletin, 84*, 852–877.

Rusbult, C. E., & Farrell, D. (1983). A longitudinal test of the investment model: The impact on job satisfaction, job commitment, and turnover of variations in rewards, costs, alternatives, and investments. *Journal of Applied Psychology, 68*, 429–438.

Rychlak, J. F. (1981). *Introduction to personality and psychotherapy* (2nd ed.). Boston: Houghton Mifflin.

Saks, M. J., & Hastie, R. (1978). *Social psychology in court.* New York: Van Nostrand Reinhold.

Salipante, P., Notz, W., & Bigelow, J. (1982). A matrix approach to literature reviews. *Research in Organizational Behavior, 4*, 321–348.

Sanislow, C. A., III, Perkins, D. V., & Balogh, D. W. (1989). Mood induction, interpersonal perceptions, and rejection in the roommates of depressed, nondepressed-disturbed, and normal college students. *Journal of Social and Clinical Psychology, 8*, 345–358.

Saranson, S. B. (1984). If it can be studied or developed, should it be? *American Psychologist, 39*, 477–485.

Saris, W. E. (1991). *Computer-assisted interviewing.* Newbury Park, CA: Sage.

Saxe, L. (1986). Policymakers' use of social science research: Technology assessment in the U.S. Congress. *Knowledge: Creation, Diffusion, Utilization, 8*, 59–78.

Saxe, L., Dougherty, D., & Cross, T. (1985). The validity of polygraph testing. *American Psychologist, 40*, 355–366.

Scarr, S. (1981). *Race, social class, and individual differences in IQ.* Hillsdale, NJ: Erlbaum.

Scarr, S. (1985). Constructing psychology: Making facts and fables for our times. *American Psychologist, 40*, 499–512.

Scarr, S. (1988). Race and gender as psychological variables: Social and ethical issues. *American Psychologist, 43*, 56–59.

Schlenker, B. R., & Bonoma, T. V. (1978). Fun and games: The validity of games for the study of conflict. *Journal of Conflict Resolution, 22*, 7–38.

Schmidt, F. L. (1992). What do data really mean? Research findings, meta-analysis, and cumulative research in psychology. *American Psychologist, 47*, 1173–1181.

Schmidt, W. C. (1997). World Wide Web survey research: Benefits, potential problems, and solutions. *Behavior Research Methods, Instruments, & Computers, 29*, 274–279.

Schneier, B. (1993, February). Data guardians: How strong are the software locks on 24 security products? *Macworld,* pp. 145–151.

Schnelle, J. F., Kirchner, R. E., Macrae, J. W., McNees, M. P., Eck, R. H., Snodgrass, S., Casey, J. D., & Uselton, P. H., Jr. (1978). Police evaluation research: An experimental and cost-benefit analysis of a helicopter patrol in a high crime area. *Journal of Applied Behavior Analysis, 11*, 11–21.

Schoeneman, T. J., & Rubanowitz, D. E. (1985). Attributions in the advice columns: Actors and observers, causes and reasons. *Personality and Social Psychology Bulletin, 11*, 315–325.

Schofield, J. W. (1982). *Black and white in school.* New York: Praeger.

Schofield, J. W., & Pavelchak, M. A. (1989). Fallout from *The Day After:* The impact of a TV film on attitudes related to nuclear war. *Journal of Applied Social Psychology, 19*, 433–448.

Schofield, J. W., & Whitley, B. E., Jr. (1983). Peer nomination vs. rating scale measurement of children's peer preferences. *Social Psychology Quarterly, 46*, 242–251.

Schuerger, J. M., Zarella, K. L., & Hotz, A. S. (1989). Factors that influence the temporal stability of personality by questionnaire. *Journal of Personality and Social Psychology, 56*, 777–783.

Schuler, H. (1982). *Ethical problems in psychological research*. New York: Academic Press.

Schultz, D. P., & Schultz, S. E. (1994). *Psychology and work today* (6th ed.). New York: Macmillan.

Schuman, H., & Presser, S. (1996). *Questions and answers in attitude surveys*. Thousand Oaks, CA: Sage.

Schuman, H., Walsh, E., Olson, C., & Etheridge, B. (1985). Effort and rewards: The assumption that college grades are affected by quality of study. *Social Forces, 63*, 945–966.

Schwab, D. B. (1985). Reviewing empirically based manuscripts: Perspectives on process. In L. L. Cummings & P. J. Frost (Eds.), *Publishing in the organizational sciences* (pp. 171–181). Homewood, IL: Irwin.

Schwarz, N. (1999). Self-reports: How the questions shape the answers. *American Psychologist, 54*, 93–105.

Schwarz, N., & Clore, G. L. (1983). Mood, misattribution, and judgments of well-being: Informative and directive functions of affective states. *Journal of Personality and Social Psychology, 45*, 513–523.

Schwarz, N., Hippler, H. J., Deutsch, B., & Strack, F. (1985). Response scales: Effects of category range on reported behavior and comparative judgments. *Public Opinion Quarterly, 49*, 388–395.

Schwarz, N., Strack, F., Müller, G., & Chassein, B. (1988). The range of response alternatives may determine the meaning of the question: Further evidence on informative functions of response alternatives. *Social Cognition, 6*, 107–117.

Sears, D. O. (1986). College sophomores in the laboratory: Influence of a narrow data base on social psychology's view of human nature. *Journal of Personality and Social Psychology, 51*, 515–530.

Secord, P. F., & Backman, C. W. (1974). *Social psychology* (2nd ed.). New York: McGraw-Hill.

Seligman, C., Finegan, J. E., Hazlewood, J. D., & Wilkinson, M. (1985). Manipulating attributions for profit: A field test of the effects of attributions on behavior. *Social Cognition, 3*, 313–321.

Seligman, M. E. P. (1975). *Helplessness*. San Francisco: Freeman.

Senior, C., Phillips, M. L. Barnes, J., & David, S. (1999). An investigation into perception of dominance from schematic faces: A study using the World Wide Web. *Behavior Research Methods, Instruments, & Computers, 31*, 341–346.

Shadish, W. R. (1996). Meta-analysis and the exploration of causal mediating processes: A primer of examples, methods, and issues. *Psychological Methods, 1*, 47–65.

Shadish, W. R., Jr., & Sweeney, R. B. (1991). Mediators and moderators in meta-analysis: There's a reason we don't let dodo birds tell us which psychotherapies should have prizes. *Journal of Consulting and Clinical Psychology, 59*, 883–893.

Shaffer, D. R., & Kerwin, J. (1992). Reply to Whitley and reaffirmation of our conclusions. *Personality and Social Psychology Bulletin, 18*, 685–689.

Sharf, B. F. (1997). Communicating breast cancer on-line: Support and empowerment on the Internet. *Women & Health, 26*(1), 65–84.

Sharf, B. F. (1999). Beyond netiquette: The ethics of doing naturalistic discourse research on the Internet. In S. James (Ed.), *Doing Internet research* (pp. 243–256). Thousand Oaks, CA: Sage.

Shaw, M. E., & Costanzo, P. R. (1982). *Theories of social psychology* (2nd ed.). New York: McGraw-Hill.

Shedler, J., & Block, J. (1990). Adolescent drug use and psychological health: A longitudinal study. *American Psychologist, 45*, 612–630.

Sheets, V. L., & Braver, S. L. (1999). Organizational status and perceived sexual harrassment: Detecting the mediators of a null effect. *Personality and Social Psychology Bulletin, 25*, 1159–1171.

Sherwood, J. J., & Nataupsky, M. (1968). Predicting the conclusions of Negro-White intelligence research from biographical characteristics of the investigators. *Journal of Personality and Social Psychology, 8,* 53–58.

Shortell, S. M., & Richardson, W. C. (1978). *Health program evaluation.* St. Louis, MO: Mosby.

Shotland, R. L., & Heinold, W. D. (1985). Bystander response to arterial bleeding: Helping skills, the decision-making process, and differentiating the helping response. *Journal of Personality and Social Psychology, 49,* 347–356.

Shrauger, J. S., & Osberg, T. M. (1981). The relative accuracy of self-predictions and judgments by others in psychological assessment. *Psychological Bulletin, 90,* 322–351.

Shulman, A. (1973). A comparison of two scales on extremity response bias. *Public Opinion Quarterly, 37,* 407–412.

Shweder, R. A. (1975). How relevant is an individual difference theory of personality? *Journal of Personality, 43,* 455–484.

Shweder, R. A., & D'Andrade, R. G. (1980). The systematic distortion hypothesis. In R. A. Shweder (Ed.), *Fallible judgment in behavioral research* (pp. 37–58). San Francisco: Jossey-Bass.

Sieber, J. E. (1992). *Planning ethically responsible research.* Newbury Park, CA: Sage.

Sieber, J. E. (1993). The ethics and politics of sensitive research. In C. M. Renzetti & R. M. Lee (Eds.), *Researching sensitive topics* (pp. 14–26). Newbury Park, CA: Sage.

Sieber, J. E., & Saks, M. J. (1989). A census of subject pool characteristics and policies. *American Psychologist, 44,* 1053–1061.

Sieber, J. E., & Stanley, B. (1988). Ethical and professional dimensions of socially sensitive research. *American Psychologist, 43,* 49–55.

Sigma Xi. (1986). *Honor in science* (2nd ed.). Research Triangle Park, NC: Author.

Signorella, M. L., & Vegega, M. E. (1984). A note on gender stereotyping of research topics. *Personality and Social Psychology Bulletin, 10,* 107–109.

Simon, R. W., Eder, D., & Evans, C. (1992). The development of feeling norms underlying romantic love among adolescent females. *Social Psychology Quarterly, 55,* 29–46.

Simonton, D. K. (1994). *Greatness: Who makes history and why?* New York: Guilford.

Simpson, J. A., Campbell, B., & Berscheid, E. (1986). The association between romantic love and marriage: Kephart (1967) revisited. *Personality and Social Psychology Bulletin, 12,* 363–372.

Singer, J. E., & Glass, D. C. (1975). Some reflections upon losing our social psychological purity. In M. Deutsch & H. A. Hornstein (Eds.), *Applying social psychology* (pp. 15–31). Hillsdale, NJ: Erlbaum.

Singleton, R., Jr., & Straits, B. C. (1999). *Approaches to social research* (3rd ed.). New York: Oxford University Press.

Slavin, R. E. (1986). Best-evidence synthesis: An alternative to meta-analytic and traditional reviews. *Educational Researcher, 15*(9), 5–11.

Smith, A. C., III, & Kleinman, S. (1989). Managing emotions in medical school: Students' contacts with the living and the dead. *Social Psychology Quarterly, 52,* 56–69.

Smith, M. A., & Leigh, B. (1997). Virtual subjects: Using the Internet as an alternative source of subjects and research environment. *Behavior Research Methods, Instruments, & Computers, 29,* 496–505.

Smith, M. F. (1989). *Evaluability assessment.* Boston: Kluwer.

Smith, M. L., & Glass, G. V. (1977). Meta-analysis of psychotherapy outcome research studies. *American Psychologist, 32,* 752–760.

Smith, S. S., & Richardson, D. (1983). Amelioration of deception and harm in psychological research: The important role of debriefing. *Journal of Personality and Social Psychology, 44,* 1075–1082.

Snyder, M. (1986). *Public appearances/private realities: The psychology of self-monitoring*. New York: Freeman.

Snyder, M. L., & Mentzer, S. (1978). Social psychological perspectives on the physician's feelings and behavior. *Personality and Social Psychology Bulletin, 4*, 541–547.

Solomon, J. (1988, December 29). Companies try measuring cost savings from new types of corporate benefits. *Wall Street Journal*, p. B1.

Sommer, R. (1991). Literal versus metaphorical interpretations of scale terms: A serendipitous natural experiment. *Educational and Psychological Measurement, 51*, 1009–1012.

Spector, P. E. (1976). Choosing response categories for summated rating scales. *Journal of Applied Psychology, 61*, 374–375.

Spector, P. E. (1992). *Summated rating scale construction*. Newbury Park, CA: Sage.

Spence, J. T., Helmreich, R. L., & Stapp, J. (1975). Ratings of self and peers on sex-role attributes and their relation to self-esteem and conceptions of masculinity and femininity. *Journal of Personality and Social Psychology, 32*, 29–39.

Spielberger, C. D., Vagg, P. R., Barker, L. R., Donham, G. W., & Westberry, L. G. (1980). The factor structure of the State-Trait Anxiety Inventory. In I. G. Saronson & C. D. Spielberger (Eds.), *Stress and anxiety* (Vol. 7, pp. 95–109). Washington, DC: Hemisphere.

Sprecher, S., McKinney, K., & Orbuch, T. L. (1987). Has the double standard disappeared? An experimental test. *Social Psychology Quarterly, 50*, 24–31.

Stake, R. E. (1995). *The art of case study research*. Thousand Oaks, CA: Sage.

Stanton, A. L., & New, M. J. (1988). Ethical responsibilities to depressed research participants. *Professional Psychology: Research and Practice, 19*, 279–285.

Steers, R. M., & Rhodes, S. R. (1978). Major influences on employee attendance: A process model. *Journal of Applied Psychology, 63*, 391–407.

Stein, J. A., Newcomb, M. D., & Bentler, P. M. (1987). An 8-year study of multiple influences on drug use and drug use consequences. *Journal of Personality and Social Psychology, 53*, 1094–1105.

Steininger, M., Newell, J. D., & Garcia, L. T. (1984). *Ethical issues in psychology*. Homewood, IL: Dorsey Press.

Steptoe, A. (1981). *Psychological factors in cardiovascular disease*. New York: Academic Press.

Sternberg, R. J. (1986). A triangular theory of love. *Psychological Review, 93*, 119–135.

Sternberg, R. J. (1993). *The psychologist's companion* (3rd ed.). Cambridge, England: Cambridge University Press.

Stewart, D. W., & Kamins, M. A. (1993). *Secondary research* (2nd ed.). Thousand Oaks, CA: Sage.

Stewart, D. W., & Shamdasani, P. N. (1990). *Focus groups*. Newbury Park, CA: Sage.

St James-Roberts, I. (1976). Cheating in science. *New Scientist, 72*, 466–469.

Stogdill, R. M., & Coons, A. E. (Eds.). (1957). *Leader behavior: Its description and measurement*. Columbus: Bureau of Business Research, Ohio State University.

Stokols, D. (1972). On the distinction between density and crowding: Some implications for further research. *Psychological Review, 79*, 275–277.

Straits, B. C. (1967). Resume of the Chicago study of smoking behavior. In S. V. Zagona (Ed.), *Studies and issues in smoking behavior* (pp. 73–78). Tucson: University of Arizona Press.

Stratton, P. (1997). Attributional coding of interview data: Meeting the needs of long-haul passengers. In N. Hayes (Ed.), *Doing qualitative analysis in psychology* (pp. 115–142). Hove, England: Psychology Press.

Stricker, G. (1991). Ethical concerns in alcohol research. *Journal of Consulting and Clinical Psychology, 59*, 256–257.

Strube, M. J. (1991). Small sample failure of random assignment: A further examination. *Journal of Consulting and Clinical Psychology, 59*, 346–350.

Stryker, S., & Statham, A. (1985). Symbolic interaction and role theory. In G. Lindzey & E. Aronson (Eds.), *Handbook of social psychology* (3rd ed., Vol. 1, pp. 311–378). New York: Random House.

Sudman, S., & Bradburn, N. M. (1982). *Asking questions.* San Francisco: Jossey-Bass.

Sudman, S., Bradburn, N. M., & Schwarz, N. (1996). *Thinking about answers.* San Francisco: Jossey-Bass.

Summary report of journal operations, 1998. (1999). *American Psychologist, 54,* 715–716.

Susman, G., & Evered, R. (1978). An assessment of the scientific merit of action research. *Administrative Science Quarterly, 23,* 582–603.

Swanson, H. L., & Sachse-Lee, C. (2000). A meta-analysis of single-subject-design intervention research for students with LD. *Journal of Learning Disabilities, 33,* 114–136.

Swazey, J. P., Anderson, M. S., & Lewis, K. S. (1993). Ethical problems in academic research. *American Scientist, 81,* 542–553.

Swets, J. A., & Bjork, R. A. (1990). Enhancing human performance: An evaluation of "New Age" techniques considered by the U.S. Army. *Psychological Science, 1,* 85–96.

Swets, J. A., Dawes, R. M., & Monahan, J. (2000). Psychological science can improve diagnostic decisions. *Psychological Science in the Public Interest, 1,* 1–26.

Szanton, P. (1981). *Not well advised.* New York: Russell Sage Foundation.

Tabachnick, B. G., & Fidell, L. S. (1996). *Using multivariate statistics* (3rd ed.). New York: Harper Collins.

Taffel, C. (1955). Anxiety and the conditioning of verbal behavior. *Journal of Abnormal and Social Psychology, 51,* 496–501.

Tajfel, H., Billig, M., Bundy, R., & Flamant, C. (1971). Social categorization and intergroup behavior. *European Journal of Social Psychology, 1,* 149–178.

Tesser, A. (1990, August). *Interesting models in social psychology: A personal view.* Invited address presented at the meeting of the American Psychological Association, Boston.

Tetlock, P. E. (1979). Identifying victims of groupthink from public statements of decision makers. *Journal of Personality and Social Psychology, 37,* 1314–1324.

Thompson, B. (1995). Stepwise regression and stepwise discriminant analysis need not apply here: A guidelines editorial. *Educational and Psychological Measurement, 55,* 525–534.

Thompson, R. A. (1990). Vulnerability in research: A developmental perspective on research risk. *Child Development, 61,* 1–16.

Thorne, B. (1988). Political activist as participant observer: Conflicts of commitment in a study of the draft resistance movement of the 1960s. In P. C. Higgins & J. M. Johnson (Eds.), *Personal sociology* (pp. 133–152). New York: Praeger.

Thurstone, L. L. (1929). Theory of attitude measurement. *Psychological Bulletin, 36,* 222–241.

Tinsley, H. E. A., & Tinsley, D. J. (1987). Uses of factor analysis in counseling psychology research. *Journal of Counseling Psychology, 34,* 414–424.

Tittle, C. R., & Hill, R. J. (1967). Attitude measurement and prediction of behavior: An evaluation of conditions and measurement techniques. *Sociometry, 30,* 199–213.

Tomarken, A. J. (1995). A psychometric perspective on psychophysiological measures. *Psychological Assessment, 7,* 387–395.

Treadway, M., & McCloskey, M. (1987). Cite unseen: Distortions of Allport and Postman's rumor study in the eyewitness testimony literature. *Law and Human Behavior, 11,* 19–26.

Tremper, C. R. (1987). Organized psychology's efforts to influence judicial policy-making. *American Psychologist, 42,* 496–501.

Tunnell, G. B. (1977). Three dimensions of naturalism: An expanded definition of field research. *Psychological Bulletin, 84,* 426–437.

Unger, R., & Crawford, M. (1992). *Women and gender.* New York: McGraw-Hill.

U.S. Bureau of the Census. (1992). *Statistical abstract of the United States* (112th ed.). Washington, DC: U.S. Government Printing Office.

U.S. Department of Health and Human Services [DHHS]. (1992). *Protection of human subjects* (45 CFR 46). Washington, DC: U.S. Government Printing Office.

U.S. Public Health Service. (1971). *The institutional guide to DHEW policy on protection of human subjects* (DHEW Publication No. NIH 72-102). Washington, DC: U.S. Government Printing Office.

Velten, E., Jr. (1968). A laboratory task for induction of mood states. *Behaviour Research and Therapy, 6,* 473–482.

Vidmar, N. (1979). The other issues in jury simulation research: A commentary with particular reference to defendant character studies. *Law and Human Behavior, 3,* 95–106.

von Békésy, G. (1960). *Experiments in hearing.* New York: McGraw-Hill.

Vredenburg, K., Flett, G. L., & Krames, L. (1993). Analogue versus clinical depression: A critical reappraisal. *Psychological Bulletin, 113,* 327–344.

Walker, H. M., & Buckley, N. K. (1968). The use of positive reinforcement in conditioning attending behavior. *Journal of Applied Behavior Analysis, 1,* 245–250.

Wampold, B. E. (1996). Designing a research study. In F. T. L. Leong & J. T. Austin (Eds.), *The psychology research handbook* (pp. 59–72). Thousand Oaks, CA: Sage.

Wampold, B. E., Davis, B., & Good, R. H., III. (1990). Hypothesis validity of clinical research. *Journal of Consulting and Clinical Psychology, 58,* 360–367.

Wanous, J. P., Sullivan, S. E., & Malinak, J. (1989). The role of judgment calls in meta-analysis. *Journal of Applied Psychology, 74,* 259–264.

Webb, E. J., Campbell, D. T., Schwartz, R. D., Sechrist, L., & Grove, J. B. (1981). *Nonreactive measures in the social sciences* (2nd ed.). Boston: Houghton Mifflin.

Weber, R. P. (1990). *Basic content analysis* (2nd ed.). Newbury Park, CA: Sage.

Weber, S. J., & Cook, T. D. (1972). Subject effects in laboratory research: An examination of subject roles, demand characteristics, and valid inference. *Psychological Bulletin, 77,* 273–295.

Wegner, D. M., & Vallacher, R. R. (1977). *Implicit psychology.* New York: Oxford University Press.

Wegner, D. M., Wenzloff, R., Kerker, R. M., & Beattie, A. E. (1981). Incrimination through innuendo: Can media questions become public answers? *Journal of Personality and Social Psychology, 40,* 822–832.

Weick, K. E. (1985). Systematic observational methods. In G. Lindzey & E. Aronson (Eds.), *Handbook of social psychology* (3rd ed., Vol. 1, pp. 567–634). New York: Random House.

Weigel, R. H., Loomis, J. W., & Soja, M. J. (1980). Race relations on prime time television. *Journal of Personality and Social Psychology, 39,* 884–893.

Weiner, B. (1986). *An attributional theory of motivation and emotion.* New York: Springer.

Weiss, C. H. (1984). Increasing the likelihood of influencing decisions. In L. Rutman (Ed.), *Evaluation research methods* (2nd ed., pp. 159–190). Beverly Hills, CA: Sage.

Weiss, C. H. (1998). *Evaluation* (2nd ed.). Upper Saddle River, NJ: Prentice Hall.

Weiss, C. H., & Bucuvalas, M. J. (1980). Truth tests and utility tests: Decision-makers' frames of reference for social science research. *American Sociological Review, 45,* 302–313.

Weiss, R. S. (1994). *Learning from strangers: The art and method of qualitative interview studies.* New York: Free Press.

Welch, N., & Krantz, J. H. (1996). The World Wide Web as a medium for psychoacoustical demonstrations and experiments: Experience and results. *Behavior Research Methods, Instruments, & Computers, 28,* 192–196.

Wells, G. L. (1978). Applied eyewitness-testimony research: System variables and estimator variables. *Journal of Personality and Social Psychology, 36,* 1546–1557.

Wells, G. L., Malpass, R. S., Lindsay, R. C. L., Fisher, R. P., Turtle, J. W., & Fulero, S. M. (2000). From the lab to the police station: A successful application of eyewitness research. *American Psychologist, 55,* 581–598.

Wells, G. L., & Windschitl, P. D. (1999). Stimulus sampling and social psychological experimentation. *Personality and Social Psychology Bulletin, 25*, 1115–1125.

West, S. G., Aiken, L. S., & Krull, J. L. (1996). Experimental personality designs: Analyzing categorical by continuous variable interactions. *Journal of Personality, 64*, 1–48.

Wexley, K. N., Yukl, G. A., Kovacs, S. Z., & Sanders, R. E. (1972). Importance of contrast effects in employment interviews. *Journal of Applied Psychology, 56*, 45–48.

Wheeler, M. (1976). *Lies, damn lies, and statistics*. New York: Dell.

White, K. R. (1982). The relation between socioeconomic status and academic achievement. *Psychological Bulletin, 91*, 461–481.

Whitley, B. E., Jr. (1982). Degree of defendant responsibility for a crime and assigned punishment. *Replications in Social Psychology, 2*(1), 29–32.

Whitley, B. E., Jr. (1988). Masculinity, femininity, and self-esteem: A multitrait-multimethod analysis. *Sex Roles, 18*, 419–431.

Whitley, B. E., Jr. (1990a). College student contraceptive use: A multivariate analysis. *Journal of Sex Research, 27*, 305–313.

Whitley, B. E., Jr. (1990b). The relationship of heterosexuals' attributions for the causes of homosexuality to attitudes toward lesbians and gay men. *Personality and Social Psychology Bulletin, 16*, 369–377.

Whitley, B. E., Jr. (1992). Units of analysis, measurement scales, and statistics: A comment on Kerwin and Shaffer. *Personality and Social Psychology Bulletin, 18*, 680–684.

Whitley, B. E., Jr., & Greenberg, M. S. (1986). The role of eyewitness confidence in juror perceptions of credibility. *Journal of Applied Social Psychology, 16*, 382–409.

Whitley, B. E., Jr., & Gridley, B. E. (1993). Sex role orientation, self-esteem, and depression: A latent variables analysis. *Personality and Social Psychology Bulletin, 19*, 363–369.

Whitley, B. E., Jr., McHugh, M. C., & Frieze, I. H. (1986). Assessing the theoretical models for sex differences in causal attributions of success and failure. In J. S. Hyde & M. Linn (Eds.), *The psychology of gender: Advances through meta-analysis* (pp. 102–135). Baltimore: Johns Hopkins University Press.

Whitley, B. E., Jr., & Schofield, J. W. (1986). A meta-analysis of research on adolescent contraceptive use. *Population and Environment, 6*, 173–203.

Wholey, J. S. (1987). Evaluability assessment: Developing program theory. In L. Bickman (Ed.), *Using program theory in evaluation* (pp. 77–92). San Francisco: Jossey-Bass.

Wicker, A. W. (1985). Getting out of our conceptual ruts: Strategies for expanding conceptual frameworks. *American Psychologist, 40*, 1094–1103.

Wicklund, R. A. (1975). Objective self-awareness. In L. Berkowitz (Ed.), *Advances in experimental social psychology* (Vol. 8, pp. 233–275). New York: Academic Press.

Widom, C. S. (1988). Sampling biases and implications for child abuse research. *American Journal of Orthopsychiatry, 58*, 260–270.

Wilcox, B. L. (1987). Pornography, social science, and politics: When research and ideology collide. *American Psychologist, 42*, 941–943.

Willson, V. L. (1981). Time and the external validity of experiments. *Evaluation and Program Planning, 4*, 229–238.

Wilson, E. O. (1978). *On human nature*. Cambridge, MA: Harvard University Press.

Wilson, T. D., & Linville, P. W. (1982). Improving the academic performance of college freshmen: Attribution theory revisited. *Journal of Personality and Social Psychology, 42*, 367–376.

Winick, M. (1979). Malnutrition and mental development. In M. Winick (Ed.), *Human nutrition* (Vol. 1, pp. 41–59). New York: Plenum.

Wolchik, S. A., Braver, S. L., & Jensen, K. (1985). Volunteer bias in erotica research: Effects of intrusiveness of measure and sexual background. *Archives of Sexual Behavior, 14*, 93–107.

Wolfgang, M. E. (1974). The social scientist in court. *Journal of Criminal Law and Criminology, 65*, 239–247.

Wright, R. E. (1995). Logistic regression. In L. G. Grimm & P. R. Yarnold (Eds.), *Reading and understanding multivariate statistics* (pp. 217–244). Washington, DC: American Psychological Association.

Wylie, R. C. (1989). *Measures of self-concept.* Lincoln: University of Nebraska Press.

Yammarino, F. J., Skinner, S. J., & Childers, T. L. (1991). Understanding mail survey response behavior: A meta-analysis. *Public Opinion Quarterly, 55*, 613–639.

Yeaton, W. H., & Sechrest, L. (1987a). Assessing factors influencing acceptance of no-difference research. *Evaluation Review, 11*, 131–142.

Yeaton, W. H., & Sechrest, L. (1987b). No-difference research. In D. S. Cordray, H. S. Bloom, & R. L. Light (Eds.), *Evaluation practice in review* (pp. 67–82). San Francisco: Jossey-Bass.

Yin, R. K. (1993). *Applications of case study research.* Newbury Park, CA: Sage.

Yin, R. K. (1994). *Case study research* (2nd ed.). Thousand Oaks, CA: Sage.

Young, D. R., Hooker, D. T., & Freeberg, F. E. (1990). Informed consent documents: Increasing comprehension by reducing reading level. *IRB: A Review of Human Subjects Research, 12*, 1–5.

Yu, J., & Cooper, H. (1983). A quantitative review of research design effects on response rates to questionnaires. *Journal of Marketing Research, 20*, 36–44.

Yuille, J. C., & Wells, G. (1991). Concerns about the application of research findings: The issue of ecological validity. In J. L. Doris (Ed.), *The suggestibility of children's recollections* (pp. 118–128). Washington, DC: American Psychological Association.

Zaitzow, B. H., & Fields, C. B. (1996). Using archival data sets. In F. T. L. Leong & J. T. Austin (Eds.), *The psychology research handbook* (pp. 251–261). Thousand Oaks, CA: Sage.

Zeller, R. A., & Carmines, E. G. (1980). *Measurement in the social sciences.* Cambridge, England: Cambridge University Press.

Zimbardo, P. G. (1973). On the ethics of intervention in human psychological research: With special reference to the Stanford prison experiment. *Cognition, 2*, 243–256.

Zimring, F. E. (1975). Firearms and federal law: The Gun Control Act of 1968. *Journal of Legal Studies, 4*, 133–198.

Zuckerman, M. (1990). Some dubious premises in research and theory on racial differences: Scientific, social, and ethical issues. *American Psychologist, 45*, 1297–1303.

CREDITS

Chapter 1 Table 1–2 From "Aggression pays," by A. H. Buss in *The control of aggression*, J. L. Singer, ed., 1971, Academic Press. Reprinted with permission.

Chapter 4 Box 4–2 Adapted with permission from Fred Leavitt, *Research methods for behavioral scientists*. Copyright © 1991 Wm. C. Brown Communications, Inc., Dubuque, Iowa. Times Mirror Higher Education Group, Inc., Dubuque, Iowa. All rights reserved.

Table 4–2 R. Rosenthal, "Replication in behavioral research," in J. W. Neuliep, (Ed.), *Handbook of replication research in the behavioral and social sciences* [Special issue]. *Journal of Social Behavior and Personality*, 5(4), 1–30. Copyright © 1990 by Select Press, Corte Madera, CA.

Fig. 4–3 B. E. Wampold et al., "Hypothesis validity of clinical research," *Journal of Consulting and Clinical Psychology*, 58, 360–367. Copyright © 1990 by the American Psychological Association. Adapted with permission.

Chapter 5 Table 5–1 Adapted from *Research design explained*, second edition, by Mark Mitchell and Janina Jolley. Copyright © 1992 by Holt, Rinehart and Winston, Inc. Reproduced by permission of the publisher.

Table 5–3 From J. P. Robinson et al., "Criteria for scale selection and evaluation," in J. P. Robinson et al., (Eds.), *Measures of personality and social psychological attitudes*, 1991, Academic Press. Reprinted by permission of the publisher.

Chapter 8 Fig. 8–3 From *Introduction to measurement theory* by M. J. Allen and W. M. Yen. Copyright © 1979 by Wadsworth Publishing Company. Reprinted by permission of Wadsworth, an imprint of the Wadsworth Group, a division of Thomson Learning. Fax 800 730–2215.

Fig. 8–7 From J. P. Meyer and A. Mulherin, "From attribution to helping: An analysis of the moderating effects of affect on expectancy," *Journal of Personality and Social Psychology*, 39, 201–210. Copyright © 1980 by the American Psychological Association. Adapted with permission.

Fig. 8–9 From S. Scarr, "Constructing psychology: Making facts and fables for our time," *American Psychologist*, 40, 499–512. Copyright © 1985 by the American Psychological Association. Adapted with permission.

Fig. 8–10 From S. J. Breckler, "Application of covariance structure modeling in psychology: Cause for concern?" *Psychological Bulletin*, 107, 260–273. Copyright © 1990 American Psychological Association. Adapted with permission.

Chapter 9 Fig. 9–1 From R. K. Yin, *Case Study Research: Design and Method*, second edition, p. 51. Copyright © 1994 by Sage Publications, Inc. Reprinted by permission of Sage Publications, Inc.

Fig. 9–2 From H. M. Walker and N. K. Buckley, "The use of positive reinforcement in conditioning attending behavior," *Journal of Applied Behavior Analysis, 1*, p. 247, fig. 2. Copyright © 1968 Journal of Applied Behavior Analysis. Reprinted with permission from the publisher.

Fig. 9–3 Reprinted with permission from *Behaviour Research and Therapy*, Volume 12, P. M. Miller, M. Hersen, R. M. Eisler, and J. G. Watts, "Contingent reinforcement of lowered blood alcohol levels in an outpatient chronic alcoholic," pp. 261–263. Copyright © 1974 Elsevier Science Ltd. With kind permission from Elsevier Science Ltd., The Boulevard, Langford Lane, Kidlington, OX5 1GB, UK.

Fig. 9–5 From M. R. Bornstein et al., "Social-skills training for unassertive children: A multiple-baseline analysis," *Journal of Applied Behavior Analysis, 10*, p. 190, fig. 3. Copyright © 1977 Journal of Applied Behavior Analysis. Reprinted with permission from the publisher.

Fig. 9–6 From T. H. Ollendick, *Behavior Modification*, Vol. 5, No. 1, p. 82. Copyright © 1981 by Sage Publications. Reprinted by permission of Sage Publications, Inc.

Fig. 9–7 From K. Dyer et al., "The role of response delay in improving the discrimination performance of autistic children," *Journal of Applied Behavior Analysis, 15*, p. 235, fig. 1. Copyright © 1982 Journal of Applied Behavior Analysis. Reprinted with permission from the publisher.

Fig. 9–8 From T. H. Ollendick et al., "Reducing stereotyped behaviors: An analysis of tentative procedures utilizing an alternating treatments design," *Behavior Therapy, 12*, 570–577, 1981. Reprinted with permission.

Fig. 9–9 From R. M. Foxx and A. Rubinoff, "Behavioral treatment of caffeinism: Reducing excessive coffee drinking," *Journal of Applied Behavior Analysis, 12*, p. 339, fig. 1. Copyright © 1979 Journal of Applied Behavior Analysis. Reprinted with permission from the publisher.

Figs. 9–10, 9–13 From A. E. Kazdin, *Research Design in Clinical Psychology*, third edition. Copyright © 1998 by Allyn & Bacon. Adapted by permission.

Fig. 9–12 Reprinted from *Journal of Behaviour Therapy and Experimental Psychiatry*, J. E. Martin and D. E. Sachs, "The effects of a self-control weight-loss program on an obese woman," pp. 155–159. Copyright © 1973 Elsevier Science Ltd. With kind permission from Elsevier Science Ltd., The Boulevard, Langford Lane, Kidlington, OX5 1GB, UK.

Chapter 10 Fig. 10–2 From *Research Methods in Social Relations*, sixth edition, by Charles M. Judd, Eliot R. Smith, Louise H. Kidder. Copyright © 1991 by Holt, Rinehart and Winston, Inc. Reproduced by permission of the publisher.

Fig. 10–4 Reprinted from 1970 Nebraska Symposium on Motivation by permission of the University of Nebraska Press. Copyright © 1971 by the University of Nebraska Press. Copyright © renewed 2000 by the University of Nebraska Press.

Fig. 10–5 From F. E. Fiedler et al., "Increasing mine productivity and safety through management training and organizational development: A comparative study," *Basic and Applied Social Psychology, 5*, 1–18, 1984. Reprinted by permission of Lawrence Erlbaum Associates.

Fig. 10–7 From R. F. Bales, *Interaction Process Analysis*, 1950, p. 9, University of Chicago Press. Reprinted with permission from the publisher.

Box 10–3 From *Approaches to Social Research*, third edition, by Royce A. Singleton, Jr. and Bruce C. Straits. Copyright © 1998 Oxford University Press, Inc. Used by permission of Oxford University Press, Inc.

Box 10–4 From L. A. Joy et al., "Television and children's aggressive behavior," in T. M. Williams, (Ed.), *The impact of television*, 1986, Academic Press, p. 340. Reprinted with permission from the publisher.

Tables 10–1, 10–2 From M. H. Gonzales and S. A. Meyers, *Personality and Social Psychology Bulletin*, Vol. 19, no. 2, p. 135. Copyright © 1993 by the Society for Personality and Social Psychology. Reprinted by permission of Sage Publications, Inc.

Chapter 11 Fig. 11–4 From E. R. Babbie, *Survey research methods.* Copyright © 1990 by Wadsworth Publishing Company. Reprinted with the permission of Wadsworth, an imprint of the Wadsworth Group, a division of Thomson Learning. Fax 800 730–2215.

Fig. 11–5 From *Mail and Telephone Surveys* by Don A. Dillman. Copyright © 1978 John Wiley & Sons, Inc. Reprinted by permission of John Wiley & Sons, Inc.

Table 11–2 From *Research Methods in Social Relations*, sixth edition, by Charles M. Judd, Eliot R. Smith, Louise H. Kidder. Copyright © 1991 by Holt, Rinehart and Winston, Inc. Reproduced by permission of the publisher.

Table 11–6 From R. Christie and F. L. Geis, *Studies in Machiavellianism*, Academic Press, 1970, pp. 17–18. With permission from the publisher.

Chapter 13 Table 13–2 From B. E. Whitley et al., "Assessing the theoretical models for sex differences in causal attributions of success and failure" in J. S. Hyde and M. Linn, (Eds.), *The psychology of gender: Advances through meta-analysis*, 1986, p. 106. Reprinted by permission of the Johns Hopkins University Press.

Table 13–3 Adapted from *The Social Psychology of Prejudice* by J. Duckitt, 1992, p. 48. New York: Praeger. Copyright © 1992 by John Duckitt. Adapted by permission of the Greenwood Publishing Group, Inc., Westport, CT.

Chapter 14 Fig. 14–2 From K. I. Howard et al., "The dose-effect relationship in psychotherapy," *American Psychologist*, *41*, 159–164. Copyright © 1986 by the American Psychological Association. Adapted with permission.

Chapter 15 Fig. 15–2 From K. I. Howard et al., "The dose-effect relationship in psychotherapy," *American Psychologist*, *41*, 159–164. Copyright © 1986 by the American Psychological Association. Adapted with permission.

Table 15–1 From A. E. Kazdin, *Research Design in Clinical Psychology*, third edition. Copyright © 1998 Allyn & Bacon. Adapted by permission.

Table 15–2 From Emil J. Posavac and Raymond G. Carey, *Program Evaluation: Methods and Case Studies*, fifth edition, p. 175. Copyright © 1997 Prentice–Hall. Adapted by permission of Prentice-Hall, Upper Saddle River, NJ.

Fig. 15–6 From A. J. McSweeney, "Effects of response cost on the behavior of a million people: Charging for directory assistance in Cincinnati," fig. 1, p. 49, 1978, *Journal of Applied Behavior Analysis*, *11*, 47–51. Copyright © 1978 Journal of Applied Behavior Analysis. Reprinted with permission.

Chapter 17 Fig. 17–1 From *Research Methods* by F. C. Dane, Brooks-Cole Publishing Company, 1990. Copyright © 1990 by Francis D. Dane.

Box 17–2, Box 17–3, Text pp. 550, 552 From D. J. Bem, "Writing the empirical research report," in M. P. Zanna & J. M. Darley, (Eds.), *The Compleat Academic*, 1987, pp. 171–201. Reprinted with permission from Blackwell Publishers.

Figs. 17–2, 17–4, 17–6 From R. A. Baron, "'Sweet smell of success'? The impact of pleasant artificial scents on evaluations of job applicants," *Journal of Applied Psychology*, *68*, 709–713. Copyright © 1983 by the American Psychological Association. Reprinted by permission.

Box 17–4, 17–5, 17–7, 17–8, 17–9, text pp. 565, 567 Adapted from *Research Design Explained*, second edition, by Mark Mitchell and Janina Jolley. Copyright © 1992 by Holt, Rinehart and Winston, Inc. Reproduced by permission of the publisher.

NAME INDEX

Abbott, B. B., 15, 290
Abelson, R. P., 433
Abramson, L. Y., 16, 18, 20, 95, 99, 133, 175, 186, 228, 230
Adair, J. G., 460
Adams, K. A., 462, 594
Agnew, N. M., 10, 117, 435
Aiken, L. S., 241
Ajzen, I., 230, 253, 366, 433
Albee, G. W., 605
Alexander, S., 601
Alfred, R. H., 315, 316, 320, 321
Allen, M. J., 227
Allgeier, E. R., 86, 346, 347, 404
Allison, P. D., 509
Alloy, L. B., 16, 99, 133, 175, 186, 228
Allport, G. W., 39, 43
Al-Zahrani, S. S. A., 557
American College of Sports Medicine, 77
American Psychological Association, 58, 59, 66, 71, 75, 82, 84, 548, 549, 555, 559, 575, 583, 584, 585, 586, 603, 604, 607
Amir, Y., 109
Anastasi, A., 130
Andersen, M., 38
Anderson, C. A., 329, 470
Anderson, M. S., 592
Anderson, N. H., 139, 357
Annas, G. J., 71
Applebaum, M. I., 44, 48
Aragon, A. S., 67, 407
Archer, D., 113, 508
Arellano-Goldamos, F. J., 71
Argyris, C., 36, 457, 460, 468
Arnold, J., 376

Aronson, E., 70, 83, 113, 140, 141, 143, 169, 170, 174, 177, 178, 189, 190, 300, 302, 303, 399, 400, 401, 402, 404, 408, 409, 457, 459, 508
Atkinson, D. R., 441
Attridge, C., 335
AuBuchon, P. G., 172

Babbage, C., 590
Babbie, E., 344, 371, 372, 373, 374, 379
Bachman, J. G., 370
Back, K. W., 293
Backman, C. W., 467
Baer, D. M., 295, 296
Bailey, R. D., 411, 413
Bakeman, R., 127
Baker, K., 601
Bales, R. F., 330, 331
Balogh, D. W., 460
Baltes, P. B., 44, 48
Bamberger, E., 500
Banaji, M. R., 471
Bandura, A., 19
Bangert-Downs, R. L., 530, 533
Banister, P., 34
Banks, W. C., 470
Barb, K, H., 242
Barber, T. X., 176, 457
Barker, L. R., 466
Barlow, D. H., 264, 265, 266, 274, 493
Barnes, J., 411
Barnett, P. A., 249
Barnett, W. S., 505
Baron, R. A., 553, 554, 555, 559, 561, 563, 565, 566, 567, 571, 572

Baron, R. M., 247, 439
Barrett, G. V., 131
Barrett, R. P., 284, 286
Bart, P. B., 357
Basow, S. A., 10, 11, 37, 191, 464
Bass, B. M., 360
Baumeister, R. F., 606, 610
Baumgardner, M. H., 522
Baumrin, B. H., 609
Baumrind, D., 74
Baxter, J. C., 141, 318
Baxter, L. A., 330
Baxter, P. M., 101, 147
Beattie, A. E., 401
Bechtel, H. K., 592, 593
Beck, A. T., 148, 351
Becker, B. J., 540
Belar, C. D., 2
Bell, C. H., 314
Bell, P. A., 329
Bell, R., 591, 592
Bellack, A. S., 281, 282
Bem, D. J., 253, 548, 549, 550, 551, 552, 553, 555, 568, 592
Bem, S. L., 242
Benjamin, L. S., 332
Bentler, P. M., 47
Berscheid, E., 464
Berkowitz, L., 313, 327, 469, 472
Bermant, G., 465
Bernstein, A. S., 457
Bernstein, D. A., 142
Bersoff, D. N., 26
Bertera, E. M., 504, 506
Bertera, R. L., 504, 506
Beutler, L. E., 59
Bickman, L., 30
Bigelow, J., 528

Billig, M., 432
Biner, P. M., 25, 456
Binik, Y. M., 413, 420, 421
Binning, J. F., 131
Birnbaum, M. H., 411, 412, 415, 417
Bjork, R. A., 603
Black, D. J., 316, 717, 319
Blalock, H. M., 393
Blanchard, F. A., 84
Blank, T. O., 464
Block, J., 607
Blumer, C., 255
Bochner, S., 302, 303, 304, 305
Boersma, F. J., 408
Bogardus, E. E., 364, 365
Bogdan, R., 319, 320
Bohrnstedt, G. W., 248
Bolger, N., 247
Bollen, K. A., 242
Boller, F., 306
Bond, M. H., 462
Bonoma, T. V., 461
Booth-Kewley, S., 13
Borden, V. M., 246, 353
Bordens, K. S., 15, 290, 354
Borgida, E., 26
Borkovec, T. D., 142
Bornstein, M., 281, 282
Boruch, R. F., 498
Botivin, G. J., 244
Bouchard, T. J., 160, 301, 315, 457
Bounds, W. G., 99
Boyle, G. J., 230
Bradburn, N. M., 345, 346, 348, 349,
    350, 367, 371, 373
Bramal, D., 99
Brandt, D., 509
Bransford, J. D., 5, 184, 185, 186, 188,
    203, 427, 428, 431
Braver, M. C. W., 161
Braver, S. L., 161, 443, 459
Bray, R. M., 462
Breckler, S. J., 248, 252, 253
Brehm, J. W., 71, 173
Brehm, S. S., 71, 173
Breuning, S., 591, 595, 596
Brewer, M. B., 74, 75, 300, 330, 336,
    354, 472
Broad, W., 590, 593, 594, 595, 596
Brody, J. L., 67, 82, 407
Broman, C. L., 570
Brown, A. S., 585
Brown, C. E., 559, 560, 569
Brown, D. R., 356, 489, 490
Brunswik, E., 452
Buchanan, T., 418
Buckley, N. K., 278, 279
Bucuvalas, M. J., 113

Bullock, R. J., 531
Bundy, R., 432
Burbach, D. J., 79
Burger, J. M., 531, 533
Burgess, A., 600
Burman, E., 34
Burns, D., 432
Burt, C., 592, 595
Bushman, B. B., 470
Bushway, D. J., 245
Busk, P. L., 246
Buss, A. H., 13, 14
Butler, D. L., 25, 402, 558, 569
Butzin, C. A., 139, 357

Cacioppo, J. T., 143
Calder, B. J., 31, 113, 116, 469
Calhoun, K. S., 172
Cameron, K., 604
Cameron, P., 604
Campbell, B., 464
Campbell, D. T., 23, 75, 83, 133, 134,
    157, 159, 160, 178, 250, 307,
    310, 328, 452, 453, 473, 490,
    491, 498, 500, 501, 528
Campbell, J. P., 132, 468, 576, 577
Campion, M. A., 581
Cannell, C. F., 325
Capasso, D. R., 457
Capitanio, J. P., 383
Caplinger, T. E., 442, 488
Carey, R. G., 478, 498, 499, 500, 501,
    504, 507
Carli, L. L., 6, 7, 96, 118, 157, 458,
    467
Carlsmith, J. M., 70, 140, 169, 175,
    190, 300, 303, 399, 400, 457
Carmines, E. G., 132
Carr, T. S., 466
Carver, C. S., 12, 150, 228, 229
Cascio, W. F., 44, 130, 132, 360
Cash, T., 532
Catania, J. A., 607
Catlin, E. C., 352
Cerny, J. A., 493
Chafetz, J. S., 9
Chapanis, A., 591
Chapanis, N. P., 591
Chassein, B., 367
Chemers, M. M., 314
Chen, H. T., 486
Cherulnik, P. D., 456
Childers, T. L., 379
Chitwood, D. D., 607
Cho, H., 411, 416, 420, 421
Chow, S. L., 433
Christensen, L., 76, 81, 173, 408
Christian, W. P., 283, 283

Christie, R., 362
Cicchetti, D. V., 359
Clark, R., 383
Clark, R. P., 31
Clarke-Stewart, K. A., 602
Clore, G. L., 187
Coates, T. J., 607
Cobben, N. P., 48, 50
Coffman, T. L., 467
Cohen, J., 225, 226, 232, 233, 239,
    242, 250, 396, 397, 398, 444
Cohen, P., 225, 226, 232, 233, 239,
    250
Cohen, R. J., 134
Cohen, S. P., 330
Cohn, A., 605
Cohn, E. S., 141
Cole, D. A., 134
Coles, M. G. H., 142
Collis, J. M., 367
Committee on Government Opera-
    tions, 592, 595, 596
Condon, J. W., 246, 247, 253
Connell, D. W., 500
Converse, J. M., 345
Cook, S. W., 66, 84
Cook, T. D., 23, 139, 168, 169, 250,
    307, 444, 446, 452, 453, 473,
    494, 498, 500, 501, 506, 523,
    528, 530, 532, 533, 534
Cooney, N. L., 497
Coons, A. E., 11, 12, 228
Cooper, H., 378, 379
Cooper, H. M., 517, 539, 540
Cooper, J., 96, 112, 446, 592
Cooper, M., 211
Cooper, W. H., 368
Coovert, M. D., 248
Cordray, D. S., 499
Cormier, W. H., 99
Costanzo, P. R., 21
Cota, A. A., 457
Council, J. R., 376
Council of National Psychological
    Associations for the Advance-
    · ment of Ethnic Minority Inter-
    ests, 108
Cowles, M., 429
Cox, D. L., 408
Cox, E. P., 359
Coyne, J. C., 462
Craig, J. R., 470
Crandall, C. S., 228, 229
Crandall, R., 63, 65, 66, 70, 73, 76,
    83, 109, 110, 112, 600, 602, 604,
    606, 608, 609
Crano, W. D., 74, 75, 246, 247, 253,
    330, 336, 354, 472

Crask, M. R., 379
Crawford, M., 10, 22, 23
Crego, C. A., 594
Critchfield, R., 39, 319
Cronbach, L. J., 130, 133, 135, 459, 466, 469, 474, 509
Cross, T., 27
Crosse, S., 498
Crossen, C., 508
Crowder, R. G., 471
Csikszentmihalyi, M., 140
Cummings, L. L., 579

Daft, R. L., 577
Dalal, R., 411, 413, 414, 418
D'Andrade, R. G., 139
Dane, F. C., 405, 407, 408, 550
Danziger, K., 264
Darley, J. M., 141, 170, 400, 456, 462, 612
David, S., 411
Davis, B., 105, 107
Davis, C., 429
Davis, R. N., 418
Davison, M. L., 353
Dawes, R. M., 4, 44, 364, 371
Dawis, R.V., 362
Dayson, K., 211
Deaux, K., 26
DeJong, W., 201, 202, 461
DeLamater, J., 365
Delaney, H. D., 243
D'Emilio, J., 464
Dempster, F. N., 112, 116
Denmark, F. L., 118, 437
Depue, R. A., 465
Deutsch, B., 367
Deutsch, M., 74
DeVellis, R. F., 136, 375
Diaz, T., 244
DiCecco, J. V., 246, 353
Diener, E., 63, 65, 66, 70, 73, 76, 83, 600, 602, 604, 606, 608, 609
Diesing, P., 7, 117, 434
Dill, C. A., 80
Dillman, D. A., 371, 373, 375, 379
Dion, K. L., 457
Dipboye, R. T., 54, 459, 471
Dishion, T. J., 490, 491, 494
Dobson, K. S., 151, 159, 240
Dodson, C. L., 266, 267
Donham, G. W., 466
Donnerstein, E., 469, 472, 604
Doob, A. N., 394
Dooley, D., 25, 329
Dougherty, D., 27
Douglas, R. J., 580
Dovidio, J. F., 31

Downs, C. W., 324
Doyle, C., 172
Doyle, M. M., 244
Drew, C. J., 449
Duckitt, J., 435, 436
Dudley, K. A., 31, 609
Duncan, D., 94
Dunkel-Schetter, C., 249
Dunkle, J., 498
Durlak, J. A., 102, 521, 534, 540
Dworkin, R. J., 66, 71
Dwyer, C. A., 137
Dyer, K., 283, 285

Eagly, A. H., 6, 7, 96, 118, 157, 458, 467, 540–544
Ebbesen, E. B., 94
Ebbinghaus, H., 264
Eberhardt, A. A., 435
Eder, D., 276
Educational Testing Service, 4
Edwards, W., 152, 484, 485
Eichler, M., 117, 118, 438
Einstein, A., 18
Eisler, R. M., 279, 280
Elig, T. W., 462
Ellard, J. H., 415, 418
Elliot, A. J., 251
Elliott, R., 112, 115, 572, 573
Ellsworth, P. C., 70, 140, 169, 190, 303, 306, 399
Endler, N. S., 459
Epperson, D. L., 245
Epstein, J. A., 244
Epstein, S., 455
Erlebacher, A., 310
Estes, W. K., 581, 610, 611
Etheridge, B., 223
Evans, C., 274
Evans, I. M., 459
Evans, J. D., 95, 293
Evered, R., 32
Exline, R. V., 141
Eyer, D. E., 602
Eysenk, H. J., 230

Fabrigar, L. R., 254
Farh, J., 97
Farha, J. G., 79
Farkas, G. M., 459
Farrell, D., 19, 24
Faust, D., 44
Fazio, R. H., 112, 211, 212, 213, 446, 592
Feather, N. T., 235, 237
Feldman, R. A., 442, 488, 489, 500
Feldman, R. S., 202, 461
Festinger, L., 112, 175

Feuerstein, M. J., 142
Fidell, L. S., 225, 226, 239, 244, 245, 246, 254, 255, 256, 309, 461
Fiedler, F. E., 11, 12, 314, 327
Fields, C. B., 383
Fillenbaum, S., 173
Fine, M., 33, 34, 583
Finegan, J. E., 301, 404
Fink, A., 346
Firebaugh, G., 329
Fischhoff, B., 601, 607
Fishbein, M., 230, 253, 366, 433
Fiske, D. W., 133, 134, 576, 577, 578
Fiske, S. T., 26, 31, 318, 319
Fitzgerald, M. P., 520
Flamant, C., 432
Flanagan, M., 54, 459, 471
Flay, B. R., 444
Flett, G. L., 472
Floyd, J., 459
Floyd, K., 411
Fogg, L., 576, 577, 578
Folger, R., 74, 75, 81, 82, 83, 172, 173, 178, 300, 531
Fong, K. T., 611
Fontana, A. M., 352
Foote, W. E., 411
Forgas, J. P., 462
Forsyth, D. R., 166
Fowler, F. J., 322, 323, 324, 373
Fowler, R. L., 444
Fox, R. J., 379
Foxx, R. M., 287
Freeberg, F. E., 71
Freedman, B., 598
Freedman, E. B., 464
Freedman, J. L., 41, 96
Freeman, H. E., 478
Friedman, H. S., 13
Friedman, P. J., 594, 596, 597, 598, 599
Friedman, S., 552, 555
Friend, R., 99
Frieze, I. H., 8, 117, 118, 429, 438, 462
Fromkin, L. H., 461
Frost, P. J., 579
Furby, L., 509
Furlong, M. J., 431
Furman, W., 242

Gaertner, S. L., 31
Gaiser, T. J., 411
Gannon, L., 117, 458
Garbin, M. G., 148
Garcia, J., 522
Garcia, L. T., 69, 600
Garfield, E., 591

Garfield, S. L., 575
Geis, F. L., 362
Gergen, K. J., 464
Gescheider, G. A., 352
Getter, H., 497
Ghiselli, E. E., 132
Gibson, D. R., 607
Gilbert, D. T., 456, 568
Gilbert, G. N., 109
Gilden, E. R., 80
Gillen, B., 432
Gilligan, C., 137
Gilovich, T., 2, 22, 117
Giusti, L. M., 423
Glantz, L. H., 71
Glass, C. R., 255
Glass, D. C., 97
Glass, G. V., 530, 544
Gluck, J. P., 67, 407
Gold, R. L., 315
Goldberg, L. R., 4, 44
Goldman, A. E., 326
Goldman, B. A., 147
Gonzales, M. H., 70, 140, 169, 190,
    303, 336–338, 399
Gonzalez, R., 306
Good, R. H., 105, 107
Goodall, J., 38
Goodyear, R. K., 594
Gordon, M. E., 460
Gotlib, I. H., 249, 462
Gottfredson, S. D., 577
Gottman, J. M., 127
Graham, S., 117, 458, 610, 611
Green, B. F., 521, 532, 595
Greenberg, J., 74, 75, 81, 82, 83, 94,
    172, 173, 178, 243, 300, 307,
    308, 310, 500, 501, 531
Greenberg, J. S., 80
Greenberg, M. S., 462
Greene, E., 160
Greenwald, A. G., 102, 192, 193, 196,
    431, 432, 444, 522
Gridley, B. E., 566, 567
Griffin, K. W., 244
Grisso, T., 58
Gronlund, N. E., 128
Grove, J. B., 328
Gruder, C. L., 444
Gruenewald, P. J., 500
Gruenfeld, D. H., 327
Gunst, R. F., 240
Gutek, B. A., 380
Guthrie, R. V., 458
Guttman, L., 364
Guzzo, R. A., 518, 531, 545

Hackman, J. R., 19, 24, 268, 272, 485,
    486, 519, 520, 523

Hagenaars, J. A., 48, 50
Halberstadt, L. J., 230
Hall, G. S., 264
Hall, J. A., 521, 532
Hallahan, M., 327
Halvorsen, K. T., 537
Hamilton, D. L., 370
Hamilton, V. L., 570
Hammonds, A. D., 457
Haney, C., 470
Hanselka, L. L., 80
Harackiewicz, J. M., 251
Harcum, E. R., 444
Harvey, D. F., 356, 489, 490
Harris, F. C., 169
Hartlage, L. C., 599
Hastie, R., 25
Hastorf, A. H., 201, 202, 461
Hatfield, E., 432, 464
Hay, L. R., 170
Hay, W. W., 170
Hayes, S. C., 502
Hays, W. L., 431
Haynes, S. N., 168, 169
Hazlewood, J. D., 301, 404
Hearnshaw, L. S., 592, 595
Hearold, S., 97, 525
Hedges, L. V., 517, 527, 530
Heilman, M. E., 26
Heinold, W. D., 70
Heinsman, D. T., 312
Heinsson, R. K., 255
Helmreich, R. L., 242, 459
Hendrick, C., 457, 466
Hennigan, K. M., 444
Henninger, M., 102
Henshel, R. L., 470
Herbert, J., 335
Herek, G. M., 237, 383
Hersen, M., 264, 265, 266, 274, 279,
    280, 281, 282
Herzog, T., 327
Hewson, C. M., 415
Higgens, R. L., 469, 470
Hill, P. C., 80
Hill, R. J., 364
Himmelstein, J. L., 383
Hippler, H. J., 367
Hoch, H. M., 205, 206, 207, 209, 210,
    211, 212, 213, 214
Hochschild, A. R., 10
Hodgins, H. S., 555
Hoffman, W. S., 570
Holden, C., 591
Hollenbeck, J. R., 19
Holmes, D. S., 82
Holsti, O. R., 336
Hooker, D. T., 71
Hopkins, K. D., 312

Horn, W. F., 168, 169
Hotz, A. S., 127
Houts, A. C., 7, 472
Hovland, C. I., 364
Howard, K. I., 463, 483
Hoyt, W. T., 333
Hubbard, M., 82
Huberman, A. M., 294
Huck, S. W., 99, 103, 105, 163, 166,
    180
Hughes, E. F. X., 506, 507
Humphreys, L., 58
Hunter, J. E., 138, 534, 540
Hunter, R., 138
Huxley, A., 600
Hyde, J. S., 13
Hyde, K. R., 255

Ilgen, D. R., 472
Imber, S. D., 65
Impara, J. C., 147
Innes, C. A., 112, 113, 115, 116, 455,
    465, 480, 571
Irvine, A. A., 31, 609
Iwamasa, G., 611

Jackson, G. B., 517, 519, 524, 525, 526
Jackson, S. E., 518
Jacob, T., 59, 63, 67, 474, 560
Jacobson, N. T., 433, 493, 510
Jamieson, D. W., 171
Janis, I. L., 37, 273
Jensen, K., 459
Jette, R. D., 531
John, O. P., 567
Johnson, B. T., 540–544
Johnson, C. G., 85
Johnson, M., 211
Johnson, M. K., 184, 185, 186, 188,
    203, 427, 428, 431
Johnston, M. W., 594
Joinson, A., 369, 381, 413, 418
Jolley, J., 135, 556, 562, 568, 570, 571
Jones, R. A., 75, 317, 318, 466
Jones, S. K., 402
Joswick, K. E., 101
Joy, L. A., 334
Joynson, R. B., 595
Judd, C. M., 2, 143, 310, 311, 326,
    329, 359, 377, 382, 600, 608

Kadden, R. M., 497
Kahn, R. L., 325
Kallman, W. M., 142
Kamin, L., 607
Kamins, M. A., 383, 384
Kanter, R. M., 37
Kaplowitz, S. A., 557
Karlins, M., 467

Kashy, D. A., 247
Katz, B. F., 71
Katzell, R. A., 518, 531
Kazdin, A. E., 64, 65, 141, 143, 184, 265, 267, 271, 287, 288, 289, 292, 295, 457, 465, 484, 488, 492, 493, 495, 496, 502
Keith-Spiegel, P., 64, 67, 68, 71, 76, 78, 80, 85, 245, 583, 584, 585, 597, 598, 612
Kellehear, A., 326, 327
Kelly, J. A., 242
Kelman, H. C., 600
Kendall, P. C., 59
Kendler, H. H., 604
Kenny, D. A., 247, 439
Kerker, R. M., 401
Kerkhoff, A. C., 293
Kerns, M. D., 333
Kerr, N. L., 74, 462
Kerwin, J., 600
Kessler, R. C., 465
Kessler, S., 457
Kidd, G. R., 192, 193
Kidder, L. H., 2, 33, 34, 143, 310, 600
Kidder, T., 273
Kiesler, S., 413
Kilmann, R. H., 2, 8
Kim, J., 379
Kim, Y., 306
Kimball, M. M., 334
Kimble, G. A., 7, 11, 472, 604, 605
Kimmel, A. J., 65, 601, 602, 607, 608
Kinsey, A. C., 85
Kite, M. E., 244, 245
Klein, H. J., 19
Kleinman, S., 170, 268, 274, 294
Klitzner, M., 500
Klosko, J. S., 493, 496
Knerr, C. R., 86
Knight, L. A., 255
Knoke, D., 248
Knowles, E. S., 69, 403, 560
Koeske, R., 8, 117, 438
Koestner, R., 555
Konecni, V. J., 94
Koocher, G. P., 59, 64, 67, 68, 70, 71, 76, 78, 85, 583, 584, 585, 597, 598, 612
Kopta, S. M., 463
Korn, J. H., 71
Kosecoff, J., 346
Kovacs, S. Z., 196
Krahn, G. L., 59, 474, 560
Krames, L., 472
Krantz, J. H., 411, 413, 414, 415, 418
Krasner, L., 7, 472
Krause, M. S., 463
Krosnick, J. A., 359, 369, 370

Kraemer, H. C., 397, 398
Kratochwill, T. R., 265, 266, 267, 268, 269, 271, 272
Krauss, R. M., 74
Kremer, J. F., 203, 204
Krippendorf, K., 336
Krishef, C. H., 296
Krueger, R. A., 380, 381, 382
Kruglanski, A. W., 174
Krull, J. L., 241
Kuhn, T. S., 18
Kurdek, L. A., 583

Lahey, B. B., 169
Lamal, P. A., 112
Lambert, M. J., 478
Landy, D., 189
Landy, F. J., 12, 114, 128
LaRose, R., 411, 416, 420, 421
Larson, R., 140
Lassiter, G. D., 31, 609
Latané, B., 141, 170, 400, 462
Latham, G. P., 10, 13, 15, 16, 17, 18, 19, 24, 95, 99, 113, 114
Lau, R. R., 327, 336
Laurant, D., 415
Lawshe, C. H., 129
Leak, G. K., 67
Leavitt, F., 102, 117
Lee, F., 326, 327
LeFan, J., 459
Leigh, B., 412, 413, 414, 415, 417, 420, 421
Leippe, M. R., 522
Lemke, K. M., 539
Lennenberg, E. H., 40
Leonard, K., 59, 67, 474, 560
Leonhard, C., 502
Lepper, M. R., 82
Levin, J. R., 265
Levine, R. J., 63
Leviton, L. C., 506, 507, 523, 530, 532, 533, 534
Lewin, M., 347, 358
Lewis, K. S., 592
Lewis, O., 39
Lewontin, B. C., 607, 609, 610
Lickert, R., 361
Lidz, C. W., 67
Liebow, E., 37
Light, R. J., 517, 518, 520, 521, 522, 524, 525, 533, 535
Lindsay, J. J., 470
Lindsey, D., 577
Linville, P. W., 16
Linz, D., 604
Lipsey, M. W., 102, 397, 478, 498, 499, 501, 502, 503, 517, 521, 526, 534, 540

Litt, M. D., 497
Locke, E. A., 10, 13, 15, 16, 17, 18, 19, 24, 95, 99, 113, 114
Lofland, J., 293, 294, 321
Lofland, L. H., 293, 294, 321
Loftus, E. F., 4, 139, 160, 605, 606, 607, 608
Loher, E. F., 520
Loo, C., 611
Loomis, J. W., 327
Lowen, A., 470
Luce, S. S., 283, 285
Luchetta, T., 117, 458
Lunney, G. H., 246, 353
Lydon, J., 249
Lykken, D. T., 124
Lyon, D., 94

Macauley, J., 313
MacCallum, R., 248, 254
MacCorquodale, P., 365
MacCoun, R. J., 74, 438, 472
MacDonald, G. E., 394
MacDonald, W. S., 610, 611
Mackie, D., 96, 436
Mah, K., 413
Mainieri, T., 71
Malfese, D. L., 410
Malinak, J., 527
Mangione, T. W., 322, 323, 324, 344, 379
Maracek, J., 33, 34
Marascuilo, L. A., 246
Maris, R. W., 328
Marks, G., 516, 531
Marlatt, G. A., 469, 470
Marlin, N. A., 593
Marshall, C., 293
Martin, C. J., 408, 416
Martin, E., 324
Martin, J. E., 288, 291
Mason, R. L., 240
Masters, J. C., 518, 573
Masters, K. S., 478
Matlin, M. W., 461
Matsumoto, D., 462
Matter, C. F., 69, 403, 560
Maxwell, S. E., 243
Maynard, M., 383
McCall, R. B., 44, 48
McCloskey, M., 99
McCord, J., 490
McDonald, S. S., 326
McFatter, R. M., 213
McGrath, J. E., 54, 473, 524
McGuire, C. V., 244
McGuire, M., 465
McGuire, W. J., 95, 96, 244, 253, 457
McHugh, M. C., 8, 117, 118, 428, 438

McKenna, W., 458
McKinley, W., 465
McKinney, K., 213
McNemar, Q., 471
McRae, J. A., 383
McSweeney, A. J., 502, 503
Medewar, P., 595
Meehl, P. E., 44, 133
Meier, S. T., 255
Mendel, G., 9
Mentzer, S., 612
Metalsky, G. I., 16, 99, 133, 228, 230
Meyer, J. P., 16, 247, 248, 253
Meyers, S. A., 336–338
Michalak, E. E., 417, 420, 421
Michell, J., 353
Middlemist, R. D., 69, 70, 403, 405, 560
Milavsky, J. R., 464
Miles, M. B., 294
Milgram, S., 58, 65, 75, 77, 80, 81, 82, 169, 170, 400, 401, 462
Mill, J. S., 3
Miller, D. T., 431, 432, 470
Miller, N., 516, 519, 531
Miller, P. M., 279, 280, 290
Millman, S., 466
Mills, J., 82, 83, 408
Mills, J. L., 590, 592
Mirvis, P. H., 67
Miskevich, S. L., 412
Mitchell, C., 47, 62, 66
Mitchell, M., 135, 556, 562, 568, 570, 571
Mitroff, I. I., 2, 8
Moeller, N. L., 520
Money, J., 435
Monohan, J., 4, 605, 606, 607
Monroe, S. M., 465
Monteith, M. J., 557, 558
Mook, D. G., 433, 445, 469, 470
Mooney, K. M., 141
Morris, W. N., 201, 202, 461
Morrow, L., 306
Morrow-Bradley, C., 112, 115, 572, 573
Mott, S. E., 266, 267
Muehlenhard, C. L., 423
Mulherin, A., 16, 247, 248, 253
Mulkay, M., 109
Mullen, B., 519, 524, 532, 537, 540
Müller, G., 367
Murphey, L. L., 147
Murphy, D. R., 585
Murray, H. A., 401
Musch, J., 415
Myers, J. L., 246, 353
Myers, R. H., 240

Nance, J., 37
Nataupsky, M., 437
National Commission for Protection of Human Subjects of Biomedical and Behavioral Research, 58
National Opinion Research Center, 383
Neisser, U., 37, 40
Nelkin, D., 610
Nelson, R. O., 170
Nesselroade, J. R., 44
Neuliep, J. W., 109, 110, 112
New, M. J., 78, 84
Newcombe, M. D., 47
Newell, J. D., 69, 600
Newman, J. R., 152, 484, 485
Newstead, S. E., 367, 376
Newton, I., 18
Nezu, A. M., 494, 496
Nickel, G. S., 255
Nicks, S. D., 71
Nielson, J., 419
Nisbett, R. E., 139
Noe, R. A., 520
Nolen-Hoeksema, S., 243
Norman, D. A., 22
Notz, W., 528
Nye, R. D., 9

Oakes, W., 469, 471
O'Connor, E. J., 360
Oden, C. W., 610, 611
Ogles, B. M., 478
Ogloff, J. R., 71, 72
Oldham, G. R., 19, 24, 268, 272, 485, 486, 519, 520, 523
Olkin, I., 527, 539, 540
Ollendick, T. H., 268, 283, 284
Olson, C., 223
O'Malley, P. M., 370
Orbuch, T. L., 213
Orlinski, D. E., 463
Orne, M. T., 171, 173
Osberg, T. M., 169
Osborne, R. E., 568
Osgood, S. E., 365, 366
Otto, R. K., 71, 72

Palmer, J. P., 4
Pardie, L., 117, 458
Parker, I., 34
Parker, J. D. A., 459
Parks, M. R., 411
Parsonson, B. S., 295, 296
Pasveer, K. A., 415, 418
Patrick, D., 314
Patton, M. Q., 294, 489, 490, 495, 507

Paulhus, D. L., 151, 170, 171, 368, 369
Pavelchek, M. A., 306, 308, 310
Pearson, W., 592, 593
Pedhazur, E. J., 240, 241, 243, 248
Pembroke, M., 306
Penner, L. A., 248
Penrod, S., 4, 139, 604
Perkins, D. V., 460
Perri, M. G., 494, 496
Perry, N. W., 2
Peterson, C., 326, 327, 336
Pettigrew, T. F., 113, 508
Petty, M. M., 500
Pfeifer, M. P., 598
Pfungst, O., 175
Phares, V., 96, 117
Phelps, J. L., 423
Phillips, L. W., 31, 113, 469
Phillips, M. L., 411
Phillips, S. M., 134
Piliavin, I. M., 170, 301, 303, 304, 305, 306
Piliavin, J. A., 31, 170, 301
Pillemer, D. B., 517, 518, 520, 521, 522, 524, 525, 533, 535
Pinto, J. N., 255
Plake, B. S., 147
Platz, S. J., 205, 206, 207, 209, 210, 211, 212, 213, 214
Plous, S., 415, 418, 419
Podasakoff, P. M., 97
Pogue, D., 575
Polivy, J., 172
Pollard, J., 498
Pomeroy, W. B., 85
Pope, K. S., 245
Popovich, P. M., 255
Popper, K. R., 21
Porter, A. C., 309, 310
Posavac, E. J., 478, 498, 499, 500, 501, 504, 507, 571, 572, 573, 574
Poulin, F., 490
Powch, I. G., 423
Pratkanis, A. R., 522
Prentice, D. A., 431, 432, 470
Presser, S., 345, 346, 357, 369, 371, 372
Preston, J., 327
Price, R. L., 571, 573
Pyke, S. W., 10, 117, 435

Quinn, R. P., 380, 381

Rabinowitz, V. C., 33
Rafferty, Y., 99
Rasinski, K. A., 348
Raudenbush, S. W., 309, 310

Rauma, D., 570
Redfield, R., 39
Reed, J. G., 101, 147
Reese, H. W., 44
Reips, U. D., 412, 413, 414, 415, 418, 419
Reisenzein, R., 248
Reiss, A. J., 316, 317, 319, 321
Resnick, J. H., 71, 73
Reynolds, P. D., 602, 603, 604, 606, 607, 608
Rhodes, K., 117, 458
Rhodes, S. R., 94
Richardson, D., 83, 174
Richardson, W. C., 482
Richter, M. L., 191
Riger, S., 8
Riordan, C. A., 593
Rivlin, A., 605
Robbins, S. P., 40
Robinson, J. P., 127, 147, 148, 149, 363
Robinson, W. S., 329
Rodin, J., 170, 301
Roese, N. J., 171
Rogers, C., 5, 600
Rogosa, D. R., 509, 510
Rokeach, M., 5
Roman, M. B., 595
Rose, S., 607
Rosen, F. P., 202, 461
Rosenblatt, A., 243
Rosenthal, M. C., 521
Rosenthal, R., 39, 111, 166, 174, 176, 177, 371, 430, 431, 433, 456, 457, 458, 524, 526, 597, 610
Rosnow, R. L., 166, 174, 177, 371, 430, 431, 433, 458, 610
Ross, L., 82, 83
Ross, R. R., 86, 346, 347, 404
Rossi, J. S., 397, 430, 527
Rossi, P. H., 478, 479, 480, 484, 487, 504, 506, 508
Rossiter, C., 500
Rossman, G. B., 293
Rousseau, D. L., 7, 593
Ruback, R. B., 112, 113, 115, 116, 455, 465, 466, 480, 571
Rubanowitz, D. E., 328
Rubens, W. S., 465
Rubin, H. J., 322
Rubin, I. S., 322
Rubin, Z., 47, 62, 66
Rubinoff, A., 287
Rumenik, D. K., 457
Rusbult, C. E., 19, 24
Rushe, R., 474
Russell, D., 327, 336

Russo, N. F., 118, 438
Rychlak, J. F., 40

Sachs, D. A., 288, 291
Sachse-Lee, C., 531
Saks, M. J., 25, 66
Salas, E., 519
Salipante, P., 528
Salo, C., 465
Sanders, R. E., 196
Sandler, H. M., 103, 105, 163, 166, 180
Sanislow, C. A., 460
Saranson, S. B., 610, 611
Saris, W. E., 380
Saunders, J. L., 147
Saxe, L., 27, 603
Scarr, S., 250, 251, 434, 435, 606, 610, 611
Schlenker, B. R., 461
Schmidt, F. L., 112, 138, 516, 522, 534, 540
Schmidt, W. C., 411, 413, 415
Schmitt, N., 460
Schneider, W., 460
Schneier, B., 85
Schnelle, J. F., 505
Schoeneman, T. J., 328
Schofield, J. W., 37, 117, 169, 171, 306, 308, 310, 318, 503, 504, 520, 521
Schuerger, J. M., 127, 128
Schuler, H., 71
Schultz, D. P., 600
Schultz, S. E., 600
Schuman, H., 223, 236, 345, 346, 357, 369, 371, 372
Schwab, D. B., 577
Schwartz, R. D., 328
Schwartz, T., 71, 73
Schwarz, N., 187, 346, 367, 368
Sears, D. O., 54, 412, 458, 459, 461, 468, 472
Seashore, S. E., 67
Seay, M. B., 191
Sechrist, L., 328, 444
Sechzer, J. A., 118, 438
Secord, P. F., 467
Segrist, D., 117, 458
Seilhamer, R. A., 474
Seligman, C., 301, 303, 304, 305, 404, 405
Seligman, M. E. P., 18, 20, 95, 327
Senior, C., 411
Shadish, W. A., 312, 519, 530, 532
Shaffer, D. R., 600
Shamdasani, P. N., 380, 381
Shapiro, E. S., 284, 286

Sharf, B. F., 411, 412, 420, 421
Sharma, A. R., 353
Sharon, I., 109
Shaver, P. R., 127, 147, 149, 363
Shaw, M. E., 21
Shedler, J., 607
Sheets, V. L., 443
Sherif, M., 364
Sherman, G., 599
Sherwood, J. J., 437
Shotland, R. L., 70
Shortell, S. M., 482
Showalter, D., 359
Shrauger, J. S., 169
Shulman, A., 370
Shweder, R. A., 139, 319
Sieber, J. E., 60, 62, 63, 65, 66, 68, 70, 73, 74, 75, 76, 80, 82, 83, 407, 596, 598, 607, 610, 611
Sigma Xi, 596, 599
Signorella, M. L., 459
Simon, R. W., 276, 294
Simonton, D. K., 327
Simpson, J. A., 464
Sine, L. F., 459
Singer, J. E., 97
Singleton, B., 500
Singleton, R., 332
Skinner, B. F., 5, 600
Skinner, S. J., 379
Slade, L. A., 460
Slavin, R. E., 535
Smeyak, G. P., 324
Smith, A. C., 170, 268, 274, 294
Smith, E. R., 2, 143, 310, 600
Smith, J. L., 418
Smith, M. A., 412, 413, 414, 415, 417, 420, 421
Smith, M. F., 480
Smith, M. L., 530
Smith, S. S., 83, 174
Smith, T. L., 371
Snodgrass, G. L., 598
Snyder, M. L., 228, 369, 611
Soja, M. J., 327
Solomon, J., 505
Sommer, R., 306
Spector, P. E., 136, 360, 363
Spence, J. T., 242
Spielberger, C. D., 466
Sprague, R., 596
Sprecher, S., 213, 432, 464
Stake, R. E., 34, 295
Stanley, B., 610
Stanley, J. C., 157, 159, 160, 178
Stanton, A. L., 79, 84
Stapp, J., 242
Statham, A., 141

Steer, R. A., 147
Steers, R. M., 94
Stein, J. A., 47, 48
Steinberg, S., 552, 555
Steininger, M., 69, 70, 600, 604, 606, 608
Stephens, L., 203, 204
Steptoe, A., 142
Sternberg, R. J., 516, 548, 568, 580
Steuerwald, B. L., 558, 569
Stewart, D. W., 380, 381, 383, 384
Stipp, H. H., 464
St James-Roberts, I., 594
Stobart, G., 498
Stogdill, R. M., 11, 12, 228
Stokols, D., 3
Strack, F., 367
Strahan, E. J., 254
Straits, B. C., 330, 332, 333
Stratton, P., 322
Streufert, S., 461
Stricker, G., 59, 67
Strube, M. J., 194
Stryker, S., 141
Suci, G. J., 365
Sudman, S., 345, 346, 347, 348, 349, 350, 367, 368, 371, 372, 373
Sullivan, S. E., 527
Summer, G. F., 457
Swerdlik, M. E., 234
Susman, G., 32
Swanson, H. L., 531
Swazey, J. P., 592, 599
Sweeney, R. B., 519, 530
Swets, J. A., 4, 603
Swift, M. B., 141
Szabo, A., 417, 420, 421
Szanton, P., 270

Tabachnick, B. G., 225, 226, 239, 244, 245, 246, 254, 255, 256, 309, 461
Taffel, C., 71
Tajfel, H., 432
Tannenbaum, P. H., 365
Tassinari, R., 493
Tassinary, L. G., 143
Taylor, M., 34
Taylor, S. G., 31, 318, 319
Teasdale, J. D., 18, 20, 95
Tesser, A., 95
Tetlock, P. E., 327
Thiemann, S., 397, 398
Thompson, B., 236
Thompson, R. A., 64, 71
Thorne, B., 315, 317, 319, 321
Thorpe, J. S., 79
Throckmorton, B., 411

Thurstone, L. L., 363, 364
Tindall, C., 34
Tinsley, D. J., 255
Tinsley, H. E. A., 255
Tittle, C. R., 364
Tomarken, A. J., 143
Treadway, M., 99
Tremper, C. R., 26
Truax, P., 433, 493, 510
Tubbs, M. E., 531
Tunnell, G. B., 467
Tybout, A. M., 31, 113, 469
Tyrer, P. J., 359

Udolf, R., 605
Unger, R., 10, 22, 23
Urbani, S., 130
Urtunski, P. B., 306
U.S. Bureau of the Census, 433
U.S. Department of Health and Human Services, 58, 59, 60, 61, 62, 66, 69, 71
U.S. Public Health Service, 58

Vagg, P. R., 466
Vallacher, R. R., 2
Valliant, G. E., 327
Vegega, M. E., 459
Velten, E., 172, 174, 175
Vidmar, N., 453, 455, 464
Viscusi, D., 175, 186
Vogel, C. M., 415
von Békésy, G., 577
Vredenburg, K., 472

Wade, N., 590, 593, 594, 595, 596
Walker, H. M., 278, 279
Walsh, E., 223
Walsh, J. T., 380
Walters, G., 467
Wampold, B. E., 40, 105, 107, 427, 431
Wanous, J. P., 527, 532, 533, 534, 536
Warman, R. E., 245
Watts, J. G., 279, 280
Webb, E. J., 328
Weber, R. P., 336
Weber, S. J., 139, 168, 169
Wegner, D. M., 2, 254, 401
Weick, K. E., 335
Weigel, R. H., 327
Weiner, B., 16, 18, 95, 237, 247
Weiss, C. H., 32, 113, 478, 481, 482, 485, 486, 490, 502, 506, 507
Weiss, R. S., 322
Welch, N., 415
Welljams-Dorof, A., 591
Wells, G. L., 95, 113, 190, 460, 472
Wenzloff, R., 401

Weseen, S., 33
West, S. G., 241, 243
Westberry, L. G., 466
Wexley, K. N., 196
Wheeler, M., 347, 386
White, J. B., 246, 353
White, K. R., 522, 523, 524
Whitley, B. E., 96, 117, 202, 237, 238, 428, 429, 439, 446, 460, 461, 462, 503, 504, 520, 521, 566, 567, 600
Wholey, J. S., 480, 486
Wicker, A. W., 95
Wicklund, R. A., 456
Widom, C. S., 391, 423, 432
Wilcox, B. L., 608
Wilkenson, M., 301, 404
Willerman, B., 459
Willett, J. B., 509, 510
Willson, V. L., 463
Wilson, D. B., 517, 526, 540
Wilson, E. O., 436
Wilson, T. D., 16, 139
Windschitl, P. D., 190, 460
Winick, M., 46
Winkler, J., 4, 139
Wodarski, J. S., 442, 488
Wolchik, S. A., 459
Wolfgang, M. E., 605
Wright, R. E., 244
Wrightsman, L. S., 127, 147, 149, 363
Wundt, W., 264
Wylie, R. C., 129

Yammarino, F. J., 379
Yeaton, W. H., 444
Yen, W. M., 227
Yin, R. K., 37, 265, 266, 267, 268, 269, 270, 271, 272, 273, 274, 276, 292, 502
Young, D. R., 72
Young, V., 242
Yu, J., 378, 379
Yuille, J. C., 472
Yukl, G. A., 196

Zabrack, M. L., 324
Zaitzow, B. H., 383
Zakrajsek, T., 255
Zarella, K. L., 127
Zedeck, S., 132
Zeller, R. A., 132
Zimbardo, P. G., 63, 65, 78, 81, 470
Zimowski, M., 509
Zimring, F. E., 508
Zuckerman, M., 439, 606, 610, 611

SUBJECT INDEX

Note: Numbers in **boldface** indicate pages on which key terms are defined.

Actuarial prediction, 39, **43**–44
Additivity, **223**–224
Affirmative assent, **71**
Aggregate data, **329**
Alpha level. *See* Type I error
Alternative explanation for effect of independent variable, **3**–4, 111, 156, 301, 567
   in archival data, 329
   in case study research, 38, 270–271, 295
   and causality, 3–4, 41, 182
   in correlational research, 41–43
   in nonequivalent control group designs, 308–312
   in path analysis, 250–253
   use of control condition to rule out, 102, 186–187
American Psychological Association, 58, 75, 84, 574
Analysis of covariance (ANCOVA), **309**–310
Analysis of variance (ANOVA), 183, 246
   factorial, 206
   multiple regression analysis as an alternative to, 241–243
   one-way, 203–204
   nested design, **312**
   random effects model, 191
   See also Factorial designs
Anchors in numerical rating scales, 357–360

Application of research results, 25–27, 447, 517, 566, 567–568, 608
   design issues, 113–116
   ethical issues, 600–602, 608
   relation to research, 25
   relation to theory, 25
   See also Research, applied; Utilization of research results
A priori contrasts, **204**, 211
   See also Planned comparisons
Archives, 326–327
   of survey data, 383–384
Artifact, **156**, 516
Assumptions, 9–10, 103, 117
Attenuation of correlation coefficient, **224**
Attrition, 415
   See also Mortality

Between-subjects designs, **192**–195, 212
Bias
   in formulating research questions, 116–119
   in interpreting data, 435–438
   in publication, 441–443
      and integrative literature reviews, 522, 533, 537–538
   researcher, **39**, 43, 102, 413
      in case study research, 39
      in integrative literature reviews, 524, 536–537
      in observational research, 176, 318–319
      in qualitative data analysis, 295

   See also Experimenter expectancy effects
   in theories, 118
Bivariate regression, **231**
Blind review, **576**
Blocking on extraneous variables, **217**
Boundary conditions, 96, **112, 452**

Carryover effects, **196,** 199, 286
Case studies, 33, **37**–40, 43, 85, 272–277
   control cases, **270**
   embedded, **274**
   in evaluation research, 502
   test cases, **270**
   validity of, 273–274
   See also Single case research
Catalog of U.S. Government Publications, 101
Causality, 3–4, 35, 182, 440
   in case study research, 38
   in correlational research, 41, 43
   in nonequivalent control group designs, 311
   reciprocal, **42**
   reverse, **42**
Change, 492–494
   measurement of, 509–510
   rate of, and evaluation research, 482–483
   in research findings over time, 464
   See also Evaluation research; Research, developmental
Change in R^2, **239**
Chi-square analysis, 183, 244, 246
Clinical significance, 433
   See also Practical significance

Coding systems, 180, **329–336**
  characteristics, 330–334
  developing, 335
  reliability, 335–336, 527
Cohort effects, **47**
Comparison groups, 185–187
  See also Control groups
Condition blindness, **178, 180**
Confounds, 102, **156,** 157–159, 180
  measurement, 159
  natural, 157–158
  treatment, 158–159
  See also Internal validity, threats to
Construct. *See* Hypothetical
  construct
Constructionism, **434–435**
Construct validity, **23,** 24, 141
  of archival data, 328–329
  in field experiments, 305
  of manipulation of independent
    variable, 102, 187–188, 401,
    404, 442, 500–501
  of measurement, 131–134, 141,
    143, 442
  of research, 23, 102
Content analysis, **336–338**
Context effects
  between questionnaires, 376
  within questionnaires, 372–373
  See also Reactivity
Control groups, 102, 184–187, 278
  contamination of, **500**
  and internal validity, 164–165,
    180
  no-treatment, 64–65
  role-play, 174–175, 180
  and single-case research, 269–271,
    286
Control series design, **314–315**
Convenience survey, **344**
Convention presentations, 100,
  580–581
  See also Publication
Correlational analysis,
  bivariate regression, **231**
  differences in correlation
    coefficients, 232–233
  partial, **233–235**
    as control for measurement con-
      found, 159
  simple, 231–233
  See also Chi-square analysis;
    Correlational research; Latent
    variables analysis; Logistic
    regression analysis; Multiple
    regression analysis; Multi-
    way frequency analysis; Path
    analysis

Correlational research, **40–44,** 53
  assumptions underlying, 223–224
  and causal inferences, 41–43, 222
  considerations in conducting,
    224–228, 230–231
  and factorial designs, 212–213
  See also Correlational analysis
Corresponding author, **576**
Costs of intervention program, 494–
  495
  cost-benefit analysis, **505**
  cost-effectiveness analysis, 505–
    506
Counterbalancing, **197**
  of order of questionnaires, 376
  in within-subjects designs, 197–
    199
Covariation (as a criterion for causality), **3,** 41, 43, 182, 222
Cross-generational problem, **48**
Culture, 462

d (effect size indicator), 526
Data
  cooking, **591**
  discarding, 591–592
  forging, **591**
  qualitative, **32–34,** 291, 292–295,
    531
  quantitative, **32–34,** 291,
    295–296, 531
  snooping, 178, 180
  torturing, **592**
  trimming, **592**
Data analysis, 98
  open-ended data, 329–336
Data collection, 406
  in case study research, 275–277
  in survey research, 377–383
  See also Internet research; Inter-
    views; Measurement modali-
    ties; Questionnaires
Debriefing, **81–84,** 406–408
  components, 82–83, 407
  functions, 81–82, 406–408
  in Internet research, 421
  potential harm from, 83–84
  steps in 408–409
  See also Post-experimental
    interview
Debugging research procedures, 403–
  405
Definitions (in theories), 13
Dehoaxing, **82,** 83
Demand characteristics, **171–175,**
  180
  controlling, 174–175
  detecting effects of, 172, 175, 404

Dependent variable, **14,** 35, 113–115,
  116, 236, 300–301, 442–443
  dichotomous, 246
Desensitization, **82–83**
Design flaw analysis, **528–529**
*Directory of Unpublished Experimental
  Measures,* 147
Discriminant validity, 94, 187
Dissertation Abstracts International,
  101

Ecological fallacy, **329**
Ecological validity, 103, **300, 453,**
  454, 455, 519–520, 523–524
  assessing, 467–468, 470–471
  of laboratory research, 468–473
  of measurement, 353–354, 484
  research participants and, 459–460
  of research procedures, 461–462
  of research settings, 457–458
  See also External validity; General-
    izability
Editor of journal,
  action, **576**
  copy, **579**
  production, **579**
Educational Resources Information
  Center (ERIC), 100, 101
Effect size, 397–399, 431–433, 526,
  532, 533, 534
  critical, **397**
  and practical significance, 432–433
Eigenvalue, **256–257**
Empiricism (as a scientific value),
  5–6, 439–440
Epistemology, **7–8,** 117, 472–473
  See also Constructionism; Human-
    ism; Logical positivism
Errors in research, 109, 596–600
  See also Professional responsibili-
    ties; Scientific malpractice
Error variance, **183,** 217–218
Ethical issues. *See* Application of
  research results, ethical issues;
  Ethical treatment of research
  participants; Evaluation research,
  ethical issues; Field experiments,
  ethical issues; Internet research,
  ethical issues; Professional responsibilities; Publication, ethical issues; Scientific malpractice;
  Utilization of research results,
  ethical issues
Ethical treatment of research participants, 37, 189, 271, 328, 405
  children, 63–64, 71, 75, 80, 85–86
  coercion, 66–67
  compensation of control groups, 84

confidentiality of data, 84–86, 277
 certificate of confidentiality, 86
 in Internet research, 421
deception, 72–76, 141
 alternatives to, 74–75
 in Internet research, 420
 in observational research, 170,
  315, 316
deprivation, 64–66
discussion of in research report,
  560–561
in field research, 68–70, 81
general principles, 58
government regulations, 58, 59, 60,
  61, 68, 69, 71
harm, 62–66, 75–76, 77–79, 597
 in Internet research, 421
 See also Ethical treatment of research participants, risk
inducements to participate in research, 67–68
informed consent, 68–72, 74,
  80–81, 172
 behavioral consent, 68
 competence to give, 71, 420
 consent form, 71–72
 to deception, 75, 76
 in Internet research, 420
 withdrawal of, **80**–81
 and internal validity, 72, 80–81,
  172, 174
in Internet research, 418, 420–421
psychological problems of participants, discovering, 79
responsibility for, 59–62
 researcher, 59–60, 71
 sponsoring institution, 60–62
risk, 62–66
 categories of, 62–63, 64
 in debriefing, 83–84
 from deception, 74, 76
 minimal, **63**, 72
 screening for, 63, 77, 79
 unanticipated, 66, 77–79
 use of deception to minimize, 74
risk-benefit analysis, 59, **65**, 76, 78
 benefits of research, 65–66
subject pools, 66–67
voluntary participation, **66**–68, 174
 in Internet research, 418, 420
See also Debriefing; Post-experimental interview
Evaluability assessment, **479**, 480–
  487
Evaluation apprehension, 139, 141,
  167–168, 170
Evaluation research, **32**, 51, **478**
 effectiveness criteria for, 492–495

efficiency analysis in, 504–506
ethical issues, 64–65
formative evaluation, **487**–492
internal validity, 487, 499–501
null results in, 502–504
process evaluation, **487**
research designs
 client and program variation,
  496–497
 comparative outcome, **495**–496
 constructive, **497**
 dismantling, **496**
 parametric, **497**
 program package, **495**
research questions, 478, 495–497
research strategies, 497–502
summative evaluation, **487**,
  492–506
theories in, 478, 485–487, 497
unintended effects in, 490–491
See also Stakeholder
Experimenter expectancy effects,
  176–177, 180, 413
Experiments, 30, **35**, 41, 222
 and causality, 35–36, 182
 characteristics of, 182
 conditions of
  comparison, 35, 185–187
  control, **35**, 64–65
  experimental, 35
 in evaluation research, 498–499
 See also Between-subjects designs;
  Factorial designs; Field experiments; Manipulation of
  independent variable; Multiple group designs; Quasi-
  experiments; Within-subjects
  designs
Expert witness, 605–606
Explanation building, **292**, 293–
  295
External validity, **23**, 24, 103,
  452–474
 assessing, 466–468
 components of, 453–455
  conceptual, **455**, 465
  functional, **454**–455, 464–465
  relationships among, 466, 471
  structural, **453**–454, 455–464
 and internal validity, 473–474
 threats to, 456
 See also Ecological validity; Generalizability

Factor (in factor analysis), **253**
 factor loading, **257**–259
 factor score, **259**
Factor analysis, 241, **253**–259

in developing Likert scales, 254,
  362
interpreting, 257–259
Factorial designs, 205–218, 309
 interaction effects in, **205**,
  207–212, 229, 241, 564
 and generalizability, 218, 467
 interpreting, 209–212
 and meta-analysis, 532
 main effects in, **205**, 209
 mixing between- and within-
  subject independent variables
  in, 212
 mixing manipulated and correlational independent variables
  in, 212–213
 possible outcomes of, 206–209,
  213
 uses of, 214–218
Fallacy of the mean, **438**–439
Fatigue effects, **196**
Field experiments, 52, **301**–306
 ethical issues, 70, 302
 and laboratory experiments, 302
Figures, 209, 565–566
Focus group, **380**–381
Fraud. *See* Scientific malpractice

General Social Survey, 344, 383
Generalizability, 53, 54, 103, 189,
  218, **440**, 441, 452, 454,
  487–488, 567
 assessing, 466–467
 of natural-setting research, 471
 overgeneralization, 601–602
 and integrative literature reviews,
  517, 519
 in single-case research, 266, 281
 See also Ecological validity; External validity

History (threat to internal validity),
  48, **150**, 267, 281
 local history, **501**
Humanism, **7**, 8, 9, 33
Hypotheses, **3**, 5, 103, 132
 formulating, 40, 90–108,
  background for, 90
 research, **105**, 107, 427–428
 statistical, **105**, 107, 430–431
 and theoretical propositions, 14
 See also Research questions
Hypothetical constructs, **10**–13,
  439
 and criterion-related evidence of
  validity, 131
 as independent variables, 187–188,
  190

Hypothetical constructs (*continued*)
    measurement of, 123–124,
        131–133, 140, 361
    multidimensional, **11,** 12, 363
    multifaceted, **12,** 228–230
    unidimensional, **11,** 12, 363, 364
    See also Operational definitions

Independent groups designs, **192**
    See also Between-subjects designs
Independent variable, **15,** 35, 183,
        222, 236, 239, 442
    in applied research, 113–115, 116
    in field settings, 300–301,
        304–305
    levels of, 103, 201–203
        and external validity, 461
    qualitative, 203
    quantitative, 200–203, 242–243
    in single-case research, 272
    See also Confounds; Experiments;
        Manipulation of independent
        variable
Inference, 17, **23**–24, 107, 180, 426,
        427, 430, 434–440
    and behavioral measures, 140–141
    in coding systems, 180, 333
    and criterion-related evidence of
        validity, 131
    in measurement, 123
    and physiological measures, 142–
        143
Institutional Review Board (IRB),
        60–62, 78
Instructions to research participants,
        402, 404
    in questionnaires, 374
Instrumentation change, **161**
Integrative literature review, **516**
    best evidence approach to,
        534–536
    criteria for evaluating, 538–539
    and ecological validity, 523–524
    and generalizability, 519
    generalizability of conclusions, 520
    hypothesis testing vs. exploratory
        approaches to, 520–521
    level of analysis in, 529–530,
        543–544
    mediating variables in, 532
    moderator variables in, 516, 518,
        519, 527–528, 532, 537
    narrative, **531**–536
        comparison with meta-analysis,
            535
    purposes, 516
    research questions in, 518–521
    researcher bias in, 532–533
    steps in, 517, 521–538

uses, 517
    See also Literature review; Meta-
        analysis
Interaction effect. *See* Factorial de-
        signs, interaction effects in
Intercept, **231**
Internal validity, **23,** 24, 102, **156,**
        189, 323, 413, 487, 523
    effects of ethical requirements on,
        74
    enhancing, 180
    and external validity, 473–474
    role of control groups in, 164–165
    of single-case research, 266–272
    threats to, 159–167, 499–501
        analyzing patterns of, 528–529
Internet, 100, 101, 104
Internet research, 411–421
    advantages, 412–414
    disadvantages, 414–415
    ethical issues in, 418, 420–421
    forms of, 411–412
    and internal validity, 413, 418
    participant recruitment, 411,
        416–418
    Web sites, 418, 419
Interviews, 33, 321–326
    elements, 324–325
    information provided by, 322
    types
        group, 326
        semistructured, 323
        structured, 323
        unstructured, 322–323
        See also Focus group
    standardization of, 323–324
Item analysis, **363**

Journal articles, 99, 100, 574–580
    reviewing, 581–583
    See also Peer review; Research
        reports

Latent variables analysis, **248**
    See also Path analysis
Latin square design, **198**–199
LISREL analysis, 248
Literature review
    as background for research, 91,
        97–104, 218
    in research reports, 553–555
    sources of information for, 99–103
    See also Integrative literature re-
        view; Meta-analysis
Logical positivism, **7,** 8, 9, 33,
        116–117, 182, 434
Logistic regression analysis, 244, 246
Logit analysis, **245**–246
Log-linear analysis, 245, 246

Main effect, **205**–206, 209
Manipulation check, **187**–188, 404,
        407–408
Manipulation of independent vari-
        able, 103, 158, 184–191, 442,
        500–501
    acute, **466**
    chronic, **466**
    and deception, 73
    experimental condition, 184–185,
        278
    and external validity, 461
    in field experiments, 303, 304–305
    multiple stimuli in, 190–191
    reliability of, 188–189, 401–402
    salience of, 188, **189**–190, 442
    strong, 188, **189,** 442
    See also Comparison groups; Con-
        trol groups
Masked review, **576**
Maturation (threat to internal valid-
        ity), **160**–161, 267
Measurement, 48, 122–152, **350,** 438
    confounds in, 159
        See also Validity of measurement,
            discriminant levels of,
            350–354, 438
    and ecological validity, 353–354
    interval, **351**
    nominal, **351,** 356
    ordinal, **351,** 355, 356, 357
    ratio, **351**–352
    and statistical tests, 352–353
    reactivity in, 47, 73, **167**–171, 180
    role of theory, 131–134, 136–137,
        138, 148–150
    scales of. *See* Measurement, levels
        of
    sensitivity of, 188, **357**–358, 361,
        443
    in single-case research, 267–269
    steps in measurement process,
        136–137
    See also Change, measurement of;
        Coding systems; Measurement
        error; Measurement modali-
        ties; Measures; Rating scales;
        Reliability of measurement;
        Validity of measurement
Measurement error, 124–125
    random, **124,** 162–163, 183
    systematic, **125**
Measurement modalities, 138–145,
        265
    behavioral, **140**–141
        controlling reactivity in, 73, 170
    comparisons among, 143–144
    physiological, **142**–143
    self-report, **138**–140, 141

controlling reactivity in, 73,
170–171
use of multiple, 143–145, 361, 565
Measures,
criteria for evaluating, 148–152
locating, 147–148
normed, **146**
norms, 149, 151
psychometric tests, **146**
research measures, **146**
ad hoc, **146**
developed, **146**
See also Coding systems; Measurement; Rating scales; Reliability of measurement; Validity of measurement
Median split, **242**–243
Mental Measurements Yearbook, 147
Meta-analysis, 397, **531**–536, 537
comparison with narrative literature review, 535
how to read, 539–544
interpretation of main effects in, 542
Models, **16**
Mortality, 166–167, 180, 415
differential, **167**
Multicollinearity, 240–241
Multiple correlation coefficient (R), 238, 239
Multiple group designs, 200–204
interpreting results of, 203–204
Multiple operationism, 143–145, 565
Multiple regression analysis, 236–243, 246
and analysis of variance, 241–243
hierarchical, **237**
simultaneous, **236**–237
stepwise, 236
See also Logistic regression analysis; Multicollinearity
Multitrait-multimethod matrix, 134
Multiway frequency analysis, 244–246

Natural experiments, **306**–315
Needs assessment, **479**–480
Nonequivalent control group design, **307**–312
Nonspecific treatment effect, **184**
Novelty effect, **168**–169
Null hypothesis, **440**
accepting, 444–445
prejudice against, 441–443, 522, 538
Null results, **440**–445, 502–504

Observational research, 33, 170, 176, 315–321

effects on observer, 320–321
ethical issues, 68–70, 81, 170
over the Internet, 412, 420, 421
nonparticipant, 317–318
participant, 170, **315**–317
records in, 319
Office of Technology Assessment, 517
Operational definition, **13**, 94, 102, 103, 131, 132, 140, 142, 439, 559
and external validity, 460–461
of goals in evaluation research, 481–484
in integrative literature reviews
of study outcome, 525–527
of variables, 516, 529–530, 537
Order effects, **196**–200
controlling, 197–199
detecting, 214–216
differential, **199**
Outcome
distal, **484**
proximal, **484**
social impact, **484**
Outlier, **225**–226, 533

Page proofs, **579**
Paradigm, 9–10
Partial correlation. *See* Correlational analysis, partial
Passive research strategy, **40**
See also Correlational research
Path analysis, **247**–248
Pattern matching, **292**, 293
Peer review, **576**–577
being a reviewer, 581–583
Pilot studies, 180, **403**–405
Placebo effect, **184**
Plagiarism, **585**
Planned comparisons, 204, **430**–431
See also A priori contrasts
Population parameters, **344**
Populations
client, **480**
research, 301
study, **390**
target, **53**, 390
of an intervention, **487**–488
Poster session, **581**
Postexperimental interview, 187, **406**–409
See also Debriefing
Post-hoc analysis, **204**, 211
Practical significance, 103, **433**, 493–494
See also Statistical significance
Practice effects, **196**
Preexperimental designs, 501–502
Primary source, **99**
Privacy, 69

Privileged communication, 86
Professional responsibilities, 598–599, 606–608
See also Errors in research; Expert witness; Publication, ethical issues; Research assistants; Scientific malpractice; Utilization of research results, ethical issues
Program evaluation. *See* Evaluation research
Propositions, **13**–14
Psychological Abstracts, 101
PsycINFO, 101, 570
Publication,
censorship of, 610–612
errors in, 599–600
ethical issues, 583–586
See also Convention presentations; Journal articles; Peer review
Publicness (as a scientific value), **6**–7, 413–414

Quasi-experiments, **307**–315, 499
See also Nonequivalent control group designs; Time series design
Questionnaires, 139, 170, 180
administration, 377–383
comparing methods of, 381–383
computer, 381
focus group, **380**–381
group, 377–378, 407
interview, 379–380
mail, 378–379
telephone, 380
See also Internet research
context effects in, 372–373, 376
design of, 371–376
instructions in, 374
use of existing measures in, 374–376
Questions (in questionnaires),
closed-ended, 345, 373
double-barrelled, **347**
leading, **348**
loaded, **348**
open-ended, 345
response formats, 354–360, 375–376
sequencing of, 372
wording of, 346–350, 404
Quota matrix, **392**, 393

R. *See* Multiple correlation coefficient
Rating scales, 354–371
ambiguity in, 366–367, 368, 371
comparative, **354**–355

Rating scales (*continued*)
  graphic, **357, 358**
  Guttman, **364**–365
  interpreting responses to, 371
  itemized, **356**–357, 367
  Likert, **361**–363
  multi-item, **360**–366
  numerical, **357**–360, 368
  paired comparison, **354**
  rank-order, **354**–355
  semantic differential, **365**–366
  summated, **361**
  Thurstone, **363**–364
  visual analog, 357
  See also Questions; Response bias
Reactivity, 73, **167**–171, 180, 286,
    327, 456–457
  controlling, 169–171
  in longitudinal research, 47
  in observational research,
    169–170, 319
  in self-report measures, 170–171
  test, **47**
Regression analysis. *See* Bivariate re-
    gression; Multiple regression
    analysis
Regression coefficient, **238**–239
Regression equation, **43**
Regression to the mean. *See* Statisti-
    cal regression
Rehearsal of research procedures, 177,
    180
Reification, 11
Relationships between variables,
    200–201, 427–431
  assessing nonlinear, 201–202
  curvilinear, **200**–202, 223, 224,
    241, 443
  linear, **200**–201
  negative, **200**–201
  positive, **200**–201
Reliability of measurement, **124**–128,
    137, 323, 361, 363, 364
  alternate forms, **126**
  choosing among forms, 127
  and correlational research, 224
  Cronbach's alpha, 127, 149
  of difference scores, 509–510
  interrater, **126**–127, 335, 527
  internal consistency, 127
  and measurement error, 124–125
  split-half, **127**
  standards for, 127–128, 149, 151
  test-retest, **125**–126, 149
  and validity of measurement, 125,
    126
Reliable change index, **510**
Repeated measures designs, **192**
  See also Within-subjects designs

Replication research, 7, 81, **109**–112,
    555
  conceptual, **109**, 453, 454
  considerations in conducting,
    110–112
  and errors and malpractice in re-
    search, 109, 594
  exact, **109**
  and external validity, 466–467
  in nonequivalent control group de-
    signs, 311
  replication and extension, 110
  results of, 110
  in single-case research, 269
Research,
  action, **32**, 33
  analog, **471**–472
  and application, 25–27
  applied, **30**–32, 452–453, 465,
    609–610
  archival, 326–329
  artificiality in, 36, 460
  basic, **30**–32, 452, 609–610
  cohort-sequential, **48**–49
  criteria for evaluating, 23
  cross-sectional, **45**–47, 180
  developmental, **44**–49
  field, 52–54, **300**
    See also Field experiments; Nat-
      ural experiments; Quasi-
      experiments
  ideas for, 95–97
  idiographic approach to, **39**, 264
  longitudinal, **47**–48, 85
    retrospective, 327–328
  naturalism in, 37–38, 54, 472–473
  nomothetic approach to, **39**, 264
  primary, **517**
  prospective, **49**–51, 249–250
  purposes, 30–32
  realism in, 400–401
    experimental, **400**
    mundane **400**, 457
  relation to theory and application,
    24–25
  restrictions on, 610–612
  steps in research process, 23–24
  strategies, 35–44
    case study, 31, 33, **37**–40, 43
    comparisons among, 44, 45
    correlational, 31, **40**–44
    experimental, 30, **35**–37
    and research settings, 52–53
    See also Case study research;
      Correlational research;
      Experiments
  and theory, 24, 30–31
  topic, 91–92
  tradeoffs in, 54–55, 398, 402

  uses of, 25–27
  See also Evaluation research; Repli-
    cation research; Utilization of
    research results
Research assistants, 59, 409–410
Research participants, 102
  assignment to conditions of the in-
    dependent variable
    in field experiments, 303,
      304–305
    matched nonrandom, 310, 311
    matched random, **194**–195
    nonrandom, 165–166
    simple random, **192**–194
    use of preexisting groups,
      308–312
  children as, 63–64, 71, 75, 80,
    85–86
  and external validity, 458–460,
    464
  in Internet research, 412–413, 414,
    415, 416–417
  roles, 172–174
  volunteer, 165, 166, 458–459
  See also Populations; Sampling
Research proposal, 91, 108, 403
Research protocol, **60**, 61
Research questions, 447
  characteristics, 93–95
  formulating, 92–95
  for evaluation research, 478,
    495–497
  for integrative literature reviews,
    518–520
Research reports, 277, 548–574,
    606–607
  abstract, 570, 572
  authorship, 583–584
  common problems in, 577
  content of, 549
  criteria for evaluating, 102–104,
    582
  discussion section, 566–569, 570,
    571, 582
    See also Inference; Interpretation
      of research results
  introduction, 552–557, 566, 582
    See also Literature review
  method section, 556, 557–562,
    582
  and nonresearchers, 552, 571–574,
    585
  results section, 552, 562–566, 568,
    569, 582
  structure of, 549, 550, 551
  title, 569–570
  writing style in, 550–552
  See also Convention presentations;
    Journal articles; Publication

Research sample, **53,** 149, 150,
   390–391
   See also Sampling
Research settings, 399–402
   and external validity, 103, 456–
      458
   in field experiments, 302–304
   laboratory, 30, 52–54
      and ecological validity, 468–473
      purposes of, 469–470
   natural, 31
      and generalizability, 471
   and research participants, 53–54,
      302–303
   and research strategies, 52–53
   and utilization of research results,
      115–116
   See also Ecological validity
Response bias, 149, **151,** 366–371
   acquiescence, **151,** 152, **369**–370
   category anchoring, **367**–368
   estimation, 368
   extremity, **370**
   halo, **370**–371
   leniency, **371**
   social desirability, 139, **151**–152,
      169, 170, **368**–369, 413
   See also Reactivity
Restriction in range, **225,** 443
Reverse scoring, **362**
Role-playing (as alternative to
      deception)
   active, 74–74
   passive, **75**

Sample (vs. population), 390–391
Sample size, 396–399, 443
   in pilot studies, 405
   See also Statistical power
Sample survey, **344**
Sampling, 391–395
   cluster, **393**–394
   convenience, **54**
   and external validity, 394
   haphazard, **395**
   in Internet research, 414, 416–417
   multistage cluster, 393–394
   nonprobability, **391,** 394–395
   probability, **391,** 392–394
   purposive, **395**
   quota, **395**
   random
      simple, **391**
      stratified, 392
   snowball, **395**
   stratified, **392,** 524–525
   systematic, **392**–393
   time, 463–464
Sampling frame, **392**

Scales. *See* Measurement, levels of;
      Rating scales
Science, 2–8
   goals of, 2–5
      control, **5,** 35
      description, 2–3
      prediction, **4**–5
      understanding, 3–4, 31
   values of, 5–7
Scientific malpractice, 590–596
   detection of, 594–596
   forms of, 590–593
   motivations for, 593–594
   See also Errors in research; Profes-
      sional responsibilities
Scree test, **257**
Secondary source, **99**
Selection (threat to internal validity),
      165–167, 310–312
Selective attention, **318**
Sensitization effects, **196,** 199
Significance. *See* Practical
      significance; Statistical
      significance
Simulation research, **74**
Single-case experiments, 52, 277–291
   A-B design, 278
   A-B-A design, **278,** 279
   A-B-C-B design, **279**–280
   alternating treatments design, 283
   baseline, 278, 288–291
      stability of, 290–291
      trends in, **288**–290
   changing criterion design,
      286–288
   in evaluation research, 502
   multiple baseline design, **280**–285
   reversal design, **278**
   simultaneous treatment design,
      283–286
   See also Single-case research
Single-case research
   data analysis in, 291–296
   in evaluation research, 502
   objections to, 266
   in integrative literature reviews,
      531
   in psychology, 264–266
   uses of, 266
   validity criteria, 266–272
   See also Case study research; Single-
      case experiments
Skepticism (as a scientific value), **6**
Slope, **231,** 232–233
Social activist, **603**–605, 607–608
Socially sensitive research, **610**
Social Science Citation Index, 101
Societal mentor, **602,** 603, 607–608
Sociological Abstracts, 101

Solomon four-group design, 161, 162,
      165
Stakeholder, **479,** 484–485, 508
   See also Evaluation research
Statistical conclusion validity, **23,** 24,
      102
Statistical power, 102, 396–399,
      429–430, 443, 534, 538
   and median splits, 242
   Statistical regression, **162**–163
Statistical significance, 102, 183
   and integrative literature reviews,
      525–527
   and median splits, 242–243
   See also Effect size; Practical
      significance; Statistical power
Statistical tests, 397
   inferential, **428**–430
   and level of measurement,
      352–353
   misuse of, 592, 598–599
   omnibus, **430**–431, 439
   parametric, 183
   and research design, 183
   in research reports, 563, 564,
      568–569, 573, 577
   robustness of, **353**
   in single-case research, 296
   See also Analysis of covariance;
      Analysis of variance; A priori
      contrasts; Correlational analy-
      sis; Planned comparisons; Sta-
      tistical power
Stimulus, **190,** 414
   use of multiple stimuli, 190–191
Structural equation modeling. *See*
      Path analysis; Latent variables
      analysis
Subscales, **360**

Tables, 209, 565
Tentativeness (as a scientific value),
      6, 24
Testing (threat to internal validity),
      161, 162
Test reactivity, **47**
Test sensitization, **47**
Tests in Print, 147
Theories, 4, 5, **7**–22, 94, 95, 98, 103,
      111, 292–293, 440–441, 442,
      445–446, 516, 517, 555, 566
   and application, 25, 32
   bias in, 10, 118
   boundary conditions of, **112**
   characteristics of, 15–16
   components of, 9–15
   constructionist perspective on,
      434–435
   criteria for evaluating, 21–22

Theories (*continued*)
  in evaluation research, 478, 485–487, 497
  and measurement, 131–132, 136–137, 138
  purposes of, 17–21
  and research, 24
Third variable problem, **42**–43
Time-lagged comparisons, **48**
Time precedence of cause, **3,** 41, 43, 249–250
Time series design, 296, 312–315
  interrupted, **312**–314
Treatment. *See* Independent variable
Treatment diffusion, **500**
Treatment variance, **183**
Truth test, **113**
Type I error, 110, 396, 397, 429–430, 441, 533
  See also Statistical significance
Type II error, 110, 396, 429–430, 442–443, 502–504, 527, 533
  See also Statistical power

Unit of analysis, **274**
Unit of behavior, 333–334
Utility test, **113**
Utilization of research results, 113, 506–508
  conceptual, **506**
  ethical issues, 600–608
  failure to utilize, 508
  instrumental, **506**
  persuasive, **506,** 602–606
  political context of, 507–508

and research design, 113–116
and research population, 115
and research setting, 115–116
See also Application of research results

Validity of measurement, **124,** 126, 128–138, 361
  assessing, 135–137, 149
  construct-related evidence, 130, **131**–133, 135, 149, 151
    See also Construct validity
  content-related evidence, **129**–130, 135, 137, 150, 151
  convergent, **133,** 143, 149
  criterion-related evidence, **130**–131, 132, 138
  differential, **137**–138
  discriminant, **133**–134, 135, 143, 149, 151, 159
  and reliability of measurement, 125
Validity of research, 23, 441, 597, 598–599
  and sampling procedures, 390–391
  theoretical, 523
  See also Construct validity; Ecological validity; External validity; Internal validity; Single-case research, validity criteria; Statistical conclusion validity
Variable, **10**
  criterion, **236**
  dependent, **14,** 222, 236
    and utilization of research results, 114–115, 116

See also Measurement; Multiple operationism
  estimator, **113,** 114, 116, 465
  extraneous, **156, 191,** 443
    controlling in experiments, 191–195, 216–218
    in field research, 305–306
  latent, **229**–230
    See also Latent variables analysis
  manifest, **123**–124, 131, 190
  mediating, **15,** 443, 485–486
    in integrative literature reviews, 532
    testing for, 246–253
  moderating, **15,** 103, 553, 485–486
    in integrative literature reviews, 516, 518, 519, 527–528, 532, 537
    testing effect of, 214
  policy, **113**–114, 116, 465
  predictor, **236**
    See also Independent variable
Variance inflation factor (VIF), 241
Verisimilitude, 455
Visual data analysis, **295**

Wash-out period, **199**
Within-subjects design, **192,** 195–200, 212
  compared to between-subjects design, 195–196
World-Wide Web. *See* Internet; Internet research

Zero-order correlation, **235,** 239